CADOGAN
city guides

P9-DFT-184

MOSCOW & ST PETERSBURG

Cadogan Books plc
London House, Parkgate Road,
London SW11 4NQ, UK
Distributed in the USA by
The Globe Pequot Press
6 Business Park Road, PO Box 833, Old Saybrook,
Connecticut 06475–0833

Copyright © Rose Baring 1995

Illustrations © Oleg Buryan 1995

Book and cover design by Animage

Cover illustrations by Horatio Monteverde, Animage

Maps © Cadogan Guides, drawn by Map Creation Ltd

Series Editors: Rachel Fielding and Vicki Ingle

Editing: Rachel Fielding, Chris Schüler

Proofreading: Chris Schüler, Toby Bourne

Indexing: Isobel McLean

Production: Rupert Wheeler Book Production Services

DTP: Jacqueline Lewin and Toby Bourne

UK ISBN 0–94–7754–54–7
A catalogue record for this book
is available from the British Library

US ISBN 1–56–4402–74–6

The author and publishers have made every effort to ensure the accuracy of the information in the book at the time of going to press. However, they cannot accept any responsibility for any loss, injury or inconvenience resulting from the use of information contained in this guide.

Output, printed and bound in Finland by Werner Södeström Oy on Kymexcote.

ii

About the Author

Rose Baring first fell under the Russian spell at the age of 12, in a shoe-box of a class-room known as 'The Kremlin'. Back in the 1970s no-one dreamed she would go and live in Russia, so the syllabus aimed at a fluent reading of the 19th-century classics. It wasn't until 1992, in a communal flat in Moscow, that she acquired the vital domestic vocabulary of a Russian four-year-old and a few useful phrases for older ears only. She is now living back in London.

Acknowledgements

A true list of all those who have helped in the preparation of this volume would require the felling of another tree, so this is necessarily restricted. Special thanks in Britain to Liza Hollingshead for her practical support and encouragement, Rachel Fielding and Chris Schüler at Cadogan Books for their skilful and painless editing, and to Celia de la Hay, Thaddeus O'Sullivan and Sara Harrity for making the long trek out to Russia to enjoy the cities with me.

In Moscow the web becomes more tangled. First and foremost, I owe an enormous debt of gratitude to Oleg Buryan, not only for his illustrations, but also for sharing his boundless enthusiasm for both Moscow and St Petersburg, and other places in between. The doors to his and his wife Katya's studios and flat were never closed, and the food and vodka ever-flowing. Thanks also to the inimitable song-bird Nina Kovalchuk, whose cooking is renowned in northeast Moscow and who taught me the rudiments of survival. Those who generously had me to stay include Tanya Markina, Tanya Yegorova, Lonya Bodrov and Alex Fraser. For meals, trips to the theatre, use of washing machines, advice and conversation I must add Irina Shirochenskaya, her mother Olga and aunt Nina, Lena Shibayeva, Larissa Trushevskaya, Anne McIlvoy, Marta Bruno, Phoebe Mates and Ellie Keene. A shadow has fallen over memories of sunny weekends at Peredelkino with Juliet and Rory Peck, playing cricket and mushrooming. Rory's death in October 1993, filming the fighting at Ostankino, has stolen a brave spirit from our midst.

In St Petersburg, I was welcomed into the expansive family of Sasha Kisilyov and Nellya Levitskaya, and entertained to reminiscences in the kitchen by Baba Zoya. From the hundreds of acts of kindness I would like to select Alexei Shpikovsky and Olga Yudina for tea and cakes, Yulia Pivovarova for never-ending cups of coffee in the kitchen, Natasha and MacDoppel for riotous nights fading into days, Sasha and Olga Dudarev, Masha Bozunova, Valera Katsuba, Peter and Helena Owen Edmunds, Katya Galitzine and Anna Benn.

Lastly my love and thanks to Barnaby, for his enthusiastic enjoyment of Moscow's lesser sites, for reading my drafts and offering incisive suggestions, and for encouraging me when the task seemed endless.

Contents

Travel   5–22

Practical A–Z   23–38

Maps and Plans

'Moscow... is Russia—and it is Russia's heart'.
'Petersburg is Russian, but it is not Russia'.

From the Marquis de Custine *'Letters from Russia'* 1839

Introduction

Moscow and St Petersburg, the twin capitals of Russia, could hardly be more different. Moscow's skyline, once known for its 'forty times forty churches', is still punctuated by nests of golden cupolas hemmed in by brick-red walls. In St Petersburg, the grid of streets and waterways are lined by chilly, pastel façades, eloquent and beautiful horizontals only occasionally interrupted by a golden dome or spire. While Moscow emerged as a snug defensive fortress from the untamed forests of medieval Muscovy, St Petersburg was a creation of the 18th-century Enlightenment; in the words of Dostoyevsky a 'premeditated city', planned and built on open marshland. Whereas Moscow was ever threatened by fire, raging through its curvaceous walled quarters of wooden houses and stuccoed palaces, St Petersburg's natural predator was water, which regularly flooded its granite embankments, sweeping hundreds of citizens to their deaths. Even the citizens of the two capitals are different—

or so they vociferously claim. Most of them now live in identical Soviet high-rise 'sleeping regions' on the periphery of both cities. But no self-respecting, cultured, intellectual Petersburger would ever want to be mistaken for a canny, worldly, mercantile Muscovite, or vice versa.

The mid-1990s find both cities in a state of flux. A vast country which has only ever experienced the strong-arm tactics of autocratic government has become the stage for democracy's greatest trial. Out of the shattered hulk of the despotic, atheist Soviet state a new civil society is tentatively emerging. As Muscovites and Petersburgers search for an identity beyond the failed experiment of their own life-times, they are readopting their pre-Revolutionary heritage. Churches knocked down by Stalin have been completely rebuilt to accommodate the newly faithful among their meditative modern icons and guttering candles. Books once discredited by the Communist regime are for sale on street corners, pored over in sub-zero temperatures by a highly literate population. Private galleries have mushroomed, revelling in their ability to hang everything from masterpieces of the avant-garde and modern conceptual art to exhibitions of photographs on the life of the martyred royal family.

Yet side by side with these developments, a version of Russia's early 20th-century decadence seems to be re-emerging. Close your eyes and it doesn't take much to turn the chauffeur-driven, smoked-glass Mercedes of Russia's new super-rich into the prototype motor cars and carriages driven by the liveried staff of their pre-Revolutionary namesakes. Expensive restaurants offer *blini* dripping with butter and cascading with caviar, while beyond their barred windows old women, robbed of the dignity of an adequate pension, beg for a living on the wind-chilled streets.

To the visitor, the two cities offer different aspects of the wider nation and its history. In Moscow, capital in the medieval period and again since 1918, those enthralled by Russia's medieval arts and architecture or uplifted by the idealism of socialist realism will find their spiritual home. From the highest monastery belltower to the deepest metro shaft, the city dances with decoration. As today's capital, Moscow is the business centre, a bustling market in which the place of medieval merchant guilds and turn-of-the-century industrialists has been taken by foreign businessmen and their flash and oft-times shady Russian partners. A carriage in the metro shows the diverse ethnic mix of the city—from Inuit to Central Asian; Mongolian to sandy-haired Russians. Dusty stucco palaces are shaking off the years of apathy and marching into a commercial future with a smart new coat of paint. At lunch you may find yourself tasting *nachos* and *enchiladas* in a rough-rendered pueblo interior, while by night you sink into the rustic and rowdy interior of a mouth-watering Georgian restaurant.

St Petersburg is more laid-back, and cheaper—a museum city of serene 18th- and 19th-century architecture, reflected in the still waters of canals and rivers or set off by a blanket of white snow. While Moscow shrouds itself in a heady air of mystery, St Petersburg is an intelligible, rational city. Since the Goodwill Games were held here in 1994, even some of the street signs appear in English. Yet although you can walk from Italian Renaissance painting to French furniture, from grandiose Russian Rococo to astonishing Gothic confections, the city's duplicity makes it hard to put your finger on its pulse. Camouflaged behind the European exterior, the city still beats to its emotional, quirkily Russian heart.

As far back as 1839, the Marquis de Custine observed that 'left to himself, the traveller in Russia sees nothing; protected, that is to say escorted [by a tour guide], he sees too much—which comes to the same thing.' Until the late 1980s this remained true, as all tourists were processed by the state and treated to a glut of production statistics for every factory their Intourist bus passed. Now, over 150 years after the Marquis' visit, travellers to Russia can finally explore its two great cities at their leisure. This book is written in the hope of providing an informative and practical support. Happy walking.

Best of Moscow

Essential Viewing:	The Kremlin, Novodevichy Monastery, Red Square and St Basil's Cathedral
Historic Churches:	Church of the Intercession at Fili, Church of the Trinity in Nikitniki, Old Cathedral in the Donskoy Monastery
Functioning Churches:	Yelokhovsky Cathedral, Church of the Resurrection, Cathedral of the Intercession at Rogozhskoye Old Believers' Commune, Church of the Assumption at Novodevichy Monastery

Icons:	Cathedral of the Trinity at Sergeyev Possad, Cathedrals of the Assumption and of the Annunciation in the Kremlin, Tretyakov Gallery
Frescoes:	Smolensk Cathedral at Novodevichy Monastery, Cathedral of the Transfiguration in Novospassky Monastery
House Museums:	Tolstoy House Museum, Museum of the Boyars Romanov in Zaradye, Vasnetsov's House
Art Galleries:	Tretyakov Gallery, Museum of Private Collections
Soviet Schizophrenia:	VDNKh, Ⓜ Novokuznetskaya and Kievskaya
Palaces:	Kuskovo
Markets and Shopping:	Izmailovo for junk and souvenirs, Central Market (when it reopens) for fresh caviar, Ul. Arbat for antiques and books, Ptichy Rynok for pets
Bath Houses:	Sandunovskaya Banya
Country Breathers:	Tsaritsyno, Abramtsevo, Zvenigorod

Best of St Petersburg

Essential Viewing:	Hermitage, Peter the Great's Summer Palace, Russian Museum, Peter and Paul Fortress
Historic Churches:	St Isaac's Cathedral, Kazan Cathedral, Alexander Nevsky Monastery
Functioning Churches:	Cathedral of St Nicholas
Monumental Graveyards:	Piskarovskoye Memorial Cemetery, Cemetery of the Masters of Art
Undervisited Gems:	Museum of Musical Instruments, Yusupov Palace, Museum of the Arctic and Antarctic, Museum of Applied Arts
Impressive Metro Stations:	Vladimirskaya, Pushkinskaya, Narvskaya
Soviet Memorabilia:	Cruiser Aurora, Museum of the History of Leningrad, Lenin Statue outside the Finland Station
Palaces:	Oranienbaum for authenticity, Catherine Palace at Tsarskoye Selo for sheer grandeur
Markets and Shopping:	Yeliseyev's Grocery on Nevsky Prospekt, antique shop at Ul. Bolshaya Konyushennaya 13, Kuznechny Market for fruit, vegetables and meat

Travel

By Air

From the UK

Both British Airways and the Russian airline Aeroflot fly daily to Moscow from London's Heathrow Airport. British Airways has recently begun flying daily to Moscow from Gatwick as well. Regular Apex return fares for the 3¾-hour flight are currently around £420. It is always worth booking through one of the specialist travel agents listed below, whose special tarrifs can cut these prices by over £150. British Airways currently has direct 3¼-hour flights to St Petersburg five days a week, while Aeroflot has only three direct flights a week. Prices are about £30 less than flying to Moscow. Two other possibilities are SAS (Scandinavian Airlines) or Lufthansa, both of which fly daily from London to Moscow and St Petersburg, via Stockholm and Frankfurt respectively. SAS in particular has some very good deals.

Regent Holidays (*see below*) specialize in arranging cheap fares from regional airports, often flying via Amsterdam on the Dutch airline KLM.

From Ireland

The only flights from Ireland to Russia are from Shannon Airport in County Clare, which has serviced Aeroflot for many years. There are currently direct flights six days a week to Moscow, but none to St Petersburg. Most of the time it is cheaper to fly on one of the regular Dublin or Belfast flights to Heathrow and connect with a British Airways or Aeroflot flight to Russia. Flights from Dublin are operated by British Midland, Aer Lingus and Ryanair, while British Airways and British Midland fly to London from Belfast.

From North America

Aeroflot flies direct to Moscow from New York daily, from Washington at the weekends and from Montreal twice a week. Delta Airlines also flies from New York, non-stop every other day, and via Frankfurt on the others. Prices start as low as $634.00 return. There are currently no direct flights from North America to St Petersburg. Specialist travel agents (*see* below) will be able to advise you of the best deals on European airlines, such as British Airways via London, Finnair via Helsinki and KLM via Amsterdam.

From Australasia

Aeroflot flies twice a week from Sydney to Moscow via Bangkok. You will find cheaper deals, however, by flying to Europe and on to Russia from there. Your local travel agent will be able to advise you.

In the UK and Ireland

British Airways, London: ✆ 0181 759 5511
Aeroflot, London: ✆ 0171 355 2233
SAS, London: ✆ 0171 734 4020
Lufthansa, London: ✆ 0181 750 3500
Aeroflot, Shannon Airport, Ireland: ✆ 0161 62299
British Midland, Dublin: ✆ 011 798 733
Aer Lingus, Dublin: ✆ 011 784 764
Ryanair, Dublin: ✆ 011 797 444/770444
British Airways, Belfast: ✆ 01232 240 522
British Midland, Belfast: ✆ 01232 225 151

In North America

Aeroflot, New York: ✆ 212 332 1050/1041
Aeroflot, Washington: ✆ 202 466 4080/429 4922
Aeroflot, Montreal: ✆ 514 288 2125/6
Delta Airlines: Toll free ✆ 1800 241 4141

In Australasia

Aeroflot, Sydney: ✆ 02 233 7911

In Russia

Many of these offices are only open Mon–Fri 9am–5pm, so reconfirm your return ticket between these times. You may find they insist that you travel to their office to reconfirm, but it is worth asking your hotel service bureau first.

Aeroflot, Moscow: ✆ 155 0922, 156 8019
Aeroflot, St Petersburg: ✆ 311 8072/8093 or 310 4581
British Airways, Moscow: ✆ 253 2492
British Airways, St Petersburg: ✆ 119 6222
SAS, Moscow: ✆ 925 4747
SAS, St Petersburg: ✆ 314 5086
Lufthansa, Moscow: ✆ 975 2501
Lufthansa, St Petersburg: ✆ 314 4979/5917 or 104 3432
Delta Airlines, Moscow: ✆ 253 2658/9
Delta Airlines, St Petersburg: ✆ 311 5820

Getting into the city from the airport

Neither Sheremetevo-2 nor Pulkovo-2, the international airports for Moscow and St Petersburg, are well served by public transport. Either ask your travel agent in the UK to arrange transport to your accommodation, or be prepared to haggle with the taxi drivers. Aim to pay $40 (or the rouble equivalent) to get into Moscow and $25 to get into St Petersburg. If you speak Russian and want to get out into the real world, bus No. 517 will take you from Sheremetevo-2 to Ⓜ Planernaya, whence you can make your way underground to your Moscow hotel or flat. In St Petersburg, catch bus No. 13, which will take you to Ⓜ Moskovskaya.

By Sea

From the Baltic

Arriving in St Petersburg by boat is a romantic notion, but not very practical unless you are coming from Northern Germany, Sweden or Finland. If you are, Baltic Express Line sails from Kiel, from Stockholm or Nynäshamn in Sweden and from Helsinki in Finland. To book, phone Baltic Express in Sweden ✆ 020 73 50 50, in Kiel ✆ 0431 98 20 000 or in Helsinki ✆ 90 66 57 55. For inland river cruises which take you from St Petersburg to Moscow, or vice versa, *see* p.513.

By Rail

From the UK

You can get to St Petersburg by train in 36 hours, and to Moscow in 52 hours, but it is more expensive than the cheapest flights, and currently costs around £300 return to either city, excluding the price of a couchette. For details of the route and up-to-date ticket prices, call London's Victoria Station, ✆ 0171 834 2345. Students and travellers under 26 will normally find the BIJ fares offered by Eurotrain cheaper than British Rail. Their main agent in London is Campus Travel, ✆ 0171 730 3402. InterRail passes, which allow those under 26 (or more expensively those over 26) a month's unlimited travel on Europe's train network, are not valid for the CIS or the Baltic States. If Russia is the final destination in a long journey it can be worth buying one and paying the fare from the last major station before the border.

If you are travelling via the Baltic, check carefully whether your train passes through Latvia, which still requires visas for US and Australian passport holders. Phone the embassy to find out the current situation. Transit visas for Belarus can be bought on the border, while Poland no longer requires them.

Useful Embassy Addresses

Latvian Embassy, London: ✆ 0171 312 0040
Latvian Embassy, Washington: ✆ 202 726 8213
Consulate General of Latvia, Melbourne: ✆ 03 499 6920

From Finland

Trains ply the 6 hour route between Helsinki and St Petersburg twice daily. If you haven't got a Russian visa, head for the Russian Embassy, Vuorimiehenkatu 6, 00140 Helsinki, ✆ 90 66 14 49.

From China

The famous Trans-Siberian Railway follows two different routes on its journey to and from Beijing—one via the Republic of Mongolia, the other via Manchuria in Northern China. Trains leave once a week in each direction on each route, taking about 6 days. To find out more about the trip, either phone Intourist or one of the other specialist travel agents listed below (*see* pp.12–14).

By Road

It is now the foolhardy rather than the adventurous who drive to Russia in their own car. Highway robbery, first by the traffic police, the GAI, and secondly by brigands making a living out of it, leaves many people with few possessions by the time they arrive in Moscow or St Petersburg. If you insist, contact the enterprising Russian Tourist Information Service in London (✆ 0891 516951), who will tell you the ins and outs of taking a car to Russia. Their information is as up to date as you could wish, and includes advice on insurance, obtainable through the Black Sea and Baltic Insurance Co Ltd, 65 Fenchurch St., London EC3M 4EY.

From Finland

The road from Helsinki to St Petersburg is said to be alive with highwaymen, but you will be safe on a bus. Both Finnord and Sovtransavto run daily express buses on the 7 hour trip between the two cities. Finnord can be reached in Helsinki, ✆ 90 17 61 44; Sovtransavto's number in St Petersburg is ✆ 298 1352.

Entry Formalities

Passports and Visas

Ever since the collapse of the Soviet Union, travel agents have been hoping that Russia would stop requiring all foreign visitors to obtain a visa in advance. So far, their hopes have proved fruitless. However, most of the countries surrounding Russia have recognized that visas are off-putting and, in the hope of attracting tourists away from Russia, have given them up. The exceptions are Belarus and the Ukraine, and Latvia if you are American or Australian; call your local embassy to make sure of arrangements. Always bear in mind that if you are going out of a country and back again, you will need a double- or multiple-entry visa. Russian visas come in three varieties: Tourist Visas, Business Visas and Individual Visas.

You will get a Tourist Visa if you are going to Russia in a package tour or to stay in a hotel for less than a month. It is issued against your hotel bookings, and lasts as long as they do, so it is of little interest to free-spirits who don't like to know where they are going to lay their head too many days in advance. Most independent travellers now travel to Russia on a so-called Business Visa, which is valid for up to 2 months. To obtain one you need a stamped letter of invitation from a registered Russian business organization, a service which most of the travel agents listed below can offer. This allows you to rent a flat, stay with friends or travel around without having to pre-book your accommodation. Individual Visas are granted to applicants who can show a letter of invitation from an individual Russian. Getting the letter correctly stamped in Russia can take time, so even if you are going to stay with a Russian friend, save them the hassle by paying the £15 or so extra charged by travel agents for providing you with an invitation from a business.

Obtaining a visa yourself entails queueing at your local embassy and is an inordinate waste of time. Any of the specialist Russian travel agents mentioned below will obtain the visa for you, for a small extra charge. You will need a photocopy of the relevant pages of your full passport, which must be valid for at least 6 months, three passport photographs and the right visa application form. Normal processing time for the visa, which costs around £20, is two weeks, but if you need it more quickly it can be done, at a price. The visa itself is a separate piece of paper, unattached to your passport, so take care not to mislay it.

Russian Embassies and Consulates Abroad

Australia: 78 Canberra Ave, Griffith, Canberra ACT 2603, ✆ (062) 95 9474

Canada: 52 Range Road, Ottawa, Ontario K1N 8G5, ✆ (613) 236 7220

Finland: Vuorimiehenkatu 6, 00140 Helsinki, ✆ (90) 66 14 49

Ireland: 186 Orwell Road, Rathgar, Dublin 6, ✆ (1) 711633 or 977492

Holland: Laan van Meerdervoort 1, 2517-AA The Hague, ✆ (070) 346 79 40

New Zealand: 57 Messines Road, Karori, Wellington, ✆ (4) 766 742

United Kingdom: 5 Kensington Palace Gardens, London W8, ✆ (0171) 229 8027

USA: 1825 Phelps Place NW, Washington, DC 20008, ✆ (202) 332 1483

Registration with OVIR

Until recently, all foreigners in Russia were required to register with the Visa and Registration Department (OVIR). Hotels did this automatically for their guests, but other visitors were supposed to trudge to the local office and wait to be disgorged from the bureaucratic nightmare several hours later. Many simply never registered, and threatened fines at the airport on departure rarely materialized. Registration is no longer necessary, but if you lose your visa or wish to extend or alter it to a multiple-entry visa, you will need the address of the main OVIR office in each city:

Moscow, Ul. Pokrovka 42, ✆ 208 2358/2091
St Petersburg, Ul. Saltykova-Schedrina 4, ✆ 278 3486

Customs

You will have to fill out a customs form on entry into Russia, giving details of all the money you are bringing into the country, both in travellers' cheques and cash, and any valuables such as jewellery, lap-top computers, video cameras etc. There is no restriction on the amount of money you can bring with you. Keep the stamped form throughout your trip. Theoretically you need it to change money, though it is rarely looked at. When you leave the country, customs officials may check it against the new form you fill out, to make sure you have not left—*i.e.* sold—anything, and that you are not leaving with more money than you brought in.

Leaving Russia, your baggage will be X-rayed. Photographers using slide or other sensitive film should take it out and have it examined by hand. Any works of art prior to 1945 will be confiscated. This includes all icons except the obviously modern. Most icons sold to tourists as old are really fakes, but the average customs officer is no more of an expert than you are. Theoretically you need the permission of the Ministry of Culture to export modern paintings, and if you have spent a lot of money you should make sure that the artist, shop or gallery obtain this for you. Cheaper canvasses seem to make it through, though you can never be sure what mood your officer will be in. Their favourite trick is confiscating tins of caviar bought for roubles, if you have brought more than two.

Package Tours or Individual Travel?

During the Soviet era, almost the only way to visit was on a package tour with the Soviet travel agency Intourist. Diatribes against the luxurious lifestyles of Russia's 19th-century aristocrats were interspersed with eulogies on Soviet achievement. Today, most people still visit Russia on tours organized by Intourist, whose guides are now more accurate and informative. In the off-season (from November–March) a weekend break in either Moscow or St Petersburg, or a week-long trip to the two cities can be enticingly cheap. Even if you intend to be independent when you arrive, you may find it cheaper to book a package tour and abandon the group in Russia. A number of independent companies, whose approaches tend to be more idiosyncratic, also conduct tours to Moscow and St Petersburg. The best of them are listed overleaf.

This book was written specifically for those who want to explore the twin capitals of Russia on their own. If you don't speak Russian, it won't always be easy making your own way around on your own. The cyrillic alphabet is less daunting than it at first appears, however, and with the aid of a bilingual metro map you should be able to recognize the names of the stops. Since *glasnost*, travel agents throughout the world have taken advantage of the openness to send independent tourists to stay in new, private hotels, with Russian families and in rented flats. A handful of the most experienced are listed below.

Specialist Travel Agents

In the UK

Intourist, 219 Marsh Wall, London E14 9FJ, ✆ 0171 538 8600. The old Soviet monolith has cranked itself into commercial gear, and due to its contacts and experience offers competitive package deals, from long weekends to escorted trips on the Trans-Siberian Railway. Ask for their inclusive tours department or the department for independent travel. Intourist can only book independent travellers into hotel accommodation; those who are looking for something different will be offered greater choice by the smaller agents.

Regent Holidays, 15 John St., Bristol BS1 2HR, ✆ 0117 921 1711, ✆ 0117 925 4866, are a highly informative and helpful agency, with 20 years' experience throughout the length and breadth of Russia. They are particularly useful for those flying from provincial airports or visiting the other republics of the former Soviet Union as well as Russia. Regent Holidays do not issue invitations and are therefore limited to booking you into hotels to suit your budget and requirements.

One Europe Travel, Research House, Fraser Road, Perivale, Middx UB6 7AQ, ✆ 0181 566 9424, work in tandem with **Campus Travel**, 52 Grosvenor Gardens, London SW1W 0AG, ✆ 0171 730 3402, to provide a network of services for students and other budget travellers. All One Europe's London staff are Russian speakers, and as well as arranging accommodation from as little as £12 a night in Moscow they can also send your mountain climbing in Siberia. Their buddying system, by which you pay $15 a day for a Russian to accompany you on your sightseeing, has proved very popular.

Progressive Tours, 12 Porchester Place, London W2 2BS, ✆ 0171 262 1676, have long specialized in travels to what used to be the Communist bloc. They can organize anything from school trips to personal itineraries, including issuing invitations to those who wish to rent their own accommodation or stay with a Russian family or friend.

Findhorn Ecotravels, The Park, Forres, Morayshire IV36 0TZ, ✆/✇ 01309 690995. For a more personal service, call Liza Hollingshead, something of a fairy godmother to Russian independent travel. She can issue an invitation by fax, fix up accommodation in someone's home, book you into hotels or even rent you a flat in the centre of St Petersburg. She also has experience with school or other exchanges, arranging for the like-minded, from rag-trade businesses to psychosynthesis counsellors, to meet and confer in Russia. Her speciality is ecological exchanges, sending people to spend time in environmental discussion in conservation areas in the Ural Mountains, skiing and walking, and by Lake Baikal.

Room with the Russians, 1–7 Station Chambers, High St. North, London E6, ✆ 0181 472 2694. Placing travellers with like-minded hosts, Room with the Russians can organize stays in both Moscow and St Petersburg, from long weekends to several weeks.

Noble Caledonia Ltd, 11 Charles St., London W1X 7HB, ✆ 0171 491 4752, and **Voyages Jules Verne**, 21 Dorset Square, London NW1 6QG, ✆ 0171 723 5066, are both upmarket tour operators, offering cruises between Moscow and St Petersburg on the inland waterways, passing through the medieval heartland of Russia with its kremlins and churches.

Russlang, 5–6 Fenwick Terrace, Neville's Cross, Durham City, ✆ 0191 386 9578. Over the last two years Irene Slatter and her St Petersburg partner have built up a business teaching Russian to foreigners in St Petersburg and arranging their accommodation with Russian families. They cater for everyone from university students spending a few months in Russia to those taking evening classes who want to stay for a couple of weeks. Food, accommodation and tuition cost around £125 per week, excluding flights.

In the USA

Intourist-USA Inc., Suite 868, 630 5th Ave., New York, NY 10111, ✆ 212 757 3884, runs tours throughout the year and can also book travel arrangements for independent travellers.

Pioneer East-West Initiative, 88 Brooks Ave., Arlington, MA 02174, ✆ 617 648 2020, has been arranging holidays in the ex-Communist bloc for many years.

Home & Host, 2445 Park Ave., Minneapolis, MN 55404, toll free ✆ 800 SOVIET U and the **Russian Travel Service**, P.O. Box 311, Fitzwilliam, NH 03447, ✆/✇ 603 585 6534, both specialize in putting you up with a Russian family for the duration of your stay, though they will also make any other arrangements you may wish.

Best of Russia Cruises, Ed Hogan, Zephyr Press, 13 Robinson St., Somerville, MA 02145, ☎ 617 628 9726, ✉ 776 8246, is the agent for cruises between Moscow and St Petersburg.

In Russia

In the effort to find the cheapest accommodation, you might want to try a number of agencies in Moscow and St Petersburg. Those listed below will all issue you with an invitation for your visa application, arrange accommodation with Russian families and sightseeing programmes.

Moscow

New Solutions, Ul. Volodarskaya 38, ☎ 915 6722.

Vita Agency, Ul. Staraya Basmannaya 15, ☎/✉ 265 4948.

Bed and Breakfast, ☎ 388 9549.

St Petersburg

Host Families Association, Tavricheskaya Ul. 5–25, St Petersburg, ☎ 275 1992, ✉ 332 2688.

Lingva, 7aya Liniya 36, Vasilievsky Ostrov, St Petersburg, ☎ 218 7339. In addition, Lingva can arrange Russian lessons.

Getting Around

Both Moscow and St Petersburg are increasingly badly served by their transport systems, with the shining exception of the metro, which continues to amaze visitors with its efficiency. As the cities get poorer, the number of buses, trams and trolleybuses declines, and those that remain are badly overcrowded. Trying to get onto a bus in the rush hour is worse than a rugby scrum, without a touch of sportsmanship in sight. Foreigners have been reduced to tears by the painful shoving and rudeness. The situation is particularly bad in St Petersburg, where the centre of town is less well served by the metro and you may find yourself trying to use the alternatives. In Moscow, the metro will answer most of your needs.

If you are staying long in either city, consider the advantages of monthly travel passes, which go on sale in the last week of the month in the metro stations and nearby underpasses. They are still very cheap, and mean you don't need to struggle to buy a ticket or token for each journey. A pass for the metro only is called a Проездной на метро (*proyezdnoi na metro*). A pass for all city transport costs more than twice as much and is known as a единие (*yediniy*).

While things on the ground lurch from one pothole to another, the metro systems in Moscow and St Petersburg glide swiftly underground. Russians often ponder the anomaly: if they can be so effective underground and in space, why is their life on earth such a shambles? The Moscow metro alone carries over 8 million passengers a day, more than the London and New York underground systems put together. Not only are they fast, the metros are also architectural and decorative wonders in their own right. One of Stalin's pet projects, their construction destroyed dozens of historic overground buildings, including churches, and replaced them with underground 'People's Palaces'. Marble halls, bronze torchères, mosaics, chandeliers and statues give an impression of an immensely privileged society, quite out of keeping with the insistent crowds of preoccupied and over-burdened citizens who mill beneath them. But the metro stations are more than just a transport system. In winter, when it is below freezing outside, their many benches serve as meeting points for Russians from all over the city. If you have a rendezvous in the metro and there is more than one line at the station, make sure you know at which platform you are supposed to be meeting.

For a tour of the best stations in Moscow, the older of the two systems, you should make sure you visit the bronze statues of Ⓜ Ploshchad Revolutsii, Komsolmoskaya, for its mosaics of the November parade, Mayakovskaya for its striking 1930s simplicity, Kievskaya for its mosaic glorification of the achievements of the Ukraine and Novokuznetskaya for its stern military flavour and circular entrance hall. St Petersburg's metro is deeper than Moscow's, buried way beneath the marsh on which the city is built. Most of its stations are less spectacular than the showpieces of the capital, but Ⓜ Pushkinskaya, on the earliest Kirovsko-Vyborgskaya line, has something of their grandeur. If you get obssessed with the system, there is a Museum of the Metro at Ⓜ Sportivnaya in Moscow.

The metro runs from 5.30am to 1am and can be suffocatingly busy in the rush hour, when trains come every 1–2 minutes. You will recognize the stations by the big Ⓜ lit up in red outside. Before using the metro for the first time, try to buy a dual language metro map from your hotel ooks stall. It is also a good idea to write down your route, in Roman and Cyrillic script, so you know exactly which stations you need to look for as you go. Where two or more lines meet in the Moscow system, the stations have two or more names (except on the circle line). This is not always the case in St Petersburg, and at Ⓜ Tekhnologichesky Institut there are just two platforms for the two lines; one for all northbound, the other for all southbound trains. In this book, you are often told to leave the metro via a particular station and a particular exit. This is because the entrances are often far apart above ground, and you could easily miss the start of the walk.

Moscow Metro

1	Sokolnicheskaya	5	Kaluzhsko-Rizhskaya		Line Under Construction
2	Zamoskvoretskaya	6	Tagansko-Krasnopresnenskaya		Metro Station
3	Arbatsko- Pokrovskaya	7	Kalininskaya		Transfer Station
3a	Filyevskaya	8	Serpukhovsko-Timiryazevskaya		
4	Circular	9	Lyublinskaya		

16

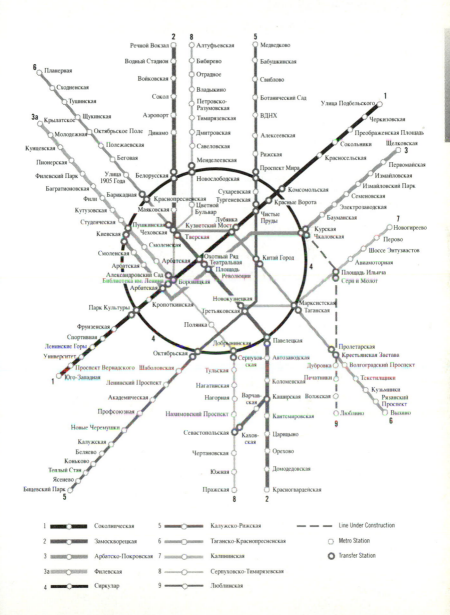

1	━━◯━━	Соколническая	5	━━◯━━	Калужско-Рижская		━ ━ ━ ━	Line Under Construction
2	━━◯━━	Замоскворецкая	6	━━◯━━	Таганско-Краснопресненская		◯	Metro Station
3	━━◯━━	Арбатско-Покровская	7	━━◯━━	Калининская		◉	Transfer Station
3a	━━◯━━	Филевская	8	━━◯━━	Серпуховско-Тимирязевская			
4	━━◯━━	Сиркулар	9	━━◯━━	Люблинская			

St Petersburg Metro

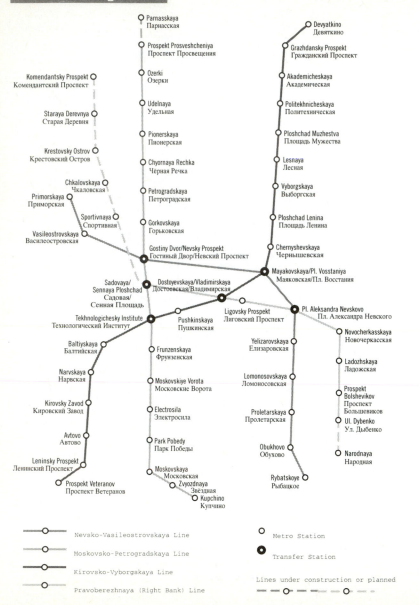

Parnasskaya
Парнасская

Devyatkino
Девяткино

Prospekt Prosveshcheniya
Проспект Просвещения

Grazhdansky Prospekt
Гражданский Проспект

Komendantsky Prospekt
Комендантский Проспект

Ozerki
Озерки

Akademicheskaya
Академическая

Udelnaya
Удельная

Politekhnicheskaya
Политехническая

Staraya Derevnya
Старая Деревня

Pionerskaya
Пионерская

Ploshchad Muzhestva
Площадь Мужества

Krestovsky Ostrov
Крестовский Остров

Chyornaya Rechka
Чёрная Речка

Lesnaya
Лесная

Chkalovskaya
Чкаловская

Petrogradskaya
Петроградская

Vyborgskaya
Выборгская

Primorskaya
Приморская

Sportivnaya
Спортивная

Gorkovskaya
Горьковская

Ploshchad Lenina
Площадь Ленина

Vasileostrovskaya
Василеостровская

Gostiny Dvor/Nevsky Prospekt
Гостиный Двор/Невский Проспект

Chernyshevskaya
Чернышевская

Sadovaya/
Sennaya Ploshchad
Садовая/
Сенная Площадь

Dostoyevskaya/Vladimirskaya
Достоевская/Владимирская

Mayakovskaya/Pl. Vosstaniya
Маяковская/Пл. Восстания

Tekhnologichesky Institute
Технологический Институт

Pushkinskaya
Пушкинская

Ligovsky Prospekt
Лиговский Проспект

Pl. Aleksandra Nevskovo
Пл. Александра Невского

Baltiyskaya
Балтийская

Frunzenskaya
Фрунзенская

Yelizarovskaya
Елизаровская

Novocherkasskaya
Новочеркасская

Narvskaya
Нарвская

Moskovskiye Vorota
Московские Ворота

Lomonosovskaya
Ломоносовская

Ladozhskaya
Ладожская

Kirovsky Zavod
Кировский Завод

Electrosila
Электросила

Proletarskaya
Пролетарская

Prospekt
Bolshevikov
Проспект
Большевиков

Avtovo
Автово

Park Pobedy
Парк Победы

Obukhovo
Обухово

Ul. Dybenko
Ул. Дыбенко

Leninsky Prospekt
Ленинский Проспект

Moskovskaya
Московская

Rybatskoye
Рыбацкое

Narodnaya
Народная

Prospekt Veteranov
Проспект Ветеранов

Zvyozdnaya
Звёздная

Kupchino
Купчино

Nevsko-Vasileostrovskaya Line

Metro Station

Moskovsko-Petrogradskaya Line

Transfer Station

Kirovsko-Vyborgskaya Line

Pravoberezhnaya (Right Bank) Line

Lines under construction or planned

If you do not have a pass, to enter the system you must buy a token (*zheton*—жэтон) from the ticket desk (касса) inside, insert it in the turnstile, and walk through the gap to the left when the light goes green. However far you travel, you pay just the flat fare. If you don't insert a token, a gate will shut painfully on your knees. If you have a pass, show it to the inspector at the end of the turnstiles. There are no maps on the platforms, so if you haven't got a map on you, you should check one before getting on the escalator or once you are in the train.

Both systems use only Cyrillic, so this is where your facility with the alphabet will be tested. As you step off the long, steep escalator, signs list the stations served by each platform. The caretaker at the bottom will help if you can't find your station. Once in the train there are few signs to tell you which station you are pulling into, so be careful to count the stops, or listen to the announcements as you arrive. As the train is about to leave, you will be politely informed to watch out, the doors are closing, and then told the name of the next station. The announcement goes like this: '*Ostorozhno, dveri zakrivayutsya! Sleduyushchaya stantsiya...*'. When you need to change lines, look for signs on the platform, often accompanied by a blue stick man running up stairs, saying переход на станцию...—*perekhod na stantsiyu...* (change to station...) or переход на...линию—*perekhod na... liniyu* (change to line...) followed by a list of stations. Scour the black Cyrillic for something that looks like yours. Some intersections have as many as four lines. If you have arrived at your destination, and are asked to leave by the twin station, you will have to use a *perekhod* again. Otherwise look for the sign saying Выход в город (*vwykhod v gorod*) which means 'exit to the city'. If there is more than one, they will give you a list of the streets served by each exit.

By Bus, Trolleybus and Tram

Stops for buses and trolleybuses are signalled by an A (for *avtobus*) and a T (for *trolleybus*) respectively, with the numbers of the routes marked beneath. Signs indicating tram stops hang from wires over the tramlines in the middle of the road.

If you haven't got a ticket, get on at the front as you need to buy some from the driver. Look for a red sign near the door or behind the driver; it will show the current cost of a single ride. The larger number below is the size of fine you will be asked to pay if you don't have a stamped ticket when an inspector comes round. Hand a note well over ten times the price of a ride to the driver (for some reason 10 tickets cost more than ten times the cost of a ride!), or get your fellow passengers to pass it all the way down if the vehicle is crowded. Amazingly, within a stop or two a strip of 10 flimsy tickets will arrive back in your hand with your change. Tear off one ticket and stamp it in one of the simple machines distributed on the wall throughout the bus, or again pass it to someone nearer who will do it for you. If you have a large piece of baggage you are expected to stamp a ticket for it too.

Getting out of a crowded vehicle has its own etiquette. Those behind you who want to leave will politely ask you if you are getting off '*Vwy vwykhoditye?*', and if they suspect you are not they will begin to push past. Many is the time you get swept off, only to have to fight to get back on the bus again.

By Train

Trains seving nearby destinations, such as those in the day trip chapters, are known as *elektrichkas*. They always leave from the part of the station known as the suburban hall (**Прыгородный зал**—*prigorodny zal*), which has its own busy ticket office. Queue up, state your destination and ask for a return ticket by adding '*tudá i abrátna*'. Write down the station's name and the words for return (*see* p.574) if you don't feel confident of speaking. Fares are still extremely low.

Getting onto the right train requires further ingenuity. You will find a chronological list of departures, identified by the station at which they terminbate and nearby a schematic map of all destinations. Get on any train which ends further down the line from your station, first checking that it will stop for you. There should be a column listing which stations the train stops at. Otherwise, before getting on board ask the driver or a number of your fellow passengers. They will happily shoo you off if you are about to make a mistake.

By Road

taxis

Official Moscow and St Petersburg taxis are normally beige or black with a chequered pattern sprayed on their doors. When you put your hand out to stop one, you may find ordinary citizens pulling over trying to make a bit of extra cash on the side. If the driver is alone, these moonlighters are usually quite safe, though you should use your common sense and get out the moment you feel uneasy. Tell them, or show them where you are going, and settle a price before you get in. For a journey in the centre of either town, you are doing well to pay under US $5.

If you are staying in an hotel, they will be able to organize a car for you. To order a cab to your door if you are living in a flat, in Moscow phone ✆ 927 0000 at least an hour in advance. In St Petersburg the number is ✆ 312 0022.

car hire

Given the availability of taxis it is unnecessary, not to say reckless, to drive in either of these cities, but if you are planning a complicated day trip you may decide to do so. Most of the car-hire firms listed below offer cars with or without drivers. Think carefully about whether a driver wouldn't make the trip more relaxing. To drive yourself, you must be over 21 and will need an international driving licence. You should keep your passport and visa with you at all times (and a wad of small denomination US$ bills for the traffic police, GAI). The rental firm will provide you with insurance. They will also brief you on the Russian highway code. What they probably won't tell you is that the other road users will be more unpredictable than any you may have encountered anywhere else. Never leave anything inside your car—not even a packet of fags—when you park, and remove the radio cassette and windscreen wipers, or you may have to buy new ones. Be careful.

Although they tend to be more expensive, it is well worth hiring a well-serviced car from a reputable company, such as those recommended by the major hotels. There is almost nothing on offer for less than US$60 a day. In Moscow try calling Avis, ☏ 930 1323 or 578 5646; Europcar, ☏ 253 2477, 971 6101 or 923 9749; MTDS-Hertz on 448 6728 or 578 7532. The best companies in St Petersburg are InNis at the Astoria Hotel, ☏ 210 5858 or Interavto-Hertz, bookable through the Grand Hotel Europe or the Moskva Hotel or on 277 4032.

It is useful to bear in mind that a number of petrol stations in each city sell fuel by credit card; few Russians have one, so there should be no long queues. In Moscow, visit Agip, Leningradsky Prospekt 61, and in St Petersburg, Moskovsky Prospekt 100.

bridges in St Petersburg

When the Neva is not frozen, St Petersburg's bridges all open for 2–3 hours in the middle of the night, allowing boats to enter and leave the system of rivers and canals which runs to Moscow and beyond. To Petersburgers, evenings either finish before the bridges go up or after they have closed again—normally the latter. Details of opening times of bridges are listed on p.526.

Travelling Between Moscow and St Petersburg

A busy schedule of Aeroflot and other flights connects Moscow's Domodedovo airport and Pulkovo-1 in St Petersburg (*see* p.7 for airline telephone numbers), and Aeroflot's internal safety reputation is improving. Overnight trains between the two cities are much more popular, however. The romance of speeding through the birch-forested countryside, with snow up to the window level or a barely darkening summer's sky, is accompanied by hot tea provided by the attendant, the *provodnik*. Sharing food is an important part of Russian travel, not to mention sharing vodka.

To book tickets for the train, either ask the service desk in your hotel to help, or set off early in the morning to beat the crowds and do it yourself. In Moscow, foreigners can buy tickets in advance, if they have their passports and visas with them, from the central ticket office at Ul. Griboyedova 6, Bldg 1, Ⓜ Krasniye Vorota (*open 8am–7pm, closed 1–2pm*). On the day, you should head for Ul. Krasnoprudnaya 1 (Ⓜ Komsomolskaya), just by the Leningradsky Vokzal. The station itself also has a tourist desk, No. 21 on the first floor. This is open 24-hours; knock loudly at night. In St Petersburg the central ticket office is at Naberezhnaya Kanal Griboyedova, across the canal from the Kazan Cathedral (Ⓜ Nevsky Prospekt). Turn right inside, and right again where it says Интурист. Up the stairs, you can buy tickets at booths No. 103 and 104. At Moskovsky Vokzal (from where the trains depart) there is a tourist desk, No. 23, off the main hall, near the sculpture of Peter the Great (*open 8am–8pm*). You will have to choose between two-berth first class compartments, known either as S.V. (pronounced *S Vay*) or *luxe* (as the French would pronounce it), or four-berth second class, known as *koopeyny*. Luxe is over four times the price of a *koopeyny*. In both, you will have to pay extra for bedding.

Several trains (the best ones are Nos. 1–6) leave both cities between 11pm and 1am, all arriving between 7am and 9am. To catch them head for Leningradsky Vokzal in Moscow (Ⓜ Komsomolskaya), and Moskovsky Vokzal in St Petersburg (Ⓜ Ploshchad Vosstaniya). There is also a new service known as the Commercial Train (Nos. 35/36). It costs more than twice as much as the others, but tickets are more readily available and can be bought from the stations themselves.

Recently, there has been a spate of apocryphal stories about robberies on the overnight trains. You could bring a long chain and padlock to add security to the door locks, though I have never had any problems. Sleep with your money and passport under your pillow, and keep your luggage under the bottom beds. A far greater threat to lone women are the unwanted attentions of drunk Russian men, and many foreign residents will not make the journey unchaperoned. Two women together should think seriously about travelling in 1st Class, since they will then have the compartment to themselves. For women alone, a four-berth compartment is probably safer than a *luxe* two-berther.

Practical A–Z

"VALIANKI"

Addresses

Finding Russians who have given you their address can be quite an ordeal. A typical set of instructions might read: Kutuzovsky Prospekt 7, korp. or stroeniye 2, kv.106. Code 274. Decoded, this means you are looking for house (*dom*) No. 7 on Kutuzovsky Prospekt, which somewhere has a second (and quite possibly a third and fourth) corpus or building (*korpus* or *stroeniye*). The flat (*krartira*) number is 106, and to get in through the main door to the block you need to press buttons 274 in succession on the entry keypad. Happy hunting!

Climate and When to Go

Both Moscow and St Petersburg suffer cold, snowy winters from November to March. Spring is short and miraculous. Within days the bare skeletons of the trees are covered with long-awaited greenery and the parks are full of picnicking groups. Only the unwise venture out in summer without a telescopic umbrella in their bag for, in Moscow particularly, bright sunshine can suddenly be interrupted by half an hour of heavy rain. It's a blessing in disguise, for when it is hot in Moscow the dust and urban pollution can make the city hard to bear. The chill of autumn makes itself felt from late August, and the golden trees are at their best in late September. While your mobility will be restricted in winter by the temperature, it is an exhilarating, dry cold, providing you are well clothed Bright blue skies and sparkling snow make it a romantic time to see the cities. The only times of the year when the weather can be miserable are November and December, and late March to early April, when a mixture of snow and thaw turns the pavements either into skating rinks or a succession of elephantine puddles.

Coastal St Petersburg has a less extreme climate than land-locked Moscow. It is both cooler in summer and warmer in winter. Bear in mind that, because of the city's northerly latitude, the number of daylight hours is limited between November and January. Conversely, around the summer solstice in mid-June, the 'White Nights' take place. Even at 3am it isn't truly dark, and for a number of weeks the city never sleeps. Even pensioners take a midnight stroll down to the Neva, while the city's younger generations sing, drink and dance for days and nights on end.

Crime and the Police

A near-hysterical campaign by the western press has tried its best to kill Russian tourism with stories of theft and mugging in both Moscow and St Petersburg. The truth is that Russians used to be too frightened to prey on tourists but now, like in any other democracy, they aren't. Things are little worse than in most capital cities in Europe, and certainly not as dangerous as in Rome, Seville or New York, for example. Unless you are intent on business, the closest you will come to the Russian mafia, if you are unlucky, is to sit near a table of them at a restaurant. After ten months living in both cities, I haven't a single personal scare story to offer. A few particular observations and guidelines will help you to have an equally hassle-free stay.

As an obvious foreigner, you will be assumed to have money about your person. Dress inconspicuously and don't wear flashing jewellery or chunky, expensive watches. Leave them and other unnecessary valuables, like your passport and ticket, in the hotel safe. Always be aware of where your valuables are (if possible in a zip-up pocket). On Nevsky Prospekt in St Petersburg and around Red Square in Moscow swarms of gypsy children use all manner of diversions to distract you while they pick your pockets and bag. It is easy to prevent them by choosing a safe place to carry money, travellers' cheques and credit cards, and keeping a firm hand on your camera and the opening of your bag.

If you are flagging down a taxi or private car for a lift, never get into one which already has anyone apart from the driver in it. If you are staying with friends, never give your full address or your telephone number to strangers. A taxi driver does not need to know the flat number, and it is easy to find out the address of a telephone number through directory enquiries.

Except during the 'White Nights' in St Petersburg, don't walk around late at night on your own. It is safe (women alone *see* p.25) to use the metro to get back to your bed at night, depending on how far you have to walk at the other end. If you are unlucky enough to get mugged, don't resist. The gun is probably real as they are very easy to get hold of. You are asking for trouble by straying into areas of organized criminal activity such as prostitution and drugs. While prostitutes picked up in your hotel may be safe, there are so many stories of punters being drugged and robbed that you should be aware of the risk.

Russia is now thought to be the major route to Europe for opiates from the Golden Triangle in Southeast Asia, and the central Asian republics keep the ex-Soviet Union self-sufficient in marijuana. It isn't easy to find out where to get them, and if you do you'll find yourself in a violent sub-culture. Don't do it.

The police (*militsia*) wear a grey uniform with red epaulettes and cap band. Their vehicles are either strident navy blue and white, or a rather insipid yellow and light blue. If you are robbed you will need a statement from them if you intend to claim on your insurance. Ask the hotel staff or your Russian host which police station to go to, and get a Russian speaker to come with you.

Electricity

Most of Russia's national grid is 220v, accessed by round two-pin plugs. The only exception to this is in some parts of the centre of Moscow, which still have a 110v power supply. If you are in central Moscow, always ask before you plug an appliance in. Be sure to bring whatever adapters and convertors you will need, as they may be hard to track down in Russia.

Embassies and Consulates

Foreign embassies are based in Moscow, but in the last couple of years many countries (but not all) have set up consulates in St Petersburg. If you don't seem to be represented yet, call your embassy in Moscow (code 8–095). You may find they already have a representative in the city, living in a hotel while waiting to move into an office.

Moscow Embassies

Australia, Kropotkinsky Pereulok 13, © 956 6070/6162/6152

Canada, Starokonushenny Pereulok 23, © 241 1111

Finland, Kropotkinsky Pereulok 15/17, © 230 2143 or 246 4027

Ireland, Grokholsky Pereulok 5, © 288 4101

Netherlands, Kalashny Pereulok 6, © 291 2954/2976

New Zealand, Ul. Povarskaya 44, © 290 1277

Norway, Ul. Povarskaya 7, © 290 3872

Sweden, Mosfilmovskaya Ul. 60, © 956 1200

United Kingdom, Sofiiskaya Naberezhnaya 14, © 230 6333

United States, Novinsky Bulvar 19/23, © 252 2451

St Petersburg Consulates

Finland, Ul. Chaikovskovo 71, © 273 7321

Netherlands, Prospekt Engelsa 101, © 554 4900

Sweden, Decyataya Liniya 11, © 213 4191 or 218 3526

United Kingdom, Ploshchad Proletarskoy Diktatury 5, © 119 6036

United States, Ul. Furshtadskaya 15, © 274 8689/8568

Gay Scene

A fragile sense of identity among Russia's male gay community was fostered by the campaign to repeal Article 121 of the penal code in the early 1990s. Under the code homosexuality, even between consenting adults, was punishable by up to five years in prison. In 1993 the campaign succeeded, and since then homosexuals have been quietly celebrating, though prejudice from their heterosexual compatriots is near universal and often violent. However, many leading figures in the artistic world in both Moscow and St Petersburg are coming out, and at the cities' more arty clubs you will find some wonderfully camp characters, as well as transvestites. Gay clubs and gay nights are well-established in Moscow and growing in St Petersburg.

Lesbians are much less conspicuous. The imported word *lesbianka* is used to describe them, and Russians tend to react as if the concept itself is some alien import. The Russian feminist movement has never had a radical, lesbian-feminist wing, and even leading feminists will tell you that lesbianism does not exist.

Health and Emergencies

Fire:	✆ 01
Police:	✆ 02
Ambulance:	✆ 03

You are unlikely to contract anything more than a bout of mild diarrhoea during your stay in Moscow and St Petersburg, but it is vital that you bear a few basic rules in mind. Foreigners travelling to Moscow and St Petersburg are currently advised to be vaccinated against diptheria, outbreaks of which have been recorded in both cities. There have also been cases of cholera.

On 11 Nov 1994 the lower house (*duma*) passed a law requiring all foreigners to test negative in an HIV test before being allowed into the country. The law has not yet been ratified and vociferous opposition to it continues.

Do not drink tap water in St Petersburg. Until recently, it was thought that water boiled for 10 minutes and left to stand for a day was safe, but now even that causes upset stomachs. The water supply, worsened by the combined flood control dam/road which has been half built across the Gulf of Finland, is alive with the virulent bacteria *giardia*. This will cause severe diarrhoea, the only cure for which is a course of specific antibiotics. Consult a doctor if you think you may be infected. In Moscow, you can drink boiled tap water, though it tastes pretty vile, and drinking bottled mineral water is undoubtedly more pleasant.

It goes without saying that you should bring any prescription or other medicines which you need with you. Previously unavailable 'luxuries', such as tampons, are now for sale in most hotels, all foreign supermarkets and most Russian pharmacies as well. I even saw a packet for sale in the lobby of the Hermitage Museum in St Petersburg! All of the medical clinics listed below have pharmacies attached, where a wide range of western drugs are available. It is useful to know the generic name for any drugs you use regularly (such as the contraceptive pill), as they go under different brand names in different countries. If you happen to go to a German-backed clinic therefore, they will be able to prescribe an equivalent drug.

Most hotels have a doctor on call at all times. If you are not staying in a hotel, or have any doubts about your treatment, ring one of the highly professional clinics listed below. Most can arrange air evacuation in the event of an emergency, or will book you into the best equipped Russian hospitals, which used to be reserved for higher Party functionaries only. None of this comes cheap. Without an appropriate insurance policy, your pocket will suffer horrendously.

Moscow

Medical Clinics

American Medical Centre, 2nd Tverskoy Yamskoy Pereulok. 10, ✆ 956 3366. A gleaming family practice, with a 24-hour emergency service, diagnostic services, a relationship with the exclusive Kremlin hospital, a pharmacy and plenty of experience in medical evacuation, this is the place to come with ailments, if your medical insurance is in order.

European Medical Centre, Gruzinsky Pereulok 3, ✆ 253 0703 (after hours and weekends ✆ 229 6536), is every bit as competent as the American Medical Centre. The doctors are French however, so you may simply find it easier to communicate with an English-speaker. Lab services and a pharmacy are available, as well as evacuation services should you need them.

Dental Clinics

Pullman Iris Hotel, Korovinskoye Shossé 10, ✆ 488 8279, is on the outskirts of town but boasts a dental clinic second to none in the city.

American Medical Centre, *see* above, also offers dental services.

Most convenient of all is **Medical Interline**, a modern, well-equipped dental clinic in the Intourist Hotel, Ul. Tverskaya 5, room 2039, ✆ 956 8493.

Oculists and Opticians

Optic Moscow, Ul. Arbat 30, Bldg 2, ✆ 241 1577, offers eye tests, glasses, contact lenses and all the associated paraphernalia.

Sana Medical Centre, Ul. Nizhnaya Pervomaiskaya 65, ✆ 464 1254, has an optician on its staff. They also make up glasses, and have a good selection of frames.

Chemists

Stary Arbat Pharmacy, Ul. Arbat 25, ✆ 291 7101, sells a wide variety of western drugs, though if you are prescribed them by a doctor in Moscow you will probably get them through one of the clinics above.

St Petersburg

Medical Clinics

American Medical Centre, Naberezhnaya Reki Fontanki 77, ✆ 119 6101 (*see* Moscow).

Medical Centre for Foreigners at Polyclinic No. 2, Moskovsky Prospekt 22, ✆ 316 6272, 110 1102 or 292 6274, has been used by St Petersburg's most privileged citizens and, until the invasion of foreign medical centres, by diplomats and tourists as well. Independent of the state system, it is now private and equipped to near western standards, with disposable syringes, modern X-ray machines etc.

Homeopathic Clinic, Ul. Prazhskaya 12, ✆ 269 5813. Most Russians take a variety of herbal cures and homeopathic medicines as a matter of course. Partly due to a lack of availability of many drugs commonly available in the West, the Russians may yet have the last laugh when we turn out to have unleashed a Pandora's box of uncontrollable viruses by our overuse of drugs. If you want to give the natural way a try, you can't do better than this, the oldest homeopathic clinic in the country. It claims to be 10 times cheaper than similar treatment in the West.

Dental Clinics

Nordmed, Tverskaya Ul. 12/15, ✆ 110 0654 (after hours ✆ 110 0401) is said to be the best private dental clinic in the city.

Polyclinic No. 2, *see* above, also offers a modern, Finnish-equipped dental clinic.

Oculists and Opticians

Visor, Lityeiny Prospekt 30, ✆ 272 7517, is an Anglo-Russian joint venture providing glasses and contact lense. It is closed at weekends.

Vision Express, Ul. Lomonosova 5, ✆ 310 1595, also British-Russian, providing the same services.

Chemists

Damian Pharmacy, Moskovsky Prospekt 22, ✆ 110 1744, is attached to Polyclinic No. 2, and fully stocked with western drugs.

newspapers

The best place to find newspapers from home is in the cities' main hotels, or at central *Troyka Press* kiosks on the street. The free *Moscow Times* (Mon–Sat) and its periodical magazines keep Moscow's English-speaking community in touch with what is going on, from the Russian parliament to the American major league baseball season. It's a strange hybrid, but a good place to read reviews of new restaurants and shows. Unless you have the patience and language skills to plough your way through *Dosug v Moskve* (*Leisure in Moscow*), which goes on sale at kiosks around the city on Friday morning, the Friday and Saturday listings in the *Moscow Times* are the best way of planning your theatre, film and concert-going. The *Moscow Times* is also available at hotels and selected shops in St Petersburg. Otherwise, the English language press in the city offers a scintillating choice between the *Neva News* and the *St Petersburg Press*, both of which used to stoop to headlines such as 'Mr Schwarz is looking for partners'. The *St Petersburg Press* has recently taken a turn for the better.

television

There are six TV channels in Moscow and five in St Petersburg. Channel 1, broadcast from Ostankino, reaches much of the former Soviet Union, while the *Rossiya* channel (2 in Moscow, 3 in St Petersburg) carries sport and news as well as dubbed American and Mexican soaps. Channel 4 is partly occupied by educational programmes, while Channel 6 in Moscow carries voiced-over CNN news. Most hotels and many bars and cafés subscribe to a cable network, offering CNN, the BBC, or more popularly MTV and Sky.

radio

Moscow's airwaves bristle with the English-language. From about 7am–10am Radio Maximum (103.7 FM) broadcasts news, reviews, business updates and consumer spots for English-speaking Muscovites. Open Radio (918 AM) alternates between the BBC World Service and Voice of America. St Petersburg's radio is almost exclusively Russian-language (except for the BBC World Service on 1260kHz/238m, but shares some good FM music stations with Moscow. Try Europa Plus (69.8 FM in Moscow; 100.5 FM in St Petersburg) or Radio Rox (103.0 FM in Moscow; 102.0 FM in St Petersburg).

Money and Banks

local currency

The rouble became Russia's national currency in 1534. Since the time of Peter the Great it has been divided into 100 kopeks. In these days of desperate inflation the rouble is known derisively as 'wooden' money, since it has as good as no metallic or real value. What the Russians now value is *kapusta* (cabbage), the slang for US dollars. For several years, dollars worked as an alternative currency, but since 1 January 1994 all transactions in Russia must, legally, be carried out in roubles.

The highest denomination rouble note currently in circulation is the 50,000. All the old Soviet notes, the largest of which was 100 roubles, have been replaced by coins and are no longer legal tender. Nor are 1000 rouble notes with Lenin on them, or pre-1993 5000 and 10,000 rouble notes. Since the beginning of another bout of inflation in October 1994, it is impossible to say at what rate the rouble will steady again on the foreign exchange. Any indication of prices in this book is made in dollars, to save it from the worst excesses of rouble inflation, even though almost all transactions in Russia must be carried out in roubles.

what money to take

The easiest currency to exchange—in banks, at kiosks on the street, in exchange bureaux, with friends—are US dollar bills. Low denominations ($1 and $5) are still useful for paying taxi drivers, for tips and for minor wheel-oiling, though you should be discreet when using them. Make sure your bills are in pristine condition. There have been a lot of forged dollar bills in circulation, so everyone is very wary, and if they doubt the authenticity of a bill they just won't accept it, even if it is your last. Remember always to take your passport, visa and your customs form with you when changing money in any form. Always change money at an exchange bureau, of which there are hundreds in each city. Don't be tempted by anyone loitering nearby offering a better rate. They *will* rip you off, probably in a big way, by sleight of hand. Hotel exchange bureaux and some banks will change travellers' cheques for roubles and dollars. You can also use major credit cards in smart hotels, restaurants and shops (take your passport), but never rely on it. You should always have enough cash on you to cover your expenditure. For enquiries about where to cash your cheques or report your lost credit card, ring:

American Express: Ul. Sadovo-Kudrinskaya 21a, ✆ 956 9000/1 in Moscow, or their office in the Grand Hotel Europe, Ul. Mikhailovskaya 1/7 in St Petersburg, ✆ 315 7487.

Eurocard/Mastercard: ✆ 284 4794 in Moscow and 312 6012 in St Petersburg.

Visa: ✆ 284 4802 in Moscow and 312 6012 in St Petersburg.

Museums and other Opening Hours

Museum opening hours are infinitely variable, and are specifically quoted in the text of this guide. The only generalizations are that they are often closed on

Mondays (or Tuesdays), and that most stick to the tradition of a *sanitarny dyen* (a 'hygiene' day) once a month, usually in the first or last week of the month.

Shops in Russia tend to stay open late, until 8 or 9pm. They are almost invariably closed on Sundays except for the western-style supermarkets, most of which are open seven days a week.

National Holidays and Festivals

With the death of the Soviet Union, which loved to celebrate milestones in the Communist year with national holidays and vast parades, the holiday situation has become rather confused. Die-hard Communists and those yearning for the stability of the old days still turn out on 7 November, the anniversary of the Bolshevik Revolution, which is still treated as a day off work by all. New holidays have been added, commemorating the historic events of *perestroika*, and old holidays have transmuted into their pre-Revolutionary form. The last few years have also seen the reinstatement of the main religious holidays as national holidays. If you are here for Russian Easter or Christmas, go to one of the all night services which start at midnight and go on until the small hours. At Easter the miracle of Christ's resurrection is celebrated each year by the lighting of a multitude of candles and the incantation 'Christ is risen!', (*khristos voskres*) to which the reply is 'Truly He is Risen!' (*voistinu voskres*).

The only regular festival which impinges on tourists is St Petersburg's White Nights (*Byeliye Nochi*) when the long hours of daylight bewitch the city into all-night revels. Pop-concerts on Palace Square and musical events of all sorts on Yelagin Island punctuate the drinking and dancing which accompanies the raising of the bridges across the Neva in the early morning.

National Holidays

New Year	31 December–1 January
International Women's Day	8 March
Spring Festival (formerly International Labour Day)	1 May
Victory in Europe Day (celebrating end of Second World War)	9 May
Russian Independence Day (1991)	12 June
National Holiday (commemorating restitution of Russian flag in 1991)	22 August
Holiday (formerly anniversary of revolution)	7–8 November

Main Religious Holidays

Russian Orthodox Christmas	6–7 January
Russian Easter	March/April

Festivals

White Nights Festival in St Petersburg   *c.* 21 June–11 July

Packing

It never gets very hot in either Moscow or St Petersburg, so even if you are coming at the height of summer bring a jersey or coat for the evening. A light mackintosh and a telescopic umbrella are also useful to combat the summer showers. In winter, with temperatures dropping as low as −20°C, you need warm clothing, including gloves, a hat, a scarf and thermal underwear. Since Russian interiors, including museums, are very well heated, it is best to dress with plenty of layers so that you can take off as many as you need to make yourself comfortable.

At all times of the year except the summer, the most important item in your Russian wardrobe will be a good pair of boots. Not only should they be warm for the winter, they must also have good grips so that you have a chance of standing upright on the icy pavements. In early spring and late autumn, it is vital that they are waterproof too, since puddles of thawing snow reach gigantic proportions and are often unavoidable. Most boots fail this test on one count or another, but perseverence in finding the right pair will pay rich rewards in warm dry feet.

In Moscow you can probably find anything you might want, but you don't want to spend your holiday shopping for the mundane. Obviously, you should bring everything you think you may need, including your own toiletries and photographic supplies. A miscellany of things you may find particularly useful in Russia include a plug for the basin, which isn't always supplied, some laundry detergent to do your own washing, a torch for badly lit streets and stairwells, toilet paper and insect repellent to fight off vicious mosquitoes. They seem to breed all through the year, in the basements of Moscow and St Petersburg apartment blocks, in water leaking from age-old heating systems, and are particularly virulent in summer and autumn. If you go out in the countryside at this time of year, you will not be able to avoid them.

The Russians are great present givers, so if you are going to be making friends think about packing some gifts that are redolent of home. Things like tights, which used to make great presents, are now easy to get hold of in Russia, so you will need to be rather more imaginative. Think in terms of tapes (not CDs) of quintessentially English/Scottish/American music, good picture books showing your native land, curiosities like Edinburgh Rock, or books of native poetry for those who speak

English. If you know people well enough, and winter is drawing in, a good supply of multi-vitamins and minerals is always pounced upon.

Photography

Flash photography is often forbidden in museums and churches, although they don't object to people using fast film and natural light. It is best to bring your equipment with you but both slide and print film, VHS cassettes and, to a lesser extent, Super-8 cassettes can be bought in hotel shops and in the shops listed in the Useful Addresses section of **Living and Working in Moscow and St Petersburg** (*see* pp.562–4).

Post Offices

The main post offices (*Glavpochtamt*) in Moscow and St Petersburg are open 9am–9pm with shorter hours on Sundays. They are at Ul. Myasnitskaya 26 in Moscow (Ⓜ Turgenevskaya/Chisty Prudy), and Pochtamskaya Ul. 9 (Ⓜ Nevsky Prospekt) in St Petersburg.

Russia's postal service is appalling. Incoming mail from abroad is often waylaid, opened for any valuables and dumped in ponds near the airport. Outgoing post takes weeks, and even that sometimes goes astray, though postcards are generally reliable. If you are in Russia for long, follow the example of the locals and give your post to someone travelling to the West, so they can post it there. If you can't find anyone and your package or letter is vital, think about using a courier company, or faxing it. There are fax services at both main post offices and in the hotel service bureaux (*see* telephones below). Call the following numbers for information about courier services:

> **DHL**: Moscow ✆ 956 1000; St Petersburg ✆ 311 2649 or 210 7654.

> **UPS**: Moscow ✆ 430 6373/6398; St Petersburg ✆ 312 2915 or ✆ 275 4405.

The queues in post offices are enough to put most people off tackling them, especially as you can normally buy stamps for postcards in your hotel. If you want to send a parcel however, you will have to go there, with the package open so that they can fill out the customs forms and pack it for you.

Religious Services

The 'when in Rome' principle works particularly well in Russia, since the services of the Russian Orthodox Church, with their moving chants, elaborate vestments and opening and closing of doors in the iconostasis, are a spectacular mystery. If you choose well, the packed, standing congregation will be overlooked by icons of transcendent beauty, the faces of all illuminated by a thousand candles (*see* introduction to each city for best working churches). For those with a greater interest in Orthodoxy, services are conducted in English every Sunday at 10am at the Danilovsky Monastery in Moscow (℃ 248 2903), by representatives of the Orthodox Church in America (Ⓜ Tulskaya).

If you want to go to your own church during your stay, call these numbers to find out where and when services are held:

Moscow

Catholic Chaplaincy, Kutuzovsky Prospekt 7/4, Bldg 5, Apt. 42, ℃ 243 9621.

St Andrew's Anglican Church, Ul. Stankevicha 8/9, ℃ 143 3562, recently graced by Her Majesty.

Protestant Chaplaincy, UPDK Hall, Ul. Ulofa Palme 5, Bldg. 2, ℃ 143 3562.

Jewish Choral Synagogue, Ul. Arkhipova 8, ℃ 923 9697.

St Petersburg

Catholic Church, Kovensky Pereulok 7, ℃ 272 5002.

Lutheran Church, Bol. Konynshennaya Ul. 8, ℃ 314 0848.

Jewish Synagogue, Lermontovsky Prospect 2, ℃ 114 1153.

Telephones

Pay phones rarely work and either need a coin you can't lay your hands on or a metro *zheton*. If, in a moment of rare synchronicity, a working phone coincides with the right coin, place the coin in the slot above before you dial. It will drop automatically when someone answers. To phone someone in another city in Russia, you need to be in a booth marked mezhdugorodny (междугородий).

The cheapest way of calling abroad is by local phone. You can now dial direct from both cities, by dialling 8, waiting for a change in the tone, then 10, then the country code and the telephone number. Country codes are as follows:

Australia:	61
Canada:	1
Finland:	358
Holland:	31
Ireland:	353
New Zealand:	055
Norway:	47

Sweden:	46
United Kingdom:	44
USA:	1

If you have trouble getting through from St Petersburg, the number for the international operator, many of whom speak English, is ✆ 315 0012. They will book a call for you, and will ask for your name and number, and the number you want to call. Ask them to make the call as soon as possible, but if they give you an unearthly hour in the morning ask for something more reasonable. Bear in mind the time difference (*see* below) as well. They will happily ring you back and tell you how much your call cost if you ask.

If you don't have access to a private phone, but can't afford the more expensive options on offer below, you will have to face a considerable wait at the Central Telephone and Telegraph Office. This is at Ul. Tverskaya 7 in Moscow, and Ul. Gertsena 3–5 in St Petersburg, both very central. In St Petersburg you pay in advance for the length of call you have specified, but in Moscow there are direct-dial phones you can use.

Hotel telephone charges are astronomical, whether you go through the reception desk or use the Business Centre. Always check the rates before you call, as there is nothing more deflating after a phone call home than to be faced by a bill that makes you feel you have been taken for a ride. Both Business Centres and the Central Telephone and Telegraph Offices listed above will send faxes for you. The difference in the price is considerable.

Time

Moscow and St Petersburg keep the same time, 3 hours ahead of Greenwich Mean Time and 11 hours ahead of Eastern Standard Time. Since the clocks go forward and back at around the same time as in the UK (last Saturday of March and last Saturday of October), they remain 3 hours ahead for most of the summer as well.

Tipping

Everybody loves a tip, but the practice is by no means obligatory. A lot of the time you will be charged over the odds for the service in question (*e.g.* in taxis) so don't even think of tipping. In restaurants good service should be rewarded as a much-needed incentive, since it is in such short supply. Some restaurants have started adding a service charge, so check before deciding on the size of your tip.

Toilets

Russian public conveniences are not for the faint-hearted, though Moscow's mayor has pledged to renovate them in time for the city's 850th anniversary in 1997. Most have recently been privatized (some have even been turned into shops) and conditions are marginally better than they used to be, with a whiff of detergent in the air. You pay as you enter and will be given some toilet paper, though it is safest to keep some with you at all times. Even smart restaurants sometimes run out.

If you are choosy, use the toilets in the smart hotels in the centre of each city.

Tourist Information and Tours

There is no such thing as a tourist information booth in either Moscow or St Petersburg. The closest thing, the Intourist office in Moscow at Ul. Mokhovaya 13, and the offices of the St Petersburg Travel Company on Issakievskaya Ploshchad 11, are cavernous offices servicing the tours run by individual hotel service desks. Most visitors end up booking a personal guide or joining a tour through their hotel. If you are not staying at a hotel, the most convenient place to book yourself a place on the regular schedule of tours is to visit the Intourist Hotel, Ul. Tverskaya 3–5, in Moscow or the Astoria Hotel, Issakievskaya Ploshchad in St Petersburg. If you want help in getting to somewhere even remotely unusual, you will have to hire a guide for yourself. With the emergence of a number of new independent companies specializing in tourism, this need not be as expensive as it sounds, and their approach is often more flexible and interesting than that of the traditional school of statistic-spouting.

Moscow

Patriarchi Dom, Ul. Ostizheva 17, Apt. 20, ✆ 299 5971. Geared more towards English-speaking residents than tourists, this enterprising US-Russian firm arranges language courses and individual lessons, interpreting services, orientation courses as well as an interesting series of excursions—walks around Bulgakov's haunts, visits to folk artists around the city, architectural walking tours. Their speciality for tourists is to teach them a bit of the language as they enjoy the city.

Art Tours Ltd, Zuborsky Balv. 16/20, ✆ 140 1860, 244 0991, 246 0159, is one of the new Russian firms offering excursions in and around Moscow and the nearby ancient cities.

St Petersburg

Service Desk, Grande Hotel Europe, Ul. Mikhailovsksaya 1–7, ✆ 312 0072, ext. 6242. At very short notice this well-organized hotel will provide you with an English-speaking guide for sightseeing trips.

Lingva, 7ya Liniya 36, Vasilievsky Ostrov, ✆ 218 7339. Ask to speak to Gulara Bernatskaya. A company that specializes in teaching Russian to foreigners, Lingva also provides English-speaking guides to St Petersburg, preferably given a day's notice.

Union of Architects, Ul. Gertsena 52, ✆ 312 0400, offers professional architects to accompany you on historical and architectural tours of the city.

Libra-Tours, Pereulok Grivtsova 22, Apt. 26, ✆ 310 9186. As well as offering guides and transport for sightseeing trips, Valentin Yemelin specializes in organizing meetings to suit your special interest. If, for example, you are involved in prison reform and would like to find out about the current state of Russia's prisons, given enough time, Valentin will arrange a visit.

Women

During the day Moscow and St Petersburg appear to be almost entirely free of sexual harassment, but at night, after the appearance of the vodka bottle, you may well find yourself prey to unwelcome attention. The good thing is that most of the men are too drunk to be any great threat, so that walking briskly away will leave them trying to focus and wondering where you have gone. Drunks in restaurants may pester you for a dance, but with luck the waiters will help to keep them away. As a woman alone you will feel conspicuous in most Russian restaurants, so it is best to stick to your hotel at night. Even when dining with another woman make sure you choose your restaurant well. Mafiosi haunts and casinos are hopping with prostitutes and men on the prowl.

If you have a long way to walk at the other end of your journey, don't take the metro at night, and don't flag down a car on your own at night either. Most Russian men will insist on seeing you home, and if you know they can't afford it you can suggest paying for the taxi to take them back home after dropping you. It is normally just as easy to say 'no' to a Russian friend who becomes amorous at the end of the bottle as it is to say 'yes'.

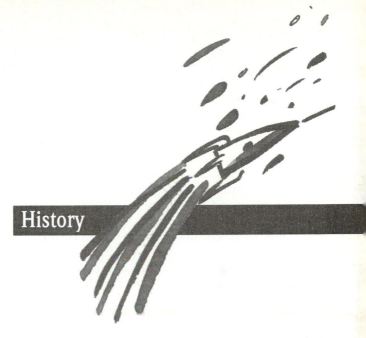

History

Until 14 February 1918, Russia followed the Julian calendar which was 13 days ahead of the Gregorian calendar then used by the rest of Europe. Throughout this book, history has been aped, so that only dates after February 1918 are given in the Gregorian calendar.

Holy Russia: the Land and its People

Russia rolls from eastern Europe to the Pacific with only one substantial ridge of mountains, the Urals, to disturb its relentless flatness. Its northernmost reaches consist of Arctic tundra, a land of permafrost and short summers in which hunting for fur and fishing have always been the mainstays of the economy. For millenia the central belt, around Moscow and St Petersburg, was blanketed by impenetrable coniferous and deciduous forests. The medieval motorways, the avenues of communication and trade, were the huge sluggish rivers, the Dvina, the Don, the Dnieper and the Volga, which meandered through the silence for thousands of miles to the Baltic and White Seas in the north, and the Black and Caspian Seas to the south. Southern Russia and the Ukraine, north of the Black Sea, are warmer, with richer soils covered in deciduous forest and vast open grasslands, the steppe. Much of the early history of Russia was played out across this fertile area, which went on to become the breadbasket of the economy but which, like the rest of the country, was entirely lacking in natural frontiers.

It was in the 6th century that the people we now think of as the Russians began to come together, when Slav tribes from the Carpathian Mountains in southeastern Europe moved east into the 'black land' along the northern coast of the Black Sea. As well as being fertile, these lower steppe lands straddled the trade routes between the ancient civilizations of the east and the emerging market in Europe. Long prone to invasion by nomadic tribesmen from the east, at this time they were dominated by the Khazars who allowed the Slavs to settle in return for an annual tribute. For 300 years this *modus vivendi* held. However, as the Slavs spread out, building some 600 settlements along the Don, the Dnieper and even the Volga, their unity dissipated until each village had its own independent government. In the 8th century, Viking longships began to navigate the Russian river system, conducting a well-organized trade in items such as amber and slaves with the Eastern potentates. The Slavs took the unusual step of inviting these fair-haired, tattooed giants to rule over them, and by the late 9th century the Rurik dynasty, who had made Kiev their capital city, had risen to pre-eminence. These red-haired Scandinavians were called Rus, from which the word Russian developed.

A century later, Grand Prince Vladimir of Kiev made one of the most important decisions in the history of the Russian nation—to convert to Orthodox Christianity. From 988 onwards, Orthodoxy became the state religion, a religion with which the Russians so identified that their word for an ordinary peasant (*krestyanin*) implies his Christianity. Until the Revolution, Orthodoxy was almost a necessary condition of being a Russian, and the Russians called themselves the 'God-bearing' people, convinced that only they carried God's true message. According to an almost legendary story, Vladimir rejected Islam because of its prohibition on drink, and

Judaism for its prohibition of pork. It was his star-struck envoys to Constantinople who made his mind up for him. 'We knew not whether we were in heaven or on earth', they said of the liturgy celebrated in Haghia Sophia. 'We cannot describe it to you. We only know that God dwells there among men. For we cannot forget that beauty.'

Meanwhile, a number of powerful principalities were also flourishing in the north. The walled city of Novgorod in the far northwest developed a properous trade with the Baltic merchant cities of the Hanseatic League, along with a reputation for unfathomable riches. To the east, on tributaries of the massive Volga river, the increasingly powerful principality of Rostov-Suzdal had established its capital at Vladimir. By the 12th century, pressure on Kiev from nomadic invaders had weakened the southern state, and many of its inhabitants were already moving north.

Moscow, not far from Vladimir, is first mentioned in 1147, when a Suzdalian prince, Yuri Dolgoruky, stumbled across a fortified homestead on a hill overlooking the Moskva River. Legend tells that he announced his intention to stay with the owner, who was foolishly less than hospitable. Yuri had him killed the following day and took his wife as a mistress. Nine years later a wooden fortress was erected where the Kremlin stands today, as a defensive outpost of Rostov-Suzdal. Looking at a map it is easy to see why Moscow was well placed to become the leading city of this vast area. Plum in the middle of European Russia, it sits at the hub of an intricate network of rivers, on a tributary of the Volga which runs into the Caspian Sea. Not far away are the upper reaches of the Dneiper and the Don, which run into the Black Sea, and of the Dvina and Northern Dvina, which drain into the Baltic and White Seas respectively. But Moscow's success arose ironically from Russia's 250-year domination by the Mongols.

The Mongol Invasion and the Rise of Moscow

When, in 1237, the Mongols flooded across the Ural Mountains by the thousand on their stocky ponies, the warring principalities of Russia were in no position to present a united defence. Unlike the waves of nomadic migrations that had gone before them, the Mongol horsemen were divided into highly-organized armies following the invasion plans of Ghenghis Khan. Despite the thick forest, great strips of which were sometimes felled like spillikins to slow their advance, it took less than two years for the entire area, except the towns of Novgorod and Pskov in the far northwest, to be conquered. It was not the Mongols' habit to rule their conquered subjects directly. Instead, they weighed heavy on local resources by demanding an annual tribute in goods and gold, ensuring its delivery with the threat of terrifying lightning raids on recalcitrant communities. The task of organizing the collection and delivery of the tribute was allotted to a prominent local leader. The Mongols were adept at choosing those whose mercenary and power-hungry personalities made them both sufficiently obsequious to their overlords and ruthless enough to extract the taxes from their neighbours. It was just such a combination of characteristics which the Mongols found in Moscow's Grand Prince Ivan I, known to history as Ivan 'Kalita' (Moneybags) (1328–40).

Moscow, still one of the smallest of the Russian principalities, had come into its own during the rule of Ivan's saintly father, Daniil (1276–1303). He had founded a number of defensive monasteries to protect the city, the first of which, the Danilovsky, bears his name to this day. He also encouraged refugees from Mongol devastation to build homes in the walled settlements that were springing up in the lee of the Kremlin. Unlike his pious father, Ivan was interested only in power and wealth. When his neighbour, the powerful Grand Prince of Tver, led a national revolt against the Mongols, Ivan cynically agreed to quash this rebellion on their behalf. Success was rewarded with the *yarlyk*, the Mongols' permission to collect the tribute from his neighbours and to act as supreme judicial authority in their disputes. Recognizing a star in the ascendancy, Metropolitan Peter, head of the Russian Orthodox Church, moved to Moscow from Vladimir, thus swinging the legitimacy of the all-important church behind the Muscovy Princes.

It was only 50 years later that the Muscovites inflicted their first defeat on the Mongols, when the heroic young Grand Prince Dmitry led an army of 100,000 into battle against 400,000 in 1380. Before leaving, Dmitry sought the blessing of the great Russian saint, Sergius, then a simple monk setting up his monastery at Sergeyev Possad outside Moscow. When he returned victorious from the battle of Kulikovo Field on the banks of the River Don, he became known as Dmitry Donskoy ('of the Don') and was later canonized. The battle was also a turning point in Russian national consciousness, since for the first time, with the blessing of God, soldiers from a variety of principalities fought together to rid themselves of a common enemy. The Trinity Sergius Monastery (full of treasures to this day) has never looked back since its part in this great victory.

To beat the Mongols in a single battle, however, was not to vanquish them forever. Just two years later they were back, and burned Moscow to the ground. By this time however, the city was rich and prestigious enough to recover quickly. Its now stone-walled Kremlin sat at the hub of a series of radiating roads which passed through a wooden outer wall (where the Bulvar Ring is now). As well as outlying monastery-forts, a second inner ring was developing to defend this wall, including the Rozhdestvensky, Sretensky and St Peter Monasteries. But it wasn't until the reign of Ivan III (1462–1505), later known as Ivan the Great, that the Muscovites felt secure enough to stop paying tribute to the Mongols. In 1480, when the Grand Princes of Moscow ruled over a kingdom stretching from the Arctic Sea in the north to the Urals in the east, they unilaterally declared the end of the 'Mongol Yoke'. With the fall of Constantinople to the 'infidel Turk' in 1453, the Russian Orthodox Church and its temporal leader the Grand Prince began to conceive of Moscow as the Third Rome, the heir to Byzantium, and of Russian Orthodoxy as the keeper of the True Faith. These sentiments were further strengthened when Ivan III married Zoë Paleologus, the niece of the last Byzantine emperor, in 1472.

Moscow's new confidence immediately made itself apparent in Ivan III's massive building programme in the Kremlin. Though Russia's period of isolation under the Mongols insured that she never became fully European, the arrival of Zoë, who had been living in Rome, brought access to some of the artistic and architectural developments that had been taking place during the Italian Renaissance. The tradition of importing foreign architects to Russia, so evident later in St Petersburg, began here, with the handful of Italians who came to express Moscow's new-found independence in stone and mortar. Many of the greatest architectural treasures in the Kremlin, including the two largest cathedrals and the swallow-tailed walls themselves, date from the reigns of Ivan III and his son Vasily III (1505–33).

The aggrandisement of Moscow continued during the reign of Ivan IV (1533–84), the first Muscovite prince to be crowned 'Tsar of All the Russias'. Moscow became one of the largest cities in Europe, with a population of 100,000. The settlement beside the Kremlin, Kitai Gorod, was enclosed by walls, and the wooden wall on the Bulvar was replaced by solid white stone. On the line of what is today the Garden Ring a further wooden stockade was erected as an outer defence. The Mongols were driven from their footholds in Kazan and Astrakhan, and the former victory was celebrated by the building of Russia's most famous landmark, St Basil's Cathedral.

By now considerable numbers of foreigners were finding their way to the city. The Englishman Richard Chancellor was looking for the northeast passage when he was blown into the harbour at Arkhangelsk on the White Sea. Brought to Moscow in 1553, Chancellor managed to secure favourable trading rights for the English. In 1556 the Russia Company was floated in London, and English merchants came to live in a house near the Kremlin that stands to this day. One hundred years later, a horrified tsar, hearing the news of Charles I's execution, expelled them. All written accounts by foreigners at the time emphasize the unparalleled power of the wealthy monarch over his subjects, the miserable lives of the majority, their lewd, crude conversation and the tendency to drunkenness. A piece of anonymous English doggerel from the early 17th century gives the gist of their opinions:

> *Churches, ikons, crosses, bells,*
> *Painted whores and garlic smells,*
> *Vice and vodka everyplace—*
> *This is Moscow's daily face.*

> *To loiter in the market air,*
> *To bathe in common, bodies bare,*
> *To sleep by day and gorge by night,*
> *To belch and fart is their delight.*
>
> *Thieving, murdering, fornication*
> *Are so common in this nation,*
> *No one thinks a brow to raise—*
> *Such are Moscow's sordid days.*

Many of these opinions, however, were simply copied from source to source, since many of the travellers actually saw little of the country and relied more on earlier accounts than on their own observations. Measured by the standards of a Europe on the cusp of the Renaissance, the political and social landscape of Russia was certainly different. The tsars had inherited many of the Mongols' autocratic traits, including the ferocity with which they dealt with enemies and even their own subjects. Women accused of cheating on their husbands, even in central Moscow, were buried with only their head above ground and left to die. Society was based on the unquestioning submission of the individual to the group. Even the aristocracy were robbed of their power; their estates were confiscated and then leased back to them in return for service to the state. Unlike in Europe, there was no powerful class to counteract the despotism of the monarchy. As Sigismund von Herberstein, envoy of the Holy Roman Emperor said in his 1549 description of Russia, 'In the sway that he holds over his people the ruler of Muscovy surpasses all the monarchs of the world.'

The Time of Troubles

The period of Russian history known as the Time of Troubles officially covers the years 1598 to 1613, but its roots lie in the reign of Ivan IV (1533–84). When his first beloved wife Anastasia died, the tsar was transformed from an enlightened leader into the man who has gone down in history as Ivan the Terrible. He had always hated the powerful *boyars* (aristocrats); deprived of. Anastasia's moderating influence, he became convinced that they had poisoned her. Thus began the first of Russia's self-inflicted reigns of terror. The National Assembly (*zemsky sobor*) became little more than a rubber stamp for Ivan's autocratic decrees. To bypass the *boyars*, Ivan established a band of agents under his personal command. Known as *oprichniki*, these black-hooded, monkish killers ran what was virtually a state within a state. They murdered whole families and depopulated entire villages and regions which had offended the tsar. The secret police had come to Russia.

As Ivan's reign continued the tsar became increasingly volatile until, one dreadful night in 1581, he killed both his the son and his daughter-in-law, who was seven months pregnant, in a ferocious burst of temper. For the remaining three years of his life the tsar was consumed by guilt, and the Kremlin was said to resound to his midnight howls of remorse.

Ivan well knew the dangers of his second, simple son Fyodor (1584–98) inheriting the throne. A man whose chief passion in life was bell-ringing was happy enough in the Kremlin, where the bells on the Ivan the Great belltower were rung on a myriad of occasions, but not fit to rule. It was as Fyodor's regent that Boris Godunov (immortalized in Mussorgsky's eponymous opera) rose to power. The little-trusted upstart had risen from his Mongol origins to a position of considerable confidence with Ivan as an *oprichnik*, and he consolidated his standing by marrying his sister Irina to the dim-witted Fyodor. Godunov's most far reaching achievement during Fyodor's life was to persuade the Patriarch of Constantinople, head of the Orthodox Church, that Russia should have its own patriarch, thereby strengthening the identification between church and state. When the tsar died childless, Godunov installed himself on the throne, and the 'Troubles' really began.

Back in 1591 another of Ivan IV's sons, the epileptic Dmitry, had been found bleeding to death. Many of the old boyar families, whose power had been fatally damaged by the reign of Ivan the Terrible, chose to believe he had been murdered by Boris Godunov, and the desire to unseat the usurper was rife. In 1603, the first 'false Dmitry' appeared, pretending to be the dead boy and the rightful heir to the throne. Seeking help from Poland, then one of Russia's enemies, Dmitry marched on Moscow, acclaimed as he went by the peasants who had faced several years of bad harvests. Conveniently Godunov died in 1605, shortly before his son and heir Fyodor II was murdered. Dmitry ascended the throne, but his arrogant Polish entourage and wife, and particularly their Catholicism, were equally unacceptable to the boyars. They led a successful revolt against them, and installed one of their number, Vasily Shuisky, on the throne. Dmitry was killed and burned, and his ashes fired in a cannon back towards Poland.

The second 'false Dmitry' was never a great threat, but the Poles took advantage of Russia's chronic instability by launching an attack of their own which took them all the way to the Kremlin. This gave rise to the only siege of the Kremlin in modern history when, ironically, it was the Russians who were trying to oust a Polish garrison from their citadel. In 1612, under the combined leadership of Minin (a butcher from Nizhny Novgorod) and Prince Pozharsky, a Russian force finally succeeded in ousting the Poles. On the back of a wave of unifying patriotic fever, the *zemsky sobor* was called, and nominated 16-year-old Mikhail Romanov, grandnephew of Ivan the Terrible's first wife Anastasia and son of the Metropolitan of Moscow, to be tsar. Not for 300 years, during another time of troubles, were the Romanov dynasty to be unseated.

The Early Romanovs

Though immense credit for the advancement of Russia is always laid at the feet of Peter the Great, the foundations for his astounding reign were built during the reigns of his father and grandfather. By the end of Mikhail's reign in 1645, during which the tsar ruled in tandem with the church (led by his father Metropolitan Filaret), Russia had recovered from her exhausting upheavals. Mikhail's son Alexei (1645–76) was a pious, hard-working leader who conquered the Ukraine from the Poles and encouraged the influx of foreign technicians—architects, mercenaries, doctors—which is so often associated with Peter. Moscow's foreign community, some 30,000 strong, was housed in a ghetto, just as it was during the years of the Cold War. In those days it was known as the German Settlement. Prints of the walled enclave show an orderly north European district with large stone houses, fountains, Protestant churches and a formal street plan. The ghetto was not far from one of the estates on which the young Peter was brought up, and would have been known to him from an early age. Today, at the heart of the region sits the infamous Lefortovo prison, where the plotters of the 1991 coup were temporarily immured; it is named after Peter's first great foreign friend, the Swiss Francis Lefort.

Two other important developments during the reign of Peter's father concerned the law and the church. With the formulation and adoption of the *Ulozheniye*, the first codification of Russian law, in 1649, Alexei slotted every one of his male subjects neatly into one of 30 divisions which exactly described his relationship to the state. This was no Magna Carta, enshrining the rights of other members to a say in the running of society, but a list of their duties. All land belonged to the tsar, and was leased in return for state service as a soldier or a bureaucrat. The *Ulozheniye* recognized, for the first time, the existence of townspeople, merchants and manufacturers, who were not a free entrepreneurial class, but bound to hand over a certain percentage of their goods to the royal household, and in addition to collect certain taxes on the government's behalf. Any nascent independence was killed off, preventing the gradual accretion of power by the aristocracy and later the bourgeoisie that took its place in western Europe. This fact was to have repercussions right up to the Revolution.

It is ironic that the greatest schism in the Russian church should have occurred during the reign of Alexei, who would retire to a monastery for months at a time and was said by his English doctor to prostrate himself as many as 1500 times on feast days. It was provoked by the appointment of Nikon as Patriarch in 1652. Nikon wanted to rid the Russian church of local traditions and bring it into line with its Greek sister church. However his reforms ran contrary to the prevailing popular opinion, which saw the Russian church as the height of piousness, the keeper of the True Faith and the uncorrupted religious heritage. In addition, his overbearing, arrogant temper did nothing to ingratiate him with his extensive opposition. Yet Nikon pressed on, his most symbolic crime being to force believers to make the sign of the cross with three fingers instead of two. This might not seem cause for a schism which still continues to this day, but to the Russians, ritual was a vital expression of spiritual values. When allied with persecution, these small changes saw a mass exodus of schismatics, known as the Old Believers (*raskolniki*) from European Russia to the south and into Siberia, where they stayed until being gradually allowed back during the late 18th century. Some villages of Old Believers in Siberia cut themselves off so thoroughly from mainstream Russia that well into the 20th century they remained unaware of the Revolution.

Nikon's arrogance also brought him into conflict with Tsar Alexei, who began to resent the Patriarch's interference in affairs of state. One look at the size and opulence of the palace Nikon built for himself in the Kremlin shows his pretensions. Sensing his unpopularity, in 1658 Nikon retired to his own mini-kingdom at the New Jerusalem Monastery outside the city, without renouncing his title as patriarch. In 1667 however, a Church Council in Moscow deposed him, though his liturgical reforms were upheld. The stage was set for Peter's further assertion of the supremacy of state power over the church.

When Alexei died in 1676, a vicious struggle for power ensued between the aristocratic clans of his two wives, the Miloslavskys and the Naryshkins. His son and heir Fyodor Miloslavsky was so frail that he had to be carried to his coronation in the Cathedral of the Assumption, and died six years later. In the ensuing rumpus, which ended with Ivan Miloslavsky and Peter Naryshkin sharing the throne as Ivan V and Peter I, the Naryshkins were accused of murdering Ivan. It was to have profound consequences for Russia's future, for it was then that Peter I, creator of St Petersburg, developed his hatred of Moscow and his distrust of its conservative, scheming society.

In a disorderly, noisy and probably drunken scrum, the *streltsy* guards marched into the Kremlin demanding to see Ivan, who was brought out onto the steps of the Red Staircase with the 10-year-old Peter. This was not enough to quell the

Streltsy's distrust of the Naryshkins, however; the family's petty provincial origins had always stuck in the throats of the haughty Muscovite families. The young Peter stood petrified at the top of the stairs, watching as the body of one of his uncles was flung like a rag-doll from pike to pike by jeering, mutinous soldiers. During a two-day witch-hunt, the *streltsy* killed another of Peter's uncles, as well as his mother's closest advisor. Ivan's sister Sophia was appointed regent to the young tsars.

Peter the Great Takes the Reins

By 1689, Peter had grown into an accomplished 6-foot 7-inch 17-year-old, and was able to wrest power from his step-sister, continuing to rule with his blind step-brother Ivan until the latter's death in 1696. By this time, the energetic Peter was in full swing, creating a modern, professional army, and a Russian navy from scratch. He defeated the Ottoman Empire and the hitherto omnipotent Swedes in the Great Northern War, making Russia the master of the Baltic Sea. As a symbol of his single-handed transformation of Russia from a medieval principality into an imperial European power, he founded the grandiloquent city of St Petersburg on the Gulf of Finland and forced his court and government to move there from Moscow. St Petersburg was built by Europeans as a western city and Peter, who visited western Europe twice, introduced a host of new ideas, fashions and techno-logical innovations to his native land. Yet Peter's legacy was not straightforward. An argument has raged ever since between the 'westernizers' and those who believe that such reforms are inappropriate to Russia's Slavic heritage. Even in Peter's day, many of his subjects believed him to be a changeling sent back from Europe to destroy Holy Russia and all that she held dear.

Peter's first fact-finding mission to Europe took place in 1697. In the early 17th century the heretics of Europe had been looked at with nothing but contempt by the Russians. However increasing numbers of young Russians were being sent abroad to acquire specific skills, and Peter wanted to see with his own eyes the technological wonders of northwestern Europe. With characteristic modesty, he travelled incognito in a party of 250, leaving the leadership of the Grand Embassy to a number of diplomats including his Swiss friend Lefort. This allowed the tsar to shed his disguise when he wished to converse with his fellow monarchs, but also to work personally in the shipyards of Holland and England, learning the skills of shipbuilding side by side with his chosen courtiers. Though Peter was ever mindful of his divine right to rule, one of his most endearing characteristics, and one which certainly contributed to his success, was his endlessly enquiring mind, his eager-ness to learn and his willingness to labour beside skilled craftsmen.

From a west European point of view, Peter's character seemed to be a mass of con-tradictions. An autocrat of unimaginable power, he was alternately excrutiatingly shy and unaffectedly natural with the royal and aristocratic women with whom he dined. He always refused the suites of sumptuously furnished rooms he was offered, prefering to sleep on a camp bed in some unpretentious garret. After King William III had arranged for the diarist John Evelyn to lend Peter his house near the shipyards at Deptford, the tsar and his Russian companions managed to destroy both the interior and the garden, using furniture as firewood and drunkenly pushing one another through the formal holly hedges in a wheelbarrow. Yet Peter recruited some 60 Englishmen, gardeners and craftsmen among them, to return with him and disseminate their knowledge in his native land.

Peter was forced into a hasty return by yet another disturbance fomented by the *streltsy*, who had been secretly corresponding with Sophia who was locked away in the Novodevichy Convent. No mercy was shown, and the leaders were hung in pairs from the city walls and left throughout the winter. From her windows, Sophia was forced to look upon the dangling corpses of no less than 190 of her co-conspirators. Almost immediately, Peter put a number of almost childish reforms into play. Whether he really thought them important or simply wanted to ruffle conservative Muscovite feathers is not clear. On the day of his return he personally shaved off the beards of the boyars who came to see him, and it soon became obvious that only those who followed suit would find favour with the tsar. It might not sound much, but the Russians believed beards to be an element of God's creation, without which the creator would not allow entry into paradise. Peter also began throwing receptions at which only Western dress could be worn. Models of clothing in the French or German style were hung from the gates of the city for anyone to copy, and men of rank trying to enter in long, traditional coats found them unceremoniously shorn at the knees.

It was Peter's slow defeat of the lion of the north, Sweden, whose army was the most powerful in Europe, which really marked Russia's emergence as a European power. It was a long war of attrition, which astonished western Europe by revealing the tenacity and resources at Russia's command. It began with Peter's search for a less ice-bound home for Russia's new navy than his only Arctic port at Arkhangelsk. The most convenient access to the open seas was through the Gulf of Finland to the Baltic, but since the Time of Troubles, the shores of the gulf had been occupied by Sweden. After a couple of disastrous engagements, the Russians began to harrass the Swedes from their positions on Lake Ladoga. First they captured the fort of Schlüsselburg which guarded the upper reaches of the Neva where it flows out of the lake. Then Peter led his troops down the river, capturing the only major Swedish fort on the way, Nyenskans, in May 1703. No sooner had he done so, securing access to the sea, than he began to build, the Peter and Paul Fortress, now in the centre of St Petersburg, on a nearby island. Though he was not yet thinking of a new capital city, he was certainly mindful of his need for a port, and made an heroic gesture of self-confidence in staking a claim to the sea route when all the surrounding land was still in Swedish hands. But Peter was right. Russia's time had come. In 1709 the Russians inflicted irreparable damage on the Swedes at the Battle of Poltava in the Ukraine, and though Sweden held back from making peace until 1721, she never seriously threatened the mighty bear again.

The Foundation of St Petersburg

Only a tyrannical autocrat could ever have got away with such an irrational display of wilfulness as to site his new capital city on an enormous bog in the far north-western corner of a country which, even then, stretched as far as Vladivostok on the sea of Japan. During the early years of construction, an army of 40,000 peasants and captured Swedish soldiers were conscripted to sink piles into the marshy ground. They were hampered by the lack of daylight, the absence of local building materials and frequent flooding when the ground was not frozen. Wolves, disease, cold and the lack of a local supply of food contributed to the mortality rate among the labourers, whose skeletons made a considerable contribution to the foundations of the city. In 1710 the imperial family and the government were conscripted to move from their warm Moscow palaces of stone and wood to the chilly, damp lathe and plaster houses of the new capital. In 1712 Peter declared St Petersburg his capital, and by the end of his life what had been the humblest of fishing hamlets had become the fulcrum of a society excitedly exploring new ideas in science and the arts, government and social life. In summer, high society retired to summer palaces which stood proud in landscaped parks round the city. They dined in pavilions where tables disappeared through the floor between courses, delighted in ingenious series of fountains and passed the White Nights in lantern-filled glades. How far they had come from Moscow. By dint of his own furious energy, Peter had managed to rid himself altogether of the capital he so distrusted. From now on, the only time the Romanovs had to go to Moscow was for their coronations.

Great emphasis has rightly been placed on Peter's reforming zeal. However he also left behind him an autocracy strengthened by a powerful secret police, a legal system that rewarded informers, and a legacy of cruelty. Though he dealt severely with all his opponents, often taking a hand in their torture himself, Peter's most repellent act of personal violence was the killing of his own son. As early as 1707 Alexei, Peter's only child by his first, spurned wife Eudoxia, found himself the focus of the traditional elements at court who opposed Peter's reforms. The young boy grew up poised between the opposition and his father. So terrified was Alexei that he even tried to blow his hand off so that he would not shame himself in an examination of his fortification planning skills by his father, and he tried a number of times to renounce his succession and retreat to a monastery. By 1717 Alexei was so afraid that he ran away to Vienna and thence to Italy, only to be coaxed back by Peter's envoy, who promised that Alexei would be rewarded with his father's 'best love'. On his return, Alexei was forced to renounce his right to the throne, after which his four-month interrogation began. Peter used Alexei as an excuse to wipe out his obvious enemies, for the young boy was so scared he would confirm the treachery of anyone the tsar suggested. After he had been sentenced to death, Alexei died in his cell in the Peter and Paul fortress, probably from wounds inflicted during torture, which his father had witnessed. Rumours at the time even lay responsibility in the hands of the tsar himself.

Strong support for Alexei had come from the Orthodox Church, against which Peter was waging a gradual campaign. He wanted to make sure that the monarch's authority would never again be challenged by that of the single spiritual leader, as it had by Nikon. At first he refused to name a new Patriarch in 1700, and then used church funds to fight his wars. In 1721, he replaced the Patriarchate with the bureaucratic Holy Synod. Headed by a layman, the Chief Procurator, the church administrations became a branch of secular government.

Peter had rationalized his government into a number of ministries known as colleges; in 1722, Peter institutionalized the meritocratic values he had employed all his life in the Table of Ranks of the Russian Empire. From now on all men of talent, whatever their birth, would be able to join one of the three branches of state service, the military, civil and court, and make their way up its 14 official ranks. Peter's own government was conspicuously full of such new men of talent, like his prime minister Alexander Menshikov. Peter's own wife and appointed successor, Catherine, was born a Lithuanian peasant. Her good looks had been noted by Peter's loyal commander Peter Sheremetev during his campaign against the Swedes, and she had been taken into his household. From there she became the mistress of Menshikov, who later introduced her to the tsar.

The Petticoat Period

After the death of Peter the Great, men occupied the throne for only ten of the remaining 75 years of the 18th century. This was the first and last time that women were to hold paramount power in Russia. It is a period remembered for its advances in the fields of architecture, the arts and sciences, which culminated in the long reign of Catherine the Great, who did so much to advance Russia's place on the international stage.

Thanks largely to Peter's wholesale tinkering with the succession, the years after his death were fraught with changes. His wife Catherine and her successor Peter II (son of the ill-fated Alexei) chose to live in Moscow, but in 1730 Empress Anna, daughter of Peter's co-tsar Ivan V, forced the court back to St Petersburg, and set about further taming of its wild northern spirit. The strong Germanic influence of Anna's advisors, brought with her from Kurland where she had been married and widowed, was resented by the Russians, and stability only really returned with the accession of the Empress Elizabeth, Peter's only remaining daughter, in 1741.

Like her father, Elizabeth was a strong but contradictory character. Her favourite pursuits were drinking and dancing, and she only fell asleep around dawn after a long session on her bed with her group of ticklers. Yet from time to time she would disappear into a convent, giving the court a much-needed breathing space from her incessant 'metamorphoses', balls at which all comers were required to cross-dress. The future Empress Catherine put this obsession down to Elizabeth's shapely ankle, which could only be fully admired in men's clothing. Matters of statecraft the attractive and energetic Elizabeth left to able male ministers, but her unmistakable interest in the arts is still felt in St Petersburg today. Some architects and patrons were made for one another, and this is gloriously true of Bartolomeo Francesco Rastrelli and Elizabeth. Between them they built three of the city's most memorable monuments: the Winter Palace, the Catherine Palace at Tsarskoye Selo and the Smolny Cathedral and convent. In each of these buildings, Rastrelli's florid Rococo embellishment of essentially simple, harmonious and rhythmical structures seems to mirror the character of the empress.

Moscow was not entirely forgotten, thanks to the frequency of coronations which had to take place in the Kremlin, but it was only Elizabeth, who loved the dowager capital, who made a point of living there for one year in three. During her reign she annulled her father's law banning the use of stone anywhere but St Petersburg and its environs, whereupon a number of new aristocratic palace appeared on the leafy bulvars of Moscow, including that of her retiring lover, and secret husband, Count Alexei Rasumovsky. Elizabeth also encouraged the development of Moscow as a place of learning, and it was here in 1755 that Mikhail Lomonosov—Russia's own Renaissance man—established Russia's first university.

Catherine the Great and the Expansion of the Empire

For such a spirited woman, Elizabeth's choice of a successor, her petty-minded, militarily-obssessed, Prussophile nephew Peter III, was surprising, though her choice of a wife for him, the minor German Princess Sophia of Anhalt-Zerbst, turned out to be inspired. Like all the German princesses who were to marry heirs to the Russian throne in the following century, she was baptized into the Russian church just before her wedding. For her Russian identity she took the name Ekaterina—Catherine. After a short honeymoon period, the marriage turned into a prison sentence for both parties, with Catherine alleging that it had never been consummated and Peter seeking refuge in the arms of his mistress Elizaveta

Vorontsova. By the time Peter came to the throne in 1761, Catherine had given birth to a son and heir, Paul, and a daughter who had died, but neither can reliably be thought to have been Peter's offspring, and many surmise that the true Romanov dynasty stopped here.

An intelligent and cultured young woman, who had worked hard to learn Russian and steep herself in the culture of her adopted country, Catherine could be forgiven for plotting with her able supporters to overthrow Peter III, who preferred drilling toy soldiers to government business. The only major piece of legislation he signed in his seven-month reign was the abolition of compulsory 25-year state service for the aristocracy in peacetime, and even that had been largely drafted by Elizabeth. When Peter threatened to divorce Catherine in the summer of 1762 and send her to a convent, Catherine's allies moved swiftly. Within days, Peter was dead and the reign of Catherine II had begun.

Immensely well read, Catherine admired the writings of the philosophers of the Enlightenment and wanted their approval as a modern ruler. She became a regular correspondent with Voltaire and Diderot, and Diderot even visited her in Russia, bringing back glowing reports of her intelligence and humanity. Between Catherine's words and her deeds, however, an ever-widening chasm opened as she confronted the realities of ruling Russia. In 1773, the success of a peasant uprising led by the Cossack Emilian Pugachev took her by surprise. The uprising, in which land- and serf-owners were murdered in droves in and around the River Volga, was quashed in 1774 and Pugachev executed. Catherine was shaken by the vehemence of feeling aroused against her, and though she had declared her opposition to serfdom, she failed to use the occasion to ameliorate their conditions. Alarmed by the American War of Independence and genuinely appalled by the regicide of the French Revolution, she backtracked so far as to ban Diderot's celebrated Enlightenment text, the *Encyclopédie,* after 1789. Her 1785 Charter of Nobility enshrined the aristocracy's right not to pay tax, and by the end of her reign courtiers were even speaking a different language to their serfs, French.

The most notorious feature of Catherine's reign was her series of lovers. It was the English cartoonists of the time who first made an issue of the empress's voracious sexual appetite as part of the propaganda war they waged as the changing balance of power between Turkey and Russia made Britain increasingly nervous. The flames were fanned by a combination of male hypocrisy (king's mistresses were accepted practice) and by their fear at the sight of a woman who had gobbled up her incompetent husband, the legitimate monarch, before assuming the throne herself. As for the rumour that she died trying to satisfy herself with a stallion…

The tsaritsa's mania for building transformed the look of St Petersburg as she marshalled the rivers and canals between granite embankments, built new neoclassical palaces for her lovers and schools for the daughters of the gentry. She also enlarged the Winter Palace to house her private art collection in the Hermitage. Though Catherine hated Moscow, which seemed to her to epitomize Russia's medieval brutality and backwardness, she even initiated a number of projects there, the most elaborate of which never came to fruition. Her Great Kremlin Palace, designed by Vasily Bazhenov, never rose above its foundations, though swathes of the ancient citadel were destroyed to make way for it. Similarly, the country palace at Tsaritsyno, also by Bazhenov, was never finished either. Moscow flourished however, with aristocrats—no longer forced to serve the state—enjoying its leisurely lifestyle in contrast to the back-biting of the capital.

Catherine earned the encomium 'the Great', as Peter had done, for her foreign policy successes. The three cynical partitions of Poland which she engineered with Austria and Prussia obliterated this proud and ancient nation, bringing hundreds of thousands of square miles and millions of new subjects into the Russian Empire. During the course of two successful wars with Turkey, in which the navy played an important role, the balance of power in the Balkans swung in favour of Russia. New lands in the southern Ukraine and round the Sea of Azov were aquired, as well as trading concessions on the Black Sea and the Bosphorus. In 1783 Catherine's lover, Prince Grigory Potemkin annexed the newly independent Crimea, thereby gaining a fertile agricultural belt and a plethora of sea-ports. By the end of Catherine's reign, Russia was poised to take up her position as a world power.

The Emperor Paul

Catherine's son and successor was in no fit state to inherit her mantle. Paul had never managed to develop an easy relationship with his powerful and energetic mother. During his lonely childhood and adolescence, he received a brilliant education which allowed him to shine when he visited the court at Versailles, but as Peter III's putative son, he was inevitably courted by Catherine's enemies. As he waited 34 years to inherit the throne, Paul became increasingly embittered and deluded. He was happiest in self-imposed exile at his military state-within-a-state at the palace of Gatchina, drilling his troops with a mania Peter III would have commended. His accession was greeted with dread by the population, who had heard stories of his draconian capriciousness: exiling officers to Siberia for wearing their caps at the wrong angle, banning the word 'snub-nosed' out of embarrasment at his own.

St Petersburg society managed to tolerate Paul until 1801 when, out of admiration for Bonaparte, he reversed Russia's established anti-French policy. Leading figures, including Catherine's last lover, Zubov, and the governor of St Petersburg Count Peter von Pahlen, acted quickly. The conspirators consulted his son and heir Alexander, who is thought to have agreed to the removal of his father from the throne on condition that he was not harmed. Paul was smothered to death in Mikhailovsky Castle on the night of 24 March, an event for which Alexander never forgave himself.

The Napoleonic Wars and the Triumph of Alexander I

Paul's eldest sons had been educated under Catherine's vigilant gaze by the best tutors that Europe could provide. When the good-looking, 24-year-old Alexander ascended the throne, it looked as if Enlightenment ideas might finally take root in the tradition-bound soil of Russia. In the early years of the tsar's reign his leading advisor was Mikhail Speransky, who even went as far as suggesting that Russia should elect a parliament (*duma*) to draft legislation. But as the threat from Napoleon grew, Speransky was overshadowed by the conservative, aristocratic inner circle. Alexander's domestic policies were entirely eclipsed by the war with France, so comprehensively described in Tolstoy's *War and Peace*. While his experienced commanders had advised caution, Alexander was determined to ride the surge in Russian patriotism and engage the enemy. Russia fought with Austria and Britain against Napoleon, receiving a crushing defeat at the battle of Austerlitz in December 1805. The price of Alexander's inexperience was 11,000 Russian dead.

Further incompetence led to the Treaty of Tilsit, signed on a raft in the middle of the River Niemen in July 1807, at which Russia became an unlikely ally of France. She was forced to join Napoleon's Continental System, which was designed to crush Britain economically by closing all continental ports to her trade. By the time Napoleon invaded with his Grand Army of 600,000 in June 1812, Russia had had time to recover her strength. It was the largest army ever assembled, but Napoleon's campaign was uncharacteristically badly planned. The French ploughed their way across the heart of Russia to Moscow, arriving there after their Pyrrhic victory at the battle of Borodino in September 1812. Relying for their provisions on the countryside they passed through, they had not bargained on the patriotism of the Russian peasants, and by the time they reached the old capital the army had dwindled to little over 100,000. Worse was to come. Alexander's commander in chief, General Kutuzov, judged that the vastness of the Russian countryside alone would defeat the invaders. The Russians abandoned Moscow and set fire to great swathes of the city. Napoleon and his troops occupied the Kremlin, horrified at the destruction of the city around them, and tried to make contact with Alexander to begin negotiations. Napoleon waited for a month, but the Russian court refused to respond, and with the onset of winter the isolated French army was forced into hasty retreat. Bowed down by booty from the Kremlin, the French made easy targets for the army. The Cossacks managed to bring back almost all the country's treasures to Moscow, and many of the weakened, freezing stragglers were picked off by the peasantry. By the time they crossed the Russian border at the River

Niemen, as few as 5000 French soldiers remained. The Russian army followed the French all the way to Paris, taking part in the allied campaign which led to the abdication of Napoleon in 1814. At the Congress of Vienna, Russia took her place as one of the five great European powers.

Over the next 20 years, an explosion of grand, Empire-style palaces and public buildings in Moscow and St Petersburg trumpeted Russia's blossoming self-confidence. Yet despite his success, Alexander was haunted by guilt for his father's murder, and became increasingly religious as his reign wore on. In the autumn of 1825, the tsar's wife fell ill and the two of them travelled to Taganrog, a spa on the Sea of Azov. In November the tsar died there of an unspecified illness, and by the time his body arrived back in St Petersburg it was said to be too decomposed to be left in an open coffin, as was the imperial practice. Rumours abounded that Alexander had not actually died, and had substituted the decomposed body of a soldier for his own. The tsar is widely believed to have lived on for half a century in Siberia, having assumed the identity of a holy hermit, Fyodor Kuzmich. A Bolshevik attempt to get to the bottom of his death by opening his sarcophagus only deepened the mystery; they found that Alexander III had substituted another coffin for the original, lending credence to the belief that the original body had not been that of the tsar.

Nicholas I: 'Orthodoxy, Autocracy, Nationality'

The turmoil caused by Alexander's death and his lack of an heir was the first moment of imperial weakness to be exploited by democratic forces. The rebels, who became known as the Decembrists, were led by army officers who had picked up liberal ideas during the European war, and who wished to establish a constitutional monarchy. When Alexander's youngest brother Nicholas was declared tsar, the officers roused their men in defence of his elder brother Constantine, who had secretly renounced his right to the throne. The rebels made their stand on what is now Decembrists' Square, already doomed to failure as they had only managed to persuade half of the St Petersburg garrison to turn against the new tsar. After a day-long stand-off, troops loyal to the tsar broke up the ice on the Neva to prevent their quarry escaping that way, and mowed down several hundred rebels before the Decembrists surrendered. The five leading figures were hanged, after personal interrogation by Nicholas I, and over a hundred were sent to Siberia.

Nicholas I, the 'Iron Tsar', never swerved from the unforgiving autocratic course he steered through the Decembrist uprising. He presided over a crackdown on dissent, with strict censorship of all publications and the establishment of a new Third Section of the Imperial Chancellery, a secret police responsible for spying on all potentially subversive citizens. Universities were forced to turn their backs on enlightened principles; their syllabuses were monitored by the state and students forced into uniform. No one was allowed abroad to study for fear they might pick up dangerous ideas. Under the slogan 'Orthodoxy, Autocracy, Nationality', coined by his Minster for Education, Nicholas tried to stifle dissent by appealing to Russia's pride in the Orthodox church, in God's chosen ruler, the tsar, and to nationalism.

After the European revolutions of 1848, repression was stepped up even further. Though everyone, including the tsar, recognized the iniquity of serfdom, Nicholas was afraid to dismantle it for fear of the unknown. Yet threats to the autocracy never came from that quarter; it was always the *intelligentsia*, chattering away in their drawing rooms in Moscow and St Petersburg, from whom the tsar had most to fear. The most famous revolutionary group to be infiltrated by the police under Nicholas I was the St Petersburg Petrashevsky Circle, exposed in 1849. Fifteen of its leading participants, including the young Fyodor Dostoyevsky, were subjected to a mock execution, pardoned at the last second by the tsar, and sent to Siberia.

Paradoxically, Nicholas' reign is also known as the Golden Age of Russian Literature, during which Alexander Pushkin, Mikhail Lermontov and Nikolai Gogol established a modern literary tradition that was to blossom for the rest of the century and into the next. Poetry became a national obsession, with new periodicals appearing regularly to cater for the ever-increasing appetite. The life of Alexander Sergeyevich Pushkin, born into the aristocracy and killed in a duel fermented at court, has therefore come to symbolize the beginnings of the Russian fight for freedom through literature. Nicholas I took on the task of censoring Pushkin's work personally.

Nicholas's greatest miscalculation was to threaten Turkey, which he called 'the sick man of Europe', by invading its vassal principalities Moldavia and Wallachia in 1853. Since the Napoleonic Wars, Russia had appeared worryingly invincible in Europe, and in 1854 Britain, France and Austria all rallied to Turkey's defence in the Crimean War. The mirage of Russian strength quickly crumbled, for though most of the fighting took place on her back door in the Crimea, she found herself embarrassingly ill-equipped. While the rest of Europe had been building railroads and reequipping their armies on the back of massive industrialization, Russia had been unable to move forward because the vast majority of her population were tied to the land by serfdom. Nicholas died in despair at the course of the war in 1855, leaving his son Alexander II, who had advised against it, to oversee its humiliating conclusion.

Alexander II: Reform and Assassination

Alexander II, described by the French ambassador of the time as 'not a great intellect but... a generous soul', is the most contradictory of Russia's 19th-century tsars. Praised by some as the 'Tsar Liberator' for his emancipation of the serfs, he nevertheless died a victim of a revolutionary terrorist's bomb. Though reform of Russia's antiquated social system could no longer be avoided, Alexander undertook the task with genuine enthusiasm, determined to abolish serfdom from above rather than wait for the 'national disgrace' to explode from below. He went on to grant a genuine element of local government by instituting rural councils (*zemstvos*), which decided on matters of local health and education. He also developed a modern legal system such as Russia has seen neither before nor since, including trial by jury. The universities were free once more to teach philosophy and literature, pupils were encouraged to study abroad and secondary education was extended to new sectors of the population. Rather than unite the population behind the tsar, these reforms merely encouraged a rush of further demands from the population. Many members of the local *zemstvos* extended the idea of representative government into calls for a *duma*, a national assembly; an idea that received ardent support from the universities. The Edict of Emancipation, passed in 1861, was riddled with its own inherent problems. Because the tsar could not afford to alienate the land-owning aristocracy, the serfs were not given land, but had to buy it off the landowners over a period of years. The land price was so high that most peasants quickly fell behind with their payments and were no better off than before, working for the same landowners in order to pay off their debts.

The turning point in Alexander II's reign, the moment when fear yet again became the prime motivation of government, came in 1866 with the first attempt on the tsar's life, just outside the Summer Garden on the banks of the River Neva. Even before this attempt, one of the seminal texts of the Russian revolutionary movement had been written from a jail cell in the Peter and Paul Fortress. Nikolai Chernyshevsky's *What is to be Done?*, passed by two censors, each of whom thought the other was supposed to suppress it, was published legally in 1863. Lenin claimed to have been converted to the revolution by it. However there was still time for the oppositionary movement to take a quaint and rather endearing turn. Mainstream dissent was led by the Populists (*narodniki*), who believed that the revolution could only take place with the participation of the peasantry. In the summer of 1874, university students abandoned Moscow and St Petersburg in droves, moving from village to village dressed in peasant clothes, preaching their sermon of socialism and justice. To their amazement their words, particularly any criticism of the tsar, fell on deaf ears. Many, reported for their subversive views by the peasants, were arrested there and then.

Out of this fiasco grew the much more aggressive faction 'People's Will', (*Narodnaya Volya*) who believed that only political assassination could advance the cause. After several attempts, in 1881 they succeeded in assassinating the tsar, the very day, ironically, that he was considering proposals for a *duma* and for the disbanding of the hated secret police, now known as the *Okhrana*. Alexander II was returning to the Winter Palace when a bomb was thrown but failed to explode beneath his carriage by the Griboyedov Canal. The tsar climbed out to upbraid the would-be assassin, only to have his legs torn off by a second bomb. Within two hours he was dead. Today, the altar of the Cathedral of the Saviour on the Blood marks the exact spot where the tsar, whose reign began with so much promise, was defeated by the inexorable clash of reform and autocracy.

The cycle of fear intensified with the accession of Alexander's shell-shocked son Alexander III. His first act was to arrest and execute as many leaders of the People's Will as he could, and for the rest of his short reign he lived in such fear of assassination that he was rarely seen in public. Alexander's fears found public expression in the person of Konstantin Pobedonostsev, procurator of the Holy Synod and Alexander's former tutor, who dominated his government. Pobedonostsev was devoted to autocratic, Orthodox Russia and an implacable enemy of what he called the 'great falsehood' of parliamentary democracy. He turned his attention to Russia's educational system, denying places in secondary schools to the children of domestic servants and small shopkeepers, and bringing the universities back under complete state control. The jury system was abolished and the press once more heavily censored. Inevitably such action led to further assassination attempts. One would-be assassin, Alexander Ulyanov, was executed in 1887—another milestone on the road to revolution for his brother, Vladimir Ilich Lenin.

To deflect criticism from the increasing levels of repression, Alexander III and Pobedonostsev encouraged the impoverished peasantry to take their anger out on local Jewish bankers. From 1881–2 pogroms against the Jews, to which the local police were largely instructed to turn a blind eye, were commonplace, culminating in a spate of attacks on their communities in 1891–2 and in Pobedonostsev's decree expelling the Jews from Moscow and St Petersburg.

If Alexander III's government made no concessions towards political modernization, Russian industry made rapid progress. An unprecedented period of peace in Europe was just what was needed by Russia's industrialists, many of them members of a new middle class who had conscientiously built family empires from modest beginnings. Their impact on Russian society was more than merely economic. Many of them were Old Believers, and became vital supporters of the turn of the century arts and crafts movement that was to have such an energizing effect on Russian art. To them too, we owe some of the great art collections—the Tretyakovs for their eponymous museum in Moscow, and the Morozovs and Sergei Shchukin for the dazzling collections of Impressionist and Post-Impressionist paintings divided between the Pushkin Museum and the Hermitage. The government's industrial policy was masterminded by the brilliant Sergei Witte, himself the son of a railway official and much derided by the rest of government. As well as encouraging the home-grown entrepreneurs, the policy sought to encourage foreign investment, and to foster 'state capitalism' through government funding. Between the death of Alexander II and 1900, Russia's railway network more than doubled in length. In the 1890s the Baku oilfields made Russia the second largest producer of oil in the world, and by the early 20th century the country was challenging France for its position as fourth industrial producer in the world. By 1914, the outskirts of both Moscow and St Petersburg were peppered with factories, many of them offshoots of German industrial giants like Siemens. Impressive though it was, this increased prosperity could not make up for Russia's age-old backwardness, and would not answer the resounding demands for political modernization which were rising from almost every corner of society except the government.

Nicholas II: Last of the Romanovs

Alexander died unexpectedly in 1894, leaving his gentle, credulous 26-year-old son Nicholas holding the reins of power. Largely educated by Pobedonostsev, Nicholas II had absorbed the reactionary lessons of his mentor and of his father's reign, and had no initiative of his own to bridge the growing rift between people and tsar. Shortly before his death, Alexander III had given his blessing to Nicholas' betrothal to Princess Alix of Hesse-Darmstadt, a granddaughter of the British Queen Victoria. Ill omens for the reign began at their coronation in Moscow in 1896. At an open-air celebration for the citizens of Moscow at Khodynka Field, 1300 people were accidentally trampled to death. Nicholas compounded the tragedy by agreeing with his reactionary uncles that he should attend the ball thrown in his honour that evening by the French ambassador, instead of declaring a period of mourning as his instinct suggested. Moscow was scandalized by his heartless behaviour.

Alexandra, as Nicholas's wife became known, was feverish in her converted zeal for Russian Orthodoxy and an unquestioning believer in the autocracy. As the troubled reign wore on, the increasingly isolated, adoring couple clung to a belief in the Russian peasants' unswerving loyalty to their tsar. This belief was strengthened between 1905 and 1916 by their infamous friendship with the extraordinary peasant 'holy man' Rasputin (*see* pp.78–80). As well as the healing powers he seemed to exert over the haemophiliac heir to the throne, Tsarevich Alexei, Nicholas and Alexandra came increasingly to believe his comforting words and even to follow his advice on the appointment of ministers. The tsarevich's disease was a closely kept secret, and the outside world was unable to understand, and deeply suspicious of, Rasputin's intimacy with the family. Politicians and courtiers despaired.

Though the underground Socialist Revolutionary Party continued to believe in the peasantry's role in the struggle ahead, the revolutionary high-ground in Russia was being hijacked by men and women of a different persuasion. Both Moscow's and St

Petersburg's populations had quadrupled in the last half of the 19th century, and the rapid industrialization had created a new force in the nation. This nascent urban proletariat meant that the kind of revolution envisaged by Karl Marx, previously unthinkable in Russia, became a possibility. Russian Marxists, most of them in exile abroad, were divided. Some believed Russia could leapfrog the stage of fully-fledged bourgeois capitalism straight to Marx's envisaged socialist workers' state. Others followed Marx's theories to the letter and believed that they would have to bide their time before the revolution could take place. This argument came to a head at the 1903 Congress of the Social Democratic Workers' Party of Russia, the leading Marxist body. The orthodox Marxists (the *Mensheviks*, 'Men of the Minority') split from Lenin's followers (the *Bolsheviks*, 'Men of the Majority') who believed that the dictatorship of the proletariat would have to be brought about by an elite party which would direct the politically unprepared workers. Living abroad, mostly in London, Lenin propagated his ideas through his newpaper *Iskra* (The Spark) which was read by Russia's left-wing expatriates and smuggled back to the motherland.

The extention of Russia's influence at the Far Eastern end of the new Trans-Siberian Railway, meanwhile, antagonized Japan. The ensuing Russo-Japanese War (1904–5) was disastrous. News of Russian defeats reached a population already demoralized by an industrial slump, and by 1905 strikes were spreading like wildfire through the factories of Moscow and St Petersburg. On 9 January, Father Gapon, a priest in charge of a police-sanctioned workers' association, organized a massive march by striking St Petersburg workers to present a petition of grievances to their 'little father', the tsar. Government paranoia turned what should have been an event of reconciliation into the beginning of the tsar's downfall. As the marchers, carrying icons and images of the emperor and empress, converged peacefully on the centre of the city, the Imperial Guard opened fire. Estimates of the dead range from 100 to 1000, and the image of an indivisible tsar and people was shattered once and for all. 'Bloody Sunday', as the event became known, was a disastrous watershed in Russian history. It set off strikes throughout the country, naval mutinies and even peasant uprisings.

The unrest, which became known as the 1905 Revolution, was exacerbated by news of the Japanese sinking of the Russian fleet at Tsushima. Nicholas was forced to accept constitutional reform and a limit to his autocracy. The October Manifesto 1905 set out plans for a bi-cameral legislature (the State Duma and the State Council) elected on wide male suffrage, with a right of veto over legislation. By the time the Duma sat, however, the tsar had reversed a number of these concessions, and right up until 1917 he treated the parliament with complete contempt, dissolving it by force whenever it brought up unpalatable subjects.

The liberal bourgeoisie, whose aspirations would have been satisfied by a genuine constitutional monarchy, banded together in the Duma to form the Constitutional Democratic (Kadet) Party. A more radical alternative was provided by the St Petersburg Soviet of Workers' Deputies. Elected from the workers and growing out of the anarchy of recurrent strikes, for a short time the Soviet became a vital arm of local government, giving working people a taste of power for the first time.

The First World War and the 1917 Revolutions

Witte's successor as Prime Minister, Pyotr Stolypin, turned his attention to agrarian reform. For the majority of the peasantry, life had become more and more difficult since their emancipation over 40 years before. Stolypin determined to provide them with cheap loans so that a productive over-class of peasantry might create a motivated backbone to Russian agriculture. In 1911 this liberal hope was gunned down at the opera in Kiev by forces within the establishment, possibly with the collusion of his enemy Rasputin. The pageantry of the 300th anniversary of the Romanov dynasty in 1913 and the burst of patriotic fervour that greeted Russia's entry into the First World War merely papered over the deep divisions in the country. By 1915, the early Russian advances into East Prussia and Galicia had been reversed. Rasputin's influence looked all the more suspicious when he and the empress were left alone in the capital while Nicholas, foolishly in view of his inexperience, took over command of the army headquarters at Mogilev. In 1916 another offensive, led by General Brusilov, was initially successful, but crumbled in the face of enormous casualties. In the midst of this demoralizing see-saw, Rasputin was murdered in December 1916 (*see* p.80). While the imperial family went into mourning, the population rejoiced. After a while, however, it must have dawned on many that Rasputin was not the cause of Russia's malaise but merely one of the symptoms.

By the end of 1916 some 3½ million Russian soldiers had been killed, wounded or captured, and the troops' morale had all but collapsed. The Germans described having to move piles of corpses before being able to advance. On civvy street there was little to celebrate either. Provisioning the army on Russia's inadequate communications network took precedence over feeding civilians. The lack of bread in the cities was becoming serious, particularly in Petrograd, as St Petersburg was now called to make it sound less German. In February 1917, strikes and bread riots were backed by a mutiny of the huge garrison of new recruits in the city. To curb the growing anarchy, the State Duma arrested the tsar's government and established a Provisional Committee. Realizing that he had no loyal troops, let alone a government, on 2 March the tsar abdicated in favour of his younger brother Mikhail. The following day Mikhail followed suit, and the Romanov dynasty came to an abrupt end. Within days the entire family were placed under house arrest in the Alexander Palace at Tsarskoye Selo.

The soldiers and workers in the city took advantage of the situation to set up Soviets of workers and soldiers deputies along 1905 lines, most important of which was the Petrograd Soviet of Workers' and Soldiers' Deputies. Lenin returned to Russia in April, given safe passage in a sealed train by the Germans who saw him as a virus which would weaken their enemy. Despite his winning slogans of 'Peace, Bread and Land' and 'All Power to the Soviets', his Bolshevik party had failed to win over the Soviets, who stuck to their moderate policy of working with the government. As 1917 progressed the Provisional Government, led from July by Alexander Kerensky, failed to reverse the course of the war or to solve the food shortages. In an incident known as the July Days, people took to the street demanding that the Soviets overthrow the government. But the Soviets were unprepared, and the Provisional Government put down the troubles. Leaders of the Soviets such as Leon Trotsky were arrested, and Lenin fled into exile again, this time in neighbouring Finland. By October, however, the Bolsheviks had taken control of the Moscow and St Petersburg Soviets, and decided on an armed seizure of power.

The ground was just right. After summer defeats, soldiers had started deserting in huge numbers and the country became increasingly ungovernable. Early on the morning of 25 October, Red Guards trained by Trotsky attacked and occupied key buildings in Petrograd in the name of Soviet power. The final battle, to arrest the Provisional Government in the Winter Palace, began late that night with a blank shot fired by naval mutineers from the cruiser *Aurora*. On Palace Square gunfire was exchanged for a number of hours, but the fight was never the heroic event filmed by Eisenstein for his film *October*. The government's only defenders were a few officer cadets and a regiment of women soldiers, and at 2.10am all except Kerensky, who had escaped in a car provided by the American Embassy, were arrested. The fight for the control of Moscow was more intense and passionate. The initial Bolshevik hold on the Kremlin was reversed three days later on 28 October. Only on 3 November did the Red Guard once more gain control, and only after considerable bloodshed throughout the city centre.

Lenin, the Civil War and the New Economic Policy

Lenin, who had only returned to St Petersburg a couple of weeks before the final showdown, now took control. One of his first decrees did at a stroke what the majority of Russia's population had been wanting for over 150 years—legitimized the seizure of land by the peasants. Yet the Bolsheviks were faced with massive difficulties: out of the whole country, the Soviets only controlled Petrograd and Moscow. Russia's allies in the West, France, Britain and particularly America, were venomous about the coup, and even more enraged by the new government's intention to abandon the war. In November 1917, a Constituent Assembly was elected by near univeral suffrage in the first and only free election in Russia until 1990. The

Socialist Revolutionaries got almost twice as many votes as the Bolsheviks, who only won a fifth of the seats. The assembly sat for just one day in the Tauride Palace in January before the Bolshevik Red Guard shut it down. To combat counter-revolution, Lenin set up the Cheka, the prototype KGB, under the ruthless command of 'Iron' Felix Dzerzhinsky. In March 1918, Lenin moved the government back to Moscow and into the Kremlin.

To fulfil the Bolsheviks' promise of peace and bread, Trotsky agreed to the punitive terms of the Treaty of Brest-Litovsk in March 1918, by which the Russians surrendered the Baltic Republics and Poland as well as recognizing both the Ukraine and Finland as independent states. Even before the cessation of hostilites, however, new battle lines were drawing themselves within Russia. Diverse groups of anti-Bolsheviks were coming together under the leadership of a handful of 'White' Army Generals in the south and east, while an allied naval force landed at Murmansk in the north in March. By 1919 the Civil War was in full swing. The Red Army was fighting off attacks from General Kolchak and the White Cossacks in Siberia, General Denikin from the Ukraine and by the Finns, Balts and the Allies in the north. One rallying point for the Whites was the Romanov family. In July 1918, as White armies drew closer, the tsar, his entire family and their small retinue were taken down into the basement at the Ipatiev House in Yekaterinburg and shot. DNA testing recently carried out on the bodies appears to have finally laid to rest the story that Anastasia, the youngest daughter, had escaped.

That the nascent Red Army managed to repel the enemy on all fronts by 1921 is more a measure of the lack of communication between the various White forces than brilliant tactics on the part of the Reds. The Allied force in the north withdrew in 1919; their deployment, after the end of the World War, was extremely unpopular at home. As the Whites were pushed back into a tiny enclave in the Crimea, those who wanted to flee the Bolshevik regime made their way south, through a land devastated by war and famine, to where French and British ships evacuated the last of the Whites to Constantinople and beyond.

The Civil War took a disastrous toll on the already tattered economy, and it is estimated that over 5 million people died of starvation in 1921–2. Lenin's economic policy, known as War Communism, by which food and armaments were simply requisitioned from peasants and factories, had been extremely unpopular. Many of those who had fought for the Revolution in 1917 became disillusioned by the Bolshevik terror. A mutiny of the previously loyal naval base at Kronstadt in 1921 was accompanied by large-scale industrial strikes. The mutiny was put down ruthlessly; troops stole across the ice to the island in the middle of the Gulf of Finland in white suits, and Trotsky did not rest until all the 'heretics' had been shot. At the 10th Party Congress then in progress, Lenin introduced the 'New Economic

Policy', a form of state capitalism by which the state would continue to finance heavy industry, banking and finance, while a measure of private business would be encouraged in both town and countryside. The peasants would be taxed in kind, but would be free to sell any excess produce from their own plot of land on the open market, while small businesses were tolerated in towns. At the same time, however, Socialist Revolutionaries and Mensheviks were imprisoned and killed, and the political model that was to serve the Soviet Union so badly for the next 70 years was instituted. All power resided in the (Bolshevik) Communist Party. Political power struggles were confined to the ladder of the party hierarchy. In 1922 Josef Stalin found himself a convenient rung from which to launch his bid for the top, as Secretary General of the Communist Party. In 1922–23 Lenin suffered a series of strokes, and finally died in January 1924.

Stalin, Collectivization and the Purges

Stalin, a Georgian whose real name was Joseph Vissarionovich Djugashvili, had been educated in a religious seminary. In a time of explosive rhetoric, his secretary described the quiet, pipe-smoking man as using 'words to conceal his thoughts'. He was sly and so obssessed by power that he developed an overriding paranoia that everyone was conspiring to deprive him of it. Many blame his violent, drunken father for setting him on the road to mass terror. By 1929, the General Secretary had used the party mechanism to promote his supporters, and had picked off all the old Bolsheviks who might in any way threaten his position. In 1925 Leon Trotsky, the fiery proponent of continuous international revolution, was removed from office by the triumvirate of Stalin, Zinoviev and Kamenev, who favoured the policy of securing 'socialism in one country' (*i.e.* the Soviet Union). In 1927 Stalin ganged up with Bukharin, Rykov and Tomsky to turn on Zinoviev and Kamenev, and in 1929 he turned on his new allies and dismissed them from office. By the end of that year, Stalin was the only member of Lenin's Politburo still in power.

In 1927 the 15th Party Congress had adopted Stalin's first Five Year Plan for the economy, reversing the liberalization of Lenin's New Economic Plan, and in 1929 Stalin unilaterally decided to radicalize it further. Instead of the voluntary collectivization of agriculture, peasants were forced to give up their land, livestock and tools to the local collective or state farm, where they would work, and from which they would receive salaries. Those who rebelled by burning their supplies and killing their livestock, particularly the richer peasants known as the *kulaks*, were killed on the spot or exiled to Siberia. Allied to bad harvests in 1931 and 1932, the forced collectivization caused a famine in which between 5 and 10 million lives were lost. In Kazakhstan alone, 1.5 million peasants, one third of the population, died during collectivization, a process which destroyed their traditional nomadic system of agriculture.

In industry too, Stalin implemented a programme of rapid reform. New mines in the east provided raw materials for huge new heavy industry plants, whose main purpose was to provide materials for the weapons industry. The annual programme for each factory, and its unrealistic output targets, were set by Gosplan, a vast central bureaucracy, and all private initiatives were shut down. Within months of the first annual plan, factory managers were cooking the books to show that they had achieved the targets set, and a chain of institutional lying was set in place. From the start, central planning was a farce. By the time it was publicly challenged for the first time in 1988, one respected economist reckoned it would take 30,000 years and full computerization, which Gosplan didn't have, to draft a thorough and workable annual economic programme.

At the 1934 Party Congress, delegates expressed their reservations about Stalin's policies by voting the Leningrad Party leader, Sergei Kirov, onto the Central Committee by many more votes than Stalin. None could have guessed that as a result, most of them would be dead or in labour camps by the time of the next Congress five years later. On 1 December 1934 Sergei Kirov was assassinated at his office in the Smolny Institute. Although Stalin was in fact the man behind his death, he fixed the blame on a terrorist cell which he claimed also aimed to assassinate him. He then began to arrest hundreds of people who might conceivably be against him, though most of his victims were loyal party members. In August 1936, at the first of the Moscow Show Trials that shocked and fascinated the world, he rid himself of his old enemies Zinoviev and Kamenev. By means of systematic interrogation by the NKVD (forerunner of the KGB), they had been forced into confessing to the murder of Kirov and were shot.

The worst period of the terror, known as the *Yezhovshchina*, was heralded by the appointment of Nikolai Yezhov as head of the NKVD in September 1936. Hundreds of thousands of loyal party members were arrested, and jails all over Moscow and Leningrad, as it was now called, as well as provinicial cities, were overflowing. The same methods of interrogation were used over and over to get people to confess to being guilty of anti-Soviet sentiments and to force them to implicate their colleagues. The 'guilty' were dispatched by the trainload to camps in the permafrost of Siberia, where they were forced to build railways or labour in mines and forests with little food and few clothes, in ceaseless sub-zero temperatures. They died by the thousand.

In June 1937 the purge of the Red Army began, a policy that was to have devastating consequences when Nazi Germany invaded five years later. Though there was no evidence of any military plot, Stalin dreaded a challenge to his power from such a powerful body and decided on preventative surgery. After the trial and execution of eight leading generals on charges of spying and treason, a further 40,000 army officers (three quarters of all officers) were purged. There was no way the army could make up that loss of experience before the war. The Great Purge, as this period became known, came to an end when Beria took over the NKVD in December 1938, but not before some 12–15 million people had been arrested and at least a million executed.

The Great Patriotic War and Stalin's Last Years

Not long after this self-inflicted bloodbath, the Soviet Union found itself embroiled in what Russians call the Great Patriotic War, during which it lost 20 million citizens, 7 million among the military, the rest during the Nazi occupation of the country. Because losses were so large, the war remains a tangible scar on the Russian psyche to this day. Stalin thought that the Nazi-Soviet non-aggression Pact, signed in August 1939 by Molotov and Ribbentrop, the two foreign ministers, would safeguard the Soviet Union from invasion. It divided central Europe into German and Soviet spheres, and in 1939–40 the Soviets made the most of it, marching into Eastern Poland (now Belorussia), Lithuania, Latvia and Estonia, and attacking Finland. Then, in June 1941, Hitler invaded the Soviet Union without a declaration of war. Though his intelligence had been warning him of such a move, Stalin was so shocked he was temporarily incapacitated. His voice was not heard on the radio, and it took several days for him to recover.

The Germans moved quickly. By September 1941 Leningrad was almost surrounded and by the end of the year the Germans were threatening Moscow as well. The seige of Leningrad, known to Russians as the Blockade (*blokad*), was only lifted in January 1944. Hitler had given the order to destroy the city completely, and without running water, electricity and almost without food the inhabitants of the city manned a spirited defence of its historic monuments. Though an accurate figure is hard to find, in the '900 Days', some 670,000 citizens are thought to have died and hundreds of monuments were damaged and destroyed. In winter, when it was too cold to dig graves for the dead, frozen corpses lined the streets waiting for collection.

Those hoping for a reprieve after the losses of the war were in for a shock: returning prisoners of war and other soldiers thought to have been exposed to 'foreign' ideas, including Alexander Solzhenitsyn, were sent straight to labour camps in Siberia. In 1948 the purge of 'cosmopolitans', a thinly disguised code for the Jews, was launched, while Andrei Zhdanov harangued the country's artists and writers into political orthodoxy. Stalin's swan song was the so-called Doctors' Plot of January 1953, in which nine Kremlin doctors, seven of them Jews, were accused of plotting to poison the leadership. In March 1953, in the middle of the trial, the 'Father of the People' expired.

The people of the Soviet Union wept in their millions at the news although, as the poet Yevtushenko observed, those tears were tinged with fear of the unknown. Stalin had been in power for almost 30 years, and was seen to have led the country to her finest, painful hour—victory in the war. In the economic sphere, Stalin's achievements also seem impressive at first glance. At the time of Lenin's death in 1924, the country had barely recovered from the Civil War; by the time Stalin died in 1953 the Soviet Union had become one of the two great powers. Moscow's skyline was punctuated by the needle-sharp towers of Stalin's 'Seven Sisters' sky-scrapers, a hidden allusion to the seven hills of that great, early empire, Rome. A palatial underground labyrinth, decorated with mosaics of gold leaf and marble and lit by chandeliers and massive bronze torchères, served the citizens as a glittering metro system. To achieve this, however, Stalin showed a pathological disregard for human life, and his economic development, predicated on the rapid growth of Soviet military might, entirely neglected the domestic needs of the population.

Krushchev and the Thaw

On Stalin's death, Lavrenti Beria, the sadistic and powerful head of the NKVD, seized power, only to be shot dead by his peers at a meeting of the Politburo. They were now free to pursue much needed economic and social reforms, raising the standard of living by concentrating industrial resources on the production of consumer goods—fridges, washing machines, cars. By 1955, Nikita Khrushchev had consolidated his power base in the party, and as General Secretary assumed overall control of government. A far cry from Stalin, Khrushchev was friendly and open. The greatest physical change to both Moscow and St Petersburg during his leadership was the massive new housing developments that began to spread out on the edges of the cities. Known derisively as *khrushchoby*, a pun on the leader's name and the Russian word for a slum, these box-like flats nevertheless helped to ease the urban housing crisis, made critical by wartime devastation and continuous migration from the countryside.

Though perhaps best remembered in the West as the only leader to take his shoe off and bang it on the table to express disapproval at the UN, Khrushchev is remembered by his fellow countrymen as the man who led the onslaught on the memory of Stalin. At the 20th Party Congress in 1956, Khrushchev delivered a blistering six-hour condemnation of his former boss in closed session to the shell-shocked delegates. Some 8 million victims of Stalin were rehabilitated, some posthumously, others in time to flood home from the camps in Siberia. In 1961 Stalin's embalmed body was moved out of Lenin's mausoleum and buried with other Soviet leaders beneath the Kremlin Wall behind it. In 1962, Krushchev, who is said to have read the manuscript personally, gave the go-ahead for the publication of Alexander Solzhenitsyn's *One Day in the Life of Ivan Denisovich*, an unflinching fiction based on the author's eight-year internment in the Siberian gulag. Yet all was not roses. Boris Pasternak, whose novel *Doctor Zhivago* criticized the still hallowed Bolsheviks of the Revolution and Civil War was published abroad. The author was not permitted to travel to receive his Nobel Prize for Literature, and was expelled from the Writers' Union. It was under Khrushchev too that the despicable practice of sentencing dissidents to psychiatric hospitals began.

Foreign policy was Khrushchev's most turbulent area. While in 1955 he was preaching peace with the West, in October 1956 Soviet troops were sent into Hungary to crush the revolt against Soviet control. Krushchev was not about to sacrifice the satellite Communist states of East Europe, the Soviet Union's *cordon sanitaire*, which had been hard-won in the Second World War. A brief thaw in relations with the West, during which Khrushchev made his successful trip to the United States, was followed by increased confrontation. In 1961 the Berlin Wall was erected by the East Germans, providing a tangible symbol of the opposition between the two world systems. When Soviet missiles were discovered in Fidel Castro's newly-Communist Cuba, the following year, the world came to the brink of nuclear war. Last-minute negotiations between Kennedy and Khrushchev averted a confrontation; the Soviets dismantled their arms on Cuba and a few months later America quietly stripped its own missiles from Turkey and Italy.

Khrushchev's healthy attitude to the economy is summed up by his statement that 'we must help the people to eat well, dress well and live well. You cannot put theory into your soup or Marxism into your clothes.' Sadly, the results were not as promising. To cure the country's perennial agricultural shortages, Khrushchev instituted the 'Virgin Lands' policy, which provided a new irrigated area the size of Canada's arable land in Siberia and Kazakhstan. The dry soil was not suitable for cultivation however, and severe erosion soon made it unproductive. There was still a massive lag between supply and demand for most consumer items as well. In the course of his flamboyant premiership, Khrushchev had managed to alienate many of the interest groups within the Soviet elite. In 1964, while he was on holiday, the Presidium met and agreed to overthrow him. Khrushchev was summoned back and told to retire 'on grounds of ill-health'.

Stagnation

Khrushchev was succeeded as General Secretary of the Communist Party by Leonid Brezhnev, whose 18-year premiership divides roughly in two. The first 10 years are remembered as a time of relative plenty. Thanks to incentives in agriculture and increased investment in the manufacture of consumer products, the average Soviet salary fed you, clothed you and provided a modicum of home comforts if you were prepared to queue. With inadequate infrastructure for the service or repair of domestic machinery, and the lack of spare parts, a 'second economy' began to flourish with a black market in scarce goods and services. By the early 1980s, this was estimated to account for up to 20 per cent of GNP, and even within state factories any spare capacity after the fulfillment of their quota was often used to work secretly *nalevo* ('on the left'). The agricultural crisis of 1975 and a sudden scarcity of goods put an end to this idyll, and suggested that, far from solving the country's problems, the relative hard work of the past decade had simply hidden them for a while. People began to doubt the constant exhortations that the Soviet Union was catching up with and about to overtake the economic achievements of the United States. Daily reports on the radio of this or that collective farm exceeding its agricultural targets just didn't square with empty fridges.

Brezhnev's support came from Party *apparatchiki*, whose tenure had been secured by his administrative reforms. For most of them, life was good. Their perks included the ability to shop at special shops where imported goods were readily available at subsidized prices; they also enjoyed better housing, holidays and hospital treatment. Corruption became endemic, with Brezhnev himself, and infamously his daughter Galina and her husband, receiving the lion's share. When, after Brezhnev's death, corruption in Uzbekistan was investigated, every single member of the local hierarchy—from Party to Trade Unions—was implicated. While his cronies quite literally got away with murder at times, Brezhnev took a tough stand on Jews who wished to emigrate and on political dissidents. After Solzhenitsyn was stripped of his citizenship and sent into exile in 1974, dissident activity increased, with the formation of underground groups reporting on human rights abuses, as well as an increase in the volume of *samizdat* (self-published) literature. But after the surge of protest that greeted the Soviet Union's war with Afghanistan in 1979, Brezhnev once again jammed foreign broadcasts in Russian and arrested many leading dissidents, including Andrei Sakharov, who was sent into internal exile in Gorky (now Nizhny Novgorod again). Tsarist history shows that Brezhnev was right to be scared; like that of the tsars, the Soviet regime was essentially a military dictatorship, and unpopular wars posed a greater threat to its power than anything else. Afghanistan turned out to be the beginning of the end.

Brezhnev was incapacitated by his first stroke in 1976, but such was the inertia of his government that he remained in power until 1982. A well-known Russian anecdote graphically characterizes this period of his leadership. Stalin, Khrushchev and Brezhnev are travelling together in a train when it grinds to a halt. Stalin orders the train driver and his crew to be taken out and shot and, not surprisingly, the train stays still. Khrushchev orders their rehabilitation, but to no effect. Brezhnev then pulls down the blinds on the windows, and exhorts his fellow passengers to pretend they are moving.

Brezhnev's successor Yuri Andropov was suspect in the eyes of the West as former head of the KGB, but his premiership saw a crackdown on corruption in which 40 out of 150 regional party secretaries were dismissed. He also tried to stem the national addiction to alcohol that was so costly in terms of lost working hours and health. But the aged Politburo was still trying to prevent the younger generation taking power. When Andropov died after just 15 months in office, his chosen successor, the sprightly 53-year-old reformer Mikhail Gorbachev, was passed over in favour of Konstantin Chernenko. The 72-year-old reactionary, already dying of chronic emphysema, survived for little more than a year.

Gorbachev and the Second Russian Revolution

The pace of change under Gorbachev left the Soviet Union and the world gasping for breath. The first Soviet leader since Lenin to have been to university, Gorbachev recognized that he had inherited a regime in crisis, and that radical measures were needed to avert disaster. However, not even he realized the extent of popular disillusionment. He may never have announced his famous twin policies of *glasnost* (openness) and *perestroika* (restructuring) in 1985 had he realized that he, the Communist Party and the Soviet Union itself, would be swept away by them.

At first, change was slow in coming. When one of the nuclear reactors at Chernobyl blew up in April 1986, it took Gorbachev three days to remember about *glasnost* and admit that the radiation clouds detected over Scandinavia were a result of a nuclear disaster at the plant near Kiev. Gradually, discussions opened on the subject which still haunted the country—Stalin's terror. In 1986 *Doctor Zhivago* was published for the first time in Russia and, at the end of the year, Andrei Sakharov and his wife Elena Bonner were released from internal exile in Gorky—a sign of true change. In 1987, differences began to appear in the traditionally united face of the Communist Party; as well as the hardliners, there was also a spirited radical group who called themselves the Democratic Union. Even now Gorbachev showed his loyalty to old ways by banning them from meeting. Boris Yeltsin, who made a name for himself exposing the privileges and corruption of the party, resigned from the Politburo and was sacked as head of the Moscow Communist Party.

1989 turned out to be a momentous year in European history. The new era was heralded by the March elections for the Congress of People's Deputies, in which, for the first time, a real element of choice existed between Communist and Communist-backed candidates, and those of more independent intent. Both Yeltsin and Sakharov were elected with overwhelming majorities, though at the rowdy first session of the Congress Gorbachev tried pathetically to turn the clock back by switching off the microphone as Sakharov railed against the system. In July, striking miners managed to wring real concessions out of the government, and in the autumn, sensing the disintegration of the monolith, the satellite states of Eastern Europe one by one declared the end of the Communist dictatorship and independence from the Soviet Union. Soviet troops on their soil were ordered by Moscow not to move; the motherland was too tired and bankrupt to continue policing her massive empire.

After the dismantling of the Berlin Wall, secession movements in the republics of the Soviet Union received a further boost with the widespread success of nationalist candidates and parties in the 1990 local elections. In Moscow and Leningrad, the reforming figures of economist Gavriil Popov and lawyer Anatoly Sobchak, who were to be stalwart supporters of further freedoms, took over the mayors' offices. On May Day the traditional march of Communist glory turned into a protest, and Gorbachev was jeered off the podium on Lenin's mausoleum. Shortly afterwards Yeltsin declared Russian independence from the Soviet Union and in July, in front of TV cameras at the Party Congress, he tore up his membership card. By the end of the year, 2 million other members had followed suit. In reaction to the threatened anarchy, Gorbachev and the hardliners retrenched. Eduard Shevardnadze's prophetic warning of a coming dictatorship as he resigned in December was borne out by the brutal violence used by Soviet troops trying to quash the nationalist uprisings in the Baltic Republics in January. But the tide of history was behind the secessionists, and by May 1991 Estonia, Latvia and Lithuania had all reestablished their independence. The following month, the people of Leningrad asserted their own identity by voting to restore the city's original name, St Petersburg.

It was the overwhelming victory of Yeltsin in the June elections for President of the Russian Republic, making him the first Russian leader ever to be elected, that gave him the confidence and authority to overturn the Communist system in the wake of the August coup attempt against Gorbachev. While Gorbachev was away on holiday, the country found itself under the 'protection' of a group of hardliners who had formed the 'State Committee for the State of Emergency in the USSR'. It was a shoddily planned coup, for while Gorbachev was under house arrest in the Crimea, the plotters' real enemies, the radical reformers, were never captured. Yeltsin made his way clandestinely to the White House, seat of the Russian parliament on the banks of the River Moskva, and led a three-day vigil against the threat of encroaching troops. By the second night, protective barricades were manned by upwards of 100,000 people, and the bewildered young soldiers in the surrounding tanks had been persuaded not to act. That evening three young men were crushed to death beneath the tracks of a tank on the nearby Garden Ring, but by the next day most divisions had come over to the democrats. In St Petersburg the military stayed off the streets, though a crowd of pro-democracy supporters rallied round

Anatoly Sobchak to defend the Mariinsky Palace. On the third day, the coup attempt collapsed. Some of the plotters responded in time-honoured Russian fashion by drinking themselves into a stupor; another committed suicide.

Gorbachev returned within hours, ashen-faced, as if to a new planet. Two days later on live television, he was demolished by Yeltsin, who forced him to sign a decree declaring the Communist Party, of which he was still a loyal supporter, illegal. The Russian flag flew for the first time since the Revolution, in place of the hammer and sickle. During the rest of the year, the Soviet Union disappeared as the Ukraine, Belarus, Georgia and other republics declared their independence, after which several of them allied themselves loosely with Russia again in the new Commonwealth of Independent States. Gorbachev, the emperor without an empire, resigned on Christmas Day 1991.

The Trials Begin

The last three years have been hell for Russia and her leaders. The immediate attempt to transform the command economy to a market economy with a short, sharp shock was wishful thinking on everyone's behalf. No infrastructure existed for the mechanisms of the market—no banking system, no legal safeguards, an inadequate distribution network—and most of Russian industry was not competitive anyway. On top of this the politicians who were to legislate this transformation were incapable of understanding the representative democracy within which they now found themselves operating, let alone making it work in Russia's favour. Newly entrusted with the right to oppose, they used it to the full, not realizing the importance of consensus politics, particularly in a time of national emergency.

1992 saw a 500 percent rise in the price of some foodstuffs and rocketing inflation. Savings that would have kept a couple in comfortable retirement for over 20 years were suddenly worth US$40. By December, the dynamic young Prime Minister who had overseen the attempted transition, Yegar Gaidar, was so unpopular he had to be replaced by Viktor Chernomyrdin, who turned out to be less of a hardliner than many feared. This did little to ease the deadlock which had grown up between Yeltsin and the Russian parliament. Even though the Russian people had given his policies a narrow vote of confidence in a referendum, in September 1993, Yeltsin was driven to the unconstitutional act of disbanding parliament and calling for elections in December to a new bi-cameral legislature. The speaker of parliament, Ruslan Khasbulatov, and Yeltsin's former ally Alexander Rutskoi, led the protest against what they claimed was a dictatorial encroachment by the president.

The showdown came at the beginning of October 1993, when Khasbulatov, Rutskoi and their allies in parliament were beseiged by troops in the White House, the scene of Yeltsin's triumph only two years before. Their own supporters, largely a strange mixture of old-guard Communists and Slavic nationalists known as the Red-Brown coalition, had massed outside the White House (where free vodka was reputedly being dispensed). On 3 October they stormed the nearby mayor's office and went on to try to take over the state TV and radio network at Ostankino in the north of the city. The confrontations were often violent, and in the course of the 24 hours 62 people died. Early on 4 October the government finally moved into action. Shelling of the White House set the building on fire, and at 6pm Khasbulatov and Rutskoi gave themselves up.

The results of the December 1993 elections surprised all by the strength of the vote for the erroneously named Liberal Democratic Party led by Vladimir Zhirinovsky, who attempted to capitalize on the natural xenophobia of the Russians. He ranted against the ungrateful republics who had seceded from the former Soviet Union, vowed to rebuild Russia's military strength and solve her economic problems. It never occurred to the inexperienced electorate to ask how he intended to pay for these miracles. The reformers, whose main alliance was known as Russia's Choice, blamed their in-fighting and lack of solidarity for their bad performance. In April 1994, all manner of political and social bodies, recognizing that little could be achieved by further discord, signed a Treaty of Civil Accord intended to make sure the country pulled together for its own good. The rouble, which remained remarkably stable through 1993 and the summer of 1994 began to slide in October, stirring up another bout of political manoeuvring. To make matters worse, by Christmas Russian troops were fighting in the secessionist republic of Chechnya, a bloody foretaste of other potential conflicts within the federation.

The job of converting the totalitarian country into a civil society has only just begun. The rule of law is far from established, and organized crime can only continue to proliferate in such anarchic territory. Immense investment is needed to make Russia's massive network of industry competitive on the international market, and until this is done, further gigantic sums are needed to pay for some form of welfare state as a safety net for the poor and unemployed.

Topics

Vodka

In 988, when Prince Vladimir was casting round for a religion for his people, he was forced to reject Islam because he knew that its prohibition on alcohol was an impossible condition. Since their earliest contacts with Russia, foreigners have remarked upon the symbiosis of the Russians and their tipple. In *The Travels of Olearius in Seventeenth Century Russia*, the Holsteiner Adam Olearius remarked that 'the vice of drunkenness is prevalent among this people in all classes, both secular and ecclesiastical, high and low, men and women, young and old... None of them anywhere, anytime, or under any circumstances lets pass an opportunity to have a draught or a drinking bout.' Foreign embassies were horrified to find that unless guests were made insensible from alcohol the host was not considered to have done his duty. During the reign of Peter the Great, the Danish Ambassador became so liverish that he offered to finance the building of an entire monastery if the Tsar would only stop forcing him to drink himself into a coma. Old habits die hard, as you will doubtless find out. Bear in mind the wisdom of Anton Chekhov, who remarked that though 'Vodka is white... it paints your nose red and blackens your reputation'.

For centuries, the Russians' favourite tipple has been vodka (literally the 'little water'), a distilled grain spirit which is said to have been invented by monks in the 15th century. The most common brands today are Moskovskaya or Stolichnaya, though if you know where to look you can also find *limonnaya* (lemon), *pertsovka* (red chilli) and *zubrovka* (bison grass) vodkas. Since a bottle of the real thing is often beyond the reach of the average Russian purse, home-brew, known as *samogon*, now finds its way onto the market, packaged as the real thing, only cheaper. To be sure that your purchase is genuine vodka you will have to take advice from an experienced local who will be able to tell from a number of pointers, including the speed at which bubbles travel through the liquid. Those who know they can't afford the national tipple slake their indigenous thirst on a variety of 100% proof colourless liquids known generically as 'spirit' (*spirt*). As living proof that it won't kill you, my only advice is to make sure that your shots are watered down.

Invitations to drink are often signalled by flicking the neck with your middle finger off your thumb. This is said to originate from a brilliant soldier whom Peter the Great rewarded with a tattoo beneath his beard. At the sight of the tattoo, any publican was obliged to served the soldier as much vodka as he wanted for free. Vodka should be drunk freezing cold, though no self-respecting Russian would wait if the bottle in question happened not to be. Otherwise, the etiquette varies little. The vodka is poured into small glasses, filled almost to the rim. Diluting it with tonic or orange juice is sacrilege. A toast is proposed, the shortest and most common of which is *na zdoroviye*, 'good health'. The assembled company raise their glasses and down the fiery spirit in one, followed by a *zakuska* or snack—a piece of pickled fish or mushroom, a slice of cucumber or at the very least a piece of bread.

The Mafia

You can't talk about Russia today without referring to the cabals of men and women who have hijacked the most profitable areas of business and run them as their private fiefdoms. Known collectively as the mafia, they are not one cohesive group but a myriad of power bases, best defined by their organized and illegal business practices, and the violence with which they protect their turf. They vary in size and importance from a small ring of criminals running prostitutes in a regional hotel to the networks which control the flow of radioactive materials out of Russia's nuclear installations. The mafia is so rampant that there is barely a business in the country that isn't involved, even if only by paying protection money.

The mafia is by no means a result of the official change over to capitalism and the market-economy. Just as prohibition created its own very profitable market in alcohol in the United States in the 1930s, so the empty shelves of the old Soviet Union hid a vast network of profitable markets in hard-to-obtain consumer goods, in the party membership that was vital for promotion beyond a certain level and in taboo luxury items. Unlike the 'private' mafia structures in the capitalist world, because of the centralized structure of production the extensive Soviet mafia inevitably included state officials who were bribed to procure sought-after items. In the largest exposé of public corruption, the so-called 'White-gold' cotton scandal unearthed in Uzbekistan in the 1980s, every single party and komsomol member, state and trade union employee and economic manager in the republic was shown to be implicated. They could not all be jailed and, as elsewhere, their fraternities of mutual advancement lived on, well-placed to exploit the possibilities of the new post-Soviet era.

Ironically, the widespread, secretive corruption of the Soviet mafia, which included high-ranking, die-hard Communist Party members such as General Secretary Leonid Brezhenev, was partly responsible for the demise of the Soviet system. By milking the already tottering state, weakened to a point of near political and economic bankruptcy, the mafia hastened the advent of Gorbachev's *perestroika*. The directors of new cooperative businesses continued to exploit their 'friendship' with state officials, and began to exploit the new opportunities thrown up by the changing situation. State money which had been salted away in Swiss bank-accounts found its way back into the country as the foreign contribution to joint-venture companies. Those in charge of the privatization of state assets, ignoring the obvious illegality of insider trading, have put profitable business the way of their friends and associates at knock-down prices. Protection rackets in Moscow and St Petersburg feed on new private businesses; unprotected by the ever-changing laws, the fledgling enterprises are easy prey. The contraction of the Russian armed forces and their withdrawal from the countries of the former Warsaw Pact has given rise to rampant profiteering and the sale of weapons and equipment by disillusioned officers. In late 1994, a young investigative journalist on the newspaper *Moskovsky Komsomolets*, who had uncovered evidence of corruption in the upper echelons of the ever-decreasing army, was blown up by a briefcase bomb.

As a tourist, you are very unlikely to come across the mafiosi, except in the cities' smarter restaurants where you may unwittingly rub shoulder pads. When shopping in the fruit and vegetable markets, you are inevitably dealing with the protected business of the southern republics who produce the goods—the Georgians, Azeris and Uzbeks. Beware of prostitutes, who are often controlled by groups intent on profiting from your wallet without any services rendered. The Russian mafia is now thought to play a major role in the trafficking of opiates from the Golden Triangle in Southeast Asia to Europe and USA, so you should also steer well clear of drug deals.

The wealth of the Russian mobsters is now legendary and international. An adversary of a mafia group from the breakaway republic of Chechnya has been murdered in North London, and estate agents in near-by ritzy Hampstead have reputedly been inundated by requests for million-pound pads, paid for with ready cash in suitcases.

Rasputin

Born in a village in Siberia in about 1862, Grigory Efimovich Rasputin's life ended with his murder in St Petersburg in 1916. The strange story of his rise from peasant wagoner to royal confidant is one of the best known in Russian history, and yet one of the most widely misunderstood. To call him the first Bolshevik, as did his murderer Yussupov, is only the most absurd of the myriad theories. His success can only be understood in the light of age-old Russian traditions, linked to the political climate of the early 20th century and to the specific characters involved in his drama.

Since the middle ages there has been a tradition of holy fools and wandering holy men, known as *startsi* (singular—*starets*), in Russia. Some have exerted a purely local influence, wandering from village to village dispensing wisdom and advice, whilst the fame of others has reached the ears of the highest in the land. In the 16th century Ivan the Terrible built St Basil's Cathedral over the tomb of a holy fool, Basil the Blessed, whose prophesies he had found so accurate. Even closer links between royalty and the *startsi* were forged in the 19th century. To this day there is currency in the rumour that Tsar Alexander I did not die at Taganrog but faked his demise so as to retire in solitude to Siberia. Alexander is said to have become a holy hermit in repentance for his part in the murder of his father Tsar Paul I. He is supposed to have changed his name to Fyodor Kuzmich, dying not in 1825 but in the second half of the century.

When tales of Rasputin's wisdom began to circulate in St Petersburg, it is hardly surprising that he was introduced to the devout royal couple. By 1907 Rasputin was a well-travelled 45 year-old, who had spent time in the monasteries of Mount Athos as well as the Holy Land. What is more, he was said to have powers of healing and, unbeknownst to the general population, the royal household was in dire need of such help. After the birth of four daughters, Alexandra had finally borne a son in 1904, only to discover that he had inherited the life-threatening blood-disorder haemophilia. In 1907, when Rasputin was first called to minister to the young boy, Nicholas II noted in his diary that 'Alexei was saved from certain death by his [Rasputin's] prayers'. For the next nine years, Rasputin acted as a fairy godfather to the boy, soothing him with his words and hands, and kneeling in a vigil of prayer beside his bed in times of danger. In 1912 when doctors feared for the tsarevich's life after a fall, a telegram was dispatched to Rasputin in Siberia. As soon as his reply was received the boy began to recover. 'The illness is not as dangerous as it seems', the telegram read, 'don't let the doctors worry him'. Whether you believe in such powers, or whether the holy man's effect had more to do with the family's desire to believe in his powers, there is little doubt that Rasputin did save the tsarevich on a number of occasions.

What is equally undeniable is how strange all this must have looked from outside the royal circle. Knowing little of the tsarevich's illness or the *starets's* effect upon it, the gossip of St Petersburg was Rasputin's debauched behaviour, the other side of the 'saintly' character which the tsarina so admired. At gypsy restaurants Rasputin was frequently reported leading the way in binges of feasting, drinking and dancing, foul mouthing members of the aristocracy and the government and crawling drunk into his carriage on the arm of at least one if not two voluptuous women. The list of women hypnotized into his bed by his staring green eyes and knowing looks is legendary. His flat at Gorokhovaya Ul 64 was constantly watched by the police. His last telephone number was St Petersburg 64646, not far removed from 666—the Number of The Beast.

At the beginning of the First World War, the German tsarina's popularity dipped to an all-time low. When Nicholas went off to the front, she was left in the company of the holy man, whose advice in matters of politics she passed on faithfully to the tsar, who often took it. By the end of 1916, when reverses at the front were met by starvation at home, there was a clamour to end his backward-looking influence. The ruling classes found it impossible to attack the tsar directly, and vented their anger on this strange figure who had captivated the tsar and tsarina to the point where ministers were chosen on his whim.

Vladimir Purishkevich was a member of the Duma (parliament), and held extreme monarchist beliefs. On 18 November he delivered a stinging appeal to his fellow parliamentarians to save the tsar from the 'dark forces' threatening him. Listening from the public gallery was Felix Yussupov (*see* pp.327–8). The following day he rang Purishkevich, inviting him to join him in killing the 'holy man'. Yussupov lured Rasputin to his palace on the banks of the Moika Canal (*see* pp.326–7) on the pretext of a party. He and his fellow conspirators—Purishkevitch, the tsar's cousin Grand Duke Dmitry, an army doctor called Lazovert and an officer named Sukhotin—attempted to poison the *starets*. When this failed, they tried shooting him. Then, with the connivance of the police, who shot a dog to account for the blood, Rasputin's body was taken to the far side of town and thrown under the ice of a tributary of the Neva, where it was found three days later, his hands clinging to the supports of a bridge. Where poison and four bullets had failed, drowning eventually succeeded. Yet Rasputin's death solved nothing. The licentious holy man was only a symptom of the real cause of the people's misery—the stubborn conservatism of the autocracy itself. Within months the February Revolution had dethroned the tsar and swept away the monarchy.

Icons and Iconostases

In the orthodox church an icon is a religious painting, depicting Christ, the saints, or an episode from the holy texts. The name derives from the Greek word *eikon*, meaning image. Unlike Western European religious art, icons are more than mere images. They are venerated by worshippers, who address prayers to them in the belief that they will be heard and acted upon by the particular saint in heaven.

The tradition of icon painting finds its earthly roots in the earliest painted portraits, found around the Egyptian town of Fayum and dating to the time of Christ. They are lively, intimate portraits, painted on wooden boards and buried with the deceased they represent. The idea of portable images attracted an early Christian following, since the icons could be carried away by the believers during periods of persecution.

The spiritual roots of icon painting are more complex, beginning with the legends of the portraits St Luke is said to have painted of his contemporaries. A great icon should reflect the perfect harmony of the eternal world, and to prepare themselves for this mystical task icon painters would often fast and go through long rituals of physical and spiritual cleansing before beginning an icon. In this aspect icons can act as the focus of meditation on the nature of the holy. Mirroring the belief that Jesus was God's incarnation on earth, icons are also an incarnation of the unknowable and invisible. They should act as a window on the transcendant reality of Christian beliefs. And because of the reverse perspective used by icon painters, instead of being independent of the image, the viewer or worshipper is pulled into the picture. He finds himself standing at the point of infinity, playing a vital role in the spiritual matrix which defines the boundaries of the image.

The iconostasis or wall of icons in which icons are traditionally hung in a church is like a cosmological diagram. The bottom row is known as the Local Tier, and contains icons with a specific relevance to the church—such as icons depicting the saints after whom it is named and after whom its patrons were named. At the centre of the Local Tier you will find the Royal Gates, normally decorated with panels showing the four apostles and the Annunciation, when the Angel Gabriel told Mary she had been chosen to bear the son of God. Above this comes the most important Deesis Tier, where full-length representations of the saints intercede on behalf of humanity, with Christ enthroned at the centre. To the left and right of Christ you will always find the Virgin Mary and St John the Baptist respectively, often flanked by the Archangels Mikhail and Gabriel. The rest of the tier is usually made up of disciples, apostles and local saintly bishops. Above the Deesis Tier comes the Festival Tier, in which the great feast days of the Orthodox Church are celebrated. At a minimum, these normally include scenes of the Birth of the Virgin, the Presentation of the Virgin in the Temple, the Annunciation, the Nativity, the Presentation of Christ in the Temple, the Baptism, Christ's Entry into Jerusalem, the Crucifixion, the Descent into Hell, the Ascension, the Old Testament Trinity and the Dormition of the Virgin. The upper row depicts the patriarchs and prophets of the Old Testament leaning towards a central icon of the Virgin Mary.

By the time Russia adopted Orthodoxy from Constantinople in the 10th century, strict rules had been drawn up governing the painting of icons. Since many of the early icons were said to have been painted by St Luke himself, they were holy relics. Just like any reproduction of the Bible, icons were not intended as original works of art but copies, and it was out of the question to change any detail of the original. The composition of each image had been carefully studied and given a name, depending on the exact position, dress and pose of its subject. Most of the earliest icons surviving in Russia were either imported from elsewhere or painted by foreign masters who had come to answer the needs of the new Orthodox nation. In the 15th century Russian icon painting came into its own, with a brief, superb flowering begun by a foreigner known as Theofan the Greek and continued by two native masters Andrei Rublyov and Dionisy. The best examples of their works are to be found now in the Tretyakov Gallery in Moscow, the Russian Museum in St Petersburg, and in the iconostases of the Cathedral of the Annunciation in the Kremlin (*see* p.106), and the Cathedral of the Trinity at the Trinity Sergius Monastery in Sergeyev Possad (*see* p.265). Very little is known of the lives of any of these celebrated painters, but those with a serious interest should watch Tarkovsky's film *Andrei Rublyov* for its evocation of the spirit of medieval Russian icon painting.

Until the Revolution, an icon hung in the corner of almost every room in the land, known as the Red Corner (*krasny ugol*). Very often these were directly replaced by cheaply reproduced images of Lenin, Marx and Engels, prophets of the new religion, but today you will again find small lamps burning before icons in many a home.

The Matrioshka Society

> *Man is the head of the family, but woman is the neck;*
> *which ever way the neck turns, so turns the head*

Russian proverb

For decades, the most popular Russian souvenir has been a nest of wooden *matrioshka* dolls. In a series of immaculate conceptions, the largest woman doll reveals another woman who reveals another who reveals another, to the power of 60 in the finest examples. There is an uncanny and doubtless subconscious symbolism in this pleasing and ubiquitous toy. The all-female family, a mother bringing up a child, often living with her own mother, is increasingly common in Russia, as women take the Russian proverb 'Women can do everything; men can do the rest' to its natural conclusion and cast off the dead weight of an indolent husband.

Time and again you will hear Russian women likening their husband to another child, only more demanding. On top of her own job, she must not only wash his clothes, cook for him, make his sandwiches for lunch, look after his children and clean his house, but she is also expected to capitulate to his late-night, vodka-sodden sexual advances. Divorce rates are soaring, and Russian women are learning to live without men, albeit only reluctantly. For despite the complaints, Russian society is still remarkably male-centric. The Soviet Union may have been the first society to officially emancipate women, but women have not found it easy to penetrate the ruling echelons of their society. Name a female Soviet politician if you can. Today, while 90 per cent of children's doctors are women, they make up only 6 per cent of Russia's surgeons, and less than 2 per cent of the prestigious

Academy of Sciences. Women themselves are often accomplices in the male conspiracy to keep them in their place. Indoctrinated by the pervasive old-fashioned view of the sexes, they can be seen bringing up their boys to behave just as the husband they despise. While girls are taught cookery and cleaning, boys sit and watch. Even intelligent, high-achieving Russian women tend to think feminism is a western disease, the product of a bourgeois society which turns women into power-hungry vamps seeking to compensate for their own insecurities by destroying half of the population.

In a recent survey, only 6 per cent of married Russian women claimed to be satisfied by their sex life. Others complain of their partner's consistent 'premature congratulations'. There is almost no sex education in Russian schools and 70 per cent of all first sexual experiences take place without contraceptives. Family planning services, though gradually improving, betray a societal lack of respect for the female body. The main method of contraception is still abortion, which takes place in a network of clinics across the country. Most clinics have no private operating theatres, and eight women may undergo abortions at the same time in one large room. Anaesthetic is not normally on offer and after-care extends to lying down on a bed for a couple of hours afterwards. The average Russian woman undergoes 12 abortions in her lifetime.

Things are gradually improving. If you can pay for it, family planning now offers pills and cervical smears, and *glasnost* has certainly brought sex out of the closet, most visibly in the form of pornography. It is interesting to speculate whether the advent of male *matrioshka* sets will augur in a new, nurturing Russian man, willing to do more than pay lip-service to old-fashioned gallantry by opening doors, pouring drinks, lighting cigarettes and carrying bags for his woman.

Underground

From the underground monasteries of the early Russian Orthodox Church to the vibrant Soviet counter-culture which became known as the Underground, the Russians seem to have a particular affinity with things subterranean. The country's metro systems are shining beacons of efficiency in a mire of chaos. Rumours concerning whole networks of other tunnels beneath Moscow have been rife since the reign of Ivan the Terrible. Somewhere beneath the city his invaluable library of medieval manuscripts is said to be immured, doubtless secreted off the rat-race reputedly used by his murderous henchman Maliuta Skuratov to hurry from his palace to the tsar's bedchamber. Other villains from history are widely linked with secret passages. Stalin is said to have ordered the construction of a private underground train by which he could flee the Kremlin in times of danger. Even the mild-mannered Gorbachev's home in Moscow was said to be built over several underground storeys and an underground rail link. In Dostoyevsky's horrifying short story *Notes from Underground*, the writer suggests a nest of amoral victims of Russian 19th-century society coniving and conspiring their way through 'underground' (*i.e.* invisible, unnoticed) lives.

It was only during the cultural repression of the Soviet period that the underground gained a better reputation, safe-guarding artistic freedom from the deadening depradations of socialist realism. Amongst anti-Soviet painters, poets and musicians who were banned from their 'Unions' and therefore banned from pursuing their vocations full-time, the most popular job was that of boilerman. Hidden in every district in the city are the boilers that provide the inhabitants with their heating and hot water. Often underground, the small, warm machine rooms provided studio or studying space where artists were free to create, between occasionally stoking the vast ancient boilers with coal, disturbed only by visits from their friends. The salary was enough to live on, a warm place to live and sleep was provided and in summer you could take months off at a time. There is still a community of wood-workers, poets and composers living on like unreformed hippies in these infernal refuges.

Superstitions

There are few more superstitious people in the developed world than the Russians. Every day on national television, after the evening news and weather, a serious man or woman in a donnish gown reads the nation's horoscopes to a devoted audience. Even Russian literature is said to have been saved by superstition. In 1825, as Alexander Sergeyevich Pushkin set out from his country estate to join the Decembrist Uprising in St Petersburg, a hare crossed his path in an unlucky omen. The poet and father of Russian literature returned home, and lived on to write his most important works including the epic poem *Eugene Onegin*.

To avoid a terrible *faux pas*, you may find it useful to bear the following in mind when visiting Russians. It is considered bad luck to shake hands or kiss across a threshold, and also bad luck to give even numbers of flowers, on any occasion except at a funeral. Walking around in bare socks in a flat is thought to bode a death in the family, so always accept the offer of a pair of slippers (*toofli*) that will be made. You may think it a blessing, but bear in mind that as a woman if you sit at the corner of the table it is said that you will not marry for seven years. When there is a silence in the conversation, the Russians think nothing as optimistic as that there is an angel flying overhead. To them, it means another policeman has just been born. Before you leave the house on a journey of any length, you should sit down for a minute on your bags. If you leave something behind, it is said to be bad luck to return for it.

Few words conjure up the opulent world of *fin de siècle* Europe so vividly as the name of the Russian pre-Revolutionary court jeweller Carl Gustavovich Fabergé. Of French Huguenot origin, the Fabergé family had fled persecution in 17th-century France, but it was not until the mid 19th-century that they entered the jewellery business. Gustave Fabergé opened a small shop in the Imperial capital, St Petersburg, in 1842, and four years later his son Carl, the genius of the family, was born.

Carl Fabergé studied with a leading German goldsmith and travelled to the great centres of craftsmanship in Italy and France before taking over the family business in St Petersburg in 1870 at the age of 24. Carl was gifted with a brilliant, naturalistic talent for design, incorporating and to a certain extent anticipating the trends of the Arts and Crafts and Art Nouveau movements towards an interest in materials for their own sake and not merely for their monetary value. Fabergé used rock crystal and semi-precious marbles as well as diamonds and precious metals, and even the boxes they came in, hand crafted from polished holly-wood with white silk linings, were works of art.

It comes as no surprise that the most famous jeweller of all time should have lived and worked in turn-of-the-century Russia, a land abundant with precious and semi-precious stones and metals. The first 30 years of Carl's 47-year supremacy coincided with the greatest economic boom in Russian history. In 1885 Carl became Court Jeweller to the Romanov dynasty, and though it is estimated that the income of Nicholas II, the last of Russia's tsars, was less than 25 per cent that of the British royal family at the time, the Russian royals were conspicuous spenders. As well as personal presents for friends and relatives, Fabergé designed and produced decorations and official gifts. Fabergé's fame, however, stems from the fabulous, bejewelled Easter eggs which they made for the tsars.

In 1885, Alexander III was casting round for a present for his home-sick Danish wife when he commissioned Carl Fabergé to copy an egg, containing a jewelled hen, from the Danish royal collection. So pleased was the Tsarina with her gift that Alexander continued the tradition every year, allowing Fabergé complete freedom of design and finding his family enchanted by the imaginative results. When his son Nicholas II ascended the throne, he ordered two eggs to be made every year—one for his mother, the Dowager Empress, and one for his wife. The design was a complete secret, always incorporating an element of surprise and often taking some topical event, such as the coronation or the inauguration of the new Trans-Siberian railway, as its theme. The eggs would be presented by a member of the Fabergé family in person, an occasion which came to be the focus of enormous anticipation. Of the 54 eggs crafted for the Romanovs, 47 survive. Ten are still in the Kremlin collection, the rest scattered throughout the world. The Imperial Fabergé egg record holder is the collection of the now-deceased American publishing mogul Malcolm Forbes, which includes 11 of the Imperial creations. However Fabergé also created eggs for other royal families and extravagant individuals. Anyone wanting to purchase an egg should bear in mind that the last one to come onto the market sold for US$5.5 million in November 1994. A cheaper alternative would be to visit the show-room of Fabergé's aesthetic heir, the jeweller Ananov, in the Grand Hotel Europe on St Petersburg's Nevsky Prospekt.

Tapochki

Any definition of these infuriating felt over-shoes, designed to protect the ubiquitous parquet in Russian palaces, would be incomplete without mention of their secondary, unintentional effect on their wearer's dignity. You will find yourself forced into them in most museum lobbies, and from the moment you begin to try to find a pair the right size, the battle begins. The felt is matted and grimy to the touch, the elastic looks as if it has been borrowed from pre-war knickers and if you are lucky enough to get a pair with ties, there will probably only be one of them.

Having negotiated your boots or shoes into them, you will then discover that *tapochki* have a life of their own. One way or another, when it comes to going up or down stairs your pair of pedal gloves will be lagging behind or ahead of your feet, catching themselves on the steps in a determined effort to trip you up. There is no alternative to suffering this indignity, though it may be helpful to remember the floor-polishers of yesteryear whose entire working life was spent encased in these wretched contraptions. Carrying the tools of their trade with them, they would be called to aristocratic palaces before parties to skate up and down the parquet of the ballroom, shining it with their custom-built, polish-sodden *tapochki*. As Eugenie Fraser recalls in her book *The House by the Dvina*, 'crossing one arm behind his back each man skated over the floor, the leg with the attached brush swinging back and fore in a wide sweep while the other dragged behind twisting and hopping' until 'their damp shirts clung to their backs'.

Moscow is not natural walking terrain. In the course of creating a capital fit for socialist heroes, successive Soviet governments, in particular Stalin, bulldozed wide avenues through the medieval street pattern. Lined with gargantuan apartment blocks, these endless six-lane highways reduce pedestrians to helpless ants, burrowing under-ground

Moscow: the Walks

when they want to cross the road. Only the suicidal make the over-ground dash. For those wishing to return home in one piece, the first part of the Russian highway code to learn is to recognize the sign for an underpass (Переход—*perekhod*), a white stickman running downstairs on a blue background. Having said that, there is no better way to get to know the city than walking, and once you take on board a few basic rules the secrets of Moscow, city of surprises, are yours for the taking. These walks will act as a spur to further discoveries of your own—an area of frantic street trading, a quiet courtyard café, an ancient church recently reopened for worship, or a gaggle of grannies watching indulgently over their frolicking charges while discussing the price of *kolbassa*, Russian sausage meat.

The most important pattern to slip into is to always look for the small, and you will find that after a while you won't notice the buildings of inhuman proportion. The joy of the city lies mainly in its older buildings, hidden away down side streets, dwarfed by prominent communist erections. The strange combination of power stations and factories in the heart of the city has its advantages. Certain monuments are never to be seen without a photogenic wisp of industrial cloud scudding dramatically over them. Never walk the full length of an arterial highway—the infinite vista exhausts the spirit before the feet have even begun to ache. These walks have all been constructed to lead you on and off the larger streets, dissecting them into manageable doses and explaining their relationship with the historic city around them. Before you set out on an expedition, always check that your plans won't be ruined by that idiosyncratic Russian institution, the *sanitarny dyen*. Every museum and sight is closed for its 'hygiene day' once a month, usually in the first or last week. Be extra vigilant if you are here at that time. During cold spells in winter, take taxis or public transport between the highlights of each walk, which are indicated by a snowflake on each title page. When you think you are lost, don't hesitate to ask for help from a reputable looking citizen. If they don't recognize the street name you are using, they may know the road by its old name. Refer to the list of changed street names at the end of the book, *see* pp.580–2.

Since almost everywhere else of interest in Moscow is closed on Mondays, use that day to visit the Kremlin. Walk VIII and Walk III are useful for Tuesdays, the other day when many cultural establishments close. If the relentless pavement bashing gets to you, take a short trip out to the palace of Kuskovo or the beach at Serebryany Bor described in Peripheral Attractions, or even further into the countryside on an adventurous Day Trip. As an easy reference source, you will find a list of all the interesting buildings open to the public in the Museums and Galleries chapter. Fuller descriptions are also given to sights which occur nowhere else in the book.

I: The Kremlin

Start: Ⓜ *Okhótny Ryad, following signs in the underground neon labyrinth for Red Square* (К Красной площади). *Above ground, turn right and leaving the two entrances to Red Square on your left, head for the tall wrought-iron gate into the Alexander Gardens* (Александровский сад).

Walking Time: *3 hours. Keen sightseers on fighting form could spend most of a day here, ogling the frescoes and icons.*

Sites

1 Tomb of the Unknown Soldier
   Mogila neizvestnovo soldata
   Могила неизвестного солдата

2 Grotto
   Grot
   Грот

3 Obelisk of Revolutionary Thinkers
   Обелиск

4 Kutafya Gate Tower and Ticket Office
   Kutafya bashnya i Kassa
   Кутафья башня и Касса

5 Ticket Office
   Kassa
   Касса

6 Trinity Gate Tower
   Troitskaya bashnya
   Троицкая башня

7 Palace of Congresses
   Kremlyovsky dvorets syezdov
   Кремлёвский дворец съездов

8 Amusement Rooms
   Poteshny Dvorets
   Потешный Дворец

9 Arsenal
   Арсенал

10 Patriarch's Palace
   Patriarshiye Palaty
   Патриаршие Палаты

11 Cathedral of the Twelve Apostles
   Sobor Dvenadtsati Apostolov
   Собор Двенадцати Апостолов

12 Tsar Cannon
   Tsar-pushka
   Царь-пушка

13 Senate
   Сенат

14 Presidium of the Supreme Soviet
   Zdaniye Prezidiuma Verkhovnovo Sovieta
   Здание Президиума Верховного Совета

15 Cathedral Square
   Sobornaya ploshchad
   Соборная площадь

16 Ivan the Great Belltower
   Kolokolnya Ivana Velikovo
   Колокольня Ивана Великого

17 Tsar Bell
   Tsar-kolokol
   Царь-колокол

18 Cosmos Oak
   Dub Kosmosa
   Дуб Космоса

19 Cathedral of the Assumption
   Uspensky sobor
   Успенский собор

20 Church of the Deposition of the Virgin's Robe
   Tserkov Rizpolozheniya
   Церковь Ризположения

21 Terem Palace
   Teremnoy dvorets
   Теремной дворец

22 Faceted Chamber
   Granovitaya palata
   Грановитая палата

23 Red Staircase
   Zolotaya krasnaya lestnitsa
   Золотая красная лестница

24 Cathedral of the Archangel Michael
   Arkhangelsky sobor
   Архангельский собор

25 Cathedral of the Annunciation
   Blagoveshchensky sobor
   Благовещенский собор

26 Great Kremlin Palace
   Bolshoi Kremlyovsky dvorets
   Большой Кремлёвский дворец

27 Armoury Museum/Diamond Fund Exhibition
   Oruzheinaya palata
   Оружейная палата

28 Borovitskaya Gate Tower
   Borovitskaya bashnya
   Боровицкая башня

Restaurants and Cafés

A McDonald's

B La Kantina

C El Rincon Español

D Stol Russkoy Kukhni
   Стол Русской Кухни

E Rosie O'Grady's

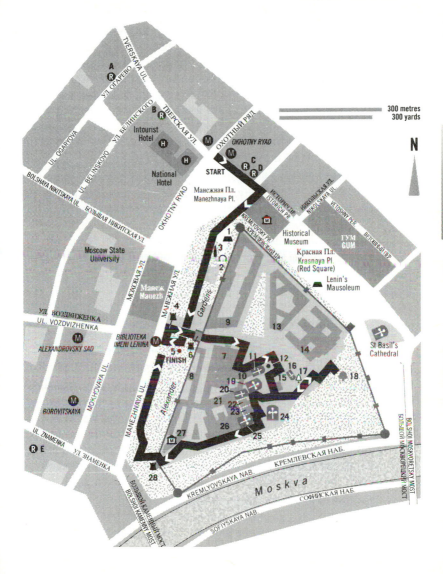

300 metres
300 yards

N

TVERSKAYA UL.

УЛ ОГАРЕВО

A R

УЛ. БЕЛИНСКОГО

B R

ТВЕРСКАЯ УЛ.

UL OGARYOVA

UL. BELINSKOVO

Intourist
Hotel

H

National
Hotel

H

H

OKHOTNY RYAD

M

ОХОТНЫЙ РЯД

M

START

C R D R

BOLSHAYA NIKITSKAYA UL. БОЛЬШАЯ НИКИТСКАЯ УЛ.

OKHOTNY RYAD

Манежная Пл.
Manezhnaya Pl.

ИСТОРИЧ.ПР.
ISTORICH.PR.

НИКОЛЬСКАЯ УЛ

VETOSHNY PER.

ВЕТОШНЫЙ ПЕР

КРЕМЛЕВСКИЙ ПР.
KREMLYOVSKY PR.

Moscow State
University

МОХОВАЯ УЛ.

Манеж
Manezh

1

3

2

Gardens

Historical
Museum

ГУМ
GUM

Красная Пл.
Krasnaya Pl.
(Red Square)

Lenin's
Mausoleum

УЛ. ВОЗДВИЖЕНКА
UL. VOZDVIZHENKA

4

МАНЕЖНАЯ УЛ.

9

13

ALEXANDROVSKY SAD

BIBLIOTEKA
IMENI LENINA

M

5 FINISH 6

7

11

12

14

St Basil's
Cathedral

MOKHOVAYA UL.

8

10

19

15

16

17

18

Alexander

20

M

BOROVITSKAYA

21 22

23

24

BOLSHOI MOSKVORETSKY MOST
БОЛЬШОЙ МОСКВОРЕЦКИЙ МОСТ

УЛ ЗНАМЕНКА

R E

УЛ. ЗНАМЕНКА

MANEZHNAYA UL.

27

M

26

25

28

KREMLYOVSKAYA NAB. КРЕМЛЕВСКАЯ НАБ.

Moskva

BOLSHOI KAMENNY MOST
БОЛЬШОЙ КАМЕННЫЙ МОСТ

SOFIYSKAYA NAB

СОФИЙСКАЯ НАБ

The earth as we all know it begins at the Kremlin... It is the central point.

Vladimir Mayakovsky

This massive, red-walled city-within-a-city needs little introduction. It is the president's place, Yeltsin's, and before that it was the general secretaries' and before that the tsars'. To most Western visitors, the fortified nerve-centre still retains echoes of the chill Cold War and before, when the decrees of Stalin rang out condemning millions of Russians to death and the thick walls symbolized intransigence and a barrier of lies. But today the blue, red and white flag of Russia flies hopefully in place of the hammer and sickle, though red stars on the towers remind that tyranny is still not far away.

Once inside the Kremlin, apart from the tourists there is an otherworldly sense of tranquillity. Few cars, the scourge of Moscow, penetrate its walls, while grass, one of the city's most embattled inhabitants, grows like a carpet in the gardens. Around you, the very buildings map out the stranglehold the supreme ruling figure had over every area of the state. It is like Buckingham Palace, the Houses of Parliament, the Old Bailey and No. 10 Downing Street, all rolled into one. Just as they were concentrated in one place, so they were concentrated in one pair of hands. Even the clutch of cathedrals here, and the Russian Orthodox Church they symbolize, were ultimately controlled by the autocrats. And yet an old Russian proverb, evidence of the people's complicity, ran 'there is nothing above Moscow except the Kremlin and nothing above the Kremlin except Heaven'.

About half of the inside of this vast irregular triangle is out of bounds to tourists, occupied either by the Kremlin garrison, the president or used only on state occasions. In total there are four cathedrals, one church, three small exhibitions and the huge Armoury Museum to be seen. If this sounds too much for you, leave out the Patriarch's Palace and cathedral, the Church of the Deposition of the Robe and, more for reasons of economy, the exorbitant Diamond Fund Exhibition.

The Kremlin precincts are open 10am–7pm (10am–5pm from Oct to April), although individual museums within begin closing earlier. It is closed on Thursdays, which makes it a good place to head on Mondays when almost everything else takes a break. Work your itinerary to coincide with one of the sessions at the Armoury Museum (*see* pp.108–10). Tourists in shorts are not welcome.

One of the major oversights of Russian tourism is the lack of even the most basic café in the Kremlin. It is the seat of government and is still revered as the most sacred place in the vast country, but if Stalin ate here the average tourist couldn't be said to be defiling the place. Remember, if you go out before you have finished, you will have to buy yourself another admission ticket. The following suggestions are divided according to which of the two working gates you should use to get to them.

Borovitskaya Gate

Rosie O'Grady's, Ul. Znaménka 9, ℘ 203 9087. One of the thousands of Irish pubs that have colonized the world. Guinness on tap and steaming shepherd's pie on the hot plate. Serves sandwiches too.

Trinity Gate

La Kantina, Ul. Tverskáya 5, beside the Yermolova Theatre, just beyond the Intourist Hotel (open 8am–12 midnight) is a very popular new Mexican bar and restaurant serving the usual *nachos* and *enchiladas.*

McDonald's, Ul. Ogaryova 6, if you must.

El Rincon Español, ground floor, Hotel Moskva, 2 Okhotny Ryad, ℘ 292 2893/0294). Use the front entrance of this forbidding, Stalinist monolith, looking straight on to Manezhnaya Ploshchad, to find the pearl within. Cold San Miguel or extortionate sangria wash down the tapas, paella and specials of the day.

Stol Russkoy Kukhni, Hotel Moskva, Manezhnaya Ploshchad entrance. Those with tighter budgets can bypass the Spanish food in favour of the Russian cafeteria on the floor above.

Like all important Russian medieval towns, Moscow began with a Kremlin (Kreml), a fortified stronghold in which the local ruler could defend himself. The first Kremlin on this site was built by Yuri Dolgoruky, Prince of Suzdal, in 1156 as an outpost for his nearby kingdom. In 1238 the Mongols burned it to the ground. However the natural advantages of the site, at the heart of the river system that linked Russia from north to south, guaranteed its survival. In 1272 Daniil, son of St Alexander Nevsky, came here from Novgorod and founded the principality of Moscow, governing from a wooden Kremlin. But the Kremlin really took off during the avaricious reign of his son Ivan I 'Kalita' (Moneybags), who ruled from 1328–40.

As the local tax collector for the Mongols he earned riches and the title of Grand Prince, his leadership legitimized when the head of the Russian Orthodox Church moved here from Vladimir. On a wave of gold and confidence, Ivan built the first stone churches inside his fortress.

In the late 14th century the fort was for the first time walled in stone, but the current walls date from a century later. It was then, under Ivan III, 'the Great' (1462–1505), that many of the more magical structures, those which give the place its Thousand and One Nights feel, were built. Influenced by his Byzantine wife Zoë, who had brought all manner of foreign scholars, craftsmen and objects with her, Ivan sent to Italy for architects. Between 1475 and 1509, by which time his son, Vassily III had ascended the throne, the majority of those buildings which we think of as the quintessence of Russia—the Cathedral of the Assumption, the red-brick towers and walls, the Faceted Palace, the Cathedral of the Archangel Michael and the Ivan the Great Bell Tower—were all built by Italians. Their contribution to Russian architectural *savoir faire* can be judged by comparing them with the Church of the Deposition of the Virgin's Robe and the Cathedral of the Annunciation, both built at the same time by Russians from Pskov. Vassily's other major contribution to the Kremlin was the addition of a wide moat outside the wall on Red Square, as much to ward off fire as enemy armies. The other two sides of the fort were protected by the rivers Moskva and Neglinnaya, the latter now piped beneath the Alexander Gardens.

Of all the ironies, the greatest siege the Kremlin ever withstood pitted a Polish army on the inside against Russians trying to get them out. During the weakness of the Russian successsion crisis known as the Time of Troubles, the Poles used a series of pretenders to further their influence in Russia. In 1611–12 they found themselves trapped in the Kremlin, driven to cannibalism in one of the most miserable of sieges. The arrival of the Romanovs on the throne in 1613 heralded a spate of palace building, but within a century they had abandoned the Kremlin for St Petersburg.

It was the psychological revulsion of one of the dynasty's strongest monarchs for the Kremlin that reversed its fortunes. In 1682 a young Peter the Great stood on the Red Staircase, the processional entrance to the Faceted Chamber. Below him the Kremlin guard (*streltsy*), in league with his half-sister Sophia, killed his uncle and his advisor Artamon Matveev, tossing their bodies like rag-dolls from pike to pike. From that moment on Peter loathed the Kremlin, a fact which made it easier for him to transfer his government to boggy St Petersburg. Throughout the 18th century, while building raced ahead in St Petersburg, the monarchs paid little attention to their old capital. A small wooden Kremlin palace built by Rastrelli for Elizabeth was burned in 1812, and when Catherine the Great came to Moscow for her coronation in 1762, the royal quarters were so damp and neglected that she sequestered the house of Prince Golitsyn to live in instead. As a result, she later commissioned a monumental palace from Bazhenov, one of two Moscow projects she initiated with him only to cancel them after building work had begun. However the master of neoclassicism, Matvei Kazakov, did manage to build his triangular Senate (1776–90), which stands today.

The Kremlin's second foreign invasion came in 1812, when Napoleon's troops occupied it for five weeks. They took out priceless furniture to burn on their camp fires, stripped the Uspensky Cathedral alone of an estimated 5 tons of silver and several hundred pounds of gold and used 183,000 pounds of gunpowder in their attempt to destroy it as they left. Luckily heavy rain and prompt action by the Russians limited the damage to a section of wall, three towers, the Ivan the Great Bell Tower and the Arsenal. During restoration the Alexander Gardens were created and the moat on Red Square was filled in. The rest of the 19th century saw the addition of the massive but architecturally dubious Great Kremlin Palace (1839–49) and Arsenal Chambers (1849–51), commissioned by Nicholas I from Konstantin Thon.

During the October 1917 Revolution, the Bolsheviks lost control of the Kremlin for several days. Passions raged among the revolutionary leaders in St Petersburg, as rumours reached them that its monuments had been destroyed. In fact the week's fighting did far less damage than Lenin's decision to move the seat of government back here in March 1918. By the mid-fifties, when the Kremlin reopened to tourists, the ancient Convent of the Assumption and the Monastery of the Miracles, dating back to the 14th century, and the 19th-century Nicholas Palace, had all been destroyed. In their place stands the pseudo-classical Presidium of the Supreme Soviet. The most recent addition, the Palace of Congresses (1960–61) has been used for little, since the demise of the Communist Party, other than showing second-rate ballet and opera.

As a prelude to the fortress itself, the **Alexander Gardens** *beneath its towering walls give little away. Peeping above the walls, the long yellow façade of Peter the Great's much rebuilt Arsenal overshadows the* **Tomb of the Unknown Soldier**.

The flame has burned here in memory of the 20 million or so Russians who died in the Second World War since it was brought from the Field of Mars in St Petersburg in 1967. Each red granite plinth commemorates a 'hero-city' whose role in the war was particularly bloody. Until 1961 Volgograd had been known as Stalingrad, and you can still see the marks where its plinth was amended after Stalin had been posthumously denounced. The war so devastated the country and was so heavily used as a propaganda tool by the Soviet regime that newlyweds still come here to lay flowers in memory of the dead. Nearby is a half-hearted grotto with a curious classical colonnade, dating from the original construction of the gardens in 1822, when the Neglinnaya River which used to flow here was channelled into a pipe underground. The cast list on the **Obelisk to Revolutionary Thinkers** read very differently when it was first erected in 1913 to commemorate 300 years of the Romanov dynasty with a list of the tsars and tsarinas. Today pride of place is taken by Marx, Engels and, curiously, amongst others, Thomas More.

> *Ticket offices for the Kremlin can be found beyond the red-brick bridge or round to the right, up the stairs by the stylish Baroque bastion, the* **Kutafya Tower***. Ask for tickets to all (всё—vsyo), and you will be given rouble tickets to everything but the* **Armoury and Diamond Fund Exhibitions***, which you buy inside. Bear in mind that all this is changing, and that you may now be able to buy them here too.*

> *As you enter the Kremlin through the solid* **Trinity Gate***, you are greeted by the plain glass and stone walls of the Palace of Congresses.*

Stalin lived with his wife and two children just down the only surviving street in the Kremlin, to the right before the palace, in the building with a protruding fourth-floor bay. The intimately-proportioned, yellow stucco houses recall the early centuries of the Kremlin, when much of the population lived within its walls; unfortunately, they are out of bounds. Stalin's house originally belonged to a boyar family, and owes its survival to the fact that it was taken over by the Romanovs in the late 17th century as the **Amusement Rooms** (*Poteshny dvorets*). Here the first court theatre was established. Some 250 years later it was the scene of a tragic drama when, after a series of disagreements with her husband's policies, and with his infidelity, Stalin's wife Nadezhda killed herself in 1932. Their daughter Svetlana was only six and a half, but understood the chilling reality of 'this thing called death' when she and her brother were moved into a smaller Kremlin apartment to live only among nannies and governesses. Stalin himself lived elsewhere.

Most of the other residential streets disappeared beneath the vast yellow **Arsenal** on the other side of the road, started by Peter the Great in the early 18th century and regularly rebuilt in the following century. Its military purpose is still recalled by the bristling row of French artillery pieces—captured during the Napoleonic Wars—lining its walls, and by the occasional khaki jeep screeching through the archway. On either side of the entrance are plaques commemorating (on the left) soldiers killed during the Second World War, and (on the right) 'comrade-soldiers' killed defending the Kremlin after the October Revolution.

> *Just past, but attached to, the Palace of Congresses is a much older building, painted a blushing pink. Typical of the 17th century are its three-storey walls, barely decorated except for a few relief details, and its*

*secretive lack of windows. It was the Patriarch's Palace, with its domestic Cathedral of the 12 Apostles beneath the squat domes at the far end. It now houses a **Museum of 17th–Century Life and Applied Arts**; largely displaying religious objects and ambassadorial gifts.*

While there had been a primate's residence here since the arrival of Metropolitan Peter from Vladimir under Ivan I, this lavish spread was appropriately completed by Patriarch Nikon who led the church from 1652 until his resignation in 1658. He was the Russian Church's most arrogant and effectual leader (*see* p.46), and felt that the earlier building, and the small Church of the Deposition of the Virgin's Robe round the corner, were too meagre for the second-most, if not the most, powerful man in the country. In the entrance hall are vestments belonging to Nikon himself.

The first room on the right gives you some idea of the scale of his pretensions. Known as the **Hall of the Cross** (*Krestovaya palata*), its enormous painted, unsupported vault was the first of its kind in Russia, and as a reception room the hall rivalled the tsar's own banqueting hall in the Faceted Palace.

After Peter the Great abolished the Patriarchate in 1721, replacing it with a governing Holy Synod, this became the Moscow Synod building. The magnificent marble range for making holy oil, miro, was given to the church by Catherine the Great. It is covered by a gilded canopy and decorated with the images of the saints, and though it looks as good as new was used every Thursday for a good 100 years. The rest of the room contains magnificent vessels for use at the altar and at home—chased metal cups, vases, jewel-embedded crystal and jade made into bowls, beakers and perfume bottles. To the left of the entrance hall, leading to the chapel, is a room containing ecclesiastical vestments and cloths, in immaculate condition considering that they are at least 300 years old. In the chapel itself the paintings have disappeared from the walls, remaining only on the ceiling and in the dome. The golden iconostasis, dating from 1700, was moved here in the 1930s from the Monastery of the Miracles, one of those destroyed to make way for the Supreme Soviet building on the far side of the Great Kremlin Square.

*Walk on along the side of the Patriarch's Palace and resist the temptation to nip through the arches beneath it and into Cathedral Square. Beyond the triple apse of the cathedral stands a massive cannon, the **Tsar Cannon** (Tsar-pushka), and a pile of its 2-ton cannon balls. Cast in 1586 in Moscow, with an impression of the reigning Tsar Fyodor I, it was designed to protect the Saviour's Gate on Red Square but was probably never used. It was mounted on its over-ornate carriage in 1835.*

Across the open cobbled space beyond, out of bounds and behind the fir trees at their apex, march the yellow perspectives of the two visible sides of the triangular **Senate** building. From this angle and distance it is difficult to appreciate why its architect, Matvei Kazakov, who built it between 1776–90, was so proud of it, though the admirable use of a difficult site is obvious from a plan of the Kremlin. It was his favourite project, designed to house the Moscow Senate who governed for the monarch, and has been in almost continuous use by the highest echelons of government ever since. In the mid-19th century it became the court offices and law courts and from March 1918 the headquarters of the Soviet government. Lenin's flat within has only just been dismantled, during the recent renovation work. The building's *pièce de résistance* is its central rotunda, known as the Sverdlov or Catherine Hall. Painted blue and white, and decorated inside with bas-reliefs and Corinthian columns, it is still used on important state occasions and supports the Russian flag which waves continuously over Red Square.

> *The undistinguished yellow building to the right of the Senate was built for Stalin, in the style derisively referred to as 'too-late' Classicism, in 1932–4. In 1938 it became the offices of the Presidium of the Supreme Soviet, and is now used as government offices. To make way for it, several ancient buildings of unique significance were destroyed. Among them were the Convent of the Ascension, in which female members of the royal house lived and were buried, and the Monastery of the Miracles, which provided the churches of the Kremlin with their staff. The royal corpses were transferred to the Cathedral of the Archangel Michael before their graves were built over, but to this day there are no monks or priests assigned permanently to the Kremlin's churches. The Cathedral of the Assumption sometimes has services on important church holidays, but otherwise the open churches serve as museums. To find the rest of them walk into the Kremlin's main* **Cathedral Square,** *which beckons with its bunches of gleaming golden domes.*

The contrast between fume-ridden Moscow beyond the walls and this serene expanse of white stone paving, surrounded by soaring edifices, seems almost untenable in one city. And yet if the nation's consciousness is taken up with the anarchic struggles of everyday life without, it is just this kind of powerful fairytale, this childish, spiritual vision which occupies the centre of her subconscious. Following Dostoyevsky's maxim that you should judge the Russian people 'not by what it is, but by what it would like to become', you will understand as much if not more of her character by letting the spirit of this confident space seep in. It seems to speak of her aspirations: pride, strong government verging on autocracy, and power, all in the sight of God.

Today, this is the oldest part of the Kremlin, almost entirely surrounded by buildings from the reign of Ivan III (1462–1505) and his son Vassily III. You can sadly no longer climb the 265ft **Belltower of Ivan the Great** (Marco Bono 1505–8) but the ground floor, which was once two chapels, is now open as an exhibition space, showing selected pieces from the Armoury Museum. A ticket bought here will also admit you to the main museum (*see* pp.108–10).

The belltower's strange, aesthetically flawed architectural configuration results from it being built in three stages. The oldest and most beautiful part is the high tower, for long the tallest in Moscow, which replaced a church built by Ivan I in honour of his patron saint Ivan Lestvichnik (St John of the Ladder). Ivan III built a two-storey tower, to which Boris Godunov added the third, short octagonal piece and the crowning round section which grows out of the band of *kokoshniki* gables. The inscription at the top of the tower, beneath its golden dome, reads 'by the Grace of the Holy Trinity and by order of the Tsar and Grand Prince Boris Fedorovich, Autocrat of All Russia, and of his son, the Orthodox Great Lord Fyodor Borisovich, Tsarevich and Prince of All Russia, this church was finished and gilded in the second year of their reign [1600]'. The central section of the belltower, which was built in the mid-16th century, contains the largest of the 21 bells which hang here. Known as the Holiday, or Uspensky (Assumption) Bell, it was cast in the 19th century from a number of older bells. Its bass voice rang out on church holidays, and to acknowledge major events of state. The third, tent-roofed, section was built in the 17th century and rebuilt after Napoleon had tried to blow it up.

Behind the belltower the massive **Tsar Bell** is marooned on its granite plinth. Fifteen times the size of Big Ben and the world's largest bell, it has never tolled. Two years after it was cast, fire swept through the foundry where it still lay and water poured over to cool it caused the triangular fault. It was commissioned by the Tsarina Anna in 1735, and bears her relief portrait to the left of the hole, beneath images of Christ, the Virgin Mary and St Anna. The bell is something of a *matrioshka* among bells, since it contains within it a number of others. On the other side of the fault is a portrait of Tsar Alexei Mikhailovich, whose bell was melted down for inclusion into the Tsar Bell. His bell in turn was said to contain the famous bell from Novgorod, which the Muscovite princes brought to their Kremlin as a symbol of their subjection of the northern principality in 1477. Interpret as you will a country which displays with pride a bell which never rang and a cannon which never fired.

While you are here, you might like to cross the cobbles to the gardens from which the large sedentary **sculpture of Lenin** has recently been removed. Maybe the monument to Alexander II which it replaced will be reinstated. Apart from Moscow's best grass, and apple trees in season, the gardens also contain the **Cosmos Oak**, planted on 14 April 1961 to commemorate the first manned space flight by Soviet hero Yuri Gagarin two days earlier.

> *Return to Cathedral Square, and cross diagonally to the entrance to the* **Cathedral of the Assumption** *(Uspensky sobor), formerly the*

coronation church of the tsars. It is hidden round the corner on the west
façade. The tsars and their families used the door on the square, to which
they processed in solemn splendour from their palaces on the west side
of the square, down the Red Staircase.

This was the first of the cathedrals which Ivan III commissioned, to replace an ear-lier Cathedral of the Assumption on the site, and it was completed in 1479 by Aristotle Fioravanti. From the outside it looks largely Russian, for the Bolognese architect was sent by the tsar on a tour of Russia's great medieval churches in the winter of 1475–6 and instructed to pay particular attention to the Cathedral of the Assumption in Vladimir. Its massive rectangular stone walls are divided into a series of soaring arches by full-length pilasters and decorated with a blind arcade running round them like a belt. The building is crowned by five substantial drums, which are closely grouped beneath chunky, golden, helmet-style domes.

The only other decoration on the external walls, apart from the unobtrusive apses on the eastern (altar) end, are some frescoes. Guarding the tsars' door on the square are the Archangels Michael and Gabriel. Above them, a row of bishops dec-orates the arcade beneath a depiction of the Virgin and Child. It is to the Virgin, or rather to her assumption into heaven, an important feast day in the Orthodox church, that this and many other major Russian cathedrals are dedicated. The Byzantine tradition of dedicating principal cathedrals to St Sophia, the personifica-tion of Holy Wisdom, died out as the church spread north into Russia and her more down-to-earth, less educated population. They needed a less esoteric manifestation of the female aspect of their church.

It is inside that you realize what a fine building this is; how different from the small, cluttered and dark churches the Russians would have been used to. A tremendous feeling of space, lit by the windows in the domes and barely disturbed by the four supporting pillars or the human tapestry of frescoes on the walls, ends with a magnificent and lofty iconostasis.

The Iconostasis

The impression of uniformity given by this screen of icons is due to the fact that all the icons except those in the bottom layer were painted at the time of its erection in the mid-17th century by the monks of the Trinity Sergius Monastery. The bottom row, by contrast, held, and still holds, a changing array of images. While now they change because of restoration, during the cathedral's 500-year working history they would also have changed as new icons were acquired through con-quest or when a new tsar wished his patron saint to be represented. The acquisition of great icons from Novgorod, Vladimir and Suzdal by the Muscovite princes was felt to confer, or symbolize, the legitimacy of Moscow's gradual assumption of leadership of the country. And, in fact, from 1395 the original

Cathedral of the Assumption, built by Ivan 'Kalita' I, housed the most important of all Russia's symbolic icons, the Virgin of Vladimir, which also graced this iconostasis until 1930. The icon, mythically attributed to the hand of St Luke the gospel writer, is in fact a Byzantine work which appeared in Kiev in the 12th century. With the fall of Kiev as the political and spiritual capital of 'Rus', it was moved to Vladimir and from there to Moscow, as each in turn became pre-eminent. Brought here to protect Moscow from Tamerlane, the icon is Russia's most holy, and now hangs in the Tretyakov Gallery.

A number of icons are currently being restored, allowing a glimpse of some of the few remaining frescoes from the church's original painting. The work was led by one of the greatest Russian painters of the time, Dionisy. The faces of his saints can be seen peering out across the centuries through holes in the bottom row of the iconostasis, from their place on the pillars. Of the icons themselves, the second icon to the right of the Royal Gates is a 15th-century depiction of the cathedral's feast day, the **Assumption of the Virgin** (or the Dormition as it is also known). It shows the Virgin on her death bed, with Jesus holding her soul, represented by a babe in swaddling clothes, as white as the driven snow. The luminous, cream-coloured sky is dotted with angels bringing the apostles and saints to her bedside on clouds, like pendulous birds. In the centre of the sky, the virgin is being carried to heaven in a round rainbow by four angels.

To the left of the Assumption is the **Christ Enthroned**, an icon brought here from the Cathedral of St Sophia in Novgorod after Ivan III sacked the city in 1477. Though typical of the 12th-century Novgorod school, with its bold and angular use of scarlet, legend has it painted by the Byzantine Emperor Manuel I, who saw this image of Christ after he had wounded an innocent priest. Between the two doors to the right of the Assumption is a **deesis** icon which unusually depicts Christ in the priestly vestments of the Orthodox Church and Mary as some Orthodox queen. John the Baptist, needless to say, is still a half-dressed hairy hobo, barefoot and clad in a bit of cloth. To the left of the Royal Gates, over the first subsidiary door is an icon known as the **Saviour with the Stern Eye**, which was commissioned for the earier cathedral here in the 14th century. It is a profoundly distressing image, for not only his accusing eyes but also every muscle on Christ's face seems to reproach mankind for taking so little notice of his suffering. The famous 12th-century icon of **St George the Warrior** from Novgorod should be back in its place in a glass screen to the left of the Royal Gates in mid-1995. It too was pillaged during Ivan III's conquest in 1477, and is one of the earliest images to survive.

Other Icons

Of the icons displayed around the walls, the most famous is the 15th-century Muscovite copy of the **Virgin of Vladimir** (*see* above), the central of the three icons to the right of the main entrance as you look at it. On the south wall, fourth from the west, is an image attributed to Dionisy showing **Metropolitan Peter**, the prelate responsible for moving the leadership of the Russian Orthodox Church to Moscow. He is dressed in gorgeous green robes, with scenes from his life, including once showing the foundation of the original Cathedral of the Assumption, painted round the edge of the icon. To its left is another 15th-century icon painted by Dionisy for this cathedral. Called **In Thee Rejoiceth**, it illustrates an ode to the Virgin, who sits at the centre of an harmoniously united heaven and earth. In the upper, heavenly sectors one sees an image of paradise in the fruiting and flowering trees and the whimsically domed church. In the foreground are representations of human life on earth. On the opposite wall, seek out the icon of the **Trinity**, which shows three angels sitting round a table. A small patch, the head of the right-hand angel, has been cleaned to illustrate the way in which icons were overpainted and given the gloss of a new period, almost as if they had become unfashionable. At the bottom of the icon, small servants are slaughtering cows and kneading dough for their important celestial guests.

Thrones and Sarcophagi

As well as coronations, this cathedral also saw the anointing of new Metropolitans and Patriarchs, and their burial. The tombs of every man to head the Russian Church, from Metropolitan Peter in 1326 to the Soviet period, lie somewhere within its walls, most of them in underground crypts and the chapels behind the iconostasis. The most splendid of those in the nave of the church is that of **Patriarch Germogen**, who died of starvation in the Monastery of the Miracles when the Poles occupied the Kremlin in 1611–12. He was canonized and buried in the monastery until 1913, when his sarcophagus was moved into the birdcage-like, open-work bronze reliquary in the southwest corner. This was designed in 1625 in full-blown Russian style with a tent-roof and *kolkoshniki* gables, to house the cathedral's important relics, including a piece of Christ's robe. In the north-western corner, an impressive gold and silver classical pediment supported on columns marks the grave of **Metropolitan Iov,** Russia's first Patriarch. To the far right of the iconostasis is the sarcophagus of **Metropolitan Philip**.

Other structures of note are the various thrones to the front of the church. The massive, wooden, pavilion-like **Throne of the Monomakhs** in the southeast corner was built for Ivan the Terrible in 1551, out of black walnut. It is intricately carved, topped with a double-headed eagle, supported on dogs biting their own backsides. Its name derives from one of the carvings on its ceiling, which illustrates the Byzantine Emperor Constantine IX Monomachus giving the so-called Crown of Monomakh to Grand Prince Vladimir Monomakh in the early 12th century. Attached to the nearby pillar is the 17th-century stone **Patriarch's Seat**, also ornately carved, and painted, while the second pillar supports the back of a 17th–19th century giltwood and velvet throne in which the tsaritsa would worship.

Frescoes

The walls are covered with frescoes, but the lightness of their ochre ground—probably a memory of an earlier gilding—prevents the space from seeming cluttered. The majority of the frescoes have now been restored to their mid-17th century form. The bottom row on the north and south walls glister with the golden halos of the bishops attending the **Ecumenical Church Councils**, at which early Christian dogma was thrashed out. Above them, biblical tales concentrate on the **Life of the Virgin**, only appropriate in her cathedral, though the relative lack of halos here makes one wonder if the Muscovite Princes didn't want to paint the earthly church as rather more holy than its founders. The pillars portray some of the saints of old Byzantium, mixed in with the saints and martyrs of the Russian church. **God the Father, Christ and the Emmanuel** can be seen in their usual positions in the domes. As was customary in Orthodox churches, the **Last Judgement** greets you as you leave, reminding you of the fiery torment awaiting sinners. This composition is thought to echo the original 15th-century design by Dionisy.

> *The entrance to the **Church of the Deposition of the Virgin's Robe** (Tserkov Rizpolozheniya) is directly opposite that of the Cathedral of the Assumption.*

Sandwiched between palace and cathedral, the church served the Metropolitans and Patriarchs until their new palace was built in the mid-17th century. Built by craftsmen from Moscow and the northern city of Pskov, who began work five years after the completion of the cathedral (1484–6), it is typical of its period, and commemorates the placing of the relic of the Virgin Mary's robe in a church in Constantinople in 458. Though much prettier than the cathedral from the outside, you can imagine how awe-inspiring the latter's interior must have seemed.

Once the church was relinquished by the prelates who created it, it was used by the Romanovs, and particularly by the women, as a route to the cathedral. It is divinely innocent and child-like in its whiteness, surrounded by large buildings intent on suggesting their power. Ogee gables, delicate blind arcading on its rounded apses and simple brick friezes on façade and dome are its only decoration. The wide stone staircase on its southern façade recalls the building's roots in wooden architecture, when all churches were raised on wooden socles to save them from the snow.

Another smaller entrance leads into a covered loggia adjoining the church, in which a few early wooden religious carvings are displayed. Relatively little has survived, but there are examples here from as early as the 14th century, and as you look at them bear in mind than until the early 18th century Russian woodworkers used only axes and knives as tools. The murals in the body of the church date from 1644, and were painted by the same team as those in the cathedral. The churchmen cheekily carried their fight with the tsar for supreme authority right onto the twin pillars in the nave. One is covered in portraits of Russian princes; the other men of the church. Without either, they imply, the roof would fall. The four rows of murals on the wall tell the story of the **life of the Virgin** as it is recounted in the apocryphal gospel of St James, which is now little known to catholic and protestant Christians. Over the door on the back wall, and to the left and right, you will recognize the stories of Gabriel's annunciation of the birth of Christ to Mary, the Christmas story, with the arrival of the Wise Men on magnificent horses and the flight into Egypt. The single dome, flooded by light from its four windows, is decorated with the face of the **Saviour**. Apart from the local (bottom) tier, the icons in the iconostasis date from 1627 and are by a well-known painter from the Metropolitan's workshop, Nazary Istomin. They stand out for their understated yet luminous use of colour and for the serenity lent to the ensemble by the echoing lines which describe the successive figures. In the local tier, to the right of the Royal Gates, is an icon showing the **Deposition of the Robe**, and to its right is an image called the **Tikhvin Virgin**. The massive, coloured candle-holders by the iconostasis are themselves made of wax.

> As you leave the church, the phalanx of buildings behind and beside it were all **Royal Palaces**, built at various times. Just behind it, the crowd of golden cupolas, rising on drums decorated with tiles, mark the private chapels in the **Terem Palace**. Lining the west of the square is the impenetrable white face of the **Faceted Chamber**, looking distinctly like a building from Renaissance Florence. Designed as a banqueting and reception hall, inside it is more Russian, with massive vaults supported only on one central pillar. It was here that the coronation banquets were held, the tsars returning to them from the Uspensky Sobor via the **Red Staircase**. This staircase, destroyed in the 1930s to make way for a delegates' dining room, is one of the first architectural casualties of the Soviet period to have been rebuilt. The fourth side of the square is occupied by the **Cathedral of the Archangel Michael** (Arkhangelsky sobor), 1505–8, where almost every tsar from the early 14th to the late 17th centuries lie buried. Michael was the guardian of the Moscow princes, here invoked to spread his protective wings over them in death as in life.

If any building round the square looks really out of place it is this one, with its elaborate Italian Renaissance decorations. The *forte* of its architect, Alevisio Novi, was decoration rather than building, and the pilasters, capitals and deep cornices of the exterior, though absolutely not Russian, are exhilarating. It is the use of shell motifs under the gables, however, which really distinguishes this cathedral from anything that had gone before it in Russia. If you removed the five, bunched domes and the triple apse from the outside, this could almost be a two-storey secular structure.

However, the painting of the Last Judgement over the cathedral's western entrance warns that this is a place of burial; and the interior proves far more sombre. Unlike the interior of the Uspensky Sobor, the cathedral's space feels crowded by its dark frescoes and mass of tombs. Originally of carved white stone, the sarcophagi were encased in bronze at the beginning of the century. The nearby map will help you identify where the commissioner of the cathedral, Ivan III, was buried, in pride of place. Ivan I 'Kalita' was reburied here when his original church was rebuilt. As well as the local rulers, also buried here are a number of saints associated with them. The best known are St Michael of Chernigov and his companion Boyar Feodor, who went to pay tribute to the Mongols in Kazan in 1246, refused to walk through their pagan, sacred fire and were killed by being trampled beneath boards. Brought back to Moscow in the 17th century, they were canonized and buried here by Tsar Aleksei Mikhailovich. Buried nearby is Ivan the Terrible's unfortunate epileptic son St Dimitri, whom Boris Godunov was falsely accused of murdering.

The frescoes were painted between 1652–66, by a team of royal painters the most famous of whom is Simon Ushakov. In addition to tales from the New and Old Testaments, the pillars and part of the south wall of the cathedral show images of the princes buried beneath, not in portrait form but as figures whose prime message, conveyed through jewels and fabrics, is their power and glory. Both northern and southern walls also contain scenes showing the military might of the Archangel Michael. The 1680–1 iconostasis was gilded in the Baroque style in 1813. Its most interesting image is that of the Archangel Michael, both dynamic and peaceful at the same time. Legend has it that it was commissioned by Evdokia, wife of Dmitri Donskoy, to commemorate her husband's defeat of the Mongols at the battle of Kulikovo Field in 1380.

> By leaving the small white and gold church opposite the Archangel Michael until now, we have kept the best till last. The **Cathedral of the Annunciation** (Blagoveshchensky sobor) was built in 1482–90 on the site of an earlier church, but was much altered in the following 100 years. Its resulting convoluted shape makes exploring it an adventure. From jasper floor to golden roof, it is a jewel, decorated with painting and carving fit for the christenings, marriages and everyday devotions of the royal family.

Though it now has nine domes, when Ivan III commissioned this building from the finest builders from Pskov in northwest Russia, it was built with a mere three. The minimal external decoration comprised a high, blind arcade on the apses, a confection of gables leading up to the drums and the typically Pskovian brick, relief frieze beneath the golden domes. After fire devastated the building in 1547, Ivan the Terrible ordered four chapels to be added to each corner during the restoration, each surmounted by a many-gabled roof and dome of its own. What had been an open loggia on the three sides was enclosed to connect them. Two further domes were also added. When Ivan ignored the dictates of the Orthodox church and married for a fourth time in 1572, he was obliged to add a separate entrance for himself on the south east corner, leading to a porch from which he was allowed to follow the service, outside the main building. He went on to marry seven times in all.

The intricate **carved portals** leading from the loggia into the main church date from Ivan the Terrible's restoration. Though there was a tradition of stone carving in Russia at the time, it was much cruder, and these magnificent deep bands, painted blue and gold, owe a great deal to Italian Renaissance influence. The chased and gold-inlaid copper doors in the north portal, showing the Annunciation, were brought here by Ivan the Terrible from Rostov Veliky. Before being enticed within, take a look at some of the **frescoes** in the loggia. Over your head is the **Tree of Jesse**, the genealogy of Christ, as descended from King David, which Isaiah had prophesied: 'And there shall come forth a rod out of the stem of Jesse [David's father], and a Branch shall grow out of his roots: and the spirit of the Lord shall rest upon him'. It gives the impression that you are walking beneath a Mediterranean grape trellis. A number of other frescoes date from Ivan's restoration. On your left in the north gallery is the dynamic story of **Jonah and the Whale**. In a country with little seashore and no maritime tradition, it is not surprising that the whale looks more like an overgrown fresh-water carp. The movement of time is abandoned, with Jonah being eaten, disgorged and marvelled at all in the one picture. In the western gallery to the left of the door is a representation of **In Thee Rejoiceth**, a hymn to the Virgin Mary, and to its right **The Trinity**, both calm and gentle but difficult to make out. They were uncovered during restoration when later layers were stripped off, but whether or not to retouch them is a contentious subject.

Walking onto the warm earthy red floor of the central church, made of jasper presented to the tsar by the Shah of Persia, the **iconostasis** immediately demands attention. It is one of the three finest in Russia, for many of its images date from the golden era of icon painting in early 15th-century Moscow. They were commissioned from some of the greatest masters who ever lived, the elderly Theophan the Greek, the devout young monk Andrei Rublyov and Prokhor, from the monastery at Gorodets, for the earlier church on this site. For hundreds of years they were thought to have perished in the 1547 fire in this building, but in the 1920s they were discovered beneath layers of paint by ecstatic restorers. Finest are the icons of the **Deesis Row**, where the Virgin, John the Baptist, the Archangels, selected Apostles and bishops plead with a central enthroned image of Christ for the souls of mankind. The old Byzantine master Theophan created most of them, the dynamic Christ, enthroned against a red diamond on a dark globe, the blue-robed Virgin, John the Baptist and the dark Archangel Gabriel. The young Rublyov, suffused with the rigorous preparation of the Trinity Sergius Monastery in Sergeev Passad, created the red-cloaked Archangel Michael and St Peter to the left. While Theophan seems to rely on colour and sharp definition for effect, the works of Rublyov are more rounded and soft, making their impact with a sense of almost sensual spirituality. In the small holiday tier above, the same suffused religiosity inhabits the paintings on the left, most of which are by Rublyov, while the right-hand images by Prokhor use sudden bands of dark colours to dramatic effect.

As in other cathedrals, the local (bottom) tier of the iconostasis often housed icons brought in from elsewhere. To the right of the royal doors, a 14th-century **Christ** sits enthroned on a bejewelled red chair, staring unforgiving at his worshippers. To its right hangs a 17th-century copy of the 12th-century **Ustuig Virgin** from Novgorod. The original of this almost embarrasingly shy portrayal of the Virgin is in the the Tretyakov Gallery.

Some of the murals in the main nave are even earlier than those in the loggia, and date from 1508. The 40 martyrs, Roman soldiers killed in Armenia for their beliefs, decorate the roof and figures of Russian and Byzantine princes cover the two piers, upholders of the church both physically and metaphysically. The north side of the north pillar pairs Dmitri Donskoy with his son, builder of the first Annunciation Cathedral, Vasily I. Female members of the royal family would watch the services from the small choir balcony which they support, while Ivan the Terrible watched through the south door. Today a further exhibition of impressive icons and bejewelled, enamelled icon covers graces the southern loggia and Ivan's porch beyond.

Behind the Cathedral of the Annunciation tower the unsubtle, Russo-Byzantine, yellow walls of the **Great Kremlin Palace**. *Built for Nicholas I by the architect Konstantin Thon in 1838–49, its 125m façade is as much of it as you will see, as it is closed to the general public along with the earlier royal palaces beyond it. During the Soviet period two of its massive halls were converted into the gargantuan meeting place of the Supreme Soviet, in which Russia's rowdy deputies now meet. The* **Armoury Palace** *beyond is open to the public however, and has housed Moscow's richest museum since it was built for the same man, by the same man and in the same style as its neighbour. It has two entrances, the first directly to the Diamond Fund Exhibition, the second to the ticket office of the Armoury Museum itself. You can get from one to the other inside. If you have not bought a ticket for the Armoury Museum in the Ivan the Great Belltower, and want to see the extortionate Diamond Fund as well, go to the first door, buy your ticket and see the jewels before walking down-*

stairs and through the vaulted cloakrooms to the Museum ticket office. If you only want the museum, you will probably have to queue outside for a while. Visits to the Armoury Museum take place in four 1½-hour daily sessions, so to have a long look arrive before or close to 10am, 12am, 2.30pm or 4pm, when the sessions begin.

The **Diamond Fund Exhibition** is disappointingly small, although its highlight, a small selection of the Russian Crown jewels, is undeniably impressive. Most of the exhibition is made up of forearm-sized nuggets of gold, sculpted by nature to look like, say, a horse's head, and small maps of the former USSR made of diamonds. The jewellery windows contain a dazzling display of beautifully set stones making up brooches, earings, necklaces and necklaces of office. The centrepiece is Catherine the Great's French-made crown and sceptre. The crown is made of almost 5000 diamonds, with a pearl band across the top, and finished off with a huge, fruit-gum of a ruby. Her sceptre contains the 190-carat Orlov Diamond, brought by her lover Grigory Orlov from an Armenian gem-dealer, which was once the eye of a god in an Indian temple. The miniature portrait of the playwright Griboyedov and the beautifully cut Shah Diamond beside it tell a strange tale. During the 1829 treaty negotiations with Persia, Russian demands provoked the storming of the Russian embassy and the death of almost all inside it. The diamond was given to Nicholas I by the Shah of Persia as compensation for the death of his Ambassador Griboyedov in Tehran.

The **Armoury Museum** occupies two floors. Though this building dates only from the 19th century, the royal collection was housed on this spot from the 14th century. It developed in tandem with the Kremlin workshops, in which arms, precious metals and jewels, fine cloth and icons were fashioned for royal use. True to his belief that Russia could be transformed through education, Peter the Great opened the collection as a museum. Today the top floor displays religious objects, precious domestic artefacts and ambassadorial silver gifts, while the tsars' and tsarinas' clothes, regalia, carriages and thrones are on the lower floor.

Room 1 on the top floor shows early Russian ecclesiastical objects in gold and silver. Particularly impressive are the gold dish, given by Ivan the Terrible to his second wife, with its swirling central composition and engraved, inlaid border, and the church-shaped censer, in which incense was burned, given to the Cathedral of the Archangel by Irina Godunova. Also to be marvelled at are the bejewelled gospel covers, icon frames and crosses ranging from the 12th–16th centuries. **Room 2** houses Russian work from the 17th to the 20th centuries. Particularly fine is the collection of late 17th-century enamelware whose colours are reminiscent of Italian majolica—an ornate gospel cover, a golden chalice and a loving-cup, given by Patriarch Nikon to Tsar Alexei Mikhailovich. Russians would drink in turns from such cups, known as *bratina*. Somewhat out of place in this room is the cabinet of contemporary work by Russia's leading jewellers.

Room 3 displays arms and armour (15th–19th century), with oriental exhibits from Iran and Turkey on the right, and European, particularly Russian, examples on the left. Every flat ring on Boris Godunov's set of armour is engraved with the mantra 'God is with us, no one is against us' and nearby is a full set made for a child. Two rooms lead off from here. In **Room 4** look out for the remnants of the 13th-century helmet of Alexander Nevsky's father. A number of pieces were obviously not designed for battle, like the golden, jewel-encrusted weapons' cases and maces, carried during court displays.

Room 5 contains one of the finest collections of Western European gold and silver anywhere in the world, displayed according to country of origin. The collection of 16th and 17th-century English silver in the first central cabinet is virtually unique; both Cromwell and the Royalists melted down so much Tudor and Jacobean silver to pay their armies that there is little more elsewhere. England developed an early trading relationship with Russia and most of the collection is gifts from traders and ambassadors. Much of it dates from Elizabeth I's diplomatic refusal of Ivan the Terrible's proposal of marriage to her. The largest collection is of 17th-century Swedish ware, but its accumulated effect can dazzle. Don't miss the stranger objects—a massive German crystal jug on a crystal plate and the embellished coconuts and ostrich eggs. The extensive Sèvres service in the final cabinet was given by Napoleon to Alexander I in 1807 in commemoration of the Treaty of Tilsit. Known as the Olympic Service, it was no doubt in the palaces of St Petersburg and missed the irony of Napoleon's occupation of the Kremlin five years later.

In **Room 6** downstairs is an immense collection of royal and ecclesiastical clothing. In the central display are Romanov wedding and coronation clothes. The tsarinas wore silver embroidered dresses at coronations, the most tasteful being Catherine the Great's at the far end of the room, covered in double-headed eagles and finished with fine lace at the neck and on the sleeves. Along the right-hand wall hang ecclesiastical vestments, the early ones made from imported cloth, mostly from Constantinople, as there was no cloth industry in Russia until the 18th century. The second cassock is 14th-century Byzantine, its blue silk almost obliterated by golden embroidery. After the fall of Constantinople to the Turks in 1453, the material begins to take on non-figurative Moslem characteristics. Patriarch Nikon's pearl and gold costume with its gold, pearl and enamel crown is only eclipsed by that given to Metropolitan Platon by Catherine the Great. Its apricot velvet and jewel-encrusted beauty sparkles almost opposite its donor's coronation robe. The other side of the room shows male court costumes, including the massive boots of the giant Peter the Great.

The earliest of the thrones in **Room 7** is Ivan the Terrible's ivory seat. Boris Godunov's golden throne, dotted with over 2000 precious and semi-precious stones, was given to him by the Shah of Persia. The central double throne was built for the 16-year joint minority of Peter the Great and his sickly half-brother Ivan V. Their advisors would prompt the boys' responses through the open panel, hidden by a curtain. The ornate putti-festooned gilt and velvet confection crowned with an 'EI' is typical of Tsaritsa Elizabeth's rococo tastes. Opposite it, a selection of royal crowns glisters with filigree gold and jewels. The most important is the mercifully simple crown of Monomach in front, with its sable band. Its legendary history, that it was given to an early grand prince by his grandfather the Byzantine Emperor Constantine IX, was used to strengthen Russia's claim as the heir to Byzantium, but ignores the fact that Constantine died 50 years before Vladimir even became Grand Prince.

The last two rooms deal with horse harnesses and carriages. The majority of the harnesses in **Room 8** are Turkish and Iranian, with some Russian work immediately on the left, and West European on the right. Confirming the suspicion that the best royal gifts are the product of war, the most impressive pieces here were given to Catherine the Great by the Turkish sultans after the treaties of 1774 and 1792. **Room 9** is the museum's most popular, with its collection of royal coaches, ranging from winter coaches on sleighs to Peter the Great's childhood carts which were pulled by ponies. The most ornate belonged to the Tsarina Elizabeth, and include the French 1757 coach decorated with paintings by Boucher. Catherine the Great's are marginally more restrained and dignified, though the last richly gilded, English-made, summer coach given to her by her lover Grigory Orlov seems distinctly out of character with this substantial and serious monarch.

> The **Borovitskaya Gate**, next to the museum, takes you back into the Alexander Gardens. Turn right for Aleksandrovsky Sad metro station, which is just before the entrance to the Kremlin, on the left.

After this mammoth tour, it might seem a relief that it has only just scratched the surface. For below ground in the Kremlin is a huge network of crypts, storehouses and tunnels which many would give their eye teeth to examine. Built for storage, as escape routes and as conduits for water during times of siege and trouble, they fascinate the contemporary Moscow psyche, which seems to equate their very existence with the sly, underhand way in which they have been governed for so long. Most intriguing is Ivan the Terrible's world-famous library which is said to be immured somewhere below ground. One late 19th-century German scholar even surmised that it might contain the earliest written manuscripts of Homer, given to Ivan III by his Byzantine wife as part of her dowry. It's a toss-up now as to whether the library 'would renew for Europe the times of the Medici, Petrarch, and Boccaccio, when from the dust of libraries was extracted the unknown treasures of antiquity,' or whether it would merely yield a heap of soggy paper.

II: Kitai Gorod and Red Square

Start: Ⓜ *Lubyanka. If you came to the connecting* Ⓜ *Kuznetsky Most, follow signs underground saying* 'Переход на станцию " Лубянка"'.

Walking Time: *2½–3 hours.*

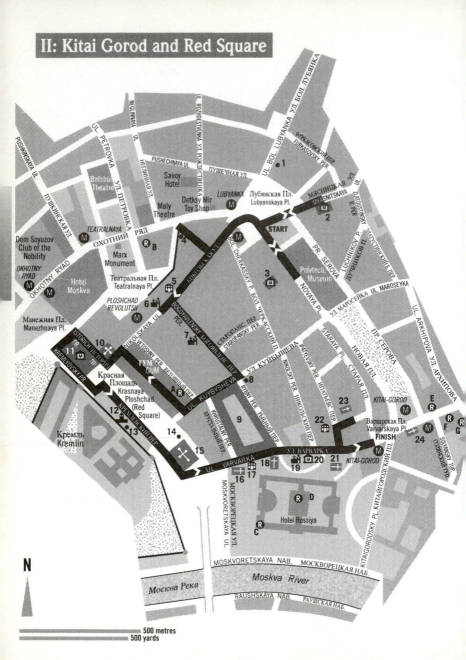

II: Kitai Gorod and Red Square

PUSHKINSKAYA UL.

UL. PETROVKA

NEGLINNAYA UL.

UL. ROZHDESTVENKA УЛ. РОЖДЕСТВЕНКА

UL. BOL. LUBYANKA УЛ. БОЛ. ЛУБЯНКА

УЛ. БОЛ. ЛУБЯНКА

FURKASOVSKY PER

ФУРКАСОВСКИЙ ПЕР

Bolshoi Theatre

ПУШКИНСКАЯ УЛ.

УЛ. ПЕТРОВКА

PUSHECHNAYA UL. ПУШЕЧНАЯ УЛ.

Savoy Hotel

● 1

MYASNITSKAYA

ZLATOUSTINSKY B. PER.

ZLATOUSTINSKY PER. ЗЛАТОУСТИНСКИЙ Р.

ЛУЧНИКОВ П.

Maly Theatre

Detksy Mir Toy Shop

LUBYANKA Ⓜ

Lubyanskaya Pl.
Лубянская Пл.

МЯСНИЦКАЯ

Ⓜ 2

TEATRALNAYA УЛ.

ОХОТНЫЙ РЯД

START

Dom Soyuzov
Club of the
Nobility

Ⓡ B

БОЛ. ЧЕРКАССКИЙ Р. БОЛ. ЧЕРКАССКИЙ

PR. SEROVA

Polytech. Museum

OKHOTNY RYAD

OKHOTNY RYAD

Marx
Monument

● 4

Ⓜ 3

NOVAYA PL.

UL. MAROSEYKA UL. MAROSEYKA

UL. ARKHIPOVA УЛ. АРХИПОВА

Hotel Moskva

Театральная Пл.
Teatralnaya Pl.

5 🏛

PR. SEROVA

Манежная Пл.
Manezhnaya Pl.

Ⓜ

PLOSHCHAD
REVOLUTSII

6 🏛

BOGOYAVLENSKY PER. BOGOYAVLENSKY PER.

STAROPANS. PER.

STAROPANSKY PER.

NOVAYA PL.

STARAYA PL. STARAYA PL.

ISTORICH. PROEZD

10

11

IVERSKY PR.

NIKOLSKAYA UL.

NIKITNIKOV PER. ВЕТОШНЫЙ ПЕР.

7 🏛

ИЛЬИНКА

UL. KUYBYSHEVA

RYBNY PER.

NIKOLSKY PER.

STARAYA PL.

● 8

 SHATYEV. PER.

ИЛЬИНКА

Красная
Площадь
Krasnaya
Ploshchad
(Red
Square)

TSUM GUM

Ⓡ
A

UL. KUYBYSHEVA УЛ. КУЙБЫШЕВА

RYBNY PER.

RYBNY PER. РЫБНЫЙ ПЕР.

NIKOLSKY PER. НИКОЛЬСКИЙ ПЕР.

23

KITAI-GOROD

Ⓜ

E
Ⓡ

12

9

22

Варварская Пл.
Varvarskaya Pl.
FINISH

Ⓜ

Ⓡ G
F Ⓡ

КРЕМЛЕВСКИЙ ПЕР.

13

14 ●

15

KRISTIANNY PER. ХРИСТИАННЫЙ ПЕР.

UL. VARVARKA

УЛ. ВАРВАРКА

18 †

19 🏛 Ⓜ 20

21

24

SOLYANSKY TUP. СОЛЯНСКИЙ ТУП.

Кремль
Kremlin

16
17

UL. VARVARKA

KITAI-GOROD

Ⓜ

KITAIGORODSKY PL. КИТАЙГОРОДСКИЙ ПЛ.

MOSKVORETSKAYA UL.
МОСКВОРЕЦКАЯ УЛ.

Ⓡ D

Hotel Rossiya

Ⓡ
C

MOSKVORETSKAYA NAB. МОСКВОРЕЦКАЯ НАБ.

N

Москва Река

Moskva River

RAUSHSKAYA NAB. РАУШСКАЯ НАБ.

━━━ 500 metres
━━━ 500 yards

Sites

1   Lubyanka
    Лубянка

2   Mayakovsky Museum
    Muzei V. V. Mayakovskovo
    Музей В. В. Маяковского

3   Museum of the History of Moscow
    Muzei istorii goroda Moskvy
    Музей истории города Москвы

4   Gate in Kitai Gorod Walls

5   Old Printing House
    Stary pechatny dvor
    Старый печатный двор

6   Monastery of the Saviour Behind the Icons
    Zaikonospassky monastir
    Заиконоспасский монастырь

7   Monastery of the Epiphany
    Bogoyavlensky monastir
    Богоявленский монастырь

8   Stock Exchange
    Birzha
    Биржа

9   Gostiny Dvor
    Гостиный двор

10 Kazan Cathedral
    Kazansky sobor
    Казанский собор

11 Historical Museum
    Istorichesky muzei
    Исторический музей

12 Lenin's Mausoleum
    Mavzolei V. I. Lenina
    Мавзолей В. И. Ленина

13 Kremlin Wall Cemetery
    Nekropol Kremlyovskoy steny
    Некрополь Кремлёвской стены

14 Lobnoye mesto
    Лобное место

15 St Basil's Cathedral
    Khram Vasiliya Blazhennovo
    Храм Василия Блаженного

16 Church of St Barbara
    Tserkov Velikomuchenitsy Varvary
    Церковь Великомученицы Варвары

17 English Merchant's House
    Angliyskoye podvorye
    Английское подворье

18 Church of St Maxim the Blessed
    Tserkov Maxima Blazhennovo
    Церковь Максима Блаженного

19 Nunnery of Our Lady of the Sign
    Znamensky monastir
    Знаменский монастырь

20 Museum of the Romanov Boyars in Zaradye
    Muzei boyar Romanovikh v Zaradye
    Музей бояр Романовых в Зарадье

21 Church of St George
    Tserkov Georgiya
    Церковь Георгия

22 Ushakov's House
    Dom Ushakova
    Дом Ушакова

23 Church of the Trinity in Nikitniki
    Tserkov troitsy v Nikitnikakh
    Церковь троицы в Никитниках

24 Church of All Saints in Kulishki
    Tserkov vsekh svyatykh na Kulishkakh
    Церковь всех святых на Кулишках

Restaurants and Cafés

A   Rostik's Restaurant
    Ростик

B   Hotel Metropol
    Гостиница Метрополь

C   Tokyo, Hotel Rossiya
    Токио, Гостиница Россия

D   Café in Hotel Rossiya

E   Karina
    Карина

F   Micro-café
    Микро-кафе

G   Khinkalnoe Café
    Кинкальное Кафе

This walk threads its way through the area of the city east of the Kremlin, which was walled in the 16th century to accommodate the overflow from the royal fortress. It was and is known as Kitai Gorod, not—as modern Russian would suggest—meaning Chinatown, but rather a medieval reference to the 'defended city'. Within its walls lived the first English merchants and European doctors, side by side with Russian traders and even the future royal family, the Romanovs. Today, with its walls gone and street-trading run riot, the modern translation seems more appropriate.

During the 19th century, Kitai Gorod lost its residential quality with the building of the Stock Exchange and other large commercial premises. When government moved back to Moscow in 1918 many of these were taken over by government and party offices. Today, on its short narrow lanes, civil servants on their way to work mix with the shoppers headed for GUM, the State Department Store, an indoor mall with several kilometres of shop front.

As well as the churches and museums of Kitai Gorod, this walk also braves Red Square, site of the mind-bending St Basil's Cathedral and the erstwhile parade ground of the Communists. While the memories of the soldiers, workers and children who marched twice a year beneath a sea of red banners are fading slowly, the body of Lenin, the Sleeping Bolshevik, still lies in his crystal coffin nearby.

The best time to walk this is at the weekend, when everything is open. Start by 11am to catch Lenin on display. Any other day of the week you will miss at least one of the sites (see text for detailed opening times).

---

lunch/cafés

There is a dearth of places to grab a quick bite to eat on this route, with the best coming at the very end.

Metropol Hotel, Teatralny Proezd 1/4, ✆ 927 6029. For a princely breakfast before you start, the magnificent mosaic Metropol Hall serves an expensive all-you-can-eat buffet. There is also a lunch-time buffet. There are three other restaurants in this extravagant Style Moderne hotel, built by an English architect, Walcott, between 1899–1903. During recent refurbishment, most of the interior was reduced to almost standard international hotel style, but the exterior has kept its high, tiled frieze by the tormented painter and ceramicist Vrubel. Entrance to the Teatro Trattoria and Lobster Bar is on Teatralny Proezd.

Extortionate but delicious Russian food is served in the Boyarsky Zal, through the main entrance at the back of the building.

Rostiks Restaurant, in GUM, furthest row from Red Square, 1st floor, ☎ 921 1529. Serves fried chicken, chips and other Americana from 10am–10pm.

Tokyo, Hotel Rossiya, entrance off Red Square, far right, ☎ 298 5707, 298 5374. Apart from coffee and snacks on the 13th floor (*see* p.486), this delicious but expensive Japanese restaurant is the only place where lunch is worth eating in the entire 3000-room hotel.

Karina, Solyansky Proyezd 1–3, ☎ 924 0369. There are few places to sit down at the end of this walk, so if you are exhausted this might be the place for you. The food is traditional Russian, well-prepared, and the soups and stews are particularly good.

Micro Café, Solyansky Proezd 6. This little hole in the wall serves sugary milky coffee, very restorative however you usually drink it, and delicious homemade cakes.

Khinkalnaya Café, Ul. Solyanka 2. Run by the same people as the above, this wins the Restaurant of the Walk award with its good, cheap food. Look for the sign saying (Хинкалная), dive in, join the queue in peak times and order by pointing to the salads and other cold dishes. Of the hot dishes, the *khinkali* (хинкали), from which the place gets its name, are large, meatfilled dumplings served with a spicy tomato sauce. They taste much better than they look. Also good if it's on is *solyanka*, a meat soup. The only disadvantage here is that the tables are made for standing.

Leaving the metro, turn left outside the swing doors, and take the first exit 'На Мяцницкую улицу', *to Myasnitskaya Ul. On reaching the surface, turn for a moment to look back on Lubianskaya Ploshchad.*

Lubyanka Square was the site of some of the most symbolic pictures to come out of the aftermath of the August 1991 coup. It was from the island in the middle of the traffic that the statue of 'Iron' Felix Dzerzhinsky was precariously dismantled. A Polish nobleman, he was the first head of the KGB, then known as the Cheka. Of all the Soviet institutions, this one, in its orangy-yellow headquarters next door to you, was the most hated. Within the monolith of a building, with its impenetrable granite foundations, is a prison in which hundreds of thousands of people got their first taste of torture. The KGB has split into five agencies, the main one being the friendlier Ministry of Security, but its rather grisly contribution to glasnost, a conducted tour of the building, seems to have folded.

*The **Mayakovsky Museum** is a little way up Myasnitskaya Ul. on the right, signposted beneath a dark colonnade by a blank staring head of the poet and a terrifying red wedge sculpture. Entrance is in the bizarre sloping structure behind (open every day 10am–6pm, Thurs from 1pm; closed Wed and last Fri of the month).*

Recently overhauled by a group of theatre designers, this radical and surreal representation of the life and work of Vladimir Mayakovsky (1893–1930) sits incongruously between two KGB buildings, in the house where the poet lived from 1919. He dubbed himself 'the drummer of the October Revolution', and his jarring, declamatory style sought to express its turmoil and determination. But the Party-led terror overseen by the KGB led to his disillusionment and contributed to his suicide.

The exhibition, conceived in Mayakovsky's own Futurist style, surrounds the visitor with the jarring dynamism of Suprematism and Constructivism, the new proletarian art which took so much of its inspiration from industrialization and science. The first rooms, showing Mayakovsky's Georgian origins and early poetry, lead up to the actual room in which he committed suicide in 1930, preserved as a simple, reflective shrine. The metallic maze continues with a collection of propaganda posters he produced for the windows of the Soviet Press Agency and copies of original manuscripts of poems and letters, all set behind angular glass sheets. Documents of the period of disillusion, as the Revolution failed the aspirations of the workers and fell into the hands of the Party bureaucrats, lead to a sepulchral sculpted deathbed.

But the main cause of his suicide was the disintegration of his love affair with Lily Brik, whom Mayakovsky had shared with her husband for 15 years of anguish. Her picture can be seen on his deathbed, and it was she who provided the muse for some of the most heart-rending love poetry in the Russian language. His last, unfinished poem begins 'She loves me? She loves me not? I wring my hands and then scatter my fingers as they are broken off, like the petals of wayward daisies in the May breeze.'

*To get to the **Museum of the History of Moscow** go back into the underpass, turn left at the bottom of the stairs and at the very end of the corridor take the left-hand exit. The museum is housed in the green-roofed, red and white church building some 50m ahead on your right (open 1am–6pm, Wed and Fri 12 noon–8pm; closed Mon and the last day of the month).*

Before it became a museum, this was Church of St John the Divine, built in 1825. Like many Russian museums these days, this one has had to sublet most of its premises to commercial enterprises. Just one room remains, but this is sufficient to give an impression of what a fairytale world Moscow must have seeemed to the first foreigners who came here. It is on the left as you enter the museum, and portrays Moscow's lifestyle and buildings as the city spread out from the Kremlin through the ages. Particularly graphic are the paintings by turn-of-the-century Slavophile painter A. M. Vasnetsov, which show the city all wooden and brightly coloured with a fleet of glittering domes. If you would like to buy a modern painting or print of Moscow to remember your trip by, the gallery here has the best, most affordable selection in the city. The waxwork exhibition is dull even if you understand Russian.

> *Retrace your steps and walk past the B-movie Metro entrance with its sci-fi double arches to turn left down Ul. Nikolskaya.*

Were this the early 1920s we would now be entering Kitai Gorod through the Vladimirsky Gate. All but stretches of the walls (by the Hotel Rossiya and behind the Metropol Hotel) were destroyed, so to get some idea of how it would have looked, dive first right down Tretyakovsky Proezd and look back at its triumphal **red gate**. This was only built in 1871, mimicking the medieval walls it joined, by a rich textile merchant who wanted a short cut from his home on Nikolskaya to the banks across Teatralny Proezd.

Nikolskaya Ulitsa was also known as the 'Street of Enlightenment', for it was here that Russia's first printing press and her largest secular school were located. The site of the printing house in which Ivan Fyodorov, Russia's Caxton, printed the country's first book, the Acts of the Apostles, in 1564, announces itself with a flamboyant Gothic façade. The aquamarine and white fantasy (No. 15) incorporates hectic columns twisted with vegetable carving, Gothic windows, metal porches, two bronze sundials and a lion and a unicorn. It was here too that Russia's first newspaper, *Vedemosti*, was published in 1703. Known as the **Synodal Printing House**, it was rebuilt after the 1812 fire and continued to print religious literature for the Holy Synod.

Of the street's two monasteries, only the cathedral (1661) of the **Monastery of the Saviour behind the Icons** (*Zaikonospassky monastir*) has survived, in a decrepit state of repair, inside the courtyard of No. 7. Its curious name refers to the icon selling for which Nikolskaya Ulitsa was also famous, but what is left of it barely merits the walk. Some 80 years after it was founded, in 1687, the monastery incorporated the Slavo-Graeco-Latin Academy, the first higher school in the capital, where both Lomonosov, 'the Father of Russian Science' and Bazhenov the architect were educated.

In 1292 Daniil, the first Muscovite prince, founded the fortified the **Monastery of the Epiphany** (*Bogoyavlensky Monastery*) to give some protection to the inhabitants of the area which was then unwalled. Nothing survives but its much later cathedral, on the right down Bogoyavlensky Pereulok. Today even that is just a haunting mass of crumbling red brick, decorated in typical Moscow Baroque style with lace-like details in white stone, and partially covered in scaffolding. It was built in 1693–6, and until the cholera epidemic of 1771 when burial within the city walls was outlawed, was the chosen repository of the aristocratic Golitsyn family.

The end of Bogoyavlensky Perevlok is marked by the proud civic entrance to the former Stock Exchange, built in the classical style in 1838. On the opposite corner, the Trading Courtyard for visiting merchants, *Gostiny dvor*, is well worth penetrating. It was finished in 1805 to designs by one of Catherine the Great's favourite St Petersburg architects, the Italian Giacomo Quarenghi. The yellow and white paint on its external classical façade may be peeling, but its enormous inner courtyard seems even more forgotten. Offices occupy the storerooms which were once overflowing with trade items. The intriguing collection of ramshackle buildings in the centre are reputed to be a secret Metro junction, ready to whisk incumbents of the Kremlin to destinations unknown in the event of catastrophe.

> *Leave Gostiny Dvor via the same entrance and turn left towards Red Square. A healthy sign of the arrival of civil society in Russia, the square, which often used to close for no apparent reason, is now normally open to all comers. Before visiting Lenin, indulge in a little window shopping in* **GUM**, *the State Deparment Store. Its multiple entrances are in the last block on the right before the square.*

The huge covered trading area of GUM has just celebrated its centenary, though trading took place on this spot for several hundred years before the present building was erected. It consists of three parallel passages of shops on two floors. The most chic is the passage closest to Red Square. The luxuriant furs and embroidered textiles sold here before the Revolution were replaced by cheap mass-produced cotton during the Soviet period. In today's free-market Moscow, the superior buying power of Benetton, Galleries Lafayette and Karstadt have assured that the city's most prestigious shop front no longer offers the curious fascination of a showcase of Soviet austerity. If you look hard a few pockets of austerity still exist, but if your feet are aching, follow signs up to the Business Centre on the 1st Floor where you can get peace, coffee, snacks and a powerful view of the Mausoleum.

> *Leaving GUM at the far end, you come face to face with the* **Kazan Cathedral**, *the second Soviet-destroyed monument of national importance to have been completely rebuilt. It was reconsecrated in November 1993 in the presence of Boris Yeltsin. It was originally built by Prince Pozharsky in 1625, in thanks for Russia's deliverance from the Poles, and for the help given her by the miraculous Icon of the Virgin of Kazan,*

which was moved from here to St Petersburg in 1710. Since the Revolution the icon has completely disappeared, reputedly into the vaults of an American collector.

*Beyond the Kazan Cathedral, the gate church of the Iberian Virgin is currently being rebuilt, adjoining the deep red mass of the Historical Museum to its left. An unsuccessful attempt to balance St Basil's at the other end of Red Square, built by an English architect in the 1880s, the museum has been closed for a long time. **Lenin's Mausoleum**, on the other hand, is currently open 10am–1pm, closed Mondays and Fridays.*

Red Square is beset by a terrible schizophrenia. As an open space beside the tsar's palace it originally combined the functions of market-place and place of proclamations and executions. Most pre-Revolutionary pictures show it teeming with walkers and carriages, moving between 'huts of painted wood... filled with cherry-trees in blossom, with roses of all kinds', while earlier prints might people it with rows of corpses hanging from gibbets. Recently the world was accustomed to two images: of elderly leaders watching a monotonous metallic current of soldiers and military hardware march by on May Day and the anniversary of the Revolution, and of long queues of citizens waiting for the chance to pay their belated respects to Lenin. Today a trickle, albeit constant, of people visit Lenin, but there is talk of closing him down, and otherwise groups of tourists wander forlornly across the massive space, which dwarfs everything but St Basil's Cathedral. The square is so huge, built on its hilltop, that it gives the illusion that you can perceive the curvature of the earth on its surface. It cries out to be crammed with people or broken up by some activity, but years of Communism and leaders who still like to show their power by occasionally closing the whole place keep it echoing and silent. 'Red' it is by virtue of the buildings on three sides of it, but 'beautiful', as it was originally called, it only becomes at night beneath a silent full moon.

When Lenin died in 1924, his wife Nadezhda Krupskaya came out strongly against the 'outward veneration of his personality. Do not raise monuments to him, or palaces to his name.' And yet every town in the USSR named streets after him, and his embalmed corpse was placed in a makeshift wooden mausoleum on this spot. Two of the great architects of the time, Melnikov and Shchusev, were charged with designing his sarcophagus and mausoleum respectively. The final red and black granite version was erected in 1929.

These days people visit for the most curious of motives, some crossing themselves continuously and invoking God's protection, some to see just how deteriorated the old boy's left hand is. However hard you tell yourself he's just an ordinary bloke, the building itself successfully disabuses you. After stumbling down a dark staircase, you are released with a sense of elation into his orangy-pink presence. The curious triple reflection of his head in the crystal coffin momentarily confers on him the dignity of Van Dyke's triple portrait of Charles I. As a charm against the hallowed hellishness of the place, think about the guards' gym and canteen buried below it. An anecdote which did the rounds when Khrushchev was heard to mention that he wouldn't mind lying here, after Stalin had already inveigled his way in, has Lenin sitting up and bleating petulantly: 'What do you think this is, a dormitory?' The removal of its famous guards, talk of burying 'Leecy' (Baldy) beside his wife, and of American offers to buy the place, suggest that Lenin himself may not be on display for much longer.

After his posthumous disgrace, in 1961 Stalin was taken out and buried in the Soviet Union's second most prestigious plot, the **Kremlin Wall**, punctuated by the glacial fir trees behind the mausoleum. It's a sorry reminder of the Russians' love of autocrats that his grave always has more flowers on it than any other. Various other Communist worthies are buried on either side of him beneath imposing busts, including Dzerzhinsky, Zhdanov, Brezhnev, Chernenko and Andropov. In one of the first groups on the left is Lenin's lover, Inessa Armand. Lenin and his wife had no children, and Inessa's daughter (father unknown), is alive today. She became a dancing teacher after being a pupil at the school Isadora Duncan set up in Moscow when she was married to the poet Yesenin. The ashes of Yuri Gagarin, hero of the cosmos, and the writer Maxim Gorky are among those immured behind plaques in the wall. Alongside these heroes are a number of foreign Communists, including John Reed, the American journalist famed for his account of the October Revolution, *Ten Days that Shook the World*, and Arthur MacManus, one of the founders of the British Communist Party.

Before you get sucked into the alluring St Basil's Cathedral (*open 11am–4pm, closed Tues and first Mon of month*) cast a glance at the elevated round platform in the square, the **Lobnoye Mesto** or Place of Skulls. This particular structure was designed by Kazakov in the 1780s, but for hundreds of years before that major new laws and decrees had been read out from earlier platforms on the same spot. It owes its name to the fact that executions took place around it. The massive **Statue to Minin and Pozharsky** has been moved into the cathedral precincts from the centre of Red Square. Put up in 1818, it gives thanks to a butcher, Minin, and a prince, Pozharsky, who galvanized the Russians to form a united army and expel the Poles during the Time of Troubles (1598–1613). One of the last battles routed the enemy from the Moscow Kremlin itself, in 1612.

No amount of tourist brochures can prepare you for the colourful other-worldliness of **St Basil's** (Храм Василя Блаженного—*Khram Vasiliya Blazhennovo*); the experience is like coming across a bowl of oriental fruits after a diet of apples. Surely this can't be... bricks and mortar? The fruity, faceted cupolas so dazzle the senses that you are in no fit state to work out even the basic plan of the cathedral. It is in fact quite regular. The central *shatyor*, or steep, tent-roofed tower, is surrounded by four octagonal chapels in the shape of a cross with smaller chapels in the four corners. Wide porches cover the stairways that lead into the building from two corners and painted floral designs further enliven the exterior.

The original name given to this church by Ivan the Terrible, who commissioned it in 1552, was Pokrovsky Sobor (the Cathedral of the Intercession). For it was on the feast of the Intercession, 1 October, that he finally routed the Tartars from their stronghold in Kazan, 700km east of Moscow. This building was to be a joyful commemoration of the victory, but while Ivan was beseiging the town, the ragged holy fool, Basil the Blessed, died in Moscow. The tsar, who took a personal interest in Basil on account of his accurate prophecies, ordered that he be buried near the Church of the Trinity, which was pulled down to make way for the cathedral. In 1579 Basil was canonized and a chapel was built over his grave, which had been incorporated into the new cathedral.

Legend has it that Ivan, on seeing the completed cathedral, had its architects, Postnik and Barma, blinded to stop them from achieving such dizzying heights for any other patron. They took their inspiration entirely from Russia's traditions of wooden architecture, turning their backs on the Byzantine and Italian legacy, and as a result built the most quintessentially Russian of all buildings. The interior is poky and warren-like, the ground floor housing some armour from Ivan's battle for Kazan and a range of paintings and engravings of St Basil's through history. Climbing up the steep steps to the central Chapel of the Intercession, you find yourself in a tall frescoed space with a leather-covered, gilded 19th-century Baroque iconostasis. Thanks to Napoleon's treatment of the building, which he tried to blow up along with the Kremlin before leaving, little of the original decor survives, though the quasi-pagan brick swirl at the apex of the ceiling has doubtless always been visible. The surrounding chapels are even smaller, linked by a narrow passageway which blooms with colourful floral murals.

Exploration of the interior suggests that Ivan's intention was to build an external statement of secular might rather than a glorious setting for the worship of God. In the 20th century his statement got in the way of Stalin's, the Red Square parades. It was almost as if the two autocrats were competing for the prize of 'Dictator of Dictators' across the centuries. Stalin was only stopped from pulling the building down by the threat of a famous architect to slit his throat on the steps of the cathedral if demolition began.

*From St Basil's you cannot miss the vast **Hotel Rossiya**, completed in 1971, largely to accommodate out-of-town party functionaries on their visits to the twice-yearly, rubber stamp of a legislature, the Supreme*

Soviet, or the annual Communist Party congress. Take the intriguing road leading down its left side, Ul. Varvarka, whose cluster of domes makes a thought-provoking contrast to the 3000-room monstrosity.

Most of what was razed to build the hotel was a run-down residential area, the Zaradye (beyond the trading rows), populated by poor craftsmen and Jews. However the strangled horror of Moscow's conserving classes somehow penetrated the apathy of the Brezhnev administration and prevented the destruction of the buildings on Ulitsa Varvarka. Since the 14th century it had been one of the main arteries of the city, and by the mid-20th had amassed a veritable outdoor museum of architecture. Dating principally from the 17th century, they offer a glimpse of the low-rise city as it was, all domes, bell-towers, steep pitched roofs and elaborate chimney pots. The one exception is the first pink and white **Tserkov** the **Church of St Barbara** (*Velikomuchenitsy Varvary*), built in the classical style around 1800. Like most the the buildings here, it now houses a souvenir stall as well as offices.

Next to the church is one of the oldest civilian structures in the city, a **merchant's house** built in the early 16th century, which was given to English traders from the 'Moscow Company' by Ivan the Terrible. In 1553 a certain Richard Chancellor was all but wrecked in the mouth of the Northern Dvina while searching for a northern passage over Russia. He was brought to Moscow where Ivan, keen to buy arms from the English, sent him back to Queen Elizabeth with the promise of exclusive trading rights in Russia in return. For almost a hundred years English merchants stored, traded and recuperated from selling trips in this building, recently restored right down to its A-line wooden roof. Horrified by the regicide of Charles I, Tsar Alexei Mikhailovich turned the merchants out of their protected lair in 1649.

The yellow and white building just before the first raised driveway to the hotel was once the **Church of St Maxim the Blessed** (*Tserkov Maxima Blazhennovo*). Another holy fool like St Basil, Maxim was blessed with the gift of clairvoyance, and was buried here. The church also functioned as the belltower for the neighbouring monastery, but now houses the 'Nobility League Art Salon', which feeds a home-grown fascination with Russia's pre-Revolutionary leading families. Here you can buy macabre modern group portraits of the tsar and his family, on canvas, on Easter eggs and in ceramic, as well as the usual souvenirs.

> *Before taking the stairs to get to it, down from Ul. Varvarka after the hotel drive, you might like to take in the fairytale **view of the Kremlin**, and a snack or a shot of vodka, from the hotel. Take a lift to the 12th floor. At the desk turn left and walk to the end of the grim, red-carpeted corridor. The buffet here (open 10am–10.30pm) is dominated by the myriad golden domes of Cathedral Square. At newsworthy moments, foreign TV crews book rooms here for the backdrop.*

Back outside, head down the staircase and take a quick look inside the brick and green-tiled cathedral, all that remains of the **Nunnery of Our Lady of the Sign** (*Znamensky Monastir*). Although this building dates from the 1680s, the nunnery was founded by the father of the first Romanov tsar, who had become a monk, shortly after his son's accession in 1613. It is named after the Romanov family icon, the Znamenskaya Virgin, but its guts were ripped out during the Soviet period, when it served as a warehouse (basement) and concert hall (1st floor). Still to be seen are a few commemorative stone plaques in the walls of the basement chapel, and Baroque wall decoration in the concert hall, including the pretty starburst in the dome. A little earlier painting still clings to the window indents. Outside the upper chapel there are brick benches for the elderly who had tired of standing through the long Orthodox services. A busy icon workshop occupies the other room. There is an enormous demand for their work to replace those icons destroyed and sold abroad in Soviet times, or jealously guarded by museums.

The monk Filaret chose this spot to found the nunnery because his family home was next door, and indeed became the abbott's residence. Today, much reconstructed, it is open as the **Museum of the Romanov Boyars in Zaradye** (*Muzei Boyar Romanovykh v Zaradye*) (*open 10am–6pm, 11am–7pm on Wed, closed Tues and first Mon of month*). Despite its towering four-storey structure and bogus architectural eclecticism, the museum within is informative and cosy, and shows the warren-like conditions in which even the richest of families lived in the 16th and 17th centuries. Thick walls insulated the building against the winter cold.

The only original part of the house is the least successful, the basement. Its trunks, simple wooden storage vessels and a few armaments do little to conjure up the spirit of a 17th-century cellar. The 19th-century reconstructions on the top two floors are much more fun. The walls of the low-vaulted living apartments are covered in painting, the windows glazed with mica. The boyar's study is lined with painted embossed leather, and was heated by a pretty tiled stove. Furniture, costumes and accoutrements of everyday 16th- and 17th-century life bring the rooms, including the top-floor women's quarters, to life.

The last church along this narrow slice of history is the **Church of St George**, built by the community of merchant traders from Pskov in 1658 beneath gold-starred cupolas. The front porch and powder blue belltower are Baroque additions dating from 1818. Unless you feel like shopping, the interior is not worth paying the entrance fee demanded by yet another souvenir shop within. A stretch of the redbrick Kitai Gorod wall remains standing beyond.

The last treat of Kitai Gorod, the **Church of the Trinity in Nikitniki** (*Tserkov troitsy v Nikitnikakh*), once towered over the one and two-storey houses of the area. Now dwarfed by former Communist Party buildings up Ipatievsky Pereulok opposite the Church of St George, its jewel-like interior is a museum (*open 10am–6pm, 12 noon–8pm on Wed and Thurs, closed Tues and first Mon of month*). Until the mid-1950s the church was lived in by a number of families, so severe was the housing crisis. After a decade of restoration it opened in 1968. Just before you turn onto Nikitniky Pereulok, notice on the right the first of two obviously older, pink and white buildings. Though it was altered in the 18th century, this is where Simon Ushakov, the greatest 17th-century Moscow icon and fresco painter lived. Not surpisingly, he was chosen to lead the work on the Trinity Church, which now rises colourfully round the corner.

This confection of red brick, saturated with contrasting, white, decorative motifs, coloured tiles, green cupolas and a tent-roofed bell tower, is the best-preserved example of a mid-17th century Moscow church. Here you see the Byzantine tradition of the simple, cube-shaped church completely swamped by the traditions of Russian wooden architecture and an almost child-like enjoyment of colour. It was built between 1635 and 1653 by the merchant Grigory Nikitnikov, a man of great wealth who was not only a member of the highest Russian guild, the *gost*, but also served as a financial adviser to the first two Romanov tsars. There were only 30 members of the *gost*, including the tsar himself, and not only were they exempt from import or customs duties, they were the only citizens in the land with the right to unlimited foreign travel.

Before ascending into the interior, notice the high stone basement on which this merchant church is founded. Valuable goods stored in God's house were thought to have His added protection from thieves. All the doorways in the church deserve special attention for their bold sculptural forms. The entrance to the inner narthex for example, is through a complex sculpted and painted stone gateway with fine 17th-century metalwork gates, incised with mythical beasts and bird of fate. The tent-like, painted wooden **choir stalls** within are very rare. They exert the same sort of appeal that the fanciful shapes and colours of a fairground do to children. The walls around them are decorated with deep rich bands of fresco.

The main chapel offers a breathtaking panorama of religious images. The soaring, gilded **iconostasis** dates largely from the 1640s, and contains a number of particularly interesting paintings, as usual located in the bottom, 'local' tier. In the **six roundels of bishops and saints** just above them, painted in 1658 by Simon Ushakov, a distinct element of realistic portraiture, usually absent from Russian iconography, can be seen.

To the far left of the local tier is a copy of the **Vladimir Virgin** as painted by Simon Ushakov, sitting over a depiction of the Ascension Cathedral in the Kremlin and surrounded by the family tree of the Russian royal family and saints, among them the reigning Tsar Alexei Mikhailovich, his wife and son. Just to the left of the royal doors is an icon contemporary with the church, an image of the **Annunciation** by Simon Ushakov with the collaboration of Jacob Kazanets and Gabriel Kondriatev. The icon of the mysterious **Trinity**, the church's name icon, in its customary place to the right of the Royal Gates, is of the same date. The icon to its right shows the **Descent of the Holy Spirit** upon the Virgin and the 12 disciples.

The walls, painted under the direction of Ushakov, are covered with stories from the New Testament. On the south wall, a melancholic comic-strip version of the Passion recounts Christ's last days and death, while on the back wall a number of famous parables, all particularly relevant to a merchant community, are depicted. Over the entrance arch the wise and foolish virgins are arrayed, all in 17th-century Russian costume. The wise are shown with their sleeves rolled up as proper working Russians, while the foolish are all wearing the impractical long-sleeved gowns worn only on festive occasions. On the left is the parable of Lazarus, the rich man, who was condemned to eternal damnation for not letting the poor eat even a crumb from his table, and on the right is the story of God's forgiveness made flesh in the Prodigal Son. See if you can also make out **Jesus curing the sick**, and **turning water into wine** at the marriage at Cana, above. The wine flagons are in the lower right hand corner.

Through the stone portal in the southeast corner is the **memorial chapel** of the founding Nikitnikov family, beneath which lies their vault. The earliest icon in the church is a 16th-century depiction of St Nikita the Martyr which stands guard over them on the altar. It was saved from the earlier wooden Church of St Nikita which stood on this site. The walls are covered with scenes depicting the persecution of Christians.

Return to Ulitsa Varvarka and turn left towards Ⓜ *Kitai Gorod. The station, beside the red-brick* **Church of All Saints in Kulishki** *(see p.213), marks the end of mercantile Moscow and of this walk. It sits on the line of the former Kitai-Gorod walls. Those with boundless energy could continue straight on with Walk VIII; those with less can seek solace in the cafés and restaurants of Solyansky Proezd.*

III: Prechistenka

Start: Ⓜ *Borovitskaya. Take the exit to Mókhovaya and Znamenka Ul.* (К улицам Моховая, Знаменка).

Walking Time: *3½ hours or more, depending on how absorbed you become by the Pushkin Museum of Fine Art and the Museum of Private Collections.*

III: Prechistenka

Restaurants

A   Rosie O'Grady's

B   Patio Pizza
Патио-пицца

D   Snack Hut

E   Tren Mos Bar and Bistro
Трэн-мос Бар и Бистро

F   U Margarity
У Маргариты

H   Kropotkinskaya 36
Кропоткинская 36

I   Fast Food Booth

K   Guria
Гурия

Shops

C   Photo Centre
Фото-центр

G   Beriozka (books and snacks)
Берёзка

J   Progress Books
Прогресс

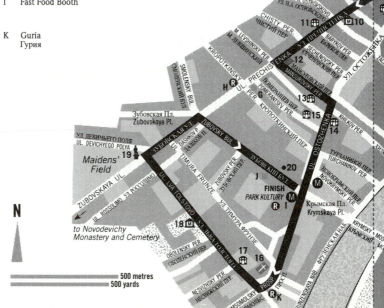

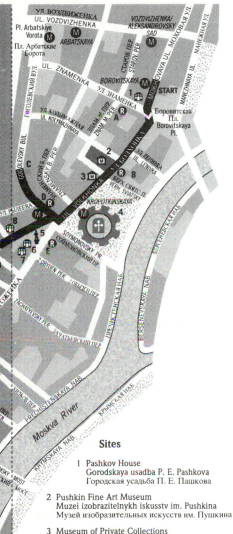

4 Moscow Swimming Pool/Christ the Redeemer
   Bassein Moskva/Khram Khrista Spasityelya
   Бассейн Москва/Храм Христа Спасителя

5 Statue of Engels
   Pamyatnik Friedrichu Engelsu
   Памятник Фридриху Энгельсу

6 Golitsyn Manor House
   Palata Golitsyna
   Палата Голицина

7 Lopukhin Manor House
   Lopukhinsky korpus
   Лопухинский корпус

8 Orlov's House
   Dom Orlova
   Дом Орлова

9 Pushkin Memorial Museum
   Muzei A. S. Pushkina
   Музей А. С. Пушкина

10 Tolstoy Memorial Museum
   Muzei L. N. Tolstovo
   Музей Л. Н. Толстого

11 Isadora Duncan's House
   Dom Isadori Duncana
   Дом Исадоры Дункана

12 Academy of Arts
   Akademiya khudozhestv
   Академия художеств

13 Bulgakov's House
   Dom Bulgakova
   Дом Булгакова

14 Turgenev's House
   Dom Turgeneva
   Дом Тургенева

15 Yeropkin Palace
   B. Dom P. Yeropkina
   Б. Дом П. Еропкина

16 Church of St Nicholas of the Weavers
   Tserkov svyatitelya Nikolaya v khamovnikakh
   Церковь святителя Николая в хамовниках

17 Weavers' Guild House
   Palati Khamovnovo dvora
   Палаты Хамовного двора

18 House Museum of Lev Tolstoy
   Muzei-usadba L. N. Tolstovo
   Музей-усадьба Л. Н. Толстого

19 Statue of Tolstoy
   Pamyatnik L. N. Tolstovo
   Памятник Л. Н. Толстого

20 Food Depot
   Proviantskiye magaziny
   Провиантские магазины

Sites

1 Pashkov House
   Gorodskaya usadba P. E. Pashkova
   Городская усадьба П. Е. Пашкова

2 Pushkin Fine Art Museum
   Muzei izobrazitelnykh iskusstv im. Pushkina
   Музей изобразительных искусств им. Пушкина

3 Museum of Private Collections
   Muzei chastnykh kollektsy
   Музей частных коллекций

Here is a walk for all tastes. Heading southwest from the centre of the city it begins with a world-class collection of European art and ends up looking into the wardrobe and larder of one of the greatest novelists of all time, Lev Nikolaevich Tolstoy. The route is strewn with the ghosts of Russia's literary heritage, both through the houses they lived in and museums in their honour. Behind the façades of the palaces which line Ul. Prechistenka lived their aristocratic heroes and heroines, squandering their lives in the style for which Moscow was famous. Far from the ambitious bustle of imperial St Petersburg, the world of Dostoyevsky's arrogant but insecure ministers and poor, demented clerks, 18th- and 19th-century Moscow society was cushioned from life by inherited fortunes. In the 'capital without a court', life was one long ball.

A few timing provisos. To walk this on a Monday would be madness, as almost everywhere is shut. The two Tolstoy museums are also closed on the last Friday of the month. On Wednesdays and Thursdays, don't start before 10.30 or 11.

---

lunch/cafés

Rosie O'Grady's For something before you start, *see* p.488.

Patio Pizza, Ul. Volkhonka 13a, ✆ 201 5000. Open 12noon–12 midnight. Down a small track opposite the Pushkin Museum of Fine Art is a place to warm the cockles of any western suburbanite. With a bulging salad bar, the only difference between this busy eaterie and the one at home is that its pizzas, cooked in a wood-fired oven, are a cut above the average.

Snack hut in the centre of Gogolievsky Bulvar garden, behind Kropotkinskaya metro station. A particularly bracing stop on a cold winter's day; order a coffee and cognac, and a toasted sandwich to take away to a nearby bench.

Tren Mos Bistro and Bar, Ul. Ostozhenka 1/9, ✆ 202 5722. Italo-American pasta joint.

Kropotkinskaya 36. Since the street name was changed this, the oldest of Moscow's co-operatives, has been at Ul. Prechistenka 36, ✆ 201 7500. For an expensive lunch, book a table downstairs, which is as cosy as upstairs is coldly formal. The food is excellent, particularly the soups, and the fluffy *blini*, though the caviar is absurdly overpriced.

Guria, Komsomolsky Prospect 7, ✆ 246 0378. Hidden behind the large house with a sign saying **Dom Modeli** (Дом Модели) on the roof. Go down Ul.

Timura Frunze and cut behind it across the mud. *Open 12 noon–11pm*. With a menu in English, reasonable prices and good everyday Georgian food—quite apart from the fascination of what is happening in the private dining booths—this is a good spot though you may have to queue for a table. Order cheesy bread (*khachapuri*) with mutton soup (*kharcho*) or *solyanka*, a meat soup with pickled cucumbers and other vegetables.

Profiteering in Russia's 'Wild East' is not exclusively a 20th-century malaise. During the reign of Peter the Great, Prince Matvei Gagarin enriched himself by using his post as Governor of Siberia to traffick in state grain and diamonds. But Peter's valet, Igor Pashkov, informed on him. The prince was hanged, and the valet rewarded with riches, vast tracts of land and several thousand 'souls'—not to mention Gagarin's licence to sell spirits. Pashkov's son even took over the job of Governor of Siberia.

> *From the metro station, turn right and walk beneath the steep double staircase of the **Pashkov House**, the arrogant, magnificent palace commissioned by Igor Pashkov's son from the architect Vasily Bazhenov.*

Bazhenov must have been pleased with this 1784 commission, for the site overlooks the Kremlin's Borovitskaya Gate, inside which he was to have built Catherine the Great a grandiloquent palace of her own. In 1775, she had suddenly cancelled the project, three years into its building. After she cancelled another major project of his ten years later, it must have been satisfying to erect such a visible monument to his talents on her back doorstep. Stylistically, the Pashkov House provides a bridge between Rastrelli's Petersburg Baroque and Kazakov's Moscow classicism. From 1861 Bazhenov's lavish building housed the Rumiantsev Museum of paintings and manuscripts collected by the heirs of one of Catherine's colonels. After the Revolution the collection was divided between various museums, and the house became an annexe of the Lenin Library, now known as the Russian State Library.

> *Cast your gaze back onto the Kremlin. There has long been a mischievious but intriguing rumour, particularly believable when you see them illuminated by night, that the vast **red stars** on the towers, some as much as 3.75m across, are made of low-grade rubies. Cross Ul. Znamenka and carry straight on slightly to the left, along Ul. Volkhonka.*

After the Hermitage in St Petersburg, Russia's finest collection of non-Russian art can be found in the somewhat confusingly named **Pushkin Museum of Fine Art** (*Muzei izobrazitelnykh iskusstv imeni A. S. Pushkina*), Ul. Volkhonka 12 (*open 10am–7pm every day except Mon*). Roman Klein's purpose-built neoclassical museum was originally conceived by a group from Moscow University as a place where copies of great classical and European art and architecture could be studied. It opened in 1912, serenaded by a choir of 700 in the presence of Tsar Nicholas II. Its first director was Professor Ivan Tsvetayev, whose daughter Marina Tsvetayeva was to become the great poet.

After the 1917 Revolution, the vast, 'nationalized' European collections of the Romanovs and exiled aristocratic and merchant families were divided between Russia's various museums, including the Pushkin. To this day, the museum's highlights are still the fruits of three tsarist-era collectors. Shortly after it opened the Egyptologist Vladimir Golenishchev donated his astonishing collection, which ranged from a 4000-year-old alabaster jar to a group of 2nd-century Fayyum portraits, with which the art of two-dimensional portraiture is thought to have begun. Also at the turn of the century, two Moscow merchants, Sergei Shchukin and Ivan Morozov, were amassing world-class collections of Impressionist and Post-Impressionist French paintings. They were particularly perspicacious in their early recognition of the talents of Matisse and Picasso, from whose studios they regularly bought new works as well as commissioning paintings.

*From the cloakroom downstairs, ascend and turn left into **Room 14**.*

Here the museum still fulfills its original remit, showing copies of Greek and Middle-Eastern art from the 5th–4th centuries BC. These include a reduced copy of the Erechtheion on the Athens Acropolis and a small corner of the Parthenon itself, scaling both floors. In addition, there is a massive Achaemenid capital, made from two half bulls some 6m high.

*Walk through rooms 3, 4 and 2 to arrive at **Room 1**.*

This magnificent Egyptian room is an aesthetic treat. The well-labelled exhibits begin at the far end of the room with flint arrowheads and a 3rd-millenium BC alabaster jar. One of the most astonishing exhibits is the 14th-century BC relief sculpture of mourners at a funeral, whose ululating despair is expressed in the fluid flailing of their arms. In the centre of the room near the door are an exquisite pair of 15th-century BC wooden sculptures, of a priest in a pregnancy smock and a fantastically shapely priestess. Distinctly unnerving is the mummified head of a woman, teeth intact—it gives you an idea of who would have inhabited the beautiful, black and gold, person-shaped sarcophagus nearby.

Room 2 is ostensibly devoted to the ancient civilizations of the Middle East, though it also covers a multitude of cultures that fit nowhere else. Most impressive are the massive plaster casts of Assyrian gates and the 9th-century BC ceramic courtyard friezes from the palace of King Ashuriazirpal, featuring scenes of hunting, waging war and the taking of slaves. Also on show are tablets encrusted with the earliest of all written languages, Sumerian; Hindu sculptures; and Meso-American ceramics.

To keep some form of chronology it is better to visit **Room 3** now, with its arresting Fayyum portraits, well-preserved Coptic embroideries and Byzantine icons. Found in the Fayyum oasis near Cairo, the portraits of men and women were painted on panels of cypress wood with a wax-based encaustic paint, and wrapped with the shrouded dead in their sarcophagi. Two examples, one of a man one of a woman, show that the Egyptians also painted their shrouds at this period. Of the embroidery for which the Christian Copts of Egypt are particularly famed, the most vigorous of the samples here is an image of the local God of the Nile. Staring at the Fayyum portraits from the opposite wall are six 14th-century Byzantine icons.

Returning to **Room 4** we enter the world of medieval European art: Italian paintings of the 13th–15th centuries and slightly earlier French Limoges enamelwork. Having just seen the Byzantine icons, it is interesting to study the three paintings of the Virgin between the doors, to watch the arrival of realism with the Renaissance. The central image dates from late 13th-century Florence, and shows all the standard features of Byzantine iconography—the static, formal expression of the face, exaggerated and schematic folds in the cloths and the traditional blue shawl encircling the Virgin's head in a neat series of folds. On the left is a 14th-century Venetian Madonna whose facial features are less exaggeratedly formal and her clothing more naturalistic despite the crown. The third, 15th-century Madonna has come full circle to just plain Mary, the girl from Galilee, seen without any throne, wearing a simple rust-coloured shift and blue overgarment with her naked child on her lap. This is the very point at which Western European painting and that of Orthodox countries such as Russia diverged.

In **Room 5** Italian paintings continue along side German and Dutch, and with the arrival of the 16th-century comes that of background landscape. Among the highlights here are Botticelli's Annunciation, the small Breughel the Younger Winter Landscape, with a simple but lethal looking bird-trap and people curling on the river. The Italian 16th-century paintings in **Room 6** include the tiny Veronese of Minerva and a distressing Pieta by Cima de Conegliano in which Mary runs her fingers through Christ's hair with a look on her face that suggests she doesn't yet fully realize he is dead. Also on display is a stylish walnut chest.

Taking in **Room 7** and its classical antiquities on the way, the exhibition of paintings continues in **Room 10** with 17th-century Dutch art, the central place given to Rembrandt, his pupils and contemporaries. In general the pictures are notable for their realistic attitude to everyday life in contrast to the portrayal of myths and religious subjects that had gone before. Having said that, one of the most affecting pictures in the room is Rembrandt's *Christ Cleansing the Temple* of its vivid-faced money-lenders. Another Rembrandt shows a bejewelled Esther with her husband King Ahasuerus and his minister Haman, who had ordered a pogrom of the Jews. By Esther's intervention, her people were saved.

Flemish and Spanish art of the 17th century in **Room 11** is represented by works by Rubens, David Teniers the Younger, José Ribera and the ghostly figures of Bartolome Murillo. Particularly suitable to Rubens' style is his grotesquely depraved Bacchanalia, in which a fleshy Silenus, Bacchus's tutor, pours wine mindlessly onto the ground. Teniers paints intimate peasant scenes while the Spaniard Ribera has pulled off a hauntingly straitforward portrayal of St Paul and St James. **Room 12** returns to Italian painting, with a poignant picture entitled *The Old Coquette* by Bernardo Strozzi. An elderly woman, her wrinkled breasts thrust blowsily upwards, sits in front of the mirror preparing to go out, oblivious to the years that have passed. Also here are paintings by Tiepolo father and son, and a doubtful Canaletto. Three centuries of French painting (16th–19th) and furniture are displayed in **Room 13**, with examples of the work of Poussin, David, Fragonard and a pair of early Watteaus. Boucher's Head of a Young Girl, with her head thrown back and lips parted with an extatic smile must, in its time, have been every bit as suggestive as Marilyn Monroe standing on the air vent in hers.

Take the stairs to the second floor in **Room 15**, where Michaelangelo's *David*, a Gothic choir stall from Germany and the Golden Entrance to Freiburg Cathedral are all reproduced. **Room 16a** at the top of the stairs contains copies of small statuettes and objects from the Greek and Aegean world of 3000–600 BC.

The top floor of the gallery is divided between reproductions at the back, and more Western European paintings at the front. Walking anti-clockwise round the floor, you can breeze through the reproductions and arrive at the chronological start of the painting section. **Room 16**, when not displaying temporary exhibitions, shows reproduction 5th-century BC Greek statues and friezes. **Room 29** is devoted to Michaelangelo, and **Room 28** to Italian Renaissance sculpture and applied art. Here you can see copies of Ghiberti's doors for the Baptistery in Florence, which were copied by the Russians for the Kazan Cathedral in St Petersburg. Rooms 27, 26, 25 and 24 continue the art history lesson with German sculpture, the European Middle Ages, Ancient Italy and Greece respectively.

The first room of painting, **Room 23**, is indicative of the rest of this collection in its preponderance of French works, here of the 18th and early 19th century. These begin with Antoine Jean Gros' *Portrait of Prince B. N. Yussupov*, an ancestor of one of Rasputin's assassins, dressed in pointed boots and curved sword as befits his Tartar ancestry. There is also a serene Ingrès, a series of windy and cold looking landscapes by the masterful Corot, and the only English painting permanently on show in the gallery, a romantic portrait by Thomas Lawrence.

In July 1993 the curators were threatening to rehang the pride of the collection, its Impressionist and Post-Impressionist works, but these are at least well labelled in English. **Rooms 22 and 21** between them contain works by Manet, Monet,

Renoir, Pissarro, Degas and a sprinkling of sculptures by Rodin. You should find the startlingly unfamiliar Van Goghs in **Room 18** with a number of works by Cézanne, Gauguin and Toulouse-Lautrec. The last large room, **Room 17** dazzles with a colourful and decorative collection of Matisses, side by side with graver works from Picasso's early period.

The Pushkin Museum has recently expanded to include a **Museum of Private Collections** (*open Wed–Fri 10am–4pm; Sat and Sun 12 noon–6pm; closed Mon and Tues*) in the green and white palace next door, Ul. Volkhonka 14. This annexe was a palace of the Golitsyns and was commandeered by Catherine the Great for the duration of her coronation in 1762. There is a certain historical resonance in its use as a museum extension; in the mid-19th century it became the first private house to be opened to the public when Prince Sergei Mikhailovich Golitsyn, a noted philanthropist, enjoyed sharing his Leonardo da Vinci, Rubens and marble sculptures with a wider audience. Today it houses beautifully planned exhibition halls on three floors. By creating the museum, Russia has managed to persuade a number of emigrés as well as ex-Soviet citizens to leave their collections to the state. Paintings and sculptures are displayed collection by collection, in homage to those brave enough to collect paintings proscribed by the state. Were it not for them, far fewer works by the cream of the avant-garde would have survived—their work was condemned in the late 20s and 30s as 'formalism'.

Between the Pushkin Museum and the Museum of Private Collections, a small road leads back to the **Roerich Museum** in the last yellow and white palace on the left, two buildings behind the museum (*open 11am–7pm; closed Mon, Wed, Fri and Sun*). Inside, paintings by the Russian Buddhist Nikolai Roerich and his family are on show beside photographs detailing their lives, and press coverage of Roerich's successful attempt to get an international pact safeguarding important cultural monuments in times of war adopted by the League of Nations.

> *Walk back and on along Ul. Volkhonka. Construction work is now taking place on the site of what was the largest heated outdoor swimming-pool in the world.*

It took 44 years, between 1839 and 1883, to build the **Cathedral of Christ the Redeemer** (*Khram Khristá Spasítyelya*) here as a monument of thanksgiving for the Russian defeat of Napoleon between 1812–14. Funded by public subscription and designed by Nicholas I's favourite architect Konstantin Thon, the cathedral was the most lavishly decorated church in the Moscow, but also a rather lumpen building in an unflattering eclectic style. Photographs taken before it was blown up in 1939 show it pompously dwarfing the surrounding city. The Soviet regime planned to replace it with an even more pompous glorification of the Soviet Union, a 1378ft high Congress of Soviets, intentionally taller than any skyscraper in

America, topped by a 230ft statue of Lenin. Construction began, but the bedrock was not strong enough to support the envisaged mass of stone, and eventually, in 1959, the plan was abandoned. In its place, a swimming pool was excavated.

Ever since the church was blown up, reputedly burying a number of its monks who refused to leave their underground cells, it has been a focus of spiritual opposition to the atheist Soviet regime. The fact that the Soviets were unable to build on the site was seen as God's justice, and many Muscovites are determined to see the resurrection of the church. In today's economic climate it seems folly to many, but if anyone can do it maybe the Russians can.

> *Ul. Volkhonka ends at Kropotkinskaya Ploshchad, beneath the stern gaze of the only statue of Engels in the city. Turn right and walk a little way up the boulevard to take a look at the* **Photo Centre**, *8 Gogolievsky Bulvar (open 12 noon–8pm, closed Mon), where excellent exhibitions of both Russian and foreign photography are staged. A shop has recently been set up within offering the best selection of original Soviet posters in the city, plus other miscellaneous Soviet memorabilia. Prices are not cheap. Now return and make your way across the Bulvar Ring, at its most peaceful here, past the elegant arches of* Ⓜ *Kropotkinskaya.*

Though the 17th-century Golitsyn and Lopukhin manor houses marked on the map show that the area ahead had been settled by noble families for some time, it was in the late 18th and 19th century that it became one of the most fashionable areas of Moscow. The outstanding collection of classical and Empire-style houses now occupied by a constellation of embassies were the homes of the old Moscow nobility. As ordered, they had followed their tsar to the new capital, St Petersburg in 1712, but by the end of the century many found themselves out of style with the developments of government and social life that had taken place. Back they came, to familiar Moscow where, as Prince Pyotr Kropotkin judiciously surmised, 'they looked with a sort of contempt and secret jealousy upon the motley crowd of families which came "from no one knew where" to take possession of the highest functions of government.' Moscow became a rather laid-back social centre, where indolence was endemic and the throwing of a couple of balls every winter obligatory. It was a famously hospitable place; you could drop in on friends and not be surprised to stay for the rest of the day, if not several, being lavishly fed and amused. Walking along Prechistenka today, between the shabby but potent façades of its palaces, it is easy to imagine their inhabitants, visible through the brightly lit windows, waltzing the evening away or losing another estate at cards.

But nowhere in this period of Russian history do you find reactionaries without reformers. A considerable number of aristocrats were deemed political 'trouble-makers' and exiled from court to Moscow. The secret societies which met here to discuss constitutional reforms did so in an atmosphere of greater freedom than those of their co-conspirators in St Petersburg. Throughout the Soviet period, Ul. Prechistenka was named after one of their aristocratic number, the fiery anarchist, Prince Pyotr Kropotkin, who lived at Kropotkinsky Per. 26.

> *The length of Ul. Prechistenka is lined with impressive façades. A plaque on No. 10 commemorates the Jewish Anti-Fascist Committee, whose members worked tirelessly here for the Russian war effort in the Second World War. They continued to meet until 1952, when they fell victim to Stalin's terror.*

The house was once lived in by Count Mikhail Fedorovich Orlov, a descendant of Catherine the Great's lover Grigory. Despite his heroic role in the rout of Napoleon, the count was exiled to Moscow by Alexander I in 1822 after he was reported to have suggested marching against the government.

> *The refined Empire palace at Ul. Prechistenka 12 (there is also a confusing 'No. 2' on its wall) is now a **Pushkin Memorial Museum**—this time, as its name suggests, housing material relating to the poet and his period, although the house itself has no connection with Pushkin (open 12 noon–8pm Tues–Thurs, 10am–6pm Fri–Sun, closed Mon). The entrance is on Khrushchovsky Pereulok, where the yellow and white portico and bold relief medallions of the Prechistenka façade are repeated.*

Inside, ten rooms have been restored with painted ceilings and parquet floors, each bedecked with lithographs, prints, watercolours and objects illuminating the poet and his times (1799–1837). There are a few English labels, but it's worth whizzing round as the self-assured Empire furniture and contemporary views of Moscow and St Petersburg help to create the feel of Russia in Prechistenka's heyday. Throughout the museum the poet's manuscripts are displayed. The last room is devoted to Pushkin's lasting influence, with foreign-language editions of his works, designs for operas and plays from his stories, and stills from films based on his life and works.

> *The literary giant **Lev Tolstoy** (1828–1910) is also represented on Prechistenka by a memorial museum, across the road behind the more modest, dark yellow and white, late-Empire façade of No. 11. We will visit the house where he lived later in this walk; this museum concerns itself with the environment from which his writing sprung. (Closed Mon, open 11am–5.30pm on Thurs, Sat and Sun, 12 noon–8pm other days).*

A series of copies of portraits of the novelist, including the oil painting by Repin showing the old man looking beyond this world for inspiration, greet the visitor. **Room 2** is hung with the portraits of his parents on the immediate left, as well as contemporary views of Moscow and the Caucasus, where he spent a period as a volunteer in the army. **Room 3** shows life on the estate where he was born, Yasnaya Polyana, some 200km from Moscow. Tolstoy set up and taught in a local school for the peasant children there, and among the photographs is one taken in the 1920s showing four of his former pupils as grown men, sitting formally on a bench. Playing on his legendary libido (he fathered 13 legitimate children, all of whom were educated in Moscow) an anecdote asks why he established the school. To educate his own children, comes the reply.

Room 4 is devoted to *War and Peace*, the novel Tolstoy wrote about the life of two Russian families during the Napoleonic period. A lithograph shows the Kremlin being set alight by French soldiers in 1812 and there is also a portrait of Tolstoy's relative, Prince Volkonsky, the model for his character Prince Bolkonsky. This is the main room of the house, which belonged to the noble Lopukhin family, and is decorated with a serene painted ceiling and a number of mirrors. **Rcom 5** explores Tolstoy's family life and his thoughts on the family, as revealed in all his novels, particularly *Anna Karenina*. Portraits of his relations hang beneath the barrel-vaulted ceiling. In **Room 6** are excerpts from his philosophical writings, while the documents in **Room 7** relate to his rejection of Orthodoxy and adoption of pacifism and his own simple moral code as the solution to the world's problems.

Rooms 8 and 9 cover his last years and death. By this time, to the embarrassment of his wife, he had rejected the frivolity of a social life. Having already renounced his right to royalties from his most successful novels, he transferred his estate to his wife and children. But the domestic rift only continued to widen, and one October night in 1910 he stole away from the estate with one daughter and a doctor, but caught a chill and died two days later in the stationmaster's house at Astapovo.

> *Turn left as you leave the Tolstoy Museum. As you pass No. 20 on the other side of the road, spare a thought for the fate of the American dancer* **Isadora Duncan** *and the Russian poet,* **Sergei Yesenin.**

Duncan and Yesenin, a notorious hell-raiser, lived here during their brief marriage in 1922. Without a language in common, they travelled the world on a wave of high living before their incompatibility surfaced. Neither lived long after this tempestuous bout. He took his own life in 1925; two years later in the south of France, she was strangled when her scarf wrapped itself around the wheel of the car she was driving.

> *There may be an exhibition showing at the* **Academy of Arts** *at Ul. Prechistenka 21, the pink house adjoining the much finer, disintegrating classical palace at No. 19.*

Before the Revolution the house containing the Academy belonged to Ivan Morozov, whose collection of French Impressionists so enlivens the Pushkin Museum of Fine Art. After his emigration it continued to be displayed here until

1948. Opposite is the symmetrical façade of a notable Style Moderne apartment block (1904–06), lent fluidity by the varying designs of its wooden window frames, its organic mushrooming roof and the elaborate grey metal balustrades which stand out against the façade.

> *Hug the end of the Academy of Arts and walk down Mansurovsky Pereulok. The small, wooden, mustard-coloured house at No. 9 is an unlikely looking pilgrimage spot, but you may not be the only person being barked at by the dog behind the gate; the novelist and playwright* **Mikhail Bulgakov** *(1891–1940) lived here in the basement for a while.*

If you've seen the staircase of Bulgakov's flat in Walk IV, you'll know that he has quite a following. Bulgakov plays with a host of Moscow locations in his most famous novel *The Master and Margarita*, and has the Master living here when he first meets Margarita, the woman he has been in love with all his life. For those who haven't yet been seduced by Bulgakov's quirky charms, here is a nugget:

'She only came through the gate once a day, but my heart raced at least ten times every morning with the false alarms. Then, when both hands were pointing to twelve, my heart continued to pound until her shoes with their black patent-leather straps and steel buckles drew level, almost soundlessly, with my basement window.'

Peering through the gate you can see the windows in question.

> *At the end of the street, the grey-blue wooden house with its well-proportioned columned balcony, Ul. Ostozhenka 37/2, was lived in between 1839–51 by Varvara Turgeneva, mother of another writer,* **Ivan Turgenev**. *Turn right on Ul. Ostozhenka.*

Turgenev spent half his life abroad, but when in Moscow, it was here that he would stay. His acutely observed novellas *First Love* and *Torrents of Spring*, are crafted with all the skill of the finest miniaturist, while his novel *Fathers and Sons* illustrates the arguments which beset the different generations of 19th-century reformers.

The enormous palace almost opposite the Turgenev's modest home belonged to one of Catherine the Great's generals, Yeropkin. Pompous as it seems for a private residence, it is difficult to begrudge him it. For during the worst of the Moscow cholera epidemic of 1771 it was Yeropkin who kept some sort of order in the old capital: enforcing quarantines, arranging for the burial of up to 900 dead a day in new graveyards and making the sensible suggestion that large-scale manufactures be located away from the city centre. He was building this house at the time, but when he died in 1805 its immense size was immediately seized upon and transformed into a school. With the onset of the Communist regime, the decoration on the pediment was transformed into a hammer and sickle crest.

*The so-called Garden Ring road is one of the unavoidable realities of Moscow. Tackle its roaring, hooting traffic as best you can, aiming for Ⓜ Park Kultury, the busiest in Moscow. An underpass runs from beside the elegant Classical **Food Depot**, now in use by the army.*

Outside Ⓜ **Park Kultury** is a hive of trading activity, people selling fruit and vegetables, pies and pizzas. The pavement along Komsomolsky Prospekt is lined with kiosks, most selling just the same as the one before, since blocks are normally controlled by one trading group, or 'mafia'. Before August 1991, the few kiosks in the city were state-run, and sold newspaper or cigarettes. Now there must be many tens if not hundreds of thousand. Imagine the sudden wealth of the people who made them.

*As you continue along Komsomolsky Prospect, the bold colours of the Church of **St Nicholas of the Weavers** (Tserkov svyatitelya Nikolaya v khamovnikakh) take you by surprise.*

This is another of Moscow's 17th-century guild churches, commissioned and paid for by the members of the weavers' guild whose workshops were concentrated in the area. You can imagine the various guilds spying on one another's creations, each vying to build the most spectacular church. Rather than go for the latest in architectural savoir-faire, the weavers decided to build (in 1676–82) a large, traditional, cubic church with a fashionably Baroque bell tower, and to embroider its exterior with paints of green and orange, studding it with countless ceramic tiles. The effect, with its five golden domes, is of an oriental fairytale palace. If you've ever wondered why there is no bird-shit on the domes, train your eyes on the crosses and you will see that anywhere a pigeon might sit is covered with spikes. For a long time the Russians feared heresy if they ate a pigeon, since the Holy Ghost is represented by a dove. A rich Russian household was not complete without a pigeon house 'to amuse the family'.

St Nicholas's has been kept alive with worship during the Communist period, and as a result its interior is intact, if not as it was originally decorated. In the 19th century, the walls were repainted, and beneath these very images the family of Lev Tolstoy would pray when they were living in their house nearby. The church is particularly known for an icon of the Virgin called the **Helper of all Sinners**, which has been credited with curing a number of people. A copy of it is lodged in the iconostasis (local tier) to the left of the royal gates. As usual, the icon two to the right of the royal gates is the church's name icon, in this case that of St Nicholas.

Turn right up Ul. Lva Tolstóvo immediately after the church. Another relic of the weavers in the area stands not far along the street on the right. A recently restored, whitewashed building with a steep shingle roof, it dates—like the church—from the end of the 17th century. It was a

Weavers' Guild House,
where material was woven and embroidered.
As you near Tolstoy's house, you may notice your fellow-pedestrians
weaving pitifully along the pavement, just as they did in the writer's time.
For next door to his house beer has been brewed for well over 100 years
and today, to afford a drink, the city's poorest alcoholics collect empties
and bring them here to the brewery to exchange them for a bottle or two
more of oblivion.

The sombre-looking **House Museum of Lev Tolstoy** (*Muzei-usadba L. N. Tolstovo*) sits behind its high decorative wooden fence at Ul. Lva Tolstovo 21. It is the most atmospheric writer's house in Moscow, hugging its period to the extent that it remains without electricity (*open from 10am–6pm, closed Mon and the last Friday of the month*). As well as the house there is the stable yard, a souvenir shop in the shed where Tolstoy's printing press was housed, and the novelist's beloved wooded green garden beyond the house. It is presided over by a gaggle of Tolstoy buffs who, amidst the clothes and crockery of the old man's family, seem to come here to escape the realities of contemporary Moscow. Their conversation is still more likely to be about Old Moscow and the literary culture of Russia than the price of sausage. Notes in English explain the function of each of the 18 rooms.

Living principally at the family estate of Yasnaya Polyana, the Tolstoys spent the winters here between 1882 and 1901. It was not the most tranquil of times for the family. Tolstoy had married Sophia Andreyevna in 1862, and was at first blissfully happy, fathering 13 children and launching into the most successful creative period of his life. By 1878 however Tolstoy had published his *Confession*, the first statement of his personal creed of an ascetic Christian morality, stripped of mysticism and worldliness, committed to the rights of the individual and nonviolence. He came to condemn his own great novels *War and Peace* (1863–9) and *Anna Karenina* (1874–76) as artistically worthless on account of their artifice and sophistication, and, while living here, wrote the more moralistic *The Death of Ivan Illych, The Kreutzer Sonata* and *Resurrection*. He retreated from the social whirl he had formerly inhabited, living a simple life, dressed in peasant's clothes, dining on vegetarian food and suffering the steely disapproval of his wife and sons. Only occasionally would he venture into the upstairs drawing room to listen to one of the virtuoso Russian musicians, Rimsky-Korsakov, Rachmaninov or Anton Rubinstein, when they played at a family soirée.

Otherwise he occupied the small suite of two rooms at the kitchen end of the house, rising with the whistle of the neighbouring brewery, keeping fit with his dumb-bells, on his bicycle or by chopping wood in the stable courtyard. As well as his clothes and his large desk, some of the shoes that Tolstoy himself made are also on show. As time went on the strength of Tolstoy's convictions led him to attack the state for subverting humanity by destroying individuality, accusing the Church of being her handmaiden. In 1901 he was excommunicated from the Russian Orthodox Church by the Holy Synod, his letter of response being the last he ever wrote from this house.

From 1901 Tolstoy lived only at Yasnaya Polyana, concerning himself with the education of the peasants on his estate and the development of his ethical system. Like any guru, he attracted a steady stream of acolytes who milled around the estate, much to the irritation of his wife. Through one particular South African correspondent and admirer, Tolstoy's theory of non-violence went on to affect the course of history. The inquiring letters were signed by one Mahatma Gandhi.

> *Continue to the end of Ul. Lva Tolstovo, where it meets Bolshaya Pirogovskaya Ul. On the other side of the road a recent (1972) stone statue of Tolstoy marks the end of a large triangular park, known as the Maidens' Field. Its name derives from the legend that this was the place were young virgins were left as part of Moscow's tribute to the Tartars. From here the energetic can take trolleybus No. 5 or 15 from the other side of the road to the Novodevichy Monastery (see p.242). Otherwise, walk back to the Garden Ring road and either take a trolleybus (Nos. 5 or 15) from this side of Bolshaya Pirogovskaya back to Ⓜ Kropotkinskaya or turn right and walk back to Ⓜ Park Kultury. On the way, pop in to the first floor of* **Progress Books** *at Zubovsky Bulvar 17. Open 10am–2pm and 3pm–7pm every day except Sunday, specializes in foreign-language editions. Among the more technical material you can always find bargain translations of the Russian classics.*

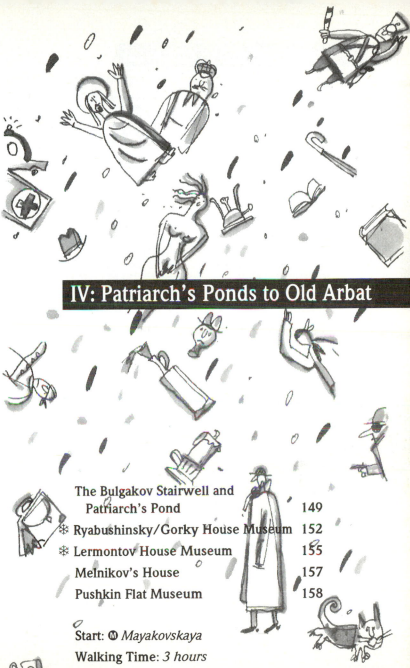

IV: Patriarch's Ponds to Old Arbat

Start: Ⓜ *Mayakovskaya*

Walking Time: *3 hours*

IV: Patriarch's Ponds to Old Arbat

Sites

1 Tchaikovsky Concert Hall
Konsertny zal im. P. I. Tchaikovskovo
Консертный зал им. П. И. Чайковского

2 Theatre of Satire
Akademichesky teatr satiry
Академический театр сатиры

3 Mossoviet Theatre
Teatr Mossoveta
Театр Моссовета

4 Bulgakov Stairwell
Bulgakovskaya lestnitsa
Булгаковская лестница

5 Patriarch's Ponds
Patriarshiye prudy
Патриаршие пруды

6 Morozov Mansion
Osobnyak Z. G. Morozova
Особняк З. Г. Морозова

7 Ryabushinsky/Gorky House Museum
Muzei-kvartira A. M. Gorkovo
Музей-квартира А. М. Горького

8 Arsenal
Арсенал

9 Church of the Great Ascension
Tserkov 'Bolshoe Vozneseniye'
Церковь 'Большое Вознесение'

10 Bobrinsky Mansion
Osobnyak Bobrinskovo
Особняк Бобринского

11 Statue of A. N. Tolstoy
Pamyatnik A. N. Tolstovo
Памятник А. Н. Толстого

12 Gnessin Musical Academy
Musikalnaya akademiya im. Gnessinykh
Музыкальная академия им. Гнесиных

13 Lermontov House Museum
Dom-muzei M. Yu. Lermontova
Дом-музей М. Ю. Лермонтова

14 Church of St Simon Stylites
Tserkov Simeona Stolpnika
Церковь Симеона Столпника

15 Statue of Gogol
Pamyatnik Gogolya
Памятник Гоголя

16 Morozov House
Osobnyak A. A. Morozova
Особняк А. А. Морозова

17 Ministry of Defence
Ministerstvo oborony
Министерство обороны

18 Vakhtangov Theatre
Teatr im. Ye. Vakhtangova
Театр им. Е. Вахтангова

19 Tsoy Memorial Corner
Memorialny ugol V. Tsoya
Мемориальный угол В. Цоя

20 Melnikov's House
Dom Myelnikova
Дом Мельникова

21 Church of St Saviour on the Sand
Tserkov Spassa na Peskakh
Церковь Спаса на Песках

22 Spasso House
Osobnyak 'Spasso'
Особняк 'Спасо'

23 Pushkin Flat Museum
Muzei-kvartira A. S. Pushkina
Музей-квартира А. С. Пушкина

24 Ministry of Foreign Affairs
Ministerstvo inostrannykh dyel
Министерство иностранных дел

Shops

A Colognia Supermarket

B Lavash bakery
Лаваш

D Garden Ring Supermarket

G Knigi Bookshop
Книги

Restaurants and Cafés

C Voyage Café

E Moskovskiye Zori
Московские Зори

F Café Margarita
Кафе Маргарита

H U Nikitskikh Vorot
У Никитских Ворот

I Vareniki
Вареники

J Praga
Ресторан Прага

K Café Arba
Кафе Арба

L Baskin Robbins

M Café Ogni Arbata
Кафе Огни Арбата

N Restaurant Bar Italia

O Mzuri Georgian Restaurant
Мзуры

P No. 44 Arbat Café

Q McDonald's

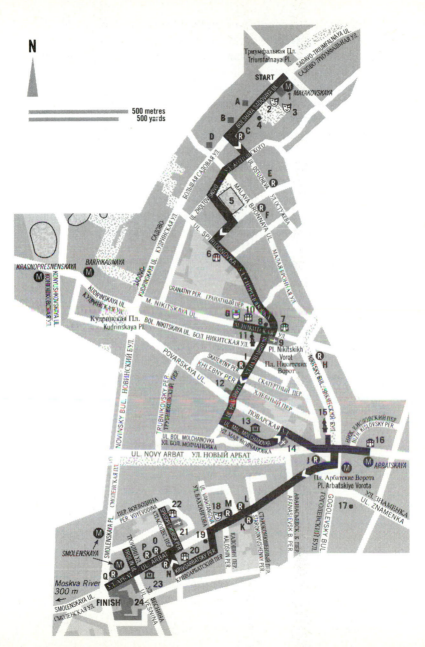

N

500 metres
500 yards

Триумфальная Пл.
Triumfalnaya Pl.

START

МАЯКОВСКАЯ
MAYAKOVSKAYA

A
B
C
D

SADAVO-TRIUMFALNAYA UL.
САДОВО-ТРИУМФАЛЬНАЯ УЛ.

BOLSHAYA SADOVAYA UL.

Большая Садовая Ул.

Садово-Кудринская Ул.

Садово-Кудринская Ул.

САДОВО-
КУДРИНСКАЯ УЛ.

MALAYA BRONNAYA UL.

МАЛАЯ БРОННАЯ УЛ.

УЛ. СПИРИДОНОВКА

UL. SPIRIDONOVKA

УЛ. ЗНОУПОВО

УЛ. СТУДЕ...

UL. OBUKHA

E

F

5

6

KRASNOPRESNENSKAYA
КОНЮ: USHKOVSKAYA УЛ.
KONYUSHKOVSKAYA UL.

BARRIKADNAYA
БАРРИКАДНАЯ

M

Kudrinskaya Ul.
Кудринская Ул.

NOVINSKY BUL.

НОВИНСКИЙ БУЛ.

GRANATNY PER. ГРАНАТНЫЙ ПЕР.

M. NIKITSKAYA UL.

Кудринская Пл.
Kudrinskaya Pl.

BOL. NIKITSKAYA UL. БОЛ НИКИТСКАЯ УЛ.

10

11

УЛ. НИКИТСКАЯ

7

8

9

Pl. Nikitskikh
Vorot
Пл. Никитских
Ворот

R

H

POVARSKAYA UL.

Skatertny Per.

KHLEBNY PER.

12

УЛ. ПАЛАШЕВСКИЙ

СКАТЕРТНЫЙ ПЕР.

ХЛЕБНЫЙ ПЕР.

ПОВАРСКАЯ

13

TRUBNIKOVSKY PER.
ТРУБНИКОВСКИЙ ПЕР.

UL. BOL. MOLCHANOVKA
УЛ. БОЛ. МОЛЧАНОВКА

UL. MAL. MOLCHANOVKA
УЛ. МАЛ. МОЛЧАНОВКА

14

15

NIKITSKY BUL. НИКИТСКИЙ БУЛ.

PER. N. KISLOVSKY PER.

16

UL. NOVY ARBAT УЛ. НОВЫЙ АРБАТ

R

M
ARBATSKAYA
АРБАТСКАЯ

Пл. Арбатские Ворота
Pl. Arbatskiye Vorota

GOGOLEVSKY BUL. ГОГОЛЕВСКИЙ БУЛ.

UL. ZNAMENKA
УЛ. ЗНАМЕНКА

17

SMOLENSKAYA PL.
СМОЛЕНСКАЯ ПЛ.

PER. VOYEVODINA
ПЕР. ВОЕВОДИНА

22

ETOSLEV. PER.

SIVTSEV VRAZHEK

21

UL. VAKHTANGOVA
УЛ. ВАХТАНГОВА

18

M

R

K

L

KRIVOARBATSKY PER.

SMOLENSKAYA
СМОЛЕНСКАЯ

M

P

O

P

R

R

UL. ARBAT

20

19

23

N

KRIVOARBATSKY PER.
КРИВОАРБАТСКИЙ ПЕР.

KALOSHIN PER.
КАЛОШИН ПЕР.

STAROKONYUSHENNY PER.
СТАРОКОНЮШЕННЫЙ ПЕР.

AFANASIEV. B. PER.
АФАНАСЬЕВ. Б. ПЕР.

Moskva River
300 m

SMOLENSKAYA UL.
СМОЛЕНСКАЯ УЛ.

FINISH

24

УЛ. ВЕСНИНА
UL. VESNINA

145

From the 18th century, west and northwest Moscow, inside the Garden Ring, was the city's Upper East Side—the place to live. Anyone with even a passing acquaintance with Russian literature will be familiar with the lifestyles of its aristocratic inhabitants. But at the turn of the century it also housed a group of people known as 'the forgotten class', who were just coming into their own on the eve of the Revolution. They were self-made industrialists and businessmen, who eschewed the suicidal frivolity of St Petersburg and the court for Moscow, the heart of the nation. Their intelligent patronage, which was to have a profound effect on Russian art, can be seen in the startling houses that scatter this walk.

This is, then, an amble through the 'might have been' of Russian history; what might have been if gradual constitutional change had brought this alienated but financially important group into the political arena. A New Year's toast by one of their number, Pavel Ryabushinsky, sums it up:

'To the bourgeoisie... to the rising power which, because of its spiritual and material riches, has overtaken the degenerating gentry and the ruling bureaucracy. We... welcome creative egoism, striving towards self-perfection and the well-being of each of us. The sound, constructive egoism of the State and of the individuals who constitute the State is the foundation for a new and powerful Russia.' How wrong they turned out to be.

The walk also links a wide range of Russian writers from Pushkin, the universally acknowledged fount of modern Russian literature, through the romantic Lermontov, master of the short story, to Mikhail Bulgakov whose surreal imaginings were hot-housed by the absurdities of Soviet rule. You should avoid doing this walk on a Monday or Tuesday when the museums devoted to them are closed. The Ryabushinsky House is also closed on the last Thursday of the month. On Wednesdays and Fridays don't start before 12.30.

---

lunch/cafés

Voyage Café, Ul. Bolshaya Sadovaya. *Open round the clock.* Contrary to its name, this glorified kiosk does not serve coffee. It will give you a shot of spirits, a beer or a soft drink, and you can buy something to eat—chocolate, fruit—from the shops on either side. In summer they have umbrella-shaded tables on the pavement. Shame about the eight-lane highway next to them.

Picnic food could easily be bought in one of the two hard-currency stores on the other side of Ul. Bolshaya Sadovaya—the Irish Garden Ring Supermarket (No. 1) or the German Colognia (No. 5/1). The latter has a particularly good salami and cheese deli, at a price. Buy bread in the bakers (*see* map) who specialize in Georgian flat bread—*lavash*.

Café Margarita, Ul. Malaya Bronnaya 28. *Unreliable hours from around 1pm— 11pm*. This very popular, small restaurant used to be a bikers' café. A no-booking policy means that at peak times you have to stand around outside trying to swing it with the bouncers. The food is hearty and well-prepared, particularly the stews. They also serve Turkish coffee, but not without a meal.

Moskovskiye Zori, Maly Kozikhinsky Pereulok* 11, ✆ 299 5725/292 6260. *Open 12 noon–3pm, 5–10pm*. If you plan this walk for an afternoon, it is worth booking a table here for a lunch to fortify you, particularly if the weather is good. In a quiet backstreet, they have a few tables outside in the garden. Specify '*chisty stol*' if you don't want a range of starters waiting, although this can put them off accepting your booking. The main courses are not revolutionary but they are well cooked. Inside, the wooden cabin is cosy.

U Nikitskikh Vorot, Ul. Gertsena 23, opposite Tass building. ✆ 290 4883. Popular underground bistro serving plain Russian fare.

Vareniki, corner of Ul. Paliashvili and Skaterny Pereulok. *Open 12 noon–9pm*. This fast and popular Ukrainian co-op specializes in the eponymous *vareniki*, dumplings filled either with meat or with fruity jam. Both are well-prepared, as is the rest of the menu. Order at the counter and the food will be brought to you.

Praga, Ul. Arbat 2, ✆ 290 6171. Don't let Cold War nostalgia tempt you to infiltrate this gargantuan restaurant, where only bribery will put you together with its lousy fare. Thank *perestroika* for the fact that there are now at least a dozen small co-ops to choose from on this street, and *glasnost* for the fact that as a foreigner you are welcome.

Café Arba, Ul. Arbat 11, serves good, strong coffee '*po vostóchnomu*', in the eastern manner (Turkish coffee heated up in a tray of sand), and snacks.

Café Ogni Arbata, Ul. Arbat 12, is tiny but serves a good cheap hot lunch.

No. 44 Arbat has a mass of tables outside in the summer and serves reasonable food but no coffee.

Mzuri is in the basement of the Georgian Cultural Centre, Ul. Arbat 42, and not surprisingly specializes in the spicy cuisine of the Caucasian mountain state. Their soups are particularly invigorating.

Restaurant Bar Italia, Ul. Arbat 49, ✆ 241 4342. Tables outside in the summer, bland international decor all year round. The food here very nearly tastes Italian, the Italian wine is better, the menu is in English and it may be just what you feel like at the end of the walk.

Those with a star-spangled tooth can celebrate here too. Both **McDonald's** and **Baskin-Robbins** have colonized Ul. Arbat, at Nos. 52 and 20 respectively.

Ⓜ *Mayakovskaya is one of the best decorated and least complicated in the city, with just one set of escalators. Turn right at the top of them to come out onto* ***Triumfalnaya Ploshchad****.*

This so-called 'square', in fact a seething mass of badly-tuned cars hemmed in by a miscellany of buildings, is a good example of Russia's colossal appellation crisis. It got its name from the temporary triumphal arches which were erected here to welcome the tsars' family to the city when they came from St Petersburg. In 1935 it was renamed Mayakovsky Square, and in the 1950s a statue of the poet was erected here. In 1992 the old name of the square was restored, though there are no triumphal arches on show, and the stern and disapproving statue of Mayakovsky still gazes on. Objections have been voiced to all name changes, but the last round, proposed in 1993, has met with particular hostility. This attempt to get back entirely to pre-Revolutionary street names has ousted such genuine literary luminaries as Pushkin and Chekhov from their squares and streets in favour of long-vanished monasteries and other remote historical associations.

Mayakovsky himself is a particularly ironic victim of Soviet iconography. Although at first he wrote 'to accept or not to accept? There was no such problem for me... It was my revolution,' by the time of his suicide in 1930 he was disillusioned by the anti-individualism of the Bolsheviks. The disapproval on his face, one can imagine, is directed at the fawning propaganda department who, following Stalin's declaration that he had been 'the greatest Soviet poet', disregarded his less than perfect record and made a Soviet hero of him (*see* p.116).

> *Turn left and walk beneath the massive colonnade of the Tchaikovsky Concert Hall. Posters on the doors tell you about forthcoming performances, and a ticket office back round the corner on Tverskaya Ul. may be able to sell you tickets for anything you fancy. It's a mercurial business, ticket buying, however (*see p.519*). As well as the concert hall, this side of the square is lined by two theatres, the* **Theatre of Satire** *and the* **Mossoviet Theatre**, *behind its railings and garden. The rest of the square straddles the misnamed Garden Ring road, part of which disappears here in an underpass, and is overseen by the benign, beige wedding cake of the* **Peking Hotel** *and its blue clock.*

Not far along this side of Ul. Bolshaya Sadovaya is our first appointment with literature. In the beige building with jutting balconies, sited confusingly between Nos. 8 and 14, presumably No. 10/12, the young doctor from Kiev, Mikhail Bulgakov lived from his arrival in Moscow in 1921 until 1934. You will recognize its rounded archway by the fantastical bronze bas relief which hugs the wall, illustrating his masterwork *The Master and Margarita*. Its inscription is the first line of the book: 'One spring day, at a time of unusually warm weather in Moscow...'.

The stairwell at the back of the yard on the left has become a graffiti memorial to both writer and book. It's a strange and uniquely Russian phenomenon, which could only happen in a country where for almost 200 years literature has been the most consistent vehicle for the expression of political opposition. The novel stretches Bulgakov's unique talent to perfection by combining a satirical fantasy about the Devil in his contemporary Moscow with a realistic account of the interrogation of Jesus by Pontius Pilate. Bulgakov used his own flat, at the top of the stairs on the left, as the location for the Devil's sensational ball at which figures from the underworld mingle with contemporary Muscovites. In a typical, diabolic Bulgakov touch, the flat becomes enormous, embellished with sweeping staircases and other decorative flourishes which the author culled from a brief visit to the residence of the American ambassador.

The Master and Margarita, finished in 1938, was only published in 1966, and even then in a severely censored edition. Since the devil's main purpose in Moscow seems to be the disruption of the self-seeking, corrupt lives of the lower levels of the Soviet élite, the novel attracted a cult following among the underground opposition. When the authorities refused to erect a memorial to Bulgakov, who died in 1940, his fans 'occupied' the stairwell to his first flat here with their graffiti. Long negotiations to turn the flat into a memorial museum failed amid bitter arguments, so fans are restricted to the stairwell.

> *A little further along Ul. Bolshaya Sadovaya cut through the garden behind the Voyager kiosks and turn right at the end to reach the Patriarch's Pond, where* The Master and Margarita *opens on that spring day. This is the very corner on which, at the end of Chapter III, Mikhail Berlioz slips on a pool of sunflower oil and falls under the screeching wheels of a tram.*

This single square pond is all that remains of an area of the city, known as the Patriarshaya Sloboda, the Patriarch's Quarter, which was given to and governed by the head of the Russian Orthodox Church in the 17th and 18th centuries. Just as the houses of Muscovite nobles were never complete without a fish pond, so the patriarch had three ponds dug to supply his table. The one which remains, with its elegant yellow and white pavilion, is still the focus of fishermen's hopes, but the tiny fish which emerge from its stagnant waters are only for feline consumption, if that. The park which surrounds it, with its mature trees and shaded benches, is a favourite spot with almost any Muscovite you ask, and its easy to see why in the remorseless sprawl. With a little more attention to the growing of grass and a regular clean of the pond it would be delightful by anyone's standards.

> *The top end of the pond is a favourite haunt with local children and their carers, often grannies or granddads who look after them while both parents work. They play around an uninspired statue of the inspired children's fabulist, Ivan Andreevich Krillov (1769–1844), in a playground decorated with free-standing bronze screens illustrating his tales.*

Ever since the 19th century, when the area was colonized by Moscow's bohemia, the houses round about have been popular with the intelligentsia—academics, musicians and writers—now much depleted by emigration, particularly to Israel. After the war the area also attracted the acquisitive gaze of the Communist Party. They settled high-ranking military officers in the Classical building with the lion-topped gateposts behind Krillov, and built high-quality apartment blocks and a hotel for themselves nearby. Gorbachov, for example, lived nearby before his elevation to the Kremlin. The area is still inhabited by the ghosts of the previous élite, the flats having passed to their children, once known as the 'golden youth' (*zolotnya molodyozh*), such as Galina Brezhnev.

> *For some reason, you can always tell these Party buildings by the pale, beige bricks used in their construction. There is one at the end of Ul. Adama Mitskevicha, on Ul. Spiridonovka. Turn left at this junction.*

Although Moscow's turn-of-the-century industrialists bought up and built houses all over the city, two of their most impressive commissions to survive are both on this street. Even today you can get an idea of why they wanted to build these grand, free-standing houses here, for the atmosphere is more that of a calm and peaceful suburb than the centre of a major city. During the Soviet period most of the buildings were turned into offices, or were taken over by one of the few aristocracies of the regime, the diplomats.

> *A little way down Ul. Spiridonovka to the left, your attention will be drawn to the neo-Gothic grandeur of Savva Morozov's house.*

This domestic cathedral was built between 1893–98 for Morozov's wife Zinaida, the daughter of one of his machine operators. Its architect, Fyodor Shektel, was on the verge of a 10-year period in which his designs were to mark him out as one of the most remarkable architects of the international movement known variously as Arts and Crafts, Art Nouveau, Jugendstil and in Russia as Style Moderne. The inside, if we could but visit it (it is currently used by the Foreign Ministry to receive visiting heads of state), expresses in every aspect the 'mood' which Shektel felt it was important a house should evoke. The attention to detail which was a hallmark of this era of architecture can also be seen on the exterior. Inspired by medieval English Gothic, it includes gargoyles at the head of each drainpipe, a soaring vaulted porch, dark brown stone-carved detailing and a baronial cast-iron railing, each spike topped with the head of a griffin.

 The Morozovs were one of Moscow's top mercantile dynasties, self-made cotton millionaires whose business had expanded to include banking and newspapers as well as sponsorship of the arts. They belonged to the schismatic Orthodox sect, the Old Believers (*see* p.249), who seem to have played an analogous role in Russia to that of the Quakers in the English industrial revolution. They combined an uncanny industrial knack with a quasi-socialist attitude towards the physical and mental well-being of their employees. Savva secretly funded the paper Lenin published in exile, *Iskra* (*The Spark*), and was known to hide revolutionaries in the dark recesses of his fantastical home. When the interest generated by the theme mansion reached the ears of the tsar, he sent a representative to inspect the building. Morozov agreed to his visit, but only in his absence, such was his aversion to the old power structure. During the period of massive strikes following Bloody Sunday in 1905, the conflict between his interests as an industrialist and his loyalties as a supporter of reform became too much for Morozov to bear, and the passionate patron blew his brains out.

Morozov's protegé Fyodor Shektel was born in Saratov. He came to Moscow at the age of 16 with his mother, who worked as housekeeper to the art collector Pavel Tretyakov and his family. Fyodor completed just one year at the Moscow Architecture School before being lured into the world of theatre design, where he developed a close friendship with the playwright Anton Chekhov. Within a few years he was designing country estates for the industrial and merchant class from which the Tretyakovs stemmed; his imaginative eclecticism was the ideal style to express their rebellion against the established order. Then came the Morozov commission and fame in the centre of Moscow. Shektel is quoted as saying he loved Moscow as a man loves a woman, and his surviving buildings do seem to beautify her body like unexpected jewels. With the Revolution, his style of architecture was condemned as bourgeois, and he died in poverty in 1926. The wheel turns, and in 1993 one of Shektel's descendants entered Moscow's Architectural Institute.

*Walk on down the street to the point where it curves sharply to the right. Opposite each other, round the corner, are a Shektel masterpiece dating from 1900–02 and a **17th-century arsenal**, distinguished by its characteristic high-pitched roof and small windows, ornamented by a plain brick relief surround. It was sited here, outside the white walls of Moscow which at that time followed the line of the bulvar ring, to minimize the spread of fire if its volatile munitions were to go up in flames.*

The entrance to the museum in the **Ryabushinsky House**, whose address is 6/2 Ul. Kachalova, is actually from Spiridonovka Ul., signalled by a red plaque (*open 10am–5pm Thurs, Sat and Sun; 12 noon–7pm Wed and Fri; closed Mon, Tues and last Thursday of the month. English-language guided-tours can be arranged by calling © 290 5130 in advance; allow three quarters of an hour to get to this point of the walk*). The museum is officially known as the House Museum of Maxim Gorky (*Muzei-kvartira A. M. Gorkovo*), who bears the dubious honour of being known as 'the father of Soviet literature' (1868–1936). A writer who compromised his second-rate talents with revolutionary moralizing, he left the country in 1921 after disagreements with the Bolsheviks. When he returned in 1931, he was given this house to live in. But the staff who work here are not deceived. They revel in the inventive architectural genius of Shektel, not the mundane domesticity of Gorky, who even allowed a 'Party member' to remove one of the original Shektel fireplaces from the building. They are keen to open more of the house than the ground floor, which is all that is currently on show.

Shektel was commissioned to design this house for a member of the Ryabushinsky banking dynasty, Stepan Pavlovich, a profoundly religious member of the Old Believers' sect with one of the finest collections of icons in the country. One of the highlights of the building, his mosaic-lined chapel upstairs, is closed to visitors. It hardly matters though, as the mood of the ground floor, with its varied and detailed craftsmanship, is reward enough. Shektel involved the house with the spirit of nature, most dramatically in the central staircase, whose banisters appear to rise from the sea, racing in waves up the stairs, illuminated by a terrible dripping sea monster of a lamp. It is a particularly suitable theme for the Style Moderne, which was distinguished above all by an obssession with the fluid. The hall leads into the panelled dining room where the wave pattern continues on the parquet floor. Next door the ceiling of the library is adorned with plaster bas reliefs of flowers and snails, and a small mural of snails and sunflowers. The range of textures encountered in the house—wood, brick, plaster, tile and marble—are another hallmark of Style Moderne. Every ceiling and every window in the house is different. Unfortunately the last rooms, the author's study and 'bedroom', are overawed by the tacky oriental taste of Gorky.

The outside of the house is rather different. At first it gives the impression of being a solid cube, but the more you look, the more you notice its curves, introduced via the metalwork, the wooden window frames and the rounded plaster porches. The railings echo the interior with their waves. Beneath the overhanging eaves is a dream–like tile mosaic of massive purple orchids.

These two houses hold a looking-glass to a unique period in Moscow's history, which was both partially responsible for and annihilated by the Revolution. With government and the court in St Petersburg, Moscow's industrial millionaires were free to create a society of their own devising, and creative they were, particularly in their patronage of the arts. There were the Tretyakovs, whose collection of Russian art, bequeathed to the city, still forms the kernel of the Tretyakov Gallery. It was Savva Morozov who funded Stanislavsky's pioneering Moscow Arts Theatre, where the works of Shektel's friend Chekhov were appreciated for the first time. Meanwhile, out at Abramtsevo (*see* pp.261–4), the railway millionaire Savva Mamontov was supporting a clutch of artists and architects, encouraging the diverse talents of Vrubel, Nesterov and Vasnetsov as well as throwing the commission for Yaroslavl Railway Station in Shektel's direction. This was a profoundly encouraging milieu, without which the Russian avant-garde art of the 10s and 20s would have been a pale shadow of its vibrant, confident self. And yet most of its players were in one way or another ruined by the events of 1917.

> Opposite the Ryabushinsky House sits the impressive stone portico of the **Church of the Great Ascension** (Tserkov 'Bolshoye Vozneseniye'), a large, late-Empire church of confident and satisfying simplicity.

Though work began in 1798, the church was only completed in 1840. It is particularly dear to Muscovites for an event that took place in its unfinished shell in February 1831, the romantic marriage of Pushkin. The poet had long boasted that he was going to marry the most beautiful woman in Russia, and eventually settled upon Natalya Goncharova, daughter of an impoverished nobleman. Goncharov père at first turned down Pushkin's suit, convinced that his daughter's legendary beauty could land her a more reliable husband During the service a crucifix crashed to the ground, and the candles blew out ominously. Small wonder, it was later surmised, that Pushkin died defending his wife's honour in a duel. The church is once again a place of worship, and has become a centre of the monarchist revival. However its interior, stripped of its original fittings, is a disappointment.

> *A short shopping detour up Ul. Kachalova passes the **Bobrinsky Mansion** at No. 12. This exquisite late 18th-century classical palace was built by the Dolgoruky family.*

Until the Revolution, it was inhabited by the descendants of Catherine the Great's illegitimate son by Grigory Orlov, Count Bobrinsky. Its delicate yellow and white façade, whose bas-relief details were redone when the metal porch was added after 1812, is set back behind a garden sporting statues of Helen of Troy and Paris.

Our aim is **the bookshop**, at No. 16, beneath a sign which reads 'КНИГИ'. In its second-hand foreign language department you can pick up a novel, a Russian dictionary or a children's book in English, and the shop also sells antiques, jewellery, icons, china and other trinkets.

> *Returning and turning right before Pushkin's church, the garden on your right contains a **statue of the writer Alexei Tolstoy,** who lived nearby.*

A distant relative of the better-known Lev Tolstoy, Alexei Nikolaievich is fast being eclipsed by his grand-daughter, Tatyana Tolstaya, as well. Tolstoy fought for the White Army during the civil war and went into exile where he began his well-known trilogy about the Revolution, *The Road to Calvary*, as an anti-Bolshevik novel. He returned to Russia in 1923, only completing the trilogy in 1941. By then its politics was unrecognizable and in 1942 it was awarded the Stalin Prize. Stalin called him 'our proletarian prince'.

> *If the Ryabushinsky House has wetted your appetite for the Style Moderne, venture off Ul. Paliashvili as you walk down it, into Skaterny, Stolovy and Khlebny Pereuloks.*

They are dotted with more town houses of Moscow's turn-of-the-century commercial aristocracy, the descendants of the aristocratic palaces like the Bobrinsky Mansion. The names of these lanes—Tablecloth, Table and Bread—recall earlier inhabitants, settlements of bakers, lace-makers and the like, who lived and worked here in the 17th century, servicing the royal household in the Kremlin.

> *In summer, as you cross Ul. Vorovskovo, you may hear music floating through the open windows of the **Gnessin Musical Institute**. This is Moscow's second-best music school, after the Conservatoire. Carry*

straight on along Bolshoy Rzhevsky Pereulok and first left down Ul. Malaya Molchanovka. The charming, two-storey, pink and white wooden house at No. 2 is the **House Museum of Mikhail Lermontov** *(Dom-Muzei M. Yu. Lermontova). (Open 11am–6pm, 2–6pm Wed and Fri, closed Mon and Tues.)*

Lermontov (1814–41), a romantic poet regarded as second only to Pushkin, is best known to the English-speaking world for the series of connected short stories he wrote at the age of 25, a pattern-book for the romantic era called *A Hero of Our Time*. Ten years earlier he lived here with his grandmother, from 1829–32, while attending the educational Noble Pension in Moscow. His mother had died when he was two, escaping a marriage made unhappy by her husband's drinking and mistresses. His rich grandmother wrested him from his father from that moment, bringing him eventually to Moscow for the benefit of his education. This house they rented from a merchant who had built it after the 1812 fire.

Like many of the great figures of 19th-century Russian literature, Lermontov was no mean painter; indeed this house will familiarize the visitor more with his visual skills than with his written genius. In the first room, his granny's, his first watercolour, a classical scene painted at the age of 15, hangs to the left of the door. The fine tapestry hunting scene was also his work. A portrait of Lermontov hangs on the right-hand wall. The next two rooms, a formal small sitting-room and a large drawing-room, are both furnished with Empire sofas and tables of the period. The piano and violin in the drawing-room indicate another of the poet's talents. In Russia to this day poetry is often set to music, known as 'romances', and Lermontov is thought to have composed music for his poems. Also in the room is a portrait of his mother, the dark-haired woman, and of Lermontov at about the time she died of tuberculosis. The other woman is his kindly-looking granny.

Upstairs is Lermontov's study, a serious-looking place for a 15–18 year old, but by this time Lermontov was already translating Byron, whose portrait dominates the room. On the easel is Lermontov's own portrait of his father, while one of Pushkin hangs over his desk. It is for a poem he wrote on the death of Pushkin (1837) that Lermontov first attracted official censure. In it he clearly accuses the court of connivance in his death:

> *'You, hungry crowd that swarms about the throne,*
> *Butchers of freedom, and genius, and glory,*
> *You hide behind the shelter of the law,*
> *Before you, right and justice must be dumb!*
> *But, parasites of vice, there's God's assize…'*

The poem was circulated in hand-written copies, an early example of the *samizdat* (self-publishing) which was so much a part of the Soviet literary scene. Inevitably in closely knit St Petersburg, it was brought to the attention of the tsar, and Lermontov was exiled to the Caucasus. An etching of those mountainous lands, with which he had been familiar from childhood, hangs beside his desk. When he lived here as a boy, they constituted a symbol of freedom to him. By the time of his death, in that most 'romantic' of gestures, a duel, he was enduring his second period of exile there. In the last room downstairs, a number of his own paintings show a meticulous attention to detail.

> Carrying on down the road you hit Ul. Vorovskovo again, and continue right to the picturesque **Church of St Simon Stylites** (Tserkov Simeona Stolpnika), named after the saint who withdrew from the world up a 60ft pillar, from which he was said to be able to fly.

It was here, in the 18th century, that Count Nikolai Sheremetev married his serf-actress Prasokovia Zhemchugova-Kovaleva (see p.196). Since its restoration in the 1960s, this church has been an exhibitions hall for the Society for the Preservation of Nature and a craft shop, but it is now a working church. The interior is a white shell, but the exterior, typical of 17th-century Moscow, is composed of a cluster of cupolas rising from clouds of kokoshniki gables. Walk on past and you will see how the church is marooned against the horror of Novy Arbat, the wide highway cut through the city in the 1960s, in accordance with the 1935 plan for Moscow's redevelopment. Though the avenue contains some of the best food shopping in Moscow, its monumental proportions make it unbearably inhumane.

> Arbatskaya Ploshchad ahead teems with pedestrians and vehicles. Before plunging into the underpass, turn left onto Nikitsky Bulvar to visit the courtyard of No. 7, where Gogol wrote and burned the second volume of Dead Souls in his last months of life. The langorous pose of the 1909 sculpture epitomizes the depressed writer, and its pedestal is ornamented with characters from his stories. Now take the underpass beneath the bulvar and onto Ul. Vozdvizhenka.

A cousin of Savva Morozov, whose Gothic mansion by Shektel we saw on Ul. Spiridonovskaya, commissioned the eclectic fantasy of a house at No. 16, the most unusual in the city. The commission is said to have begun in a drunken conversation on a railway platform in Portugal, when Arseny Morozov told his architect friend Mazyrin to replicate the 16th-century castle they had just seen. When it was finished Morozov's mother is said to have anguished: 'I know you are crazy, but now everyone else will know it too.' Unfortunately the interior, now occupied by an institue afffiliated to the European Commission, is closed to visitors. Each room is decorated in a different style, from English Gothic to ancient Greek.

> Retrace your steps to the bulvar, and take the underpass diagonally under Arbatskaya Ploshchad, to emerge opposite the vast semi-circular end of

the Praga Restaurant. The subway here serves as an unofficial petshop, where Muscovites show off puppies and kittens for sale, cutely tucked in baskets or peeping out from unbuttoned coats. Despite tiny flats and problems with food, pets are incredibly popular in Moscow. There is no such thing as tinned petfood, and I've known dogs eat meat that their owners can't afford for themselves. Ironically, people have been trying recently to turn exotic pedigrees to financial gain by breeding from them, at the very time when fewer people can afford to buy them.

Mention the word **Arbat** to a Muscovite and you will get a strong reaction, mostly of the 'it's not what it used to be' variety. Architectural historians lament its aristocratic heyday in the early 19th century when the district was known for its wooden Empire palaces. Elderly residents remember with affection its civilized, intellectual milieu before the Second World War. Former members of the underground tell how it has been downhill since the risky days before and just after the beginning of *perestroika*, while Moscow's young *kapitalisti* bemoan Yeltsin's decision to move them off the pedestrian street, where until mid-1993 they traded very profitably in tourist tat. By the time you arrive they may have inched their way back among the portrait painters, buskers and poets who still use the pavement. Bar a complete reversal of politics however, all these old Arbats are lost for ever to the dull and debilitating process of cultural homogenization: Baskin-Robbins, McDonalds and Benetton are already installed, and you are now as likely to hear the strains of a South American pipe band as a lone guitarist struggling with an inimitable ballad by Vysotsky.

That is not to say that the Arbat isn't still fun, the only place in the city with a genuine café culture, at least in the summer. Since its origins as the road from Smolensk in the 15th century, it has always been associated with trade, and today there is an intense concentration of *kommissiony* antique shops where the occasional gem is still to be found. Look for signs reading Антиквариат.

Shortly after the heavy portico of the Vakhtangova Theatre on the right, Krivoarbatsky Pereulok leads off to the left with a fanfare of graffiti and a dose of grunge. Since the death of the young Korean-Russian pop star, Viktor Tsoy, in a car crash in 1989, his fans have been gathering here to remember him. Tsoy was the lead singer of one of Russia's most popular bands, *Kino*. Continuing along the lane past the graffiti, photographs, flowers and candles, you turn the corner and on the right is the unique **Melnikov House** (No.10), hopefully divested of its coat of scaffolding. Built in 1927 by one of the greatest Constructivist architects, Konstantin Melnikov, it consists of two interconnecting white cylinders pierced by seemingly random hexagonal windows. At the height of his favour Melnikov designed Lenin's glass sarcophagus in next to no time, revealing later that he was told he would be killed if he didn't complete it by the deadline. The individualist architect managed to live on in this house himself until his death in 1974, no mean feat for a man whose sparse Futurist style was anathema to the New Soviet Rococo favoured by Stalin. Today, the house is inhabited by his son, who has been valiantly trying to save the building since his father's death.

*Walk back onto the Arbat and take a swift detour down Spassopeskovsky Pereulok, past the **Church of the Saviour on the Sand** which was built in 1711 and is slowly returning to its original purpose thanks to local dedication. The lane ends at the grand, neo-Empire **Spasso House**.*

With its semi-circular portico, this is an example of a very different approach to architecture by the 'forgotten class'. Despite its 19th-century look, it was in fact built by a banker and industrialist, Vtorov, in 1913. It is now used by the American Embassy for entertaining.

Stalin's planners destroyed two monasteries and ten churches in the Arbat area, but there are still stretches where you can see what the whole area must have looked like in the 19th century. Long three-storey buildings line the street, and down side streets detached wooden houses stand defiantly apart. The mansion in which Pushkin lived for three happy months after his marriage, so happy that he wrote not a word of poetry, is one of the best preserved and prettiest in the street. You can now penetrate beyond the powder blue and white stucco façade (No. 53) into the **Pushkin Flat Museum** within, which until some 15 years ago was, like most of central Moscow, communal flats. The interior has been painstakingly restored and contains exhibits of Pushkin's Moscow, before and after the great fire of 1812, the story of his courtship and wedding, a replica of the poet's library and, upstairs, early 19th-century objects donated to the museum. The fact that Tchaikovsky, probably better known outside Russia than Pushkin, also lived here (in 1875) goes without mention.

Most Muscovites look upon the pedestrianization of the Arbat with civic pride, a sign of a user-friendly city. Cynics note that the kilometre-long street begins at the Defense Ministry and ends with the Foreign Office and draw their own conclusions. Tales of underground communications, better serviced without cars trundling over, abound.

Beyond the Pushkin Flat Museum, the Arbat meets the Garden Ring road beneath the stern gaze of one of Stalin's Seven Sisters, in this case MID, the Ministry of Foreign Affairs. Ⓜ Smolenskaya is behind McDonald's, on the right. At the trolleybus stops in front of the MID building you can catch Nos. Б or 10 which travel in both directions around the Garden Ring.

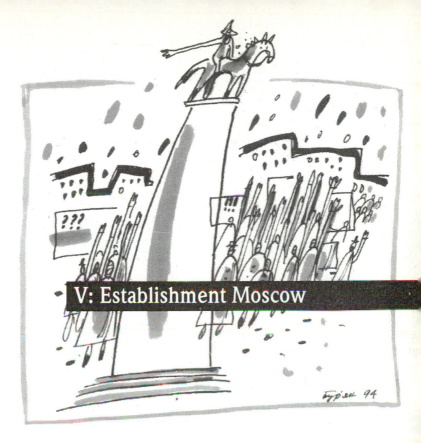

V: Establishment Moscow

Start: Ⓜ *Vozdvizhenka/Aleksandrovsky Sad.*

Walking Time: *2½ hours, more for enthusiasts of oriental art.*

Sites

1 Russian State Library
Rossiskaya Gos. Biblioteka
Российская Гос. Библиотека

2 Manezh
Манеж

3 Old University Buildings
Stariye zdanii universiteta
Старые здании университета

4 Hotel Moskva
Gostinitsa Moskva
Гостиница Москва

5 Menshikov Mansion
Dom S. A. Menshikova
Дом С. А. Меншикова

6 Tchaikovsky Conservatoire
Konservatoria im. P. I. Chaikovskovo
Консерватория им. П. И. Чайковского

7 Mayakovsky Theatre
Teatr im. Vl. Mayakovskovo
Театр им. Вл. Маяковского

8 Inter-Tass Building
ТАСС

9 Museum of Folk Art
Muzei narodnovo iskusstva
Музей народного искусства

10 Stanislavsky House Museum
Dom-muzei K. S. Stanislavskovo
Дом-музей К. С. Станиславского

11 Church of the Resurrection
Tserkov Voskreseniya
Церковь Воскресения

12 Moscow Arts (Chekhov) Theatre
MKhAT im. Chekhova
МХАТ им. Чехова

13 Church of Ss Cosmas and Damian
Tserkov Kosmy i Damiana
Церковь Космы и Дамиана

14 Lenin Institute of Marxist-Leninism
Institut Marxisma-Leninisma
Институт Мархизма-Ленинизма

15 Statue of Yuri Dolgoruky
Pamyatnik Yu. Dolgorukovo
Памятник Ю. Долгорукого

16 Moscow City Council
Mossovet
Моссовет

17 Yeliseyev's
Magazin G. G. Yeliseyeva
Магазин Г. Г. Елисеева

18 Literary Institute
Literaturny institut
Литературный институт

19 Pushkin Theatre
Dramatichesky teatr im. A. S. Pushkina
Драматический театр им. А. С. Пушкина

20 Moscow Arts (Gorky) Theatre (MKhAT)
MKhAT im. Gorkovo
МХАТ им. Горького

21 House Museum of Maria Yermolova
Muzei-kvartira M. N. Yermolovoy
Музей-квартира М. Н. Ермоловой

22 Church of the Great Ascension
Tserkov 'Bolshoye Vozneseniye'
Церковь 'Большое Вознесение'

23 Museum of Oriental Art
Muzei iskusstva narodov vostoka
Музей искусства народов востока

Restaurants and Cafés

A Gyro Express Café
Гиро-экспрес Кафе

B Stanislavskovo 2
Станиславского 2

C Ristorante Artistico
Ресторан Артистико

D Oladi
Олади

E Stolishniki Café
Столишники кафе

F Aragvi
Арагви

G M. B.
М. Б.

H Tsentralny Restoran
Центральный Ресторан

I Pizza Hut

J McDonald's

K U Nikitskikh Vorot
У Никитских Ворот

Shops

L Alesia Antiques

M Oriental Crafts

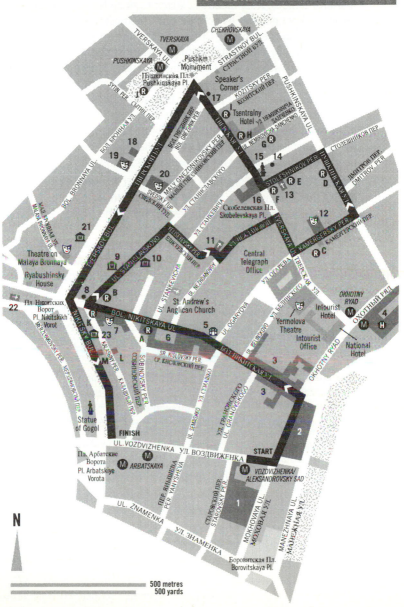

TVERSKAYA

CHEKHOVSKAYA

TVERSKAYA

PUSHKINSKAYA

STRASTNOY BUL.
СТРАСТНОЙ БУЛ.

Pushkin
Monument

PUSHKINSKAYA UL.

Пушкинская Пл.
Pushkinskaya Pl.

SYTIN PER. СЫТИН ПЕР.

Speaker's
Corner

17

KOZITSKY PER.
КОЗИЦКИЙ ПЕР.

Tsentralny
Hotel

UL. NEMIROVICHA-DANCHENKO
УЛ. НЕМИРОВИЧА-ДАНЧЕНКО

G

H

18

BOL. BRONNAYA UL.

BOL. GNEZDNIKOVSKY PER.

15   14

STOLESHNIKOV PER.

СТОЛЕШНИКОВ ПЕР.

19

MALY GNEZDNIKOVSKY PER.
МАЛЫЙ ГНЕЗДНИКОВСКИЙ ПЕР.

STOLESHNIKOV PER.

E

DMITROV. PER.

20

SVEDK. T. TUP.
СВЕДК. Т. ТУП.

UL. STANISLAVSKOVO
УЛ. СТАНИСЛАВСКОГО

R

F

13

D

16

УЛ. СТАНКЕВ

Скобелевская Пл.
Skobelevskaya Pl.

12

UL. MALAYA BRONNAYA
УЛ. МАЛАЯ БРОННАЯ

21

TVERSKOY BUL.

YUSSKAYA
ЕПШ. ТЕЗ. КИН ПЕР

11

UL. NEZHDA

TVERSKAYA

KAMERGERSKY PER.
КАМЕРГЕРСКИЙ ПЕР.

Theatre on
Malaya Bronnaya

UL. TSKATSINSKOVO

9

10

Central
Telegraph
Office

UL. OGAREVA

C

Ryabushinsky
House

8

B

R

UL. STANKEVICHA

UL. OGARYOVA

St. Andrew's
Anglican Church

Intourist
Hotel

OKHOTNY
RYAD
ОХОТНЫЙ РЯД

22

Пл. Никитских
Ворот
Pl. Nikitskikh
Vorot

R

K

23

7

A

5

Yermolova
Theatre

M   H

BOL. NIKITSKAYA UL.

G

BOL. NIKITSKAYA UL.

Intourist
Office

4

NIKITSKY BULV.

M

L

SR. KISLOVSKY PER.
СР. КИСЛОВСКИЙ ПЕР.

OKHOTNY RYAD

National
Hotel

Statue
of Gogol

SOBINOVSKY PER.
СОБИНОВСКИЙ ПЕР.

KASHI PER.

UL. SEMASHKO
УЛ. СЕМАШКО

UL. GRANOVSKOVO
УЛ. ГРАНОВСКОГО

3

3

FINISH

2

Пл. Арбатские
Ворота
Pl. Arbatskiye
Vorota

UL. VOZDVIZHENKA УЛ. ВОЗДВИЖЕНКА

START

M   ARBATSKAYA

M

VOZDVIZHENKA/
ALEKSANDROVSKY SAD

N

1

UL. ZNAMENKA УЛ. ЗНАМЕНКА

MOKHOVAYA UL.
МОХОВАЯ УЛ.

MANEZHNAYA UL.
МАНЕЖНАЯ УЛ.

STAROVSKY PER.
СТАРОВСКИЙ ПЕР.

Боровицкая Пл.
Borovitskaya Pl.

500 metres
500 yards

Though the highlights of this walk range from illuminating icons to Buddhist tankras, from theatrical kitsch to retail fantasy, an aura of respectability underlies its eclecticism. The musical establishment is represented in the Moscow Conservatoire; the former ideological establishment by the Lenin Institute of Marxist-Leninism; and the 18th-century aristocratic establishment by their Empire mansions. The walk weaves through leafy backstreets with children's playgrounds and antiques emporia, but sadly it is the inhuman monumentalism of Tverskaya Ulitsa which stays in the mind. There is no way to regain the street for the common man, but at least now we can celebrate the passing of an establishment which expected people to enjoy shopping on the banks of a motorway.

There is no point walking here on Monday or Tuesday, or starting earlier than lunchtime, as many of the sights do not open until 1–2pm. Otherwise *cave* only the last Friday of the month, when the Museum of Oriental Art is shut.

---

lunch/cafés

Gyro Express Café, beside the Conservatoire, Bolshaya Nikitskaya Ul. 15. A fast food joint next to a nicer, typical Russian café.

U Nikitskikh Vorot, Bolshaya Nikitskaya Ul. 23. In peak times this cheap underground bear's lair, complete with long wooden tables, is popular for its simple, nourishing fare. Choose a few *zakuski* followed by mushrooms in *smetana* or grilled chicken.

Stanislavskovo 2, Ul. Stanislavskovo 2, ✆ 291 8689. Said for a while to be the best Russian restaurant in town, its unfriendly owners and a sharp rise in prices have dented its reputation. You won't be disappointed by the food if you can get a table, but the bill may take some of the shine off it.

Ristorante Artistico, Kanergersky Per., opposite the Moscow Arts Theatre, ✆ 252 4042 (*open 12 noon–12 midnight*). Serves Russified Italian food in the dignified surroundings of an old Style Moderne café.

Oladi, Ul. Pushkinskaya 13. This little stand up serves cheap *blini* (pancakes), flavour of the day, warm pizza, sandwiches and juice.

Stolishniki Café, Stoleshnikov Pereulok 4. Look out for the metallic awning covering the stairs down to this basement warren. At tables in alcoves you will be served soups and stews with, supply permitting, champagne or soft drinks.

Aragvi, Ul. Tverskaya 6, entrance on Sovietskaya Ploshchad, ✆ 229 3762. Moscow's longest-running Georgian restaurant. Its painted walls bring homely succour to large parties of (almost entirely male) Georgian 'business men'/mafiosi, who sensibly tuck into *lobio* (spicy bean stew) and chicken *satsivi* (with a walnut and coriander sauce).

MB, Ul. Nemirovich-Danchenko 3, ℡ 292 9731, a new addition to the stable of Indian restaurants in Moscow. Be cautious and stick to the tandoori dishes, *nan* bread and *raita*, washed down either with Heineken or a refreshing lime *nimbu pani*. Tummies have been known to be upset.

Tsentralny Restoran, Tverskaya Ul. 10, ℡ 229 0241. Located beneath the Tsentralny Hotel, which in its pre-war guise as the Hotel Luxe was the hotel for foreign Communists, the formula in this large dining hall is as old as its crumbling ceiling but has lasted better. The *blini* and caviar are standard, among the cheapest in town; the rest of the menu, though not as good, is equally authentic.

Pizza Hut, Tverskaya Ul. 12. The fare is familiar, though the salad bar is a bit limp. There is a restaurant and a take-away window for inveterate walkers.

McDonald's, Ul. Bolshaya Bronnaya 29, Pushkinskaya Ploshchad. Everyone knows what to expect, and the fabled queue at this, the first branch in Russia, has shrunk with inflation to a quite manageable size.

The interchange between Ⓜ *Vozdvizhenka and* Ⓜ *Aleksandrovsky Sad is a veritable warren: take care to take the exit* 'На Улицу Воздвиженка и Военторгу'. *Turn right outside, with the brooding neoclassical **Russian State Library** (formerly known as the Lenin Library) on your right.*

The library is a typical product of the 'peoples' palace' era of the 1930s; its shoddily-built cellars cracked up when the metro was constructed beneath, so that some of the book stores are flooded and too dangerous to enter. The library is the Russian equivalent of America's Library of Congress, and yet tragically thousands of its 36 million books, including some unique manuscripts, are said to have been ruined. The Russian combination of a highly literate population and an under-developed publishing industry means that demand for the library's services is enormous; all the reading space fills up early in the morning.

*Disappear into the underpass ahead and turn left below ground under Ul. Vozdvizhenka. Come out with a large stretch of tarmac separating you from the rounded brick and white bastion which hides the main entrance to the Kremlin. Turn left and walk along fume-ridden Ul. Mokhovaya, hemmed in on the far side by the arcaded walls of the **Manezh**.*

This massive stone and stucco hall was built in 1825 as a military riding school, or *manège*, part of a general redesign for the Alexander Gardens and this side of the

Kremlin. Since 1957 it has served as the Central Exhibition Hall. It was here, in December 1962, that an explosion took place which signalled the end of the Khrushchev thaw. Following the humiliation of the Cuban Missile Crisis in October, Khrushchev could no longer afford to ignore the dissatisfaction of Party and military hard-liners with his liberal leadership. Visiting an exhibition of abstract art, he fulminated that the artists must all be homosexuals, and that even a donkey could do better with its tail. The sculptor, Ernst Neizvestny, who publicly argued back, fell into disgrace, but when Khrushchev died in 1971 his will expressly commissioned Neizvestny to sculpt his headstone, now in the Novodevichy Cemetery (see p.244). Entrance to the exhibition hall (currently under restoration) is at the far end of the building, overlooking Manezhnaya Ploshchad.

On either side of the beginning of Ul. Gertsena you will notice the grand old buildings of **Moscow University**. Opened in 1755, it is the oldest in the country. The courtyard of the first building contains a statue of the university's founder, that renaissance man of science and letters, Mikhail Lomonosov, who was born the son of a poor fisherman and first came to Moscow barefoot in search of an education. The second building, beyond the street, is one of Matvei Kazakov's classical masterpieces, complete with portico and dome. It was completed in 1793, destroyed by the 1812 fire, and subsequently restored. Statues here commemorate two 19th-century graduates of the university who played a leading role in the creation of a revolutionary ideology, Herzen and Ogaryov. Most faculties are now housed in the Soviet Disneyland Moscow State University building far away on the Sparrow Hills.

> Before turning up Bolshaya Nikitskaya Ul., cast an eye over the monumental façade of the **Hotel Moskva** at the far end of Manezhnaya Ploshchad. While the central section is symmetrical, the wings are of two different designs. When the plans for the building were shown to Stalin in the early thirties, they covered a double-page spread, showing an either/or design, one on each page. Stalin failed to notice the differences and okayed both by signing across the divide, thus condemning the building to its schizophrenic existence. The gaping hole between you and the hotel is destined to be an underground shopping mall.

Ul. Bolshaya Nikitskaya was one of Moscow's main arteries in the early days, the road to the independent principality of Novgorod. From the Middle Ages it was settled by aristocratic boyars, grouped around the Nikitsky Monastery. After Peter the Great moved the capital to St Petersburg in 1712, most of their houses suffered a period of disintegration. Today it is relatively quiet, a narrow street lined with dusty 18th- and 19th-century mansions which commands ever better views back over the Kremlin as it climbs to the bulvar ring. Its Soviet-era name, Ul. Gertsena, commemorates Alexander Herzen (1812–70), whose statue we have just seen. After a spell in jail he was sent into exile in 1847 for his revolutionary socialism. His magazine, *Kolokol* (*The Bell*), was the most important mid-19th century mouthpiece of radical politics, edited in exile in London and smuggled into Russian.

Two of the most impressive mansions on this street were originally designed by the architect of the university building, Matvei Kazakov. The darling of both crown and aristocracy in Moscow at the end of the 18th century, Kazakov was a natural choice for new houses on one of the city's smartest thoroughfares. Here his clients were those scions of the Establishment, Prince Sergei Menshikov, grandson of Peter the Great's right-hand minister, and Princess Ekaterina Vorontsova-Dashkova, a close supporter of Catherine the Great.

Menshikov's blue and white residence, the front courtyard of which originally gave straight onto the street, is now squeezed behind a polyclinic off Ul. Ogaryova, diminishing the effect of its fine proportions. After the 1812 fire its porticoed front was restored in the fashionable Empire style, with plaster decoration and delicate wrought-iron work. The curved wing at the far end is all that remains of the symmetrical wings which embraced the courtyard. Someone with a cruel sense of humour alloted this divine building to the municipal housing department. Or perhaps they though it might inspire the bureaucratic planners to better things.

Princess Dashkova's mansion (No. 13) is even less recognizable. Since 1870 it has housed the Moscow **Tchaikovsky Conservatoire**, the country's largest music school, and all that really survives from the 18th century is the semi-circular rotunda in the central façade. The conservatoire was set up in 1866 by Nikolai Rubinstein, whose more famous composer brother Anton had done the same in St Petersburg four years earlier. Tchaikovsky taught here from its beginning, while later pupils included Rachmaninov, Skriabin, Oistrakh and Khachaturian. The courtyard sports a statue of Tchaikovsky, the railing behind embellished with musical notes. Today the massive building includes two concert halls, in the larger of which the annual International Tchaikovsky Piano Competition is held. If you enjoy classical music it is well worth deciphering the posters and checking with the box office inside, though most concerts are sold out well in advance.

It is hard to imagine when Princess Dashkova (1744–1810) had time to enjoy her Moscow home. Beguiled by the ambition and charm of the future Catherine the Great, she was a leading supporter of the 1762 coup against Peter III, despite the facts that she was only 19 and her sister was Peter's mistress. It is not surprising that the two women were attracted to one another; they both stand out as bright, determined and relatively independent in the man's world of 18th-century Russia. Princess Dashkova travelled abroad, making friends with Diderot and Voltaire among others. When she returned in 1783, Catherine made her head of the Russian Academy of Arts and Sciences, a post she held until her mentor's death in 1796.

However she was prissy about the fast turnover of men in Catherine's bed, and was thought by the empress to be in touch, through her brothers, with potentially subversive liberals. When the two of them did quarrel, it must have been useful to have a place in Moscow, a city which Catherine loathed almost pathologically.

Walking on up the street you pass the **Mayakovsky Theatre**. In the 1920s this was home to Meyerhold's Theatre of the Revolution, the theatrical equivalent of poetic Futurism and artistic Constructivism. Meyerhold's insistence on the primacy of the director's vision contrasted sharply with the realistic acting of the Moscow Arts Theatre and Stanislavsky. Under the cultural dictatorship of Socialist Realism in the 1930s, Meyerhold was accused among other things of staging the plays of the poet after whom the theatre is now named, and died in prison.

> The **photographs** in the windows of the press agency Inter-Tass, the last building on the right before the bulvar, are always worth a glance. They are likely to include a breath of fresh air from rural Russia, a new angle on an old Russian theme, evidence of yet another environmental disaster and a few pompous politicos.

> Take a break from the sightseeing and browse the **bookstalls** in front of the building, a good place for cheap coffee-table tomes in English. For an eclectic selection of **antiques**—icons, heads of Lenin, hats, posters and 19th-century Russian diplomats' uniforms—walk a little way down Kalashny Pereulok to **Aksia** on the left. The trail then continues along Ul. Stanislavskovo to the **Museum of Folk Art** at No. 7. (Open Tues and Thurs 2pm–8pm, rest of week 11am–5pm; closed Mon and last day of month.)

This 18th-century house was bought, and its exterior completely remodelled in the Neo-Russian style, by the merchant and art patron Savva Morozov in 1900, expressly as a Museum of Folk Art. The porch, steep roof and relief decoration all date from then. The one-room display includes both modern souvenirs for sale, wooden toys, painted trays, materials and scarves, and a changing exhibition of the crafts of Russia—clothing one month, toys the next.

Almost opposite, at Ul. Stanislavskovo 6 (entrance from courtyard), is the **Stanislavsky House Museum** (Dom-muzei K.S. Stanislavskovo, open Wed and Fri 2–9pm, Thurs, Sat and Sun 11am–6pm, closed Mon, Tues and last Thurs of month). It is housed in the Empire mansion in which the actor-turned-director lived from 1920 to his death in 1938. Stanislavsky was originally a textile merchant called Alekseyev; with his change of career came a new surname and a shot in the arm for the acting profession. His theory of 'method' acting, first employed by the actors of the Moscow Arts Theatre which he co-founded (see p.168), remains highly influential to this day. Stanislavsky converted the ballroom into a theatre with a temple-like stage. Here, beneath the meticulous painted ceiling, he rehearsed his Opera Dramatic Group. Their first production was Tchaikovsky's *Eugene Onegin*. Following the ballroom are a library with stained-glass fronted bookshelves, the director's study, bedrooms and the family dining room. Down in the much older cellar you will find highly theatrical folk costumes.

> *Walk on along Ul. Stanislavsky, enjoying the relative calm, and take the first right down Yeliseyevsky Pereulok which leads to the Church of the Resurrection (*Tserkov Voskreseniya*), the focus of a leafy square.*

Around this quiet square in the 1920s, blocks of relatively luxurious flats were built for the musicians, singers, dancers and actors of the numerous nearby theatres. This policy of housing by profession, initially no doubt a response to the housing crisis and the importance of performers in Soviet society, became the tool of a policy of divide and rule. Even if the doorman was not at his post when someone slipped in or out, it was unlikely that some other resident, all of whom knew each other, would not notice. Privileges also were easier to administer to favoured citizens if they lived together in one block. Even in these days of freedom, there is a preponderance of performers living here, and doubtless a number of old actresses who can remember the productions of Stanislavsky and even Meyerhold.

The terracotta and white **Church of the Resurrection** (*Tserkov Voskreseniya*) is said to mark the spot where the first Romanov tsar, Mikhail, welcomed his father Patriarch Filaret back from imprisonment in Poland in 1619. Though the first church burned down, the main body of the church of today, surmounted by a single cupola on a saint-emblazoned drum, dates from 1629, only 10 years later. Its authentic 17th-century features have been obscured beneath a neat 19th-century plaster job, which took place after the single-storey classical refectory and bell-tower were added. The interior of the church, which remained in service during the Soviet period, is embued with a devotional air and the walls are encrusted with icons. When the surrounding churches and monasteries were destroyed or turned into recording studios, some of the most precious icons were spirited to safety here. The image to the left as you enter the refectory, **Our Lady of the Passion**, came from the Strastnoy (Passion) Monastery on Pushkin Square. Its name derives from the symbols of the crucifixion, the spear and sponge, carried by the angels on either side of the Virgin.

The **chapels** in the refectory are dedicated to St Nicholas the Wonderworker (on the left) and the Prophet Elijah (on the right). The passageway between them is hung with a late-16th century copy of the **Virgin of Kazan**, an icon which was believed to have helped the Russians oust the Poles in 1613, encased in a silver frame. Opposite it is an icon of **St George** which is attributed to a foreign hand as it breaks with the Russian tradition of always depicting the patron saint of Moscow either fighting the dragon on horseback, or at least as a warrior-saint with a sword.

The crucifix in front of the iconostasis is said to have been carved in the 17th century by a blind man whose sight was restored when he had finally finished it. His act of devotion echoes across history in today's blind priest.

Walk on along Ul. Nezhdanovoy, beside the church, to emerge through a high archway onto **Tverskaya Ul.,** *Moscow's main drag. You need to cross the road and turn right downhill, so take the nearest underpass.*

Throughout the twenties and thirties all manner of ambitious plans were put forward to transform Moscow into a city worthy of the capital of the world's first proletarian utopia. Luckily, Le Corbusier's scheme to flatten the centre and start again was rejected. In 1935 however, a plan masterminded by Kaganovich and future General Secretary Nikita Khrushchev was adopted. Its main characteristic was to iron out the kinks which had been etched into the city by its 800-year history, by rationalizing the inner ring around the Kremlin and straightening the roads that radiated out from it. Tverskaya Ulitsa suffered worst of all.

Were it not for all the shop signs and advertisments, late 19th-century photographs show an almost medieval, curving street, with varying roof levels and façades jutting onto the pavement. Today it is a straight six-lane highway lined by massive eight-storey Stalinist apartment buildings. Their chief characteristics are tiny, beady windows and a minimum of vestigial, classically-derived decoration. The ground floors are occupied by shops. Advertising, in its plastic 20th-century variation, has returned with the advent of beauty retailers such as Nina Ricci, Estée Lauder and Yves Rocher, and even the former Soviet retailers have begun announcing themselves with brightly-coloured signs.

Our aim is the first turning off to the left, Kamergersky Pereulok, and the **Moscow Arts Theatre** *(Moskovsky khudozhestvenny akademichesky teatr or MKhAT), conceived by Stanislavsky and Nemirovich-Danchenko in 1897 (see p.166).*

Though already a theatre, it was redesigned by Fyodor Shektel, the genius of the Moscow Moderne movement (*see* p.151), who paid particular attention to the interior. The exterior he merely tinkered with, adding six pendulous, square lanterns complimented by three entrances, the main one topped by a plaster bas-relief of an androgynous human figure emerging from a wave. The box office within is *open 12 noon–7pm (closed 3–4pm)*, and though the direction here is no longer Moscow's most interesting, theatre buffs may want to admire the simple interior and sit in a theatrical legend.

This building symbolizes the synthesis and novelty which made the turn-of-the-century Russian arts scene at so important worldwide. For it was here that the plays of Anton Chekhov found their voice under the direction of Stanislavsky, who refused

to build his productions around one star role, insisting on the importance of the background and psychology of every character. It was as if the playwright, with his subtle characterization, and director where made for one another. Chekhov's *The Seagull*, a failure in St Petersburg where it premiered, was the Arts Theatre's first production, and an enormous success. After that, Shektel's graceful seagull which you see on the façade became the theatre's logo. Chekhov went on to write his three further masterpieces, *Uncle Vanya*, *The Three Sisters* and *The Cherry Orchard*, for the Arts Theatre before his death in 1904.

Amid the airline offices which seem to have colonized this street, keep your eyes skinned for interesting looking shops or cafés, particularly opposite the theatre. The very dusty-looking secondhand bookshop sells antiques as well. Turn left on Pushkinskaya Ul. and left again onto steep Stoleshnikov Pereulok.

Before reaching the square at the top of the hill you pass the simple, white octagonal drum and single cupola of the **Church of Ss Cosmas and Damian** (*Tserkov Kos'my i Damiana*). The interior has long been a factory, though services are now occasionally held in some part of the building. More interesting is the story of its Arabian patron saints. They were doctors, persecuted and eventually beheaded for their Christian beliefs by Diocletian in 287, but not before drowning, burning and stoning had all failed. A wooden church to them stood here long before it was rebuilt in stone in 1626. The octagonal drum dates from the early 18th century.

Tverskaya Ploshchad has been ruined. Adorned with a summer café and benches, it might perhaps have provided some relief from the traffic on Tverskaya Ul., but 20th-century architectural additions have so overshadowed it that people scurry as fast as possible across its stone and tarmac. Even the **horseback statue** of the founder of Moscow, Yuri Dolgoruky, seems insignificant. Placed here in 1954 to commemorate the city's 800th anniversary, Dolgoruky's outstretched arm is a pun on his surname, which means 'long-armed'.

Behind Dolgoruky, the glass monolith of the **Lenin Institute of Marxist-Leninism** (1927) stares out blindly; its impenetrable façade seems embattled now that its creed has incurred such ignominy. The state philosophy was originally so entrenched, the basis of every branch of learning, that a popular joke told of a medical student asked in an exam to write all he could about the medical history of two given corpses. Knowing little about medicine but well-drilled in political correctness, he simply answered that they must be Marx and Lenin. In front, what was once a pretty three-storey, 18th-century palace built by Matvei Kazakov and used by the governors of Moscow, is now an arrogant five-storey monument to Soviet power, housing the **Moscow city council**. Not only were the lower portico, fanfare entrance and two bottom storeys added, but the entire building was moved back to fit in with the new alignment of the street.

> *Turn right up Tverskaya Ul., window shopping and popping into book and jewellery shops at will. Don't however miss Moscow's smartest state food store, **Yeliseyev's**, at No. 14 on the right-hand side.*

In the late 19th century the merchant Yeliseyev, purveyor of fine foods to the aristocracy of St Petersburg from his shop on Nevsky Prospect, decided to open a branch in provincial Moscow. He chose one of the finest classical mansions in the city, built by Kazakov in 1790 and graced by Pushkin in the 1820s, and transformed its ground floor into a soaring consumer paradise with chandeliers, floribund pillars, glass display cases, mirrors and gilt. After the Revolution it stayed as it was, becoming an early, unintentional 'people's palace'. Instead of selling finest imported foodstuffs it catered for everyman, with its staples of Soviet sausage, root vegetables, frozen fish and in times of plenty caviar and champagne. Mirroring Moscow as a whole, today you will find a mixture of imported and home-produced goods for sale.

> *Where Tverskaya Ul. meets the bulvar ring, turn left onto Tverskoy Bulvar.*

No amount of 20th-century city planning could ruin the pleasure of this ribbon of trees, the **bulvar** which encircles the city centre (*see* p.176), though the traffic these days does its best. Shut out the diesel and noise and watch Muscovites enjoying this unique urban green belt as they always have—conducting romantic trysts and drunken arguments, walking dogs and children. Much of the 18th- and 19th-century stucco may be crumbling, balconies leaning at improbable angles, but these buildings are being bought up and restored by the dozen.

Behind light iron railings supported by sturdy round stone pillars on the right-hand side of the bulvar stands the much altered yellow and white classical building of the **Literary Institute** (No. 25), set up by Maxim Gorky in 1933. Its establishment stance, teaching a succession of would-be writers how to please Stalin with Socialist Realism, led Bulgakov to use the house as the location of MASSOLIT, the corrupt, self-serving writers' union in his novel *The Master and Margarita*. It is also known as 'Herzen House' as it was here that Herzen was born in 1812, while his family stayed with his father's brother. A statue of the revolutionary thinker stands in the courtyard garden. Next to the institute is the **Pushkin Theatre**, nothing to buy tickets for, though in the first half of the century, under the direction of Tairov, it was the place to see new foreign plays by challenging European playwrights such as Brecht and O'Neill.

The reddish-brown modern building almost opposite is the breakaway **Moscow Arts Theatre** named after Gorky (*imeni Gorkovo*), to distinguish it from the parent theatre named after Chekhov (*imeni Chekhova*). The split arose out of theatrical politics, with the better-known actors remaining with the director Oleg Yefremov and the bit-part actors going in search of better work here with director Tatiana Doronina. Productions at both theatres, needless to say, are variable.

Muscovites have long taken their theatre, and its stars, very seriously, and at Tverskoy Bulvar 11 you can step into a shrine to one of the leading actresses of her time in the **House Museum of Maria Yermolova** (1853–1928) *Open 1pm–8pm, 12 noon–7pm on Sat and Sun; closed Tues and last Mon of month.* Yermolova was the first person to be awarded the Soviet distinction of being a 'People's Artist'. She lived here for the last half of her life and, as a great actress might wish for, seems to live on in its heavy, sentimental atmosphere.

If you were writing a novel about Moscow or its theatrical life at that time, this would be an obligatory stop. As well as a number of camp *tableaux* reconstructions, such as the actress's dressing room, there are copious photographs of the star in her many roles. The main rooms, particularly the winter garden and the drawing room, are most interesting today, as they evoke the rather formal dignity of the unimaginable, a private bulvar house in bygone Moscow.

> At Ploshchad Nikitskikh Vorot, named after the Nikitsky Gates which gave entrance to white-walled Moscow at this point, you will recognize the Inter-Tass building from earlier in the walk. Opposite it is the **Church of the Ascension** (Tserkov Voznesenii) in which Pushkin was married. Continue straight onto Nikitsky Bulvar.

About half way down on the left, the **Museum of Oriental Art** occupies the austere yellow and white Empire mansion at 12a Nikitsky Bulvar. *Open daily 11am–8pm, closed Mon and last Fri of month.* The building is best seen from the bulvar garden, where its simple, porticoed confidence and the amputation of one of its wings becomes apparent. It was built between 1818–22 by D. I. Giliardi, initially for General Lunin, though even before it was completed, in 1821, he sold the central part to the Commercial Bank. Inside, don't fail to take in the painted ceilings of the main exhibition halls.

As with so many Russian museums, the collections from Communist and formerly Communist countries are particularly strong. The rarest collection is the bequest of Indonesian Buddhist 'icons' given to Khrushchev by President Sukarno. The unseen depths of the museum's collection, including countless shamanistic artefacts from the length and breadth of Siberia, are put to good effect in an ever-changing programme of exhibitions. On permanent display is an extensive collection of compellingly grotesque and humorous Japanese miniature sculptures known as *netsuke*, worn hanging from the girdle of a kimono, which exert the same repellent fascination as trolls. A small part of the museum is occupied by a semi-permanent exhibition about the life and work of Nikolai Roerich

(1874–1946). A painter and designer who began his career in St Petersburg, Roerich's amateur archaeology led him gradually further east, both physically and metaphysically. The spiritually-charged landscapes shown here were painted in exile in the Himalayas.

> *Just beyond the museum is a small shop selling modern oriental handicrafts—ceramics, carved wood and silk cushions. This establishment trail peters out where Nikitsky Bulvar meets Novy Arbat in a cloud of diesel fumes. Beyond lie the dangerously bohemian dominions of the Moscow underworld—Arbat.* Ⓜ *Arbatskaya awaits to whisk the weary home, while those with the inclination can slough off the stuffiness of the walk in the bars and restaurants of Arbat* (see *p.157*).

GOGOL BULVAR

VI: The Bulvar Ring

Start: *The statue of Pushkin on Pushkinskaya Ploshchad.* Ⓜ *Pushkinskaya/Tverskaya/ Chekhovskaya.*

Walking Time: *4 hours, excluding time spent in the Sandunovskaya Banya.*

VI: The Bulvar Ring

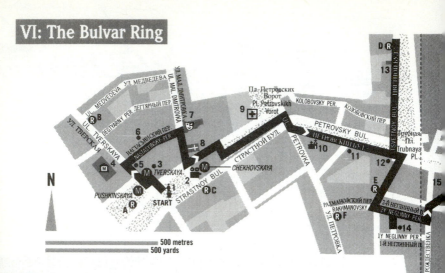

Sites

1. **Pushkin Monument**
   Pamyatnik A. S. Pushkina
   Памятник А. С. Пушкина

2. **Rossiya Cinema**
   Kino 'Rossiya'
   Кино 'Россия'

3. **Izvestia Building**
   Zdaniye 'Izvestia'
   Здание 'Известия'

4. **Museum of Revolution**
   Muzei Revolyutsii
   Музей Революции

5. **Sytin Building**
   Zdaniye Sytina
   Здание Сытина

6. **Credit Bank**
   Ssudnaya kazna
   Ссудная казна

7. **Lenkom Theatre**
   Teatr Lenkom
   Театр Ленком

8. **Church of the Nativity of the Virgin in Putinki**
   Tserkov rozhdestva Bogoroditsy v Putinkakh
   Церковь рождества Богородицы в Путинках

9. **Catherine Hospital**
   Yekaterininskaya bolnitsa
   Екатерининская больница

10. **Monastery of St Peter on the Hill**
    Vysoko-Petrovsky monastir
    Высоко-Петровский монастырь

11. **'The Iron'**
    'Utyug'
    'Утюг'

12. **Former Hermitage Restaurant**
    Bwivshy restoran 'Ermitazh'
    Бывший ресторан 'Эрмитаж'

13. **Old Moscow Circus**
    Stary Tsirk
    Старый Цирк

14. **Sandunovsky Baths**
    Sandunovskaya banya
    Сандуновская баня

15. **Convent of the Nativity of the Virgin**
    Rozhdestvensky monastir
    Рождественский монастырь

16. **Ministry of Fisheries**
    Ministyerstvo rybolovstva
    Министерство рыболовства

17. **Cathedral of the Vladimir Virgin**
    Vladimirsky sobor
    Владимирский собор

18. **Printers' Church of the Assumption**
    Tserkov Uspeniya v pechatnikakh
    Церковь Успения в печатниках

19. **Statue of Krupskaya**
    Pamyatnik N. Krupskoy
    Памятник Н. Крупской

20. **Dom 'Rossiya'**
    Дом 'Россия'

21. **Academy of Painting and Sculpture**
    Uchilishche zhivopisi, vayaniya i zodchestva
    Училище живописи, ваяния и зодчества

22. **Perlov's Tea Shop**
    Magazin 'Chai' A. Ya. Perlova
    Магазин 'Чай' А. Я. Перлова

23. **Bove Mansion**
    Gorodskaya usadba Bova
    Городская усадба Бова

24. **State Statistical Service**
    Gos. statisticheskaya sluzhba
    Гос. статистическая служба

25. **Statue of Griboyedov**
    Pamyatnik A. S. Griboyedova
    Памятник А. С. Грибоедова

26. **Central Post Office**
    Glavpochtamt
    Главпочтамт

27. **Church of the Archangel Gabriel**
    Tserkov arkhangela Gavrila
    Церковь архангела Гавриила

28. **Church of St Fyodor Stratilit**
    Tserkov Fyodora Stratilita
    Церковь Фёдора Стратилита

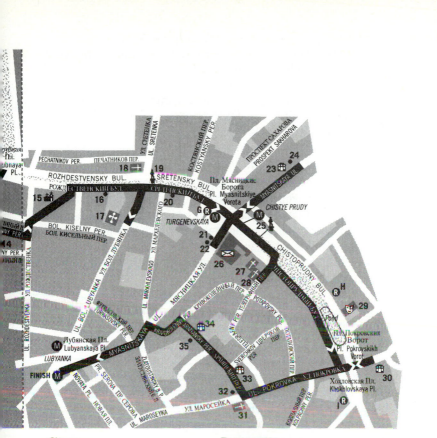

Sites

29 Sovremmyenik Theatre
Teatr Sovremmyenik
Театр Современник

30 Apraksin Mansion
Gorodskaya usadba M. F. Apraksina
Городская усадба М. Ф. Апраксина

31 Church of Ss Cosmas and Damian
Tserkov Kosmy i Damiana
Церковь Косьмы и Дамиана

32 Belarussian Embassy
Belorusskoye posolstvo
Белорусское посольство

33 Gagarin Mansion
Gorodskaya usadba I. S. Gagarina
Городская усадба И. С. Гагарина

34 Miloslavsky/Matveyev Mansion
Palaty Miloslavskikh
Палаты Милославских

35 Armenian Embassy
Armyanskoe posolstvo
Армянское посольство

Restaurants

A   McDonald's

B   Baku-Livan
Баку-Ливан

C   Blinchiki
Блинчики

D   Central Market
Tsentralny rynok
Центральный рынок

E   Café Samarkand
Кафе Самарканд

F   Kofeinya
Кофейня

G   Na Sretenke
Ресторан на Сретенке

H   Sovremmyenik Café
Кафе Современник

I   Don Quixote

Given the choice, wait for a gentle breezy day, ideally a leafy summer's weekend, to make your acquaintance with this Muscovite experience, the bulvar garden. A semi-circular slice of green, it is as quintessentially Moscow as the Grand Canal is Venice, or Central Park New York. From joggers to drinkers, there's not an inhabitant of the city who can't remember some odyssey of self-discovery or self-obliteration which took place along its sinuous lengths. And yet at 6½ miles long and on average some 20 yards wide, it must be the strangest shaped park in the world.

The history of this slice of land explains everything. In the 14th century an earth rampart was thrown up along it to defend the city, reinforced in the late 16th century by white stone walls. A handful of gates, topped by chapels and towers and each bearing a sacred icon gave entrance to the area within—'Bely Gorod', the White Town. When these were razed, bit by bit, in the late 18th century, gardens sprung up in their stead.

Deviating regularly from the bulvar, this walk visits a number of historical buildings, from defensive medieval monasteries to later aristocratic palaces. In the middle, you are encouraged to rest a while in Russia's answer to the doctor, beauty therapist and shrink rolled in to one, the *banya* (*see* p.183). Pack a towel, soap and shampoo, and plastic slippers or flip-flops if you have some. Otherwise you can rent them with the sheet you will need to wrap round you. If you hate communal nudity, go on a Tuesday when the *banya* staff take a rest and the *banya* are closed. The Museum of the Revolution is closed on Mondays and the last day of the month.

---

lunch/cafés

McDonald's, Pushkinskaya Ploshchad, needs little introduction. Just as clean, safe and anodyne as anywhere else in the world.

Baku-Livan, Tverskaya Ul. 24, ✆ 299 8506. The take-away section of this Lebanese-Azerbaijani restaurant offers falafel and delicious houmus with pine nuts, as well as chips.

Blinchiki, Pushkinskaya Ploshchad. Near the entrance to Chekhovskaya metro station; look out for the sign saying 'Блинчики', and order a couple of pancakes with savoury or sweet filling and a glass of fruit juice.

Kofeinaya, Ul. Petrovka 28. A little way below the monastery, a good place for a quick coffee. Look out for the sign 'Кофейная'.

Central Market, Tsvetnoy Bulvar. Closed for renovation, but when it reopens the place to buy picnics of caviar, sour cream, smoked eel and fruit.

Café Samarkand, Ul. Neglinnaya 29. In the summer, a few tables decorate the terrace beside this Uzbek restaurant, where you can eat *shashlik* or meatballs. The interior feels like a nest of mafiosi.

Na Sretenke, Turgenyevskaya Ploshchad 2/4, entrance on Frolov Pereulok. This clean Caucasian joint serves good red bean *lobio, kyufta* (a herby broth with meatballs) and *dolma* (stuffed vine leaves) in a creamy garlic sauce. The nearby escort agency and preponderance of all-male groups of diners make it unadvisable for a woman on her own.

Sovremmenik Café, Chistoprudny Bulvar 15, *Open 11am–10pm (closed 4pm–5pm)*. This dark hovel seems to attract its own, very particular brand of anarchic teenagers and twenty-somethings. Good coffee.

Don Quixote, Pokrovsky Bulvar 4/17, ✆ 297 4757. The only place you might want to book, this is slightly off the route of the walk, towards the end. The standards of Spanish cuisine, *gazpacho* and *tortilla,* can be washed down with tangy *sangria*, or you can try something more adventurous. They also offer a set lunch menu.

If you arrive at 🚇 *Chekhovskaya, follow the signs below ground to either* 🚇 *Pushkinskaya or Tverskaya. Take the escalator from there and turn immediately left outside the swing doors. Ahead rises the* ***Pushkin Monument,*** *where you will normally find a handful of people awaiting a rendezvous. In summer the whole square mills with Moscow's youth, hanging out, and throughout the year the statue is used as a designated meeting point.*

It is no surprise that it should be Pushkin (1799–1837) who graces this important square at the junction of Tverskaya Ul. and the bulvar ring. While foreigners tend to lionize Tolstoy or Dostoyevsky as the presiding genius of Russian literature, Russians confer that honour on Pushkin. He holds this unique position not just by virtue of his writing, but because he created the very language of Russian literature, synthesizing the lofty tones of earlier written Russian with the more informal everyday language of the people. In the words of Gogol, Pushkin's work 'was a fire tossed out of the sky, from which lesser poets of his day, like candles, came alight.' His influence lasts to this day, and his poetry is quoted daily by millions of Russians.

Take the word of an old Pushkin family servant that this statue is a good likeness. At the unveiling ceremony in 1880 he admitted as much to Dostoyevsky adding, 'except that Alexander Sergeevich was not nearly as tall as that.' The jamboree

surrounding the unveiling of the monument turned into an event in itself. Literary luminaries from all over the country assembled in Moscow, divided as they were by that time into two irreconcilable camps. When the Slavophiles who gravitated around Dostoyevsky collided with the Westernizers led by Turgenev, snarls unfurled from curled lips. Tolstoy, by this time increasingly anti-social, refused point blank to join the circus, leaving Turgenev and Dostoevsky to battle for the position of top literary dog. Turgenev, who lived in Paris, was at first heaped with praises, including an honorary doctorate from the university for his 'talented mastery of Pushkin's language'. But it was for Dostoyevsky's speech—'an event in our literature' according to the Slavophile journalist Ivan Aksakov—that the proceedings were eventually remembered.

Until the 1930s, the towering belfry of the Strastnoy Convent, the Convent of the Passion, rose on the site of the Rossiya Cinema, the huge glass edifice behind the statue of Pushkin. And after the Revolution the square became the Soviet Fleet Street, housing a number of important newspapers including the national *Izvestiya,* whose offices are still in the buildings on Pushkin's right. The troubles *Izvestiya* faced in 1993 after they had unilaterally declared themselves independent of the state show the fragility of freedom of expression in Russia. Pressure was exerted on their printers to stymy production, while parliament schemed to get their hands back on this traditional organ of conservatism. The placing of Russia's first McDonald's here in the 1980s was a media sensation of a rather different nature. To some it symbolized Russia's return to the world community, to others its position within sight of Pushkin summed up the terrifying threat to Russian culture.

Return to the underpass, turning left by the swing doors to the metro and right at the far end of the passage beneath Tverskaya Ul. A hundred metres up on the left is the red and white palace, Tverskaya Ul. 21, which now houses the **Museum of the Revolution** *(open 10am–6pm, 11am–7pm Wed and Fri; closed Mon and last day of month).*

As if there wasn't enough of a contradiction between this 18th-century mansion, with its portico and lion-bedecked gateposts, and its role as a museum of the Revolution, the exhibition within suffers from its own disconcerting but endearing schizophrenia. For as well as a standard Soviet chronicle of the glorious events of the 1905 and 1917 Revolutions, with passport-sized photographs of hundreds of long-forgotten participants, you will now find an exposé of Stalin's genocide and pictures of the Muscovites' heroic stance against the coup in August 1991. The tram in the front courtyard was one of those used to block the path of the plotters' tanks outside the White House.

Unfortunately, none of the labelling is in English so you have to work hard to orient yourself. The first rooms are self-evidently the official story. Things begin to get more interesting in Room 9, with Sovietabilia such as a communist v. capitalist chess set and *palekh* boxes lauding the agro-industrial achievements of the Five Year Plans. In Room 11 the *gulags* are exposed. If it all gets too much, you can always raise your eyes to the paintings that adorn the vaulted ceilings, as they did when the palace housed the English Club. The club started as a haven for foreigners living in the city, but by the time it moved here in the 1830s its membership was drawn largely from the upper echelons of Russian society. Like the London clubs on which it was modelled, it functioned as an informal talking shop for statesmen, generals, men of science and of letters. Tolstoy and Pushkin were both members, and both made use of the building in their works of fiction. Here men of the world would get down to the serious things in life, like eating, talking and gambling, without the distraction of the giddy fairer sex, except in the compliant form of gypsy singers and dancing girls.

As you leave the museum, notice the yellow brick building opposite, Tverskaya Ul. 18, now a showroom for American gas-guzzlers.

In 1866 a poor young 15-year-old boy, Ivan Sytin, went to work in a bookshop. At the turn of the century, he commissioned this Style Moderne building to house his printing empire, the largest publishing business in Russia. Its coloured tiles, rounded windows and balconies were finished in 1904. The building continued to house publishers after the Revolution, and became the first premises of the Communist Party paper *Pravda*.

Unless there is a lull in the traffic, to cross the road you will have to return to the underpass, and turn left before the swing doors into the metro.

Walk back up to the Sytin printing house and turn immediately right down Nastasinsky Pereulok.

You can't miss the **Credit Bank**, a little way down on the left. It was built in 1914–16, a high temple to the extravagance of pre-Revolutionary capitalism. It is an extraordinary aquamarine and stone confection of medieval Russian, Renaissance Venetian, European Gothic and Moorish architecture. The steep-pitched roof and wings recalls a Russian palace, while the central section, with its Gothic windows above a 16th-century Russian porch, pulls your imagination in all directions.

The end of the lane faces the green and white façade of the **Lenkom Theatre**, an angular *moderne* interpretation of classicism. Originally built in 1907 as an exclusive club for Moscow's rich, the Merchants' Club, it became a theatre in the 1920s. Since Brezhnev's time, it has been under the direction of Mark Zakharov, whose daring, topical productions have made it one of Moscow's most popular theatres. However, chronic financial troubles and the recent withdrawal of state funding have taken the building full circle, and by night the theatre hosts an expensive, Irish-run night club, 2 x 2.

*Turn right onto Ul. Chekhova to find one of Moscow's most extravagant local churches, the **Church of the Nativity of the Virgin in Putinki** (Tserkov Rozhdestva Bogoroditsy v Putinkakh)*

Originally sited just outside a gate in the white walls of medieval Moscow, legend tells how a first wooden church was commissioned by a noblewoman who gave birth in her carriage on the spot. It burned down in the mid-17th century, but the congregation successfully petitioned Tsar Alexei Mikhailovich to help them rebuild it. Behind it was a rest house in which travellers, *putiny*, could tidy themselves up before making their entrance into the capital.

Everything about the church seems exaggerated. In characteristic 17th-century style it is fantastically asymmetrical, with two main chapels forming an L-shape, and a possibly later refectory filling in the corner to make an oblong building. Deeply indented *kokoshniki* gables top the walls, which are pierced by windows framed variously and elaborately by brick columns and pediments. A series of no less than six tent roofs, five of them culminating in blue cupolas and golden crosses, add the final touch. Sadly the church is rarely open, though there are apparently still some 17th-century frescoes on the walls.

Turn first left at the end of the street. After 100m you can cross the road to walk along the garden of Strastnoy Bulvar.

Today the bulvar is dominated by 20th-century buildings, but in its 19th-century heyday it was lined with palaces. Their aristocratic inhabitants, having slipped through the net of state service in St Petersburg, lived a life of famous gluttony and sloth, spying on one another through the trees and sending servants across to penetrate the pretty stucco façades. Ironically it was Catherine the Great, who hated both Moscow and its lazy, backward inhabitants, who set the creation of the bulvar in motion by ordering the destruction of the great white city walls which had followed this line since the late 16th century. Doubtless she felt that if she made enough of a mark on the city, she might come to like it a little more.

Today the garden is so well used that the grass barely gets a chance to grow, what with childrens' playgrounds, cafés, bars, benches, lovers, dogs and drunks. The last great yellow and white stucco **palace** on the left as you walk down Strastnoy Bulvar is now a hospital. Built by the great Moscow classical architect Matvei Kazakov for the Princes Gagarin, it housed the English Club in the early 19th century, before it moved to the palace on Tverskaya Ul. Cast a glance down Ul. Petrovka on the right at the end of the garden. The proud octagonal belfry topped by narrow drum and dome signals the **Monastery of St Peter on the Hill** (Vuisoko-Petrovsky Monastir).

> *To get into the monastery grounds, walk across the rough ground after the first buildings on the right on Petrovsky Bulvar.*

Although this agglomeration of buildings has been a religious enclave for over 500 years, the spirit has been all but ground out of it by recent years of secular use as a museum of literature. However it now houses the Moscow Patriarchate's Department for Religious Education and Catechism and, money forthcoming, has some chance of regaining its sacred aura. Established in the 14th century as one of the city's protective fortified monasteries, it was enclosed within the white walls in the 16th century and blossomed in the late 17th when its patrons, the Naryshkins, married into the royal family. It was to this haven that Peter the Great escaped from the *streltsy* uprising with his mother, Natalya Naryshkina, in 1682, and it is to this period that the present-day monastery owes the majority of its buildings.

The one great exception is the small, red-brick, octofoil cathedral which stands alone in the centre of the grounds, surmounted by a large octagonal drum and a tartar-helmet of a dome bristling with tiles. A rare surviving example of such pillar-type constructions, it was built in 1514–17 to replace an earlier **Cathedral of Metropolitan Peter**. While building work went on all round it in the late 17th century, the cathedral was renovated, its outer walls painted with lavish Baroque ornament, and it was reconsecrated. For a long time it was though to date from that period too, but recently it has been attributed to the 16th-century architect involved in the Kremlin, Alevisio Fryazin. The cathedral has recently been renovated to its original aspect.

The first church on the left as you enter the enclave, the **Church of the Icon of the Virgin of Bogolyubovo**, has been so mucked about that it is barely recognizable as a church at all. It was built in 1684–5 over the graves of Peter the Great's Naryshkin uncles, Ivan and Afanasy, who died at the hands of the *streltsy* in 1682. Much more impressive is the **Refectory Church of Sergei Radonezhsky**, standing high on its arcaded foundations beyond the Cathedral of Metropolitan Peter. It was commissioned by Peter the Great himself and built in 1690–94. Its clean Baroque exterior has been well restored, with white scallop shells decorating the top band of the central cube, leading to a roof with five tall drums topped by cupolas. Services take place here from 8am on Sunday mornings, and at 6pm on Mondays and Saturdays. Only beyond the arcade, in the second, southern courtyard, do you get any feel of what the monastery must have been like. Completely walled in, with a small church over its southern gate and the monks' quarters hidden behind their Baroque windows over the arcade on your right, it is a peaceful, contemplative spot.

> *Return to Petrovsky Bulvar and the garden walk. Notice as you go by the strange multi-coloured brick building at Krapivensky Pereulok 4.*

Known as the iron (*utyug*) because of its wedge shape, it narrows to a single window's width on its bulvar façade. It is an apartment block, built in 1892 as a commercial venture round the perimeter of the grounds owned by the Church of St Sergei. Beyond it, at Petrovsky Bulvar 12, Moscow's biggest artistic community has been squatting round the courtyard for many a year, always under imminent threat from commercial developers. The squat shelters some of Moscow's most extravagant eccentrics, and they sure know how to throw a party. The recent 80th birthday of one of the inhabitants, who paraded down a Tatlin-esque tower in a ball-gown to shame the Paris collections, came to a climax with the lighting of a 30ft, petrol-soaked 'candle' and the arrival of the fire-brigade.

Squatting has long been a major feature of non-conformist life in both Moscow and St Petersburg. During the days of the *propiska*, when you could only live where this stamp in your passport said you could, people with the freedom of spirit to rebel took over ruined buildings, hooked into the national grid and the nearest telephone wire, did their own plumbing and lived for free, souls lost by the massive bureaucracy. If any local official should prove too nosey, the odd bottle of vodka normally did the trick. These squats acted like magnets on other elements of Soviet society's dispossessed, attracting orphans escaped from childrens' homes, patients released from mental hospitals. To experience the sense of community which held these Babels together was to understand not only why the theory of Communism appealed so strongly to the Russian people, but also how they managed to survive it in practice.

> *Continuing down Petrovsky Bulvar you are disgorged into Trubnaya Ploshchad, once a hub of exoticism, now merely a knot of traffic. As if life*

wasn't bad enough, a 1993 decree by the city council to make various roads round the Kremlin one-way seems to have paralysed the traffic throughout central Moscow.

But enough of that. Trubnaya Ploshchad is named after the *truba* (pipe) through which the river Neglinnaya flowed under the white walls of the city at this point. You can feel yourself in its valley, though the entire flow is now channelled underground. Before the Revolution, Tsvetnoy (Flower) Bulvar to your left was the site of the old flower market which, like London's Covent Garden, was a hot-bed of prostitution. On your right, the theatre building on the corner of Petrovsky Bulvar and Ul. Neglinnaya housed the Hermitage Restaurant. Moscow's finest, it was starred and listed first in Baedeker's 1914 guide book. Run by the French chef Olivier, it was host to all manner of gastronomic excesses, including Tchaikovsky's ill-fated wedding party. Within 11 weeks the composer and his bride had separated.

Even if the weather is not good enough for a picnic, pop up Tsvetnoy Bulvar to see if the **Central Market** (Tsentralny Rynok) has reopened. Prices here were always the highest in the city; although it purported to be a place for local farmers to sell their excess produce, it was actually one of the most visible 'mafia' enclaves in the city, controlled by traders from the the southern ex-Soviet republics who bribed officials in the city council. The odd anti-corruption drive or bout of institutional racism pared down their numbers, but never for long. Whatever you are tempted by, the only advice is to ignore the endemic sexism if you are a woman, and bargain like hell—offer half the initial asking price. If the weather is good, buy fresh or tinned caviar and eat it with the unleavened Georgian bread, *lavash*, which is usually on sale towards the front. Or tuck into tomatoes, smoked fish, pickles and fruit. The highlight of the market is its 'milky ladies'. Walk right through the main market and go into the building behind it on the right. Behind the tiled counter of the dairy section white-coated women, their faces and arms like buttery incarnations, sell home-produced butter, sour cream (*smetana*), curd cheese (*tvoróg*), hard cheese and fresh cream (*slivki*). They go into a frenzy at the sight of foreigners, proffering a taste of everything, as do the neighbouring honey sellers, who stock several distinct types including lime, mustard and meadow honeys.

Right next to the market, on the way back to the bulvar, is the Moscow Circus building. If you fancy a visit to this very traditional entertainment, you could see if there is a tout about as you pass (otherwise see p.522). Another sensual treat, the Russian banya, *awaits hedonists on the other side of the bulvar ring. Cross Trubnaya Ploshchad and head straight down Ul. Neglinnaya, taking the second lane on the left, 2nd (Vtoroy) Neglinny Pereulok. The entrance to Moscow's most atmospheric Russian sauna, the* **Sandunovskaya Banya***, is down the first cul-de-sac on the* *right (open 8am–10pm; closed Tuesdays). Buy your birch switch from the vendor outside, and turn to p.546 if you don't know what to do with it.*

As you would expect, men get the pick of this early 19th-century complex, including the cold plunge pool. Women should not despair however, as their part has a certain genteel post-war charm to it. Little seems to have changed here for decades, but if current rumours about an Italian joint-venture face-lift are correct, everything may be different by the time you get there. With any luck they will at least have had the taste to keep the stunning Empire-style marble benches in the washroom. They may well be originals, first installed when the baths were created by the famous actor Sandunov in 1808. If this is not the first walk you have done, a pedicure may be in order before you continue pavement bashing, and you should certainly rehydrate with several cups of blackcurrant tea.

On leaving the banya *continue up 2nd Neglinny Pereulok, turn left on Ul. Rozhdestvenka and cast a glance up Bolshoy Kiselny Pereulok as you pass. The large modern building on the right is the former Party hospital, just one of the ways in which some people were more equal than others in the Soviet Union. The tiered belltower ahead advertises the otherwise secretive existence of the* **Convent of the Nativity of the Virgin** *(*Rozhdestvensky Monastir*). An arch before it on the right lets you into the complex of buildings.*

This convent was founded a little after the Monastery of St Peter on the Hill, in the 1380s, by the daughter-in-law of Ivan 'Moneybags' I. From medieval times right into the 20th century, unmarried female members of the royal family and widows were expected to tidy themselves away into religious communities. Most convents were founded under these circumstances. The two free-standing churches at the centre of the convent are, in the order in which you come to them, the **Church of St John Chrysostom**, built in the 1670s and the working **Cathedral of the Nativity** which dates back to 1501–05. If the cathedral is open, walk in to visit a miraculous icon rediscovered in the 1980s. The priest at the monastery appealed for help in the reconstruction of the cathedral, and a building firm promised to give him some wood. One old door aroused his suspicions and on cleaning it off he found the icon of the Virgin, which now hangs on the far left of what counts for an iconostasis. For the first few months the Virgin is said to have wept tears of sap. Before leaving the building, glance up in to its single dome to see the swirling, celestial brick pattern with which it is decorated.

Beyond the cathedral is an early 20th-century, dark brick **refectory church** which is now used by members of the Moscow Institute of Architecture. They were given the building in the seventies in return for helping restore the convent, but lack of money hampered serious work and in the 1990s a feud has developed between the church, who want to take over the entire complex, and the architects. The other buildings in the complex have been squatted by artists, homeless students and poets.

> *At the far end of the architects' building, steep steps lead down onto Rozhdestvensky Bulvar, which climbs out of the Neglinnaya valley. In general the houses lining the bulvar from now on tend to be later and less attractive than before, with exceptions such as the pretty 18th-century palaces at 16, 14 and 12 Rozhdestvensky Bulvar. Today these house the Russian Ministry of Fisheries.*

Until this century the junction of the bulvar and Ul. Sretenka/Bolshaya Lubyanka was marked by the Sretensky Gate, a monumental three-storey structure with church and tapering spire which had originally been part of the white walls of the city. Today the **Printers' Church of the Assumption** (*Tserkov Uspeniya v Pechatnikakh*) on the corner with Ul. Sretenka recalls the 17th and 18th centuries when Moscow's master-printers lived and worked just outside the gate. Much more interesting, thanks to its frescoed interior, is the **Cathedral of the Vladimir Virgin**, all that remains of the Sretensky Monastery (*open 9.30am–6.30pm*).

> *To find it turn right down Ul. Bolshaya Lubyanka. It is set back from the road, some 100 yards down on the right.*

This important monastery was originally founded on the spot where the people of Moscow formally welcomed the miracle-working icon, the Virgin of Vladimir, when it was brought here from Vladimir in 1395. The most highly venerated of all the icons in Russia, it has been kept in Moscow ever since (*see* p.201). It is believed to have saved the city on numerous occasions, in particular from Tamberlane's attack that year. In the 16th century, the monastery was moved to its present location on the spot where Muscovites welcomed another icon from Vladimir. The cathedral, which is all that remains today, was built in 1679 on the orders of Tsar Feodor Alexandrovich.

The frescoes date from 1707 and are the work of masters from the monastery at Kostroma, some 200 miles northeast of Moscow, who were particularly famed for their painting. Until well into this century the interior was also adorned by a marvellous mid 18th-century wooden screen, carved with a detailed scene of the crucifixion, inlayed with coloured glass, tin and foil. Today it is mouldering in some museum vault while the cathedral is the busy base for an evangelical wing of the Russian Orthodox Church, so if there is an English-speaker present, you may well be approached.

> *Return to the beginning of Sretensky Bulvar where you will find a towering statue of a woman, looking like a Roman swathed in a toga.*

This is supposed to represent one of the least favourite figures of early Soviet history, **Nadezhda Krupskaya**, Lenin's wife, but was in fact modelled on a famous prostitute of the seventies. Behind her, on the two tall carved plinths, are quotations showing Krupskaya's appreciation of the Revolution. Most of the right hand side of the bulvar is taken up by apartment blocks erected by the Rossiya Insurance Company before the Revolution. Known as **Dom Rossiya** (Russia House) they became something of a byword for bourgeois housing standards in the era of the dreadful prefabricated 'Khrushchobi' flat blocks, though to this day many of them are still *komunalki*, communal flats.

> *Turgenevskaya Ploshchad is a massive expanse of tarmac, a site of whole-sale architectural butchery entirely out of keeping with the intimate dimensions of the bulvar. Marooned at its far end is the 1930s entrance to ⑩ **Chistye Prudy**, which was used by Stalin as a bomb shelter during the war.*

The square is known to all as the home of Moscow's main **Post Office** (Glavny Pochtamt), the grey building on the far right corner. Other than that, the only building of any interest to survive the overland onslaught which brought the underground miracle of the metro in the 1930s is the vast classical building set back on the right, currently obscured by scaffolding. Built by Bazhenov in the 18th century, from 1844 it was the **Academy of Painting and Sculpture** and after the Revolution **VKhuTeMas** (the Higher Artistic and Technical Workshop), where many of the geniuses of Soviet design were nurtured. The painter Ilya Glazunov, something of a mega-star among Russian artists despite (or perhaps because of) his right-wing affiliations, has plans to reestablish an art school on the premises when restoration has finished.

> *It is worth walking down Ul. Myasnitskaya, named after the butchers* (myasniki) *who traditionally plied their trade here, to see the **tea-shop** at No. 19, next to the art school.*

This piece of overblown chinoiserie was designed in 1893 for Mr Perlov, an importer of china tea, and to this day stocks tea and coffee as well as biscuits and western sweets. In the aesthetic wasteland which is the Soviet legacy in shop design, its rather crude black and red laquered decor seems a haven of taste and individuality.

> *In the other direction, between Myasnitskaya Ul. and Prospekt Akademika Sakharova, named after the nuclear scientist turned human rights campaigner Andrei Sakharov who died in 1989, is the only building in Moscow by the great Swiss architect Le Corbusier (see p.168).*

Behind its neglected acres of glass façade works the **State Statistical Service**. In the days when its product was at its most implausible, it is said to have issued 30,000 million questionnaires a year. From Prospect Sakharova it appears like a brooding brown stone ship of a building, its semi-circular 'bridge' supported by simple concrete columns. Although it looks rather tired and worn today, it is important to remember that it was built in 1929–36, one of the first modernist buildings in the country. The other side, on Myasnitskaya Ul., was supposed to be the back entrance. A more formal, less adventurous straight glass façade, it sits in monumental contrast to the neighbouring pink and white classical mansion by Bove.

*Return to the neoclassical metro station and continue the bulvar walk, past the draped statue of the playwright and diplomat **Griboyedov**. Hop over the right hand fence—watching out for trams—and nip down Telegraphny Pereulok to the **Church of the Archangel Gabriel**.*

In the early 18th century this region of Moscow was the estate of Alexander Menshikov, Peter the Great's closest advisor, a man so powerful that later monarchs felt secure only after exiling him to Siberia. In 1705 he commissioned Ivan Zaradny, a Ukrainian sculptor and painter recently turned architect to design him a magnificent church with a spire taller than any in the city. The resulting building marks the exact moment at which purely Russian architecture was eclipsed by the techniques of European classicism. Zaradny, with his sculptor's sense of volume and a painterly theatricality, created this lavishly decorated terracotta and white Baroque tower, with its deep cornices, garlands, urns, pillars and exaggerated buttresses in the form of scrolled volutes. The tower was crowned a spire, surmounted by a statue of the archangel holding a cross. Inside, picked out in a contrasting pale blue and white, caryatids and putti hold up the ceiling from a voluminous balcony.

All that has changed are the frescoes and the height of the tower. The original was destroyed by lightening in 1723, by which time Menshikov, like the rest of the aristocracy, was taken up with building projects in the new capital St Petersburg. It was eventually rebuilt in 1780, without the spire and shorter by an entire octagonal tier. Today it is topped by a twisting golden cupola, which still seems very high, even though it is now hemmed in by more recent buildings.

*Protecting the church's courtyard from the street is the early 19th-century quasi-Gothic structure of the **Church of St Fyodor Stratilit**, built as a belfry and winter church. Return to the bulvar, trying to ignore the central glass eyesore which once housed an Indian restaurant.*

Sadly it ruins the effect of the **pond** beyond, from which Chistoprudny (Clean Pond) Bulvar gets its name. The adjective may seen inappropriate in the 1990s, but when Menshikov took over the district he cleared the pond of the guts and carcasses which butchers had been dumping into it for centuries. In winter the ice here buzzes with skaters. To the left of the pond is the white semi-rotunda entrance to the **Sovremmenik Theatre**, which has lost its pioneering reputation and tends to stage safe European classics. Beyond the pond on the right, **Chistoprudny Bulvar** 14 is decorated with strange, monstrous animals—

double-headed winged beasts, birds and half-vegetable, half-animal beings—whose Scythian, Georgian, Viking and even Greek origins are fitting decoration for the city where east meets west.

It proves much more difficult to admire the architectural splendours of the Baroque **Apraksin Mansion** at Ul. Chernyshevskovo 22, opposite the end of the bulvar to the left, than to chuckle at the frivolous charm of the figures in the window of the hairdressers to the right. The palace has been so hedged about by other buildings that the detail and proportion of its pale blue and white façade are quite lost.

> *Bidding adieu to the bulvar, turn right down Ul. Chernyshevskovo, past the hairdressers. If you are hungry, look out for the discreet bistro-style café some 100 yards down on the left.*

On the far corner of the junction with Starosadsky Pereulok purrs the perfectly proportioned, rounded classicism of the **Church of Ss Kosmas and Damian**. The interior, like many in the city, was converted for secular use after the Revolution, with false ceilings and corridors which crucify the proportions. In the words of Michael Ignatieff, 'a country too poor to replace [old buildings] lived out the drama of the new in the tattered stage sets of the old'. The church was built by Matvei

Kazakov, the great architect of Moscow Classicism, in 1791–3, and in fact this crossroads is something of a Kazakov corner. The overly busy, blue and white eclectic façade of the **Belarussian Embassy** opposite hides an original Kazakov palace and was commissioned by the same man as the church, Colonel Khlebnikov, in 1780.

> *Now turn down the right hand side of the Belorussian Embassy, along Armyansky (Armenian) Pereulok.*

The lane is distinguished by a number of well-preserved urban palaces. This is not in itself unusual in Moscow, but what makes the place so evocative is that it has escaped being turned into a major thoroughfare. The palaces have kept the stone arches, pillars, vases and in some cases the railings which delineated their forecourts. It is still possible to imagine a procession of carriages clattering over the planks laid down to counteract Moscow's infernal mud, and swinging into the torchlit court-yard of the Gagarins or the Lazaryevs to let down fur-wrapped revellers.

> *The first of the palaces is situated some 30m down on the right, at **No. 11**.*

This is yet another Kazakov building, and a divine one at that. Built in 1790, it comprises three blue and white storeys centred on a columned loggia and balcony. It was commissioned by Prince Ivan Gagarin, a naval captain, and from 1810 was lived in by the family of the poet Fyodor Tyutchev (1803–73). Now, after restoration, it houses the offices of the Russian Children's Fund.

> *Further down on the left is the grandest of all the palaces in the lane, and the reason it got its name.*

During the reign of Catherine the Great (1762–96) an Armenian of staggering wealth from Persia arrived in Russia and set up a thriving business manufacturing silks and brocades. His name was Lazar Lazarian, which was Russified to Lazaryev. It was he who sold Grigory Orlov the 190-carat diamond which Orlov gave to Catherine the Great and which stars in the Diamond Exhibition in the Kremlin. Admitted to the nobility in recognition of his wealth and charity, he settled here, building a house and church for himself at **3 Armyansky Pereulok**. This was vastly aggrandized by his sons in 1815–23, who had their serfs build the porticoed edifice with its wide sweep of steps which is now the Armenian Embassy. The obelisk in the courtyard thanks the Lazarev brothers for leaving their house to the Armenian community, who turned it into an Insitute of Oriental Languages.

> *Almost opposite the embassy, obscured by trees, is an earlier 17th-century building, part of the **manor house** either of the aristocratic Miloslavskys, or of their neighbours and rivals the Matveyevs.*

The enmity between these two families constituted an important episode in Russian history. The Miloslavskys were the family of Tsar Alexei Mikhailovich's first wife

Maria; the upstart Matveyevs introduced the tsar to his second. After the death of Maria Miloslavskaya, her father Ivan watched in horror as his son-in-law socialized with his neighbour Artamon Matveyev, whose Slav sensibilities had been so diluted by admiration for the West that he had even married a Scots woman, Mary Hamilton. At their house, the tsar met Natalia Naryshkina, who became his second wife. When Alexei died in 1676, the throne was contested between Sophia, his daughter by his first wife, and his son by his second wife, the eventual victor Peter the Great. Apart from a brief period after the *streltsy* rebellion of 1682, when Artamon Matveyev was torn to pieces in the Kremlin, the Miloslavskys fell from favour, victims of the eternal Russian struggle between Slavophiles and Westerners.

Nowadays the house is supposed to house the electrifying Museum of Moscow Street Lighting, and certainly the garden is dotted with old lamp-posts. Whether the exhibition inside is ever open is anyone's guess.

> *On that illuminating note, this walk finishes. All that remains is to turn left at the end of Armyansky Pereulok, curve round to the right and find yourself on Myasnitskaya Ul. The entrance to* **Ⓜ** *Lubyanka is down to the left.*

ZAMOSKVORECH'E

VII: Zamoskvarechiye—Across the River

Start: Ⓜ *Paveletskaya*.

Walking Time: *4–5 hours, depending how long you stay in the various museums.*

Sites

1 Bakhrushin Theatre Museum
Teatralny muzei im. A. A. Bakhrushina
Театральный музей им. А. А. Бахрушина

2 Paveletsky Railway Station
Paveletsky vokzal
Павелецкий вокзал

3 Church of St Nicholas the Blacksmith
Tserkov Sv. Nikolaya v kuznetskoy slobode
Церковь Св. Николая в кузнецкой слободе

4 Church of the Trinity in Vishnyaki
Tserkov Troitsy v Vishnyakakh
Церковь Троицы в Вишняках

5 Church of St Clement
Tserkov Klimenta
Церковь Климента

6 Empire Mansion
Ampirskaya usadba
Ампирская усадьба

7 Tolstoy Museum
Muzei L. N. Tolstovo
Музей Л. Н. Толстого

8 Church of St John the Baptist in the Pine Wood
Tserkov Ioanna Predtechy pod borom
Церковь Иоанна Предтечи под бором

9 Museum of Modern Glass
Muzei sovremennoy stekly
Музей современной стеклы

10 Church of the Chernigov Martyrs
Tserkov Chernigovskikh chudtvortsev
Церковь Черниговских чудотворцев

11 Cultural Centre of Pan-Slavism
Kulturny klub panslavisma
Культурный клуб панславизма

12 Church of the Resurrection
Tserkov Voskreseniya
Церковь Воскресения

13 Empire Mansion
Ampirskaya usadba
Ампирская усадьба

14 Dolgov House
Usadba Dolgovikh
Усадьба Долговых

15 Church of the Virgin of All Sorrows
Tserkov Bogomateri vsekh skorbyashchikh radostey
Церковь Богоматери всех скорбящих радостей

16 Tretyakov Gallery
Tretyakovskaya galeria
Третяковская галерия

17 Demidov House
Usadba Demidovikh
Усадьба Демидовых

18 Ministry of Atomic Energy
Ministerstvo po atomnoy energii
Министерство по атомной энергии

19 Church of St Gregory of Neocaesarea
Tserkov Grigoriya Neokesariiskovo
Церковь Григория Неокесарийского

20 Church of the Assumption
Tserkov Uspenia v kazachey slobodye
Церковь Успения в казачьей Слободе

21 Tropinin Museum
Muzei V. Tropinina
Музей В. Тропинина

22 Church of St Catherine
Tserkov Yekaterini
Церковь Екатерины

23 Art Moderne Gallery
Galereya sovremennovo iskustva
Галерея современного искусства

24 Ostrovsky House Museum
Dom-muzei Ostrovskovo
Дом-музей Островского

25 Convent of Ss Martha and Mary
Marfo-Mariiskaya obitel
Марфо-Мариинская обитель

26 Church of St Nicholas in Pyzhi
Tserkov Nikoly v Pyzhakh
Церковь Николы в Пыжах

Restaurants

A Beriozka Café
Кафе Берёзка

B Lazagne
Ресторан Лазагна

C U Tretyakovki
У Третьяковки

D Dorian Gray

E Co-op Café Yakimanka
Ко-оп Кафе Якиманка

F Traktir Zamoskvarechiye
Трактир Замоскваречье

G U Babushki
У Бабушки

Shops

H Taxidermist

I Australian Bakery

J Confectioner

K Art Salon of the Moscow Cultural Fund

L Bookshop

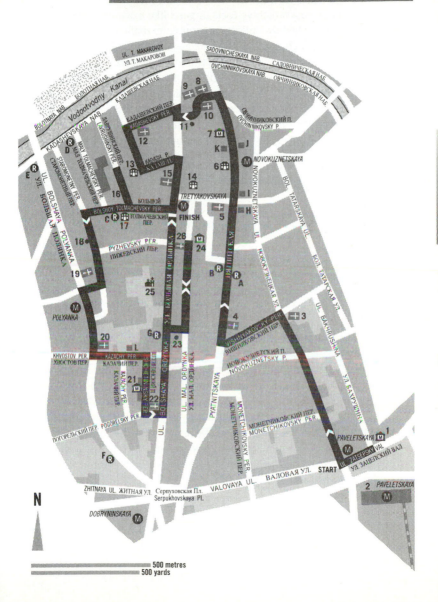

UL. T. MAKAROVOY
УЛ. Т. МАКАРОВОЙ

SADOVNICHESKAYA NAB
САДОВНИЧЕСКАЯ НАБ
OVCHINNIKOVSKAYA NAB ОВЧИННИКОВСКАЯ НАБ

BOLOTNAYA NAB
Vodootvodny Kanal
БОЛОТНАЯ НАБ

KADASHEVSKAYA NAB
КАДАШЕВСКАЯ НАБ

9 8

KADASHEVSKY PER
КАДАШЕВСКИЙ ПЕР.
KADASHEVSKY PER

10

11

OVCHINNIKOVSKY P.
ОВЧИННИКОВСКИЙ П.

KADASHEVSKY PER.

12

7

K   J

MALY TOLMACHEVSKY PER
МАЛ. ТОЛМАЧЕВСКИЙ ПЕР.

STAROMONETNY PER
СТАРОМОНЕТНЫЙ ПЕР.

KRUSHINSKY PER
КРУШИНСКИЙ ПЕР.

13

KADASH. PER
КАДАШ. ПЕР

6

NOVOKUZNETSKAYA

15

14

16

NOVOKUZNETSKAYA

UL. BOLSHAYA POLYANKA
УЛ. БОЛЬШАЯ ПОЛЯНКА

BOLSHOY TOLMACHEVSKY PER
БОЛЬШОЙ
TRETYAKOVSKAYA

БОЛЬШОЙ ТОЛМАЧЕВСКИЙ ПЕР

ТОЛМАЧЕВСКИЙ
ПЕР.

17

FINISH

5

BOL. TATARSKAYA UL.
БОЛ. ТАТАРСКАЯ УЛ.

18

PYZHEVSKY PER
ПЫЖЕВСКИЙ ПЕР.

26

24

NOVOKUZNETSKAYA UL.
НОВОКУЗНЕЦКАЯ УЛ.

19

B

A

R

PYATNITSKAYA
ПЯТНИЦКАЯ

25

POLYANKA

4

3

UL. BAKHRUSHINA

UL. MAL. ORDYNKA
УЛ. МАЛ. ОРДЫНКА

UL. BOLSHAYA ORDYNKA
УЛ. БОЛЬШАЯ ОРДЫНКА

VISHNYAKOVSKY PER
ВИШНЯКОВСКИЙ ПЕР.

NOVOKUZNETSKY P.
НОВОКУЗНЕЦКИЙ П.

20

G

23

KHVOSTOV PER
ХВОСТОВ ПЕР.

KAZACHY PER
КАЗАЧИЙ ПЕР.

L

KADASHEVSKY PER
КАДАШИЙ ПЕР.

21

22

UL. BOLSHAYA ORDYNKA

PEREKERSKAYA

POGORELSKY PER.
ПОГОРЕЛЬСКИЙ ПЕР. POGORELSKY PER.

PYATNITSKAYA
ПЯТНИЦКАЯ

MONETCHIKOVSKY PER.
МОНЕТЧИКОВСКИЙ ПЕР.

MONETCHIKOVSKY PER.
МОНЕТЧИКОВСКИЙ ПЕР.

PAVELETSKAYA

1

F

R

MONETCHIKOVSKY PER
МОНЕТЧИКОВСКИЙ ПЕР.

UL. ZATSEPSKY VAL
УЛ. ЗАЦЕПСКИЙ ВАЛ

START

N

ZHITNAYA UL. ЖИТНАЯ УЛ.   Серпуховская Пл.
Serpukhovskaya Pl.

VALOVAYA UL.   ВАЛОВАЯ УЛ.

2   PAVELETSKAYA

DOBRYNINSKAYA

500 metres
500 yards

193

This is Moscow at its most archetypal, displaying all the qualities for which partisans love the city. Though only a stone's throw from the Kremlin, Zamoskvarechiye feels in parts like a country village. Largely untouched by Stalinist planning, its roofline is mostly two to three storeys high, interrupted by a good handful of the churches for which Moscow was once world-renowned. Behind the rational streets lies a jumble of courtyards and smaller houses, the stage on which the dramas of childhood, courtship, drunkenness and old age are played out, just as the local playwright Ostrovsky recorded them in the mid-19th century. The mass renovation of the district's old mansions has revealed the simple timber structures behind their stucco façades, much as walk through this district will strip away the pompous veneer of the capital, introducing outsiders to the Moscow of the Muscovites.

As this walk weaves its course from museum to church and back again, it cannot help but bring the everyday life of Moscow to your attention. Mothers and daughters check out the price of tomatoes from street vendors, while a misshapen queue worthy of an audition for stage villain snakes along the pavement outside the booze shop. Huddles of workers disgorge from the print factory for a smoke, while the staff of the right-wing pan-Slavic culture centre discuss last night's concert. And through it all, coach-loads of tourists pass unseeing, focussed only on the riches of the Tretyakov Gallery, the greatest collection of Russian art in the world.

This may look more like a marathon than a walk, but it is worth staying the course; there is no better place to begin to understand the hidden essence of the city. As with most walks in Moscow, if you do this on a Monday or Tuesday you will miss a slice of the attractions. On Wednesday and the last working day of the month the Tropinin Museum is closed. Beware also the last Friday of the month, when both the Ostrovsky House Museum and the small Tolstoy Museum are shut.

---

lunch/cafés

Beriozka Café, Pyatnitskaya Ul. 37. Nothing to write home about, but at least it offers sustenance.

Lazagne, Pyatnitskaya Ul. 40, ✆ 231 1085. You could use this co-operative for a light snack though it urges you to linger over something more elaborate. The food is good, if not quite as Italian as it would like to be, but beware of exorbitant extras such as bread and fruit juice. In summer however, you can sit outside here, a rarity in Moscow.

U Tretyakovki, Bolshoy. Tolmachevsky Per. 3, ✆ 230 3075, is a quiet spot just beside the Tretyakov Gallery, to the right of the Demidov Palace. Food from the Russian menu is good though prices are a bit steep.

Dorian Gray, Naberezhnaya Kadashevskaya 6/1, ✆ 237 6342, is an extortionate Italian restaurant beyond the Tretyakov Gallery, whose clients seem to arrive exclusively in Mercedes. The only advantage to being fleeced here is that the menu is in English.

U Babushki, Ul. Bolshaya Ordynka 42, ✆ 239 1484. It is well worth making a reservation at this co-operative to coincide with the end of your walk. Run by a pair of retired actresses, it is small enough, with only six tables, to allow the staff to make you feel wanted. Service is excellent, the food and wine too, and if you've still got room, do have a pudding. The best value restaurant in the city.

Traktir Zamoskvarechiye, Ul. B. Polyanka 54, ✆ 230 7333. A traditional Russian basement restaurant where the Russian food can be excellent. Go for anything with mushrooms in it, particularly the medallions of beef, and the *zharkoe* with its baked-bread crust.

Co-op Café Yakimanka, Ul B. Polyanka 2/10 (enter from Yakimanskaya Naberezhnaya), ✆ 238 8888. Open from 2pm (4pm on Sun). The Uzbek food here attracts a wide clientèle, from homesick Uzbeks to foreigners desperate for some culinary variety. Try the stuffed vine leaves (*dolma*), giant dumplings (*manti*) or the *plov*.

Zamoskvarechiye's unusual history began in the 13th century, when embassies from the enemy Mongol tribes would pitch camp here during negotiations and while collecting tribute from their Muscovite vassals. The first Muscovite settlements were military, regiments of the *streltsy* living in fortified compounds on continuous alert against raiding bands of Mongol cavalry. By the mid-17th century, the bend in the river was dotted by walled settlements, each inhabited by members of one guild of craftsmen or another: barrel-makers, tanners, weavers and sheepskin curers. As the guilds became richer, the churches they built became prominent landmarks. Each settlement was governed by a *mirsky soviet*, a group of elected elders whose meetings were often held in the narthex of their guild church, while the whole district was overseen by a nobleman who acted as judge and jury, as well as the all-important coordinator of fire-prevention policy.

The areas between the settlements filled in as merchants, who continued to trade in Kitai Gorod over the river, built their increasingly impressive mansions here. Small artisan manufactures blossomed during the late 1800s, encouraging an influx of workers who lived in courtyard slums hidden behind the impressive façades. Today, printers and brewers still work down the side-streets, but the spirit of the area is monopolized by antique dealers, restorers and the painters of the Zamoskvarechye school of realism, never far from the inspiration of the Tretyakov Gallery.

*Leave the metro via the '*К Павелецкой Площади*' exit. Facing you across acres of tarmac is the low-slung* **Paveletsky Railway Station,** *from which trains still leave in the direction of the former Tartar strongholds on the Lower Volga. Turn left and first left up Ul. Bakhrushina for the* **Bakhrushin Theatre Museum,** *named after the theatre-lover who started it in 1894, at No. 31 (open 12 noon–7pm, Wed and Fri 1pm–8pm; closed Tues and last Mon of the month).*

There are a handful of fascinating exhibits in this otherwise rather dusty and reverential museum, an uneasy marriage between a sombre 19th-century interior and the dramatic extravagance of the theatre. It begins in the study of A. A. Bakhrushin himself, his rounded Art Nouveau desk surrounded by his collection of theatrical memorabilia. The entire basement is dedicated to the the great Russian bass, Fyodor Ivonivich Chaliapin (1873–1938), whose operatic career began under the patronage of Savva Mamontov (*see* p.204) and his Moscow Operetta Theatre. On Mamontov's piano is a sombre tribute to the millionaire industrialist from Chaliapin: 'He spent money on the theatre, and died in poverty...'. As well as photographs of Chaliapin in various roles, there are set and costume designs for Mamontov's operas by artists such as Viktor Vasnetsov and Nikolai Roerich. The far room deals with Chaliapin's work in Paris, both during the Russian seasons there in 1909 and 1913, and then in self-imposed exile after the Revolution until his death. The four costumes, from right to left, are for the roles of Prince Galitsky in Borodin's *Prince Igor*, of Boris Godunov in Mussorgsky's eponymous opera and two of Mephistopheles' costumes in Gounod's opera *Faust*.

Returning upstairs, the next room is the best in the museum, with models of early European theatre, engravings of the earliest Russian public fireworks displays and fairs, paintings of entertainers and puppet shows, as well as an extravagant dolls' house and puppets. The far wall shows the beginnings of Russian theatre in St Petersburg, while the right-hand wall includes a model of Moscow's late 18th-century Petrovsky Theatre. The costume designs flanking it were for the Sheremetev family theatre, whose place in popular annals was assured by the legendary romance between Prince Nikolai Sheremetev and his serf-actress Praskovia Zhemchugova-Kovaleva (*see* p.156). The next room houses temporary exhibitions.

The heart of the museum is a room devoted to the sentimental world of the 19th-century Russian theatre. Faces call out for recognition from the walls, each isolated in their sepia sea. Among the highlights, at the far end of the room are some *Style Moderne* set, costume and poster designs by Annisfeld, Bakst and Kainer for Diaghilev's *Ballet Russe*, seasons of Russian ballet featuring Nijinsky, which captivated Paris with their daring new fluidity. Nearby are Nijinsky's ballet shoes. The photographs on the far wall form a comic strip of the early history of the Moscow Arts Theatre, dominated by productions of Chekhov.

Approach the last room, which tells the story of post-Revolutionary avant-garde theatre, from the main entrance hall. After the cosy self-importance of the 19th-century memorabilia, the excitement and dynamism of the period leaps out. The coercion of the theatre to the cause of the Revolution is spelled out by a quotation from Lunacharsky, the first Soviet Commissar of Education: 'The Revolution has said to the theatre: Theatre I need you… I need you as a helper, as an accomplice, as an advisor… I want you to light up my mistakes.' Much of the theatre of the 20s and early 30s was indeed revolutionary. Plays by writers such as Mayakovsky were directed by Meyerhold and Stanislavsky, on sets designed by artists such as Rodchenko and Malevich, and set to music by the young Shostakovich. The alluring energy of these performances is well captured in photographs. However Mayakovsky's 'lighting up' of the bureaucratic stupidities of life under Stalin in his last play *The Bathhouse* soured his relations with the government by the time of his suicide in 1930, while Meyerhold died in captivity in 1940.

> *Retrace your steps back past the metro station. The street to the right after it is Novokuznetskaya Ul. The quiet of this leafy thoroughfare is interrupted every now and again by the heavy rumble of a tram, while its gracious 18th- and 19th-century mansions linger in a state of limbo. Scandalized local residents point out one which, with the neighbouring church, is undergoing development into a… casino.*

The church of **St Nicholas the Blacksmith**, opposite Vishnyakovsky Pereulok, is set back beside its beige and white belltower. Built in 1681 and rebuilt in the 19th century, it is better known as St Nicholas of the Miracles because of the many wonder-working icons it contains. If you are there when it is open, check out the pulling power of these paintings, most of them older than the church itself.

> *Turn left down Vishnyakovsky Pereulok, and right onto Pyatnitskaya Ul. round the **Church of the Trinity in Vishnyaki**, built in the 1820s with Empire-style porticoes on three sides and a red and white belltower of diminishing tiers.*

Despite the traffic, Pyatnitskaya Ul. is one of Moscow's most charming. Almost untouched by 20th-century planning fiascos, it is still lined with two-storey warehouses and shops, and taller Empire town houses and mansions. As the street progresses a number of intriguing shops, pleasing façades and a couple of churches present themselves for inspection. Wander through arches to look at the courtyards into which families of labourers were crammed in the 19th century, or to find lone wooden cottages, testimony to a vanished bourgeoisie.

The cluster of towering star-studded cupolas on the left signals the **Church of St Clement**, Pope of Rome, on Klimentovsky Pereulok. Foreign in name, it also feels foreign in nature, with its triffid-like cast-iron fence and ornate white decoration on a Renaissance-Italian blood-red body. It was, appropriately, built by an Italian, who was commissioned by Empress Elizabeth's favourite Alexei Bestuzhev-Riumin to commemorate her seizure of the throne on the feast day of St Clement, 23 November 1741. It was finished in 1774.

On the other side of Pyatnitskaya Ul., at No. 31, is a curious shop specializing in skins and taxidermy, just across the lane from the popular Australian Bakery at No. 29. The impressive circular pavilion of Novokuznetskaya metro station hints at one of the most lavishly decorated interiors of the entire system. Though by no means an eyesore, it did replace the 16th-century building from which the street gets its name, the church of St Paraskeva Pyatnitsa. Opposite the station stands a noble yellow and white **Empire mansion**, No. 18, typical of the self-assured architecture with which Moscow celebrated Russia's defeat of Napoleon on the blank canvas left by the 1812 fire. Interesting souvenirs, art and antiques can sometimes be bought next door at No. 16, the **Art Salon of the Moscow Cultural Fund**. Two houses down (No. 12), is a little-known **Tolstoy Museum**, which was being repainted in 1994 (advertised as open 11am–6pm, closed on Mon, Tues and the last Fri of the month). Lastly, Pyatnitskaya Ul. 9 has been a **confectioners** since the last century, and its shop fittings have been preserved almost intact.

> *From the metro station onwards, the diminishing perspective of Pyatnitskaya is punctuated by a three-tiered belltower belonging to the* **Church of St John the Baptist 'in the Pinewood'** *(Tserkov Ivan Predtechy 'pod borom').*

The tower was built in 1781 in the grounds of the Monastery of St John, founded here in the 14th century when the city of Moscow was hemmed in by forest. Its early Classicism and light green and white paint combine to give the tower a floating quality. Sturdy Doric columns support the lowest tier, Ionic ones the second, while the top tier is decorated with the lightest of Corinthian pilasters. The ponderous swathed vases seem like a later addition. One of the monastery churches survives along Chernigovsky Pereulok, a 17th-century whitewashed brick structure with an 18th-century red and white refectory. Today its voluminous interior is occupied by a **Museum of Modern Glass**, which claims to be open every day (*10am–6pm, though it has few visitors and it might be advisable to ring © 231 2516*) if you are a particular fan. The objets are undoubtedly ingenious, perhaps even good if you like that sort of thing. Beneath the single dome are a few fragments of the original frescoes.

This narrow lane, whose proportions and wealth of old buildings hint at the feel of medieval Moscow, also contains another **church** directly opposite, dedicated to two 13th-century Russian martyrs. Prince Mikhail Chernigov and his companion Boyar Fyodor went as envoys to the Tartar Orda. When they refused to renounce their Christianity, Baty Khan devised an ignominious end for them, and had them trampled to death beneath wooden boards. Their bodies were brought back to Moscow on the orders of Ivan the Terrible, and were eventually buried alongside the tsars in the Cathedral of the Archangel Michael in the Kremlin. This cubic brick building with its decorative porches and five green-tiled cupolas was built in 1675 and replaces an earlier wooden memorial church. The interior was used as a warehouse until 1993, but has recently been reclaimed by the local congregation.

The secular cherry on Chernigovsky Pereulok's distinctly clerical icing is the porticoed pink mansion round the corner, set back from the road behind garden railings. It began life in the late 17th century as the town house of one of Peter the Great's trusted officers in the newly-formed Preobrazhensky regiment, Vasily Timofeevich Rzhevsky. The domestic quarters around the courtyard on the left date from that incarnation. From the early 18th century it passed through a variety of mercantile hands, undergoing successive alterations. The decoration on the pediment, a girl with a book and one with a lyre, give a clue to its 20th-century use as a girls' school, first under the patronage of the Dowager Empress Maria Feodorovna and then during the Soviet period. Today it serves as the **Cultural Centre of Pan-Slavism** (*open 11am–6.30pm, closed Mon*), appealing to those on the right of the post-Soviet political spectrum, but by and large well to the left of Zhirinovsky and the 'Liberal Democrats'. Its exhibitions, talks and concerts, often monarchist in subject matter, are impressive and well-funded.

> *Continue along Chernigovsky Pereulok to Ul. Bolshaya Ordynka, whose name recalls its role as the main road to the Tartar Orda, or headquarters. Turn right for a few yards, cross the busy one-way street and head for the* **Church of the Resurrection** *down 2nd (Vtoroy) Kadashevsky Pereulok.*

The lane on which this church stands is named after the guild of barrel-makers, or *kadashi*, who lived here. Before the church was built, however, they were replaced by a settlement of weavers. The weavers were officially the employees of a state enterprise, but once they had delivered their statutory 4000 yards of cloth to the Kremlin each year, they were allowed to sell material on the open market. The proceeds paid for this early Baroque masterpiece, built between 1687 and 1713.

The church, currently inaccessible and used as a restoration centre for wooden religious artifacts—iconostases and sculptures—is one of the finest in central Moscow. The money lavished by the weavers allowed the unknown architect to transform the traditional 17th-century Muscovite style of church. The white sculptural decoration is refined, *kokoshniki* gables have been replaced with an almost classical broken pediment, and the whole building seems to soar towards the heavens. Its cupolas sit on tall, thrusting drums, and the fine octagonal belfry, from which the church gets its nickname 'the candle', tapers ever upwards. Two porches, decorated with a white tracery of traditional Russian motifs, lead into the building beneath the belltower.

> *Now walk on around the end of the church and down to 3rd (Trety) Kadashevsky Pereulok. On the corner is a pleasing blue and white Empire-style mansion, No. 14. Back on Ul. Bolshaya Ordynka, turn right and pause beside the rounded yellow and white apse of the bulbous Church of the Virgin of All Sorrows.*

The merchant Dolgov, who originally commissioned the church from his son-in-law Vassily Bazhenov in the 1780s, had the yellow and white classical palace at No. 19 built for himself at the same time. Unfortunately both structures were severely damaged by the 1812 fire, but they were rebuilt in the 1820s and 30s by the architect heading the Commission for the Rebuilding of Moscow, Osip Bove. The round belfry is the only survivor of the 18th-century work. The apse and dome of the reconstructed church which jut out into the pavement, balanced by porti-coes on either side, are one of Bove's most brazen pieces of Empire-style building in the city. Exploring the interior, renowned for its choir and for the wonder-working icon of the Virgin in the left chapel of the refectory, is like being inside a blue and white Wedgwood cup. The iconostasis in the main round chapel is surrounded by a colonnade and lit by shafts of light from the dome's abundant windows.

> *Continue down Ul. Bolshaya Ordynka to the next lane on the right, Bolshoy Tolmachevsky Pereulok.*

The street name is another reference to Zamoskvarechiye's association with the Mongols. Negotiations between them and the Muscovite princes were conducted through *tolmachi*, interpreters, whose settlement stood here. Opposite Lavrushinsky Pereulok, stands the imposing wrought-iron entrance to a beige and white porticoed classical house, its pillars topped with huge marble urns. This house belonged to the **Demidovs**, a family whose legendary wealth was built on mines and metallurgy plants in the Urals. In the late 18th century Nikolai Demidov travelled to Europe to study mining, and while in Florence gave so much money to the arts that a sculpture of him stands to this day in the Piazza Demidov.

Some hundred years later the Demidov's neighbour, Pavel Tretyakov, was busy patronizing the arts rather closer to home. Walk down Lavrushinsky Pereulok to the **Tretyakov Gallery** (Государственная Третьяковская Галерея)*, which began as his private collection of Russian painting and is now the greatest collection of Russian works of art in the world (open 10am–8pm, closed Mondays).*

In the mid-19th century, Pavel Tretyakov and his brother Sergei used their family textile fortune to become important collectors of art. Pavel in particularly patronized the *Peredvizhniki* ('the Wanderers'), a group of painters who rebelled against the classical teaching of the St Petersburg academy and sought to bring Russia, her landscape, history and experience, to the centre of their art. He opened his house to the public in 1856, and built a new gallery for his paintings in the 1870s. Eventually, in 1892, both brothers bequeathed their collections to the city. In 1901–2 the Board of Directors of the museum commissioned the neo-Russian painter Viktor Vasnetsov to design a fitting façade for the gallery. His answer was to employ the motifs of medieval Russian architecture: ogee arches, low colourful porches, ceramic tiles, Slavonic inscriptions and the patron saint of Moscow, St George. By the 1980s the collection stood at some 50,000 pieces, and more space was desperately needed. New wings have now been constructed on either side of the original gallery, and since late December 1994 the Tretyakov Gallery has once more been open. Post-Revolutionary works and other temporary exhibitions from the Tretyakov Collection are housed in the 'New' Tretyakov Gallery in the Central House of Artists (*see* p.229).

Early Icons

The Tretyakov Gallery owns the finest collection of Russian icons in existence, including the famous Virgin of Vladimir. This icon inspires great reverence; flowers are laid beneath it, and you will often see people crossing themselves and praying in front of it. It is one of the most tender and human portrayals of the relationship between Christ and Mary, physically united by the gold of his robe and the golden border of her deep red veil. Mary's sad face looks directly out, asking the viewer to consider the tragic fate of her son. The icon's value was enhanced by the legend that it was painted by St Luke. It was in fact created in Constantinople, during the golden age of Byzantine art early in the 12th century, and taken immediately to Kiev. With the demise of Kievan Rus, the icon found its way to the Cathedral of the Dormition in Vladimir. By the 14th century it had come to symbolize of the true spirit of Russian Orthodoxy, and the house of Rurik in Moscow needed it to legitimize their growing ascendency. In 1395 Grand Prince Vasily I had it brought to the Kremlin, where it hung in the Cathedral of the Assumption and was credited with saving Moscow from invasion by the Mongols on several occasions. Since

1930, when it was brought to the museum, it has been discovered that only the faces of the mother and child date from the original painting.

Rublyov and the Moscow School

After the advent of the marauding Mongols in 1237, the bulk of Russian icons were produced in the northern towns of Novgorod and Pskov, which lay beyond their reach. The Tretyakov offers examples of the dynamic Novgorod style, with its striking use of red, and a number of Pskovian works which tend to show a more worldly interest in great saintly bishops.

As the Mongol threat receded, Russia entered her greatest period of icon painting with the development of the Moscow School, and particularly the works of the greatest icon painter of all, Andrei Rublyov. His most famous work, the *Old Testament Trinity*, resides at the Tretyakov. It was painted in the early 15th century for the Cathedral of the Trinity at the monastery in Sergeyev Passad, where Rublyov was a monk. It depicts the Old Testament visit of the three angels to Abraham and Sarah, which was interpreted as a prefiguration of the Trinity. The harmony of the figures, their clothes, the incline of their heads, the crooked elegance of the landscape and the luminosity of the painting combine to make this an extraordinarily serene image of God. Words always fail great icons, but the mountain symbolizes the universe and therefore God the Father, the tree is the tree of life and therefore the Holy Spirit, and the house of Abraham is thought to contain the wisdom of Christ. Some people also believe that Rublyov intended the angels to be recognizable as the ethereal God on the left, Christ in the centre in earthly imperial purple, and the Holy Spirit on the right.

The remains of Rublyov's *Zvenigorod Deisis*, painted in 1410 and rediscovered at the monastery in Zvenigorod (*see* p.273) only in 1918, should also be on display. Only three panels have survived the centuries, depicting the Archangel Michael, Christ and the Apostle Paul. With their combination of tenderness and humanity they feel utterly approachable, and yet something about their rhythmic serenity tells you that these figures have been inspired by a source close to divine. Coming face to face with Rublyov's Christ feels like coming across a portrait of someone you have heard about for years but never seen. He appears to be looking round from behind a door, a friend who visited Rublyov often, rather than the hieratic figure he is so often depicted as being.

While here you shouldn't miss the work of two other great painters. A large *deisis* row survives from the hand of Dionisy, who worked slightly later than Rublyov and is thought to have been the first major icon painter not to have been a monk. As such he was able to devote more time to his art, and technically his paintings are much more sophisticated. Note for example his use of highlights, swirling drapery and dynamic background colours to create dramatic characters. Theophanes the

Greek arrived in Novgorod from Constantinople at about the same time that Rublyov was born. There is a dynamic painterliness, a feeling of experience, to his *Transfiguration*. In it celestial blue rays of light, signs of his new godliness, emanate from Christ on top of Mount Hermon. Theophanes shows them physically bowling over the disciples Peter, James and John, conveying their awe at Christ's majesty. Theophanes is also thought to be responsible for the small icon known as the *Don Virgin*, which Dmitry Donskoy carried into the first victorious battle over the Mongols, on the banks of the River Don in 1380. It saved Moscow again in 1571 when the Crimean Tartars attempted to raid the city. On the eve of the battle it was taken to where the attack was expected, and on the following morning the Russians woke to find the enemy retreating. It is strongly influenced by the Virgin of Vladimir, except that it shows the Virgin looking tenderly at her son, instead of out at the viewer.

Early 19th-century Secular Painting

Just as Peter the Great dragged his country, kicking and screaming, away from medievalism into the 'enlightened' 18th century, so he forced the wide range of realistic Western European painting traditions on its artists. The Tretyakov's exhibits from the 18th and early 19th centuries, by and large express the spirit of the new capital St Petersburg, with its drawing schools and Academy of Fine Arts modelled on their Western counterparts. The first generation of secular painters, who turned exclusively to the genre of portrait painting, are represented by Antropov and Argunov, and the slightly later Rokotov. Works by the two great figures of 18th century painting, Dmitry Levitsky (1735–1822) and Vladimir Borovikovsky.

Late 19th and Early 20th-Century Painting

In 1863 the St Petersburg Academy of Arts set Odin in Valhalla as the theme for its annual gold medal, precipitating a rift in the Russian artistic community. Many artists were already champing under the Academy's rigid orthodoxy, and that year 13 students resigned in anger at the irrelevance of the topic. They grouped together under the leadership of Ivan Kramskoy, and in 1870 formed the Society of Wandering Exhibitions (*peredvizhniki*). Their credo, influenced by the revolutionary and Slavophile ideologies then gaining ground, was to take exhibitions around the country, provoking debate about social issues affecting the motherland with their realistic portrayals of Russian life. The Tretyakov has a magnificent collection of works of Kramskoy and his followers, pictures of ordinary experience, the Russian countryside and Russian history, for it was the Wanderers whom Pavel Tretyakov principally patronized. Perov's thoughtful *Dostoyevsky* and Kramskoy's portrait of *Tolstoy*, caught up in his inner world, sit happily at the heart of a positive reappraisal of the value of Russian culture. Somewhere on view should be Kramskoy's portraits of Pavel Tretyakovsky, his patron and the founder of this museum. Other works to look out for are the almost modern, ghostly religious works of Nikolai Ge, the quintessentially Russian landscapes of Isaac Levitan and the work of Russia's greatest turn-of-the-century realist, Ilya Repin, particularly his honest portrait of the dying, alcohol-riddled composer *Modest Mussorgsky*. His huge canvas at the centre of the back wall is called *They Did Not Expect Him*, and daringly if a little melodramatically depicts the moment when a political prisoner arrives back home, unannounced, from exile in Siberia.

Works of the Abramtsevo circle, patronized by Savva Mamontov (*see* p.196), are also well represented. The paintings by Serov (1865–1911) encapsulate the move away from realism towards Symbolism. Compare for example his sunny portrait of Mamontov's daughter sitting at a table in Abramtsevo, entitled Girl with Peaches, with his painting of the *Kidnap of Europa*, a mythological tale in which even the landscape is highly stylized. Look out too for paintings by one of Russia's most visionary painters, Mikhail Vrubel (1856–1910). Haunted throughout his life by *The Demon*, Vrubel painted many images of his tormenting muse, but never managed to complete the final great work which he envisaged. And yet his sketches for it show a revolutionary attitude to painting techniques, with their fractured sense of colour dancing in the light. The inalienably emotional quality of his work allows the viewer to glean a sense of Vrubel's complex character: here a lyrical love of times gone by (*Pan*), there a sense of mystical premonition and foreboding. Vrubel's unstable genius led him inexorably to the lunatic asylum, while the fate of his paintings would not have amused him. It was Vrubel, in the spirit of the Moderne movement, who said that 'a museum is a morgue'. He preferred to paint a fresco or to design a ceramic frieze to adorn a living environment.

Avant-Garde

For a long time very little of the Tretyakov collection of avant-garde painting has been seen, so it is hard to know what to expect. Certainties are works by two leading members of the Jack of Diamonds movement, Mikhail Larionov and Natalia Goncharova, his lover and a descendant of Pushkin, who went on to found Rayonism, the first truly abstract school of painting in Russian art. Their earlier pictures are redolent of the neo-primitivism that was so much a part of the Russian Symbolist movement. In his painting of a slumped soldier and hers of Jewish women on the porch you can feel the influence of Russian popular prints (*loubki*) as well as that of simple wooden sculpture and icons. Paintings by Kandinsky which attempt to convey the hidden dynamism in everyday life—the electricity, the noise, the refraction of colour out of light and even the emotion implicit in every event, are also likely to be on show, as well as works by Malevich and Tatlin.

> *Leaving the Tretyakov, turn left and continue along Lavrushinsky Per. to the drainage canal. A new bridge heads straight over it to a sculpture of Repin. Turn left before the canal and second left down Staromonetny Pereulok, named after the old mint that used to operate here.*

Today it is a rather forbidding back street, with grimy buildings secreted behind high walls topped with barbed wire. The imagination runs riot as you pass the **Ministry of Atomic Energy**, a stern looking building on the right. There are some 13 institutions in greater Moscow licensed to experiment or use nuclear fuel, and reports on their safety standards are alarming. One told that laboratories were dumping radioactive materials in any hole they could find. Muscovites survive however, so there is little to worry the tourist.

> *Just after the ministry, on the right, you pass the triple apse at the back of the* **Church of St Gregory of Neocaesarea** *(1667–69), also called the Wonder Worker.*

St Gregory was the first saint to whom the Virgin is recorded as having appeared, in the early 3rd century. She and St John the Baptist apparently gave Gregory a statement of doctrine on the Trinity. The church has a closely grouped bunch of five cupolas, but its most notable feature is the glorious ceramic frieze which runs beneath the roof. The floral design of the tiles, reminiscent of a peacock's feathers, gives the church its nickname, the 'Peacock's Eye'. The tiles were made by the most famous 17th-century Muscovite potter, Stepan Polubes, whose masterpiece was the ceramic interior of the cathedral at the New Jerusalem Monastery (*see* p.275). His work can also be found closer to hand at the Potters' Church of the Assumption (*see* p.217). Just after the next house (No. 32), you can wiggle through the courtyard to look at the church's festive front porch and tent-roofed belltower on Ul. Bolshaya Polyanka. Most porches which jut out over the pavement like this were destroyed during the Soviet rationalization of the city. If the doors are open it is worth looking at the fine carved brick inner portal, and the few frescoes which survive around it.

> *Turn around and walk back down Ul. Bolshaya Polyanka until you come to the* **Church of the Assumption in the Cossack Settlement** *(* Tserkov Uspenia v Kazachay Slobodye*) on the left.*

By the mid-17th century this area of swampy ground had been enclosed by Cossacks loyal to the tsars, and in 1695 they began the church, which was considerably remodelled in 1797. The older, single-domed white brick church is hidden at the back, behind the 18th-century lemon yellow and white refectory and bell-tower. The original Cossacks were descendants of the Mongol invaders, whom the Russian princes managed to woo over to their side. By the time of Napoleon's invasion they had become the pride of the Russian army, their loyalty to the tsar rewarded with social and political freedom in their homelands on the borders of the Russian Empire. During the Soviet period the Cossack communities were decimated, and their populations moved wholesale onto alien lands. Beneath the surface however, they kept their traditions and folklore alive, and recent years have seen a strident reaffirmation of their nationhood. Their leader, the ataman, has repossessed his ancestral palace on the Don, after years spent as an intellectual and a poet in St Petersburg. If you catch a glimpse of men with impressive moustaches in old-fashioned army uniforms, you can bet your last thousand roubles they are Cossacks. They make up the backbone of the monarchist revival.

> *The lane leading off to the left after the church is 1st (Pervy) Kazachy Pereulok. For those with good Russian, there is an excellent co-operative **bookshop**, selling highbrow publications, in the small wooden house opposite 2nd (Vtoroy) Kazachy Pereulok. Others should meander on, taking time to savour the sense of village life in these back streets. Turn second right down Shchetininsky Pereulok to No. 10, the **Tropinin Museum** (Музей В. Тропинина) (open Mon, Thur, Fri 12am–6pm; Sat and Sun 10am–4.30pm, closed Tues, Wed and last working day of the month).*

Everything within this immaculately kept, two-storey, sky blue and white house conjures up the late 18th and first half of the 19th century, the period when the portrait painter Vasily Tropinin (1776–1857) was active. Tropinin was born a serf, but showed such talent that he was sent to study at the Academy in St Petersburg. While many artists of the time were from rich, urbane families, and painted only their peers, Tropinin chose to depict a strata of society previously ignored by portraitists—merchants and craftspeople. His milieu was the back lanes of Zamoskvarechiye, where stucco-on-wood merchants' houses rubbed shoulders with small workshops, and the courtyards were stuffed with peasant families newly moved to the city to find employment.

The basis of this museum is the collection of Felix Vishnevsky (1902–1978), the enterprising son of an artistic family who welcomed the Revolution and managed to carry on collecting throughout the Soviet period. It begins with 18th-century portraits, including one of Catherine the Great, and a number of rare naive portraits from the 19th-century, the like of which you will not find elsewhere. The highlights however are a collection of watercolour portraits by Sokolov from first half of the 19th century, and Tropinin's oil portraits. Throughout the museum's five or six rooms are good pieces of furniture and objets, vases, chandeliers and lamps, many of them in the Empire style. To further set the scene there are drawings and watercolour landscapes of Moscow at the time.

> *Turn right out of the museum and left at the end of the road, passing the* **Church of St Catherine**, *surrounded by a wooded garden.*

A wooden church was originally built here by the cosmetic makers' guild. Their wares were so lavishly applied by Russian women that foreigners always remarked upon it, particularly their habit of blackening the teeth. After the church burned down, Catherine the Great paid for the architect Karl Blank to build another church to her patron saint on the spot, in the 1760s. Though it was altered in the 1860s, the Baroque feel of the architecture has survived, though subdued by the all-white exterior. If restoration is complete, go in to admire the frescoes.

> *After the church we come again to Ul. Bolshaya Ordynka. Cross the road and turn left. Just before the third lane off to the right is a well-kept former church, now the* **Art Moderne Gallery** *(open 11am–7pm, Sat and Sun 11am–6pm. Closed Mon). Ring the bell for admission. There are three floors here, and the exhibitions look great in this clean white space, with fragments of original frescoes, but when you look closer the art is often something of a disappointment. To continue turn right immediately after the church, down Iversky Pereulok, and then left on Ul. A.N. Ostrovskovo, named after Russia's best-known 19th-century playwright.*

The small wooden house in which Ostrovsky was born, Ul. A.N. Ostrovskovo 9, has been turned into a **museum** in his honour (*open 1pm–8pm daily; closed Tues and the last Fri of the month*). Set in its own courtyard garden, with tie-back curtains at the windows and a host of chatty *babushki* within, it seems every bit the gossipy milieu inhabited by the bourgeois characters of his plays. Though the museum occupies the entire house, the Ostrovsky family only rented the two rooms on the far left, into which Alexander arrived on 31 March 1823. It gives a good idea of how simply the Russians have always lived, since his family was far from poor, his father being a lawyer and his brother going on to become a Minister of Culture. When Ostrovsky was three, the family moved, but he grew up nearby, a Zamoskvarechiye boy through and through.

In the ground-floor drawing room are pictures of actors from the Maly Theatre in Moscow, where Ostrovsky worked from 1853 until his death in 1886. Beside them are views of a Moscow which has long since disappeared. Upstairs are more photographs of performances and actors, and personal effects—make-up cases and ostrich-feather fans among them—donated by actors. Among Ostrovsky's own possessions, you will find the divine black velvet embroidered hat with which he covered his bald head, and a carpentry work-bench, on which he made presents for friends and family.

Retrace your steps back to Iversky Pereulok and turn right on Ul. Bolshaya Ordynka. A whitewashed archway closed with a forbidding metal gate hides the **Convent of Ss Martha and Mary,** *Ul. Bolshaya Ordynka 34a. Just beyond it a small door leads to the caretaker's lodge. He can usually be persuaded to allow you into the tranquil compound.*

The convent was founded by Grand Duchess Elizaveta, sister of the Empress Alexandra, in 1908. She had lived a saintly, loveless married life with her reactionary, autocratic husband, Grand Prince Sergei (Nicholas II's uncle). After his assassination in 1905, she decided to retire into a convent of her own making, and hired some of the great talents of the time to build and decorate it. The stunningly simple central Church of the Intercession of the Virgin was built between 1908–12 by A. V. Shchusev, better known for Lenin's mausoleum. As inspiration he took the medieval churches of northern Russia, the geometric relief ornaments on the exterior being particularly reminiscent of Novgorod. The interior, which has been used as an icon restoration workshop for some years, is painted with frescoes by Mikhail Nesterov, a protegé of Savva Mamontova and his neo-Russian circle at Abramtsevo (*see* p.261). Nesterov also designed the light grey and white wool habits worn by the sisters. Despite her popularity in Moscow nursing the sick and wounded, the day after the death of the tsar and his family, in another part of the Ural mountains, the Grand Duchess was pushed down a disused mineshaft with other members of the royal family. Grenades and heavy timbers were thrown in after them, but when a peasant crept up afterwards, he heard hymns wafting from the abyss.

A little further up the road on the other side is the small five-domed **Church of St Nicholas in Pyzhi,** *Ul. Bolshaya Ordynka 27a.*

This highly ornamented, whitewashed building was first built inside the settlement of the *streltsy*, part-time soldiers, in 1657–70. The bare interior, only recently reclaimed by the church, is scarcely worth a visit.

Dropping with fatigue but hopefully exhilarated too, you now have only two sensible options: Ⓜ *Tretyakovskaya just beyond St Nikolai, or— providing you have reserved a table—the restaurant U Babushki, back down the road just after the Convent of Ss Martha and Mary.*

Start: Ⓜ *Kitai Gorod*

Walking Time: *4 hours*

VIII: Inner Walls to Outer Monasteries

Sites

1   Church of All Saints in Kulishki
    Tserkov Vsyekh Svyatakh na Kulishkakh
    Церковь Всех Святах на Кулишках

2   Solyanka Gallery
    Galereya 'Solyanka'
    Галерея 'Солянка'

3   Ivanovsky Convent
    Ivanovsky monastir
    Ивановский монастырь

4   Church of St Vladimir
    Tserkov Vladimira v starykh sadakh
    Церковь Владимира в старых садах

5   Shiusky Manor House
    Shiuskiye palaty
    Шуские палаты

6   Church of St Nicholas
    Tserkov Nikoly v Podkopayevye
    Церковь Николы в Подкопаеве

7   Entrance to Salt Caves

8   Site of Khitrovo Market
    Rynok Khitrova
    Рынок Хитрова

9   Church of Ss Peter and Paul
    Tserkov Petra i Pavla
    Церковь Петра и Павла

10 Holy Trinity Church of the Silversmiths
    Tserkov Troitsy v serebryanikakh
    Церковь Троицы в серебяаниках

11 Stalinist Skyscraper
    Vysotnoe Stalinskoye zdaniye
    Высотное Сталинское здание

12 Church of St Nikita Beyond the Yauza
    Tserkov Nikity za Yauzoy
    Церковь Никиты за Яузой

13 Count Bezukhov's House
    Gorodskaya usadba Bezukhova
    Городская усадьба Безухова

14 Old Wooden House

15 Rakhmanov House
    Gorodskaya usadba Rakhmanova
    Городская усадьба Рахманова

16 Stalinist Apartment Block
    Mnogokvartirny dom
    Многоквартирный дом

17 Potters' Church of the Assumption
    Tserkov Uspeniya v goncharakh
    Церковь Успения в гончарах

18 Church of St Nicholas of the Hatters
    Tserkov Nikoly na bolvanovkye
    Церковь Николы на болвановке

19 Taganka Theatre
    Teatr na Tagankye
    Театр на Таганке

20 New Monastery of the Saviour
    Novospassky monastir
    Новоспасский монастырь

21 Krutitskoye podvorye
    Крутицкое подворье

Restaurants and Cafés

A   Karina
    Ресторан Карина

B   Micro-café
    Микро-кафе

C   Khinkalnoye Café
    Хинкальное Кафе

D   Restaurant Vladimir
    Ресторан Владимир

E   Moscow Commercial Club
    Moskovsky kommerchesky klub
    Московский коммерческий клуб

F   Skazka Restaurant
    Restoran Skazka
    Ресторан Сказка

G   Taganka Gastronom
    Tagansky Gastronom
    Таганский Гастроном

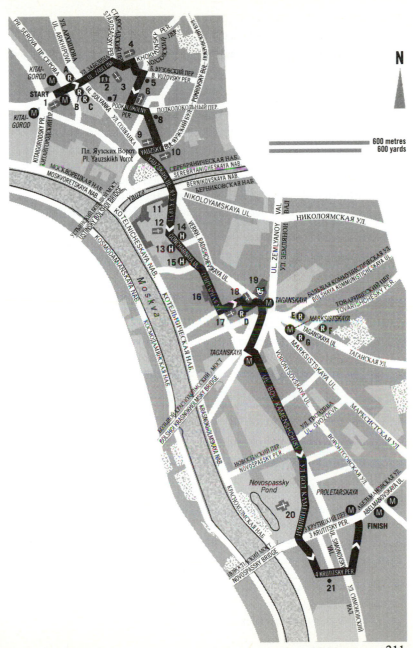

N

600 metres
600 yards

211

This southeasterly amble, parallel to the River Moskva, covers ground unthought of by the average tourist. Beginning at the edge of Kitai Gorod, it meanders among the steep inclines, narrow lanes and low development of what once served as kitchen gardens and orchards to Moscow high society. From the 15th to the18th centuries these attractive hillsides were seeded with the manor houses of rich *boyars*. Even today, when the area houses a mixture of civil service offices, educational establishments and private enterprises, it offers welcome relief from Moscow monumentalism. As the walk dips down to the Yauza River and beyond, echoes of the artisans who plied and hammered out their trades here reverberate through the names: Silversmiths' Lane, the Churches of the Assumption in the Potters' Settlement and of St Nikita on the Sewing Hill, and a whole series of Boilermakers' Lanes. From the late 18th century it became increasingly residential; today, the newly refurbished classical mansions are dwarfed by monumental Stalinist apartment blocks.

Throughout the four-hour walk the only buildings you will be visiting are churches. A number of these are overseen by formidable *babushki* (grandmothers) with strong ideas about decorum in churches. Women are advised to wear a skirt, or at least long trousers, and to have a scarf at the ready to put over their heads. The pilgrimage ends at a semi-working monastery and the extraordinary palace of the Metropolitan of Moscow, in their heyday defensive outposts far beyond the boundaries of the city.

---

lunch/cafés

Karina, 1–3 Solyansky Proyezd, ✆ 924 0369 (*see* p.115)

Micro Café, 6 Solyansky Proyezd (*see* p.115)

Khinkalnaya Café, 2 Ul. Solyanka (*see* p.115)

Restaurant Vladimir, Pyaty Kotelnichesky Pereulok (closed 3–5pm), has tables outside in the summer and serves standard Russian fare: soups, tomato and cucumber salads, *kotleti* etc.

Taganka Gastronom, situated between Taganskaya Ul. and Marksistskaya Ul. on Taganskaya Ploshchad, in the ground floor of the massive purple-decorated high-rise block. There are several fast-food outlets in here, serving everything from coffee to roast chicken and pizza. Alternatively, put together a picnic here to eat overlooking the Novospassky Pond.

Moscow Commercial Club, Bolshaya Kommunisticheskaya Ul. 2A, ✆ 274 0081. For those who would rather pretend they weren't in Moscow, this compound with two restaurants—one Russian, one Scandinavian—is the place.

Skazka, Tovarishchevsky Pereulok 1, ✆ 271 0998. The food here, a mix of traditional Russian and European, is good and the service a miracle. It's open 12 noon–4pm and 5–11pm (closed Sun), and should be booked in advance. The table will be laden with expensive *zakuski* when you arrive, unless you book a *chisty stol* (clean table). On the ground floor there is also a rouble café (open 10am–6pm).

Making it to the right exit from the metro station involves following signs 'На Славянскую Площадь' *from the platform, turning right in the underpass and looking for the exit* 'К Китайскому Проезду… Гостиницу Россия'. *You emerge right beside one of the few remaining pieces of the crenellated Kitai Gorod wall, and should turn briefly left to the highly-decorated, red-brick* **Church of All Saints in Kulishki** *(*Vsyekh Svyatakh na Kulishkakh*).*

This soft, tactile building was erected in the 15th century and enlarged in the 17th, and is thought to mark the site of the graves of heroes of Dmitri Donskoy's victory over the Tartars at Kulikovo in 1380. Its recently reopened interior is still enriched by a number of old frescoes, but restoration is proceeding with such verve that soon it will be difficult to tell old from new.

Turn back, away from the enticing cupolas of Ul. Varvarka which are visited in Walk II.

Beyond the metro, Solyansky Proezd, as its suggests, led to Moscow's all important salt market from the 16th century. The precious commodity was stored underground, fuelling the Muscovites' paranoia about the secret network of tunnels that undermines, both physically and metaphysically, their city (*see* p.83). Later, the old salt caves were used by Moscow's pre-Revolutionary Fortnum and Mason's, Yeliseev's. If you are a mole by nature, you can find the entrance slightly off the route, through the soaring archway before Ul. Solyanka 3. Be warned that you enter a twilight zone here, for a number of the cellars are occupied by homeless youngsters. One night dancing down here to a car stereo, we were almost laid into by a motorbike-riding, self-appointed group of vigilantes, the Night Wolves, who mistook high vodka spirits for a drug-induced frenzy. Only in Moscow!

Otherwise walk straight uphill up Ul. Zabelina, setting your sights on the Church of St Vladimir in the Old Gardens ahead. To distract you on the way visit the **Solyanka Gallery**, once run by the district government but now leased by two women who originally exhibited an eclectic mix of work, from tapestry to painting. Hopefully rumours that they have succumbed to pressure to use the space more commercially are untrue. See for yourself, just down the first lane on the left.

Though its interior has only just been reclaimed and is still in the whitewash and plyboard stage, the **Church of St Vladimir** is in parts the second oldest surviving parish church in Moscow. The original church was built in the early 16th century by the Italian Alevisio Novy, the architect of the Cathedral of the Archangel Michael in the Kremlin. Between 1677 and 1689 it was largely rebuilt, to a brief that must have included instructions to make it look old. It still has a 16th-century feel, though only the foundations and porch date from Novy's building. The arched porch is highly decorated with melons and sheaves of wheat, while the drums of the five domes are traced with bas-relief hearts.

While you are up on the hill on which it stands, look back at the Renaissance-style **Church of St Elizabeth**, built in the 1870s. It forms the centrepiece of the **Ivanovsky Convent**, founded in the 15th century and rebuilt after it burned down in the great fire of 1812. Its history is doom-laden and at two separate periods its grounds, which now hold the Moscow Region Archives and a Law School, were associated with imprisonment. In the 18th century 'problem' noblewomen were locked up within its confines. Some, such as Darya Saltykova, richly deserved it—she had murdered 138 of her serfs, mostly for minor domestic slips. Others did not. Catherine the Great had her rival to the throne, 'Princess Tarakanova', imprisoned here from 1772 for the rest of her reign and more, under the pseudonym of Sister Dosifeya. She had done nothing more than be born to the Empress Elizabeth and her lover Count Razumovsky, who may have been secretly married. At the height of Stalin's Terror the convent was again used as a prison. The brick and stone towers flanking the original entrance are now home to more trees than the average Moscow courtyard, and look particularly sad and decrepit, as if mourning the horrors they have witnessed.

> *Walk down the road beside the convent. Over on the left, No. 5/2 Podkopaevsky Pereulok is a much rebuilt example of one of the **manor houses** which once dotted this area.*

From the end of the 16th century this land had belonged to the Shiusky family, though the earliest part of the red and white building, the downhill part, was not built until the mid-17th century. As a result of later additions, considerable imagination is required to reconstruct its original form. On the land around it they would have kept chickens and other livestock for the table of their palace in town, and grown vegetables and fruit. The blood-red belltower and khaki **Church of St Nicholas** below form another hybrid, built in stages between the 17th and 19th centuries.

Turn left and walk uphill to the junction of five roads.

Before the Revolution this was one of the poorest areas of the city, known as the **Khitrovo Market**. Labourers would congregate here in the hope of being hired for the day, only to have their wages taken from them by the owners of the flea-ridden slums and lodging houses nearby. In his play *Lower Depths,* Maxim Gorky depicted this milieu, and the memory of its ragged, shivering, faces launched Tolstoy on a path which progressively alienated him from family and society. Convinced that the existence of tens of thousands of have-nots was a continuous crime on the part of the haves such as himself, Tolstoy gradually withdrew from society. Nothing of this mire remains in today's rather tidy buildings.

> *The second road right, Petropavlovsky Pereulok* (Петропавловсий Пер.)*, aims for the silhouette of a turquoise and white Baroque belltower beyond, but is in fact named after the* **Church of Ss Peter and Paul** *which sits off to the right towards its far end.*

Built in 1700–02 on a prominent hill beside the Yauza, this church is a modest example of the Moscow Baroque. Its distinctive features are the lace-like white stone details—cornices, window frames, doorways and attached columns—against the red-brick structure. The belltower was added during the reign of Catherine the Great and is in the more austere classical style she preferred. The inside of this church is in an excellent state of repair, with a mid 19th-century iconostasis and unusual late 19th-century mosaics and frescoes. If the main body of the church is not cordoned off, go to the glass case to the left of the iconostasis to see the icon of the Virgin Bogoliubskaya, renowned for its healing powers. During the 1771 cholera epidemic, instead of saving the people who flocked to it, it caused a riot in which 100 of them were trampled to death. The Metropolitan of Moscow, Amvrosii, was a later victim. Fearing the consequences of mass gatherings at a time of rampant contagion (900 people were dying daily), he took down the icon from the city wall, only to be sought out and murdered by an angry mob.

> *The bulvar ring ends just beyond the church in massive, indeterminate, vehicular chaos, which continues on the other side of the River Yauza. With your wits about you, make your way to the unmistakably Stalin-era 'wedding-cake' block of flats, taking in the closed turquoise and white* **Holy Trinity Church of the Silversmiths** *as you go.*

This pretty sea-blue 18th-century church claims the distinction of being commissioned by the grandfather of Pushkin's wife. Its squat, uneven octagonal drum and wave-like cornice are highly unusual in the canon of Russian architecture of the time. The detached belltower achieves its upward momentum by means of a clever architectural conceit: each tier is upheld by pillars of increasing lightness, ending with mere pilasters beneath its soaring cupola.

In its own way, the monumental Stalinist complex soars too, but you could hardly call it light. It is one of the Seven Sisters Stalin ordered to be erected round the city, and was built between 1949 and 1953 with 30 storeys and a profusion of decorative details. Its ground floor cinema, *Illuzion*, shows foreign films.

Take the steep road past the fiery, mustard coloured house to the small white **Church of St Nikita on the Sewing Hill***.*

Now housing a fledgling monastery, this confusing church was built in five stages, in the 15th century, in 1595, and in the 17th, 18th and 19th centuries. The earliest part is the cubic church with *zakomar* pointed gables leading to the decorated drum and cupola. It was commissioned by a wealthy member of the sewing guild, Savva Yemilianov, in 1595, to repair an earlier church which was damaged by a bolt of lightning in 1543. The spot, highly visible from all directions until Stalin's building programme, made the church a local landmark (*closed 12 noon–2pm*).

High over the River Moskva, Goncharnaya Ul. was an ideal position for grand architectural shows of wealth. Two impressive classical mansions here have recently undergone extensive restoration, restoring them to more or less their original appearance. Both were initially built by rich merchants, but were quickly sold to members of the nobility. **No. 12** was built by Moscow's greatest classical architect, Matvei Kazakov, in 1788 and was once as famous as the Dashkov House opposite the Kremlin. Its view was so good that the roof was specially built as an observation platform. It suffered extensive damage during the fire of 1812, but was then rebuilt, and is thought to have been the model for the house of Count Bezukhov, Pierre's father, in Tolstoy's *War and Peace*. Opposite is another old house on a much more modest scale, a little wooden dwelling with lacey carved window-surrounds and tiny buttresses of wood beneath the eaves. Only a handful of these houses still exist, in a city which for centuries was filled with them.

The second, smaller and later mansion stands behind handsome gates at **No. 16**. Originally built in 1800, it received its fine Empire detailing between 1816–23, when it belonged to the merchant Rakhmanov. Particularly extravagant is the frieze and decoration of the pediment over the Ionic portico.

*Further along Ul. Volodarskovo, walkers are dwarfed by the solid wall of a high Stalinist block of flats. Diagonally opposite the end of it is the tiny but exquisite **Potters' Church of the Assumption** (* Церков Успения в Гониарах—Tserkov Uspeniya v Goneharakh*). The craftsmen located on this side of the Yauza tended to be those, such as boilermakers and potters, whose work involved the use of high temperatures. The idea was that the river would stop fire spreading to the centre of the city.*

This tiny rising cube of a church, with its central golden dome and surrounding blue, star-spangled cupolas, looks like a child's study in Russian church architecture. Built in 1654, it belongs to the same, exuberant period of Muscovite architecture as the Church of the Trinity in Nikitniki, when Russia had colourfully adapted her Byzantine heritage but had yet to Westernize it with the advent of the Baroque. What distinguishes it from other churches is its use of tiles, made by the master potters who commissioned it. As well as the visible frieze beneath the eaves of the refectory, there is even better tilework on the far side. Beyond the copy of the icon of the Virgin of Three Hands in a chunky ceramic frame is a courtyard with ceramic saints adorning a cupola and old green and yellow tiles set into the wall. These last were made by the 17th-century master-craftsman Stepan Polubes, and were donated by his family after his death as a memorial. The belltower dates from the middle of the 18th century.

Within the church, undisturbed holiness reigns beneath the wide vaults; worship has continued here relatively uninterrupted. The main iconostasis is 18th-century; to the right of the royal gates an icon of the Dormition and Assumption of the Virgin commemorates the feast after which the church is dedicated.

*Turn right out of the church, down Pyaty Kotelnichesky Pereulok. The towering, uninhabited red, tent-roofed church at the far end is the **Church of St Nicholas of the Hatters**. It dominates not only this small street but also a number of the monumental avenues leading into Taganskaya Ploshchad just beyond it. Cut round it to the right.*

Of all the institutions around this massive square the **Taganka Theatre**, with its new redbrick stage on Verkhnaya Radishchevskaya Ul., is the best known. Under the directorship of Yuri Liubimov it provided Moscow theatregoers with a frisson of danger during the Brezhnev era. His star actor Vladimir Vysotsky played Hamlet as an honest young man incapable of overcoming the hypocrisy and corruption of the establishment. He entered the empty stage from the back, sat down with his legs dangling over the edge and, accompanied by his guitar, sang Pasternak's Hamlet poem from *Dr Zhivago*, at that time unpublished in the Soviet Union. It was this subtle determination not to be silenced, voiced on millions of bootleg copies of his own husky, Dylanesque ballads, that made him the most popular musician of his time, a voice in almost every household. His funeral, though hushed up by the government, was attended by tens of thousands of weeping mourners.

By 1993, arguments between Liubimov and the more traditional members of the theatre showed how much had changed. Liubimov was accused of spending too much time abroad, and many workers and actors feared that his plans to keep the theatre alive would jeopardize their permanent salaries. The fight over who controlled the theatre went to court, and the first few nights of Liubimov's new production of *Dr Zhivago* fell by the wayside as a result.

> *Taganskaya Square, the hub of a phalanx of routes leading into Moscow's southeastern suburbs, is another amorphous area of asphalt to be negotiated. Your goal is the road leading off diagonally opposite the corner with the theatre, at the far side of the island of greenery marooned amid traffic. It is a wide highway called Ul. Bolshiye Kamenshchiki. One mile down here on the right is the unmissable yellow and white belltower over the entrance to the* **The New Monastery of the Saviour** *(Novospassky Monastery). Open daily 10am–5pm.*

The Novospassky Monastery was founded here high above the river in the 1460s, as one of the ring of fortified monasteries protecting the outer reaches of the city from the Tartars. It gets its designation 'new' from the fact that it was moved here from its original position in the Kremlin, when Ivan the Great's grandiose plans for the fortress required more space. Its status was assured by the fact that the Romanovs had chosen it as their place of burial *before* their elevation to the throne in the 17th century; little of what you see today predates them. In 1812 Napoleon's troops plundered the monastery, putting up both men and horses in its holy buildings, while during the Soviet era the place was occupied by restoration workshops. Today the monastery is again lived in by a handful of monks, who share it with the restorers.

Once through the high archway beneath the mid 18th-century belltower, you come face to face with the main **Cathedral of the Transfiguration** (Spasso-Preobrazhensky Sobor). The small neo-Russian porch to the right of the main entrance gives a clue as to its history. The coats of arms on either side of the door, flanking the mosaic of the Saviour, are those of the Romanovs (on the right), and the Sheremetevs (on the left). Members of both families lie buried in the vaults below. It was Michael Fyodorovich, the first Romanov tsar, who began work on the cathedral over his mother's grave in the 1640s. Although it is modelled on the Uspensky Cathedral in the Kremlin, the preponderance of low details on the outside prevents the church from soaring like its prototype.

Within, however, the **frescoes** which cover every inch of the walls are beyond criticism. They date from the late 17th century. Just inside the inner door at the top of the stairs on the ceiling, Princess Olga and Prince Vladimir, who brought Christianity to Russia, are watering the Rurik family tree. The point of the fresco was to stress the legitimacy of the Romanovs by recalling their link with the earlier dynasty through the wife of Ivan the Terrible, Anastasia Zakharina. Most of the right hand wall in this outer gallery is taken up with portrayals of the seven ecumenical councils which decided the doctrine of the early church. That nearest the door is in fact the seventh, the first being right round the corner in the second side of the gallery. Looking at each in turn, you sense that the purpose of these depictions was to provide a portrait of each of the crowned heads who initiated and led the seven councils. Again the Romanovs wanted to show the legacy to which they felt themselves heirs, in this case as leaders of the 'True' Orthodox Church.

The gate into the nave is guarded by the two archangels, Michael, the warrior with his sword, and the peaceful Gabriel. If it is open, or you can find a monk to let you in, you will find it completely covered in frescoes. The soaring **iconostasis** includes some surprisingly modern icons in the local tier.

Walking anti-clockwise round the outside of the cathedral, you will see a small ruined brick chapel covering the site of a holy well, before coming upon a second, unusual octofoil building attached to the cathedral. This is the neoclassical **Church of the Sign** (*Znamenskaya Tserkov*) which was built by the Sheremetev family in 1791–5 with a white stone portico and shallow dome. The wall of the monastery opposite is lined by what were once the **brothers' quarters**, the ground floor still pierced by the tiny, deeply recessed windows of their cells. These are now restoration workshops.

By now you will have reached the far wall of the monastery, where a gate leads out to a pond and a view over the river—an ideal site for picnics. Continuing on round the monastery you walk between the monastic **bakery** on your left and the **kvass chamber** on your right. In the Middle Ages, when this was an isolated fortification, the monks would have been completely self-sufficient, and no self-respecting monastery would have been without its *kvass*, a refreshing, mildly alcoholic drink made with rye bread. The last of the four interlinked buildings at the centre of the monastery is the triple-domed **Refectory Church of Pokrov**. The **abbot's quarters**, standing white and alone in the last corner of the monastery, are once again occupied by clerics. Before leaving the monastery, peer through the metal gate to the left of the main entrance. You should be able to make out a low white tent-roofed chapel, the final resting place of Princess Tarakanova, whom Catherine the Great locked up for so long in the Ivanovsky Convent. Only after death was she acknowledged by her Romanov relatives.

> *Turning right out of the monastery, walk straight down the hill, across the road and up 4th (Chetvyorty) Krutitsky Pereulok opposite. At the end of*

> *the lane turn right and find yourself back in 18th-century Moscow, on cobbled streets lined with one- and two-storey wood and stucco buildings. This overgrown backwater, an almost forgotten corner, is one of the most peaceful places in the city.*

This is the **Krutitskoye Podvorye** containing Moscow's most memorable façade. Mention is first made of a monastery here in the 12th century, but today's edifices date from its use by Moscow's premier churchman, the Metropolitan, after he moved here from the Kremlin to make way for the newly created Patriarch in the 16th century. The buildings you see now were built as his church and palace in the 17th century. On the left rises the red brick hulk of the **Cathedral of the Assumption** (*Uspensky Sobor*), with its five domes and tent-roofed belfry. Behind it a massive covered arcade leads to the astounding façade of the *teremok*, with its carpet of green, yellow and blue tiled decoration. Tiled columns with vines and grapes in deep relief support the Baroque broken pediments above the windows, above which rises the steeply pitched, tiled roof. This single-storey room was built in 1693–4, and the two frescoes over the double arch beneath it still cling faintly to the plaster. They show a *deisis* with the Virgin Mary and John the Baptist flanking Christ, and the Dormition of the Virgin.

Walk through the gates into what was the formal garden of the Metropolitan's palace, the Palace of the Cross, on the right. By contrast, the only decorations on its walls are raised brick bands around the windows and a decorative cornice beneath the wooden eaves. Soon, the palace should reopen as a museum. The barbed wire and raised look-out ahead signal the military prison which still occupies monastery buildings. Indeed in the 19th century, after Napoleon had sacked it, the entire complex served as a prison, housing, among others, the radical Alexander Hertzen. Walking on round towards the river, the only other building is the small, one-storey early-18th century **Embankment Palace**, used by the Metropolitan in summer.

> *As the crow flies, it is only some 3½ miles since the beginning of the walk. Having risked your very existence twice and faced one of the relentless Moscow avenues, it will doubtless feel a lot longer. For the truly superhuman, the Simonovsky Monastery (see p.258) is only another half-hour's walk away. Mere mortals can either hold out a weary arm for a taxi, or head for Proletarskaya metro station, straight across Ul. Simonovsky Val and up Ul. Krutitsky Val.*

Moscow: Museums and Galleries

MUSEY COSMONAVTIKI

The Lenin Museum in the old Duma building at the heart of Moscow has admitted its last visitors, more a victim of economics than political correctness. Entrance was free, and the wages of the formidable phalanx of old female Leninists who guarded the old man's replica flat, Rolls Royce and funeral video must have mounted up. Its neighbour, the massive Historical Museum, has been closed for years, ostensibly for renovation, but it would be a brave place to reopen in the current economic climate. It seems the days of that larger-than-lifesize phantasmagoria, the Soviet museum, are numbered. This list is a comprehensive gazetteer of those which survive, including brief entries on museums and galleries described elsewhere (with page references) and more detailed information on museums not lying on the route of a walk or included in peripheral attractions. Depending on mood you will want to choose between the inimitable House Museums of the culturally famous, museums of historical, religious or special interest or one of particularly Muscovite alternatives. The museum listings are divided accordingly. Under art galleries and museums you will find a list of the major state galleries and non-commercial exhibition spaces in the city, though commerce is creeping into even the most unexpected corners.

House Museums

Chaliapin's House, Novinsky Bulvar 25, ☎ 205 6236 to book a tour. Ⓜ Barrikadnaya *Open 10am–7pm Tues and Sat, 11.30am–7pm Wed and Thurs, 10am–5pm Sun; closed Mon and Fri.*

The most famous Russian singer of the 20th century, barring perhaps the brassy Alla Pugachova, was the legendary bass Fyodor Chaliapin (1873–1938). He lived here between 1910 and 1922, when he left Russia for a Paris which he had already charmed, and never returned. His eldest daughter, Irina, lived on in this house until her death in 1978, hemmed in by neighbours in the other rooms but cherishing a desire one day to see the house turned into a museum to her father's memory. Two years after her death it was indeed designated a museum, and opened after careful restoration in 1988. Only Chaliapin's youngest daughter was alive to witness the transformation back into the house of her childhood. But it was thanks to Irina's plans and careful hoarding of what possessions she could that the house retains its authenticity.

The rooms of Chaliapin's wife and children vividly evoke his family life. In 1898 he married an Italian ballerina, Iola Tornagi; their photograph, beside mementos of their wedding, shows the massive bass towering over his diminutive bride. To complete the picture are photographs of the five children. When on tour Chaliapin would send his family the humorous illustrated letters on display here.

The rest of the house is dedicated to the singer himself, his career and his collections. The dining room is hung with landscapes by his friend Konstantin Korovin, and in the blue-walled study you will find two impressionistic sketches by Chaliapin, of himself in the role of *Don Quixote*, an opera created specifically for him by Jules Messenet. There is also a portrait of an elderly Lev Tolstoy by Leonid Pasternak, father of the poet and novelist Boris, and a portrait of Chaliapin's contemporary Chekhov. In the singer's bedroom enormous costumes and sketches of him in different roles remind you of his immense physical presence on stage, while his bathroom contains his dressing room table and make-up mirror.

The climax of the tour comes in the White Hall however, where in the presence of a huge oil portrait of the singer (by Korovin and Serov) you can listen to a 1931 Paris recording of Chaliapin singing Massenet's *Elegy*, accompained by a cello. Chaliapin claimed to have learned to sing from the cello, for 'it is the closest to the human heart'.

Chekhov House Museum, Sadovaya Kudrinskaya 6. Ⓜ Barrikadnaya. *Open 11am–6pm, 2–8pm Wed and Fri; closed Mon and last day of month.*

This small pink house was the home of doctor turned writer Anton Chekhov (1860–1904) between 1886–90. It was here that he first achieved success as a writer with a book of short stories and one-act plays like *The Bear* and *The Proposal*. His brass plate on the door suggests that he saw his patients here as well. There is a hint of period feeling, and serious fans will no doubt extract something from the photographs of Sakhalin at the time Chekhov's journey there in 1891, and the myriad copies of the comic papers to which he contributed. The layman will only really get a kick out of the wonderful photos of Chekhov with Tolstoy. Each room is explained by an English text.

Dostoyevsky's Memorial Flat, Ul. Dostoyevskovo 2. Ⓜ Novoslobodskaya/ Mendeleyevskaya. *Open 11am–6pm Thurs, Sat and Sun, 2–9pm Wed and Fri; closed Mon, Tues and last day of month.*

This dark, vaulted ground floor flat, in which Dostoyevsky (1821–81) lived until 1837, says reams more about the writer than his bourgeois flat-museum in St Petersburg. It is still part of a hospital, then the Mariinsky Hospital for the Poor, and was only opened in 1983, so little of the furniture is original. But as you walk round you can imagine the writer's father, a melancholic, quick-tempered surgeon at the hospital, listening unsmiling to his son's Latin of Biblical recitations. And looking out onto the hospital courtyard, you are staring at the site of one of the events which made the greatest impression on young Fyodor. One of his few friends, a nine-year-old girl, was raped here and died a few day later. A consumptive air of wretchedness must have clung to the building, and indeed Dostoyevsky's mother contracted and died of the disease while the family lived here. To make things worse, there was a collecting point nearby for prisoners on their way to Siberia; with a monotonous regularity, these ghostly figures would march past the family windows. There are just three rooms: the writer's bedroom, which he shared with his brother Mikhail; the drawing room, strewn with wooden toys and a reverentially neat desk where young Fyodor studied, and the parlour.

Gorky House Museum, *see* Ryabushinsky House Museum.

Kuskovo Palace, Ul. Yunosti 2, ℂ 370 0260. Ⓜ Ryazansky Prospekt. Palace of the princes Sheremetyev. *Oct–March 10am–4pm, closed as below and in very cold weather. Rest of year 10am–6pm Wed–Fri, 10am–7pm weekends; closed Mon, Tues and last Wed of the month (see p.256).*

House Museum of Mikhail Lermontov, Ul. Malaya Molchanovka 2, ℂ 291 5298. Ⓜ Arbatskaya. His childhood home. *Open 11am–6pm Thurs, Sat and Sun, 2–6pm Wed and Fri; closed Mon and Tues (see p.155).*

Mayakovsky Museum, Proezd Serova 3/6, ℂ 921 6607. Ⓜ Lubianka/ Kuznyetsky Most. *Open 10am–6pm Fri–Tues, 1–6pm Thurs; closed Wed and last Fri of the month (see p.116).*

Museum of the Romanov Boyars in Zaradye, Ul. Varvarka 10, ℂ 298 3706/ 3235. Ⓜ Kitai Gorod. *Open 11am–7pm Wed, 10am–6pm otherwise; closed Tues and first Mon of the month (see p.123).*

Ostrovsky House Museum, Ul. A. N. Ostrovskovo 9. Ⓜ Tretyakovskaya/ Novokuznyetskaya. *Open 1–8pm daily; closed Tues and last Fri of the month.* Memorabilia from the playwright's childhood home (*see* p.207).

Pushkin Flat Museum, Ul. Arbat 53, ℂ 241 3010. Ⓜ Smolenskaya. *Open 12 noon–6pm Wed–Fri, 11am–5pm weekends; closed Mon, Tues (see p.158).*

Ryabushinsky (Gorky) House Museum, Ul. Kachalova 6/2, ℂ 290 0535. Ⓜ Arbatskaya. The best, easily accessible interior in the *Style Moderne* in the city. *Open 10am–5pm Thurs, Sat and Sun, 12 noon–7pm Wed and Fri; closed Mon, Tues and last Thurs of the month (see p.152).*

Scriabin Museum, Ul. Vakhtangova 11, ℂ 241 0303. Ⓜ Arbatskay or Smolenskaya. *Open 10am–5pm Thurs, Sat and Sun, 12 noon–7pm Wed and Fri; closed Mon, Tues and last Fri of month.*

The deathly calm which grips the moment you enter the home of the composer seems strangely at odds with his music, but the semi-darkness which contributes to it was apparently his own idiosyncracy. Alexander Scriabin hated direct light. Unless you are a serious music fan, or addicted to interiors in aspic, this one, dating to 1913–15 when Scriabin lived here, is not for you.

Stanislavsky House Museum, Ul. Stanislavskovo 6. Ⓜ Pushkinskaya/Tverskaya/ Chekhovskaya. The director's personal possessions and costumes from his Moscow Arts Theatre productions. *Open 2–7pm Wed–Sat, 11am–6pm Sun; closed Mon, Tues and last Thurs of the month* (*see* p.166).

Tolstoy House Museum, Ul. Lva Tolstovo 21, ✆ 246 6112. Ⓜ Park Kultury. The house museum to beat all house museums. *Open 10am–6pm; closed Mon and last Fri of the month* (*see* p.141).

Vasnyetsov's House, Pereulok Vasnyetsova 13, ✆ 281 1329. Ⓜ Sukharevskaya, followed by a short walk. *Open Wed–Sun 10am–4.30pm; closed Mon, Tues and last Thursday of the month.*

Anyone with no time to visit the countryside near Moscow, and particularly the turn of the century artists' colony at Abramtsevo, should visit the cosy wooden home of the painter Viktor Vasnyetsov. A central member of the Slavophile arts and crafts set which gelled around the patron Savva Mamontova at Abramtsevo, Vasnyetsov designed this steep-roofed log cabin for himself. Ceramic tiles made by Vasnetsov's colleagues from Abramtsevo decorate the stoves, matched by some of the finest contemporary Russian furniture you will see anywhere. If you return to Ⓜ Sukharevskaya, notice the tall green-tiled building on the far side of the square. This too was designed by Vasnyetsov.

Yermolova House Museum, Tverskoy Bulvar 11. Ⓜ Pushkinskaya/Tverskaya/ Chekhovskaya. House of well-known actress Maria Yermolova (*see* p.171).

Historical Museums

The Kremlin. Ⓜ Alexandrovsky Sad. *Open 10am–7pm (Oct–April 5pm); closed Thurs. Armoury Museum sessions at 10, 12, 2.30 and 4.30* (*see* p.89).

Lenin's Mausoleum, Red Square. Ⓜ Ploshchad Revolutsii. *Open 10am–1pm; closed Mon and Fri* (*see* p.119).

Museum of the History of Moscow, Novaya Ploshchad 12, ✆ 924 8490. Ⓜ Lubianka/Kuznyetsky Most. *Open 10am–6pm, 12 noon–8pm Wed and Fri; closed Mon and last day of the month* (*see* p.116).

Museum of the Revolution, Ul. Tverskaya 21, ✆ 299 6724. Ⓜ Pushkinskaya/ Tverskaya/Chekhovskaya. *Open 10am–6pm, 11am–7pm Wed and Fri; closed Mon and last day of the month* (*see* p.179).

Borodino Panorama and Kutuzov's Hut, Kutuzovsky Prospect by the Triumphal Arch. Ⓜ Kutuzovskaya. *Panorama closed for renovation but hut open 10am–6pm Sat and Sun, otherwise 10.30am–5.30pm; closed Mon, Fri.*

Following the indecisive battle of Borodino portrayed in this panoramic painting, General Kutuzov took the tactical decision to abandon Moscow in a hut on this spot. A horseback statue of the general is surrounded by a relief depicting his generals and heroes of the various regiments. A replica hut has been built with two rooms, one the room in which they deliberated, the other housing 1812 memorabilia. The former is decorated as a peasant house of the time, with its brick stove, popular coloured prints (*lubki*) and birch bark pots and shoes. Whether the panorama is open or not, the expensive military toy shop within is well worth a browse. Cannons around the building were captured from Napoleon, while the nearby triumphal arch, erected originally on Ul. Tverskaya to celebrate the eventual Russian victory, was re-erected here after WWII in a fit of patriotic pride. It had been taken down from Tverskaya in the 1930s, victim of a road widening scheme.

Monasteries and Churches

Church of the Trinity in Nikitnikakh, Nikitniky Pereulok. Ⓜ Kitai Gorod. *Open 10am–6pm, 12 noon–8pm Wed and Thurs; closed Tues and first Mon of the month.* 17th-century Moscow church with intact murals (*see* p.124).

Church of the Intercession in Fili, Ul. Bolshaya Filievskaya at the intersection with Ul. 1812 Goda. Ⓜ Fili. *Open 11am–5pm; closed Tues and Wed.* Moscow Baroque at its most decorative (*see* p.245).

Danilovsky Monastery, Ul. Danilovsky Val. Ⓜ Tulskaya. *Services weekdays 7am and 5pm, weekends and holy days 9am and 5pm.* Centre of the Russian Orthodox church. Few buildings are open except during services, though you can enjoy the calm any day. More important historically than aesthetically (*see* p.236).

Donskoy Monastery, Ul. Donskaya. Ⓜ Shabolovskaya. A heavenly wooded, walled cemetery containing three contrasting churches and some remnants of its days as part of the architectural museum. *Open 11am–6pm; closed Mon, Sat and last Thurs of the month* (*see* p.234).

Kolomenskoye, Prospekt Andropova 39, ✆ 115 2713. Ⓜ Kolomenskoye. An ideal retreat on a hot summer's weekday. *Open 11am–5pm, 12 noon–8pm Wed and Fri from May–Sept; closed Mon and Tues* (*see* p.237).

Novodevichy Convent, Novodevichy Proezd. Ⓜ Sportivnaya. Moscow's most picturesque collection of religious buildings. *Open 10am–5.30pm; closed Tues and first Mon of the month* (*see* p.242).

Novospassky Monastery, Ul. Bolshiye Kamenshchiki. Ⓜ Prolyetarskaya. Go when the central frescoed cathedral is open. *Daily 10am–5pm* (*see* p.218).

St Basil's Cathedral, Red Square. Ⓜ Ploshchad Revolutsii. *Open 11am–4pm; closed Tues and first Mon of the month* (*see* p.120).

Spasso-Andronikov Monastery, Ploshchad Pryamikova 10, ✆ 278 1489. Ⓜ Ploshchad Ilicha. *Open 11am–6pm; closed Wed* (*see* p.253).

Bakhrushin Theatre Museum, Ul. Bakhrushina 31. Ⓜ Paveletskaya. *Open 12 noon–7pm, 1–8pm Wed and Fri; closed Tues and last Mon of the month* (*see* p.196).

Central Museum of the Soviet Armed Forces, Ul. Sovietskoy Armii 2, ✆ 281 1880. Ⓜ Novoslobodskaya/Mendeleyevskaya. *Open 10am–6pm: closed Mon and last Tues of the month.*

This anachronistic collection of military hardware includes the wreckage of the U2 spy plane in which Gary Powers was shot down over Siberia in the 1960s, and a notable portrait of Josef Stalin.

Glinka Museum of Musical Culture, Ul. Fadeyeva 4, ✆ 251 1066. Ⓜ Mayakovskaya or Novoslobodskaya. *Open 11am–6pm; closed Mon. Free on Sun.*

Until you have been to a Russian music museum, it is hard to understand the point of one without music, but infact the delight of row upon row of musical instruments from around the world is their pleasing sensuality and aesthetics. The museum has recently been reorganised but you should still find sections devoted to the great Russian 19th-century composers. While you are here you could walk a further 15 minutes to the Museum of Cosmonauts (*see* below).

Museum of Cosmonauts, Alleya Kosmonavtov, ✆ 283 7914. Ⓜ VDNKh. *Open 10am–7pm; closed Mon and last Fri.*

You can't miss the 100-metre high titanium Space Obelisk which marks the start of Cosmonaut's Alley, a sixties hymn to the excitement and energy of the space race. In the museum in the obelisk you can examine rockets, satellites and space suits at close quarters, as well as watching documentary footage of early flights.

Museum of Decorative and Applied Arts, Ul. Delegatskaya 3, ✆ 921 0139. A 15-minute walk from Ⓜ Tsvetnoy Bulvar. *Open 10am–6pm, Tues and Thurs 12.30pm–8pm; closed Fri and last Thurs of month.*

If you are lucky and the museum is fully open, this is *the* place to study Russian costumes, laquerware, Palekh boxes, wooden toys and porcelain. The highlights are the costumes and the Soviet propaganda porcelain. Temporary design exhibitions are also mounted here.

Museum of Folk Art, Ul. Stanislavskovo. Ⓜ Pushkinskaya/Tverskaya/Chekhovskaya. A one room exhibition of crafts and toys. *Open 11am–5pm; 2–8pm Tues and Thurs; closed Mon and last day of the month* (*see* p.166)

Museum of Oriental Art, Nikitsky Bulvar 12a. Ⓜ Arbatskaya. *Open 11am–8pm; closed Mon and last Fri of the month* (*see* p.171).

Polytechnical Museum, Novaya Ploshchad 3/4, © 223 0756. Ⓜ Lubianka. To find the entrance to the museum turn left out of ticket office, left round corner of building and continue to central door. *Open 10am–6pm; closed Mon. To see models working be here at 11am, 1pm, 3pm and 5pm.*

Nothing more and nothing less than a vast, 3-D, 1950s, *World of Wonder/Boy's Own* magazine. There are collections of every thing from clocks to space rockets in this massive survey of mainly Soviet technology, but everything has a low-tech sepia bakelite feel. Every two hours the museum comes to life with model mines, robots, pianolas and early sound equipment.

Pushkin Museum, Ul. Prechistenka 12, © 202 3293. Ⓜ Kropotkinskaya. *Open 12 noon–8pm Tues–Thurs, 10am–6pm Fri–Sun; closed Mon (see p.137).*

Tolstoy Museum, Ul. Prechistenka 11, © 202 3091. Ⓜ Kropotkinskaya. *Open 11am–5.30pm Thurs, Sat and Sun, 12 noon–8pm otherwise; closed Mon (see p.137).*

Puppet Museum, Obraztsov Puppet Theatre, Ul. Sadovaya-Samotyochnaya 3, © 299 0904. Ⓜ Tsvetnoy Bulvar. *Open 45 minutes before performances.*

This labyrinth of glass display cabinets contains many of the characters developed by the theatre's inspired founder, Sergei Obraztsov, who died in 1992, alongside puppets from Japan, American and 19th-century Russia.

Off-beat Alternatives

Museum of Vandalism, Ul. Spiridonovka 8A, hidden in the trees opposite the junction of Spiridonovka and Granatny Pereulok. Ⓜ Pushkinskaya. *Open when the self-appointed curator Sergei Alexandrov is around.*

Originally the studio of Tomsky, sculptor by appointment to the Soviet regime. Alexandrov has been squatting here, doing his own sculpting amongst the disembodied remnants of Tomsky's work, for some years now. The door is ajar for passing visitors, and the collection of Soviet 'heroes' augmented by gifts and finds.

Cat Museum, Ul. Malaya Gruzinskaya 15, © 141 5455 to hear about special events such as feline fashion shows and the like. Ⓜ Barrikadnaya/ Krasnopresnenskaya. *Open 10am–5pm; closed Mon.*

As well as living examples of rare species, you can find out more than you thought possible about cats, followed by thei paintings, photographs and sculptures.

Museum of Horse Breeding, Timiryazevskaya Ul. 44, © 976 1003. Bus 72 or trolleybus 35 from Ⓜ Novoslobodskaya. *Open Thurs and Sat 10am–4pm.*

This strange collection grew out of the paintings of a stud farmer, but now includes representations of horses in all media, plus carriages, harnesses and toys.

Museum of Popular Nutrition, Bolshoy Rogozhsky Pereulok 17. Ⓜ Marxistskaya and a 15 minute walk.

A school kitchen of a museum with a sobering account of food supply during the Second World War. Foodies will be disappointed.

Moscow Metro Museum, Ⓜ Sportivnaya, ✆ 222 7309. Coming from the city centre, take the right hand escalators and ask at the top. *Open 9am–4pm Tues–Fri, 11am–6pm Mon: closed weekends.*

As conditions above ground deteriorate, the efficient running of the metro becomes ever more miraculous. Here you can see photographs of the building of the system, one of the old turnstiles and a working scale model.

Moscow City Planning Museum, 2nd (Vtoraya) Brestskaya Ul. 6, ✆ 209 3442/220 3442. Ⓜ Mayakovskaya. *Open 10am–6.30pm Mon–Fri; closed weekends.*

Lovers of architectural models will find this heaven. Once funded by the City Building Council and now struggling to keep going, these spacious premises are the memory bank of the city. From 17th and 18th century maps to a scaled architect's vision of the city 10 years hence, you can trace the evolution of the Moscow and see buildings from angles you never get on the ground. The masterpiece of the museum, a 12x12m model of the city centre on which urban planners try out their new projects, can only be seen by prior appointment.

Art Galleries and Museums

Central Exhibition Hall in the Manezh, Manezhnaya Ploshchad, ✆ 202 9304. Ⓜ Alexandrovsky Sad. *Open 11am–7pm; closed Tues.*

Massive changing exhibitions in the former indoor military riding school range from the politically important to the artistically dubious.

Central House of Artists and New Tretyakov Gallery, Krimsky Val 10. Ⓜ Oktyabrskaya. *Central House of Artists open 11am–9pm, New Tretyakov Gallery open 10am–8pm; both closed Mon.*

Housed together in a monstrous modern concrete hanger opposite Gorky (Central) Park, between them these galleries constitute a lot of hanging space. The Central House of Artists often curates fascinating exhibitions, spanning folk art to masterpieces of the Russian avant-garde in private hands. On the first floor are contemporary commercial exhibitions and offices belonging to art auction firms. The New Tretyakov Gallery (entrance on the righthand side of the building) has an exhausting permanent collection of Soviet painting and puts on temporary exhibitions both from the vaults of the Tretyakov collection (*see* p.201) and from abroad.

While you are here, wander over to look at the church of **St John the Warrior**, which holds services every day at 8am and 6pm and is often open in between. You can see the octagonal belltower and towering dome, both tipped with gold cupolas, from the entrance to the New Tretyakov Gallery. It was designed by Ivan Zarudny and built between 1709–13, blending west European Baroque with the 16th-century Moscow version.

House of Moscow Sculptors, 1st (Pervy) Spasonalivkovsky Pereulok 4. Ⓜ Oktyabrskaya or Polyanka.

New in 1993, this charming house in Zamoskvarechye had a rather dull retrospective on a medal maker the only time I visited. Posters of previous exhibitions in the corridors looked promising however.

Exhibition Hall of the Cultural Ministry of Russia, Staraya Baumanskaya Ul. 15a. Ⓜ Baumanskaya. *Open 12 noon–7pm; closed Mon.*

An out-of-the-way cultural outpost near the Yelokhovsky Cathedral, with the clout of a government ministry behind it, this gallery tends to show a side of Russian cultural life wiped out by the amnesia of the Revolution. Walking out into 20th-century Moscow was a debilitating experience after an exhibition about the growth of the country estate in the 18th and 19th centuries.

Moscow House of Artists, Kuznetsky Most 11, ✆ 925 4264. *Open 12 noon–7pm; closed Tues.*

This grim building is hardly conducive to aesthetic fireworks, but from time to time what you find inside is pleasantly surprising.

Photo Centre, Gogolievsky Bulvar 8, ✆ 290 4188. Ⓜ Kropotkinskaya. Often excellent exhibitions of photographs. *Open 12 noon–8pm* (see p.136).

Museum of Private Collections, Ul. Volkhonka 14, Ⓜ Kropotkinskaya. *Open Wed–Fri 10am–4pm; Sat and Sun 12noon–6pm; closed Mon and Tues* (see p.135).

Pushkin Museum of Fine Art, Ul. Volkhonka 12, ✆ 203 9578/7998. Ⓜ Kropotkinskaya. *Open 10am–7pm; closed Mon* (see p.131).

Russian Academy of Arts, Ul. Prechistenka 21, ✆ 201 3704. Shows academic Russian painting. *Open 12 noon–8pm: closed Mon, Tues* (see p.000).

Tretyakov Gallery, Lavrushinsky Pereulok 10, ✆ 230 1116/7788. Ⓜ Tretyakovskaya. *10am–8pm; closed Mon* (see p.201).

Tropinin Museum, Shchetininsky Pereulok 10. Ⓜ Polyanka. *Open 12 noon–6pm Mon, Thurs and Fri, 10am–4.30pm Sat and Sun; closed Tues, Wed and last working day of the month* (see p.206).

Moscow: Peripheral Attractions

Moscow: Peripheral Attractions

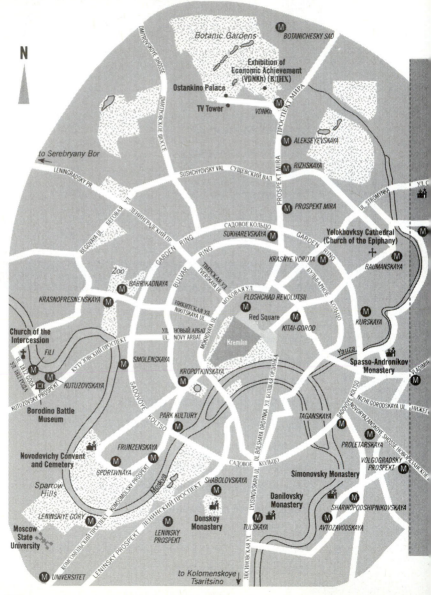

N

Botanic Gardens

Ⓜ BOTANICHESKY SAD

Exhibition of
Economic Achievement
(VDNKh) (ВДНХ)

Ostankino Palace

TV Tower

VDNKh

DMITROVSKOYE SHOSSE

ДМИТРОВСКОЕ ШОССЕ

Ⓜ ALEKSEYEVSKAYA

to Serebryany Bor

LENINGRADSKY PR

Ⓜ RIZHSKAYA

SUSHCHYOVSKY VAL   СУЩЕВСКИЙ ВАЛ

УЛ. ЛЕНИНГРАДСКИЙ ПР

БЕГОВАЯ UL.

Ⓜ PROSPEKT MIRA

ПРОСПЕКТ МИРА

UL. STROMYNKA

Ⓜ

САДОВОЕ КОЛЬЦО
SUKHAREVSKAYA Ⓜ

GARDEN

Yelokhovksy Cathedral
(Church of the Epiphany)
✝
Ⓜ

BEGOVAYA UL.

Zoo

KRASNE VOROTA

RING

BAUMANSKAYA

KRASNOPRESNENSKAYA Ⓜ

BARRIKADNAYA Ⓜ

НИКИТСКАЯ УЛ.
NIKITSKAYA UL.

ТВЕРСКАЯ УЛ.
TVERSKAYA UL.

БУЛЬВАРНОЕ КОЛЬЦО

BULVAR

МОХОВАЯ УЛ.

МОХОВАЯ УЛ.
PLOSHCHAD REVOLUTSII Ⓜ

KURSKAYA Ⓜ

Church of the
Intercession
FILI

Red Square Ⓜ

KITAI-GOROD

УЛ. 1812 ГОДА
УЛ. 1812 ГОДА

Ⓜ SMOLENSKAYA

УЛ. НОВЫЙ АРБАТ
UL. NOVY ARBAT

Kremlin

Yauza

Spasso-Andronikov
Monastery

Ⓜ
KUTUZOVSKAYA

КУТУЗОВСКИЙ ПРОСПЕКТ

SADOVOYE

KROPOTKINSKAYA Ⓜ

VLADIMIR

Ⓜ

Borodino Battle
Museum

КУТУЗОВСКИЙ ПРОСПЕКТ

SADOVOYE

KOLTSO

УЛ. БОЛЬШАЯ ОРДЫНКА УЛ. БОЛЬШАЯ ОРДЫНКА

PARK KULTURY Ⓜ

TAGANSKAYA Ⓜ

САДОВОЕ КОЛЬЦО

НИЖЕГОРОДСКАЯ УЛ. НИЖЕГОРОДСКАЯ UL.

NOVORYAZANSKOYE SHOSSE

Ⓜ PROLETARSKAYA

Novodevichy Convent
and Cemetery

FRUNZENSKAYA Ⓜ

SPORTIVNAYA

МОСКВА

ЛЕНИНСКИЙ ПРОСПЕКТ

САДОВОЕ   КОЛЬЦО

SHABOLOVSKAYA Ⓜ

Simonovsky Monastery

VOLGOGRADSKY
PROSPEKT Ⓜ

Sparrow
Hills

КОМСОМОЛЬСКИЙ ПРОСПЕКТ

Danilovsky
Monastery

SHARIKOPODSHIPNIKOVSKAYA Ⓜ

LENINSKIYE GORY Ⓜ

Donskoy
Monastery

TULSKAYA

AVTOZAVODSKAYA Ⓜ

Moscow
State
University

КОМСОМОЛЬСКИЙ ПРОСПЕКТ

LENINSKY
PROSPEKT

ЛЕНИНСКИЙ ПРОСПЕКТ

ЛЫСИНСКАЯ УЛ.

ПЫЖНИНСКАЯ УЛ.

Ⓜ UNIVERSITET

to Kolomenskoye
Tsaritsino

By the end of the 19th century, Moscow had become a burgeoning industrial and trading centre. Peasants and their families, attracted by the prospect of employment, found themselves working in dark, dangerous and unhealthy conditions, without so much as a place to call home. They lived in dormitories or extortionate, rat-infested lodging houses, often using beds in rotation. To make good the housing shortage, the 20th century has seen the construction of mile upon mile of flat-blocks flanking radial roads and leading inexorably to high-rise suburbs known as 'sleeping regions'. In the push for decent housing, scant regard was paid to historic buildings, and the sights listed below are all isolated islands of interest in a sea of brick and concrete.

УЛ. СТРОМЫНКА
Nikolsky Old Believers' Commune
IZMAILOVSKY PARK
SEMYONOVSKAYA Ⓜ to Izmailovo
Ⓜ Ⓜ
ELEKTROZAVODSKAYA
Ⓜ
VLADIMIRSKOYE SHOSSE. ВЛАДИМИРСКОЕ ШОССЕ
Ⓜ PLOSHCHAD ILICHA
Rogozhskoye Old Believers' Commune
...КАЯ УЛ. НИЖЕГОРОДСКАЯ УЛ.
to → Kuskovo
...SS. НОВОГИРЕЕВСКОЕ ШОССЕ
Ⓜ

What has survived tends to fall into four categories: parks, old royal and aristocratic estates, defensive monasteries and a few isolated churches, many of which once formed the heart of Old Believer communities, forced to live outside the city limits. The Old Believers are an introverted sect and can be unfriendly to outsiders, but their churches, and particularly the icons, are worth the risk of a rebuff. You'll stand a much better chance of being given a guided tour if you speak Russian, or take a Russian speaker with you. The oldest church in Moscow forms the centrepiece of the calm Spasso-Andronikov Monastery, and here there is a museum of spectacular icons for all to see.

You can take a complete break from sightseeing on Serebryanny Bor, an island in the Moskva River, or combine a walk in the park (and a swim?) at Kuskovo with a tour of the exquisite palace. Unlike so many of the palaces round St Petersburg, its wooden interior is not a reconstruction, and the spirit of the 18th century remains ingrained in its materials. At Izmailovo market a thick snake of people weaves between stalls selling icons painted yesterday to pay for the living expenses of tomorrow. After witnessing the lonely struggle for existence in the centre of the city, it is liberating to see families enjoying themselves over a tree-shaded barbecue, or taking in a gentle draught of culture in a monastery or palace.

Donskoy Monastery (Донской монастырь)

The Donskoy Monastery was founded in the early 16th century in honour of the icon of the Donskaya Virgin, which was credited with twice protecting Russian troops from the Tartars. The image was carried by Prince Dmitry during the Battle of Kulikovo near the River Don in 1380, the first Russian victory over the horde since its arrival in the early 13th century. It also frightened off an army intent on sacking Moscow in 1571. The story goes that the Tartar leader, Kaza Girei, was asleep in on the eve of battle when he dreamed that the icon floated over his army's encampment, raining fiery arrows down upon his tent. The khan ordered a retreat, and the walls of Moscow were left untouched. Twenty years later Tsar Fyodor expressed the city's thanks by founding this monastery on the place whence Prince Dmitry, now known as Donskoy, had set off with his troops over 200 years before.

Though there are a number of interesting churches to be visited here, the real joy of this walled enclosure is its peaceful shaded cemetery, which became fashionable after 1771, when burial within the city walls was outlawed because of a cholera epidemic. For over 50 years during the Soviet period, the monastery was part of the Shchusev Museum of Architecture, and the more monumental sculptures dotted around the cemetery date from that period. As you sit in dappled shade on a summer's day, the only things to disturb your reveries are the occasional tolling of a bell and the insistent birdsong.

Getting There

Ⓜ Shabolovskaya. Turn right and right again round the back of the building for a short cut through to Ul. Akademika Petrovskovo. A short walk to the left takes you to the Church of the Deposition of the Lord's Robe.

The **Church of the Deposition of the Lord's Robe** was built in 1701, in a simplified version of Moscow Baroque. The corner pillars and window surrounds inject elements of classical calmness into the underlying Byzantine structure, a distended square with a bulbous projecting triple apse. Inside, frescoes adorn the ceiling and walls, interrupted by gilded icon frames and iconostases. Many of the icons are in bad shape, but are housed in a highly theatrical, Rococo environment, garlanded with gilded cherubs and swags of material. The icon depicting the event after which the church is named is set alone in front of the main iconostasis to the right. It commemorates a specifically Russian event in the church calendar, when the Shah of Persia gave a piece of Christ's robe in a golden casket to Tsar Mikhail Romanov and his father, Patriarch Filaret, in 1625. The icon, a copy of the original ordered by Patriarch Filaret, shows him with his son presenting the relic at the altar in the Cathedral of the Assumption in the Kremlin.

> *From the church, a right turn down Donskaya Ul. takes you towards the bulging domes of the monastery's New Cathedral. The entrance is round to the right—follow the massive red walls past the Baroque **Gate-Church of the Virgin of Tikhvin** to the 18th-century belltower (open 10am–6pm, 10am–5pm Oct–April; closed Mon and Fri).*

You enter the complex through the squat arch beneath the tiered and columned bell-tower, immediately coming face to face with the red-brick **New Cathedral of the Donskaya Virgin**, built in 1684–93. The building is cruciform, raised on a high plinth and surrounded by a single-storey gallery. Yet, despite its height, the church seems disappointingly rooted to the ground. Under the influence of Ukrainian masters who had recently arrived in the capital, the four outer cupolae on the roof form a cross, instead of sitting on the corners of the building as is more usual in Russian architecture. Restoration work is taking place inside. If you can get in you will be struck by the smallness of the main chapel in relation to the size of the building. It makes up for its size with the grandeur of its decoration. The iconostasis, which also dates from the end of the 17th century, leads your gaze ever upwards over its seven tiers. The frescoed walls and pillars were painted some 100 years later by an Italian artist, Antonio Claudio, and are far more life-like than the hieratic frescoes of the Russians.

To the right of the New Cathedral, hidden among the trees, you will find the original, **Old Cathedral of the Donskaya Virgin**, a small green-roofed, red and white building. Originally, it consisted of just the multi-gabled cube with its single blue cupola; the surrounding side chapels, narthex and bell-tower were added in 1670. Far from spoiling the effect of the church, these additions contribute to the mystery of the sculpted, cave-like interior. This was one of the few churches where services continued throughout the Soviet period, and hundreds of years of worship have polished the stone floor to a smooth rink, interrupted by reminders of mortality in the form of dark bronze memorial plaques decorated with sombre skulls. The icons have a luminous antiquity. A copy of the tender Donskaya Virgin hangs to the left of the Royal Gates, and a haunting John the Baptist in a simple classical silver and gold iconostasis, to the right. The Teutonic metal cask against the left wall of the inner chapel holds the body of Archbishop Ambrosius of Moscow, who was killed in the New Cathedral by a mob during the cholera riots in 1771 (*see* p.215). The mitre of Tikon, one of the Soviet Patriarchs, is visible through the window into his golden coffin in the narthex on the right.

Coming out of the old cathedral, walk up the path that veers slightly left to the neo-Russian porch of the otherwise exquisitely classical **Church of the Archangel**

Michael, formerly the burial chapel of the Golitsyn family and now the repository of the best of the funerary sculpture from the cemetery. Nearby is the red and white building which housed the monks' cells. On the far side of the New Cathedral stands a stone plinth, part of the old triumphal arch which welcomed visitors to the city on Tverskaya Ul. Look out for the bits and pieces left behind by the Shchusev Museum of Architecture. The series of massive bas-reliefs set into the bottom wall are part of the decoration of the Cathedral of Christ the Redeemer which Stalin blew up in 1934 (*see* p.135), and which is now being rebuilt. The group on the far left appropriately shows St Sergei Radonezhsky blessing Prince Dmitry Donskoy before he left to defeat the Tartars at Kulikovo.

*It is about a 15-minute walk on from here to the Danilovsky Monastery (*see *below for precise directions).*

Danilovsky Monastery (Даниловский монастырь)

The spiritual credentials of the Danilovsky Monastery are impeccable. It was the first monastery in Moscow, founded by Prince Daniil in the 13th century, and is now the seat of the head of the Russian Orthodox Church, the Patriarch of Moscow and All Russia. Within its thick whitewashed walls, built in the 17th century and wide enough to hold a covered walkway, an open expanse of paving is scattered with religious buildings. However, something seems to be missing; there is none of the burnished patina of worship which is ingrained into so many of Russia's monasteries. From the 19th century it served as a borstal for young offenders, closing briefly after the Revolution only to reopen as an orphanage, and later as a juvenile prison. Then it was hurriedly restored, over a period of less than five years from 1983, so that it could serve as the centre of festivities surrounding the Millenium of Christianity in Russia in 1988.

Getting There

Ⓜ Tulskaya. As you leave the station, keep your eye on the flats over shops on the other side of the main road, and walk to the right. At the busy crossroads, turn right, following Ul. Danilovsky Val for 200 metres until you reach the monastery walls. To walk here from Donskoy Monastery, turn left out of the gates and follow the walls of the neighbouring crematorium round to the left again. The vast, red piece of very late classicism houses the People's Friendship Patrice Lumbaba University, founded in 1960 to train students from friendly communist countries in Africa and Asia. At the end of the street, cross over into tree-lined Serpukhovsky Val, crossing the major intersection at its end (Lusinovskaya Ul.), and continuing straight on along Ul. Danilovsky Val for 200m. Alternatively, take either a 38 or 39 tram until you see the fortified white walls and towers on your right.

The Patriarchate has its own hotel, the Danilovsky Hotel Complex (Гостиничный комплекс Даниловский), Bolshoy Starodanilovsky Per. 5, ✆ 954 0503, a green building just to the south of the walls. The restaurant on the ground floor serves excellent Russian food from a multilingual menu, though foreigners may find themselves faced with absurd bills. If you don't want to risk it, take the lift to the 5th floor, turn right and find the café down the corridor on the right. It serves coffee, sandwiches and other snacks, and a good selection of Georgian wine and champagne.

The entrance to the monastery (*open Mon–Fri 6.30am–6.30pm, weekends 8.30am–6.30pm*), beseiged by elderly beggars, runs beneath the solid pink and white gate chapel of St Simon the Stylite, topped by a bell-tower and golden cupola. The monastery bells are new—the old set toll at Harvard University. Straight ahead is the arcaded drinking fountain built to commemorate the restoration and the millenium in 1988. After the death of Prince Daniil, the monastery was neglected until, according to legend, the ghost of the by then canonized St Daniil appeared to one of Ivan the Terrible's courtiers. He asked that Ivan honour his memory, which he did by building the whitewashed cathedral on the left, the **Cathedral of the Holy Fathers of the Seven Ecumenical Councils**, in 1565, on the site of St Daniil's original church. It was added to in the 17th century, when the central rectangular building was obscured by the galleried walkways which surround it on two storeys. Only fragments of its 17th-century frescoes remain, in the ground floor chapel and on the first floor. It is worth visiting during a service (*7am and 5pm weekdays, 9am and 5pm weekends and holy days*). The icons in the upper chapel are by one of the most highly-regarded contemporary icon painters, Zennon.

The yellow and white classical **Church of the Holy Trinity**, built by Osip Bove in 1838, is said to be open on certain high feast days. If you can't get in, you can at least admire its solidly satisfying architecture, topped by a drum pierced with eight windows to give top-lighting to the interior. The modern building at the far end of the complex, its central entrance presided over by a mosaic of a strangely uncertain looking Christ, is the Patriarch's residence. Against the wall opposite the Church of the Holy Trinity, you will find a curious stone cross, carved in Armenia in the 13th century and given to the monastery by the Armenian church. The gate on the other side of the church leads out to a very busy baptismal church the Church of the Resurrection. The walk-in font is a rarity.

Kolomenskoye (Коломенское)

Kolomenskoye, named after the people who settled here to escape Mongol attacks on the town of Kolomna, was a favourite royal estate from the 14th century at least. Although the most important building to survive dates from the reign of Vassily III (1505–33), the estate is largely associated with Tsar Alexei Mikhailovich (1645–76), father of Peter the Great, who had a fairytale wooden palace built here in 1666–7. He was, by all accounts, passionate about agriculture and hunting, particularly falconry, and it was on his estates around the capital that he experimented with crops and medicinal herbs, while also growing grain, vegetables and fruits for the royal table. His falconers are said to have kept 300 birds of prey, supplied with food from a larder of 100,000 live doves. Today, Kolomenskoye has been turned into a park-museum, with wooden buildings brought here from northern Russia. Parts of the original royal estate are still standing, principally churches and a gatehouse. Sitting high on the banks of a bend in the river Moskva, a half hour's metro ride from the Kremlin, this is the ideal tourist escape from the bustle and pollution of downtown Moscow.

Getting There

Ⓜ Kolómenskaya. Turn right out of the train if coming from centre, left outside the swing doors and right at the end of the underground passage. Emerging into an area of housing, head straight for the trees ahead and walk on through them parallel to the road. The blue domes of the Church of the Virgin of Kazan will appear to the left in front of you. Bring a picnic.

Visitors enter the park (*open 11am–5pm, May–Aug, Wed and Thurs 1–8pm; closed Mon and Tues*) from what used to be Alexei's orchards through the Saviour Gate, a 17th-century wood-roofed, whitewashed structure. The Church of the Virgin of Kazan on the left is thronged with worshippers. Started by Alexei's father Mikhail but finished by the son, its busy external details and rising cuboid mass prefigure the arrival of the Moscow Baroque while its tent roofed porch and belfry refer back to the golden age of Russian wooden architecture. Inside low ceilings, frescoes in the inner chapel and glittering contemplative icons add to the busy sense of worship. The copy of the icon, of the Virgin of Kazan (*see* p.118), which helped rid Russia of the Poles in 1613, can be seen to the left of the royal gates in the main iconostasis.

Alexei's royal palace, adorned with tent roofs, kokoshniki gables, bulbous cupolae and intricate carved details, was joined to the church by a passageway. It straddled today's path, though the bulk of it was to the right. It took just one year to build its 250 rooms and 3000 windows, but the decorative work carried on into 1668. This was entrusted to Simon Ushakov, the pre-eminent church muralist of the time, and the windows were of glittering mica. One of many foreign visitor to the palace described how its interior 'appears to have emerged from a jewel-box'. Others remembered the tsar's throne more clearly. Alexei Mikhailovich would receive foreign ambassadors flanked by gilded copper lions who could be made to roll their eyes and roar by means of an invisible mechanism. Sadly, this Gothic splendour was torn down by Catherine the Great in 1768. Thankfully she had a model of the palace made; you can see a copy in the museum.

Way over to the right are two wooden buildings, the cabin in which Peter the Great lived in Archangel, where he was supervising ship-building, and a 1690 tower from the Nikolo-Karelsky Monastery on the banks of the White Sea. Inside Peter's hut, which you must pay to enter, you will find his simply-furnished bedroom and dining room, and the minute servant's quarters, everything dating from the early 18th century.

The next major building is the whitewashed brick **gatehouse**, originally the main entrance to the royal enclosure, built shortly after the palace in 1672. The clock over its double archway has been working since Peter the Great's time. Tickets for the museum within, and for guided tours around the Church of the Ascension beyond, are available from the window in its far façade. The museum houses primarily religious artifacts, with a good explanatory text introducing each room in English. The first few highlights are secular however, and include a model of the wooden palace, with a picture of its mid-19th century maker, and mica windows similar to those which would have adorned it. There is also a recreated 17th-century interior. The second part of the museum, housed in former administrative quarters adjoining the gates, contains a plethora of sculpted lions symbolizing the tsar's power. In the first room is the most impressive of the museum's exhibits, a wooden crown which hung above the altar in the cathedral of the island Monastry of Solovki in the White Sea. It took six months of 1677 to make and was originally gilded and adorned with two plates on each façade depicting saints. The treasure was evacuated from the monastery when it became one of the first post-revolutionary concentration camps in 500 separate pieces. Its octagonal shape symbolizes the eight points of the compass. Upstairs you will find ceramic tiles and stoves, including a fireplace by the arts and crafts master Mikhail Vrubel, depicting two knights, their horses and the birds of fate. Also displayed are fine decorative items and furniture painted in tempera, and icons.

The jewel of Kolomenskoye is the Church of the Ascension, which rises majestically on the banks of the river beyond. Built in 1532 for Vassily III, to celebrate the birth of a son (later Ivan the Terrible) after 25 years of waiting, it was one of the earliest translations of the Russian wooden tower-churches into brick. The slightly earlier Kremlin cathedrals were all built on the square, Byzantine model, but this harmonious creation points the way towards that quintessentially Russian building, St Basil's on Red Square. The style was short-lived; 120 years later these tent-roofs were banned by Patriarch Nikon, who wanted a return to Byzantine traditions. As well as the obviously wood-derived kokoshniki gables which lead up to the central shatyor (tent roof), there are decorative elements which celebrate the translation into stone. Perhaps the finest is the lattice web spun across the roof, but there are also classical elements in the pilasters and capitals which adorn the doors of the open-sided gallery. Other sculpted stone details adorn the various entrances to the church and the tsar's chair, which looks out over the river onto the fields beyond. It is said that Ivan the Terrible would sit here watching his soldiers massing for battle against the Tartars across the river, while a century later Tsar Alexei Mikhailovich would listen to petitions from his subjects after services. He normally used the Church of the Virgin of Kazan, but on important holy days would process here for the service. Even in high summer the bare interior is absolutely freezing, lit from above by windows in the tent roof. Thanks to the proliferation of arches which make up the internal structure, the acoustics are extraordinary.

The two buildings not far from the church are the redbrick **Water Tower**, which once contained a mechanism for bringing water up from the river, and the now silent **St George Belltower**, the only remnant of the Church of St George, which sits isolated and purposeless without its bells. There is one more architectural curiosity, the **Church of the Decapitation of John the Baptist** at Dyakovo, across the ravine beyond the belltower. Walk down through the ancient oaks, some reputedly planted by Peter the Great, and scramble up the hill to this riot of octagonal chapels joined together beneath a single octagonal roof. It was built by Ivan the Terrible, who spent much time at Kolomenskoye, to celebrate his adoption of the title tsar and the birth of his son in 1547.

Tsaritsyno (Царицино)

Tsaritsyno's romantic Gothic palace ruins are set beside lakes and woods, in which hidden garden follies and pavilions stand abandoned, played on by children, and families hire rowing boats to explore tumbling bridges on islands. Catherine the Great bought the estate—then known as Chornaya Gryaz (Black Mud)—in 1775, and commissioned Vassily Bazhenov to build palaces here for herself and her son Paul, in the 'Moorish-Gothic' style. Only two years earlier, the empress had cancelled work on Bazhenov's Great Kremlin Palace, but the architect was able to come up with an imaginative interpretation of the brief. The plans were agreed and building was well-advanced by the time Catherine drove out to see the new royal estate in 1785, and she stopped work on it there and then. This second royal volte-face, and the snub of having his rival Kazakov take over the job, sent Bazhenov into terminal hibernation on his estate. Luckily the resumption of the Turkish war soon put a stop to Kazakov's work, and apart from the ruins of his main palace and the earlier 18th-century church, the rest of the buildings follow Bazhenov's inspired and harmonious design. The complex was never entirely finished, and recent work has restored it much to its former state of dereliction. Unfortunately the main palace, already badly damaged, was used for mountaineering training until recently; the picks, nails and crampons have done little for its towering walls.

Getting There

Ⓜ Oryékhova (Орехова). Before you get on the metro in central Moscow, be aware that this line splits, and either ask or check that the sign on the front of the train says Krasnogvardyéiskaya (Красногвардейская), not Kakhovskaya. Don't be tempted by Tsaritsyno metro station, which leads to miles of high-rise housing. This approach is much more attractive. Leave the train and take the staircase to the left, signposted Киеcoпapкy. Turn left out of the station, which leads straight to a hole in the park fence.

lunch

In summer bring a picnic, including meat to barbecue if you want to blend in with the riotous Russian *shashlyk* parties. In winter try to lay your hands on skates, skis or a toboggan.

Wandering through the penumbra of the woods from the metro station, you approach the hollow, sobering arches of the palace from the back. To get a better view of the palace itself walk through the exotic arch which sprouts with sharp white teeth like stone barbed wire. The large, complete square building on the left is the so-called **Bakery** (*Khlebny Dom*), from which the domestic side of the palace was to be run. The magnificently decorative octagonal building behind you, the **Octahedron**, with its roof-line of lacey open arches and blown-up, decorated spade gables was servants' quarters. The building of the palace administration to the right, also by Bazhenov, is currently being repaired. Plans to use the buildings at Tsaritsyno to house a national Gallery of Modern Art are shakily afloat, but almost no important contemporary Russian art has been bought yet for lack of funds. The first church to be built in the Soviet period was erected in nearby Tsaritsyno in 1988 as part of the celebrations of the Millenium of Russian Christianity, but the 1722 whitewashed church here is still very busy. Beyond it is the Figourny Bridge, intended as the main entrance to the palace.

Most of the park, laid out in the naturalistic English manner made so fashionable in the mid-18th century by Capability Brown, lies behind the palace above the lake. Hidden among the trees are a very ruined classical belvedere looking out onto the lake, and beyond it a folly in the shape of a ruined Gothic arch. Further on, on an island in the lake are the remains of another arch, this time classical. Walk on round the lake to reach the jetty where you can hire boats in summer, and either return to the palace via the causeway between the two lakes or walk on into the high-rises ahead to find Ⓜ Tsaritsyno.

Novodevichy Convent and Cemetery (Новодевичий монастырь и кладбище—*Novodevichy monastir i kladbishche*)

If you only have time for one of Moscow's religious complexes, visit Novodevichy Convent, the most picturesque and lyrical of them all. Situated in a bend of the River Moskva not far from the centre of the city, the tree-strewn enclosure hides a clutch of exhibitions and churches within its delicate crenellations. The cemetery next door is considerably less interesting, but lovers of graveyards will find plenty to satisfy their various tastes.

Novodevichy Convent (The New Convent of the Virgin) was founded by Vassily III in 1524 in thanksgiving for his recapture of Smolensk from the Lithuanians in 1514. Part of the city's defensive ring, it was badly damaged in the early 17th century during the Time of Troubles, and most of the present buildings date from that most delicate period of Russian architecture, late Moscow Baroque, at the end of the 17th century. It was here that the most powerful woman of the time, Tsarevna Sofya Alexeyevna, the older half-sister of Peter the Great and effective regent, chose to live. Under her patronage the convent blossomed into the powerful yet lace-like ensemble it is today. The decoration of the 12 bastions which top the walls show that by the time they were erected in the 1680s the convent's primary purpose was no longer military. It had become a gilded paddock in which female members of the royal family and aristocracy, following Irina Godunov who retired here after the death of her husband Tsar Fyodor in 1598, were put out to grass.

In 1994 the convent gained its first nun since 1922, the 80-year-old Abbess Seraphinia. Granddaughter of the Metropolitan of Petrograd, who was shot by the KGB in 1937, the Abbess is a former professor of science. She says that she drifted into the church because she had nothing to do at home after she retired.

Getting There

Ⓜ Sportivnaya, or trolleybus 5 or 15 from Ⓜ Kropotkinskaya. Entrance to the convent grounds is on Pl. Novodevichovo Monastyrya and to the adjacent cemetery on Luzhnetsky Proezd down the left-hand wall.

lunch

U Pirosmani, 4 Novodyevichy Proezd, ✆ 247 1926 (cc), *open 12 noon–4pm, 6–10.30pm.* Once an oasis in a culinary desert, this old favourite serves Georgian food in whitewashed surroundings looking out onto the convent. Concentrate on the vegetable appetizers and spicy mutton soups (*kharcho*), as the main courses lack their subtlety. Waiters speak English and the food is good but not cheap.

Café Arena, by Hotel Arena on corner of Ul. Usacheva and Ul. 10-letia Oktyabrya, ✆ 245 2972, is a down-market Georgian establishment where you can pick up a cheap salad and *shashlyk.*

The entrance to the convent (*open 10am–5.30pm; closed Tues and first Mon of the month*) passes through the cavernous arches below the **Gate-Church of the Transfiguration** (1687–9), which soars towards the heavens with ever taller windows, a scallop-shell cornice and five glittering golden domes.Immediately to the right inside the gate are the **Lopukhina Chambers**, where Peter the Great's first wife Eudoxia Lopukhina was tidied away when the tsar had tired of her po-faced conservatism and turned to the racier charms of the German Anna Mons. The kiosk, where you buy entrance tickets to the Smolensk Cathedral and the three exhibitions in the monastery (of ceramics, of icons and other religious artifacts, and a changing exhibition), is to the left.

Dominating everything are the bulbous cupolae of the massive white **Smolensk Cathedral** (*open May–Sept*), one of only two buildings dating back to the convent's foundation in 1524. Built on a high terrace with tall plain walls divided into several narrow sections by pilasters, the building has a strong vertical thrust, mitigated by the somewhat dumpy drums and domes. The steps leading into the cathedral will mean much to opera-lovers, for it was here that Boris Godunov, both in real life and in Mussorgsky's opera, accepted the Russian throne in 1598.

Within is a treasure trove of 16th-century decoration, including an iron grill-work screen on the left of the entrance and a carved stone portal leading into the main body of the church. Here the rich frescoes have been restored back almost to their original state. In line with the preoccupations of the cathedral's founder, Vassily III, the paintings glorify the return of Smolensk, and its famed icon, the Virgin of Smolensk, to Russian hands. The icon, which hung in the cathedral in Smolensk (except for a brief period in the 15th century) until the 1930s, was thought to have come from Constantinople via Kiev, thus legitimizing Vassily's claim that Moscow was the Third Rome, the legitimate heir to the vanquished Constantinople. Scenes from the legend of the icon occupy the bottom row of paintings on the walls. Historical princes and warrior saints of the kingdoms of Kievan Rus, symbolizing the geographical aspirations of the emerging super-state of Moscow, uphold the cathedral from their position on the pillars. The highest row of frescoes tell the biblical story of Anna, whose desire for a child was only answered very late in her life with the birth of Mary, the Mother of God. It expresses the Muscovy princes' concern with a legitimate succession. The iconostasis, commissioned by Sofya, consists of five tiers of gilded twisting grapevines. Icons commissioned by Boris Godunov hang alongside those ordered by Sofya from the royal icon-painter Simon Ushakov. Both Sofya and Peter the Great's first wife Eudoxia are buried in the cathedral.

Opposite the entrance to the cathedral stands the main church built by Sofya, the **Church of the Assumption**, a working church to this day with a busy Baroque exterior and a sentimental 19th-century interior. Services here are impressive, with an excellent choir and priestly vestments of medieval sumptuousness. Behind it is the 16th-century Church of St Ambrose, attached to which is the small palace in which Irina Godunova lived out her days. The other outstanding building in the enclosure is the six-tiered belltower, a tapering Baroque candle of the utmost delicacy with a burnished cupola for a flame. Before leaving the convent, check the map for the locations of the exhibitions to make sure you have seen them all.

> *Turning right and right again down the walls of the convent, the Novodevichy Cemetery is an overgrown wilderness of graves intersected by utilitarian tarmac avenues open 11am–4pm; closed Sun-Tues. Tickets and a plan of the cemetery in Russian (skhema—схема) can be bought opposite the entrance in the blue kiosk.*

The most prestigious Soviet graveyard after the Kremlin Wall, it contains some strange bedfellows. A constellation of stars from the 19th- and early 20th-century artistic community are swamped by the largely morose, pompous or sentimental headstones of heroes of the Soviet Union. Make sure you see Khrushchev's headstone by Neizvestny (*see* p.164), and the cluster of 19th- and 20th-century figures around Chekhov's charming black and white *Style Moderne* gravestone.

Sparrow Hills (Воробьёвые горы—*Vorobyovuiye Gory*)

This is the place to come if you want ski-jumping, tobogganing or just a panoramic view over Moscow. In front of you, unfolds the city in all its glorious disorder. Just across the river is the Central Lenin Stadium and sports complex at Luzhniki, which hosted the main events in the 1980 Olympic Games, and beyond it to the left the 16 golden domes of Novodevichy Convent. Hidden in the trees is the early 19th-century **Church of the Trinity**, a busy working church which originally served the parish of rich dacha owners who spent the summers here. As well as its obvious attractions, they were attracted here by the cachet of royal residents. Both Peter and Catherine the Great had had palaces built here, after all. The entire hill is a well-worn picnic spot and some people even swim in the river here. Considering the industrial vision before you, you would be unwise to do the same.

Getting There

Ⓜ Leninskiye Gory is temporarily closed. Trolleybus no. 7 travels between Kievskaya and Leninsky Prospekt metro stations via the Sparrow Hills. You can't miss the stop—look out for the Moscow University Building, the most imposing of the seven skyscrapers erected by Stalin round the city.

Church of the Intercession at Fili
(Церковь Покрова в Филях—*Tserkov Pokrova v Filyakh*)

This redbrick church with its fine Baroque stone decoration was commissioned by a member of Peter the Great's mother's family, the Naryshkins, in 1693. Set all alone, surrounded by wasteland, the full glory of the church is easily appreciated.

Getting There

Ⓜ Fili. Leave the station towards the front of the train, if you are coming from the centre, and turn left outside. The church is a couple of hundred yards down the road.

Three arcaded staircases lead up to the church (*open 11am–5pm; closed Tues and Wed*), which rises from a high basement shaped like a four-leaf clover, through square and octagonal tiers to a crowning golden cupola. The interior is the only one of its style and time to have survived.The chandelier itself is 19th-century, but the silver flower chain from which it hangs dates to the foundation of the church, as does the iconostasis.The pillars dividing the icons are deeply carved in a variety of styles, and the whole thing is gilded. The icons, also 17th-century, have been variously overpainted and therefore lack a uniform style. The local (bottom) tier of icons include a portrayal of the Intercession of the Virgin, her red veil held above her head to symbolize her protection. Looking up onto the roof you will see frescoes depicting the Trinity, surrounded by the heavenly host. Note how the squinches, which assist the transition from square to octagonal, are decorated, with leaf ornaments more customary in the Hindu culture. Opposite the iconostasis is an ornate black and gilt wooden tsar's box, surmounted by a crown.

*The **Borodino Panorama** and **Kutuzov's Hut** (see p.225) are not far away if you want to visit them. Walk back past the metro station, over the railway line and up the hill on Ul. 1812 Goda. You will reach Kutuzovsky Prospekt just by the Triumphal Arch. The panoramic battlescape is in the modern building to your left, with Kutuzov's Hut behind it.*

River Cruises

If your feet are rebelling against their relentless battle with the tarmac, you might want to consider a cruise on the River Moskva, though being behind dirty windows in winter can be very frustrating. Save it for summer when you can sit outside.

Between mid-April and mid-September there is a boat service every half hour between Kievsky Voksal and Novospassky Monastery, floating majestically past the Kremlin, though you may find yourself on a boat that goes only as far as Central

(Gorky) Park from Novospassky. There are several other stops on the way, the most useful in front of the Hotel Rossiya on Red Square. Services also extend slightly further in either direction during June, July and August. You can travel downstream to the Southern River Terminal, whence boats leave for destinations as exotic as Astrakhan, from Gorky Park every 1¾ hrs from 11.45am–8.30pm. The upstream run from Kievsky Vokzal, at 11.30, 2.30 and 5.30, is a bit of a damp squib.

Serebryany Bor (Серебряный бор)

It's hot, sticky and unbearably dusty in town and you want to strip off, lie in the sun, swim and feel the wind on your forehead? If you think Moscow doesn't run to it, you are wrong.

Getting There

Ⓜ Polezharskaya. Leave the station via the staircase in the direction of travel from downtown, and then take a trolleybus, Nos. 20, 21 or 65, to Serebryany Bor.

This island, upstream of the main pollutants, is sandy and covered in huge shady pine trees. Walking straight down the main road of the island takes you to the most crowded beach, which on a summer weekend rivals anywhere in the Mediterranean in August. Nudists should head upriver. For a bit more peace head off it into the woods to the left, and you should reach the main inlet on the island, known as Byezdonnoye Ozyera, Bottomless Lake. Cross the bridge and keep heading left until you come to the river. Bear in mind that there are nudist and gay stretches on the island, and choose what suits you. Everyone comes here to do their thing—from skinny-dipping octogenarians to mounted policemen grazing their horses while they take a cat-nap.

In summer a local ferry will transport you round the island; or you can hire your own boat or pedalo and spend the afternoon idly investigating.

North Moscow

Ostankino Palace (Дворец Останкина—*Dvoryets Octankina*)

Ostankino was built by Prince Nikolai Sheremetev as a summer palace and theatre for his very popular troop of serf actors. Though a number of Italian architects, including Quarenghi, were consulted about the building, it was left to the Sheremetev's serf architect, Feodor Argunov, to build. Head here for what was the most unspoiled collection of 18th-century interiors in Moscow, at that fragile and rare moment when they retain the musty patina of age but have yet to fall apart.

Since the beginning of the recent bout of restoration many of these have disappeared, but recently you could still catch the unrestored jewel-like Italian pavilion and the gallery leading to it in the left-hand wing.

Getting There

Take the metro to VDNKh, leave the station and walk to the tram stop slightly to the left up Prospect Mira. The unmistakable golden wall of the Cosmos Hotel is opposite. Tram 11 terminates just in front of the palace, which is set back behind a pond and its own topsy turvy decorative church.

lunch

In summer you could happily picnic here, or pick up a snack in the park behind the palace and eat it in a boat on the pond. The alternative is to eat in the revolving restaurant half way up the Ostankino TV tower, the tallest structure in Moscow, which you will notice in front of the palace. It is a complicated business. Once you have got to the tower you will need your passport to get up it, a reservation for one of the sittings in the **Sedmoye Nebo** (Seventh Heaven) restaurant and probably a wait. The food is not worth it, though the view on a clear day is impressive.

The pink and white classical stucco façade of the palace hides an elaborate wooden cabin, for Russians favour wood above all other building materials. There's something warm, malleable and friendly about it, and once inside you can sense it through the plaster and wallpaper. Because of the work in progress, however, it is advisable to call ① 283 1165 to see if the palace is open normal hours (*May–Sept 10am–5pm, Oct–Apr 10am–3pm; closed Tues and Wed*).

If the Italian hall is open you are in for an opulent treat. The centre of the classical room, designed by Vincenzo Brenna, soars with a great sense of space, lit by an immense crystal chandelier. In each corner is a small anteroom, so that the hall could be used either for grand or more intimate occasions. Above the intricate parquet floors the architectural details are of gilded wood, while the walls of two of the smaller rooms are hung with Italian silk. The theme of the room is taken up by a series of Italian marble sculptures, including, in the first small room on the right, a head of Aphrodite from the 1st century AD. The ceiling too is covered in frescoes, yet despite this over-decoration the room retains a sense of tranquility. The gallery leading to the hall was restored in the 1970s and 80s, with tell-tale signs such as the glittering fresh gilding and the false marble pillars. The ceiling is painted with antique scenes and Italian landscapes, linked together by daisy chains.

If it is open the central part of palace houses the theatre/ballroom in which aristocratic Moscow would while away the long summer nights in the late 18th century.

The stage could be lowered to allow for dancing after the performance. One of the actresses who appeared here was the talented Praskovia Zhemchugova-Kovalyova, who married her master Prince Nikolai in 1801. From then on, Ostankino ceased to be a place of entertainment and became the centre of their private world, away from the disapproving eyes of society. Sadly, two years after their marriage, Praskovia died in childbirth. Nikolai devoted his money to a hospital for the poor, now the Sklifosovsky Institute at Sukharevskaya, and abandoned Ostankino.

The ornate **Church of the Trinity** was built over one hundred years before the palace, displaying the flamboyant decorativeness of 17th-century Muscovite architecture. The then owner of the estate, Mikhail Cherkassy, was so stalwart a supporter of Peter the Great that he was the only courtier to be allowed to keep his beard. Inside you will find an impressive classical silver iconostasis and unexceptional 19th-century paintings on walls.

The Exhibition of Economic Achievements (ВДНХ—VDNKh)

Fasten your seat belts. You are about to step back into the never-never land of the Soviet Union, with its harmonious ethnic groups, mastery of space, abundance of food and startling industrial achievements. Once one of the Soviet Union's best-known tourist attractions, VDNKh is where friends remember being brought as children for a treat, to laugh and eat ice-cream beneath buildings labelled 'Atomic Energy' and 'Mechinization and Electrification of Agriculture'.

Getting There

Adjacent metro stations, VDNKh and Botanichesky Sad, serve these two parks, one as artificial as the other is natural. You can visit both in the same long walk by taking the left-hand exit beyond the Kosmos pavilion and lake at the back of VDNKh (pronounced Veydenkha). If you just wish to visit the Botanic Gardens, turn left outside Ⓜ Botanichesky Sad, walk towards the high rise blocks and turn first right down Ul. Selskokhozyaistvennaya. Entrance to the park is some half a mile on the left.

lunch

There are a number of restaurants inside VDNKh, particularly in pavilions behind the main drag on the right and beyond the glorious wheatear phallus of a fountain at the end. You will also find ice-cream and *shashliki* sold in abundance, and a number of kiosks serving coffee and soft drinks.

The Exhibition of Economic Achievements was opened in 1959, inheriting the grounds of the All-Union Agricultural Exhibition which, after millions had died of hunger and in the rounding up of *kulaks*, opened to educate Soviet citizens about the success of the first decade of collectivized agriculture. Today, its fountains

silent, paintwork peeling, and private entrepreneurs the only inhabitants, VDNKh resembles nothing so much as a Hollywood set left to rot after the making of some spectacular epic. The Space Obelisk and the towering sculpture of The Worker and The Collective Farmer outside the park set the scene. Inside, the Friendship of the Peoples Fountain is adorned by gilded women from each of the republics of the former union, and a massive bull stares down from the roof of The Butchery building. The Cosmos pavilion has an Aeroflot plane and rocket outside. Inside, the latest offerings from the outer limits—American cars—are now on show.

Northeast Moscow

> The three places of interest listed here are all on the same metro line and would make for a long, fascinating and varied Sunday morning. Start by visiting the Old Believers' Church for a service at 10am (there is one at 7am if you are very keen), move on to the flea-market and royal estate in Izmailovo Park and finish with lunch booked at Razgulyai near Moscow's Metropolitan cathedral.

Nikolsky Old Believers' Commune (Никольское старообрядцое кладбище—*Nikolskoye staroobryadtsoye kladbishche*)

The reclusive sect of Orthodox Russians known as the Old Believers (*see* p.151) left Moscow in their droves after they split with the establishment church in 1653, but when Catherine the Great granted them freedom of worship in 1771 a number of families returned, although they continued to live in closely-knit communities.

This unusual Gothic church was commissioned by them shortly after their arrival, in 1790, and soon filled with the holy treasures they assiduously collected. The Old Believers (among them both the Ryabushinsky and Morozov families) were formidable businessmen and traders, and much of their profit was spent on religious art.

Getting There

Ⓜ Semionovskaya. Either walk for 10 minutes down the road to the right, or take tram no. 11, 36 or 46 from the stop to the right outside the metro station for two stops. Get off and walk back to the belltower of the church of St Nicholas, its multicoloured tent roof visible above the trees. Entrance to the church is through the crenellated red walls down the lane before the tower. The grey gates at the end lead into the rather desultory cemetery.

In a city remarkable for its lack of participatory citizenship, the care lavished on the garden round the church speaks volumes for the Old Believers' sense of community. The red and white brick church, with its unusual round belltower at the west end, features elaborate reliefs, round sunburst windows, vestigial lintels, obelisks and balls, all adding to the strangely cabalistic or masonic feel of the place. Only the narthex is used for services (*8am and 6pm daily, 7am and 10am on Sundays*), divided from the rest of the building by a wooden iconostasis. Because the Old Believers venerated only icons painted before the schism in the 17th centuries, their communities became repositories of early icons, including the magnificent collection here. Many of them are older than the church itself.

Izmailovo (Измайлово)

Say Izmailovo to anyone today and they automatically think of the anarchic flea-market which appears here at weekends. Thoughts of the royal estate and even of the notorious avant-garde exhibition that was bulldozed here in the 1970s on the orders of Brezhnev have been obliterated by the sheer volume of commerce transacted here at weekends. It began in the early days of *perestroika*, as a place where underground artists came, snow or shine, to try to sell their works. From time to time they were moved off by the police, but by 1988–9 they had become a firm fixture, soon joined by antique and souvenir salesmen. Today you never know what you are going to find, except of course the ubiquitous army of matrioshkas. There are carpets and toys, homemade clothes and embroidery, military paraphernalia, guns and icons, both ancient and modern. Blond, bobby-socked American cheerleaders go through their paces while pensioners stake their hopes on selling a cup and saucer of immense sentimental, but little other, value. If you can tear yourself away, take a quick look at what remains of the royal estate.

Ⓜ Izmailovsky Park. If you are here on Saturday or Sunday you will be swept by the crowd in the direction of the market. If not, turn left and walk towards the stadium. The high-rise blocks on your left are the undistinguished Izmailovo Hotel, built to accomodate visitors to the 1980 Olympics. When water appears on your right, go over the bridge and take the right hand path round the netted sports pitch.

Here are what remains of the once imposing white walls which safeguarded a palace and two churches. Walk down to the left to find the first of the two white triple gates leading into the former royal residence. The central arch is surmounted by a pyramidal roof and flanked by two smaller low arches. Over these is an unusual terrace with columned balustrades. The square of raised brick over the central arch would originally have encased an icon.

Izmailovo was built during the reign of Tsar Alexei, as an experiment in animal and vegetable husbandry. The two rivers which flow into it were dammed into a series of ponds in which everything from fish for the royal table to medicinal leeches were bred. Alexei moved seven hundred families here to oversee the agriculture, which included all manner of different food-stuffs (some entirely new to Russia, others brought from the far reaches of the country), medicinal herb gardens and the rearing of animals, all overseen by foreign experts. This kind of scientific approach, so widespread in Western Europe at the time, was entirely new to 17th-century Russia.

The centrepiece of the estate today is a more enduring monument, the **Pokrov Cathedral**. Catherine the Great had the wooden palace demolished in 1765. Working in 1671–2, the architect seems to have ignored the prevailing fashion for the Moscow Baroque and reverted to earlier models such as the late 15th-century Kremlin Cathedral of the Assumption. Its main façade is divided into three soaring arches by attached columns. The side ones house two huge windows, the middle a traditional Russian porch derived from wooden architecture, whose delicate hanging brick arches need metal supports. Its distinguishing feature are the floral tiles made to the designs of the famous ceramicist Stepan Polubes. The inflated onion domes on the cathedral were also tiled, though now they are covered with metallic serpents' scales. The buildings on either side of the church were built in the 19th century for veterans of the 1812 war against Napoleon.

Walk round to the right of the building to find the solid redbrick bridge tower, a fortified bastion which protected one of the bridges onto the island estate, built in 1679. Reclamation has left it stranded on dry land. Its highest, octagonal layer was used as the cathedral's bell tower.

Yelokhovsky Cathedral (Елоховский собор—*Yelokhovsky sobor*)

Though the architecture of this cathedral is nothing to rave over, there are a number of other reasons to visit it. Since it was, from 1943 to *perestroika*, the seat of the Patriarch of All Russia, its importance is firmly embedded in the psyche of fervent Moscow Orthodoxy. On holy days it brims over with believers, many of them old women who religiously attended church regardless of the regime. It also attracts that less attractive aspect of Orthodoxy, anti-Semites, who have the gall to stand collecting money for the fight against the 'Zionist conspiracy' on the very steps of the cathedral. The Jews have long and vociferously been blamed for Russia's ills—under the tsars when they were largely forbidden to live in Moscow or St Petersburg for hundreds of years, and during the Soviet period they were often quietly blamed for the Revolution. Now the cat is out of the bag and Zhirinovsky's followers are openly anti-Semitic. The writing was on the wall throughout 1993, in the form of a ubiquitous piece of graffiti in Moscow which stated simply 'Yeltsin—Yid'.

Getting There

Ⓜ Baumanskaya. Turn right onto Baumanskaya Ul., cross the road and you will see the blue and white cathedral behind the big white block of flats.

lunch

Razgulyai, Spartakovskaya Ul. 11, ☎ 267 7613. A well-established co-op located in a cosy vaulted basement; the traditional Russian menu offers no surprises but the standard of the food does. There is a good selection of alcohol to enjoy with it, or you can plump for refreshing cranberry juice. A delightful end to a busy morning.

Cheaper alternatives in Ul. Staraya Basmannaya include the **Russian Café** at No. 5 where, on a good day, champagne, salad and open sandwiches are available. A few doors down Dobroslobodskaya Ul. on the right you can get toasted cheese sandwiches, tea or coffee in **Natalie**, a stand-up joint.

Just outside the metro, look up at the mosaic on the building to the right. It depicts the Nemyetskaya Sloboda, the 'German' quarter, in which most foreigners were required to live in the 16th and 17th centuries. As you can see from the mosaic, it was located outside the walls of the city, principally so that dangerous foreign ideas and customs, particularly those derived from Rome, would not spread to the population as a whole. It was here, for example, that Peter the Great's first great foreign friend, the Swiss Franz Lefort, introduced the would-be westernizing tsar to Anna Mons who was his lover for 10 years. He's gone down in local annals by giving his name to one of Moscow's most notorious, top-security prisons, Lefortovo, nearby.

Yelokhovsky Cathedral, or more properly the Church of the Epiphany in Yelokhov, was built in 1837–45 in an eclectic style by an otherwise little known architect. Renaissance and Byzantine features compete with the Classicism of the earlier 18th-century belltower. It was in the earlier church that Alexander Sergeyevich Pushkin, born nearby, was christened in 1799. Inside, the low vaulted narthex adds to the impression of space beneath the dome in the main body of the church. A host of golden iconostases glitter as you enter. The icons are mostly early 19th-century. Buried behind cordons in the left chapel is Patriarch Sergei, one of the most controversial figures in the 20th-century Orthodox Church, who died in 1944. It was he who, in 1927, wrote the 'Declaration of Loyalty' to the Soviet State, exhorting believers to faithful citizenship of the Soviet Union. Whether, as the Archbishop of York Cyril Garbett believed, Sergei was merely following Jesus's call for his followers to be 'wise as serpents' and thereby saved the church from the full force of the anti-religious onslaught, or whether he compromised the church irrevocably, has been debated ever since. Beneath the elaborate golden tent roof in front of the main iconostasis lies his successor Alexei, who died in 1971.

In leafy Baumanskaya Square in front of the church stands a statue of the Bolshevik leader N. E. Bauman, after whom the area is named. He was murdered in 1905 not far from this spot. On the right side of the square the yellow and white 18th-century palace, now a library, has a bust of Pushkin in the courtyard. After lunch you might like to visit the Exhibition Hall of the Cultural Ministry of Russia (*see* p.230).

Eastern Moscow

Spasso-Andronikov Monastery (Спассо-Андроников монастырь)

In the 14th century Metropolitan Alexei of Russia moved from Vladimir to Moscow, founding this monastery in 1359 on the spot from which he first caught a glimpse of the Kremlin. Legend tells that during the building of the monastery, Princess Taidula, favourite wife of the Mongol Khan, went blind, and called on the Metropolitan's famous healing powers. Unable to refuse the request of the Mongol overlords, Alexei put the monk Andronik, a pupil of St Sergei Radonezhsky, in charge of the building. He cured the princess of her illness, and secured the khan's promise to uphold the reign of the 10-year old Prince Dmitry. Twenty years later, the prince defeated the Tartars at Kulikovo, and a number of the Russian dead were buried here, beneath the Saviour's Cathedral. By this time, the monastery had been named Spasso-Andronikov after its central church and founding abbot.

Today the monastery combines a satisfying mix of interesting architecture and excellent exhibitions of Russian icons with the peace and quiet you will have come to expect of Moscow's old religious enclaves. Don't be fooled by its alternative name, the Andrei Rublyov Museum of Old Russian Art—the monastery only contains one fragment of the painter's work, and that is hidden behind an iconostasis.

Getting There

🄜 Ploshchad Illicha. Turn right outside the swing gates, leave the subway and double back to the main road, Tulinskya Ul. Walk down it towards the prominent church and skyscraper. Beside the church turn right and head through the trees to the white walls and twin towers of the monastery.

Tickets for the three exhibitions are on sale to the right of the entrance (*open daily 11am–6pm; closed Wed and last Fri of the month*). The **Saviour's Cathedral** (Spassky Sobor) which stands ahead of you as you enter was built in 1425–27, and is the oldest and most influential stone building in Moscow. With its Vladimir-style single drum and helmet dome, and Muscovite bunches of *kokoshniki* gables, it graphically illustrates the transition Russian architecture underwent as Moscow gained pre-eminence. While in Vladimir and before that in Kiev the church had followed the tenets of Byzantine architecture, in Moscow the Russians wrested the initiative and transformed their churches into inimitable, colourful fantasies.

Solid, self-confident porches with minimal strategic decoration lead into the cathedral, in which they sell excellent reproductions of Rublyov's greatest works. It is startlingly bare, all the more so when you realize that it was painted by Rublyov himself, with a fellow monk Daniil Chyorny. Rublyov (*see* p.254) was a monk here, probably in the last years of his life, and may even be buried somewhere beneath the hallowed turf. It was his statue, cast to coincide with the putative 600th anniversary of his birth and the opening of the museum here in 1960, that greeted you before you entered the monastery.

To the left of the cathedral is a group of buildings including an early 16th-century **Refectory**, and the **Church of the Archangel Michael**, built in 1691–1739. Despite the decorative features copied from the earlier building in an attempt to get the tiered Baroque cathedral to blend in with it, the difference between the two cannot be disguised. The church was built by the Lopukhin family, shortly after the marriage of Eudoxia Lopukhina to Peter the Great. It now houses an exhibition tracing the history and restoration of the monastery and also displaying a selection of the elegant early biblical texts copied by the monks in Old Church Slavonic.

Beyond the cathedral on the left is the former monk's building, a pink 18th-century building with a leaning first floor, disguised as something much older. Inside you can see an exhibition devoted almost entirely to icons of St Nicholas, one of the most popular Russian saints (as he is with us in his guise as Father Christmas) and the patron saint of sailors. Walking on round the cathedral, under cover against the back wall of the monastery you will see what is left of the ornate carved gravestones which once dotted these grassy slopes. The Classical building currently under restoration near the gates (themselves a reconstruction dating from the 1950s), was the seminary. Don't miss the best part of the museum, which hides in the 16th-century Abbot's House to the right of the gates as you look at them. The outside of the building is whitewashed and decorated with tiles. Inside is a dazzling display of 16th- and 17th-century works.

Rogozhskoye Old Believers' Commune (Рогожское кладбище— *Rogozhskoye kladbishche*)

Those who manage to find this reclusive community of Old Believers tucked away beyond Taganskaya will find themselves light years off the tourist track and several hundred years back in time. Against extraordinary odds, including the closing of their churches for 50 years to 1905 followed by the onslaught of the Communist campaign against religion, this sect of the Orthodox Church has managed to survive underground, only to emerge recently with their faith, and in this case their church, intact. During the brief period of open worship here between 1905 and 1917, as well as building the neo-Russian belltower in celebration, the Old Believers also established community halls and hotels for visiting co-religionists. This was their Kremlin, the centre of their orthodoxy, and the icons in the cathedral fully justify the comparison.

Getting There

From Ⓜ Taganskaya walk up Taganskaya Ul. and take a No. 106 or 169 bus, or a No. 16, 16k or 26 trolleybus up Nizhegorodskaya Ul. Get off just before the road crosses the railway line, walk over the bridge and then left under another railway line, heading for the green and white belltower. Your first move should be to find someone to take you round. For this it would be best to be with a Russian speaker. Women must cover their head on the grounds of the community, and will not be allowed into the church in anything other than respectably long skirts.

lunch

If you can't wait until you get back to Taganskaya, where the choice is greater (*see* p.212), try the Carpathian Restaurant at Pl. Abdelmanovskoy Zastavy, where Taganskaya Ul. becomes Nizhegorodskaya Ul.

In 1771, Catherine the Great had given the Old Believers the right to practice their religion freely in Moscow. The **Cathedral of the Intercession** (Pokrovsky Sobor) was built by the great classical architect Matvei Kazakov in the early 1790s, just after he had finished building the Senate in the Kremlin. Known as the summer church and closed when it is really cold, the cathedral is lit only by candles and natural light. Walking into it takes your breath away. Every inch of wall space, from ceiling to floor, is plastered with a glittering collection of icons dating from before the split with the establishment church in 1653. Some were already in the possession of members of the community when the church was built, others were added later by successful Old Believer merchants, such as the Ryabushinskys and the Morozovs. Your guide will point the treasures out with pride, amongst them the icon of the Saviour in the iconostasis, encased in a metal icon cover, its elongated features and elegant lines thought to be the work of Andrei Rublyov (*see* p.344).

Walk on past the cathedral to find the **Winter Church of St Nicholas**, the oldest church the Old Believers erected here, in 1776. With its brightly coloured exterior, tent-roof and *kokoshniki* gables, it seems more in keeping with the 17th century. The gateway to the community cemetery, established in 1771 to cope with Old Believer victims in the cholera epidemic, adjoins the church.

Kuskovo (Кусково)

If you only have time to visit one sight on the outskirts of Moscow, let it be Kuskovo. Known as the Moscow Versailles, this palace complete with lake, gardens and park may be the closest you get to a stately home now that Archangelskoye and Ostankino are not always open. It is also a must for lovers of porcelain, since the orangery houses an extensive collection of ceramics from around the world.

It was built by the Sheremetev family, who had long distinguished themselves as military leaders and diplomats. With the advent of the Romanov dynasty, to whom they were related, there was a distinct upturn in their fortunes. Count Boris Petrovich fought gallantly alongside Peter the Great at the battle of Poltava against the Swedes in 1709, and his son, Peter Borisovich, made a spectacular marriage to Varvara Cherkassakava, another relative of the Romanovs, in 1743. The newly-weds' combined landholdings amounted to some 3 million acres, worked by 200,000 serfs. No wonder they decided to rebuild the Moscow estate at Kuskovo.

Getting There

Ⓜ Ryazánsky Prospekt. Leave the platform towards the front of the train (coming from the centre) and outside the station walk a little way to the right down the road to the last bus stop. Take the 208 or the 133 for six stops. This is a food-free zone for miles around – bring a picnic or starve.

The centrepiece of this 'scaled down transfer of Eden' (Prince I. M. Dolgorukov) is the palace, a pink and white wooden building looking over the lake. Raised between 1769–77, it is a monument to the serfs of the Sheremetev workshops, who with help from western advisors not only built and decorated it, but also painted many of the pictures and made the furniture. Chief among them was the architect Fyodor Argunov, who went on to build the palace of Ostankino north of

Moscow. A cobbled drive sweeps up to the front door, beneath a sturdy portico adorned with a sky blue cartouche on which the initials PS are picked out in white.

Buy your six tickets at the office outside the gate (*open April–Sept 10am–6pm Wed–Fri, 10am–7pm Sat and Sun, Oct–March 10am–4pm; closed Mon and Tues, and the last Wed of the month. In extreme weather conditions (summer humidity and winter cold) call ℗ 370 0260 to check.* Inside, the palace decoration combines naivity with the highest aesthetic qualities. The plaster, papier-maché and wooden decorative details on floor, wall and ceiling are stunning. There are explanatory texts in English in each room, but to whet your appetite contemplate: a room of Flemish garden landscape tapestries, so vibrant in their fantastic depiction of knot gardens, luscious vegetation and fountains that you come to believe you are looking out of a series of windows; an incredibly lifelike portrait of Catherine the Great in the corner Raspberry Drawing Room, her green eyes watery and perspicacious beneath the high, intelligent forehead; tall ceramic stoves, decorated with imaginary Elysian scenes by Gzhel. Even the grandeur of the White Hall, in which balls were regularly given, is tempered by the tasteful simplicity of the materials employed to decorate it. The paintings over the doorways, pastoral scenes by Sheremetev serfs, are rather better than the majority of bad 18th-century oils on the walls. These mar what is otherwise an aesthetic delight, and it is sad to think that the paintings that hung here at the time of the Revolution are probably sitting now in the storerooms of the Pushkin gallery, gathering nothing but dust.

Just outside the palace is the dull estate church, built in 1737, opposite the kitchens. Walking round the gardens anti-clockwise you come first to the **grotto**, also built by Argunov, its ornate Baroque exterior disguising an interior decorated with shells and minerals. It overlooks a pond beyond which stands an intriguing series of **five pavilions** set in delicately fenced compounds, which once housed an orntal menagerie. The nearby **Italian Cottage** houses an exhibition of 18th-century paintings and interiors including a cosy wood-lined study and a number of pieces of Italian sculpture.

Beneath the trees beyond the Italian Cottage, strange ridges in the ground give away the location of the Sheremetev's renowned **open-air theatre**, where performances were given every Sunday and sometimes on Thursdays during the summer. For many a year Praskovia Kovaleva, the daughter of a blacksmith, sang in the choir on this stage at performances before empresses and ambassadors. But it was only in 1789 that she caught the eye of young Nikolai Sheremetev, son of Count Peter Borisovich. Their love affair is one of the most romantic stories of the 18th century. For 10 years Nikolai wrestled with social convention, unable to reject his position in society, follow his instincts and marry the beautiful serf-actress. But finally in 1799 he granted her freedom, marrying her in 1800. The couple removed themselves from the scandalized eyes of society, to live out their heroic tragedy in the palace at Ostankino (*see* p.246). A small exhibition in the first part of the **Orangery** tells their story. The rest of the building is devoted to porcelain.

The rest of the garden pavilions are currently, as the Russian language so aptly puts it, 'restoring themselves'. There certainly don't seem to be any people involved. The **Hermitage** (1765–7) is a cross-shaped Baroque building by Karl Blank in pastel tones, while the **Dutch Cottage** (1749) is painted to look like brick. Last, and least, is a **Swiss House** built much later, in the 1860s, by Nikolai Benoit.

To walk round the lake , on which Peter Sheremetev staged mock battles for the amusement of his friends, you will have to leave the museum compound. The woods on the far side, with their long straight rides, stretch for miles.

Southeastern Moscow

Simonovsky Monastery (Симоновский монастырь)

The Simonovsky Monastery was established by Dmitry Donskoy in 1370, at the height of the Mongol threat, to be the forward post in Moscow's defences. An early seal of importance was affixed to the monastery by St Sergei Radonezhsky, one of the founders of monastic orthodoxy in Russia, who stayed here when he came to Moscow with the head of the monastery Fyodor, his nephew. The few fragments of monastic buildings that survive, far from the other sites of the city, are only of interest to real fans of Moscow's monastic architecture, however.

Getting There

Ⓜ Avtozavodskaya. The monastery is a short walk north at Vostochnaya Ul. 4. Look out for the shining copper roof over one of three remaining towers.

Even today, despite being blown up in 1934 and used since then as part of the Likhachov Automobile Works, you can get a sense of the immense fortifications from the remaining Dulo Tower at the far end and the stretch of wall. Admittedly these were built in the 16th and 17th centuries respectively, in a scale commensurate with the technology of the time, but the Simonovsky had been renowned for its ferocious stands, not to mention its zealous monks, for many centuries by then.

The factory, which made the black maria Zils in which party apparatchiks moved from privilege to privilege, has relinquished its hold on the monastery, but restoration proceeds at snail's pace. The two most impressive buildings still standing are the ornate Baroque refectory, one of the best examples of its type, and the tall, thin steep-roofed palace. Though small trees sprout from the roof of the refectory, its Dutch-style pediment façade still manages to convey the building's former glory.

Day Trips from Moscow

Moscow, with its year-round pollution, spring and autumn mud and summer dust, is sometimes the one place in the world you don't want to be. Luckily within easy reach are a handful of peaceful—and not so peaceful—monasteries and country dachas in which some of Russia's greatest artists, writers and composers have found inspiration. These are been listed in a clockwise direction round the city, beginning in the northwest.

If you have no car, every one of these day trips can be reached by suburban train from Moscow, except Tolstoy's house at Yasnaya Polyana. The trains are known as *elektrichkas*, tickets for which can be bought in the Suburban Hall (Пригородный Зал—Prigorodny Zal) at the appropriate train station. With the increasing bankruptcy of state enterprises, trains in the middle of the day are becoming scarcer: it has long been inadvisable to hope of leaving between 11am and 2pm. It is also worth bearing in mind that on Friday and Sunday evenings in summer outgoing and incoming trains (respectively) are packed. In 1992 Yeltsin offered anyone who wanted it 600 square metres of land to garden, and with the threat of inflation city dwellers rushed at the chance, mindless of the possible 3-hour journey to get there. (For more information on buying train tickets, *see* p.19).

Gone, sadly, are the days of the 1914 Baedeker's guide when every railway station had its restaurant serving dinner for under a rouble. Very few of the towns and villages visited in this chapter have even the simplest of cafés. To sustain yourselves, find a convenient supermarket or market in Moscow and get used to taking a picnic. In winter you can always eat it on the train.

Klin (Клин)

Klin is an old town, founded in 1318 and the ancestral home of the Romanov family, but the main reason for treking out here is to visit Tchaikovsky's last home.

Getting There

This small town lies 2 hours by *elektrichka* from Leningradsky Vokzal, some 80 kms out along Leningradskoye Shossé. Bring your own lunch.

In the small green wooden dacha at Ul. Tchaikovskovo 48 (*open 10am–6pm; closed Wed, Thurs and last Mon of month*) the composer lived from 1885 until his death in 1893. Here he escaped from the opprobrium of a society which viewed his homosexuality as a 'vile oriental habit' to write some of his finest, most lyrical music. Two of his three great ballet scores, *Sleeping Beauty* and *The Nutcracker*, and his final (sixth) symphony, the *Pathétique,* flowed from his pen between these walls. Soon after the premier of this symphony in St Petersburg, Tchaikovsky died of cholera after ignoring advice not to drink the water during an epidemic. Rumours persist that this was a form of 'honourable' suicide, into which he was forced after an affair with a young aristocrat. If the anniversaries of his birth (7 May) and death (6 November) fit into your schedule, come then and listen to the virtuoso concerts here at his house.

Abramtsevo and Khotkovo (Абрамцево и Хотково)

These two small country villages, a couple of kilometres apart, make for an easy picnic trip into countryside beloved by Russian 19th-century landscape painters. The wooden house and estate at Abramtsevo are the main focus of the journey. They now form a peaceful museum in memory of their role as the spiritual home of the Russian arts and crafts movement known as the *Style Moderne*. The nearby convent in Khotkovo, and the old streets around it, are a mere addendum. On a long summer's day, by car, you could combine these villages with the nearby monastery at Sergeyev Possad (*see* below).

Getting There

Elektrichkas leave for Abramtsevo and Khotkovo from Yaroslavsky Station, itself one of the finest examples of Russian *moderne* architecture, commissioned by Savva Mamontov, the patron and railway magnate who lived at Abramtsevo. The architect of this overblown Russian dolls' house, with its exaggerated pitched roof, curvaceous porches and tiled strawberry decorations was none other than Fyodor Shektel, the man who turned the *zeitgeist* of turn-of-the-century, Slavophile Moscow into stone (*see* p.151). At Abramtsevo cross the railway line and walk straight ahead through the forest, where small, almost entirely faded pink signs point the way to the museum. When you reach the main road, it's left to the estate museum, standing on the hill beyond the pond, or right to Khotkovo and its convent. By car, follow Prospekt Mira onto the Yaroslavskoye Shossé and turn off after 61km, where Khotkovo and Abramtsevo are signposted.

If you are driving, **Russkaya Skazka**, ✆ 184 3436, by the 41km post on the road from Moscow offers the best food in the area. Inside the fairytale wooden building, avoid the *zakuski* and opt for the hearty country soups and stews. Don't rely on finding anything in the villages. There is a small shop opposite the entrance to the museum at Abramtsevo, but you take your chances with what you will find. A picnic by the lake would be ideal.

The roots of Russian culture, starved by the 18th-century preference for imported architects and architecture, painters and genres, theatre directors and plays, received a new draught of nutrients after the defeat of Napoleon in 1812. This victory restored Russia's confidence in her own inheritance, and gave birth to the Slavophile movement. Everything the Westernizers had spurned was re-evaluated, from the early Russian epic poems, through icon painting and medieval architecture to the age-old Russian skill of carpentry. Two important Slavophiles lived at Abramtsevo estate: first (in the 1840s–60s) the writer Sergei Aksakov, and secondly the industrialist Mamontov, who established an art school in the grounds in the 1870s. While Aksakov and his literary sons helped to thrash out the Slavophile philosophy, Mamontov turned Abramtsevo into a slowly evolving think-tank on Russian artistic culture. Here lived painters and potters, opera singers and theatre directors, encouraging the development of each other's art forms. Abramtsevo, with its wood and lakeland garden so often captured by the quintessential Russian (Jewish) landscape painter Isaac Levitan, lies at the heart of the Russian aesthetic. (*Museum open 11am–5pm; closed Mon, Tues and 30th of month.*)

The main house, originally built in 1771, contains an exhibition reflecting the ownership of both Aksakov and Mamontov. Several rooms, including Aksakov's study, the sitting room with its suite of simple birch furniture and the small writing room in which Gogol worked towards the end of his life, recall the early, literary phase. These walls once echoed to a literary legend, the first chapters of *Dead Souls*, Vol. II, which Gogol read out here, to Turgenev among others, but burned before his death. Other rooms, such as the dining room and the red sitting room, are hung with works by the Abramtsevo artists, Victor and Apollinaire Vasnetsov, Ilya Repin and Valentin Serov, who had come to Abramtsevo as an eight-year old and went on to become one of Russia's foremost painters. A copy of his most famous work, *The Girl with Peaches*, graces the dining room where it was painted. It is a delightful portrait of Mamontov's daughter Vera, who died when still quite young and is buried on the estate. Also in this room are Repin's portraits of Mamontov and his wife Elizaveta, and a still-life. The simple wooden dining furniture was produced here at the Abramtsevo workshop and was sold, from 1880, in the Abramtsevo shop in Moscow. The ceramic tiled fireplace, like others in the house, was also produced in the ceramics workshop on the estate, and is by the visionary artist Mikhail Vrubel. For him, the point of Abramtsevo was to capture 'the music of the whole man, not a sensibility disembodied by the attractions of the regimented and poverty-striken West.' A table in the red drawing room is covered with embroidered signatures of Mamontov's famous and not so famous guests. Theatre designs for Mamontov's opera company hang in the theatrical room, with its piano.

A range of buildings and sculptures dot the Abramtsevo garden, all of them part of an architectural hymn to Mother Russia. Close to the house is the kitchen, filled with an unparalleled collection of wooden domestic implements, most of which were collected by Elizaveta Mamontova and Elena Polenova for the folk art museum they set up here in the 1880s. The ceramics studio next door, with its complex wooden fretwork architectural details, contains work by Vrubel and his pupils. Not far from it, in a weather-proof hut, is his park bench, entitled 'Divan'. Some of its majolica tiles show images from Russian folk mythology, including the omnipresent woman-bird, the Siren. There seems to be an element of Vrubel's tortured soul in every fractured thing he made. The Mamontovs did not take to him when their protegé Serov first introduced him to them, but little by little his genius won them over. Vrubel was something of a conspiracy theorist, imagining himself to be the butt of most of them. When he tossed off a sketch for an interior which Serov and Korovin had been working on for days, he muttered knowingly that 'people born to paint frescoes never get the commissions.' He ended his life in a mental asylum in 1910, so perhaps someone was conspiring.

On the other side of the house two Scythian goddess carvings stand near the wooden guest hut, while beyond, in a glade, hides the famous Abramtsevo Church of the Saviour Not-Made-by-Hands. Built in 1882 to designs by the painters Victor Vasnetsov and Vasily Polenov, it seems like an immaculate dolls' cathedral. A basic square topped by a single, helmet-shaped dome, with bells hung in gaps in the wall, it recalls the early cathedrals not only of Vladimir and Suzdal but also of the northern principality of Novgorod. The ceramic tiles which decorate the exterior were made in Abramtsevo, and if you get into the interior you should find a colourful wooden iconostasis with icons by Repin (the 'martyred intellectual' Saviour), Vasnetsov (St Sergei Radonezhsky) and Polenov (the Royal Gate's Annunciation). Nearby in the woods is the Hut on Chickens' Legs, inspired by the same old Russian fairytale that gave birth to one of Mussorgsky's *Pictures at an Exhibition*. In it the witch, Baba Yaga, lives in an awe-inspiring hut built on real, massive chickens' claws, a building which stalks through every Russian childhood.

Its a long, peaceful walk to Khotkovo if the weather is good, though the Soviet era has taken its toll on the convent and there is little to see there even when the Cathedral of the Intercession (*Pokrovsky Sobor*) is open. A convent was originally founded here in 1308, but was destroyed by the Poles during the Time of Troubles in the early 17th century. Today's cathedral dates from its reconstruction, but still contains the 14th-century remains of the parents of Russia's most important saint, Sergei, whose Trinity Monastery is the main attraction of Sergeyev Possad below.

Sergeyev Possad (Сергеев Поссад)

Of the medieval cities on the Golden Ring northeast of Moscow, only Sergeyev Possad and its paramount monastery can be seen easily in a day trip from the capital. The most important religious institution in the CIS outside Kiev, it stands on a hill, master of all it surveys, boasting its eclectic selection of colourful buildings and jewel-filled museums. Until the Revolution the monastery attracted over 100,000 pilgrims a year, and no Russian aristocrat's calendar was complete without an annual visit. In the Soviet period it became a museum, but was partly returned to the church during the Second World War, when it was the home of the Patriarch and the most important seminary in the country. Today it is both tourist attraction and place of pilgrimage, with black robed monks and priests in bejewelled copes and mitres ministering to the needy and the nosey. The gaggle of misshapen beggars at the gate and fervent queues at the holy well and the tomb of St Sergius bring back ghostly memories of the central role of monasteries in Russian history. But don't be surprised if a monk whisks a set of postcards for sale from beneath his surplice. Like everywhere else in Russia, the monastery has trouble making ends meet. (*Open 10am–5pm; closed Mon. Icons and Folk Art Exhibitions also closed Thurs and last Wed of month; Early Russian Applied Art also closed Tues and last Fri of month. To book English-language tours call © 8254 45356/45350.*)

Getting There and Around

Elektrichkas from Yaroslavsky Station travel the 75km to Sergeyev Possad, or Zagorsk as it was known during the Soviet period. At the other end simply head for the visible monastery belltower, some 15 minutes' walk. To drive, take Yaroslavskoye Shossé, the continuation of Prospect Mira.

lunch

Russkaya Skazka (*see* p.262). In the town itself, **Zolotoye Koltso**, the state-run restaurant 5 minutes' walk from the monastery, back along the road to Moscow and the train station, is intensively used by Intourist and other coach groups. If you cannot get in to it, buy a makeshift picnic in the shop across the car park from the monastery entrance or bring your own.

To the left of the main road from Moscow and the town railway station, the large red brick building at Prospekt Krasnoy Armii 123 houses the **Toy Museum**, by-product of the town's *matrioshka* industry. *Open 10am–5pm; closed Mon and Tues.* Its large collection surveys the history of Russian dolls and other toys from their origins as pagan corn dollies right up to the height of Soviet kitsch and beyond. A fascinating fact emerges—the ubiquitous *matrioshka* only colonized Russia from Japan at the turn of the century.

The beggar-beseiged gateway into the **Trinity Sergius Monastery** (*Troitse-Sergeyeva lavra*) passes in painted splendour beneath the Gate-Church of St John the Baptist, which was built in the 1690s with Stroganov family money. From its foundation in the 1340s, the monastery was deluged with gifts from Russia's rich and powerful families, including the tsars. The home of Russian monasticism, it is also identified with the emergence of modern Russia from the dark ages of Mongol rule. It was founded by a charismatic hermit, Sergei Radonezhsky, whose hallowed reputation not only attracted a handful of monkish followers but also the attention of the princes of Moscow. When Muscovy faced the threat of a 400,000 strong Mongol army in 1380, it was Sergei Radonezhsky (*c.* 1321–91) who urged Prince Dmitry Donskoy to stand up to the infidel, blessing the prince and assuring him that God was on his side. Sure enough, the 100,000-strong Russian army inflicted the first defeat on the Mongols for 140 years. The Trinity Monastery of St Sergius became the head of a network of 24 monasteries, set up in the northeast of the country by Sergius' disciples. Further miracles enhanced its reputation. Sergius' body survived the 1408 devastation of the monastery by the Mongols, and he was soon after canonized. In 1608–10 the monks heroically withstood a 16-month seige by the Poles, lifting Russian morale during the Time of Troubles. By the 18th century the monastery had been bequeathed vast tracts of the countryside and owned some half a million serfs. Travellers at the time marvelled at its richness and at the worldly existence of its inhabitants. A 'meagre dinner' with the Metropolitan included 'two courses and besides caviare, fish soup, kissel (jelly) and stewed barley, we had a variety of fishes dressed in a great variety of ways… Russian Ale, a Levant Wine… and two glasses of different sweet wines' all served by 'a pretty Turkish boy… whom [the Metropolitan] seemed to treat with great tenderness' (John Parkinson, *A Tour of Russia, Siberia and the Crimea 1792–1794*).

As you enter the monastery you come face to apse with the **Cathedral of the Assumption**, the largest church in the ensemble, which was built in 1559–85 and modelled on the rather smaller Cathedral of the Assumption in the Kremlin. It is another monument, like St Basil's in Red Square, to Ivan the Terrible's rout of the Mongols from their stronghold in Kazan, which it joyfully celebrates with a bulbous collection of star-studded domes and 17th-century frescoes within (though it rarely seems to be open). To the left of the main pathway rises the refectory and **Church of St Sergius**, built in 1686–92. The fact that the building is not open to tourists matters little, as photographs of the 19th-century interior make it look unexceptional, whereas the multi-coloured exterior with its ornate Baroque stone details and vine-entwined pillars is anything but. The small Church of St Micah by the porch of the refectory was erected in the first half of the 18th century.

The two single-domed churches nearby are the oldest surviving buildings in the monastery. The whitewashed church to the right, the **Church of the Holy Ghost**, was built by Pskov architects in 1476–7. Its open drum-cum-belltower is highly unusual. The simpler stone building with its golden dome straight ahead is even older. The helmet-shaped dome gives that away, though the gold leaf doubtless dates from the Soviet period, when one Orthodox priest was heard to complain that the church was too rich. Congregations continued to give large amounts of money, but the church was forbidden to spend it on missionary work, Sunday schools or publishing. In the few working parishes, having paid the priest's salary, the only way to use the money was on the fabric of the church. And nothing used it up better than gold leaf. Known as the **Cathedral of the Trinity**, the building was erected in 1422, after the Mongols had burned the wooden monastery to the ground, as a mausoleum for the body of the recently canonized St Sergius. He lies within to this day. It is the most hallowed spot in the monastery and its interior has an aesthetic and spiritual intensity not found anywhere else in the Moscow region.

Floor, icons, walls, and even the air, seem heavy with the weight of 570 years of worship. St Sergius lies beneath the ornate silver palanquin in front of the iconostasis on the right. The small icon hanging over the nearby door in the iconostasis portrays him. The iconostasis, partly the work of one of St Sergius' monks, the famous icon-painter Andrei Rublyov and his 15th-century contemporary Daniil Chorny, is one of the greatest examples in the world. In the local tier, to the right of the royal gates, you will find a copy of Rublyov's famous icon of the Trinity, which was painted for this very cathedral but now hangs in the Tretyakov Gallery. Above, in a harmonious row, their heads inclining towards the Saviour over the gates, are the figures of the deisis row, interceding with Jesus on our behalf. The next tier, the Holiday tier, illustrates the events celebrated by great church holy days while above it are images of saints and finally the Old Testament prophets. The five-tiered iconostasis, with full-length figures in the deisis row, is specific to 15th-century Russia, when the spiritual intensity of the new monasticism produced an artistic flowering unequalled until the early 20th-century avant-garde. Standing before this unified hierarchy of the heavens, set against a luminous golden backdrop representing the world of the spirit, all the components can be seen at a glance, united in one harmonious celebration of belief. Sadly, the frescoes painted by Rublyov and Chorny do not survive though in their place are some fine 17th-century wall paintings which echo the rhythm and harmony of the iconostasis.

In the corner of the monastery, beyond the refectory and beside the Cathedral of the Trinity is the pink and white 18th-century **Metropolitan's Palace**. The long row of buildings behind the cathedral contain three exhibitions which will be discussed later. In the meantime return to the entrance to the Cathedral of the Assumption, passing an obelisk telling the history of the monastery in *bas relief*, and the colourful late 17th-century **Chapel-over-the-Well**, a Baroque tower church of three octagonal tiers, covering the monastery's sacred spring. If legend is to be believed, it was here that St Sergius smote the earth with a stick, and water miraculously poured forth, causing the foundation of the monastery. Closer still to the cathedral is the burial vault of Tsar Boris Godunov and his family.

All of this is massively overshadowed by the gargantuan blue and white, five-tiered **belltower**, built between 1740 and 1770 and deeply influenced by the contemporary Baroque buildings Rastrelli was erecting for the Empresses Anna and Elizabeth in St Petersburg. Once the roost of 40 bells, its 88 metres soar into the sky with consummate ease, culminating in a squared golden cupola. Behind it stands a Baroque rotunda, the **Church of the Virgin of Smolensk**, built while the belltower was under construction. To the left is the part tiled, tent-roof of the **Church of Ss Zosima and Savvaty**, an early 17th-century monastic infirmary chapel. You can sometimes get up into the 18th-century **Pilgrims' Gate Tower** beyond, to admire the view and walk along the immaculately restored gallery which runs inside the massive 16th-century walls.

The last building of interest in the monastery is known as the **Tsar's Chambers**, built for Peter the Great's devout father Alexei Mikhailovich. It was here that the young Peter lived when he fled from the *streltsy* uprising whipped up by his step-sister Sophia in Moscow in 1682, and where he gathered support to overthrow her regency in 1698. Built in the second half of the 17th-century with a playful use of ceramic tiles and Moscow Baroque ornaments, it has been radically changed over the years and now houses the theological college. In the monastery's heyday, the monks here learned not only about religion but were an island of aesthetic and intellectual ferment in an otherwise illiterate sea. As well as the punishing daily round of prayers and work in the fields, they were encouraged to study the strict tenets of icon-painting from inspired masters such as Rublyov, and to copy illuminated bibles in painstaking Old Church Slavonic. In 1744 the monastery was awarded the ultimate accolade of becoming one of a handful of Russian Orthodox *lavra*, the highest rank of teaching monastery.

Some of the monks' early artistic successes are still to be seen in the monastery's three exhibitions. The one in the infirmary is mostly concerned with the remarkable restoration undertaken during the Soviet period. In the Treasury next door are exhibitions of early Russian icons (14th–17th centuries) and later Russian and Soviet folk art. Though elements of the spirit of medieval Russian icons obviously do pass into the later folk art, there is something rather forced about linking these two qualitatively different exhibitions as one seamless whole. A number of the early icons, including the intense, high-browed depiction of the kindly St Nicholas, are thought to have been the personal property of St Sergius. The exhibition also contains the original 15th-century Royal Gates from the iconostasis in the Cathedral of the Trinity. In the 16th century the simple spirituality of Russia's great period of icon painting disappeared, to be replaced by a greater interest in narrative and detail. With Simon Ushakov's icon of the *Last Supper*, a masterpiece of its kind, the simple, almost symbolic 15th-century heritage is finally subsumed by the lessons of the Italian Renaissance. The folk art exhibits include Russian costumes, domestic implements and a particularly fine collection of old Russian architectural decorations such as window frames and eaves of lace-like fretwork.

The last exhibition in the monastery is in the Sacristy, behind the Cathedral of the Trinity, and contains early Russian applied art of the same period—from precious embroidered coffin palls to jewel-encrusted copes and mitres. The early 15th-century embroidery of St Sergius shows a kind, rather simian figure with the same simple intensity as the icons of the time. While icon-painting was a male preserve, it was women who performed embroidery as a sign of their devotion. The pearl-studded *podea* (icon cover) depicting the appearance of the Virgin to St Sergius, surrounded by other biblical scenes, was a gift to the monastery from Tsar Vassily III and his wife, who hoped their piety might bring them a long-awaited heir. Much of the astounding collection of early metalwork and jewellery was made by monks at the monastery. Look out for the mid to late 15th-century work of the monk Amvrosy, particularly his inlaid wooden triptych encased in golden filigree. Beside the works of the monks are articles produced in the royal workshops in Moscow, which came into their own in the 16th century. The embroidery of this period is mesmerising in its intricate detail and varying textures, and was indeed known as 'needle painting'. A number of icon cases were made at, or presented to, the monastery to protect and enhance its most precious work, the Trinity by Rublyov. While incredible objects in themselves, their outrageous opulence seems at sixes and sevens with the direct simplicity of the icon itself—expressions of worldly rather than spiritual riches. They reflect the contradiction implicit in monastic life by the 17th century, when these repositories of the nation's spirituality were also amongst its richest landowners.

Yasnaya Polyana (Ясная Поляна)

Many Russians would think it sacrilegious to call a visit to Tolstoy's estate a day trip. You make a pilgrimage to this shrine, which has come to symbolize the physical and psychic heart of Russia. Not only did this landscape give birth to the consummate novelist, but it informed his love of the Russian countryside and its inhabitants, a love for which the Soviet intelligentsia and their successors yearn with a rampant nostalgia. 'Without my Yasnaya Polyana,' Tolstoy wrote, 'I can hardly imagine Russia and my attitude to it.' Thank God for Yasnaya Polyana!

Getting There

About three hours and some 190km from Moscow, this day trip is only really feasible by car, or on a tour with Intourist or another private company (*see* p.20). Take Varshavskoye Shossé due south to Tula, find the main street, Prospekt Lenina, and follow it out of town, resisting the temptation to bear right. Tears of intellectual chagrin have already been wept over the belching smelting plant you come to some 20km later. Yasnaya Polyana, not far from this industrial behemoth, has suffered the effects of serious pollution for some years and will doubtless never be the same again, but if you have never been here before you will still find it rural and peaceful. The adventurous could try the train to Tula from Kursky Vokzal, and then a bus to the estate. Usual lunch story: bring your own or go without.

Once through the playful turrets at the entrance, you enter a complex of buildings little changed since they constituted a typical 19th-century estate, set in many acres of gladed woodland, meadows and orchards, interrupted by rivers and ponds, birch benches and bridges. Count Lev Tolstoy (1828–1910) was born and brought up here, a member of the rural nobility, and inherited the estate in 1847. The house in which he lived with his own family, just a wing of the porticoed mansion which he sold to be carted away piece by piece in 1856, functions as a memorial museum, while the Kuzminsky's house, where Tolstoy's sister-in-law and family spent many summers, is now a Literary Museum. In 1918, while Tolstoy's wife was still alive, Lenin signed a resolution placing the estate under government protection, and despite looting and burning by the Germans in the Second World War the house is still full of Tolstoy family possessions, including the writer's 22,000 tome library. (*Estate open 9am–5pm; closed Mon, Tues and last Wed of the month.*)

True to Tolstoy's earnest simplicity, there is nothing pretentious about his house or furniture. Approaching the front door your attention may be caught by the balustrade around the verandah, decorated with charming child-like cut-out figures of people, horses and cockerels. The largest room was used as a dining room and sitting room, and contains two pianos as well as a dining table. Tolstoy was a good player himself, accompanying whoever was around to sing or playing duets with his wife. In his study, you will see the Persian walnut desk, inherited from his father, at which both *War and Peace* and *Anna Karenina* were written, as well as the great leather sofa on which Tolstoy himself was born. The touching low chair on which he sat towards the end of his life conjours an image of the writer, his sight failing, crouched over the paper in front of him straining his eyes to edit the manuscript handed back to him, typed, by his secretary.

It seems sad that in these idyllic surroundings such hostility developed between the ever more humble Tolstoy and his socially-conscious wife Sofia Andreyevna. Tolstoy's vegetarianism, as he himself pointed out, was out of place with the 'silver service for twelve, two servants and roses costing one and a half roubles a piece' which she insisted on in the dining room. From 1908 he took his meals alone, and on 28 October 1910, he finally decided to renounce it all and left the house in the company of his doctor. Catching a cold at the small railway station of Astapovo, he died two days later in the station master's hut.

In the literary museum you will find exhibits illustrating Tolstoy's career and public life, as well as copies of his books in a polyglot assortment of editions. To find the writer's grave, follow the well-worn path into the wooded glade. A simple mound with no headstone surrounded by grass, it is as Tolstoy wanted it, an eloquent statement of his desire for humility.

Peredelkino (Переделкино)

Mention Peredelkino to any Russian and they will immediately think of writers. For it was here that the Soviet government allotted land to the powerful Writers' Union to build dachas for their members. And build them they did, along a rational grid-work of lanes overshadowed by towering forest, each bearing the of a different Russian literary hero. For months at a time, summer and winter, Moscow's scribes would live here, often in a state of considerable luxury, since the size of Soviet print runs and the royalty system made even second-rate writers a good living. Among them, also, worked figures who were tormented and hounded for their pains. After the smuggling out and publication of *The Gulag Archipelago* in the west in January 1974, Alexander Solzhenitsyn continued his imperative chronicling of Soviet abuses in the spare room of a writer friend's dacha here, scribbling in minute, concealable notebooks. Within a month he had been arrested and exiled.

Today, many of the dachas still conceal literary denizens, though foreigners and anyone else who can afford it are fast moving in. The point of the trip is a rest from the Moscow smog, a chance to experience the impenetrable and much loved Russian forest and a quick trip to Pasternak's *dacha* and the church.

Peredelkino, a little over half an hour from Kievsky Vokzal, is served by frequent *elektrichkas*. Bus 47, from the end of the arrival platform, will deposit you three stops on at the end of Ul. Pavelyenko, in which Boris Pasternak's dacha is to be found. If you would rather walk for 20 minutes, continue along the footpath beside the railway line and follow as it snakes up to the road. Turn left and walk past the cemetery and dachas until you come to Ul. Pavelyenko on the right, after a wide open field.

If travelling by car you should take the continuation of Kutuzovsky Prospekt, Mozhaiskoye Shossé, turning off at the signposted exit after 21km. Finding your way from there is well-nigh impossible. Just hope that you pass someone and ask for the cemetery (кладбище—*kladbishche*).

where to stay/lunch

The former Komsomol (Young Communist) resthouse was taken over by an Italian family and renamed **Villa Peredelkino** (✆ 435 1478/8184/8345, 🖷 435 1478). You will find it at the end of Pervaya Chobotovskaya Allyeya, across the railway line from the arrival platform. Turn first left down this alley; the hotel is hidden behind a concrete wall at the end. Prices for function rooms are outrageous, and the cost of genuine Italian food such as melon and parma ham is also fairly steep. In addition on my last visit, various former directors of the Komsomol had accused the Italians of ripping them off, and were threatening to close the place down. You are strongly advised to check up by booking first by phone. If the hotel has been closed down, the only alternative is a picnic or returning to the city.

To Westerners brought up on David Lean's film of *Doctor Zhivago* (the theme tune of which, incidentally, is unknown in Russia), it seems unbelievable that the novel was only finally published in Russia in 1986. Lulled into a false sense of liberalism, as many were, by the Krushchev 'thaw' of 1955–6, Pasternak brought his novel out of the closet, only to have it published in translation in 1958 and banned at home. For its attitude of disillusion at the way the Revolution had panned out, the writer was expelled from the union, and forced to decline the 1958 Nobel Prize for Literature. Two years later, he died in this dacha, now the **Pasternak House Museum** (*open 10am–6pm; closed Mon, Tues and Wed*).

The house is extremely bare, conjuring up images of post-mortem confiscations, but the guides, photographs and few paintings by Pasternak's famous father, Leonid, do their best to bring it to life In Russia, Pasternak is known as a superb translator of Shakespeare (among others) and as a mellifluous poet. *Doctor Zhivago*, his only long novel, is seen as a minor work. This, and anything else you wish to discuss, can be taken up with the enthusiastic custodians of the museum, one of whom can normally be found to speak English.

To find **Pasternak's grave**, go back to the burnished cupolas of the small 15th-century Church of the Transfiguration above the railway station. Its rather unattractive yellow ochre and white exterior entirely belies the painted jewel within, where busy iconostases vie with a multitude of saintly figures on the dark walls. The main iconostasis contains a fine icon of the Virgin to the left of the royal gates. Take the road straight out of the church to the cemetery and hug the right hand edge of the graves. A few metres before you are ejected into the open countryside, turn right to the patch of graves surrounded by small conifers. There, doubtless decked with flowers, is a gravestone with a contorted portrait of Pasternak. Nearby is the grave of an 18-year-old victim of the war in Afghanistan whose mourning mother made me wonder why I was trudging into this place of sadness to see the grave of a man I never even knew. If the stalks of the flowers are all broken off, think of it as a sign of the times. It's to stop people augmenting their income by stealing the tributes and reselling them to other visitors.

Zvenigorod (Звенигород)

Zvenigorod is commonly known as Moscow's Switzerland, but remember that everything, including hilliness, is relative. It stands on a bluff above the valley of the upper reaches of the River Moskva and was, during the Soviet period, a privileged holiday centre, where both KGB and military kept enclaves of dachas for their workforces. It's a good place to come for a hazy summer's picnic, when you can alternate swimming in the clean water of the river with a little gentle sightseeing. The air is clean out here, and the old town, uphill from the city centre, seems to represent Russian life as it has been for hundreds of years, bar the addition of electricity and mains water. Most of the cosy wooden houses you see today, individually painted and some with masterful carved wooden architectural decoration, date from the beginning of the century. However they would have replaced houses which differed very little, a good wooden house lasting well over 100 years. Chekhov lived and worked here in 1884, writing a strange early story, *Room No. 6*, about a doctor (he was one) going mad. It seems an odd subject in this healthy-setting, though quite in keeping with Chekhov's later plays in which the quietly malevolent countryside exerts a disintegrating influence on human relationships.

Getting There

Zvenigorod lies on a branch which turns off the main line railway from Belorussky Vokzal at Golitsyno station, and direct trains to the town are infrequent. If there isn't one, take a train to Golitsyno and cram onto a local bus or bargain with a car driver to take you the remaining 10km. A well-informed driver will point out that this is where Pushkin's most formative childhood influence, his nanny Arina Rodionovna, came from.

lunch

If you trawl the shops in Zvenigorod town centre you could probably rustle up a picnic of sorts, but you would be well advised to bring your own food.

Zvenigorod is one of the most ancient towns in the region, its oldest extant church older than any in Moscow. Unfortunately it is almost impossible to describe how to get to it, and you will just have to ask for help finding it along the labyrinth of paths in the tree-lined hills. Known as the **Cathedral of the Assumption** (Успенский собор—*Uspensky sobor*), it was built in 1396–9 by the local prince Yuri Dmitrivich, son of Prince Dmitry Donskoy of Moscow who had inflicted the first Russian victory on the Mongols in 1380. It is a simple, single-domed cube reminiscent of the earlier cathedrals in the Golden Ring, and if you leave Moscow early you may find it open for the morning service from 9.30am–12 noon. Otherwise you will have to beg at the priest's house next door.

Zvenigorod's main attraction, the **Monastery of Savva-Storozhevsky**, is visible from the road that winds out of town along the Moskva valley (*open 10am–5pm; closed Mon*). It was started at the turn of the 14th century by Savva, a disciple of Sergei Radonezhsky of Sergeyev Possad (*see* above), with the financial assistance of Prince Yuri, but really came into its own in the mid 17th century. Much of today's monastery was built for the pious, nature-loving Tsar Alexei Mikhailovich, who spent as much time as possible out of Moscow. This was his favourite religious retreat, and as a result became one of the most important and richest monasteries in Russia. In May 1918 the monks led a short-lived local counter revolution against the Bolsheviks, for which many of them paid with their lives. In 1919 the monastery was closed down. For most of the Soviet period it was a museum of local history, and although it is now being restored there are as yet no plans for the return of monks. There are, however, occasional services in the central, golden-domed 15th-century **Cathedral of the Nativity**, which is well worth getting inside for what has been revealed of its graceful 17th-century frescoes.

The first big building on the left is the **Transfiguration Church**, closed except for its multi-tiered belltower, which looks over the walls of the monastery to the fertile valley with its clutch of new dachas and the sinuous bends of the river. Just beyond it is the **Trinity Church**, which also dates from the 1650s but has the 19th-century classical Kazan Refectory church attached to it. It was here that icons of the Saviour, Archangel Michael and St Paul by Andrei Rublyov (*see* p.344) were discovered in 1918, and that the great director Tarkovsky filmed much of his meditation on the nature of the most famous medieval icon painter, called simply *Andrei Rublyov*. Sadly, no icons by the genius can be seen here today. The red and white single-storey building running down the left-hand wall is the **Tsaritsa's Chambers**, built for Tsar Alexei's wife in a style reminiscent of earlier, medieval buildings. In its main porch you will see both double- and single-headed eagles carved, the former the emblem of the Russian rulers, the latter of his wife's native land, Poland. Inside, the local history museum traces the occupation of the site from the Iron Age through to the establishment of the monastery with maps and pictures of participants, ending with works from an uninspiring later iconostasis.

Even if you can't get into it, it is worth admiring the nearby Cathedral of the Nativity with its tall drum, *kolkoshniki* gables and bold band of Vladimir-Suzdal-style carving running round the wall. Against the bottom wall of the monastery are the white, two-storey monks' quarters, containing exhibitions by the highly-talented local contemporary ceramicist, Ilya Kuprianov, and a strange collection of oriental objects—mostly ceramics, paintings and wood carvings—left to the museum by a local resident. The tall white building with its magnificent new pitched roof and row of tall chimneys, opposite the porch of the cathedral, was Tsar Alexei Mikhailovich's palace. A walk round the massive, forified walls reveals solid octagonal turrets with traditional wooden roofs built at the same time.

Where to Stay

If you don't want to leave the peace of Zvenigorod and return to the big smoke, call Moscow ✆ (095) 473 4428 or 3206 between 10am and 5pm weekdays, and they should be able to fix you up with a room in a former Central Party Committee health resort. Ringing a few days in advance is the only way to be sure, however.

New Jerusalem Monastery (Новоярусалимский монастырь)

This monastery, sitting on its hill surrounded by lush countryside, is unusual; while many of the others around Moscow formed part of the city's outer defences, this was built purely as an expression of the might of the church. It was the idea of Patriarch Nikon, who was invested in 1652 and whose position went rather to his head. It was he who caused the great Orthodox schism which drove the Old Believers out of the church (*see* p.46), and at every turn, not least here, he seemed to be implying that his own power was equal to if not greater than that of the tsar. For his arrogance he was stripped of his position in 1666 and exiled from Moscow.

He ended his days here in 1681, in the monastery he had been building since 1656, and is buried in the gargantuan cathedral at its heart. Building work continued into the 18th century. During the Second World War, the monastery was occupied by the Germans, who blew it up as they left. Much has now been restored, but work on the cathedral still has a long way to go. A trip to the monastery and its surroundings in summer gives you a good insight into Russian suburban life on the fringes of the countryside, and the Muscovites' obsession with gardening. In 1993, as city dwellers succumbed to panic about food prices the following winter, even the banks of the railway were planted with potatoes.

Getting There

Though trains for the monastery start from Rizhsky Vokzal, it is quicker to go to Ⓜ Voikovskaya and join the route at the nearby railway platform called Leningradskaya (Ленинградская). To find it turn left out of the underground train (if you are coming from downtown), up the stairs and then right in the underpass. Take the left hand exit onto the street, walk straight on along the road and turn right after a couple of hundred yards, just before a building with a large Aeroflot (Аэрофлот) advertising board on its roof. The station is at the end of the building, down a slope. Buy a ticket for Novaya Yerusalimskaya (Новая Ярусалимская). You'll known when to get off as you will have seen the monastery, looking more like a Buddhist stupa than an Orthodox church, rising in the distance to the right of the lines. At the station, go under the tracks to the right, turn right on the road and walk a few yards to the bus stop. Any bus will deliver you at the monastery in two stops. Drivers should take the Volokolamskoye Shossé (the extension of Leningradsky Prospekt) to the town of Istra (35km) and carry on for a further 2km. For lunch, picnic or go without.

The monastery as a whole is conceived as an architectural hymn to the holiest of cities, Jerusalem. The massive walls and towers, completed in 1697, bears like Sion, Gethsemene and Damascus Towers; you can visit almost all of them via the covered walkway round the inside of the walls. Buy tickets for all the exhibits (*dlya vsyekh*) at the office on the left outside the monastery walls. They won't sell tickets for the cathedral unless you are in a group, but you can usually find one inside and tag along (*open 10am–4pm; closed Mon, Tues and last Fri in month*).

The central **Cathedral of the Resurrection** (Voskresensky Sobor) is based on the Church of the Holy Sepulchre in Jerusalem, though its external appearance is hardly Romanesque. It seems a particular irony that the man who wished to purify the church, both doctrinally and architecturally, back to a Byzantine state of grace, should have built the biggest Russian tent-shaped roof at the apex of his monastery. Inside, the cathedral is in a very bad state, though there is an immense charm to those parts that have been restored and to the few artefacts which have been replaced. Most unusual is the extensive use of Russian tiles, originally the work of the famous 17th-century Moscow master Stepan Polubes. Between them are the remains of elaborate plasterwork and painted surfaces. The various parts of the church are named after the stations of the cross, culminating in the Golgotha Chapel, where an original 17th-century wooden sculpture of the crucifixion rises from a stone floor, in which an artificial fissure represents the earthquake which shook the world as Christ died. This iconostasis, and that in the underground chapel at the back of the cathedral, have been restored. In the central part of the cathedral you can see where the massive iconostasis would have divided the semi-circular steps on which the priests sat from the body of the church. Behind this are various small, tiled chapels. Nikon's grave, if you can get to it, is in the Chapel of John the Baptist under the Golgotha Chapel.

The monastery museum is housed in the buildings beyond the cathedral, parallel to the far wall. It begins with the history of the monastery, and moves through religious and architectural artefacts associated with it to a general exhibition of paintings and furniture from the 18th and 19th centuries, and a number of very fine icons. Behind the museum a gate in the wall leads down steep steps to a meadow known as Gethsemane Park, in which a number of wooden buildings make up a museum of wooden architecture. The buildings, brought from elsewhere, are broadly contemporary with the monastery, and include a square church, a bell-tower and a village homestead, in which you can examine the simple wooden implements of every day the life and the undoubtedly cosy stove. Off to the right as you come down from the monastery is the tall, thin 'hermitage' which Nikon built. While other Russian monks retired to caves in the woods, it seems entirely fitting that the arrogant Nikon should have used a three storey plastered building with elaborate chimneys and, by the look of things, room for servants.

Walking has been a pasttime in St Petersburg ever since foreigners first came here in the 18th century. After midday Nevsky Prospekt, the main thoroughfare of the city, would be thronged with citizens and strangers alike, some on foot, others in speeding carriages. As well as shopping, people promenaded to flirt, pick up the latest gossip, and simply to be seen. Even today, there is nothing more quintessential to the city than this seething showcase of humanity. Housewives go about their business with grim faced determination, while choleric would-be politicians harangue their opposition, artists woo potential sitters and gypsy children pick the pockets of unwary tourists. Walking the length of the street is left to you, for though a number of these walks cover parts of Nevsky Prospekt, they concentrate on leading you off into the less obvious nooks and crannies of the city. You will be able to recognize the entrance to the many art galleries, 19th-century department stores, basement bars and cafés which punctuate the ground-floor façades.

St Petersburg: the Walks

For a calmer summer introduction to the 'Venice of the North', there could be nothing better than a boat. In a city built on no less than 44 islands, the waterways once constituted an important method of transport. Just as in Venice, all of the smartest St Petersburg palaces faced a canal or river, and their liveried barges could be seen dodging the delivery vessels of Nevsky Prospekt's major retailers right up until the Revolution. Today, activity on the water is less frenetic, largely confined to the occasional tourist boat (see Peripheral Attractions). If you want to be sure of an English-language guide, or to organize something out of the ordinary, phone Akva Excursions on ✆ 314 5645 or ✆ 292 3054 between 9am–10pm.

Before setting out on any of the following itineraries, there are a few vital things to bear in mind. Make sure that your sight-seeing is not going to be scuppered by the dreaded *sanitarny dyen*, particularly if you are here in the first or last week of the month. Every museum and gallery is closed one day a month for what is supposed to be a thorough clean, and these days are all noted in the text. If it is cold or wet, take taxis or public transport (though St Petersburg's is unbearably crowded) between the highlights of each walk. These are asterisked with a snowflake on the title page of each excursion. In winter it gets dark at about 3pm, so you must start in good time in the morning. Many of the city's cultural monuments are closed on Mondays and Tuesdays. However Walks I and II are ideally suited to the first day of the week, and the labyrinthine Hermitage Museum (Walk VII) is also open on Tuesdays. Always bear in mind that if you get lost and have trouble making yourself understood, refer to the list of changed street names at the end of the book. Your helpful Petersburger may be more familiar with the old names than the new.

I: The Founding Father

Start: *Decembrists' Square (Ploshchad Dekabristov),* Ⓜ *Nevsky Prospekt/Gostiny Dvor. Leave via Nevsky Prospekt, using the Canal Griboyedova* (Канал Грибоедова) *exit. Turn right and walk down Nevsky Prospekt until you see trees stretching away to the left. Turn left onto Admiraltyesky Prospekt and right at the back of St Isaac's Cathedral. Through the trees ahead rears the horseback statue of Peter the Great on Decembrists' Square. From Nevsky Prospekt, trolleybuses 5 and 14 will take you to St Isaac's Square, on the other side of the cathedral, and bus 22 goes on to Admiraltyesky Prospekt.*

Walking Time: *3½ hours. Start after 10.15am or you may be too early for the fortress.*

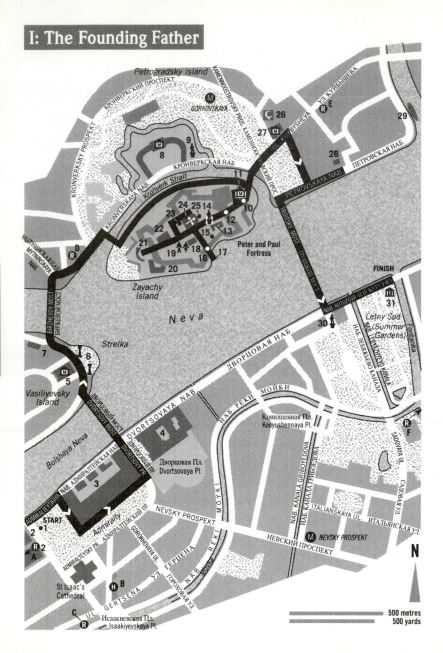

Petrogradsky Island

КРОНВЕРКСКИЙ ПРОСПЕКТ

КАМЕННООСТРОВСКИЙ ПРОС. КАМЕНООСТР.

УЛ. КУЙБЫШЕВА

GORKOVSKAYA

УЛ. КУЙБЫШЕВА

26

27

28

29

ПЕТРОВСКАЯ НАБ.

8

9

KRONVERKSKY PROSPEKT

КРОНВЕРКСКАЯ НАБ.

KRONVERKSKAYA NAB.

Kronverk Strait

11

PETROVSKAYA NAB.

ТРОИЦКИЙ ПРОС.

10

24 25 14

23

22

21

19 18

20

15 13

12

17

16

Peter and Paul
Fortress

TROITSKY MOST

МЫТНИНСКАЯ НАБ.
MYTNINSKAYA NAB.

Zayachy
Island

FINISH

НАБ. КУТУЗОВА НАБ. КУТУЗОВА

Летний Сад

31

Letny Sad
(Summer
Gardens)

БИРЖЕВОЙ МОСТ
БИРЖЕВОЙ МОСТ

Neva

30

Fontanka

7

6

Strelka

5

Vasiliyevsky
Island

ДВОРЦОВЫЙ МОСТ
DVORTSOVY MOST

ДВОРЦОВАЯ НАБ.

НАБ. ЛЕБЯЖЬЕГО КАНАЛА

SADOVAYA UL.
САДОВАЯ УЛ.

R
F

DVORTSOVAYA NAB.

НАБ. РЕКИ МОЙКИ

Bolshaya Neva

4

Конюшенная Пл.
Konyushennaya Pl.

АДМИРАЛТЕЙСКАЯ НАБ. DVORTSOVY PR.

Дворцовая Пл.
Dvortsovaya Pl.

НАБ. КАНАЛА ГРИБОЕДОВА

НАБ. КАНАЛА ГРИБОЕДОВА

ITALIANSKAYA UL.
ИТАЛЬЯНСКАЯ УЛ.

3

АДМИРАЛТЕЙСКИЙ ПР.

ГОРОХОВАЯ УЛ.

NEVSKY PROSPEKT

START

2 1

R 2
A

Admiralty

АДМИРАЛТЕЙСКИЙ ПР.

ГОРОХОВАЯ УЛ.

УЛ. ГЕРЦЕНА

НАБ. РЕКИ МОЙКИ

НЕВСКИЙ ПРОСПЕКТ

NEVSKY PROSPEKT

N

St Isaac's
Cathedral

H B

C
R

Исаакиевская Пл.
Isaakiyevskaya Pl.

UL. GERTSENA

ГОРОХОВАЯ УЛ.

500 metres
500 yards

Sites

1 The Bronze Horseman
   Medny vsadnik
   Медный всадник

2 Senate and Synod Building
   Zdaniye Senata i Synoda
   Здание Сената и Синода

3 Admiralty
   Admiralteystvo
   Адмиралтейство

4 Winter Palace (Hermitage)
   Zimny dvorets (Ermitazh)
   Зимний дворец

5 Stock Exchange/Naval Museum
   Birzha/Voyenno-Morskoy muzei
   Биржа/Военно-Морской музей

6 Rostral Columns
   Rostralniye kolonny
   Ростральные колонны

7 Pushkin House (Institute of Russian Literature)
   Pushkinsky dom
   Пушкинский дом

8 Artillery Museum
   Voyenno-Istorichesky muzei artillerii
   Военно-Исторический музей артиллерии

9 Decembrists' Monument
   Pamyatnik Dekabristov
   Памятник Декабристов

Sites inside Peter and Paul Fortress

10 Ivan Gate
    Ivanovskiye vorota
    Ивановские ворота

11 Museum of the Gas-Dynamics Laboratory

12 St Peter's Gate
    Petrovskiye vorota
    Петровские ворота

13 Engineers' House
    Inzhenerny dom
    Инженерный дом

14 Sculpture of Peter the Great
    Statuya Petra Velikovo
    Статуя Петра Великого

15 Main Guardhouse
    Gauptvakhta
    Гауптвахта

16 Neva Gate
    Nevskiye vorota
    Невские ворота

17 Commandant's Pier
    Ober-Komendantskaya pristan
    Обер-Комендантская пристань

18 Commandant's House
    Ober-Komendantsky dom
    Обер-Комендантский дом

19 Toilets
    Tualety
    Туалеты

20 Trubetskoy bastion
    Трубетской бастион

21 Alexeyevsky Ravelin
    Алексеевский равелин

22 Mint
    Monetny dvor
    Монетный двор

23 Boathouse
    Domik Botika
    Домик Ботика

24 Cathedral of Ss Peter and Paul
    Petropavlovsky sobor
    Петропавловский собор

25 Grand Ducal Burial Vault
    Usypalnitsa
    Усыпальница

26 Mosque
    Mechet
    Мечеть

27 Museum of Russian Political History
    Muzei russkoy politicheskoy istorii
    Музей русской политической истории

28 Cabin of Peter the Great
    Muzei domik Petra I
    Музей домик Петра I

29 Cruiser Aurora
    Kreiser Avrora
    Крейсер Аврора

30 Statue of Suvorov
    Statuya Suvorova
    Статуя Суворова

31 Summer Palace
    Letny dvorets
    Летний дворец

Restaurants and Cafés

A Bistro 'Le Français'

B Hotel Astoria
   Gostinitsa Astoria
   Гостиница Астория

C House of Architects Restaurant
   Dom Arkhitektorov
   Дом Архитекторов

D Café Fantasia
   Кафе Фантазия

E Café Fortetsia
   Кафе Фортеция

F Café Fontanka
   Кафе Фонтанка

On one side the sea, on the other sorrow,
On the third moss, on the fourth a sigh.

Court Jester, on the site of nascent St Petersburg

Were it not for one man possessed by a single-minded vision of his country's future, there would be no city at all here today. Peter the Great is one of the colossi of history, a controversial and pivotal figure in the development of his nation. To some he is a demi-god, to others the antichrist. Some see his dictatorial programme of Europeanization—forcing the boyars to invite women to their parties and to introduce their children to their prospective spouses six weeks before the wedding day—as a civilizing influence. Others point to his murder of his own son, his enjoyment of torture and his encouragement of denunciation to argue that Peter was just another link in a chain of despotism reaching from the mists of medieval Muscovy to Stalin's purges. What is incontrovertible is his effect on Russia's subsequent history, of which his madcap scheme to build a new capital city here, and its exquisite, timeless result, is a symbol.

This itinerary noses out the few varied buildings, dotted around the city centre, which survive from Peter's pioneering days. You will find as many Petersburgers enjoying their unique waterfront as tourists, and a clutch of buskers enlivening their patch of turf. There's jazz and violins in the Peter and Paul Fortress, which lay at the heart of the early settlement. The floor of its Baroque cathedral bristles with the sarcophagi of the ill-fated Romanovs, from Peter onwards. Peter's first home in the city, a two-room log cabin of archetypal Russian design, faces his European-looking Summer Palace built a decade later.

Elsewhere capitalism seems to be routing the communists from their bastion in the Museum of the Revolution, and does a roaring trade in souvenirs on the banks of the Kronverk Canal. At noon on Fridays the exotic turquoise mosque, one of the most northerly on earth, brings out the city's hidden Muslim population. Avoid this walk on Tuesdays, Wednesdays and the last Monday of the month. Sadly, the Summer Palace is also closed 11 Nov–30 April.

Bistro 'Le Français', Galyernaya Ul. 20, ✆ 315 2465 or 210 9622. A corner of Paris tucked away behind the Senate and Synod building at the start of the walk—try the gungy onion soup with a crust of melted cheese, followed by 'steak frites' or salmon. Alternatively, stoke up with a glass of wine or Pastis at the bar.

Hotel Astoria, St Isaac's Square. There are two entrances to this hotel. The best place to get a coffee to set you up for the walk is in the ground floor café/bar inside the door furthest from St Isaac's Cathedral. Open 9am–12 midnight, closed 2–3pm. Sit down with a frothy capuccino or an expresso and a slice of cake or an energy-giving bar of chocolate. The Winter Garden Restaurant serves a good, if rather formal, *à la carte* lunch to the tinkling of a piano.

Dom Arkhitektorov, Ul. Gertsena 52, ✆ 311 0531/4557. *Open 12 noon–10pm, closed Sundays.* The Architects' Union is one of the professional clubs to have responded to the economic squeeze by opening their doors to all comers. While some of these establishments, such as the Writers' Union in Moscow, were known for their gourmet food, the architects have always prided themselves on the decor of their dining rooms. The food is predictable—soups and cold *zakuski* followed by a meat or fish dish with potatoes—but the joy of the place is its panelled dining rooms and quiet, mixed-sex clubby atmosphere.

Café Fantasia Co-op, Zoologichesky Pereulok, Petrograd Side. *Open 8am–8pm, with a break 3pm–4pm.* Look out for the orange 'Кафе' sign. Popular with local workers and students from their nearby dormitories, this dark co-op has plenty of tables at which to devour the cheap well-cooked food. Unless you can find an English-speaking customer, you may have to resort to pointing at what looks good to order.

Café Fortetsia, Ul Kuybysheva 7, Petrograd Side, ✆ 233 9468. *Open 12 noon–midnight.* In this red velour, brothel-style interior dishes from the extensive Russian menu are carefully prepared and cooked from fresh ingredients. Bitter experience suggests you should avoid the mouth-watering fish options, so opt for steak with mushroom sauce and chips instead, after a steaming bowl of *borshch*.

Café Fontanka, Naberezhnaya Reki Fontanka 14. *Open 2pm–5am, with a well-deserved break 10pm–11pm.* For those in need of sustenance at the end of this walk, one of St Petersburg's trendiest restaurants is at hand. Soberly decorated in a strange mix of panelled wood and chrome, this small café prepares its large main courses attentively with plenty of fresh vegetables. The succulent stuffed peppers and tomatoes are a treat. Some of the friendly young staff speak English, enough to explain the short menu to you, and there is always some form of alcohol to be had. Under the same management next door, the smarter Club Ambassador, open 1pm–12 midnight, © 272 9181/3791 serves a small, very expensive menu in its mock-medieval candle-lit cavern.

There could be no better place to begin your aquaintance with St Petersburg than here in **Decembrists' Square,** *by the banks of the River Neva and Russia's most famous sculpture.*

Looking out over the broad flat waters to the water-coloured palaces beyond, it is hard to imagine the site as Pushkin describes it, before the horseback emperor ever clapped eyes on the place:

> *'...here and there,*
> *On moss-grown, boggy shores a rare,*
> *Ramshackle hut loomed dark, the dwelling*
> *Of a humble Finn.'*

Yet at the end of the tsar's reign in 1725, some 22 years later, there were 40,000 people, including all of Russia's leading families, living in stone houses on this flat marshland. Propping up their existence were many more, the skeletons of conscripted serfs, Swedish prisoners of war and convicts who had died sinking piles into the unstable, disease-infested marsh.

It was in celebration of that twin-edged achievement that an admiring Catherine the Great, Peter's granddaughter-in-law, commissioned this equestrian sculpture of the founding father from the French sculptor Etienne Falconet. By that time, the westernizing trend begun by Peter had reached such heights that Catherine consulted both Diderot and Voltaire on her choice of a sculptor. Unveiled in 1782, it shows Peter firmly in control of his unpredictable mount, Russia, her back hoof squashing the snake of Treason, his free hand outstretched omnipotently over the landscape he so brutally tamed. The two inscriptions, in Russian and Latin, state simply 'To Peter I from Catherine II 1782'. The wave-like granite base into which they are incised comes from a favourite hill of Peter's some kilometres from the city, known as Thunder Rock. This bit is said to have been split off by lightning, and it took an entire year for its bulk to be man-handled into its present position.

The sculpture towers above mere mortals much as the tsar did in his day. Peter was well over 6' 6" tall, and from early childhood his body had been spasmodically racked by terrifying physical convulsions, so that while gracious and majestic of mien he could seem severe and wild. Overall, says the Duc de Saint Simon, his 'manner announces wit, intelligence and grandeur and is not without a certain grace'. The head of the sculpture, more wild than gracious, was sculpted by Falconet's future daughter-in-law, Marie Collot.

Commonly known as the **Bronze Horseman** (*Myedny Vsadnik*), the sculpture's importance was dramatically increased when it starred in Pushkin's 1833 epic poem of the same name. The poem's human protagonist, poor Yevgeny, loses his fiancée and his mind in the terrible 1824 flood of the city, and is chased through the ravaged and empty streets of his imagination by the terrifying, clattering sculpture, symbol of the autocratic state and of the destructive potential of Peter's unnatural city:

> *'Across the empty square*
> *Yevgeny ran and seemed to hear*
> *Great, swelling, mighty peals of thunder*
> *And feel the pavement quaking under*
> *A horse's heavy hoofs. For there,*
> *Behind him, to the darkness wedded,*
> *Lit by the moon's pale ray and slight,*
> *One hand in warning raised, the dreaded*
> *Bronze Horseman galloped through the night...'*

Yevgeny is the first of the now-familiar small men of Russian fiction, hounded by the whims of tsar and state. In Pushkin's nightmarish vision of St Petersburg there seems even to be a hint of the Revolution.

Until 1925, the square was known as Senate Square, after the ordered neoclassical Senate and Holy Synod building which still surrounds the arch to the west of the Bronze Horseman. It was built in 1829–32 by Carlo Rossi, to add the finishing touches to his work on this area of the city, and like all his other important buildings is identifiable by his leitmotifs: a distinctly serious and formal apricot building with sculptural and architectural details picked out in white, including the staples of classical architecture: porticoes, friezes, pediments and mythical bas reliefs. The Senate, the supreme court of appeal and the body responsible for tax collection, occupied the northern end of the building; the ecclesiastical administration the other. Though the present building is over 100 years younger, both institutions were originally created by Peter. The Senate governed while he was away fighting, while the Holy Synod replaced the office of the Patriarch, which he abolished in 1700, thereby bringing the Church directly under his control. Today the building contains the State Historical Archives.

In 1925 however, the name was changed to commemorate the centenary of Russia's first, unsuccessful revolution, the Decembrist Uprising of 14 December 1825 which took place on this square. A group of army officers used the uncertainty over the succession after the death of Alexander I to persuade their soldiers to take up arms and to press for a constitutional monarchy. The new tsar, Nicholas I, made short shrift of the rebels. The ice on the Neva was broken by heavy artillery to cut off their escape and soldiers loyal to the tsar fired straight into the crowd of some 3000. The five ringleaders were hung and 130 others exiled to Siberia. Thus choked 'the first cry of Russian freedom' beneath the steadfast gaze of Peter who, though revolutionary in his own way, would doubtless have disapproved strongly of such attempts to interfere in the God-given task of government.

Opposite the Senate and Synod building across the square, the similarly coloured walls of the Admiralty are obscured by trees. Walk into the **Admiralty Gardens,** *away from the river.*

Nearby, a faithful Bactrian camel crouches beneath a bust of Prezhvalsky, the Russian Asiatic explorer best known to us for his discovery of the small wild horse named after him. Better known in Russia is the fact that he looks exactly like Stalin, and there have been many attempts to locate the explorer and the tyrant's mother in the same place at the appropriate moment. The only thing that can be said for certain is that Przhevalsky was in the same country at the moment of conception. Such wicked speculations have an edge to them here, in the land where the poet Osip Mandelshtam was killed for likening Stalin's moustache to a cockroach.

In front of the main arch of the Admiralty, surrounding a large round fountain, are statues of the 19th-century writers Lermontov and Gogol, and the composer Glinka, and in the garden beyond one of the Romantic poet and inspirer of Pushkin, Vassily Zhukovsky.

Appropriately the main thoroughfares of Peter's capital, Nevsky Prospekt, Gorokhovaya Ulitsa and Voznesensky Prospekt, radiate out from the **Admiralty Building**, as they did then. For one of Peter's main reasons for founding the city on the Neva was its proximity to the open sea. Peter was determined to create a navy, and was so successful that less than 70 years later under Catherine the Great the Russians were able to defeat the veteran Ottoman sailors at the battle of Chesme. The exemplary neoclassical building which stands here today was built in 1806–23, by the architect Andreyan Zakharov. However its 218ft gilded spire, topped by a sailing ship weathervane which has become a symbol of the city, replaced an earlier spire rising from the single-storey admiralty and shipyard built here by Peter, between 1704 and 1711. The original building was designed in the shape of the Russian letter P (П) for Peter, and opened onto the Neva. Arcaded workshops surrounded the central slipways on which the early Russian fleet was built. Peter, who had himself studied ship-building in the Dutch yards of Zaadam and Amsterdam and at Deptford on the Thames, felt perhaps most at home in this tough labouring environment. He had travelled abroad incognito with a seal which stated only that 'I am in the ranks of the pupils and require instruction', and is often called the 'carpenter tsar'. When he came to dine here with the Lords of the Admiralty, he would insists on eating only naval rations of smoked beef washed down with beer, to the accompaniment of fife and drums playing in the tower. This was the tsar's most attractive quality—his ruthlessness and cruelty were equalled by his dogged humility in the face of his own ignorance. He was always willing to labour next to any man in order to learn and encourage others to learn.

When the Admiralty was rebuilt in the early 19th century, it kept the same Π-shaped plan, merely adding a second Π inside the first and separating them by a canal. From the embankment this original plan has been completely obscured as the last ship was built here in 1844 and buildings have taken over the central ship-yard. However the garden façade of what is now the Dzerzhinsky Higher Naval Engineering Academy, founded in 1925, is little altered. Flanking the tall central arch are statues of three nymphs shouldering great globes, whilst the relief above depicts Neptune, in his shell vessel, handing his trident, symbol of mastery of the seas, to Peter I (*The Establishment of the Russian Fleet*). Despite the fact that the Russian Orthodox Church demanded the removal of a number of 'pagan' statues in 1860, the corners of the attic are crowned with classical heros: Alexander the Great, Achilles, Ajax and Pyrrhus. Above them, surrounding the tower, a perfectly proportioned portico supports 28 allegorical statues connected with the navy—the elements, the seasons and the muses of astronomy among them.

Opposite the Admiralty, the grey and white building at Admiraltyesky Prospekt 6 was the headquarters of the Bolshevik secret police, the Cheka, from December 1917 to March 1918 when it moved, with its boss 'Iron' Felix Dzerzhinsky and the rest of the government, to Moscow. It might seem an unlikely job for a Polish nobleman, but Dzerzhinsky got there by sheer dedication, going as far as to have his mother executed for counter-revolution.

> *Continuing along the 400-metre façade in the garden, turn left at the far corner of the building, beneath the decorative portico. The square ahead is Palace Square (see p.309), with the Winter Palace and Hermitage on the left, the General Staff building on the right. Tear yourself away and walk onto* **Palace Bridge***, over the Neva.*

During the White Nights festival in June (*see* p.530), this stretch of the Neva is at the centre of the all-night walkabout that possesses the city as the bridges go up. St Petersburg's anarchic modern art scene sometimes hijacks this bridge, hanging vast canvases—painted especially—from it. Looking right from the bridge you see the river at its widest. The right bank here quickly became the city's smartest, and to this day gives a perfect illustration of the secret of St Petersburg's architectural aesthetics. Successive generations of architects sought to make their mark on the utter flatness of the site by a judicious and rhythmical use of vertical lines—pillars, spires and statues arranged like so many musical notes on the page. It is a far cry from the traditional cities of medieval Muscovy, which centred on a fortified hill-top Kremlin, with houses looking into a central courtyard rather than out. It seems that the very size of the Neva demanded a new form of grandeur, its glassy mirrored surface crying out for the narcissistic splendour of long façades. This was no organic creation, rather—as Dostoevsky described it—a most 'premeditated city'.

In order to achieve his goal of establishing a capital here, where there was little daylight, no local building stone, a regularly flooding river and little local food supply, Peter press-ganged some 40,000 labourers every year. Thousands died of typhoid, starvation and cold, or were taken by the wolves who still roamed the streets. For 20 years it was forbidden to build in stone anywhere else in Russia, and for 56 years every carriage, boat or barge coming into the city had to bring a toll in building stone. Peter's first director of building, Domenico Trezzini, designed three standard plans for the houses of the capital, small, medium and large. These were made available to those who were gradually finding themselves forced to leave Moscow. In 1710 an Imperial *ukaz* or dictat ordered the Imperial family and the government to move to this cold northern wasteland. In 1712 Peter ordered that 'one thousand of the best families of the nobility etc. are required to build houses of beams, with lath and plaster, in the old English style, along the banks of the Neva from the Imperial Palace' (*i.e.* this bridge) to a point way beyond what the eye can see. Opposite, the merchants and traders were to build wooden houses for themselves. Because these buildings were all erected in such a hurry, none lasted long, including the first two Winter Palaces built for the tsar on the site of today's Hermitage. Foreigners visiting the city at the time describe drunken parties in rooms where the wind whistled merrily through open roofs and water cascaded constantly down the walls.

Palace Bridge leads onto **Vasiliyevsky Ostrov** *(St Basil's Island), which Peter originally intended to be his city-centre.*

Since there were no bridges in those days, this scheme stood little chance of survival. Standing on the north side of the River Neva, the island was completely inaccessible from most of Russia during autumn and spring, when the ice formed and melted, making the river impossible to navigate. By 1719 the city centre sensibly radiated out from the Admiralty.

The tip of this island, which is the largest in the Neva delta, is known as the *strelka* (point), and from the 1730s to the 1880s it served as the city's main harbour.

Today, its only useful function is as a spot for fishing and for newly-weds to have their photograph taken, come snow or shine, with the Peter and Paul Fortress as a backdrop. Directly behind the point of the island, which divides the Neva into the Bolshaya (Large) and Malaya (Small) Neva, stands the neoclassical building of the **former Stock Exchange**. It is a close copy of the famous Greek temple at Paestum in Italy, and its stocky Doric colonnade contrasts with St Petersburg's overriding use of the more ornate Corinthian order. The exchange began its life as a wooden building, with strong links to the port; it was here that the seaborne merchants came to trade their goods. In 1805–10 the present building was designed by Thomas de Thomon to house the increasingly sophisticated Stock Exchange, and the great terracotta rostral columns in the square in front were erected to balance the ensemble. These too are reminiscent of classical empires, being copies of the columns used by the Romans to commemorate naval victories. Ships' prows project from the columns, and in earlier times fires on top lit the harbour shore. The four bearded old figures sitting at the bottom of the columns represent Russia's four great rivers, the Neva, the Volga, the Dnieper and the Volkov. Fights are raging over whether the Naval Museum should be expelled from its home in the Exchange so that St Petersburg's stockbrokers can return. As yet the list of trading stocks doesn't justify a building this size—although it's fair to say that the **Naval Museum** wastes a fair amount of space too. Have a quick look at the main hall, which is awash with finely-made model boats, including Peter the Great's first childhood launch, the so-called 'grandfather of the Russian fleet'. Apart from the pre-Revolutionary uniforms on the top floor, the rest of the museum will be of interest only to a minority of technological enthusiasts (*open 10.30am–5.30pm; closed Mon and Tues*).

The two identical porticoed buildings flanking the Exchange were built some 15 years later and originally used as warehouses. To the north is now the Museum of Soil Science, to the south the Zoological Museum (*see* p.423).

> *Walk onto the bridge across the Malaya Neva, passing the **Institute of Russian Literature**, a run-down yellow neoclassical building topped by a drum and dome.*

Known as Pushkin House, it is the repository of some of the country's most valuable literary material, including most of the poet's surviving manuscripts. It seems only right that they should remain in the literary capital, a city whose extraordinary origins and 'premeditated' quality have provoked so many authors to made it an almost tangible character in their work. It is hard to imagine Dostoyevsky, Gogol or Akhmatova without the context of St Petersburg; even Tolstoy, who loathed the place, needed its social whir as an object for his disapproval. From the way Russians talk about their city on the Neva, you could be forgiven for imagining that the physical city is merely a mirage, and that what it stands for, its metaphysical self, is the reality. The Literary Museum and its manuscripts are hidden away behind signs proclaiming restoration, and by the look of it will not reopen for some time.

> *Once over the bridge, turn right and follow the banks of the river to the bridge over onto Zayachy (Hare) Island, and the **Peter and Paul Fortress*** (Петропавловская Крепость).

The fort is one of the best-preserved examples of its type in Europe, and takes the form of an irregular hexagon of massive walls, sloped against artillery attack and defended by bastions at each corner. If you are here around midday, be prepared for the single noon cannon shot, which has sounded every day (except during the seige) since a similar salute proclaimed the end of the Great Northern War on 4 September 1721.

> *Resist entering the fortress immediately, and turn left along the shore. On the other side of the Kronverk Strait, the canal which separates the fortress from the Petrograd Side, you'll see a three-storey brick horseshoe-shaped building.*

Designed in part by Nicholas I himself, the **Arsenal** was completed in 1860 to house the bulk of the Russian army's weapons, and its courtyard is still arrayed with tanks and artillery pieces. Though it never had a true defensive purpose, the building roughly followed the lines of the earlier *kronverk*, an outer series of earthwork fortifications built to protect the fortress on its most vulnerable side. Today it houses the **Artillery Museum** (*open Wed–Sun, 11am–6pm*). Beyond it a small pinkish granite obelisk commemorates the hanging place of the five leading Decembrists in 1826.

> *Continue on round the fortress until you arrive at the **Ivan Gate**, a simple rusticated triumphal arch whose date celebrates the completion of the fortifications. Turning right inside the gate, the ticket office for the various buildings and museums is concealed in this outer defensive ravelin (open 11am–6pm and until 4pm on Tues; closed Wed and the last Tues of the month). No ticket is needed to simply walk through the fort which is open 24 hours a day. Walking at night across its unchanged cobbled spaces by lamp-light is as close as you can get to time travel. There is a very basic café beyond the ticket office, and a run of the mill tourist trap, the Osteria Restaurant at the other end of the ravelin, to the left.*

The Peter and Paul Fortress, part of the *raison d'être* of Peter's city, never faced a full-scale attack. Though it was started in 1703 at the height of the Great Northern War, it was well protected by the island forts of Kronstadt and Kronschlott out in the gulf. As building progressed the fort, which had started off as an earthworks built hurriedly in one year, was embellished first with wooden and then with stone buildings and battlements. By the time it was entirely finished in 1740 the war had been over for 19 years and Russia's northern borders secured. The threat to the fortress was greatest during the October Revolution of 1917 and during the seige of Leningrad by the Germans during the Second World War. In the first, it went over to the Bolsheviks early on and served as the revolutionary field headquarters, where the attack on the Winter Palace opposite was masterminded. During the war, the spire of its central cathedral was camouflaged and damage to the fortress during the bombardments was thankfully limited to shell fragments. Such were the paucity of rations in the first months of the seige that the men who volunteered to camouflage the spire had to be given extra rations for several days to build up enough strength to scale it.

But if the fortress was never militarily important, it was the symbolic centre of political power, taking over from the Kremlin as the government prison and the burial place of the tsars. Peter hated Moscow; when he was ten, he had stood in the Kremlin and watched as three of his supporters, including his uncle, were torn limb from limb by a bloodthirsty, chanting, drum-beating mob of soldiers. When it came to the building of the Cathedral of Ss Peter and Paul in the fortress, he insisted that its spire be taller than the Ivan the Great Belltower in Moscow.

> *Before progressing into the body of the fortress, the mysteriously-named* **Gas-Dynamics Laboratory Museum** *may be of interest. It is tucked into the outer defences beyond the ticket office.*

The museum commemorates a 1930s laboratory on the site which worked on space rockets. Much of it is taken up with a dull photographic record of scientists of 'Gas-Dynamic' fame in unadulterated Soviet style, but the last exhibit, the round Soyuz command capsule, is staggering. That a man should travel so far in so little and survive!

> *You enter the fortress itself through* **St Peter's Gate,** *a Baroque triumphal arch decorated with a wooden bas relief.*

The relief—a survival from the earlier wooden gate—was designed as a charm, protecting the city with an allegory from the life of its patron St Peter. When Simon the Magician attempted to prove his pagan superiority over St Peter by flying, a mere prayer from the saint scattered the demons assisting him and the sorcerer plummetted to the ground. Should anyone be so foolish as to challenge the city, the implication goes, such will also be his fate. The central building represents the city, with Peter the Great dressed as a Roman officer to the right. Falling from the heavens is the winged figure of Simon the Magician, abandoned by his demonic assistants at the behest of the Holy Spirit personified in the tympanum above. Beneath is the double-headed eagle of the Russian Empire which has captured the ancient coat-of-arms of Moscow, St George and the Dragon, and brought it to the new capital. The statues in the niches are later and represent either the lovers Mars and Venus, with her vanity mirror, or the goddess of war Bellona and Minerva, the goddess of wisdom, with her snake.

The gate was built in 1707 and redecorated in 1717–18 by Domenico Trezzini, who was director of building in the new city from 1704–13, the first of a series of foreign architects invited by Peter to leave their cosmopolitan mark. It gave the finishing touch to the walls which he had recently built in brick, and could be closed with a portcullis.

> *Before leading to Trezzini's other major building in this ensemble, the Cathedral of Ss Peter and Paul, the main avenue of the fortress passes a yellow building on the left, a rare if undistinguished example of 1740s military architecture, known as the* **Engineers' House** *It now houses occasionally-changing exhibitions from the collection of the City History Museum, which range from early views of the city in oils, exuberant and naïve shop signs, fine early porcelain and turn of the century costumes.*

Beyond it, set behind a lawn which was once the military drill ground, the **Main Guardhouse** was neoclassicized as late as 1907–8, and it shows. What was formerly a single storey building now has two and supports a tacked-on portico, its four pillars bunched in pairs unceremoniously to the sides. On this side of the lawn a sculpted Peter the Great sits comfortably on a chair, where during his reign soldiers were made to sit on the knife-edge spine of a big wooden horse for several hours as a punishment. The sculpture was given to the city by the native sculptor Michael Shamyakin, who now lives in New York, and shows the founder of the city life size, with no hair, a small bullishly determined face on a thick neck and immense attenuated hands, legs and feet. It's a far cry, in both artistic and symbolic terms, from the heroic, god-like Bronze Horseman, and is based on Carlo Rastrelli's contemporary wax effigy of the monarch. Yet at a stroke it manages to send up the long-held Russian (and Soviet) tradition of monumental civic sculpture, to identify the pomposity that is so much a part of the official city and to wrest the place from its inhuman autocrats and return it to its mortal inhabitants.

> *Turning left at the end of the lawn leads down the side of the pink and white* **Commandant's House**.

The fortress commanders lived here until 1917, constantly enlarging their billet until it attained its present proportions in the 1890s. The first commander, true to Peter's desire to modernize his country by importing know-how, was a Scotsman, General Roman/Robert Bruce. He died in 1720 and is buried in the Commandant's Graveyard by the cathedral, beneath a sadly unreachable slab showing a soldier mourning with his horse. The trials of the Decembrists and the Petrashevsky Circle were held in the building, near to the prisons in which the accused were held. Among those tried here was the young Dostoyevsky, a natural conservative who was nevertheless not immune to the revolutionary fever that infused the city from 1825 onwards.

> *At the end of this walkway the* **Neva Gate** *pierces the curtain wall and leads onto the handsome* **Commandant's Pier**, *which was clad in granite in 1787 along with the rest of the city's riparian banks.*

As you pass through the gate to survey the magnificently horizontal view of the Neva and the palatial embankment opposite, spare a thought for all those who died in the flood-tides recorded to the right. Each plaque records a particular flood, the highest marker recording the terrible 1824 inundation when all of the fortress, Vasiliyevsky Island, the Petrograd Side and the mainland almost as far as the Moscow Station were drowned. This is the flood which so tragically deprives 'poor Evgeny' of his fiancée in Pushkin's Bronze Horseman, which in part sees Peter's bloody-minded determination to build a city on this unsuitable marsh as yet another example of the autocratic despotism to which the Russian people are fated.

In good weather, tourists on the pier are serenaded by mellow jazz. It's a measure of the penetration of 'mafia' extortion in the city that even the buskers here pay protection money. The island's main beach is to the right of the pier, round the bastion. In winter watch out for walruses, the hardy citizens who meet up for a healthy dip in the holes they make in the ice. And whatever the air temperature, if the sun is shining you may well catch someone sunbathing, sheltering from the wind deep in the corners of the fortifications.

> *Retrace your steps along the walkway to the* **Cathedral of Ss Peter and Paul**.

The cathedral, with its golden spire and cupola-topped dome, stands on the site of an earlier wooden Church of St Anne, and was designed by Trezzini in 1712. In the Russia of that time, where churches were almost exclusively squarish, topped by a forest of cupolas and with separate belltowers, its Baroque sillhouette and long, thin basilica shape would have seemed outrageously foreign. The eastern façade, minus the sculpture which once rose from it, still bears traces of the worn 19th-century fresco of Ss Peter and Paul with Jesus. The vaulted building beside the cathedral, adorned with a mosaic of Virgin and Child, is the Grand Ducal Burial Vault, where members of the Romanov family were buried between its consecration in 1908 and the revolution, and again in the 1990s. In late 1991 the angel which stands precariously atop the spire holding a 23ft high golden cross was brought down for repairs and two time capsules were discovered within. One dated back to the last known ascent for repairs in 188? and contained information on the history of the cathedral's building works; the second had been left in a lemonade bottle by some unofficial tricksters who ascended in 1957, leaving a message saying simply 'to the next ascenders'.

Before entering, spend a minute surveying the cathedral's western façade. Just 23 years after it was completed in 1733, the cathedral was struck by lightning. A massive fire broke out, and everything from the entablature upwards—roof, cupola and belltower—was destroyed. The restoration that followed was less than sensitive. The original volutes on either side of the belltower had been elegant and flowing, with a smooth downward line; their replacements are absurd, snub-nose and painfully undecorated. At the attic level, a triangular pediment concealed the base of the next level of the belltower, so that it seemed to rise from behind the façade. This was replaced by a second pair of volutes, completely spoiling the effect.

Beneath the soaring painted vaults within, white marble sarcophagi contain the bodies of all Russia's emperors and empresses after Peter, except Ivan VI, Peter III and Nicholas II, all of whom were murdered. Peter the Great's body, which lay waiting here in a sealed coffin for years until his cathedral was ready, is up near the iconostasis on the right, his tomb bedecked with commemorative medals and flowers. Mystery surrounds the coffin of Alexander I. Many believe that he did not really die in the south in 1825, but that remorse at his complicity in his father's assassination drove him to fake his death and become a mystical hermit. This alterego, known by the pseudonym Fyodor Kuzmich, lived on in Siberia into the 1880s. Further fuel was added to the rumour when the Bolsheviks opened the sarcophagus and found that Alexander III had replaced the original coffin. Above them all a riot of cherubs, painted and sculpted, adorn the ceiling which is born aloft by eight massive square piers, marblized to match the only two coloured sarcophagi, those of Alexander II and his wife. They are carved from green jasper from the Altai and rhodonite from the Urals.

Most striking of all however is the highly theatrical, gilded iconostasis, replete with wooden carved curtains drawn back and massive royal gates. It was designed by Ivan Zarudny in the 1720s and carved in Moscow, where the 43 icons were painted at the same time. Previously, iconostases had tended to be an almost solid wall of paintings, whereas here the palaquin over the communion table beyond is visible above the royal doors, themselves an unusual architectural fantasy showing the disciples coming to the Last Supper, with the Virgin Mary, the Holy Spirit in the form of a dove and the Archangels Michael and Gabriel above.

In the passage which leads into the Grand Ducal Burial Vault, and the rooms off it, there are exhibitions tracing the restoration work and the history of the mint which stands opposite the cathedral. The vault itself is a sepulchral white dome, gently lit with natural light. It was designed by a trio of architects, David Grimm, Anton Tomishko and Leonty Benois and is something of a victim of history. Designed to accommodate some 60 members of the Romanov family, the Revolution cut short its purpose at only 13, though three of the Grand Dukes killed by the Bolsheviks in 1919 have now been laid to rest here, as well as the heir to the Romanov dynasty Archduke Vladimir, who died in 1992 never having set foot on Russian soil. The reburial of the bodies of the last tsar and his family, who were killed at Yekaterinburg in 1918 and whose remains have recently been identified, was planned for March 1995, though recent doubts over the authenticity of Nicholas II's skull are holding things up.

> *You leave the cathedral complex through the fine wrought-iron fence created by Leonty Benois, inspired by the famous fence at the Summer Gardens which you will see later, and come face to face with a Baroque boathouse, marooned in a sea of pebbles. It was built to house the 'Grandfather of the Russian Fleet' which is now in the Naval Museum.*

The massive, classical building of the **Mint**, built in 1800–2 and inscribed Монстный Двор, brings to mind an apocryphal story about Russia's tin-based currency. One particularly cold winter, when temperatures fell below -86°, the entire coinage turned to white powder, as tin does under such conditions. Russia's currency was produced in the fortress from 1724, though the present building is confined to producing a galaxy of centenary and other medals which are popular collector's items and stand up against inflation far better than the rouble.

The Trubetskoy Bastion beyond the Mint and the **Alexeyevsky Ravelin**, an outer fortification protecting the end of the fort, tell of the grisly side of the fort's history—as a prison. Saddest of all is the story of Peter's son, Alexei, who became the focus of opposition to Peter. The monarch had sensitive memories of earlier treason within the royal family, and reacted with hideous ferocity. On Peter's orders—and perhaps with his participation—the terrified 28-year-old was interrogated and tortured from February to June 1718. Having been condemned to death, on 26 June the prince died in his cell in the Trubetskoy Bastion. Whether it was actually Peter who struck the final blow will never be known, but the irony of a reforming monarch bringing the bloodiest tradition in Russian history, royal infanticide, with him to his new Westernized capital is not lost. It was also Peter who struck off a law that had made unfair denunciations of others a punishable offence; thus laying the foundations for the sneaking that became such a part of the Soviet system.

Between benighted Alexei's time and 1872, when a new prison was built in the Trubetskoy Bastion, enemies of the state were held in the 'Secret House', a prison within the Alexeyevsky Ravelin. It was from there that the leading Decembrists were led to their execution. When three of the five nooses failed to work the first time round, one of the Decembrists, Muraviev Apostol, muttered mournfully, 'Poor Russia. She cannot even hang decently.' Dostoyevsky was also imprisoned there before a terrifying mock execution, from which he and his conspirators were saved by a last-second pardon from the tsar.

The **Trubetskoy Bastion** has been open as a prison museum since 1924, though it covers only the history of the building in tsarist times. As well as members of the 'People's Will' faction who assassinated Alexander II, and the radical writer Chernyshevsky who wrote the influential work *'What is to be done?'*, a utopian socialist vision of the future, Kropotkin, Trotsky and Gorky were also imprisoned here. After the Revolution it became the final holding pen for a number of members of the Romanov family before their execution. Today, the cells have been returned to their sombre 19th-century condition, and you can learn the code with which the prisoners knocked in communication with one another.

> *Return to St Peter's Gate and leave the fortress via the wood and stone bridge leading to the Petrograd side.*

It was built in 1738–40, and during restoration in 1953 it was embellished with period street lamps and iron railings. The pedestrian death-trap ahead, until recently Square of the Revolution (*Ploshchad Revolutsii*), was the heart of the city in its first few hesitant years of existence. Today it is again known by its old name **Trinity Square** (*Troitskaya Ploshchad*), though the early wooden Church of the Trinity is long gone. The square also contained the Triumphal Osteria of the Four Frigates, an inn opened by a German, which Peter the Great frequented happily alongside merchants, architects and officers. His tipple was vodka with cayenne pepper. The square took its Soviet name from its history as a place of demonstration in the revolutionary years 1905 and 1917. On Bloody Sunday, 9 January 1905, a crowd of workers marching to petition the tsar for a living wage was fired upon by panicking troops, resulting in the death of some 48 demonstrators. A further 150 died elsewhere, and what had been intended by its monarchist coordinator, Father Gapon, as a peaceful reconciliation between proletariat and tsar catapulted the country into its first revolution.

Today, trees and the traffic on Kamennoostrovsky Prospekt detract attention from St Petersburg's only **mosque** *(open daily 12 noon–2pm, particularly busy on Fridays)*. It was given to the city by the Emir of Bukhara and built between 1910–14, its roof modelled on probably the best known building in the Soviet Muslim world, the turquoise-tiled splendour of Tamerlane's mausoleum in

Samarkand. It has been undergoing restoration for some years now; the brilliant turquoise expanse reduced to dull concrete.The **Museum of Russian Political History**, Ul. Kubysheva 4 (*open 10am–6pm; closed Thurs*) is suffering from a not altogether surprising identity crisis. Until 1993 it was known as the Museum of the October Revolution. The building itself is an expansive example of Art Nouveau, or as it's called here *Style Moderne*, architecture, distinguished by the use of different textures of building materials, by fluid metalwork fantasies and coloured glass. It was commissioned at the beginning of the century by the highly successful, and upwardly-mobile ballerina, Mathilda Kshessinskaya, who had an affair with the future Tsar Nicholas II and eventually married his cousin Grand Duke Andrei. One of the last survivors of the old days, she lived in Paris, teaching ballet to future stars including Margot Fonteyn, and only died in 1971 at the age of 99. In March 1917 the Bolsheviks requisitioned the house as their headquarters, and when Lenin returned to Russia in April he came here from the Finland Station to address the crowds from the balcony facing the square.

As well as exhibitions on Russian history, and one devoted to the life of Kshessinskaya, part of the museum has been taken over by an exhibition of historical wax-works and part by a souvenir and art shop. There are 29 figures in the wax-works exhibition, entitled *Terror or Democracy*, all involved on one or other side of the tenuous line dividing those who furthered democracy in Russia and those who suppressed it with terror. An English-language guide is available, if you would like to find out what figures as diverse as Dostoyevsky or Fanya Kaplan, who was framed and executed for the attempted assassination of Lenin in August 1918, looked like. Pop in to the building, anyway, to take a look at the resplendent revolutionary red-stained-glass windows in the main hall and for a drink in the courtyard café.

Walk straight towards the River Neva, and turn left on the embankment.

This spot in the centre of the city, just downstream from the industrial centre on the Vyborg Side, is very popular with fishermen, though thankfully they never seem to catch anything. Some 100 yards down the embankment, a landing flanked by a pair of mythical Chinese Shih-Tze statues heralds Peter the Great's first home in the city. Brought back from Manchuria in 1907 during the Russo-Japanese war, these pug-like creatures are traditional temple guardians, though this humble wooden hut must seem something of a comedown for them. As has already been seen, though he founded a city which became synonymous with extravagant splendour, Peter himself was a man of simple tastes.

Hidden in a wooded garden beyond a bronze bust of Peter, the **Cabin of Peter the Great** (Домик Петра I) Petrovskaya Naberezhnaya 6, was encased in the present brick and stone superstructure by Nicholas I in 1846 (*open 10am–6pm;*

closed Tues and last Mon of the month). The central log cabin is the oldest surviving structure in the city and was built for the tsar in three days in 1703. He lived in it, when here, until 1708. Originally, it would have been plastered on the outside and brightly painted. You can get some idea of the style from the internal door surrounds, which preserve traces of plastered floral decoration. The two main rooms, a study and a dining room, are divided by a small larder and bedroom. The whole has been furnished with period pieces of simple beauty and some of the tsar's personal possessions, such as his icon of the Redemeer, but the overall impression is one of extreme puritanism and discomfort, especially as Peter was a tall man and would have had to stoop continuously beneath the low roof. The boat on display beside the house was supposedly used by Peter to save a group of fisherman on Lake Ladoga in 1690, and the exhibition explains the events of the Great Northern War. As you leave the building you can get a bearing on what's next by looking straight across the river. There, at the edge of the Summer Gardens, is Peter's next home, the Summer Palace.

> *Retrace your steps to Kamennoostrovsky Prospekt and cross the Neva on the city's most beautiful bridge, the **Trinity Bridge** (Troitsky Most).*

It was built at the end of the 19th century by Russians to a French design, to celebrate the silver wedding anniversary of Tsar Alexander III and Marie Feodorovna. Walking across it you would be forgiven for thinking you were suddenly in Paris. Its gentle curve is divided down the middle by a series of fine *Style Moderne* crucifixes from which the trolleybus lines are suspended. At the far end the bridge gives onto the Field of Mars (*see* p.313) introduced by a statue of Field Marshal Suvorov (1730–1800) whose skeletal face is unmistakable beneath his disguise as the Roman god of war.

> *Turn left along the embankment, walk over the Lebyazhy (Swans') Canal and enter the **Summer Gardens** (Lyetny Sad) through the gate in Velten's iron palisade.*

From the start of his plans for the new city Peter the Great had magnificent gardens in mind here, though what you see today is largely the product of the late 18th century and Catherine the Great's more sober classical tastes. These delicate railings for example were erected to a design by Yuri Velten in 1770–84, at the same time as the embankment of the Neva was clad in granite and the gardens separated from its banks. Their identical sections of golden-tipped spears divided by 36 granite pillars topped with urns and two gates, taps into the secret of St Petersburg architecture which had already been laid down by Rastrelli—rhythm—yet gives it a strict classical twist. Peter's gardens were modelled on a grand reverie of Versaille, and the project took on its full potential with the arrival of the French architect Alexandre Jean-Baptiste Leblond from Paris in 1715. In keeping with the frivolity of

European gardens at the time, it sang to the splashing of 50 fountains, fed by waters in a header tank on the banks of the adjacent and thus-named Fontanka River. Formal topiary set off marble and limestone sculptures imported from Italy, and were themselves framed by aviaries and orangeries. There was a grotto in which the 3rd-century Roman Tauride Venus (now in the Hermitage) presided, and even a miniature boat in which Peter's favourite dwarf rowed amongst the swans on Lebyazhy Canal.

When the 1777 floods destroyed the complex water system that fed the fountains, the present romantic, sylvan grove was laid out, and only the large Carp Pond at the far end of the gardens was left. Beside it, in the early 19th century, a vast, inappropriate porphyry vase, a present from the king of Sweden, was erected. Many of the more valuable sculptures were taken away leaving the largely 19th-century assortment which now peoples the place. In winter they are covered by individual wooden sentry boxes, packed with straw, to protect them from the frost. In summer the park is St Petersburg's favourite, a dappled haunt for old and young where busking musicians enliven the air with the ethereal sound of pipes, while nearer the Neva a brass band turns an honest rouble striking up a national anthem at the merest whiff of a tourist.

Near the corner where the Neva meets the Fontanka, surrounding the Summer Palace, are two exhibition halls, called the **Tea and Coffee Pavilions**, both erected in the 1820s, and a large bronze of **I. A. Kryllov**, which attracts children like the Peter Pan statue in Hyde Park. He was a writer of animal fables, and the

sedentary sculpture is animated by its plinth, decorated with bas reliefs illustrating a number of the most famous stories. The statue was paid for by public subscription, erected in 1855 and sculpted by Pyotr Clodt, who seems to have sculpted almost every animal (except Peter's steed) in the city.

For the first 100 years of its history, the garden was only accessible to courtiers, and it was here that one of history's most intriguing meetings, between the equally highly sexed Casanova and Catherine the Great, took place. Their chaste and courtierly conversation about sculpture and the king of Prussia is a dire disappointment, and Casanova rather uncharacteristically remarked 'who can resist making such speeches to a monarch, and above all, a monarch in petticoats.' After it was opened by Nicholas I to all 'decently dressed people' the Whit Monday marriage fair took place beneath the implacable gaze of the sculptures on the central alley. Bachelors on one side and prospective brides on the other would line up backed by their families, who bargained over their matrimonial fate.

For his **Summer Palace** (*Letny Dvorets*) Peter also chose the architect Domenico Trezzini, who worked on it in 1710–14 (*open 11am–6.30pm; closed Tues and last Mon of the month, and from 11 Nov–30 April*). Tickets can be bought at the Tea Pavilion. While grander than his wooden cabin, it is still little more than a family house and a far cry from the gargantuan state-of-the-art palaces built for his successors. Despite its lack of pretention, however, it is one of the most satisfying buildings in the city, a Dutch-influenced treat from the outside and all of a period within.

Built of brick and stucco, and with a steep-pitched roof, the primrose yellow, two-storey walls are divided by a series of pale terracotta maritime bas reliefs hinting at Peter's naval mastery over the Swedes in the Great Northern War. They are almost the only works in the city by Andreas Schlüter, a German architect whom Peter poached from Berlin to take over from Trezzini in 1713. He was one of Peter's few mistakes in his foreign recruitment drive to find architects for his new capital. Unknown to Peter, after his building of the Berlin Mint fell down, Schlüter had gone rather mad, and he died within a year of arriving in Russia. After the Peace of Nystadt in 1721 Peter went on to commission the sculpture of Peace and Plenty which is still in his garden. It shows winged Victory placing a victor's laurel crown on seated Russia, who is seen trampling on the defeated lion of Sweden.

Within, the palace has been restored as near as possible to its original decoration. Peter lived and worked on the ground floor, while his family were secreted up the staircase hidden behind the carved oak figure of Minerva in the hall. The Admiralty Chair whose dimensions, including its carved human arms, were measured for Peter himself, still presides in the corner reception room. On the walls hang portraits of the tsar's contemporaries, men who would frequently have reported to their sovereign and received his orders here, amongst them Field Marshal Count Boris Sheremetyev and Peter's right-hand man, Prince Alexander Menshikov. Snobbery was never a failing of the tsar's, and though Menshikov was a barefoot pie-seller when Peter first met him, by the end of his reign Menshikov's intelligence and energy had been rewarded with the greatest fortune in the land and unparalleled power.

In Peter's bedroom, the painted ceiling depicts Morpheus, the god of sleep, scattering the poppies of oblivion. In his workshop are the lathes (one for metal, one for wood and ivory) on which the tsar turned all manner of objects and the massive instrument for measuring the strength and direction of the wind which he ordered from Dresden. Connected to the weather vane, it works to this day. It was here, as the Danish ambassador witnessed, that Peter often conducted his affairs of state 'dressed in a leather jerkin like a workman, operating a lathe... During my visit, he from time to time left the lathe, walked to and fro, and discussed the most important affairs.' Peter's fascination with science and technology was another aspect of his interest in progress.

The palace dining room is a family affair, for Peter left Menshikov to arrange all official state banquets in his grander palace on Vasilievsky Island (*see* Walk VI, p.373). The neighbouring kitchen was the latest thing, with the only internal tap in the city disgorging water into its black marble sink and a hood over the fires, covered in finest Dutch tiles.

There are more Dutch tiles upstairs on some of the stoves which heated each room. The Green Study, the finest in the house with its trove of marquetry, is fitted with built-in glass-fronted cupboards where Peter originally displayed the collection of pickled oddities and grotesques, the Kunstkamera, which he had bought in Holland. Though most of it is now displayed in the Museum of Anthropology and Ethnography (*see* p.422), a few grisly pieces remain to remind one. The elaborate hunting scene carved in walnut above the mirror in the pink ballroom was at least partly the work of the tsar himself. It was in this suite of rooms that Peter's second wife Catherine brought up her two boys, both of whom died young, and her two surviving daughters Anna and the future Tsarina Elizabeth. In these cosy surroundings you will find the cradle, padded with leather and carved in the shape of a boat, in which she soothed her babes to sleep.

Considering his volatile temper, Peter and Catherine's marriage was a happy one; a fact which you can almost sense from the building. It was Menshikov who first met the future empress, when she was a Lithuanian prostitute following the Russian army. After she had been his mistress for a while he introduced his peasant girl to the tsar, who fell immediately for her dark intelligent charms. At first he kept their marriage a secret and liked to protect her from the prying eyes of the snobbish

Russian court, and only crowned her empress a year before he died. Yet it was said that he was unable to refuse her frequent requests for clemency on behalf of others, so that if he really wanted to execute someone he would schedule it for while she was away. He once offered a victorious general anything he chose as a reward 'except Moscow and Catherine'. After Peter's death in 1725, with the help of the former pie-seller, the former prostitute ascended the throne.

You may want to sit for a while in the gardens, and ponder this disparate and talented group of characters, who laid the foundations of the city we see today. To get back to ⓂNevsky Prospect/Gostiny Dvor, walk through to the far end of Lyetny Sad, turn right outside and walk 20m or so to Ulitsa Sadovaya. Either walk left along it or catch any tram a stop or two to Nevsky Prospect itself.

II: The Imperial City

Start: Ⓜ *Nevsky Prospekt/Gostiny Dvor*
Walking Time: *2 hours*

Sites

1 Lutheran Church and Peterschule
Lyuteranskaya Tserkov/Peterschule
Лютеранская Церковь/Петершул

2 Dutch Church
Gollandskaya Tserkov
Голландская Церковь

3 Stroganov Palace
Stroganovsky dvorets
Строгановский дворец

4 House with Columns

5 Main Staff Building
Zdaniye glavnovo shtaba
Здание главного штаба

6 Alexander Column
Alexandrovskaya kolonna
Александровская колонна

7 Winter Palace
Zimny dvorets
Зимний дворец

8 Guards' Headquarters

9 Small Hermitage
Maly Ermitazh
Малый Эрмитаж

10 New Hermitage
Novy Ermitazh
Новый Эрмитаж

11 Hermitage Theatre
Ermitazhny teatr
Эрмитажный театр

12 Marble Palace
Mramorny dvorets
Мраморный дворец

13 Field of Mars
Marsovo polye
Марсово поле

14 Former Barracks of Pavlovsky Regiment

15 Mikhailovsky Castle
Mikhailovsky zamok
Михайловский замок

16 Mikhailovsky Palace/Russian Museum
Mikhailovsky dvorets/Russky muzei
Михайловский дворец/Русский музей

17 Church of the Saviour on the Blood
Tserkov Spass na Krovi
Церковь Спас на Крови

18 Former Imperial Stables

19 Pushkin Flat Museum
Muzei-kvartira A. S. Pushkina
Музей-квартира А. С. Пушкина

20 Glinka Kapella
Khorovaya kapella im. M. I. Glinka
Хоровая капелла им. М. И. Глинка

Restaurants and Cafés

A Literary Café (and Staraya Kniga bookshop)
Literatornoye kafé (Staraya Kniga)
Литераторное кафе (Старая Книга)

B House of Scholars Café
Kafé v dome Uchenikov
Кафе в доме Учеников

C Grocery
Produkti
Продукты

D Marble Palace Café
Kafé v mramornom dvortse
Кафе в мраморном дворце

E Café Fontanka
Кафе Фонтанка

F Café Pevchesky Mostik
Кафе Певческий Мостик

G Restaurant Sankt Peterburg
Ресторан Санкт Петербург

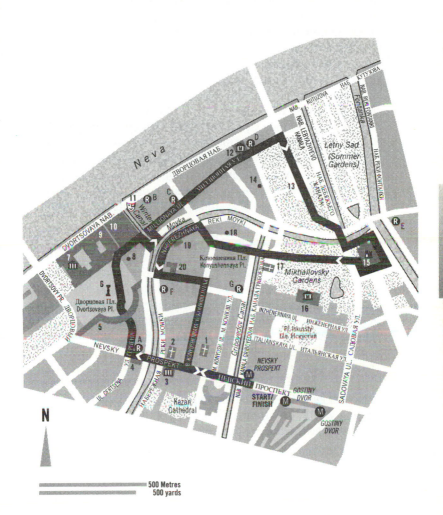

500 Metres
500 yards

Once the Romanovs had established their new capital, they lost no time in beautifying it. Within 70 years of a foundation stone being laid for the Peter and Paul Fortress on the muddy banks of the Neva, fortune-seeking architects, craftsmen, painters, choreographers, theatre directors, set designers, patissiers, milliners and dress designers were flocking to the city from Paris, Rome and London. This itinerary explores the most fashionable quarter of the city, where palaces, castles and extravagant barracks were built throughout the 18th and 19th centuries. The architecture mirrors the changing society, from the light decorative touch of the 'petticoat period', when women reigned for 65 out of 70 years, to the celebratory Empire style following the victory over Napoleon and beyond. Since 1917 most of the buildings have been colonized by offices or museums, though some were converted into communal flats. With the advent of capitalism foreign companies and Russia's home-grown *nouveau riche* have recognized the potential value of this real estate, and palatial apartments are once more gracing the ground and first floors.

Though this walk passes through Palace Square, the interior and collections of the vast Hermitage Museum in the Winter Palace are discussed separately in Walk VII. Moseying down between the palaces on Millionaire Street we find the Marble Palace which Catherine the Great built for her lover Grigory Orlov and which now houses exhibitions of Russian art from the immense collection of the Russian Museum. Royal assassinations loom large at the Mikhailovsky Castle on the far side of the immense Field of Mars, and at the nearby Church of the Saviour on the Blood. Continuing the theme, the walk finishes with a visit to the flat in which the great poet Pushkin breathed his last. To follow this itinerary on a Tuesday would be a big mistake, and bear in mind that the Pushkin Museum is also closed on the last Friday of the month.

lunch/cafés

Consider experiencing a real Russian food queue at one of the best **grocers** (Продукты) in town, on the corner of Ul. Milliónaya and Zaporozhsky Pereulok. On a good day you could find smoked salmon and champagne, though you will have to queue at different counters for them. There is always cheese, butter and sausage. Almost opposite is a **bread shop** (булочная).

Literary Café (Literatornoye Kafé), Nevsky Prospekt 18, ✆ 312 8536/8543 (*open 12 noon–11pm; unlikely to serve between 3.30 and 6pm*). After having the cheek of charging an entry fee, which they say is to pay the classical musicians who accompany your meal, the staff will do their best to ignore you. Unfortunately the whole establishment manages to rest securely on the laurels of its literary pedigree—it was once the fashionable Café Wulf et Beranger, where Pushkin met his second on the way to his deadly duel. The calm and dignified 19th-century cream interior is enhanced by eye-catching tree chandeliers and the food is just good enough, including such classic Russian dishes as caviar and *blini*. If your Russian is good enough, ask for the Russian language menu—the prices are considerably lower.

House of Scholars Café, Dvortsovaya Naberezhnaya 26, to the left of where Zaporozhsky Pereulok comes down to the embankment. Enter through the glass and wood porch of this great Florentine Renaissance palace and cross the sombre hall with its magnificent Chinese pots to find the cosy café beyond the staircase.

Marble Palace Café. Across the courtyard to the right as you leave the main door of the Marble Palace museum, an impressive selection of soft drinks and alcohol, plus a traditional Russian cafeteria serving soup and a hot main course, awaits.

Café Fontanka, Naberezhnaya Reki Fontanki 14, *open 2pm–5am; closed 10pm–11pm*, is not far off the walk by the Mikhailovsky Castle (*see* p.500).

Restaurant Sankt Peterburg, Kanal Griboyedova 5, ✆ 314 4947 *open 12 noon–5pm, 7pm–2am.* This is a slick new establishment set up with tour groups in mind. There are small intimate tables, though at night you can't avoid the somewhat dubious floor show which ingeniously manages to mix semi-nudity with Russian history. Its English-language menu is inventive but expensive. The attached café round the corner (*open 4–9pm)* serves good, ordinary Russian food, which you can choose by pointing at the samples laid out on the counter.

Pevchesky Mostik Café, Naberezhnaya Reki Moyki 26, has plenty of tables at which to devour the coffee, soft drinks, cakes and hot sandwiches on offer.

Leave Ⓜ *Nevsky Prospekt via the Kanal Griboyedova* (Канал Грибоедова) *exit and turn right down Nevsky Prospekt, over the Griboyedov Canal to pass the outstretched arms of the Kazan Cathedral (see p.333) on your left.*

After the first street on the right, the plain yellow façade of the **Lutheran Church of St Peter**, Nevsky Prospekt 22–24, currently hides a municipal swimming pool, though the city intends to give the building back to its communicants. It was built in the 1830s, but is flanked by two 18th-century buildings which date back to the earlier Lutheran church on this spot. Behind the building is one of Petersburg's oldest schools, the mid-18th century Peterschule, which still teaches its syllabus in two languages, German and Russian. 'Special' schools like this existed throughout the Soviet period, preparing citizens for work with Intourist and the Foreign Ministry, but with the collapse of the Iron Curtain they have become still more popular. Those who can afford it are even sending their children to private 'gymnasiums', modelled on their 19th-century predecessors, where Latin and Greek have been reintroduced into the curriculum. Until the Revolution the seemingly secular green building at Nevsky Prospekt 20 hid the **Dutch Church** behind its portico.

Since the foundation of the city, the banks of the River Moyka ahead have been one of its smartest addresses. In 1752–4 the Stroganov family commissioned Empress Elizabeth's pet architect Bartolomeo Rastrelli to build the green and white **Stroganov Palace** which still overlooks the river on the far side of Nevsky Prospekt. Toning down the taste for Baroque extravagance which he lavished on his imperial palaces, Rastrelli designed this private house with masterly control, though it was originally painted bright orange. Pillars are used to emphasize the plain entrance arch on Nevsky Prospekt and the centre of the façade on the Moyka, and rhythm injected into the building by the orderly use of stucco ornament around the windows. For the moment, it is impossible to get in to admire the interiors by Rastrelli, and those designed later by the Stroganov's genius serf-architect Andrei Voronykhin (*see* p.468), but the Russian Museum intends, funds permitting, to restore its halls and use them for exhibitions.

The Stroganovs, who lived here until 1917, were fabulously wealthy. 'Richer than the Stroganovs' was an expression used to describe the impossible. From the 15th-century they had been awarded vast tracts of the Ural Mountains by the tsars, where they extracted salt and iron, felled timber and traded in the abundance of animal furs. In the 16th century it was the Stroganovs not the inhabitants of the Kremlin who hired an army of Cossacks to drive the Tartar Khan from Siberia. Having supported the Romanov claim to the throne in the 17th century, they never looked back, as titles and office were heaped upon successive generations.

For an idea of just how fashionable the Moyka was, the Stroganov palace looked directly across the water towards that of his close friend the Empress Elizabeth, whose own Rastrelli palace was not finished until the 1760s. The tall pink building which now stands there, the '**House with Columns**' (occupied by the Barrikada Cinema) originally served as the home of St Petersburg's Chief of Police.

Nevsky Prospekt crosses the Moyka River over the earliest iron bridge in the city, known as **Police Bridge***. If the weather is perfect, you may be tempted to hire one of the flotilla of small boats moored down to the right for a trip round the canals (see p.427). If not, over the bridge it is worth diving into Staraya Kniga, Nevsky Prospekt 18, on the right, to admire the elegant mahogany shop fittings and sniff out a bargain amongst the books, prints and bric-a-brac. Turn right just after the shop.*

While most of Ul. Gertsena presents a unified 19th-century façade, the high grey granite building on the left, now the Long Distance Telephone Exchange, was designed as the headquarters of the Azov–Don Commercial Bank by St Petersburg's greatest *Style Moderne* architect, Fyodor Lidval, in 1908–9. The curiously angled double arch of the **Main Staff Building** anead acts as an exhilarating triumphal entrance to Palace Square (*Dvortsovaya Ploshchad*), hiding until the last minute the immense, sea-green façade of the **Winter Palace**.

For 230 years the sculptures which decorate the roof of the palace have looked down on the square, bearing indulgent witness to the follies of mankind. Nineteenth-century diplomats describe freezing on the balconies as the imperial family derived their increasingly false sense of security from another four-hour parade of soldiers. By 1879 even the square was sometimes unsafe for them, and a member of the 'People's Will' terrorist group made an attempt on the life Alexander II as he rode through it. But it was troops opening fire on a peaceful demonstration of workers on 9 January 1905, killing and wounding hundreds, that propelled the revolutionary movement into top gear and precipitated the 1905 revolution. Ironically, the gathering had been organized by Father Gapon, a monarchist who sought to prove that the tsar still had the well-being of his people at heart by allowing him to listen to and act upon their grievances. It was here too that a decisive four-hour gun battle ended with the arrest of the last members of the provisional government in the palace at 1.50am on 26 October 1917 and ushered in the rule of the Bolsheviks. John Reed, the American journalist famed for his eye-witness account of the Revolution, captures the spirit of hope which accompanied it when he wrote that that night 'on Palace Square I watched the birth of a new world.' To many Russians today, those events are known simply as the *catastroph.*

Standing in **Palace Square**, it is easy to understand how such a theatrical forum could encourage myths in an already mythomanic regime. In 1920 the third anniversary of the Revolution was celebrated with a dramatic reconstruction of the storming of the Winter Palace, in which thousands of extras rushed across the square in an heroic charge that had never taken place. Eisenstein's film *October*, shot in 1928, immortalized the image. For the first few years after 1917, May Day and 7 November (the anniversary of the October Revolution after the adoption of the Gregorian calendar in 1918) were greeted by Constructivist and Futurist canvases thousands of metres long hung from the palace roof. Impressive though the procession of the proletariat which accompanied them was, it often owed more to the promise of an extra bread ration than revolutionary fervour.

Even today Palace Square is the pulse of the city, the place where people go to hear the news. During the events of August 1991, the city's Mayor Sobchak came here from his barricaded office on St Isaac's Square to address the protesting crowd. More recently it has been the White Nights pop concerts on the square which attract the largest crowds, while strange bedfellows still congregate on the traditional Communist holidays calling for a return to the ways of sobriety—elderly die-hard reds, hard-faced Russian nationalists and hard-line Orthodox believers—the so-called red-brown coalition. At other times gypsy beggars, tourists and even massed processions of Hare Krishna devotees occupy the space.

The palace, now part of the world-renowned Hermitage Museum, was the last of the six winter homes built for the imperial family in the first 60 years of the city's history. It was commissioned by the Empress Elizabeth and built by Bartolomeo Rastrelli between 1754–62, at the same time that he was building the Catherine Palace for her at Tsarskoye Selo. With these two buildings he created a new style to express the 'the glory of all Russia', a product of his distinctive hybrid genius. Born in Italy, Rastrelli spent ten formative years from the age of 16 in Russia with his sculptor father before going abroad again to study. He used the exuberance of the Italian and French Baroque tradition in a way uniquely suited to Russia's colourful building tradition and her flat, never-ending landscape. Here, the long low façade feels surprisingly light, thanks to his use of repetition and change in the decorative motifs which are highlighted in white. In between the attached porticoes, where two-storey composite columns stand on single storey Ionic arrangements, the windows are made to dance by slight alterations in the entablature and bronze-painted decorative flourishes. Crowning all, the bronze statues and urns on the roof, oxidized to appear organically connected to the building, add an unlikely touch of the surreal. Once, as the Victorian traveller Augustus Hare was told, they shared the roof with servants, who worked amongst other tasks 'to keep the water in the tanks from freezing during the winter by casting in red-hot cannon-balls—[they] built themselves huts between the chimneys, took their wives and children there, and even kept poultry and goats who fed on the grass of the roof. It is said that at last some cows were introduced.' The central portico, surmounted by its pediment, is the only vehicular entrance into the palace's inner courtyard, which once echoed to the stacatto clatter of hoofs and the roll of royal carriage wheels.

While the Winter Palace symbolizes Russia's emergence onto the European stage as a power to be reckoned with, the **Main Staff Building** opposite marks another decisive moment in the development of the superpower mentality. Commissioned within five years of Alexander I's defeat of Napoleon in 1812–14, its architect Carlo Rossi was entrusted with a whole series of architectural ensembles in the city, each one of which uses a neoclassical idiom to express the confidence and Imperial ambitions of post-Napoleonic Russia. As in contemporary France, the style became known as Empire (*ampir*). Thanks to its graceful softening curve, the regular yellow and white edifice does not overpower the Winter Palace opposite. In the none too subtle allegory used in many capitals of the western world, the building is surmounted by a sculpture of Victory riding forward triumphant in a chariot drawn by six racing horses. To underline the point, the Alexander Column at the centre of the square was erected by his brother and successor, Nicholas I and bore the inscription 'To Alexander I from a grateful Russia'. The column is one of the tallest ever erected, a single piece of granite on a tall plinth topped by an angel whose face is modelled on that of the victorious emperor. It took two years to carve the 600-ton granite column from the rock face and a year to transport it to the city. Since 1834 it has stood on its plinth without pegging or mortar, balanced only by its own immense weight.

The third side of Palace Square is filled by a relatively small yellow and white classical building, designed as the **Guards' Headquarters**. It was built in 1837–43, the visible tip of a whole series of barracks and army staff buildings beyond.

> *Leave the square via the street between the Guards' Headquarters and the Winter Palace, Millionaya Ul.*

As its name suggests, this is St Petersburg's Millionaire's Row. In the early days, Peter I settled his many foreign friends and advisors here and it became known as the German quarter. However during the second half of the 18th century, the Winter Palace expanded further up the street, and other members of the royal family, courtiers and even court architects took up residence here.

Adjoining the Winter Palace you will find the **Small Hermitage**, built for Catherine the Great in 1764–5 by Yuri Velten, and beyond it the New Hermitage. Commissioned by Nicholas I as Russia's first purpose-built art gallery, this solid, Renaissance-inspired building, whose niches are set with statues of artists of the Renaissance and classical period, was entered via the monumental carriage porch held aloft by ten grey marble Atlantes. Today the entire palace complex has become a museum and the main entrance is on Dvortsovaya Naberezhnaya overlooking the Neva (*see* Walk VII for the interior of Hermitage Museum). Opposite the carriage porch, at the end of the 19th century a Renaissance fortress was erected to house the royal archives, though since the Soviet period it has contained the naval archive.

*Millionnaya Ul. crosses the Winter Canal (Zimnaya Kanavka), leaving the Imperial palace behind. If you look left, you will see a covered bridge near the Neva embankment which leads to the **Hermitage Theatre,** built for Catherine the Great by Giacomo Quarenghi in the 1780s.*

The gateways on the left of the street were originally the back entrances to the great palaces which line Palace Embankment (Dvortsovaya Naberezhnaya), whose façades are best appreciated from the other side of the river (*see* p.293). If you stroll through the arch at No. 29, you will find yourself in the service courtyard of the Palace of the Grand Duke Vladimir, now the **House of Scientists**. The central block, much older than his palace or the surrounding courtyard, once served as stabling for his 36 horses and 40 carriages, whose coachmen were amongst the smartest in the city in their scarlet or green uniforms, trimmed with raccoon.

As you walk down the street, there are a couple of pretty 18th-century buildings (No. 22 and the former Main Pharmacy at No. 4) but it is in the undistinguished 19th-century beige palaces that events of historical importance took place.

At Millionnaya Ul. 12, on 3 March 1917, the Romanov dynasty finally relinquished the throne of Russia in the aftermath of the February revolution. The day before Nicholas II had abdicated in favour of his brother, Grand Duke Michael, who took just one day to follow his example. The pink and white house next door, with its delicate stucco moulding, was built by the prolific German architect Stakenschneider for himself, and acted as an important international cultural salon in the mid-19th century.

*At the far end of this prestigious street, at Nos. 1–5, the **Marble Palace** (*Mrámorny Dvorets*) stands in splendid isolation, its first storey camouflaged in plain grey granite. Open 10am–6pm (Mon 5pm); closed Tues.*

It owes its name to the multi-coloured marble-clad façade above. Here in 1768 Catherine the Great ordered the previously Baroque architect, Rinaldi, to build a palace for Grigory Orlov, her lover of eight years and the father of her son Alexei Bobrinsky, using the recently discovered deposits of coloured marbles from the Urals and Siberia. She wanted to thank Orlov for his and his brothers' leading role in the 1762 coup against her husband which put her on the throne, and her generosity to her lovers was well known. Not even Catherine herself had a stone palace, and indeed at the time of its completion this was the only one in the capital. Rinaldi realized that marble was too classic a material for his beloved, curvaceous Baroque, so he built Russia's first neoclassical building instead. The handsome but severe regularity of its façades is alleviated in the portico of the courtyard entrance, where rounded columns support a pediment with a clock surrounded by garlands and swags.

Inside, the banisters and doorways are decorated in grey-blue marble. Walking up the main stairwell is like travelling through a Wedgwood pot; the powder-blue walls offset white plaster bas reliefs on a martial themes, although many of the niches gape sadly, their statues missing. Until August 1991, such holes were filled with Lenin memorabilia, for this was a branch of the Central Lenin Museum. In a grand gesture of sweeping change, one of the first exhibitions installed by the Russian Museum who now use the space was of pre-Revolutionary official portraiture—royalty, aristocrats, lawyers, government ministers and patriarchs. In the palace's Great Hall, Rinaldi's decorative genius exploited the colourful properties of the more valuable marbles to fine effect. The white marble eagle is a play on the name Orlov, which means just that in Russian. The museum shop, incidentally, is one of the best in Russia. Its postcards bear no relationship to the exhibitions, but they are the best you are likely to find.

> *Depending on the time of year, you will either want to linger amongst the lilac of the Field of Mars (Marsovo polye), or scurry across it wishing that the eternal flame at the centre of the central Monument to Revolutionary Fighters was a bit more accessible.*

The **Field of Mars** is a vast open grassy space, but ever since a frail nonagenarian Petersburger described how she was taunted and dive-bombed by a German pilot as she made her solitary way across it during the seige, it's seemed eerie and haunted to me. Beneath the paths, shrubs, benches and the heroic granite walls of the monument lie Bolshevik victims of the 1917 revolutions and the Civil War. Some 800,000 citizens are said to have shown their support for the February Revolution by massing for the first burial of 184 of its victims in late March 1917. The granite monument adorned with quotations from Commissar Lunacharsky was erected two years later and the eternal flame lit in their memory in October 1957, the 40th anniversary of the Revolution.

This open space has been used as a place of amusement and public activity since its marshy soil, the source of both the Moyka River and the Griboyedov Canal, was first drained by Peter. Its character turned predominantly martial (hence the name, after Mars, the Roman god of war) under Paul I, who obssessively drilled his troops here, and his son Alexander I who had V. P. Stasov build the immense classical Barracks of the Pavlovsky Regiment to frame its western side. Paul I had founded this regiment named after himself, and not the least of his psychological quirks was to recruit for it only men whose snub noses matched his own. The sandy parade ground, known as the Petersburg Sahara, was transformed into a garden in 1920, by 16,000 workers taking part in the Soviet institution known as a *subbotnik*, a Saturday devoted to voluntary labour. As municipal governments have less and less money to spare on cleaning their cities, so a fond longing for the days of *subbotniki* stirs in the breasts of their older citizens. A far away look glazes their eyes as they remember when Pioneers (the Soviet equivalent of the Boy Scout and Girl Guides) were marched out to clean the city's ponds after the thaw in spring.

Aim for the tall spire diagonally opposite the Marble Palace across the Field of Mars. It rises above the church in the **Mikhailovsky Castle** *(Mikhailovsky zamok) on the other side of the Moyka.*

The sad tale of Paul I's life culminates in the Mikhailovsky Castle. Paul chose to believe that he was the only legitimate son and heir of Peter III and Catherine. As a child he saw almost nothing of his mother, and when he was eight she and her lover Grigory Orlov plotted the coup which was to end in the death of his father. Rather than act as regent during Paul's minority, Catherine then usurped the throne. In the meantime, Paul's second marriage had turned out to be surprisingly happy and loving. As the Count and Countess of the North, he and Maria Fyodorovna made a European tour in 1781–2. The bright, brilliantly educated Paul was the darling of Versailles.

Catherine's reign was a long one, however, and Paul was 42 by the time he reached the throne. The 14 years of waiting, tainted by gossip surrounding his mother's successive affairs and rumours about his own legitimacy, had taken their toll. Vengeful and filled with hatred towards his mother, Paul compensated by drilling regiments of soldiers to immaculate standards. Vestiges of the sentimental idealism which had made him a loving husband remained, though they took such quaint forms that he became the laughing stock of Europe. On one occasion, in order to spare the populations of Europe the pain of war, he issued an invitation to all the crowned heads of Europe, published openly in the newspapers, to solved disagreements by personal combat in the form of duels.

Given the circumstances of his life, the dream that convinced Paul to build his home here seems like a subconscious urge to wipe out his early memories and replace them with something safe. The Archangel Michael appeared to him and told him to build a church on the site where he was born, legitimizing the destruction of Rastrelli's gay looking Summer Palace, built for the Empress Elizabeth, where he was snatched away from his mother when only a few hours old. In its place Paul ordered Bazhenov to design him a fortress, and Vincenzo Brenna to build it. The site was already protected on two sides by the Fontanka and Moyka Rivers, and the other two he dug to form a moat. A drawbridge which was raised at dusk protected the sleeping inhabitants.

Tragically, it was in this monument to emotional and physical security that Paul met his brutal death. His behaviour had become so unpredictable that a

St Petersburg cartoon showed him holding a paper marked 'order' in one hand, another marked 'counter-order' in the other, and with 'disorder' written on his forehead. He was so sensitive about his nose that he refused to have his profile on the coin of the realm and even banned the use of the word 'snub-nose'. Most dangerously of all, he distrusted the nobility and, ignoring their traditional exemptions, had them flogged in public and exiled on a whim. On 11 March 1801, just 40 days after taking up residence, Paul was smothered in his bedroom by a group of men including his mother's last lover and his own closest advisor, the Governor-General of St Petersburg.

The elegant earthy pink square building surrounds an octagonal courtyard, entry to which is through a massive granite gateway on the south side of the building. Over the gate a pediment relief depicts the Triumph of Russia. Both on the obelisks which flank the gate and all round the inner courtyard you will see plaques bearing Paul's cipher, which, in his insecurity, he insisted on having inscribed some 8000 times around the building. Outside the gateway, Paul erected the bronze horseback statue of Peter I which had been cast by Carlo Rastrelli, father of the architect, and rejected by Catherine, with an inscription directly aping his mother's on the Bronze Horseman in Decembrists' Square: 'To great grandfather, from great grandson'. Inside, the building was originally furnished with pieces confiscated from the homes of many of his mother's lovers.

Extensive restoration work is taking place here, so that it can be used for exhibitions by the Russian Museum. The handful of rooms currently open, to the left as you enter the castle, exhibit a selection of prints about the history of the building.

After Paul's death, no member of the royal family would inhabit the place, and it was eventually given over to an Academy of Military Engineering in 1823. The academy's most unlikely alumnus was Fyodor Dostoyevsky. Though he passed out third in his class, Dostoyevsky's heart was never really in his profession. 'What idiot drew this?' snarled the tsar, of a fortress he had inadvertantly drawn without doors. Today, despite the restorations, part of the building is still occupied by the naval library.

> *A walk on round the castle shows how each side differs. Facing the Fontanka the building is at its most secretive, screened by trees. Only on the northern façade is there a break in the unyielding walls—overlooking the Field of Mars and the Summer Garden a first floor terrace, supported by pillars, stands above a broad flight of steps leading to the ground. Returning to the church staircase, a gate in the railing allows you to cross Sadovaya Ul. and enter the Mikhailovsky Gardens directly opposite.*

These belong to the slightly later **Mikhailovsky Palace**, visible on the far left of the gardens. This now houses the superlative collection of native painting and crafts that makes up the Russian Museum (*see* Walk IV, pp.341–52). On the banks of the Moyka which borders the gardens to the right, the Rossi pavilion, named after the architect who designed both the palace and the Main Staff building we saw at the start of the walk, stands reflected in its waters. The far end of the gardens, dense with trees even in winter, is delineated by an exceptional early *Style Moderne* railing, florid and plastic, its floral bracts and full-blown blooms transforming themselves into all manner of imaginings at the whim of the beholder.

You can't miss the Church of the Resurrection, the fantasy pseudo-Russian confection which soars colourfully towards the sky between the gardens and the Griboyedov Canal. Better known as Spass na Krovi, the **Saviour on the Blood**, it was built between 1887 and 1907 to mark the spot where Alexander II was mortally wounded by a bomb thrown by a member of the 'People's Will' revolutionary movement on 1 March 1881. The canal has been narrowed so that the altar stands exactly where the royal blood stained the pavement.

The church manages to combine all the hallmarks of 17th-century Russian church architecture, with its use of brick, the tent-roofed central tower, *kokóshniki* gables and eight further domes including the gilded belltower. Its twisting, multi-coloured domes refer blatantly to the icon of touristic Russia, St Basil's Cathedral in Red Square. It's entirely out of place in St Petersburg, but fun.

The mosaics, both on the exterior and apparently in the interior were designed by some of the greatest artists of the late 19th century in Russia, when a movement—similar to William Morris's Arts and Crafts movement in Britain—sought to revive Russia's heritage. The interior, which has been undergoing restoration since the 1970s, shimmers with mosaic religious scenes on walls, piers and vaults, designed by Vasnetsov, Nesterov and Vrubel amongst others. For the moment however, the church is not open to the public and we must content ourselves with the transfiguration, crucifixion and resurrection scenes which adorn important parts of the exterior.

> *Beyond the Griboyedov Canal, passing round the Saviour on the Blood to the right, Stable Square (*Konyúshennaya Plóshchad*) opens up with what was the **Imperial Stables**, the vast pink and white building, on the right.*

As the internal combustion engine superseded the horse, the Leningrad Taxi Transport Company took over this early 19th-century building during the Soviet period. The taller domed section in the centre is accessible as its upper floors are a recently reopened, and hence very bare, church. Its greatest moment of glory took place between 1 and 3 February 1837, when the body of Alexander Sergeievich Pushkin, Russia's greatest poet, lay here following his death in a duel. He was brought from his last home, just round the corner at Naberezhnaya Reki Moyki 12.

> *To get there continue straight along beside the stables to the banks of the River Moyka. Turn left along the embankment until you reach No. 12, the **Pushkin Flat Museum** (Dom-muzei A. S. Púshkina). Open 11am–6pm; closed Tues and last Fri of the month. If you happen to be here on 10 February, (date of Pushkin's death according to the calendar adopted by the Bolsheviks in 1918), the place will be teeming and readings will begin shortly after the time of death, 2.45pm.*

Situated on a graceful curve of the river just behind Palace Square, the museum complex occupies buildings round a peaceful courtyard which is rarely empty of Pushkin fans here to commune with him and his muse. It is hard to describe just how dizzy a position Pushkin holds in the estimation of the Russians, but it is certainly not adequate to describe him as Russia's Shakespeare. Here Pushkin flows with the last glasses of vodka, whether you are with factory workers, artists or politicians. For Russians, poetry has been the voice of freedom through the centuries of oppression and Pushkin's death, to which he was driven partly by the contemptuous attitude of courtly society, has made him something of a martyr.

The building at the back of the courtyard was once the stables of a 1730s house built here for the Empress Anna's German favourite Biron, and predates the house in which Pushkin lived by some 65 years. The first floor gallery always has some kind of literary exhibition going on, and even if you don't read Russian they are often gloriously visual, tracing, for example, one period in Russia's unparalleled history of book illustration. The point of the visit is to see Pushkin's flat, reconstructed in the 1920s to a plan of the flat drawn, when the poet died, by his friend the poet Vasily Zhukovsky. Many of the poet's possessions, and copies of his paintings, litter surfaces and walls. If you rent an English-language cassette guide, which for once is quite good, you avoid having to be conducted in a Russian language tour.

Pushkin lived here for the last four months of his life, from September 1836, renting the flat from Princess Volkonskaya, whose brother Sergei had been exiled to Siberia for his part in the Decembrist uprising. A visit to the flat begins backwards, at the servants' door, where a copy of the last note posted to keep inquirers informed of the poet's deteriorating condition reads: 'The patient is in an extremely dangerous condition'. The irony of his death is that had Pushkin had his way and lived:

> *'...in family love*
> *contented, easeful, peaceful, quiet,*
> *ageing by our fathers' graves,*
> *at home on patrimonial lands...'*

as he longs in one of his unfinished poems, he would have escaped so pointless an end. However, Tsar Nicholas I, who barely trusted him but recognized his talent, threatened to withdraw his research rights in the state archives if he retired from the capital. So Pushkin's beautiful wife Natalia was here to provoke idle rumours about her relations with one D'Anthès, a young French cavalry officer. In the malicious, introverted society of St Petersburg, it wasn't long before anonymous letters arrived, calling Pushkin 'the historiographer of the Order of Cuckoldry'. Two months later Pushkin challenged D'Anthès to a duel at Chornaya Rechka, then outside the city. D'Anthès fired first and his bullet lodged in Pushkin's stomach, but the poet nevertheless managed to take his shot and wound the Frenchman in the hand. This was at 5pm on 27 January, and until he died two days later crowds flocked to this door for news. After that, 'multitudes of people of all ages and ranks kept gathering in crowds about his coffin—women, old men, children, schoolboys, common people in sheepskins...' and his funeral mass was packed, despite decrees ordering all staff and students of the university to attend their lessons throughout the day.

Upstairs the flat, as it did in his day, centres on Pushkin's study, the second to last room in the tour. In the second room, the sitting room, you will find portraits of Pushkin and his close friends Vyazemskoy, Zhukovsky and Odovsky and in the next, Natalia's room, a copy of the famous water-colour of her by Bryullov. After the room in which one of Natalia's sisters stayed comes the nursery where the couple's four children worked and played. It is now devoted to memorabilia of his death, including the 'cuckold' letter, the waistcoat and a glove he was wearing, and candles from his funeral.

Pushkin's study is still dominated by his library of over 4000 books, here seen in replica. His desk is strewn with papers. The inkstand, decorated with an Ethiopian, was one of his favourite objects as it reminded him of his great-grandfather Abram Hannibal, who had been brought to Russia as a gift for Peter I and became not only his friend but also his chief military engineer. The metal travelling box here belonged to him, while the letter knife, walking sticks, Turkish sabre and pipe were all Pushkin's own. The clock in this room reminds visitors eternally of the moment of his death. The last room in the flat contains the poet's death mask beside a portrait of the deceased by Kozlov and a lock of his hair which Pushkin's valet had cut off for the budding novelist Ivan Turgenev at his request. The table opposite holds a copy of the Lermontov poem on the death of Pushkin which had him exiled to the Caucasus (see Moscow Walk IV, p.155).

> To return to Ⓜ Nevsky Prospekt, continue along the banks of the Moyka, to the Glinka Kapella which was once the home of the Court Choir (No. 20). Worming your way through to Bolshaya Konushennaya Ul. via the courtyards of the Kapella, you will find yourself in archetypal Petersburg. Warrens of courtyards like this, each overlooked by the blank staring windows of a score of flats, are hidden behind even St Petersburg's most glamorous façades. Turn right along the avenue, and left when you hit Nevsky Prospekt. The station is just beyond the Griboyedov Canal.

Walking Time: *2½ hours. Try to include the interior of the Yussupov Palace by phoning © 314 7140 or © 314 3049 to arrange a tour in English, and set off 1 hour before your appointment. This will add a further ¾ hour to the itinerary.*

Start: Ⓜ *Sennaya Ploshchad (Ploshchad Mira)/ Sadovaya.*

III: A Clutch of Cathedrals

KAZANSKY SOBOR

III: A Clutch of Cathedrals

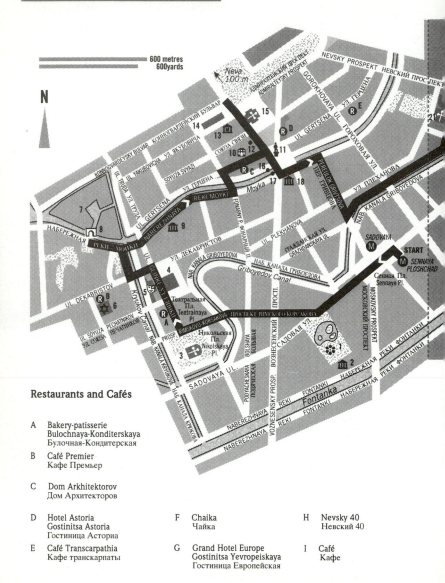

Restaurants and Cafés

A Bakery-patisserie
   Bulochnaya-Konditerskaya
   Булочная-Кондитерская

B Café Premier
   Кафе Премьер

C Dom Arkhitektorov
   Дом Архитекторов

D Hotel Astoria
   Gostinitsa Astoria
   Гостиница Астория

E Café Transcarpathia
   Кафе транскарпаты

F Chaika
   Чайка

G Grand Hotel Europe
   Gostinitsa Yevropeiskaya
   Гостиница Европейская

H Nevsky 40
   Невский 40

I Café
   Кафе

ITALIANSKAYA UL.
ИТАЛЬЯНСКАЯ УЛ

22

NEVSKY
PROSPEKT
FINISH

GOSTINY
DVOR

21

19

20

UL. LOMONOSOVA
УЛ. ЛОМОНОСОВА

SADOVAYA UL.
САДОВАЯ УЛ

SENNAYA
PLOSHCHAD

Sites

1 Children's Park (Yussupov Garden)
Yussupovsky sad
Юсуповский сад

2 Yussupov Palace (on the Fontanka)
Yussopovsky dvorets (na Fontankye)
Юсуповский дворец (на Фонтанке)

3 St Nicholas's Cathedral
Nikolsky sobor
Никольский собор

4 Rimsky-Korsakov Conservatoire
Konservatoriya im. N. A. Rimskovo-Korsakova
Консерватория им. Н. А. Римского-Корсакова

5 Mariinsky Theatre
Mariinsky teatr
Мариинский театр

6 Synagogue
Sinagoga
Синагога

7 New Holland
Novaya Gollandiya
Новая Голландия

8 Vallin de la Mothe Arch
Arka
Арка

9 Yussupov Palace (on the Moyka)
Yussupovsky dvorets (na Moyke)
Юсуповский дворец (на Мойке)

10 Nabokov's House
Dom Nabokova
Дом Набокова

11 Statue of Nicholas I
Statuya Nikolaya I
Статуя Николая I

12 Former German Embassy
Byvshoye nemetskoye posolstvo
Бывшее немецкое посольство

13 Museum of Musical Instruments
Muzei muzikalnikh instrumentov
Музей музыкальных инструментов

14 Manezh (Central Exhibition Hall)
Manezh (Tsentralny vystavochny zal)
Манеж (Центральный выставочный зал)

15 St Isaac's Cathedral
Isaakiyevsky sobor
Исаакиевский собор

16 Flood Marker

17 Blue Bridge
Sinny most
Синий мост

18 Mariinsky Palace
Mariinsky dvorets
Мариинский дворец

19 Bankovsky Bridge
Bankovsky most
Банковский мост

20 Former Imperial Bank
Byvshy assignatsionny bank
Бывший ассигнационный банк

21 Kazan Cathedral
Kazansky sobor
Казанский собор

Less than fifty years separate the building of the two cathedrals, both by Russian architects, that begin and end this walk. The earlier St Nicholas's Cathedral was designed at the height of Russia's whimsical Baroque, expressing the country's new-found confidence in a Europeanized and gilded version of Russian traditions, while the Kazan Cathedral is in the mainstream of European architecture. It consciously mimics St Peter's in Rome, ignoring the eastern roots of Orthodox church architecture and announcing Russia's emergence as a great European power. In between, Catherine the Great, with her studious energy and encouraging self-confidence had pummelled, negotiated and codified Russia out of adolescence.

Yet beneath this architectural gilding, something of St Petersburg's mythic ambivalence should be gleaned from today's contrasting locations. The walk starts in the depths of Dostoyevsky's city—Haymarket Square. In 1992 Russian men and women came back on to the streets here to drink, trade and socialize, just as their fictional forebears did between the covers of Dostoyevsky's novels. A steady stream of milling shoppers disgorges you past palatial gardens and across the leafy Griboyedov Canal into the relative quiet of St Nicholas's and the musical theatre district, bordered on three sides by canals. From here, the Moyka River sweeps back through the official 19th-century city, past mounted tsars, former embassies, grand hotels and ill-conceived monumentalities to the echoing brilliance of the Kazan Cathedral, until recently the Museum of the History of Religion and Atheism. You can walk it in a matter of hours, and yet in the 19th century you sense that people rarely crossed the bridges between these two worlds.

To make the most of the itinerary, follow it on Thurs–Sat.

lunch/cafés

Russkiye Samovary, opposite the Yussupov Palace Gardens on Sadovaya Ul., is a cheap drop in in which *blini* and *kefir*, a longevity-promoting yoghurt drink, are the standard fare.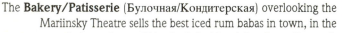

The **Bakery/Patisserie** (Булочная/Кондитерская) overlooking the Mariinsky Theatre sells the best iced rum babas in town, in the crowded stand-up café in the left side of the shop. Queue first at the till opposite, praying they have not run out, and ask for 'kófye ee room bába' (кофе и рум баба). Then present your receipt at the café, repeat the request and give extra roubles if you want sugar (sákhar/сахап).

Café Premiéra, Ul. Dekabristov 36, open 11am–10pm. This busy co-op always has a plentiful supply of exotic booze, normally including champagne, and a continuous trickle of customers for its run-of-the-mill menu.

Dom Arkhitéktorov, Ul. Gertsena 52, open 12 noon–10pm; closed Sun. Ten out of ten for decor, less for the food (*see* p.499).

Hotel Astoria, St Isaac's Square. You will find a bar inside the entrance closest to the cathedral and a café/bar and Winter Garden Restaurant, serving good *à la carte* meals for lots of roubles, inside the other.

Transcarpathian Café, Ul. Gértsena 14, open 12 noon–10pm. The sculptured wooden booths in this rouble restaurant are a lot more interesting than the food, but then finding somewhere to eat round here can get desperate.

Grand Hotel Europe, Ul. Mikhailovskaya 1–7, with its restaurants, bar and café, is not far from the Kazan Cathedral at the end of the walk (*see* p.333).

Nevsky 40, Nevsky Prospekt 40 and **Chaika**, Kanal Griboyedova 14, are both German joint ventures, more bars than restaurants though both offer an adequate microwaved menu to their often foreign clientèle.

For an authentic local café at the end of the walk, descend into the basement of **Nevsky Prospekt 42** and point at what looks interesting. Standing only.

If you have arrived at Ⓜ Sadovaya, change stations below ground to leave from Ⓜ Sennaya Ploshchad (it is still sometimes known as Ploshchad Mira). As you come out onto the mess of Sennaya Ploshchad (Haymarket Square), half building site, half market, note that we will be leaving it via Sadovaya Ul., the road to the left with tramlines running along it.

When free trading on the street was legalized at the beginning of 1992, with a certain historical inevitability **Haymarket Square** became St Petersburg's foremost flea-market, where petty salesmen and women traded everything from secondhand locks to caviar. Until the Revolution, when it assumed the pompous name Peace Square, it had been the centre of the city's most notorious slums, an inferno of cheap lodgings, brothels, sawdust and spittle ale houses, moneylenders, madmen, vagrants and animals. Here, not surprisingly, the cholera epidemic of 1831 spread triumphantly from one household to another, and here too Dostoyevsky chose to house the oppressed yet proud hero of *Crime and Punishment*, Raskolnikov. Those with a particular interest might want to see where authorities on the book reckon he lived—Ul. Grazhdánskaya 19—and where he killed the elderly moneylender at Naberezhnaya Kanála Griboédova 104.

The Church of the Saviour, for 200 years the square's central feature, was demolished in 1961 to make way for the first metro station. Now the building of the extension of the metro below ground has further destroyed the integrity of the square, with one small, porticoed early 19th-century Guard House clinging ever more tenuously to its life, surrounded by corrugated iron and the metal kiosks that represent all that is left of the traders. Outraged Soviet citizens, used to the invisible chaos of the centralized market, complained so vociferously at the visible chaos of the free market that it was closed down after only a few months.

Leave Sennaya Ploshchad via Sadovaya Ul. After a few hundred metres the **Yussupov Garden** *opens up behind railings on the left.*

Once the private garden of the pretty but crumbling Yussupov palace to the south, it opened to the public after the family moved out in the 19th century. It was here, on the 18th-century ornamental ponds, that Russian figure skating modestly began; here that several future Olympic champions etched their first figures of eight into the ice. Today it is designated a children's park, and is still a popular venue for skating in winter.

Almost opposite the entrance to the gardens, Ul. Rímskovo Kórsakova, named after the composer, leads at a diagonal over a quiet stretch of the Griboyedov Canal. Cast an eye over Naberezhnaya Kanala Griboyedova 104, which Dostoyevsky used as the model for the home of the old moneylender Aliona Ivanovna in Crime and Punishment, *before continuing to* **St Nicholas's Cathedral** *(Nikolsky sobor).*

With its five gilded domes and cupolas floating above a pale blue building, this is one of the most popular churches in the city. Open throughout the Soviet period, including the blockade, it was chosen for her funeral in March 1966 by Anna Akhmatova, the poet whose works became a mantra for opponents of the regime.

Built between 1753–62 on the site of a naval parade ground, it has always been known as the 'Sailors' Church', and on Sundays the surrounding shady garden bristles with their uniforms. The architect was Savva Chevakinsky, one of St Petersburg's first successful Russian architects who had worked with the Baroque genius Rastrelli on both the Winter Palace and at Tsarskoye Selo. Here he effortlessly fuses the characteristics of European Baroque architecture with the liturgical needs of the Orthodox Church, in which the faithful are free to walk around, praying to the various icons, and before the iconostasis. Particularly fine is the bright upper chapel and its gilded iconostasis (*normally open 10am–6pm on Sundays*), while the dark and atmospheric lower chapel is open throughout the week. To the west of the church on the banks of the Kryukov Canal (Kanál Kryúkova) rises its four-tiered Baroque bell-tower.

Due north of the cathedral, tramlines run down the centre of Ul. Glinki and into **Theatre Square** *(Teatrálnaya Plóshchad), which since the middle of the 18th century has been a centre for public amusement.*

In its early days the square was known as Carousel Square and resounded to the music of the fair-ground. Today it offers the more highbrow charms of performances in the opera studio of the Conservatoire or the Mariinsky Theatre of opera and ballet, two of Russia's most prestigious musical establishments. The Rimsky-Korsakov Conservatoire was built in 1896 to house the educational institute founded by the pianist and composer Anton Rubinstein in 1864. Its illustrious graduates include Tchaikovsky, Prokofiev and Shostakovich. A statue of Rimsky-Korsakov, who was the director of the Conservatoire for many years, sits on its left, and one of Glinka, whose opera *A Life for the Tsar* was the first Russian opera, on its right. It was in the Bolshoi Theatre on the site of the Conservatoire that this and other early Russian operas were first performed.

Opposite is the home of what has been better known in our era as the Kirov Opera and Ballet Company, from whose rigorous training the West was fortunate to receive the dissident stars Rudolf Nureyev, Natalia Makarova and Mikhail Baryshnikov. It has recently taken back the name which it was given at its foundation in 1859, the **Mariinsky Theatre** (*Máriinsky Teatr*), after the reigning Tsarina Maria Alexandrovna, wife of Alexander II. The ungainly green and white exterior hides one of the prettiest auditoriums in the world, decorated in a refined blue and gold. The Revolution transformed this splendid 1800-seat theatre into a People's Palace, the French Ambassador noting that within six weeks of the tsar's abdication in March 1917 'all the imperial coats of arms and all the golden eagles have been removed. The box attendants had exchanged their sumptuous court liveries for miserable, dirty grey jackets.' The Royal Box on that night was filled with revolutionaries recently freed from Siberia and other, closer prisons. Otherwise, little has changed and the splendidly louche stage curtain continues to punctuate performances. When a German bomber hit the building during the seige, children, many of them orphans recruited to learn the skills that would be needed to restore the city after the war was over, set to work on the ceiling in November 1943. For many of them, it was the first concrete restoration they had worked on in a life that was to be devoted to the struggle to preserve St Petersburg. While you are passing the theatre, bargain with the touts who hang around the door for tickets to the performances. Try to make sure they don't sell you one with a restricted view. Pat yourself on the back if you manage to get a seat for $15, and go to it expecting a spectacle in the old-fashioned sense, not the innovative cutting edge of production. Though the Mariinsky is currently considered better than its rival the Bolshoi in Moscow, the need to earn hard currency to keep the theatre going means the main company is often on tour abroad. While it is annoying to find yourself watching second-rate performers, imagine how irritating it is for the city's serious culture buffs never to find their own stars performing. Don't miss the charming round poster holders on either side of the theatre entrance, with their own coolie hats to keep off the rain.

The area behind the Mariinsky Theatre to the west was known as Kolomna, and housed many of the city's Jewish families at the turn of the century. Most Russian Jews were confined to a pale of settlement in Belorussia, the Ukraine and western Russia, and only those with higher education or useful professional qualifications were allowed to live in the city. During the reigns of Alexander III and Nicholas II, both of whom were markedly anti-semitic, legislation curbing Jewish freedoms of movement and ownership was accompanied by attacks on Jews and their property to which the administration largely turned a blind eye. Many Jews took part in the Revolution, and the early Soviet period was a time of unprecedented freedom, with access to higher education freely available for the first time. After the Second World War, during which many Ukrainian and southern Russian Jews had been killed by Hitler, Stalin also turned his paranoid attention towards them. With the foundation of the state of Israel in 1948, the label Zionist became synonymous with treachery, and Jews made up a disproportionate percentage of the gulag population. For the remainder of the Soviet period, they were persecuted by a restriction on their freedom to emigrate, and by discrimination in education and at work. Nowadays, most of those who wish to leave have done so, and some are even returning, pre-ferring the indisputable anti-semitism of Russia to their isolated lives on the West Bank. Sadly, with the freeing up of Russian society, anti-semitism is rampant, and long-supressed theories of the Revolution as a Jewish conspiracy, led by prominent Communist Jews like Trotsky, Zinoviev, Kamenev, Sverdlov and Radek, are too. You can visit the pseudo-Moorish looking **Synagogue**, Lermontovsky Prospekt 2, once you have secured a skull-cap from the visitor's shop.

Walking north on the banks of the Kryukov Canal, you come to the Moika River, on the far side of which lies **New Holland** *(Nóvaya Gollándia).*

This site, secreted behind tall brick walls, was originally used to store and season ship's timbers during Peter the Great's reign, and is still occupied by the Russian navy. A short distance to the left along the canal, you come upon the stone and brick arch built by Vallin de la Mothe in the 1760s–70s to give access to its internal canals. Though it is only a small industrial project in a city abounding in flamboyant palaces, this arch is one of the most satisfying and perfect. Its proportions are lofty but excellent, the combination of materials bold and the fluid use of stone highly original. Look particularly at the graceful stone drapes over and around the arch and at the roundels between the pairs of side pillars. This inspired French architect had been recruited to head the architecture department at the new Academy of Arts in 1759 and during his 16 years here had little time for private commissions.

If you retrace your steps to the Kryukov Canal and continue along the south bank of the Moyka, you come to Vallin de la Mothe's only major piece of private work, the **Yussupov Palace** *(Юсуповский Дворец— Yussúpovsky Dvoréts), Naberezhnaya Reki Moiki 94, currently occupied* *by the Union of Teachers. Visits every day except Sun, but if you have not pre-arranged a guided tour (see p.414) you will see nothing of the interior or the cellars in which the drawn-out murder of Rasputin began.*

The Yussupovs, who at the time of the Revolution were the richest family in Russia, built no less than four palaces in St Petersburg, the back of one of which we have already seen on this walk. These were just the visible tip of the iceberg—they had 37 estates strung out across the country, some of which were literally covered in a film of crude petroleum, and in 1917 their wealth was estimated at $350–$500 million (a barely imaginable sum in those days).

This palace began life as the home of the Shuvalov family. Prince Yussupov bought it in the mid-18th century and invited de la Mothe to enlarge it. It was his plan that the palace should announce itself, as it does today, with a six-column portico. The ornate carved wooden door echoes the Yussupov coat of arms plastered on the pediment of the building. Several decorative alterations and extensions to the building were made in the 19th century, particularly under Prince Nikolai Yussupov in the 1830s and then at the end of the century with the addition of a theatre.

The Yussupovs emigrated at the time of the Revolution, unable to take a fraction of their renowned collection of pictures, sculpture and furniture with them. In the post-revolutionary chaos, the house briefly sheltered the embassies of a handful of European states, before they moved, with Lenin's government, to Moscow. It then became a museum, and finally in 1925, most of the collection was transferred to state museums and the palace given over as a cultural club for teachers.

The tour of the interior comes in two parts. First, in the rather humble bachelor apartments of Felix Felixovich Yussupov, the son and heir, the characters, circumstances and events surrounding the prince's part in the assassination of Rasputin (*see* pp.78–80) are recounted. With the aid of photographs, including one of the dead monk, and a disturbing Madame Tussaud's type installation, that dark evening of 16–17 December is brought vividly to life.

Felix Yussupov was an unlikely assassin. Born to a beautiful mother longing for a daughter after the birth of three sons, he spent the first five years of his life dressed as a girl, a habit he seemed loathe to give up once he began dress himself. He regularly went out dressed as a woman, and loved eliciting the attention of other men including, on one occasion in Paris, King Edward VII of England. When he went up to Oxford University, his household included a chef, a chauffeur, a valet, a housekeeper and a groom. He returned to Russia in 1914 to marry the tsar's niece Irina, though the French ambassador describes him as 'rather too prone to perverse imaginings and literary representations of vice and death... his favorite author is Oscar Wilde... his instincts, countenance and manner make him much closer akin to... Dorian Grey than to Brutus.'

Felix only conceived the mission to kill Rasputin after partying with the dissolute holy man in the most dubious dives as well as consulting him for his healing powers. He invited the *starets* to his house on the pretext of a party, saying that they would dine first in private. Upstairs were his fellow assassins Dr Lazovert, who had doctored the chocolate cakes and wine with cyanide, Grand Duke Dmitry, a cousin of Nicholas II, Vladimir Purishkevich and an army officer called Sukhotin. When Rasputin seemed unaffected by the poison, Felix shot him in the heart. An hour or so later Felix returned to look at the body, which rose and grabbed him by the throat. Felix struggled free and ran upstairs to alert his conspirators, while Rasputin dragged himself out into the garden. Purishkevich followed and pumped three shots into him. Still Rasputin would not die, and only expired after he was pushed under the icy waters of the river.

The second part of the tour spies on the living quarters of Felix's parents and the palace's public rooms, with a great variety of interiors from the early 19th to early 20th centuries. The white marble staircase was bought in its entirety from an Italian villa. The ground floor has a wooden panelled dining room and a Moorish room with a central fountain—extremely fashionable at the end of the 19th-century and, for the Yussupovs, particularly appropriate. There is also a fascinating room with a specially constructed acoustic anomaly incorporated into the apse. Amongst other aural oddities, if you stand in the middle of the arch at the entrance to the apse and speak directly to the back wall, your voice appears wildly amplified in your ears, but not to anyone else standing about. Upstairs the public rooms begin with an enfilade of drawing rooms decorated in the Empire manner for Prince Nikolai Yussupov, the most successful of all his line. The final columned rotunda was created to show off the lush turquoise ceramic vases he was given by Louis XVIII during his ambassadorship in Paris. The chandelier in the ballroom is one of the finest in the city, while those in the massive hall next door are made of papier mâché as the suspended ceiling couldn't take the weight of bronze and crystal. The late 19th-century enfilade of rooms leading back to the jewel-like Rococo theatre of the same date housed the pride of the family art collection. Though he was not alive when this theatre was built, the successful Nikolai Yussupov was famous for his antics in his theatre near Moscow. With one wave of his stick the entire cast would appear on the stage naked. Since they were all chosen for their talent from among his serfs, his wish was their command.

> *A little beyond the Yussupov Palace, Pochtamtsky (Post Office) Bridge over the Moika is tangibly suspended. Bounce across it and turn right along Ul.*

Gertsena, one of the most fashionable streets in old St Petersburg when it was known as Bolshaya Morskaya Ul.

Ul. Gertsena 47 was the home of the Nabokovs. In this turn of the century house, with its *Style Moderne* ironwork and high floral mosaic featuring overblown lilies, the future author Vladimir Nabokov (1899–1977) was brought up. His aristocratic father, V. D. Nabokov, was a liberal member of the Duma and a minister in the 1917 Provisional Government. When Nabokov was 20, the family emigrated to Berlin and he and his brother were sent on scholarships to Cambridge. Writing first in Russian and then in English, Nabokov published his first novels in Berlin in the 1920s, under the pseudonym V. Sirin. In 1940 he moved to America where he taught and also made his mark as a lepidopterist. Butterflies and moths were an interest which began in childhood. Early photographic portraits of Nabokov by St Petersburg's leading photographer Karl Bulla show him delicately handling a book of butterfly plates. With the success of *Lolita*, his tale of sexual obssession published in 1959, he was able to devote himself solely to writing. Admired for his stylistic use of language in both English and Russian, he is also well known for his translations—of Pushkin's *Eugene Onegin* and of Lewis Carroll's *Alice in Wonderland.*

The far end of the street, beyond St Isaac's Square, was one of the most fashionable pre-revolutionary shopping streets, and china eggs with the name on still hang above the entrance to No. 24, the original Fabergé shop (*see* pp.85–6).

*First however comes monumental **St Isaac's Square** (Issákiyevskaya Plóshchad), which was named after St Isaac of Dalmatia, upon whose saint's day Peter the Great was born and to whom he built a small wooden church here. A monumental square was first mooted in 1760 though none of the large buildings today are that old, the cathedral being the fourth church on the spot, completed in 1858.*

The equestrian statue of Nicholas I in the centre was erected a year after the completion of the massive cathedral, by which time the Mariinsky Palace (1839–44) behind it was already in place. The military-loving monarch is portrayed in cavalry uniform, his prancing steed defying gravity on its two back legs. The female figures surrounding the biographical bas-reliefs on the pedestal are portraits of his three daughters and his wife who commissioned the statue, representing Faith, Wisdom, Justice and Might. It was sculpted by Pyotr Klodt, Russia's first specialist animal sculptor, whose four powerful *Horse Tamers* decorate the Anichkov Bridge over the Fontanka on Nevsky Prospect.

Moving clockwise round the triangular square, you pass the forbidding red granite, columned building of the former German Embassy (1911–12), now the St Petersburg Tourist Company offices. Strange but true, the young Mies van der Rohe, who went on to head the Bauhaus and build some astonishing modern buildings in America, was involved in the building, when he was working for its Berlin-based architect Peter Behrens. The distinctly cleansed use of period references was dubbed 'scraped classicism'. In July 1914 (according to the old Russian calendar), following the German declaration of war on Russia, a crowd of patriotic Petersburgers attacked the embassy.

Continue towards the Neva down the pavement beside the cathedral until you arrive at Issakiyevskaya Ploshchad 5, the **Museum of Musical Instruments** *(Muzei musicálnykh instruméntov). It is open 12 noon-6pm; closed Mon and Tues.*

Housed in the former palace of Count Zubov, Catherine the Great's last lover, this little-known treasure of a museum holds one of the largest collections in the world. Though you cannot hear this cacophony of horns, strings and ivories, you sense the beauty of their sound from that of their shape. They come huge and small, in birch bark and ivory, inlaid and painted, bejewelled and enamelled. In the first room there are tiny violins for keeping in your pocket, known appropriately as *pochetti*, Glinka's Fischner piano made in St Petersburg and a beautiful 17th-century painted harmonica. Upstairs are two vast horn orchestras used by the tsar's troops, and early Russian and gypsy instruments, often accompanied by prints which show them in use. Acres of balalaikas culminate in one decorated by Prokofiev. The last rooms house collections of instruments from the Eurasian landmass, stretching from Istanbul through Persia (Iran) to Japan. Before you leave, check if there are any interesting concerts here which you could attend.

Turning left out of the museum you come to Issakiyevsky Ploshchad 1, the **Central Exhibition Hall***, which occupies a riding manège where cavalrymen were put through their paces.*

Fronted by a fluteless Doric portico, it was built in 1804-7 by Giacomo Quarenghi. The aspirations of the horseguards within were symbolized by the pair of sculptures without—they show the Dioscuri, the heavenly twins of Leda and Zeus, who were thought of as the protectors of the state. The hall, which shows exhibitions of contemporary art, is open 10am–6pm; closed Thurs.

Though religious services are once again held in **St Isaac's Cathedral** *(Иссакевский Собор—Issakiyévsky Sobór), it is still a museum, open 11am–7pm; you can climb to the colonnade (kolonnada) surrounding the dome for a panorama of the city between 11am–4pm. Tickets are for sale in the kiosk to the right of the entrance on St Isaac's Square.*

Official tours of the cathedral drown you in a sea of numbers, for St Isaac's indulges the Russians instinctive awe of vastness. A pompous building, the epitome of an Imperial cathedral, it cost over 23 million silver roubles to build. In 1818 one of the young French architect Auguste de Montferrand's 24 suggested plans was commissioned by Alexander I to replace the existing cathedral. Such was its scale that it was only finished in the year of his death, 1858, long after the tsar and even his successor had died. Serfs laboured to sink wooden piles into the marsh for foundations. The massive granite columns for the porticoes were transported from their quarry in Finland on specially designed ships and a small railway built for the purpose. The dome, decorated by fire-gilding, claimed the lives of many workmen who died from inhaling mercury vapour. A host of sculptors worked on the external pediments' bas reliefs, each surmounted by one of the evangelists, on the angels at each corner and the classical figures which surround the dome. The relief over the entrance portico depicts the Adoration of the Magi, and on the far side it shows the Resurrection. The east and west pediments depicts scenes from the life of St Isaac.

The areas to concentrate on are the paintings in the dome and the iconostasis. The dome was decorated by Karl Bryullov, the first Russian painter to gain international fame, winningthe Grand Prix at the Paris Salon in 1834 for a painting entitled *The Last Days of Pompeii*, now hanging in the Russian Museum. Portraits of the apostles and evangelists are surmounted, above the windows of the dome, by the Virgin Mary in heaven with saints and angels. Recessed in the very top of the cupola, and lit by yet more natural light, hovers a white dove, symbol of the Holy Spirit. The marble iconostasis, studded with mosaic icons, is gaudy but impressive. Vertically divided by 10 massive malachite-veneer columns, the monumental royal gates are flanked by two smaller columns covered with lazurite. From behind the gates stares a wide-eyed stained glass representation of Christ Resurrected, very unusual for Russia and infact made in Munich. The mosaics were only created between 1851–1914, to replace oil paintings which were disintegrating quickly in the cold, humid environment. *Smalti* (mosaic pieces) of over 12,000 different shades, all made in St Petersburg, were used to recreate the effect of a painting. The painstaking lime-wood model of the cathedral was sculpted over 11 years by a serf, M. Salin, who was given his freedom for these labours.

On the third side of St Isaac's Square is the **Hotel Astoria.**

It occupies both its original *Style Moderne* building (1910–12) on the corner with Ul. Gertsena and what was once the Angliya (English) Hotel which continues down Ul. Gógolya. The 1988–9 campaign to save the former building, by one of St Petersburg's greatest *Style Moderne* architects Fyodor Lidval (though not his best), was one of the first examples of an open citizens' protest after *perestroika*. Though redevelopment has stripped the interior of much of its original atmosphere, the protest made its mark, if only in the collective psyche. In the 1989 election which followed, the entire slate of high Party and city officials was rejected, and reformers like the present Mayor, Anatoly Sobchak, a professor of law at the university, were given their first taste of power.

*The **Mariinsky Palace** which dominates th~ far end of the square is approached across the Blue Bridge over the Moika. This is the city's broadest bridge, wide enough to carry a bewildering number of lanes of traffic. If you feel up to it you could risk negotiating them to marvel at the hideous heights the Neva has managed to reach in its periodic floodings of the city, recorded on a cast iron flood-marker beside the river.*

The palace, built for Maria Nikolayevna, daughter of Nicholas I, in 1839–44, is the seat of local government. It is closed to tourists but were one able to penetrate its rather dour exterior, over-dominated by the high central attic, one would find the Rotunda Hall in which the artist Ilya Repin recorded the centenary of the State Council (1901) in his painting now hanging in the Russian Museum. In 1917 it housed the short-lived Provisional Government.

Turning left as you look at the palace, walk a little way along the south bank of the River Moika before turning right up Pereúlok Grivtsóva (Переулок Гривцова). The buildings become increasingly residential as the street reaches Griboyedov Canal, which always seems rather quiet.

Overlooking the junction, to the right, is a fine example of what is jokingly referred to as 'too-late' (i.e. Stalinist) Classicism. The 1952 building shows a hideous disregard for classical geometric proportions, with its tall, thin, broken portico and an absolutely vestigial use of sculptural decoration.

Turn left along the northern banks of the Griboyedov.

Just after the embankment crosses busy Gorókhovaya Ul., on the far side of the canal a mid 18th-century Baroque palace is crumbling behind its dirty terracotta and white coat of paint. Many old buildings in the centre of town were communalized after the Revolution, with several families, each living in their own often tiny room, sharing bathroom and kitchen with each other. Bulgakov wrote that 'only someone who has lived in a *kommunalka* can know the meaning of true hell'. As successive Soviet governments struggled to build housing in the suburbs, especially after the damage done during the seige, many people accepted rehousing on the outskirts in their own, albeit tiny, flat. There were never enough flats for all however, and the majority of those who remain in the centre of the city still live communally, the conditions inside little better than those outside. With the government's privatization scheme, those who can are buying their neighbours out and applying to privatize whole flats, though by and large it is the rich coming in from outside who are buying up the city's prime real-estate.

Walking on along the canal you come to Bánkovsky Bridge, suspended from the mouths of golden-winged griffins, who according to classical mythology stand guard over gold.

The bridge leads to the back of what was the Imperial Bank, whose classical façade faces Apráksin Dvor on Sadóvaya Ul. (*see* p.360). Today it is one of the most popular institutes of higher education, the University of Economics and Finance.

> *As you continue round the bend in the canal, the immense yellow stone colonnade and then the green ribbed dome of the* **Kazan Cathedral** *(Kazánsky sobór) come into view. The variegated stone was quarried nearby and was so soft it could be sawed into blocks when just excavated. On prolonged contact with the air it has become rock hard. Entrance to the Museum of the History of Religion within is down the steps into the basement on the canal side of the building. It is open 11am–6pm; closed Wed.*

Inside, you can hire an English-language cassette guide (poor quality), if you want. First impressions on emerging into the main cross-shaped body of the cathedral are of immense space, marble and a forest of pillars. Indeed when it was completed in 1811, it was the third largest church in the world. Beneath the dome, an Escher-like mosaic of marble covers the floor, and to the right of the altar as you look at it is the marble-veneered Tsar's Box, where he would attend services. Over the side doors are bas reliefs. That on the left shows Peter, sword drawn, protecting Christ from the soldiers in the garden of Gethsemane, while on the right is a depiction of Christ carrying the Cross to Calvary. Also to the right of the altar is the precious silver iconostasis containing mostly 19th-century icons. The main icons, from left to right, portray the Russian saint Sergei Radonezhsky, Mary Magdalene, the Birth of Mary (particularly fine), Jesus Christ, St John the Theologian and St Catherine.

In the north chapel is the grave of Field Marshal Mikhail Kutuzov, who led the Russian army to victory against Napoleon in 1812 and whose spirited and sympathetically modest character leaps from the pages of Tolstoy's *War and Peace*.

Buried in June 1813 he lies behind a fence adorned with his family crest and beneath the icon which he always carried into battle with him. The painting gives a clue as to why the cathedral's full name is the Cathedral of Our Lady of Kazan. It shows the victory march in Moscow following the defeat of the Poles by Prince Pozharsky in 1612, led by the protecting icon, Our Lady of Kazan. It was to glorify that icon that Paul I built this cathedral, installing what few people realized was merely a copy. Until 1904 the icon was safely in a monastery in Kazan, but it then disappeared, only to resurface in West Europe after the Second World War. It is now owned by the Russian Orthodox Church in the USA.

A series of exhibits occupies the main nave. Here you can see 19th-century painted monks' habits, torturous metal devices worn to challenge ascetics and a host of valuable silver and bejewelled church vestments and relics. More interesting is the small selection of artifacts relating to traditional Russian folk beliefs, to the right of the door as you look at it. There is a mask made from birch bark for frightening evil spirits, a doll's coffin, with which spring was encouraged and easter eggs, tradition-ally dyed a life-giving blood red, also to encourage the season of growth.

Leave the building via the basement and make your way to its front.

An elaborate double-columned semi-circular colonnade sweeps into the deep cen-tral portico, from whose pediment radiates a striking, asymmetrical, gilded sunburst. This is a show church, so much so that the Orthodox convention of having the altar in the east was entirely superseded by the need for a prestigious entrance on Nevsky Prospekt. It was Paul I, who had incidentally been to the Vatican, who set a competition for its design, and chose that of Prince Sheremetev's talented serf-architect Andrei Voronikhin. Its main doors are copies of Ghiberti's gates of the Baptistry in Florence, which are meant to have ushered in the Renaissance, yet the sculptures on either side of them have a distinctly Russian flavour—from left to right they portray St Vladimir, the first Christian king of Kievan Rus, St Andrew, John the Baptist draped in fur and Russia's warrior saint Alexander Nevsky. In the garden in front of the cathedral are statues of field mar-shals Kutuzov and Barclay de Tolly, who also fought Napoleon. This space has long been associated with popular politics, and in February 1917 the square was at the centre of the demonstrations which led to the abdication of the tsar.

Before returning to the metro on Nevsky Prospekt, beyond the canal, or into a local eatery, take a look at the Style Moderne *building opposite.*

Built as a Singer sewing-machine factory and now St Petersburg's biggest book store, **Dom Knigi**, its rounded fluidity is in complete contrast with the decorative and deeply-carved classicism of the cathedral. The globe at the top of its round tower used to light up at night, and seamstresses sat working on the marvellous American machines at the windows to encourage trade.

IV: On and Off the Nevsky

Start: Ⓜ *Nevsky Prospekt, leave via the Griboyedov Canal* (Канал Грибоедова) *exit.*

Walking Time: *2 hours, plus another two to do justice to the Russian Museum.*

Sites

1   Church of the St Catherine
    Kostyol sv. Yekateriny
    Костел св. Екатерины

2   Duma Tower
    Dumskaya bashnya
    Думская башня

3   St Petersburg Philharmonia
    Peterburgskaya Philharmonia
    Петербургская Филармония

4   Mussorgsky Maly Theatre
    Maly teatr im. M. P. Mussorgsky
    Малый театр им. М. П. Мусоргский

5   Mikhailovsky Palace/Russian Museum
    Mikhailovsky dvorets/Russky muzei
    Михайловский дворец/Русский музей

6   Shuvalov Palace
    Shuvalovsky dvorets
    Шуваловский дворец

7   Winter Sports Stadium
    Zimny stadion
    Зимний стадион

8   St Petersburg Circus
    Tsirk
    Цирк

9   Church of Ss Simeon and Anna
    Tserkov sv. Simeona i Anny
    Церковь св. Симеона и Анны

10 Sheremetiev Palace
    Sheremetyevsky dvorets
    Шереметевский дворец

11 Catherine Institute
    Yekaterinsky institute
    Екатеринский институт

12 Anna Akhmatova Museum
    Muzei Anny Akhmatovy
    Музей Анны Ахматовы

13 Beloselsky-Belozersky Palace
    Beloselsky-Belozersky dvorets
    Белосельский-Белозерский дворец

14 Anichkov Palace
    Anichkovsky dvorets
    Аничковский дворец

15 Yeliseyev's (Gastronom No 1)
    Yeliseyevsky magazin
    Елисеевский магазин

16 Alexandrinsky Theatre
    Alexandrinsky teatr
    Александринский театр

17 Russian National Library
    Rossiskaya Natsionalnaya Biblioteka
    Российская Национальная Библиотека

18 Museum of Theatre and Musical Arts
    Muzei teatralnovo i musikalnovo iskusstva
    Музей театрального и музыкального искусства

19 Bust of Lomonosov
    Byust Lomonosova
    Бюст Ломоносова

20 Apraksin dvor
    Апраксин двор

21 Former Imperial Bank
    Assignatsionny bank
    Ассигнационный банк

22 Vorontsov Palace
    Vorontsovsky dvorets
    Воронцовский дворец

23 Gostiny dvor
    Гостиный двор

24 Armenian Church
    Armyanskaya tserkov
    Армянская церковь

Restaurants and Cafés

A   Grand Hotel Europe
    Gostinitsa Yevropeiskaya
    Гостиница Европейская

B   Café Ol
    Кафе 01

C   Metekhi Café
    Метехи кафе

D   Café at Akhmatova Museum
    Кафе

E   Zakusnitsa
    Закусница

336

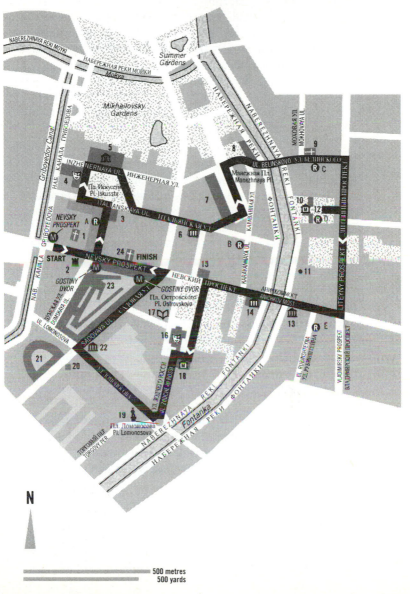

Summer
Gardens

NABEREZHNAYA REKI MOYKI
НАБЕРЕЖНАЯ РЕКИ МОЙКИ
Moyka

Mikhailovsky
Gardens

Griboyedov Canal
НАБ. КАНАЛА ГРИБЕДОВА

5
INZHENERNAYA UL. ИНЖЕНЕРНАЯ УЛ.

4

Пл. Искусств
PL. Iskusstv

ITALIANSKAYA UL. ИТАЛЬЯНСКАЯ УЛ.

NEVSKY
PROSPEKT

3

A R

M 1

7

8

UL. BELINSKOVO УЛ. БЕЛИНСКОГО

Манежная Пл.
Manezhnaya Pl.

9

R C

10

M 12

R C

НАБЕРЕЖНАЯ РЕКИ ФОНТАНКИ

КАРАВАННАЯ УЛ.

6

B R

START

2

M

GOSTINY
DVOR

NAB. KANALA
НАБ. КАНАЛА

DUMSKAYA UL.
ДУМСКАЯ УЛ.

24

FINISH

NEVSKY PROSPEKT
НЕВСКИЙ ПРОСПЕКТ

23

M

13

KARAVANNAYA UL.

11

LITEYNY PROSPEKT ЛИТЕЙНЫЙ ПРОСПЕКТ

GOSTINY DVOR
Пл. Островского
Pl. Ostrovskovo

17

ANICHKOV MOST
АНИЧКОВ МОСТ

14

13

R C

UL. LOMONOSOVA
УЛ. ЛОМОНОСОВА

16

21

22

20

SADOVAYA UL. САДОВАЯ УЛ.

UL. ZODCHEVO ROSSI
УЛ. ЗОДЧЕГО РОССИ

18

NABEREZHNAYA REKI FONTANKI
Fontanka

VLADIMIRSKY PROSPEKT
ВЛАДИМИРСКИЙ ПРОСПЕКТ

UL. RUBINSHTEYNA
УЛ. РУБИНШТЕЙНА

R C

19

Пл. Ломоносова
Pl. Lomonosova

TORGOVY PER.
ТОРГОВЫЙ ПЕР.

NABEREZHNAYA REKI FONTANKI
НАБЕРЕЖНАЯ РЕКИ ФОНТАНКИ

N

500 metres
500 yards

It is hard to think of another city in which one street is as dominant as St Petersburg's Nevsky Prospekt. If you want to shop, take in a play or film, sightsee, eat, cruise, meet up or just test the water, head for Nevsky Prospekt. In the early days it was a lifeline connecting the centre Peter had chosen for his city to the nearest existing road, which ran from the pearl-rich north to Novgorod, along what is now Ligovsky Prospekt. As the city developed, Nevsky's impressive 3km perspective was embellished with well-proportioned palaces, theatres, hotels, cathedrals and shops. From its arterial flow a network of smaller streets led off into further architectural ensembles: more palaces, museums and theatres.

There was barely a public edifice elsewhere in the city, and daily the citizens flooded Nevsky with their 'rapid phantasmagoria' (Gogol). In the morning resentful, lowly clerks scurrying to the office in threadbare overcoats were soaked by meltwater puddles aimed by the wheels of their superiors' carriages. Governesses with their charges, officers showing off on their return from the Caucasus, husbands and wives dressed as well as their purse would allow them, all promenaded past shop fronts and through gardens, gleaning the mood of the city and its gossip as they went. Brushed by their hems as they passed, drunks, beggars and madmen scrounged an existence while prostitutes hovered down sidestreets. As well as entertainment and laughter, the microcosm on Nevsky Prospekt bred resentment, envy and hard-heartedness.

After the Revolution, the Soviet regime succeeded in changing hundreds of street names, but Nevsky Prospekt never became Avenue of the 25th of October. To abolish Nevsky Prospekt was tantamount to denying St Petersburg's identity, and in 1944 they acknowledged defeat. In the sixties and seventies subtle rebellion stalked the street in the form of a pair of Italian shoes, a line from a Vysotsky song or long hair. The underground met at the Saigon Café, on the corner with Vladimirsky Prospekt, where news of poetry readings, exhibitions and meetings circulated secretly.

Today the joy and sadness of the city is out on Nevsky Prospekt for all to see. Towards the river, a consumer junket of paintings, books, Marlboro kiosks and horse rides seeks to seduce tourists while young gypsies pick their pockets. In the centre, furious political argument drowns out the sound of a jazz band as shoppers swarm into the nearby department stores. Near the Moscow station on Ploshchad Vosstaniya, drunks and the benighted former inmates of mental hospitals, closed on a massive scale because of lack of funds, grub around for a living on the street. Gogol would notice little difference.

Surprisingly, many of the buildings on this walk still serve the same purpose for which they were built: the Grand Hotel Europe, the Alexandrinsky and Mussorgsky Theatre of Opera and Ballet (formerly the Maly), the public library and the circus. Others have been turned into museums. The collection of Russian paintings in the Russian Museum is as rich and vibrant as that of the Tretyakov in Moscow and currently more accessible, hanging in rooms overlooking peaceful palace gardens. The Museum of Theatre and Muscial Arts gives a colourful lightning guide to Russian drama, while sombre greys dominate the museum devoted to the life struggle of the 20th-century poet Anna Akhmatova.

To make the most of this itinerary, its shopping and cultural possibilities, walk it on Thurs–Sat. As long as you don't start too early, you could also follow it on a Wed, when the Museum of the Theatre and Musical Arts opens at 1pm. My advice would be to give yourself two hours in the morning, have lunch after the Russian Museum and continue the rest of the walk in the afternoon.

---

lunch/cafés

Grand Hotel Europe, Ul. Mikhailovskaya 1/7, ✆ 312 0072. From 7am to 10pm you will find somewhere to graze in this top-of-the-range hotel. A brasserie, a Chinese restaurant, a café in the atrium and the quick and easy ever-changing menu at Sadkos are all good daytime possibilities.

Café 01, Karavannaya Ul. 7. *Open 12 noon–4pm, 5–11pm* Cosy and very popular, this is an ideal place to drop in for a bowl of spiced soup to keep you going. Sadly, you may find it is full.

Metekhi Café, Ul. Belinskovo 3. *Open 11am–9pm*. The better of the two adjacent Georgian cafés, Metekhi caters well for vegetarians with grilled cheese, *sir sulugumi*, and *lobio* (bean stew), beside meaty soups and entrées.

Café at the Akhmatova Museum, (*see* p.353 for directions). From the management of Café 01 comes this clean, respectable and somewhat pricey offering on the ground floor.

Zakusnitsa, Ul. Rubinshteyna 2. *Open 11am–11pm.* Little more than a hole in the basement wall just off Nevsky Prospekt. There is scant choice on the menu here, but the meat is usually exceptionally tender and well-cooked.

Leave Ⓜ Nevsky Prospekt via the exit marked Canal Griboyedova (Канал Грибоедова), emerging from an unlikely blue-and-white 19th-century façade opposite the Kazan Cathedral (see Walk III). Turn left.

Up Nevsky Prospekt on the left, the cream façade of **Church of St Catherine** (1762–83), set back from the road, provides the backdrop for a vibrant art market. Hundreds of paintings, suspended from make-shift stands, wait for passing tourists. The church was one of a clutch of foreign denomination churches on Nevsky Prospekt which earned it the name the Street of Tolerance. Designed by Vallin de la Mothe, and now under restoration, it was the hub of Catholic St Petersburg, often the focus of walks by young French governesses, for whom the priest acted as adviser on matters of marriage and employment, as well as confessor.

Next to the church is the Grand Hotel Europe, its denizens protected from the maelstrom of the street by smoked plate glass. Opposite rises the ungainly red tower of what was the Town Duma, surmounted by a coppice of aerials. Built in 1804 as a fire watchtower, it was later used to signal to the royal palaces outside the city. In the building beneath it, which runs at right angles to Nevsky Prospekt along Dumskaya Ul., the elected city council became the focus for anti-Soviet sentiments after the Revolution, but was only closed down in October 1918. Today Dumskaya Ul. is the unlikely cruising ground for the city's homosexuals, commonly known as *goluboy*, meaning light blue. Still a beleaguered minority, until the repeal of Article 121 of the penal code in 1993 they faced up to five years' imprisonment for sexual activity. The arcade beneath the tower on Nevsky Prospekt used to house rows of jewellers in the Serebryaniye Ryady (Silver Rows), but is now a mediocre art salon. The entrance is beseiged by cartoonists and portrait painters. Paintings and a few antiques, as well as theatre tickets, are for sale in the delicate yellow and white classical portico that stands alone beyond the Duma Tower.

Turn left round the corner of the Grand Hotel Europe (Gostinitsa Yevropeiskaya) into Mikhailovskaya Ul.

Though built in 1873–5 the hotel owes its character (or rather what is left of it after the recent deluxe Swedish refurbishment) to the facelift it was given by the city's most talented Art Nouveau architect, Fyodor Lidval, in 1908–10. On the other side of the street, beyond the two banks, stands one of the city's most important classical music venues, the **St Petersburg Philharmonia**. In tsarist times this building was the Nobles' Club, but from the mid 19th-century its main hall became best known for the concerts held by the Russian Musical Society. In 1893

Tchaikovsky conducted the premiere of his Sixth Symphony here before dying a few days later in suspicious circumstances, following the scandal of his latest homosexual love affair. At the turn of the century Isadora Duncan, the American dancer, made her Russian debut on this stage too. But the Philharmonia's proudest moment took place on 9 August 1942, during the Second World War seige of the city. With guns pounding just 13 km away, the orchestra, depleted by conscription and starvation, gave the first performance of Shostakovich's Seventh, 'Leningrad' Symphony, partly written in the beseiged city. The heroic concert was beamed across the Soviet Union by radio, a broadcast that still brings tears to the eyes of those who lived through the blockade.

> *As Mikhailovskaya Ul. opens out into **Ploshchad Isskustv**, Square of the Arts, one is struck by a sense of harmony.*

The whole ensemble was designed to go with the Mikhailovsky Palace, built for Alexander I's youngest brother Mikhail, which stands straight ahead. It formed part of the emperor's architectural celebration of Russia's triumph over Napoleon, coordinated by the talented neoclassicist Carlo Rossi. Such was Rossi's favoured status with the emperor that rumours that Rossi was the offspring of a liaison between Paul I and his Italian mother, gained ground. The severe classicism of the square's façades is tempered by the large central garden, which focuses on a statue of Pushkin by the popular post-war sculptor Mikhail Anikushin.

> *The main building on the lefthand side of the square is the Mussorgsky Maly Theatre. The first building on the same side (No. 5) was the site of the famous basement club known as The Stray Dog.*

In its heyday in 1913, The Stray Dog was one of the world's great bohemian clubs, for at that time there was nothing more radical than a gathering of St Petersburg's poets and painters, who were challenging the boundaries of their arts at every step. They would sit sipping coffee, or slump drunk over a table, occasionally woken from their reveries by the impromptu recitation of a few lines or a loud blast from the piano. One of its stars was the willowy poet Anna Akhmatova, who numbered herself among its 'heavy drinkers' and 'women of loose morals'. Surveying its fatalistic decadence with what Brodsky calls a 'note of controlled terror' in her voice, she seemed to prophesy imminent catastophe and the downfall of the avant-garde.

Nineteen months later, Russia was at war with Germany, and the stage set for the Revolution which ultimately and fatally rejected the daring avant-garde in favour of the saccharine platitudes of Socialist Realism. Many of The Stray Dog's habitués ended their lives in exile abroad if they were lucky, in the Siberian gulag if not.

> *Walk round the square and into the front courtyard of the Mikhailovsky Palace, now the **Russian Museum** (Gosudarstvyenny russky muzei). Open 10am–6pm; closed Tues.*

The palace was built in 1819–25. In the spirit of the age, the piers of its gates are surmounted by mock trophies of war, and the sumptuous classicism of its full-blown Corinthian portico, heroic frieze and heavily stuccoed pediment suggest an empire in the ascendancy. Within its portals however, the Mikhailovsky Palace has been associated more with culture than imperial ambition. After its completion it was Grand Duke Mikhail's wife Helen, 'a blaze of beauty and health and cheerful-ness', who infused it with her cultured, intelligent enthusiasms, bringing together artists, musicians and scientists in her 'salon'. For several years, the pianist Anton Rubinstein used rooms in the palace as a music school before founding the St Petersburg Conservatiore in 1864, and it was the Grand Duchess Helen who funded the country's first observatory, out at Pulkovo near the present-day airport. It was a time when the fabulous fortune of the royal family was fortuitously linked with good taste, and even the balls at Mikhailovsky were an artistic event. The Marquis de Custine, who attended one in 1839, recalled:

'The interior of the grand gallery in which they danced was arranged with a mar-vellous luxury. Fifteen hundred boxes of the rarest plants, in flower, formed a grove of fragrant verdure... It might have been supposed that these strange plants, including large palms and bananas, all of whose boxes were concealed under a carpet of mossy verdure, grew in their native earth, and that the groups of northern dancers had been transported by enchantment to the forests of the tropics. It was like a dream; there was not merely luxury in the scene, there was poetry.'

The palace passed out of Romanov hands for a number of decades, but was bought back by Nicholas II in 1895. His father Alexander III, a great collector, had been almost shamed into wanting to create a public gallery of Russian art in the capital after visiting the Tretyakov Gallery in Moscow, founded by a pair of rich merchant brothers. If they could do it, he certainly should too. However Alexander died before realizing his plan, and it was left to Nicholas to found it for him, calling the museum he opened here in 1898 the Russian Museum of Alexander III.

The Russian Museum owes much of its wealth to the nationalization of private col-lections which took place after the Revolution, to artists bequeathing their work to it, and to the museum's appropriation of an estimated 40,000 icons from the churches which were shut down or destroyed during the Soviet period. It con-tinues to compete with the Tretyakov in Moscow for the best collection of Russian painting, though at any one time only the tip of its iceberg is on show.

You enter the museum by a basement door, to the right of the portico. The ticket office, cloakrooms and a stygian café are all to be found in the labyrinth of corridors that leads to the stairs into the main hall. On either side of the grand double staircase you will find the museum shop, one of the few places in the city selling high quality postcards.

The following itinerary tracks a chronological course through the history of Russian painting, and to a lesser extent sculpture, weaving its way through the three interconnected buildings which make up the museum. After visiting both floors of the main palace, it passes through the Rossi Wing and up to the first floor of the Benois Building, added in 1912–16, where paintings from the 20th century are displayed. For those keen on applied and folk art, parts of the museum's collection on the ground floor of the Rossi Wing are sometimes open (as indicated on the plan). Temporary exhibitions are usually hung on the ground floor and part of the second floor of the Benois Building (again see plan).

We begin by taking the palace stairs, which sweep up to a gallery of Russian 18th- and 19th-century sculpture beneath a soaring ceiling, which is decorated with sumptuous *grisaille* murals, painted in various tones of grey and white in imitation of plaster reliefs. When Rossi built the palace he was lucky to have recourse to a fabulous circle of foreign and Russian craftsmen and decorators, attracted to St Petersburg by the lavish imperial building bonanza of the time. Many of the murals, including these, were executed by members of the Italian Scotti family who kept their artistic skills alive through several generations.

*Turn left at the top of the stairs and you will find yourself in the spiritual world of Russian **icon painting**, which occupies Rooms 1–4 (see pp.80–2 for a general discussion of icons).*

The museum's collection of sacred images begins with a few surviving icons from the 12th to the mid-14th century. The small, intense *Golden-Haired Angel* (12th century), whose peaceful, dreamy gaze bears witness to God's tenderness, was once part of a panel which showed Christ flanked by two such guardians. Also in this room is a refined mid 14th-century depiction of the first Russian martyrs, *Princes Boris and Gleb*, on a cream and gold background. The sons of Prince Vladimir of Kiev, who brought Christianity to the people of Kievan Rus in 988, they were murdered in dynastic struggles by their older brother Svyatopolk 'the accursed'. Whatever their spiritual credentials, they are depicted in worldly 14th-century Russian clothing, rendered in minute detail, down to Boris' ermine-lined cloak and the magnificent mythical birds on Gleb's smock.

Room 2 is devoted to the two great centres of icon painting from which an abundance of examples survives. They were the northern cities of Novgorod and Pskov, which were never conquered and sacked by the Mongols. The Novgorod School, represented by an icon of St George killing the dragon, and another showing the seige of Novgorod by the city of Suzdal, is characterized by bright colours, exaggerated outline shapes and a greater sense of movement. The three Pskov icons here are rigid, hieratic and formal by comparison. To appreciate the difference, compare the Novgorod and Pskov icons of the Harrowing of Hell hanging opposite one another. Both depict the moment when Christ, after His death on the cross, descended into hell on the third day to bring Adam and Eve and the godly women and men of the Old Testament with him into heaven.

Russian icon painting reached its apex in the late 14th and early 15th centuries, as the country emerged from Mongol domination. In Room 3 you will find two immense, thin panels, from the Cathedral of the Assumption in Vladimir, by **Andrei Rublyov**, arguably the greatest icon painter the world has ever seen. Depicting the Apostles Peter (left) and Paul (right) they are unfortunately not in very good condition, but they do show the definitive traits of Rublyov's hand. The figures are traced with masterly linear simplicity while their faces are a picture of gentle wisdom. Rublyov's talent lies in saturating his images with a sense of inner godliness. Also by Rublyov is the Presentation of Jesus at the Temple, which concentrates with a touching and fragile intensity on the figure of Christ, a tiny ray of hope clutched tenderly in the arms of the typically elongated, Rublyovian priest. The beautifully composed icon of St John the Evangelist receiving the word of God and dictating it to his pupil on the rocky, surreal landscape of Patmos dates from the 16th century, in the style of the Moscow School which Rublyov founded.

Work by **Dionysy** in Room 4 marks the end of the heyday of Russian icon painting. As you progress through the room you will notice that the sense of intense spirituality disppears, replaced by a concentration on physical detail and story-telling. Suddenly one's attention is grabbed by the ribbons in an angel's hair or an overpowering use of gold. The miniature icons in the octagonal display case, painted by masters of the Stroganov school, are fine examples of this later tendency.

From Room 5, English-language labelling makes it much easier to find your way around.

As you pass through the door you find yourself expelled from the spiritual world of medieval Russia. The transition to the worldly portraits of the 17th- and early 18th-century is cushioned by the fact that early Russian portraiture, known as *parsuna*, borrowed many techniques from the only indigenous art form. The portrait of Y. F. Turgenev in Room 5 is a good example, with its sharply defined, iconesque blocks of colour. This was soon to change. Peter the Great's infatuation with western Europe encouraged him to invite western painters here, and to send talented Russians to study abroad. Within decades painters such as **Ivan Nikitin** (*c.*1688– 1741) were producing works like the wonderfully informal portrayal of the strong but troubled Hetman, his collar undone and the whole picture painted at an angle.

Rooms 6–10 follow the development of Russian art during St Petersburg's formative years after the death of Peter. A brief vogue for mosaic portraits (Room 6) ran parallel to the development of a number of factories, set up with western knowhow, to produce decorative materials, such as glass, tapesteries and ceramics, for all the new palaces. See for example how the chandeliers develop from simple bronze in Room 5 to the delicate bronze, coloured glass and crystal affairs associated with the heyday of Imperial Russia. In room 7 the walls are lined with tapestries from the St Petersburg factory set up with the help of Dutch masters. The centre of the room is inhabited by a finely cast bronze of Empress Anna Ivanovna, a remote, immovable, bejewelled mass beside her delicate black slave, by **Carlo Bartolomeo Rastrelli** (1675–1744). Here too, the main ornate enfilade of the palace begins, overlooking the garden.

Room 8 is dominated by the talents of **F. S. Rokotov** (1735–1808), a serf artist trained in St Petersburg and the first Russian portraitist to try to build some psychological depth into his portraits. In Room 9 we see the beginnings of a trend which was to dominate Russian painting for almost 100 years. The foundation of the Academy of Arts in St Petersburg in 1757 encouraged a strict adherence to the principles of classicism, and portraiture lost ground to the painting of historical, biblical and mythological scenes. Coupled with the development of a proud national consciousness, this tendency could be stultifying. One of its earliest exponents was the Ukrainian **Anton Losenko** (1737–73). His canvas showing Vladimir and Rogneda tells the well-known story of how Prince Vladimir of Novgorod, rejected by Rogneda, determines to take her by force. But having killed her father and brothers, and destroyed her native Polotsk, Vladimir is beset by remorse when he finds Rogneda weeping in her room. Despite its emotive subject-matter, the picture inhabits an emotional limbo because, for the painter, the subject is purely an intellectual exercise. Room 10, in contrast, represents the peak of 18th-century portraiture. A lyrical series by **Dmitry Levitsky** (1735–1822) depicts the first graduates of Catherine the Great's Smolny Institute, a boarding school for noble girls, painted at the empress's request. As well as the three Rs, the girls were encouraged to develop their musical and dramatic talents, and often took part in performances at the royal palaces. The best loved of the portraits shows Khovanskaya, playing the part of a boy, courting her schoolfriend Khrushcheva, the shepherdess, chucking her under the chin with cheeky playfulness. Levitsky also painted the full-length allegorical portrait of Catherine the Great as Legislator at the Temple of Justice, an official work intended to emphasize Catherine's fairness as a ruler. At the height of Bolshevik madness in 1918, the city's Arts Committee had to fight a tricky battle to prevent the portrait being taken and its canvas used for a revolutionary work.

Room 11, the most sumptuous in the entire palace, is known as the White Hall. After the ravages of the seige it was restored to look just as it did when the palace was first built. The perfect white scagliola walls were the envy of the world; George IV asked for the secret, only to discover that it lay in a particularly fine white alabaster excavated near Kazan. The powdered alabaster is fixed to the wall with gesso, heated, and the hardened surface rigorously polished. The paintings on them were executed by another Italian, Vighi. Like all the original fixtures and fittings in the palace, the pale blue and gold suite of furniture, and the strange smokey blue smalt console tables were part of the master design by Rossi.

Most of the rest of the first floor of the Mikhailovsky Palace is devoted to the romantic classicism taught by the Academy of Arts. A brief respite is afforded by the virtuoso portraits by **Vladimir Borovikovsky** (1757–1825), another Ukrainian, in Room 12. Two of the massive canvasses in Room 14 by **Grigory Urgiumov** (1764–1823) illustrate turning points in Russian history and glorify the development of the nation. The first depicts the *Tartar Submission to Ivan IV* in 1552 at Kazan, the second the *Coronation of Mikhail Romanov* in 1613, which brought the Time of Troubles to an end. Room 15 is shared by two giants of Russian 19th-century painting, **Ivan Aivazovsky** (1817–1900) and **Karl Bryullov** (1799–1852), who won the Grand Prix at the Paris Salon in 1834 for the dramatic *Last Days of Pompeii*, which he painted while living in Rome. Gogol and Pushkin were amongst those overcome by the scope and talent of the painting, though today it is hard to appreciate what all the fuss was about. Bryullov's talents seem better used in the many portraits also hanging in this hall. On the wall opposite the theatrical melodrama of Pompeii rolls the meditative calm of Aivazovsky's extraordinary luminous seascapes. Aivazovsky, who lived in the Crimea on the banks of the Black Sea, is said to have painted over 6000 seascapes.

There is more light relief from the pomposity of the Grand Academic Halls in the intimate landscapes in Room 16, many painted by Russian emigrés, and the portraits by the serf artist **Orest Kiprensky** (1782–1836) in Room 17. His most famous work is the portrayal of Pushkin in the Tretyakov, but here his vision of romantic nobility is best expressed in the full-length portrait of Evgraf Davidov dressed as a colonel in the Hussars. The tousled-haired hero's resplendent uniform stands out from the moody shadows, one effete hand resting informally on his hip.

> *If the first floor of the palace belongs to portraiture and the nobility, the* **ground floor**, *with its plethora of 19th-century paintings, is the preserve of genre painting concerned with the lives of the peasantry and Russia's burgeoning middle classes.*

By the mid-19th century, the Academy of Art's proclamation that 'art must aim at revealing virtue, at immortalizing the deeds of the great men who deserve the nation's gratitude' was patently out of date. The Napoleonic Wars had revealed that it was not only the 'great men' who defended the country against her enemy, but also millions of peasants who had both fought and harrassed the enemy out of Russia. The fight was on to free the serfs, and urban sophisticates began to patronize genre painting focussing on the gentle charms of the Russian countryside.

Alexei Venetsianov (1780–1847), whose paintings hang in Room 18, was the first to take painting back to the village. He depicts peasants, whether *Cleaning the Sugar Beet* or simply resting in the fields, in a moment suspended in time; there is no attempt at narrative or psychological depth. This natural realism was popular enough for the artist to set up his own school in the countryside, in competition with the Academy. Venetsianov anticipated the move away from this institution, although it was by no means a steady flow. Such was the fickleness of artistic fashion that when Bryullov won international approval for *The Last Days of Pompeii* in 1834, many pupils deserted Venetsianov to return to the Academy. In Room 19 you will find works by some of Venetsianov's pupils, the most talented being the tragic serf-painter **Grigory Soroka** (1823–64). His works, particularly *The Fishermen*, are saturated with a sense of the unchanging tasks of the Russian peasant and the peaceful rhythm of their environment. Despite his artistic talents, Soroka was unable to free himself from the bonds of serfdom as a gardener, and became increasingly rebellious. Ironically, it was in 1864, after the abolition of serfdom had made him a free man, that he was accused of taking part in peasant disturbances; rather than face a public flogging, he committed suicide.

The portrait painter **Vasily Tropinin** (1776–1857), also born a serf, was one of the first Russian portraitists to take an interest in the urban middle classes. Room 20 abounds with faces from Tropinin's own milieu, Moscow's mercantile Zamoskvarechye district.

The works of **Alexander Ivanov** (1806–58) displayed in Rooms 21 and 22 amply illustrate the painter's strongest characteristics—his incredible technical virtuosity and his obsessiveness. Accepted by the Academy at the age of 11, Ivanov was at first taught by his academician father Andrei. In 1831 he went to Italy on a scholarship, and only returned shortly before his death. The effect of Italy, and particularly its Renaissance painting, can easily be discerned in the form and colour of his works. In 1832 Ivanov conceived the idea for his great life's work, *The First Appearance of Christ Among the People*. He worked on the painting for some 25 years, making sketch after sketch for the scene in which Jesus appeared on the banks of the River Jordan where John the Baptist was baptising the early Christians. In Room 21 you will find a clutch of these sketches, as well as an early version of the final painting. The almost identical 'original' is kept by the Tretyakov in Moscow. Other paintings by the faithful Ivanov include *Jesus' Appearance to Mary Magdalene*. He also painted secular works, including the Italianate landscapes which can be seen in Room 22.

Given the censorship that existed under the tsars, Russian art was slow to express social criticism and satire. Vasily Perov's anti-establishment attitude may well have had personal roots in his father's exile to Siberia. A quick study of his canvas

Monastery Refectory in Room 23 reveals his view of 19th-century Russia. Red-faced, pot-bellied monks ingratiate themselves with medal-encrusted grandees while ignoring the beggar woman trying to catch their attention. Not surprisingly, several of Perov's pictures were banned by the authorities. Room 24 contains a number of canvasses by the talented landscape painter **Alexei Savrasov** (1830–97). While the genre was practised by Russians living in Europe, Savrasov was one of the first to depict the Russian landscape. When first exhibited, his *The Rooks Have Returned* (in the Tretyakov), a clump of rook-strewn birches in a dirty spring landscape, caused an eruption of nationalist pride.

It was the determination to create a truly Russian school of painting, after 200 years of pervasive foreign influence, that led to the most important moment in Russian 19th-century art. Two years after the emancipation of the serfs in 1861, the Academy set yet another mythological subject for its annual Gold Medal competition. Disgusted by the irrelevance of the theme, 14 students led by Ivan Kramskoy left to set up their own assocation. They soon became known as the *Peredvizhniki*, Wanderers, and were quickly joined by others including Savrasov.

A group of penetrating portraits in Room 25 shows the talents of the group's leader, **Kramskoy** (1837–87). There is a strange sense of empathy between sitter and artist which draws you directly into the picture, as though you were there at the sittings. The radiant portrayal of Mina Moiseyev, a picture of self-assured, dignified peasanthood, shines out above the rest.

The independent spirit of Nicholas Ge (Gay), another founder member of the Wanderers, led him to experiment with several different genres before settling, under the influence of Alexander Ivanov, on biblical themes. In Room 26 you can see his marvellous portrait of the great novelist Lev Tolstoy at work, with his permanently knitted brow. Nearby hangs a painful historical scene, *Peter the Great Interrogating Tsarevich Alexei*, which captures perfectly the mutual distrust which characterized their relationship and the atmosphere of doom which hung over the event. The tsarevich, Peter's son by his first wife, had become tarnished by various plots against his father. Having fled abroad in fear of his life, Alexei was tricked into returning, only to find the full weight of suspicion still upon him. Within months of this uncommunicative scene, Alexei died during an interrogation session at which his father may have been present. Ge's dramatic portrayals of biblical events are represented by the eerie, moonlit *Jesus arriving at Garden of Gethsemene*.

The bestloved landscape painter of the second half of the 19th century was without doubt **Ivan Shishkin** (1832–98). His arboreal hymns to his native land hang in Room 27, and seem to tug at the heart-strings of most sentimental Russians. His portrait by Kramskoy a few rooms back shows a wild-haired man with subtly smiling eyes. Shishkin was known as 'the poet of the Russian forest', and his interest was so exclusive that if ever it was felt he should include a man or animal in his pictures, he would invite another artist to paint them for him.

Rooms 28–32 contain a range of lesser late 19th-century canvasses including landscapes by Fyodor Vasiliyev, genre scenes by **Vladimir Makovsky**, who champions the underdog in his portrayals of *Doss House* and *Bankruptcy*, and Karl Savitsky's highly charged set-piece *To the War*.

> *An expensive shop in Room 29 sells reproduction Russian jewellery, including the much-copied Fabergé enamel eggs.*

One of the most beloved Russian painters of all time was **Ilya Repin** (1844–1933), who came to be best known as a portraitist, though the paintings that first made him popular were bold canvasses on social and historical themes. Repin arrived in St Petersburg the very year the Wanderers boycotted the Academy. Although he studied at the Academy, he soon came to think of Kramskoy as his teacher. Dominating Room 33 is his *Barge Haulers on the Volga*, which depicts a team of ragged men struggling at every step of their back-breaking life's work. As well as betraying moral outrage at the reality of their life-threatening, medieval drudgery, which Repin captured during trips to the Volga in the summers of 1870–72, the painting also works on a subliminal level. The older men, particularly the man lagging at the back, have no chance of escape except death, but the younger recruit at the centre of the group, lit by a benevolent burst of light, is already kicking at the traces. Hope for a better future is invested in him. When he first saw it, Dostoyevsky read it as a reminder of each man's duty to his fellow men.

Rooms 34 and 35 are also devoted to Repin's work. His *Lev Tolstoy*, a famous Whistleresque full-length portrait, shows the writer in old age, barefoot and simply dressed. Other portraits from the turn-of-the-century art world include the critic *Vladimir Stasov*, the pianist *Anton Rubinstein* and the composer *Alexander Glazunov*. The ebullient picture of the *Zaporozhian Cossacks Writing a Mocking Letter to the Turkish Sultan* depicts an episode said to have taken place in the 17th century, when the high and independent spirited cossacks of Zaporozhian Republic rejected the sultan's offer to enter his service.

> *To find the other Repin* chef d'oeuvre *on show, the* Ceremonial Meeting of the State Council, 7 May 1901*, you must pass downstairs through Room 39 (see below) and turn right into Room 54.*

Some of the sketches for this official commission, portraits of individual councillors, are loaded with character despite their hurried, impressionistic execution. Look, for example, at Councillor Pobedonostsev, Chief Procurator of the Holy Synod and high priest of the systematic repression and retrenchment which took place under Alexander III.

Room 39, to which we must return, is alive with Filip Maliavin's exuberant red swirl of a peasant woman dancing. A peasant himself, **Maliavin** (1869–1940) became a monk in the Russian monastery on Mount Athos at the age of 14, and stayed for 6 years until his talent was recognized by a visiting academician who persuaded him to return to St Petersburg to study fine arts. The academy was unable to tame Maliavin's innate Russian love of colour, and though he did paint portraits it is these effusive paintings which fully express his painterly genius.

Rooms 40–41, also in the Rossi Wing, herald another important development in late 19th-century Russian painting, a further step along the path beaten by the Wanderers and their Slavophile supporters. The wealthy industrialist Savva Mamontov set up an artistic commune on his estate, Abramtsevo, near Moscow. With his encouragement, an important Arts and Crafts movement similar to those flowering throughout Europe, developed. Its roots lay deep in traditional Russian skills and the belief that the essence of Russia lay in her medieval history, literature and folk tales. Both **Alexei Ryabushkin** (1861–1904) and **Victor Vasnetsov** (1846–1926) devoted their energies to conjuring up this world in all its doom-laden, violent and colourful variety.

Walk along the corridor (Room 49) and up the stairs onto the first floor of the Benois Building.

Encouraged by Abramtsevo's multi-media approach to decorative and applied arts as well as painting, the talents of one of Russia's most individual painters, **Mikhail Vrubel** (1856–1910) flourished. Vrubel was both a ceramicist and a mural painter, and the fractured images of his paintings in Room 66 have a tactile quality normally associated with the materials of the decorative arts such as mosaic tesserae and tiles. He returned again and again to the themes of beauty and immortality that can be seen in paintings such as *The Flying Demon* and *The Six-Winged Seraphim*. The gap between his craving for these qualities and the reality of his life became unbearable to him, and Vrubel ended his life blind and confined to an insane asylum.

Another attempt to capture the essence of Russia was made by **Mikhail Nesterov** (1862–19424), whose religious mysticism hangs on the walls of Room 67. 'I love the Russian landscape,' he wrote. 'Against its background the meaning of Russian life and the Russian soul can be felt better and more clearly.' As in the 19th century, alongside this search for a truly Russian school of painting there were still painters with a more international attitude to the arts. 'Art for art's sake' was the credo of the World of Art (*Mir Isskustva*) group, whose works hang in Room 68. Their patron was the aesthete and impresario Sergei Diaghilev, who organized exhibitions of foreign art in St Petersburg, hanging French Impressionists side by side with modern Russian works and published a *World of Art* magazine. The artists in this group, who included Leon Bakst and Alexander Benois, worked on the set designs for Diaghilev's Ballet Russe, which toured Europe with great success from 1911. Their canvases are flamboyant and theatrical, and strongly influenced by Art Nouveau, known in Russia as *Style Moderne*. You can see a number of the leading figures, including Benois and Diaghilev, in the portraits they painted of one another.

Room 69 contains the eerie works of the unhappy **Victor Borisov-Musatov** (1870–1905), whose cool perception of the world around is explained by his withdrawn existence. 'When I am frightened by life I rest in art... sometimes it seems to me that I am on a deserted island. And it is as if reality does not exist.' The contrast with the Valentin Serov's worldly portraits in Room 70 could not be more marked. Among his clients pictured here were the richest of Russia's pre-Revolutionary nobility: Zinaida Yussupova (the mother of Felix Yussupov who helped to assassinate Rasputin) and the Countess Orlova. Serov, originally trained at Abramtsevo, also became involved with Diaghilev. In Room 71 you can see his famous sketch of the ballerina Anna Pavlova for the poster of Russian Season in Paris, and his nude portrait of the more risquée Ida Rubinstein who also danced for Diaghilev's company. Seeing her as a 'living bas-relief', Serov chose to paint her in the faintly monochrome style of an Egyptian stone carving.

Rooms 72 and 73 give an overview of other contemporary styles: the impressionistic landscapes of **Konstantin Korovin** (1861–1939), early Impressionist still lifes by **Mikhail Larionov** (1881–1964), and Boris Kustodiev's colourful canvases imbued with the primitive influences of folk traditions. The distinctive landscapes of **Nikolai Roerich** in Room 74, charged with his own pantheistic perception of the world, are a world unto themselves, as happy in the New Age of the late 20th century as they were in pre-Revolutionary Russia. Roerich's idealism was typified by the campaign, which he began single-handed, to press the League of Nations to sign a clause protecting cultural monuments in times of war—a clause which was eventually enshrined in the treaty of the United Nations.

Rooms 75–79 romp through the avant-garde, one of the most important periods in the history of Russian painting, and the only one to rival the 15th-century icon painters for creative innovation. Although the avant-garde had a greater impact on world art than any other group of Russian painters, they are thinly represented here. The reason for this lies in the fact that their work was consigned to the dustbin of history by Stalin. From the mid-1920s, the only form of art encouraged by the state was Socialist Realism, which replaced the heady atmosphere of experiment with an endless stream of paintings glorifying the Revolution, the Party and the People. Until the advent of Gorbachev, the Russian Museum's exhibition of 20th-century painting followed that credo. In its cellars however, it was protecting thousands of avant-garde canvases, and the new hanging is still evolving. That many avant-garde painters welcomed the Revolution and saw themselves as revolutionary painters creating a new art for the new times is all the more ironic.

Appropriating foreign artistic movements such as Cubism and Futurism as a springboard, the Russian avant-garde was propelled by its national traditions and by the Revolution to create a whole series of -isms of its own. While the works of **Pavel Kuznetsov** (1878–1968) in Room 75, **Kuzmin Petrov-Vodkin** (1878–1939) in Room 76 and **Natan Altman** (1889–1970) in Room 77 are broadly figurative and clearly emerge from the movements which preceded them, many of the works in Room 79 seem completely fresh. **Natalia Goncharova** (1881–1962) and her partner **Mikhail Larionov**, who lived abroad from 1915, were at the forefront of Russian Primitivism before Larionov branched out into what he called Rayonism. **Liubov Popova** (1889–1924) and **Vladimir Tatlin** (1885–1953) were leading exponents of a specifically Russian style known as Constructivism which, inspired by the industrial age, owed as much to architecture and stage design as it did to painting. For the moment, the museum's permanent collection of Russian art ends on this explosive note. A wealth of paintings by Suprematist **Kazimir Malevich** (1878–1935), the indefinable **Pavel Filonov** (1883–1941), Agitprop painters and photographers **Mayakovsky** (1893–1930) and **Rodchenko** (1891–1956) and the cream of the Socialist Realists have yet to emerge from the reorganisation.

> *To leave the museum, retrace your steps back into the main palace and down through the basement. Walk diagonally to the left across Ploshchad Isskustv and turn up Italianskaya Ul. passing the run-down Kommisarzhevskaya Drama Theatre on the right. Cross Sadovaya Ul. and continue into Ploshchad Manezhnaya.*

Just before the square opens out, the light blue and white, 18th-century former Shuvalov Palace today contains an institute and museum of hygiene (*see* p.423). On the left side of the square, beyond the fenced garden, stands the yellow and white edifice of the former Mikhailovsky Manezh, a riding-school which was turned into a Winter Sports Stadium and now hosts an amusement arcade. Rossi's resculpting of this area, to go with the Mikhailovsky Palace, extended as far as this building, whose neoclassical exterior echoes those on Ploshchad Isskustv. During the Revolution the building was used by the Bolsheviks' Armoured Car Detachment. The best repertory cinema in St Petersburg lies within the impressive granite building at the far end of the square. It is the House of Cinema, a club for members of the Petersburg film industry, but they sometimes let foreigners into the screenings advertised outside.

> *Between the stadium and the cinema an open-air tourist market, known as **Klenovaya Alleya** (Maple Alley), has appeared. As well as massed matrioshkas and swathes of floral scarves you may be lucky to find old musical instruments and other antiques. Having done the rounds, walk down the side of the market enclosure to find yourself on Inzhenernaya Ul., facing the guard houses of the Mikhailovsky Castle, which Rossi also adapted. Turn right; as the road bends round to the right, the porch of the late 19th-century green and white St Petersburg Circus building (closed August) looms on the far side of the street. The bridge ahead, Most Belinskovo, crosses the broad, calm reaches of the Fontanka River, which once fed the fountains in the Summer Gardens to the left.*

The waterfront in both directions is lined with 18th- and 19th-century palaces of the nobility, as far as the eye can see. The finest, with its yellow Baroque façade hidden behind elaborate railings on the far bank to the right, belonged to the Sheremetiev family. The classical portico beyond it heralds the former Catherine Institute, now a library. The building was commissioned from Quarenghi by Catherine the Great to serve as a school for young noblewomen. The **Church of Ss Simeon and Anna** straight ahead, whose single dilapidated dome rises from decorative Corinthian pilasters, is one of the oldest in the city, built in 1731–4. The entrance, beneath the three-storey classical belltower, leads into a plain green and white stucco interior, only recently reopened.

> *Continue straight up Ul. Belinskovo to Lityeiny Prospekt. It was on this corner, at Lityeiny Prospekt 45, that Sergei Diaghilev edited the influential* World of Art *magazine from 1898. In his day the street was a byword for shopping and the arts world. Since the 1930s however, Lityeiny has been synonymous with the institutional thuggery of the KGB, who meted it out in St Petersburg from their 'Bolshoi Dom' (Big House) down the street to the left. Turn right and walk through the archway at Lityeiny Prospekt 51 to come face to face with the small Teatr na Unimom. On the wall to the right, painted white arrows point the way through a series of yards to the **Anna Akhmatova Museum** (*Muzei Anny Akhmatovy), *in the large hidden courtyard behind the Sheremetiev Palace that we noticed from the bridge over the Fontanka.*

The attentive, craggy profile of Anna Akhmatova (1889–1966) is an icon of her time. Writing with deceptive simplicity, she had already become one of Russia's most popular poets by the outbreak of the First World War. Her early poems have been sifted for prophetic utternaces to show that she was always destined to be the voice of her people. Her life supplied ample material—close friends and a husband were killed, her son was imprisoned for the 'sins' of his parents, other friends fled into exile, her poetry was repressed for two long stints and she often had little more than two kopeks to rub together. That she should have lived on the street of the KGB longer than anywhere else seems entirely in keeping with her fateful life.

Anna was born on the Black Sea, but moved almost immediately with her family to Tsarskoye Selo, the town surrounding the tsar's summer palace outside St Petersburg. Her family name was Gorenko, but before the publication of her first poem her father suggested that she should not bring the shame of poetry on his respectable upper middle-class family. Anna's choice of surname shows a well-tuned poet's ear. Akhmatova was a name shared by her great-grandmother and the last Tartar khans to threaten Moscow. Where they left off with swords, she carried on with words—words which so threatened Stalin that he was forced to ban them.

Akhmatova came to live here, in the servants' quarters of the Sheremetiev Palace, with her lover Nikolai Punin, his wife and child, in 1924. She continued to live in the apartment until 1941, and again from 1944–54, always with Punin's first family. The museum (*open 10.30am–6.30pm; closed Mon and last Wed*) is on the second floor. In the course of six rooms it traces Akhmatova's life story through photographs, manuscripts, editions of her poetry, sculpture and personal effects.

Room 1 deals with Akhmatova's childhood, her courtship by fellow poet Nikolai Gumilyov, their marriage and travels in Italy and France. They founded a new poetic orientation, Acmeism, seeking clarity and rejecting the prevailing Symbolist obfuscation. There are also photographs of the in-crowd at The Stray Dog cabaret.

In Room 2, tragedy surfaces in Akhmatova's life. With the First World War came the Revolution, which she watched only half in horror, and the Civil War. Gumilev and Akhmatova, despite the birth of a son, had been drifting apart, he travelling the world while she stayed at home. In 1918 she asked him for a divorce. In 1921 Gumilev was arrested and shot for his alleged part in the Tagantsev Affair, an anti-Bolshevik conspiracy. Akhmatova steadfastly refused to emigrate, but from 1925, when for 15 years her poetry was not published, life became increasingly hard.

The sparse, dramatic intensity of Room 3, with its icon *Do Not Weep For Me Mother* and sculpture entitled *Akhmatova—Poems*, is dedicated to her great poem *Requiem*, composed in these rooms from 1940–41. To write it down could have led to the death sentence, so she would pass each fragment to a friend who memorized and then burnt it. At the heart of the poem lies her son Lev's arrest in 1935, and his disappearance into the gulag in 1939. It was while queueing to give him a food parcel that the events she describes in the preface to the poem occurred. A woman in the queue behind her whispered, 'Can you put this into words?'

> *'And I said:*
> *—I can.*
> *Then a ghost of a smile slipped across*
> *what had once been her face.'*

Room 4 is dedicated to Leningrad in the late thirties and 1940, and to those poets who died or were persecuted for their art. Amongst the exhibits are collections celebrating the lives of Akhmatova's first husband Nikolai Gumilyov, another Acmeist poet Osip Mandelshtam who died in the gulag in 1938, and Marina Tsvetaeva who committed suicide shortly after her return from exile in Paris in 1940.

Room 5, the room in which Akhmatova lived between 1938 and 1941, when she was evacuated from the beseiged city and went to live in Tashkent, contains many of her personal possessions. Above the desk is a Modigliani drawing of her, done in 1911 in Paris. Until a recent exhibition in London, when a Russian friend of mine recognized four more in the series, this was thought to be the only one to have survived. While her husband travelled, Akhmatova and Modigliani whiled away enjoyable hours sitting on park benches, reciting Verlaine. One day, Anna went to his studio to give him a bunch of flowers but the painter was not there. Finding a narrow crack of window open, she threw them in, one by one. Later Modigliani asked how she had managed to get in. He refused to believe that she hadn't arranged the way they had fallen with her own two hands. Whether they were lovers will probably never be known.

Room 6 is devoted to her epic and complicated *Poem without a Hero* written and amended countless times between 1940–62. Partly dedicated to dead colleagues, friends, the city of Leningrad during the seige and to Isaiah Berlin, it is also in part a portrait of European literature and of the role of the poet. Accompanying it you will find pictures of Leningrad during the blockade, and of Tashkent where Anna spent most of the war. The part Isaiah Berlin played in Anna's life is a perfect illustration of its extraordinary ironic drama. Berlin was visiting Leningrad in 1945 from the British Embassy in Moscow. In a secondhand bookshop on Nevsky Prospekt he bumped into a literary critic and quietly asked if Akhmatova was still alive. The critic phoned Akhmatova and the pair set off for this flat. 'We climbed up one of the steep dark staircases to an upper floor and were admitted to Akhmatova's room...' Berlin describes. 'A stately, grey-haired lady, a white shawl draped about her shoulders, slowly rose to greet us. Anna Andreevna was immensely dignified, with unhurried gestures, a noble head, beautiful, somewhat severe features, and an expression of immeasurable sadness. I bowed—it seemed appropriate, for she looked and moved like a tragic queen—thanked her for receiving me, and said that people in the west would be glad to know that she was in good health, for nothing had been heard of her for so many years.' They had not been there long when, to his horror, Berlin heard an English voice in the courtyard, shouting his name. Randolph Churchill, Winston's journalist son, had been told by Berlin's travelling companion from the British Council where he was, and wanted to know if Berlin would act as his interpreter. Everyone in the building knew that Akhmatova was receiving foreigners. Berlin left, but Akhmatova was brave enough to invite him back later that night, and the two spent all night and well into the following morning talking. It is thought that the 1946 decree vilifying her for being 'too remote from socialist reconstruction' and Zhdanov's disgusting rantings against the poet as 'half-nun, half whore' were partly a result of Churchill's blunder. The decree was only annulled in 1988, although from the 1950s until her death in 1966 Akhmatova was published again, and even travelled to Taormina and Oxford to receive prizes and honorary degrees.

> *Weave your way back to Lityeiny Prospekt, turn right and walk to Nevsky Prospekt. The enormous yellow and white neoclassical building on the other side of Lityeiny was built as a hospital by Quarenghi in 1803–4, commissioned by Emperor Paul's kindly widow Maria Fyodorovna, and serves the same purpose today. Turn right on Nevsky Prospekt and walk towards the Anichkov Most.*

On the corner of Nevsky Prospekt and the Fontanka River stands one of the city's most memorable buildings, the **Beloselsky-Belozersky** palace. Its dusky Pompeian red colour and the vigorous male torsos (atlantes) upholding its balconies are a startling, virile contrast to the delicate pilasters and pastel shades of most of the city. It was built in 1846–8, a hundred years after its Rococo style suggests, by Andrei Stakenschneider. From 1884 it was the home of Alexander III's reactionary brother Grand Prince Sergei, and his devout wife Elizabeth, whose sister Alexandra went on to become empress. The marriage was not a happy one—he banned *Anna Karenina* from her reading list on the grounds that it would encourage 'unhealthy curiosity and violent emotions'—and ended when Sergei was blown up by a bomb in the Kremlin. Until recently the offices of the local Communist party, it has now become a venue for concerts and cultural exhibitions. Guided tours are also offered. Either call ✆ 319 9990 to arrange one in advance, or chance your luck. Even if you don't manage to make it into the garish, much-gilded state rooms, the surreal white hall and staircase will give you a feel. The programme of evening concerts is advertised on Nevsky Prospekt, and tickets are sold in the hall.

The **Anichkov Bridge** and Palace, which faces the Beloselsky-Belozersky across the graceful curve of the Fontanka, take their name from the colonel and military engineer who built the original wooden draw-bridge here at the dawn of the city. For the first few decades it acted as a toll bridge, at which carts were turned back unless they were carrying a piece of stone for the building site that was St Petersburg. Rebuilt in 1839–41, it was soon adorned with the four fiery stallions rearing above their trainers sculpted by St Petersburg's resident horse sculptor Pyotr Klodt. Two conflicting tales encourage visitors to examine the animal's nether regions carefully. One professes that the sculptor sketched a profile of Tsar Nicholas I in the veins of one horse's groin, the other that the profile of the van-quished Napoleon can be recognized in another's genitalia.

The **Anichkov Palace** is not easily appreciated from anywhere, for it has been rebuilt and added to since it was designed in high Rococo style for the Empress Elizabeth's lover, Alexei Razumovsky, whom she is said to have married in secret in 1742. Continuing in the tradition, her daughter-in-law Catherine the Great pre-sented it to her lover Grigory Potemkin, who had the exterior toned down to the more fashionable classical style. Quarenghi added the bold colonnade down the Fontanka façade, and after some reconstruction it was converted into government offices in 1809–10. From 1819 the palace was occupied by the heirs to the throne, until Alexander III decided not to move out after his coronation—it contained his much-loved art collection, later the basis of the Russian Museum. His widow con-tinued to live here until shortly before the Revolution, counselling her son Nicholas II through his disastrous reign. Retiring to the Crimea, she finally left the country by boat through the Black Sea, in April 1919. Since the late 30s the palace has been given over to educating and entertaining the young, initially as the Palace of Pioneers, the politically-correct Soviet equivalent of the boy scouts and girl guides. During the summer, there are frequent concerts by military bands and choirs.

Walking on down Nevsky Prospekt, the glass façade across the road at No. 58 contains the Comedy Theatre, and on the ground floor the flamboyant Art Nouveau hall built in 1902–3 to house Yeliseyev's grocery shop.

Known officially as Gastronom No. 1 but still called **Yeliseyev's** by all, Russia's pre-Revolutionary Fortnum and Mason's is one of the city's best supplied grocers. Despite all the city has gone through since the beginning of the century, the inte-rior is resplendent. Beneath a high gilded ceiling, shoppers mill around the original wood and glass counters, eyeing home-grown and imported produce illuminated by chandeliers and lights spraying out from the walls like bunches of flowers.

*Cross back over Nevsky Propekt to admire yet another of Carlo Rossi's remarkable urban set pieces, **Ploshchad Ostrovskovo**, originally called Alexandrinskaya Ploshchad after its focus, the Alexandrinsky Theatre.*

The square is now named after 19th-century Russia's most prolific dramatist, A. N. Ostrovsky. Behind railings on the left, the Anichkov Palace gardens are linked to the ensemble by their two pavilions designed by Rossi. This area is a favourite meeting place for the city's outdoor chess enthusiasts. When new pipes were laid beneath the square, rather than abandon their places players merely perched their chess sets on top of abandoned diggers, and their bottoms on concrete drains.

Against the backdrop of the Alexandrinsky Theatre, a building of truly imperial splendour commissioned by her grandson, is the city's only statue of Catherine the Great. Though she did so much to foster the spirit of the city, she was only finally awarded a statue in 1873. In an allegory of her reign, the empress stands on a plinth surrounded by the clutch of figures without whom the obscure German princess would never have become Empress of All the Russias. Walking anti-clock-wise round the monument you can identify the field marshals who masterminded Catherine's victories over the Turks, P. A. Rumyantsev and the skeletal A. V. Suvorov, separated by their fellow-soldier, Catherine's lover and advisor Grigory Potemkin. Her chancellor and foreign minister A. A. Bezborodko is sculpted in earnest conversation with fellow-statesman Ivan Betskoi. Beneath the fluid metal waterfall of the empress' cloak are Admiral Chichagov and Grigory Orlov who, with his brothers, masterminded the coup d'état which brought Catherine to the throne. On the empress' right is poet Gavriil Derzhavin, while another conspirator and President of the Academy of Sciences, Ekaterina Dashkova, reads beside him.

The right hand side of the square is occupied by the **Russian National Library**, commonly referred to as the 'publichka'. Established in the reign of Paul I (1796–1801), it was extended by Rossi at the same time as he built the Alexandrinsky Theatre. The façade sports statues of philosophers by St Petersburg's most prolific sculptors of the time, Pimenov and Demut-Malinovsky, ranged beneath the godess of wisdom, Minerva. Perhaps the library's greatest hour came during the seige of Leningrad, when most of the city's public institutions closed down. Day in, day out, librarians kept their doors open, helping members of the public search their precious treasure to find ways of manufacturing matches, recipes for candles, and clues for converting wood into an edible substance and creating artificial vitimins. If you are interested in consulting its 25 million tomes, in a variety of languages, all you need to take along is your passport, a photograph of yourself and to pay a small rouble fee. Be warned that this is not a lending library, and reading space is scarce.

Looking at the handsome **Alexandrinsky Theatre** (known as the Pushkin Theatre in Soviet times), it comes as no surprise to find out that theatre ran in Carlo Rossi's blood. His mother was a ballerina, and the building resembles a three-dimensional stage design, a backdrop for the drama of autocratic imperial life. Built in 1828–32 and named after Nicholas I's wife Alexandra Fyodorovna, it is adorned with straight-forward dramatic metaphors—the chariot of Apollo on the roof and statues of the muses Terpsichore (lyric poetry and dancing) and Melpomene (tragedy) on either side of the main façade. These external decorative touches, which run right round the building enlivening the porticoed façades, were again executed by Pimenov and Demut-Malinovsky with the help of Triscornia.

In the far left hand corner of the square, the **Museum of Theatre and Musical Arts**, *Ploshchad Ostrovskovo 6, overlooks the Alexandrinsky.*

Its four rooms are plastered with the history of the dramatic arts in Russia, in a floor-to-ceiling display of photographs and theatrical posters. The origins of Russian theatre—in churches, serf theatres and the early imperial theatres—pave the way for turn-of-the-century developments, including Mayakovsky's avant-garde approach in St Petersburg and the establishment of the Moscow Arts Theatre (MKhAT) by Stanislavsky and Nemirovich-Danchenko. Revolution breaks out in Room 3, with a riot of Constructivist designs and experimental photographs of leading activists such as Meyerhold, photographed by Rodchenko. While the world-renowned bass singer Fyodor Chaliapin's St Petersburg flat is being restored, the last room provides a home for some of the maestro's effects. The gramophone in the golden cabinet was a gift from his Anglo-American recording company.

The street leading away from the back of the Alexandrinsky Theatre has been renamed in honour of the creator of its symmetry, Ul. Zodchevo (master builder) Rossi. Looking back from the far end, you can appreciate the perfection of its proportions. The buildings are exactly the same height as the width of the street, while the street is exactly ten times as long. The precision appeals to some, while others feel threatened by its unerring regularity. However tired your legs, spare a thought for the denizens of the Vaganova Ballet School, hidden behind the blank windows of the left-hand building as you walk down. Following in Russia's demanding tradition, their eyes are on the heights attained by previous pupils of their *alma mater*, Pavlova, Nijinsky, Nureyev, Baryshnikov and Makarova. Like them, they may end up seeking work in the West, though they will be choosing New York or London for economic reasons without the palaver of having to seek political asylum.

Rossi's work continues in the crescent of creamy yellow buildings at the far end of the street. Formally Ploshchad Lomonosova, with a bust of the scientist looking towards the decorative Lomonosov Bridge over the Fontanka, it is affectionately known as the *vatrushka*, after the much-loved round cheese pie of the same name.

Turn right, walk through the arch and down Ul. Lomonosova. There's a good stand-up café in the last arch on the left before you hit Sadovaya Ul.

Between Nevsky Prospekt and Sennaya Ploshchad on Sadovaya was once the hub of commercial St Petersburg, boasting three major department stores excluding the four market buildings on the square itself. Today trading continues, but it's a far cry from its heyday of precious furs and jewellers' arcades.

Turn left briefly on Sadovaya, opposite the grand neoclassical crescent of what was once the Imperial Bank, to dive into **Apráksin Dvor** *(formerly Apraksin Market) and enter the lower depths of its poverty-driven flea market, Veschovy Rynok. Turn on your heels to continue the walk.*

Just beyond Ul. Lomonosova on the right rises the former **Vorontsov Palace**, which is sadly inaccessible. Built by Rastrelli in 1749–57 for the father of Elizaveta Vorontsova, Catherine the Great's competitor for the affections of the feckless Peter III, its charming, light three-storey central corpus is flanked by two-storey wings, all in pale yellow and white. Somewhat heavy iron railings separate the palace's front garden from the pavement. It was once chosen by Paul I as the headquarters for the Knights of the Order of St John of Malta, gaining a delightful chapel by Quarenghi in the process. Chased from their island habitat by Napoleon and facing extinction, the Catholic order found an unlikely ally in the Orthodox Russian emperor. Paul became Grand Master of the Order in 1798, though his election was not legal. Russia's involvement finished with the emperor's assassination, suggesting that the snub-nosed madman was driven more by his love of dressing-up than by a desire to provide Russia with a naval toehold in the Mediterranean. From 1810 the building sheltered the Corps of Pages, educating the sons of high-ranking army officers. Whatever the regime, it has remained a military school to this day.

On the other side of the street running all the way to Nevsky Prospekt is the arcade of **Gostiny Dvor**, St Petersburg's main bazaar since it was erected in 1761–85 by Vallin de la Mothe. Now a department store, its relentless gloom, despite an abundance of goods, makes you forgive the worst excesses of commercial fever in the West. Dive into one of the doors and follow its corridors for as long as you can, keeping an eye out for occasional gems: stationary, scarves and children's toys.

Far more absorbing, even if you don't understand a word, is the street theatre which takes place in front of the building on Nevsky Prospekt. Here, knots of citizens practise their right to free speech by haranguing one another. Using humour to win over your audience has yet to take off. Arguments are fast and furious, often involving racist attitudes you would be arrested for airing in London or New York.

Before disappearing into Ⓜ *Nevsky Prospekt, use the underpass to visit the heavenly blue and white Armenian Church, recently reopened.*

Set back from the street, the church was built in 1771–80 and is an excellent example of its architect Yuri Velten's light, decorative neoclassical style. Its pillared interior is in serious need of repair but with their motherland bankrupt it is hardly a priority for the city's Armenian population. Light a candle for their sake.

Ⓜ *Gostiny Dvor and* Ⓜ *Nevsky Prospekt are both at hand to whisk you to your hotel. Alternatively revitalize yourself in one of the handful of bars and cafés nearby (see p.501).*

Start: Ⓜ *Chernyshevskaya.*

Walking Time: *2 hours.*

V: Tauride Palace and Smolny Region

SMOLNY SOBOR

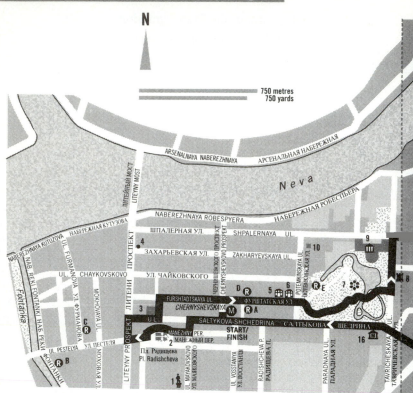

Sites

1   Bust of Mayakovsky
Byust Mayakovskovo
Бюст Маяковского

2   Cathedral of the Transfiguration
Preobrazhensky sobor
Преображенский собор

3   Former Church of St Anna
Tserkov sv. Anny
Церковь св. Анны

4   Bolshoi Dom
Большой дом

5   Ignatieff House
Ignatievskaya usadba
Игнатиевская усадба

6   Spiridonov House
Spiridonovskaya usadba
Спиридоновская усадба

7   Tauride Gardens
Tavrichesky sad
Таврический сад

8   Ivanov Tower
Ivanovskaya bashnya
Ивановская башня

9   Tauride Palace
Tavrichesky dvorets
Таврический дворец

10   Horticultural Exhibition Hall
Vystavochny zal 'Tsvety'
Выставочный зал 'Цветы'

11   Kikin Chambers
Kikiny palaty
Кикины палаты

12   Smolny Convent and Cathedral
Smolny monastir i sobor
Смольный монастырь и собор

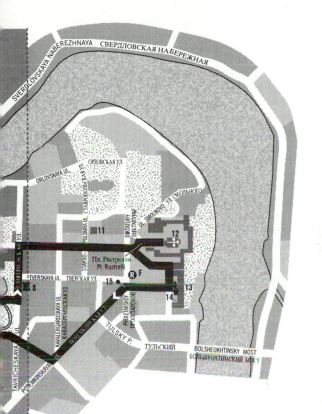

13 Smolny Institute
   Smolny institut
   Смольный институт

14 Statue of Lenin
   Pamyatnik V. I. Lenina
   Памятник В. И. Ленина

15 Square of the Dictatorship of the Proletariat
   Ploshchad proletarskoy diktatury
   Пл. пролетарской диктатуры

16 Suvorov Museum
   Muzei A. V. Suvorova
   Музей А. В. Суворова

Restaurants and Cafés

A   Café Baghdad
    Кафе Багдад

B   Café Fontanka
    Кафе Фонтанка

C   Café Kameya
    Кафе Камея

D   Café Parakar
    Кафе Паракар

E   Tauride Park Café
    Café v. Tavricheskom sadu
    Кафе в. Таврическом саду

This spacious corner of St Petersburg, beyond the concentric canals which hem in the centre, remained a region of aristocratic country estates right up until the mid-19th century. Most of it is well over four metres above sea level, saving it from the unhealthy marshy miasma and the floods which have left such a psychological scar on the rest of the city. In the last 150 years these estates have been built over to create a series of stately streets. The houses themselves now shelter consulates or public services such as the register offices for marriages and births. In between, examples of much later architecture, apartment blocks in the self-important eclectic and *Style Moderne* styles, make many of the streets into an illustrated textbook of Petersburgian styles.

On the far side of the Tauride Gardens, much to the region's misfortune, Lenin decided to turn the Smolny Institute, then Russia's foremost school for the daughters of the nobility, into the Bolshevik Party headquarters in 1917. With such revolutionary credentials the area was doomed to a busy life as a communist heartland. Older, characterful buildings were flattened to create the Square of the Proletarian Dictatorship, a construction as clumsy and ugly as its name. Somehow Rastrelli's neighbouring masterpiece, the Smolny Cathedral, manages to ignore the concrete and tarmac hell with the aloof superiority of a proud 18th-century courtier. Together, the square and cathedral are an eloquent statement of the extreme nature of Russia, her people and their history.

Weaving your way between these two worlds, a varied crowd will accompany you. Furshtadskaya Ul. has the self-confident air of private business and foreign embassies, the gardens are the province of local children, while poor Smolny is still overrun by state employees. Avoid this itinerary on Thursdays, when the Smolny Cathedral is closed. As it is the only building you will be spending any time in apart from restaurants, a windy wet day would be miserable.

lunch/cafés

This area of town is low on eating places, but the two that do exist are at least good, and there's a fast food open-air possibility in summer too. If it is warm, consider bringing a picnic to eat in the Tauride Park. The two restaurants mentioned at the end of this list are not actually on the itinerary, but both are a five minute walk from the metro station.

Café Baghdad, Furshtadskaya Ul. 35, ✆ 272 2355/3533, open daily noon–11pm. Look for the gaily painted street level windows. This bright basement cooperative resounds bearably to the beat of MTV and serves spicy food from the middle eastern republics, tea and alcohol. Their soups are original hot creations, though sometimes a little greasy, and the shashliks are excellent. If the spicy meat soup (харчо) is on, go for it.

Café Pogrebok, Ploshchad Proletarskoy Diktaturi 5, open daily noon–11pm; closed 4–5pm. Just to confuse, this is one of the cafés which doesn't serve coffee, or even tea. Wash down the normal fare of soups, cold starters and meat dishes with the alcohol and soft drinks of the day.

Café Parakar, beneath the trees of the central pedestrian avenue, Furshtadskaya Ul. In summer this is the best place in the city to watch the passing crowds over a drink and light snack.

Tauride Park Café, in a garden rotunda, past the statue of Lenin in the park itself. Sitting pretty on top of a small rise, this café only operates in summer.

Café Kameya, Ul. Furmanova 32, open noon–11pm; closed 4–5pm. This café epitomizes the Russian tendency of making it feel like night in restaurants all day long. The Russians traditional Russian menu is well-cooked and there are plenty of large tables which you can share.

Café Fontanka, Naberezhnaya Reki Fontanki 14, open 2pm–5am; closed 10–11pm (*see* p.500).

> *Turn left on Chernishevskaya Ul. outside the metro and right at the T-junction with Ul. Saltykova-Shchedrina, named after the 19th-century satirical journalist.*

In the 1860s and 70s Mikhail Saltykov-Shchedrin collaborated with the poet Nekrasov in publishing an important radical literary periodical, *Notes from the Fatherland*, from a flat on Lityeiny Prospekt. It was between its covers that both Dostoyevsky and Tolstoy first came to the attention of the wider public. His own literary fame rests on one masterpiece, *The Golovlevs*, which depicts a family from the rural gentry falling apart after the emancipation of the serfs in 1861, hailed by the Soviets as a truthful exposé of the rotten core of the upper classes.

> *Crossing the road, take the first left onto Ul. Mayakovskovo, named after another writer, this time the poet Vladimir Mayakovsky.*

Assured of his reputation by Stalin's posthumous praise of him as 'the greatest Soviet poet', he had welcomed the Revolution and devoted himself to writing poetry appropriate to the new world it had created. It was partly because of events that took place on this street that he committed suicide in 1930. For seventeen years he was in love with the married Lily Brik, and even lived here, at No. 52, *à trois* with her and her husband Osip. The social realist portrait bust of him further down the street conveys his strength and commitment but not his idiosyncrasy, which towards the end of his life was attacked by the conformism of writers under Stalin.

> *If you go to look at it, you will have to return to turn down Manezhny Pereulok, which leads down to the back of the **Cathedral of the Transfiguration** (Преображенский Собор—Preobrazhensky Sobor).*

This delightful Empire-style five-domed, yellow and white cathedral is surrounded by a small garden and handsome chain fence, which you can enter through a gate opposite the lane. The cathedral was built in 1827–29, and the fence is suspended from Turkish cannons captured in the Russo-Turkish war of 1828. Each cannon is decorated at the top with a tugra, a piece of heraldic calligraphy created in the Topkapi Palace in Istanbul to be the signature of each new sultan. Presumably cannons were thought suitable for inclusion since this building, by the Moscow-trained V. P. Stasov, replaced St Petersburg's foremost military church which had burned down in 1825. It was here in 1741 that the future Empress Elizabeth rallied the guards to support her coup d'état against the infant Ivan VI, and in memory of their support she built a wooden church on the spot, naming it the Church of the Transfiguration after the Transfiguration (Preobrazhensky) Regiment. Until the Revolution the interior of the church dripped in guards' memorabilia: captured standards, keys of fortresses, the uniforms of several tsars and even the sword worn by Tsar Alexander II at his assassination. The bronze and crystal chandeliers were made specially for the building, echoing the religious element in the external decorative reliefs: Moses' tablets, along with angels and crosses. The dramatic iconostasis was built to a design by Stasov himself, its royal gates, enclosed in a classical apse, surmounted by a brilliant gilded sunburst. There are a number of fine icons in the church, and appropriately perhaps the best hangs off a side column to the right, showing the Transfiguration of Christ. It tells of the moment on Mount Hermon when Peter, James and John witnessed the transfiguration of Jesus, and saw the prophets Elijah and Moses appear to talk to him. Jesus is portrayed on the mountain top abounding in glory while the disciples cower in terror at its foot.

> *Leave the cathedral through its main door and portico, giving what you can to the beggars who normally lie in wait here, and walk straight on to busy Lityeiny (Smelting) Prospekt.*

This was one of the first streets in the city, named after the armaments foundry built in 1711 on the river, and connecting it with Nevsky Prospekt. This century 'on Lityeny' has come to mean something more sinister, as the KGB headquarters and prison are located in **Bolshoi Dom**, on the site of the former foundry.

*Turning right and right again back onto Ul. Saltikova-Shchedrina, the first building to command attention is the turquoise and white former Lutheran **Church of St Anna**, some 100 metres up on the left.*

Unfortunately there is nothing to be seen in the interior as the church was converted into a cinema, the Spartak, in 1939. It was built in 1775-9 by Yuri Velten, the man responsible for girding the Neva with granite banks. Appropriately for the designer of a Lutheran church, Velten had trained in Germany. If you cut through beside the church you will come to its elegant eastern end, where the internal apse is mirrored externally by a graceful semi-circular Ionic portico topped by a cupola.

You are now on Furshtadskaya Ul., which is rapidly regaining its feel as one of St Petersburg's smartest streets, with a boulevard atmosphere and a smattering of embassies.

Furshtadskya Ul. was already a fashionable street by the time the Duma (parliament) began to sit in the nearby Tauride Palace in 1905; but finding itself within the metaphorical sound of the division bell, it soon gained several parliamentary residents. Turning right, one walks through a living manual of St Petersburg architecture, containing everything from low, crumbling Petrine houses (No. 34) to disintegrating concrete Constructivist flat blocks (No. 26). In between there are contrasting examples of northern *Style Moderne* in the functional pale brick building at No. 24, which borrows and modernizes various 'Empire' motifs, and the aquamarine and white building at No. 28 which is much more flamboyant. But the majority of the buildings date from the second half of the 19th century, when eclecticism in architecture saw a neo-Russian 'medieval' construction rise side by side with a piece of pseudo-classicism. Two of the finest examples lie at the end of the street, at Nos. 52 and 58, and were the town houses of the aristocratic Ignatieff and Spiridonov families respectively. Both were built in the late 1890s and now serve to record important rites of passage: the first as a Palace of Weddings and the second as the local registry for births. In his admirable reconstruction of his family saga *The Russian Album*, Michael Ignatieff enumerates the household as it was on the night in February 1917 when the revolutionary mob marched past on their way to the Duma. Aside from the family, there were 21 servants living in the house, ranging from young messenger boys to an English governess and a French tutor. Two years later the family, accompanied only by the English governess, were lucky to find passage on a boat across the Black Sea to Istanbul, where they lived in two rooms of a cheap boarding house. The ghosts of the revolutionary upheaval seem particularly vivid on Furshtadskaya Ul.

*An entrance to the **Tauride Gardens** (Tavrichesky Sad), designated a children's park, opens opposite the end of the street. Threaded with would-be streams and lakes and landscaped with small hills, in winter it is* *criss-crossed by the swish of diminutive skaters, skiers and toboggans. While exploring, bear in mind that you should be heading for a gate straight across the park, directly opposite where you came in.*

This park was once the private garden of Catherine the Great's influential lover, the one-eyed Grigory Potyomkin, for whom she had the gardens and neighbouring **Tauride Palace** (Tavrichesky Dvorets) built in 1783–9. Following Crimean victories against the Turks, she crowned her gift of thanks by making him Prince of Tauris (a contemporary name for the Crimea) in 1787, but it was only after his death in 1791 that she named the palace and gardens after him. This park was laid out in the informal style of landscaping preferred by Catherine, by an Englishman called Gould. Striding past one of the last statues of Lenin in the city at the entrance, on the left is the only original garden pavilion remaining, now a small café. Reading of the park's well-tended gazebos, islands and grottos of yesteryear, it is tempting to echo Catherine's words as she walked mournfully through the gardens less than a year after Potyomkin's death. 'Everything here used to be charming' she murmured wistfully, 'but now everything is not right'. Despite the modern concrete open-air theatre and caged sports pitches, the park is still undulating and sylvan. Near the centre, a **Monument to the Young Defenders of Leningrad** during the 1941–4 seige faces the back of the palace across a lake, its three conspirators leaping stealthily out of a camouflage of stone. A poignant story is told of the adolescent girls who volunteered to look for mines, barefoot, after the German retreat. Suzanne Massie, in her book on Pavlovsk tells how 'in the morning the girls would go out to work singing songs, and in the evening would return in silent formation, carrying a wounded or dead friend on a field stretcher.' All occupied areas round the city were scattered with mined toys—dolls, rabbits, elephants and cars—designed to continue the German reign of terror over the children of the city well after they had gone.

From this angle, the most prominent feature of the palace is the roof of its conservatory. These popular features of Russian houses were known as **Winter Gardens**. Now distinctly dishevelled, this was one of the most splendid ever conceived: the 18th-century French traveller C. P. Masson describes how 'the delicious temperature, the scented plants and the voluptuous silence of this magic spot throw the soul into gentle dreams and carry away one's imagination to the woods of Italy. The enchanted illusion is only destroyed by the view out of the windows onto icicles and frosts.' In the middle of the 19th century it was used as the imperial kitchen garden, where one visitor noted 15,000 pots of strawberry plants. After radical reconstruction, it was here that the Duma held their parliamentary sessions from 1906–17. This large auditorium went on to be used by the Petrograd Soviet and for congresses of both the Soviets and the Communist Party, before becoming an elite Higher Party School. It is now used as offices and for meetings between the representatives of the different nations of the CIS, and is sadly closed to tourists.

Leaving the park by the Tavricheskaya Ul. exit, turn left. There will doubt-less be a queue on the other side of the road, insisting itself through the doors of Karavanaya, a popular Scottish bakery.

Like carrying low-grade lignite to Newcastle, this company has imported the 'know how' for tasteless, nutritionless white bread to a country which bakes the most delicious bread in the world. It sells because of the rare novelty value and the inno-vative smear of psychedelic icing on the buns.

On the top floor of the round tower on the corner with Tverskaya Ul., the uncrowned king of the pre-Revolutionary St Petersburg's literary scene, the Symbolist poet Vyacheslav Ivanov, presided over his Wednesday salon, known as The Tower (*Bashnya*) which was renowned for its intellectual punch throwing. The battle of the time was between the Symbolists who had rather run out of steam and the younger generation of poets, the Acmeists, amongst them Nikolai Gumilev, Anna Akhmatova and Osip Mandelshtam. The young Akhmatova remembers being taken there at the age of 21 and reciting a recent poem to the 'Tauride Sage', who responded 'with indifference and irony: "What pure Romanticism."'

*Continue to the end of the park and turn left on Ul. Shpalernaya to come to the front of the **Tauride Palace.***

On the left, opposite a 19th-century brick water tower, are the severe neoclassical portico, sweeping drive and single storey wings of the main façade. The architect chosen by Catherine in 1783 to laud her conquering hero was Ivan Starov, one of Russia's first home-grown architects. Starov had followed his studies in Moscow by travelling to France and Italy. A passionate disciple of the neoclassicist Palladio, he was the obvious choice for a building which Catherine wanted to be inspired by the Pantheon in Rome. This muse explains the flattened dome atop a circular hall. On the other hand the inspiration for the colour scheme, a hopeful spring-like yellow, green and white, could only be the long grey Russian winter.

Potyomkin was a bold strategist, shrewd advisor and passionate lover, Catherine's 'greatest, most bizarre and most entertaining of eccentrics'. The palace's finest moment, a year or so after its completion, was the great party Potyomkin threw for his former lover, now respected friend, in April 1791. Preparations took months, and the seven hour extravaganza was said to have cost 150,000 roubles. It began with Catherine's arrival greeted by a fanfare from 300 musicians and continued with ballets, a comedy, a costume ball and more music. The highlight was a sit-down dinner for a select 600, served on gold and silver platters, with the rest of the guests eating standing up. In the meantime the gardens and rooms were ablaze with light and covered with sparkling reflective stones, mirrors, crystal pyramids and globes. When the empress eventually left for bed past midnight, Potemkin, according to Masson, 'threw himself at her feet, took her hand and burst into tears.' Within six months Potyomkin was dead, and Catherine honoured his memory by living in the palace during the spring and autumn. After her death her son Paul, who hated his mother and desecrated all her favourite places, gave the palace over to a regiment of the horse guards, who used the halls as stables.

> *Beyond the palace, on the corner with the street named after Grigory Potyomkin (Ul. Potyomkinskaya), there is a promising looking garden-centre and* **horticultural exhibition hall**, *supposedly open every day except Sunday and Monday. Further, the road leads past the Tsarist Detention Centre at No. 25 Shpalernaya Ul. and on back to the KGB, or rather the Russian Security Ministry as it is now known, on Lityeiny.*

> *The walk continues in the opposite direction, and is spectacularly punctuated by Rastrelli's greatest surviving masterpiece, the* **Smolny Cathedral**, *(Смолный Собор—Smolny Sobór) rising beatifically straight ahead.*

Before getting to the cathedral, you will pass a statue of 'Iron' Felix Dzerzhinsky (*see* pp.63–4), first head of the Bolshevik secret police, the Cheka, which means lynchpin. Beyond, your attention will be drawn to the highly decorative **Kikin Chambers** (Kikiny Palaty) on the left. One of the city's earliest surviving structures, it was built in 1714 for Peter the Great's naval advisor, A. V. Kikin, one of the bright young men whom he had sent to Europe to study, in this case shipbuilding in Holland. Granted a piece of what was then open countryside, Kikin planned this building in the Petrine Baroque style favoured by his master, but with grandiose embellishments such as the double staircase entrance. It was perhaps just such tactless foolishness that led to him being dismissed from the Admiralty while the house was still being built, and eventually to his execution in 1718 after he saw some advantage in championing the cause of Peter's hated son and heir, Alexei. From 1718–27 the palace housed Peter's collection of nature's curiosities, his Kunstkamera, and his scientific library, Russia's first museum. Such was Peter's enthusiasm for education that he encouraged visitors with the enlightened bribe of a pie and a shot of vodka before they left. After the collections were moved to their present locations on Vasilievsky Island, the building became barracks and hospital to a regiment of the horse guards. It was greatly added to and it is largely due to heavy damage during the Second World War that the original house was rediscovered and restored to its current striped originality in the 1950s. The chambers are used by a local children's music school and out of bounds to tourists.

The Smolny ensemble ahead grew out of the 'petticoat period', or era of empresses, when in an unprecedented and unrepeated 71 years (1725–96), Russia was ruled by women for all but five of them. Successive empresses added to this female enclave, which began with a convent for female orphans and grew to include a school for the daughters of the nobility and a home for widows. This feminine tradition was sharply disrupted in 1917 when the Petrograd Soviet requisitioned the Smolny Institute and, dominated by the Bolsheviks, went on to direct the October Revolution from here. Doubtless no-one at the time worried about the symbolism of such a move, but with the benefit of hindsight it seems the early Communists subconsciously began as they intended to continue. For all the talk of equality, the well-being, both physical and mental, of women has for 70 years been one of the most forgotten corners of the socialist utopia.

Empress Elizabeth first commissioned a nunnery for poor orphans here, at what had been the naval tar yard ('Smolny Dvor'), which served Peter's nascent fleet. Bartolomeo Francesco Rastrelli began the **cathedral** and encircling convent buildings in 1744. Rarely do patron and artist appear so well suited, a fact Elizabeth had already acknowledged by making him Chief Architect in 1736. Like Rastrelli's cathedral building, Elizabeth was a mixture of worldliness and piety. She loved to adorn herself with exquisite ornaments (she was said to have had 15,000 gowns), adding a judicious smattering of jewellery, and to flirt and chatter in a superficial manner, yet she was also one of Russia's most pious monarchs. It is even said that she thought of retiring here in penitence at the end of her life. For all its decoration, pilasters, sunbursts, architraves and capitals, the building, with its five cupolas crowned by golden crosses reaching into the sky, is a brilliant homage to the creator. Its master stroke is the light grey leaded rooves, which allow the cupolas and dome to float at one with the predominantly overcast St Petersburg sky.

The stern interior shows the vigorous, no-nonsense body onto which the building's baroque ornament was once grafted. It was only completed, to Rastrelli's plans by Stasov in 1835, but seventy years of Soviet rule have robbed it of all decoration, save the contrasting grey marble floor and yellow marble steps leading up to the altars. Everything else is long since gone, and the cathedral is used as both a choral concert hall and a space for exhibitions about the city. It is open everyday except Thursdays, 11am-6pm but closes an hour earlier on Wednesdays and concert days. Included in the price of the ticket is a fascinating climb into the upper ducts and arteries of the building for a magnificent view of the city and river.

The original **convent buildings**, which Catherine partly used when she set up her Institute for the Education of Well-born Young Ladies in 1764, form a square around the cathedral, leaving a peaceful processional way between. At each corner tall thin domes rise to ornate cupolas. The buildings were used as Party offices until the downfall of the Communists in 1991, and now house, one suspects, the same former party members in disguise as impartial civil servants.

> *Walking away from the cathedral entrance, across the square on which Rastrelli planned to build the highest tiered bell-tower in Russia, you pass other buildings in Rastrelli's style dating from the 1860s. Turn left and*

*hug the convent walls on Quarenghi Lane, named after the Italian architect of the **Smolny Institute**, whose yellow classical façade appears ahead.*

Whether as one of its teachers remarked early in his career, its 'only concern is dancing, singing and curtseying' or as he eulogized with hindsight it transformed the girls 'from a piece of sweetmeat or pie filled with physical delights, into thinking, noble beings', Catherine's school was a great success. In the early 19th century it was enlarged under her grandson and new buildings, commissioned from Quarenghi, were built in 1806–8. Born in Italy in 1743, he had been at the forefront of the neoclassical movement under Catherine. His long porticoed building is prefaced by one of the earliest and most human statues of **Lenin**, sculpted by V. V. Kozlov and erected in 1927. It commemorates the six months during which Lenin headed the government here before moving the capital back to Moscow in 1918. More dramatically, it was here that Sergei Kirov, head of the Leningrad Communist Party, was assassinated on the orders of Stalin in December 1934, giving the paranoid Georgian an excuse for his purge of the Party, which resulted in an unbelievable 1.5 million deaths. Today Mayor Anatoly Sobchak is trying to turn the city's fortunes round from his office in the Institute.

*A processional avenue runs from the Smolny Institute, between busts of Marx and Engels, to a pair of 20th-century classical gatehouses inscribed with an exhortation to the workers of the world to unite, and an announcement of the Soviet of Proletarian Dictatorship. Ahead lies the massive expanse of the **Square of the Proletarian Dictatorship**.*

Almost all the buildings in sight were used by the Party. A graphic illustration of the self-importance of Soviet bureaucracy is given by the building at the end of the square on the left; its hideous grandiosity housed nothing more than the executive committee of the local district deputies.

Taking your life in your hands cross the imposing tarmac onto Suvorovsky Prospekt and take the third right down Ul. Saltikova-Shchedrina.

Arriving at the corner of the Tauride Park, the splendid fortified pseudo-Russian castle of a building on the left houses the **Suvorov Museum**, which has not been open for some time. Nominally its opening hours are 11am–5pm; closed Mon. General A. V. Suvorov spanned the 18th and 19th centuries, and was one of Russia's greatest military figures. Under Catherine the Great he campaigned successfully against the Turks; under her son Paul I he defeated the French. The external mosaics represent, on the right, Suvorov's recall from retirement in Konchanskoye by Paul I, and on the left his crossing of the alps on the Italian campaign.

To regain Ⓜ Chernyshevsky, follow Ul. Saltikova-Shchedrina along the edge of the park. Fourth right after the park is Chernyshevsky Prospekt, and the station is down it on the right.

VI: Vasilievsky Island

Start: Ⓜ *Vasilieostrovskaya*

Walking Time: *2½ hours*

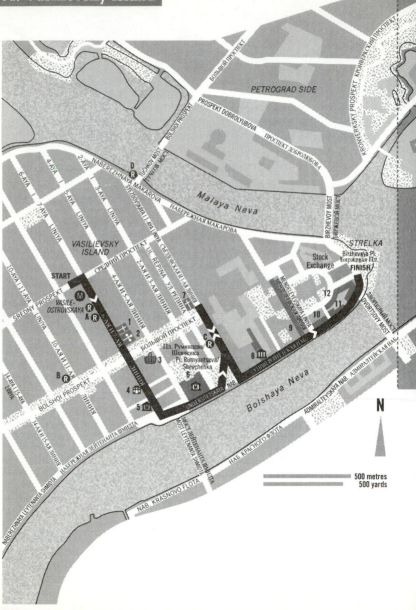

Sites

1   Church of the Three Saints
    Tserkov tryokh svyatiteley
    Церковь трёх святителей

2   Cathedral of St Andrew
    Andreyevsky sobor
    Андреевский собор

3   Vasileostrovsky Market
    Vasileostrovsky Rynok
    Василеостровский Рынок

4   Trezzini House
    Dom postroyen Trezzini
    Дом построен Трезини

5   Pavlov's Flat in Academicians' House
    Dom Akademikov
    Дом Академиков

6   Academy of Arts
    Akademiya khudozhestv
    Академия художеств

7   Church of St Catherine
    Tserkov sv. Yekateriny
    Церковь св. Екатерины

8   Menshikov Palace
    Menshikovsky dvorets
    Меншиковский дворец

9   Twelve Colleges
    Dvenadtsati kollegii zdaniye
    Двенадцати коллегий здание

10 Academy of Science
    Akademiya nauk
    Академия наук

11 Kunstkamera/
    Museum of Anthropology and Ethnology
    Kunstkamera/
    Muzei antropologii i etnografii
    Кунсткамера/
    Музей антропологии и этнографии

12 Museum of Zoology
    Zoologichesky muzei
    Зоологический музей

Restaurants and Cafés

A   Café/Bar
    Кафе/Бар

B   Fregat
    Кафе Фрегат

C   Sirin-Bar
    Сирин-Бар

D   Hotel Ship Peterhof
    Gostinitsa Petergof
    Гостиница Петергоф

Wedged into the mouth of the River Neva, Vasilievsky (St Basil's) Island is both integral to St Petersburg's central riverfront façade and a quiet residential backwater, far from the hurly burly of downtown Nevsky Prospekt. The river divides as it hits the island's picturesque pointed tip, the Strelka, flowing as the Bolshaya (Large) and Malaya (Small) Neva round the ever-widening landmass. At its far end the island buffers the Gulf of Finland with a long, low shoreline.

The far reaches of the island, subsumed by the port of Gavan, are of little interest to visitors, even those billeted there in the massive Pribaltiskaya Hotel. This walk concentrates on the historical sector of the island, close to the centre. Peter the Great originally envisaged the area as the centre of his new city, but the disadvantages of siting a capital on an island in the middle of a powerful river, at times alive with the groans of breaking ice, were made manifest when the tsar's own physician drowned. The scheme was dropped, and the first bridge over the river was only erected after the tsar's death. Even then it had to be taken down each autumn until after the thaw in the following spring.

Instead of becoming the centre of the capital, within the lifetime of Peter the Great Vasilievsky Island began to take on its present-day character as an area of learning, St Petersburg's Bloomsbury. The country's first permanent museum was sited here in 1718, doubling as an observatory. In the early 19th century the Twelve College buildings designed to house Peter's civil service were given to the fledgling St Petersburg University. Today, the joy of the area is its clutch of architectural survivors from the 18th century, including the highlight of the walk, the recently restored palace of the first governor of the city, Prince Menshikov.

Russia's industrial revolution in the late 19th century made itself strongly felt on the island. A number of large factories were built on its far reaches, with nearby accomodation to house the work-force. By the early 20th century, reactionary government ministers could hardly bear to think about the island, with its explosive mix of radical students and discontented workers. With better shopping at this end of the island, today workers and students still mingle in the shadows of its historic buildings, much as they have for 300 years.

To make the most of this walk, plan to do it on Tues–Thurs or Sun. You should also bear in mind that Menshikov Palace is closed between noon and 1pm. Since tours there are conducted on the half hour in Russian, it's worth getting someone to ring ✆ 213 1112 to see if they can give you an English-speaking guide at a particular time. If you do this, start the walk about ¾ hour before your alloted tour round the palace. Of minor interest is the memorial museum to physiologist Ivan Pavlov, which is closed on Thurs, Sat and Sun. If you are intent on including it in your itinerary, ring ✆ 213 7234 to make an appointment.

---

lunch/cafés

Vasilievsky Island is a desert as far as food is concerned. In summer, a picnic can be assembled at the market, Bolshoi Prospekt 16, which you will pass early in the walk. The gardens by the Rumyantsev Obelisk are the best place to eat it.

If you complete the walk and then want to eat, you are almost as close to the better restaurants on the Petrograd Side than you are to some of the questionable options listed below. Demyanovaya Ukha (see p.503) and Tbilisi (see p.503) are a walk or taxi drive away for example.

Café/Bar. For an energizing snack or drink at the beginning of this walk, drop into either the café in the large wooden kiosk behind the metro station or the bar at 7-ya Liniya 40.

Fregat, 11-ya Liniya 14, on the corner of Bolshoi Prospekt, is a long narrow restaurant, immured from sunlight, like so many, by dark glass and drapes. In the gloom you can eat from the reasonable Russian menu. Soups and *kotleti* are staples, and don't miss the opportunity to sample the punch and *kvas* on offer here. Such drinks were common in Russia from medieval times, and their demise is still lamented by the thirty-something generation who remember them from their Brezhnev childhoods *Open 12 noon–11pm.*

Sirin-Bar, 1-ya Liniya 15, ✆ 213 7282, open 11am–11pm, is another stygian basement bar and restaurant, enlivened by a wide choice of drink and a lengthy well-cooked Russian menu.

Hotelship Peterhof, Naberezhnaya Makarova, ✆ 213 6321. For a break from the reality of the streets, walk up Syezdovskaya and 1-ya Liniya to this floating hotel by the Tuchkov Bridge. The *à la carte* menu is overpriced, but the restaurant offers an inexpensive set lunch, and in summer you can eat out on deck at the grill bar.

Leaving Ⓜ Vasileostrovskaya, turn right and first right down the street known as 6-ya and 7-ya Liniya (6th and 7th Line).

Whoever came up with the bright idea of giving most of the north-south streets on the island two names, one for each side of the road, should be awarded a medal for lateral thinking, even if it does make things rather confusing at first. As a rule of thumb, remember that the even numbered 'lines' refer to the east side of the streets. True to the name, the street pattern is very linear, like a mini Manhattan, a grid that dates back to Peter's original plans for the city centre. Inspired by the tsar's admiration for Amsterdam, his French architect Jean-Baptiste Leblond came up with a scheme to chequer the island with a mass of parallel and intersecting canals. When Peter came to inspect the work in 1718 he found that they had been dug too narrow for two vessels to pass and, fuming, ordered them to be filled in.

These street are still peppered with two-storey 18th-century façades, although most of the buildings are in the eclectic 19th-century style, with a smattering of *Style Moderne* apartment blocks thrown in. As you walk down the street, look out for the shop at 7-ya Liniya 40, on the right hand side of the road. Beneath the 'Грамиластинки' sign, you can buy cheap records and CDs.

As the street nears the intersection with Bolshoi Prospekt an old plaque, inlaid into a façade on the left side of the street and inscribed in distinctive curly Georgian script, marks the **Church of the Three Saints**. It is the oldest surviving church on the island, so-run down that it is hard even to recognize its original function. It was built in 1740–60 by Domenico Trezzini, the by then elderly Italian architect whom Peter had recruited from the Dutch court to oversee the construction of his capital. The inscription commemorates the burial here of a Georgian prince.

*The pink and white **Cathedral of St Andrew** next door, on the corner of Bolshoi Prospekt, is in much better shape. Beneath its cupolas lies one of the best kept aesthetic secrets in the city, its unrestored mid-18th century iconostasis. You can usually get in through the door on Bolshoi Prospekt.*

The cathedral was built in 1764–80 by a little-known architect on the sight of an earlier wooden church which had burned down. Its more recent history is typical of religious buildings throughout the country. Until 1937 it remained open, serving the increasingly embattled spiritual needs of the local community until the height of Stalin's terror, when its priests were taken out and shot by the NKVD, forerunners of the KGB. For the rest of the Soviet period it was given over to the Museum of Ethnography of the Peoples of the USSR, who used it to store skulls and bones. Services are now held in its partially repaired blue and white interior, beneath a dome upheld at its four squinches by the Apostles Matthew, Mark, Luke and John. You can identify them by their attributes—an angel for Matthew, a lion for Mark, an ox for Luke and an eagle for John.

The glory of the church is its iconostasis, which is one of the few 18th-century gems in and around the city which has not been over-restored by the Soviets. The spirit of this staggeringly beautiful, delicate Baroque masterpiece simply soars, entirely unnoticed by tourists. The fine wooden tracery of the doors is surmounted by a filigree sunburst, and the icons, though of differing ages, nestle happily amongst the gilding, mottled with the patina of age.

It was at a ceremony in the earlier church here that Mikhail Lomonosov (1711–65) was installed as professor of chemistry in the nearby Academy of Sciences in 1745. Lomonosov personified the spirit of 18th-century Russia, particularly the intellectual daring embodied by the early buildings on Vasilievsky Island itself. Born the son of a fisherman on the north coast of Russia near Archangel, the teenage Lomonosov is said to have walked barefoot to Moscow in search of an education. He was an astounding polymath: after studying philosophy in Germany he turned to science, returned to Russia, ran the country's first chemistry laboratory, wrote works on Russian history, systematized the Russian language and its grammar, set up factories for the production of ceramics and mosaic *tesserae* and in 1755 founded Moscow University. Lomonosov's rise from peasant to Imperial advisor signalled the arrival of the enlightenment on Russian shores and the introduction of rational science to its superstitious, religious and intellectually backward people.

Within a few hundred feet of this intersection lie a number of other 18th-century buildings.

The most prominent is the low arcaded yellow and white building on the opposite side of Bolshoi Prospekt, which was built as trading rows for the island's merchants. Traders still occupy the **market**, as well as the less pleasing 1950s building next door. Outside, citizens sell anything they can get their hands on. Inside is strictly the preserve of food sellers. Depending on the season you might want to buy fruit, vegetables, pickled cucumbers and garlic, cured meats or cheese for your picnic. There is also a café serving soup and sandwiches near the meat counters.

Once you have done your shopping, continue down 6-ya and 7-ya Liniya towards the River Neva. The mid-19th century **pharmacy** at 16 7-ya Liniya has been partly turned into a museum, its floor to ceiling Empire cabinets used to house old bottles, pharmaceutical instruments, Chinese pots and pestels and mortars (*open 8am–9pm; closed Sun*). It was established by the city's leading pharmacist, Alexander Vasilievich Pel (1850–1908). One of the oldest houses in the city is the pink and white two-storey building at 12 7-ya Liniya, built by Trezzini in 1720–6. As first director of building in the city, he designed three basic house plans which the population, conscripted from their cozy wooden Moscow homes, were obliged to follow when building their new residences. Peter the Great was taking no chances with his European capital. This now undistinguished building followed the scheme for the so-called 'House for the Distinguished', and long functioned as an out-building of the Alexander Nevsky Lavra at the far end of Nevsky Prospekt.

On the building at the corner of 7-ya Liniya and Naberezhnaya Leytenanta Shmidta, 26 memorial plaques commemorate the distinguished scientists who have lived here, in **Academicians' House**, since the foundation of the nearby Academy of Sciences in the 18th century. The apartment of the most famous, Ivan Pavlov (1849–1936), whose work on conditioned reflexes netted him a Nobel Prize in 1904, has been turned into a memorial museum. Son of a country priest, Pavlov began his education in a seminary but went on to university and was made head of the Institute of Experimental Medicine in St Petersburg. In his most famous experiments, which gave us the term 'Pavlovian reaction', his dogs became accus-tomed to being fed after hearing a particular bell. Pavlov went on to ring the bell without providing food, and observed that the dogs salivated nonetheless.

> The embankment is named after Lieutenant Pyotr Schmidt, one of the leaders of the 1905 naval mutiny which pressurized Nicholas II into agreeing to the election of the Russian parliament, the duma. If you look right you will see the five green domes of the late 19th-century **Church of the Nativity**, built with mock Byzantine grandeur, silhouetted against a background of belching factory chimneys.

These are the only hint you get on this walk of Vasilievsky Island's other face. The industrial suburb, so close to the centre of the city, gave the island an ominous repu-tation during the unsettled years before the Revolution. It is no coincidence that in Andrei Bely's novel *Petersburg*, set in 1905, the first revolutionary we meet lives on the island. The population is described as 'industrial and coarse', a 'many-thousand human swarm which shuffled in the morning to the many-chimneyed factories'. Into the mouths of the bourgeoisie, living on the other side of the river, Bely inserts the entreaty: 'Don't let the crowd of shadows in from the islands! Black and damp bridges are already thrown across the waters…If only they could be dismantled…'.

> Turn left towards 4-ya and 5-ya Liniya. Here, on 9 January 1905 (later known as Bloody Sunday) a 6000-strong 'crowd of shadows' was halted abruptly by a hail of gunfire and charging soldiers as they marched peace-fully to petition the tsar. The bridge opposite, Most Leytenanta Shmidta, was the first permanent link with the mainland, completed in 1850. Just beyond, a pair of sphinxes punctuate the granite embankment.

Excavated in Thebes, the sphinxes are the oldest architectural features in the city, dating from the 14th century BC. Their inscription celebrates Pharoah Amunhotep III, 'ruler of Thebes, builder of monuments rising to the sky like four pillars holding up the vault of the heavens.' They were moved here in 1832 to glorify the river approach to the **Academy of Arts**, Universitetskaya Naberezhnaya 17.

The Academy itself had been built in 1763–88, designed by Vallin de la Mothe and overseen by Alexander Kornilov. Its dusty yellow façade marks the very beginning of the classical revival under Catherine the Great; the only decoration is a minimal frieze showing the tools of the three major arts—sculpture, architecture and painting. Inside the building there is a museum of the academy but, with no-one around to tell you where to go, you feel rather like a trespasser if you try to find it. Don't be put off. Having admired the circular courtyard at the centre of this massive square building, walk up the magnificent pillared staircase. Wander through the round red senate room and turn left to see paintings by past and present pupils of the Academy. Further on you will come to the plaster casts and copies of Renaissance paintings and sculpture, which the pupils copied in turn to learn their skills. On the second floor you should find architectural models of many of St Petersburg's most notable buildings. Although the great mid 19th-century revival of Russian art initiated by the group of painters known as the Wanderers took the form of a rebellion against the classical focus of the Academy, many of its practitioners were nevertheless trained here. Among them were the painters Karl Bryullov and Ilya Repin, the serf architect of the Stroganov family, Andrei Voronikhin and the 19th-century sculptor Pyotr Klodt, who executed almost all the equestrian statues in the city.

For the rest of this walk we will carry on along the Universitetskaya Naberezhnaya, looking across to monumental St Petersburg on the far side of the lugubrious Neva.

The wooded square beside the Academy of Arts is the best place for summer picnics. It is known, incongruously, as both **Rumyantsev** and **Shevchenko Square**, after a Russian general and a Ukrainian poet respectively. Both of them studied in neighbouring institutes. In the 18th century Rumyantsev, leader of numerous successful battles against the Turks under Catherine the Great, was educated at the Military Cadet School housed in Menshikov Palace beyond, while Shevchenko studied at the Academy of Arts in the middle of the 19th century. The granite obelisk at the centre of the garden, between two broken fountains, is inscribed 'to the victories of Rumyantsev', and topped by a golden eagle. It was moved here in 1818 from the Field of Mars.

Those seriously interested in church architecture could walk diagonally through the park and up 1-ya Liniya back to Bolshoi Prospekt.

The classical green and white **Church of St Catherine** at the beginning of the avenue was designed by Yuri Velten, a native of St Petersburg and the first director of the Academy of Arts. The interior is occupied by recording studios for the Melodiya record label. St Catherine's was a Lutheran church, serving the city's foreign community, many of whom lived on the island in the early days. As well as architects, they included mercenaries employed in the army and navy, portrait painters and doctors. Indeed, it became a habit for the Russian Imperial family to employ a Scottish physician. Catherine the Great's regular physician was Dr John Rogerson, whom she grew to distrust. 'It seems to me that who ever falls into Rogerson's hands is already a dead man' she inveighed in 1783. At the height of a smallpox epidemic in 1768, Catherine the Great sent to London for Dr Thomas Dimsdale, whose 1767 treatise on inoculation had been a runaway success. The treatment was then at the forefront of medicine, and most people considered it too risky, Catherine was determined to be inoculated herself however, and when she survived her son Paul, and later her grandchildren, were also inoculated.

*Alternatively, skip the church and carry on along the embankment, across 1-ya and Syezdovskaya Liniya to **Menshikov Palace** (Дворец Меншикова—Dvoryéts Menshikova) Universitetskaya Naberezhnaya 15.*

The first thing you see is the end wing, a latter addition to the yellow stucco palace. Beyond it stands Menshikov's original palace, with its porticoed porch flanked by two gabled projecting bays. Restored since 1967 almost to its original look, the palace was the earliest stone structure on Vasilievsky Island and, topped with statues and coronets, the most extravagant building in the city. Since 1967 it has been restored to a near-original condition. Started in 1710 by an Italian architect and finished in 1716 by a German, it was built for Prince Alexander Menshikov. This legendary figure rose from humble beginnings as the son of an ordinary soldier to become Peter the Great's prime minister, military commander, pimp, rumoured lover and governor of St Petersburg. At the time, the rest of the island was a building site, a chequerboard of canal trenches and boggy streets on which people were still devoured by wolves in broad daylight. The tsar was away when it was completed; his reaction on his return is subject to much speculation. Was he angered by his favourite's scene-stealing grandeur, or had he expressly told Menshikov to build a palace in which the tsar could also work and entertain? Certainly, Menshikov's countryside extravaganza, the palace at Oranienbaum, provoked Peter to build himself a great palace at Peterhof in friendly rivalry.

Menshikov, vain and addicted to corruption on a huge scale, was not destined to outlive his master long. He oversaw the accession of Peter's wife and his own former mistress, Catherine I, to the throne in 1725, and acted as her principal advisor. Unfortunately for Menshikov, she died after a reign of little more than two years. Her successor Peter II (Peter the Great's 12-year-old grandson by his first wife) was less fond of grandfather's old crony, and packed him off to Siberia. Within two years Menshikov was dead. His palace was taken over by the state and in 1732 became the school for military cadets, which Rumyantsev attended. It was at this time that the wings were added to the building to house the hundreds of potential officers. Most of the boys were of noble birth. They entered the school at the age of five, when their parents signed away their rights to see them for 15 years, except at public functions.

Entrance to the palace is through a door in the basement of the first wing. Mind your heads in the low vaulted cloakrooms. Open 10.30am–12 noon, 1–4.30pm; closed Mon.

The collection of interiors, costumes, furniture, prints and portraits within goes under the title **Russian Culture 1700–30**, and memorably includes a beautifully shaped Italianate staircase and a suite of rooms decked out in blue and white Dutch tiles. You start in the kitchen, lined with huge wooden vessels, where you can see the enormous clothes of Tsar Peter. In the main reception room, Italian tapestries and sculptures compete with massive German cupboards. The room opens into the hall, from which one of the oldest wooden staircases in the city rises in two to meet in a single flight and double back onto the next floor. Its wrought-iron balustrade is of the utmost delicacy, entwined to include the initials PP (Petrus Primus) and AM (Alexander Menshikov), in Latin rather than Cyrillic script.

The first floor rooms begin with the vestibule and study in which the virtually illiterate Menshikov and his secretary would oversee the affairs of state. The German desk contains many a secret drawer beneath its busts of Roman emperors. Next come a series of outrageously tiled bedrooms, originally revetted entirely with 18th-century Delft tiles. The Russian appetite for Dutch tiles was enormous, and when the bills became too dizzy, Menshikov simply imported two masters from Delft. The products of the Russian kilns they set up are charmingly naive; those over the far door in the third room are decorated with fine line drawings of household implements, isolated pieces of architecture and cherubs. Menshikov's walnut office is a jewel of inlaid woodwork, highlighted by gilded Corinthian capitals. With the help of a secretary the Prince oversaw much government paperwork, though he never learned to write more than his signature. Finally we come to the Great Hall, decorated later in the early classical style. The 18th-century clock and organ at the far end were designed as a single piece of furniture. The organ is still used for concerts, but the clock has long since ceased to function. The tour reaches its conclusion through a room displaying 18th-century Chinese wall-hangings which were given to Peter. In the final room you can recognize the portrait of Peter's father Tsar Alexei, wearing what looks like a dunce's cap.

Leaving the palace, turn left on the embankment, passing the disintegrating building of the military cadets' former riding school (No. 13) which is occupied by the army to this day. Next comes the university's Faculty of Languages, housed in a green and white 18th-century building, and beyond it the more intimate proportions of the Rector's Wing (No. 9).

A plaque on the wall states that the Symbolist poet Alexander Blok was born here in 1880. His grandfather, a botanist, was rector of the university at the time. The heart of the university beats in the extraordinary, long early Baroque terrace which runs at right-angles to the embankment from here. To get a good look at it you will need to walk all the way round. The interior is a warren of subdivided spaces.

Started during the reign of Peter the Great to house part of his revamped civil service, the tsar intended the building to line the embankment, but while he was away Prince Menshikov changed the brief so that it would not dwarf the façade of his own nearby palace. Perhaps because of this setback, work on the **Twelve Colleges**, as it became known, progressed slowly, and the terrace was only completed in 1742. In 1819 it was given over to the new University of St Petersburg.

The street in front of the terrace is named after one of the university's most distinguished alumni, Dmitri Mendeleyev (1834–1907). He formulated the Periodic Table, known to pupils of chemistry throughout the world, and in so doing was able to predict the existence of a number of elements which were only subsequently discovered. One of them, Element 101, is known as mendelevium. Another student who had an even greater impact on the world was Vladimir Ilyich Lenin, who graduated with honours from the Faculty of Law in 1891.

Lenin was only one of a string of revolutionaries to be educated here. Almost from the beginning of the university's existence, the authorities were terrified by the beast they had created, closing it down regularly to quell surges of political radicalism. On the day of Pushkin's funeral in January 1837, orders were received that all professors and students must be present at lectures. The authorities feared that the students 'might band together and carry Pushkin's coffin—they could 'go too far' (Alexander Nikitenko, *The Diary of a Russian Censor*). The regime was right to fear the university, but only for as long as tsarism refused to reform itself. Had the Romanovs agreed to reign as constitutional monarchs earlier, it is likely that the sons of the enlightenment at the university would have been their staunchest supporters. As it was, these educated and talented free-thinkers, their career paths dictated by an outdated hierarchical structure, became their implacable foes.

> *Back on the embankment, we quickly bypass the **Academy of Science**, built in 1784–7 by Catherine the great's favourite classical architect Quarenghi, to house the institution set up by Peter the Great in 1724. Initially, the Academy was staffed by 17 German scientists, but soon home-grown scientists of the calibre of Mikhail Lomonósov began to take their seats here. Since 1934 the headquarters of the Academy has been in Moscow, and this building has become the St Petersburg branch.*

The large green and white building which now houses the **Museum of Anthropology and Ethnography** (Музей Антропологии и Этнографии—

Muzei Antropologii i Etnografii) was the city's first purpose-built museum (*open 11am–5pm; closed Fri and Sat; entrance in the alleyway before the building).* Don't confuse this place with the Museum of the Ethnography of the Peoples of the USSR (*see* p.421). It was designed to showcase the pickled human and animal freaks which Peter the Great had begun to collect in 1714. Peter decided to house his grotesque collection on this spot when he noticed a curious pine tree, one branch of which had grown back into the main trunk, standing here. The building was begun in 1718 and was always erroneously known as the **Kunstkamera** (German for 'art chamber') after the museum in Dresden which Peter had so admired. As well as the pickled wonders, it sheltered a library, an anatomy theatre and an observatory in the tower. Peter encouraged his subjects to preserve any curiosities they came across in vodka and bring them in, and encouraged visitors with a free shot of the spirit and a pie.

The large collection of artefacts from all over the world now housed in the building is a paean to man's practicality and his ceaseless spiritual quest. There is little here that is not directly useful, either physically, or as a tool for communicating with God. The ingenuity with which man has used the materials available to him, the care which he has lavished on the aesthetics of everyday objects and the imagination he has shown in his different approaches to the divine are heart-warming.

The first rooms you enter contain exhibits from the continent of North America, beginning with the Inuit tribes of the northern reaches and travelling southwards towards the Pueblo Indians of New Mexico. Waterproofs made of fish skins, an elk-skin quiver vivid with red painted hunting scenes, and shamanistic masks give way to birch-bark canoes, dioramas showing scenes from Indian religious rituals and magnificent woven baskets which held water when saturated and could be heated by dropping in stones from the fire.

Beyond the Japanese collection to the left, the central rotunda was once the forum for anatomical dissections, which visitors and students watched through the gaps in the ceiling now occupied by gesticulating dummies dressed in native garb. Today it houses Peter's Kunstkamera, in all its grisly B-movie sci-fi glory. The curiosities are none the better for the 275 years that have elapsed since he bought the bulk of them, and there is little pleasure in ogling the pickled two-headed calf and human Siamese twins. They should revive the practice of giving out a shot of vodka here, to stiffen the resolve before taking a look. Less sickening are Peter's personal surgical instruments in the cabinet. Beside them lie teeth that the tsar himself extracted. He is said to have greatly enjoyed playing dentist; from the look of the teeth, when the urge took him he extracted them whether healthy or unhealthy.

The African room comes next, with an exquisite Azandi harp and bronze cast objects from Benin. The pride of the collection, a magnificent cast head, was stolen in 1993. The exhibition continues upstairs with a room devoted to Australia and Oceania, in which you can see the mummified head of a Tahitian chieftain, complete with traditional tattoos, bought by James Cook shortly before his death in Hawaii. His sailors presented it to the governor of the far eastern Russian province of Kamchatka in recognition of his hospitality. In the centre of the room are the cloak and helmet of a Hawaiian king, made from luminous feathers. The rooms beyond, which cover Indonesia, India, China, Tibet and Mongolia may well now be open, as may the memorial museum to Mikhail Lomonósov, the talented poet, scientist and linguist who worked here from 1741 until his death in 1765. With the help of the telescope in the tower above the museum, he and other astrologers created an early planetarium, known as the Great Academic Globe. Spectators got into the globe which revolved around them, with models of the planets giving an inaccurate, but at the time thrilling, impression of the movement of the heavens.

Retracing your steps to the entrance of the museum, turn left on the embankment to reach the last museum on this extensive trail, the **Museum of Zoology** *(Зоологический музей—Zo-ologíchesky muzei) next door (open 11am–6pm; closed Fri). It can be unbearably crowded during the school holidays. You will know if you have hit it at the wrong time, not necessarily by the crowds outside, but by the fact that you simply can't buy a ticket. They will all have been pre-booked.*

Inside you will be faced with one of the largest collections of stuffed animals in the world, often placed together in dioramas recreating their natural habitats. The mammoths unearthed from the permafrost in Siberia in the course of this century are the most unusual sight, though there is plenty to keep you gasping—blue whales, polar bears and tray upon tray of insects. A number of the animals once belonged to Peter the Great, including the horse he rode at the battle of Poltava.

Leaving the museum, a left turn takes you onto the tip of the island (the strelka*) with its majestic view of St Petersburg's main waterfront.*

Directly ahead the golden spire of the Ss Peter and Paul Cathedral, burial place of the Romanovs, pierces the sky from within the sombre confines of the Ss Peter and Paul Fortress. On the right bank of the river, Palace Embankment unfurls in an endless succession of extravagant façades. Starting with the countless columns of the Winter Palace it extends through Renaissance and Classical exteriors to the smooth veneer of the Marble Palace.

The walk is at an end, and you are unfortunately miles from a metro station. Either flag down a taxi or catch a bus or trolleybus from the stop in front of the former stock exchange (Birzha), which looks onto the strelka *through the brick-red rostral columns. Bus No. 44 and Trolleybus Nos. 1, 7 and 10 will all take you over Dvortsóvy Most to* 🅜 *Nevsky Prospekt.*

HERMITAGE

Walk VII: The Hermitage

Start: *Ticket Hall, Hermitage Museum*

Walking Time: *3 hours for each walk*

There could hardly be a less appropriate name for this priceless labyrinth of a museum with its superlative collection of works of art housed in a series of Baroque and classical palaces once inhabited by the tsars. No self-respecting hermit would go near a place that attracts 3 million visitors a year. To Catherine the Great in the 1760s, it seemed entirely appropriate to call the small building, which she had commissioned to adjoin the Winter Palace, her 'hermitage'. This was the place where she retreated from the affairs of state to admire her latest artistic acquisitions in selected company.

Since the Revolution, when the royal collection was augmented by the confiscation of private art treasures, the whole ensemble of buildings has been open to the public. It is said that to spend one minute looking at every piece, displayed in over 10 kilometres of halls and corridors, you would need to put aside six days a week in the museum for nine years. The visitor with just a day or less must therefore approach the place with surgical precision. Simply to cover the highlights of the museum—the state rooms and masterpieces by Rembrandt, Leonardo, Picasso and Matisse—will take a good day. At some point a trip should also be made to the small Special Collection, where the opulent but contrived baubles of the Romanovs vie with the raw energy of the golden belts, scabbards and amulets worn by Scythian princes some 2000 years earlier. With less than a day to spare, you will have to choose between the two suggested itineraries, each of which is enough to fill three hours with spectacular images and impressions. Those who have a further particular interest should refer to the gazetteer, under What is Where in the Hermitage (*see* p.411).

Dvortsovaya Naberezhnaya 36. Open 10.30–6; closed Mon.

---

lunch/cafés

Hermitage Buffet, Room 77, first room on right in dark corridor at bottom of Jordan Staircase, serves Russian hamburgers and soft drinks to a never-ending but bearably-sized queue.

Café, House of Scholars, Dvortsovaya Naberezhnaya 26, is the closest café to the Hermitage, and serves tea, coffee, alcohol and simple snacks in its cosy interior overlooking the Neva.

Pevchesky Mostik Café, Naberezhnaya Reki Moyki 26, is almost within site of Palace Square. Drinks proliferate—coffee, tea, alcohol and soft drinks—but food is minimal—cakes and hot sandwiches.

Literaturnoye Café, Nevsky Prospekt 18, ℂ 312 8536/8542 (*Open 12 noon–11pm; unlikely to serve between 3.30–6pm*) For those in search of real sustenance at lunch-time, this old chestnut will serve it slowly and at a price (*see* p.498). The restaurant has an associated cheap café just round the corner, inside the first door on Naberezhnaya Reki Moyki, where salads, pizzas and mushrooms in sour cream come quick and tasty.

Practical Hints

The queues outside the Hermitage and the number of tour groups queue-barging, particularly in summer, can become irritating for the individual tourist. You will notice people leaving the museum via the nearby door from the basement. Take your revenge by slipping in through here and walking left through the cloakroom, and you will find yourself in the ticket hall immediately. Here you may have to queue too, but there is no avoiding that. Tickets are valid for all but the Special Collection and occasional visiting exhibitions. If the Special Collection is open and you have not pre-booked a guided tour through the service bureau in your hotel, take the stairs up out of the ticket hall to the excursion bureau and buy yourself a place (or ℂ 311 3725 in advance). The Special Collection is popular, and access is restricted, so there is no guarantee that you will be able to visit it on the same day.

Great efforts are being made to bring the Hermitage displays up to the standard of other great museums of the world in time for the tricentenary of the city in 2003, but there is a serious lack of cash for the job. One day in 1993, museum staff could be seen wandering everywhere with heavy sacks in their arms. In an attempt to make up for their meagre wages, the administration was giving everyone a couple of kilos of sugar. Many of the less popular departments have been closed to visitors for years (*see* What is Where), and you can never tell when others will be temporarily out of bounds for restoration or through lack of staff. These unexpected closures could disrupt the itineraries below, in which case you will have to use the maps to negotiate your way to the next open area.

Occasionally you will come across signposts in Russian and English pointing to different collections. Treat them with caution, as they frequently point in the wrong direction. The artworks themselves are labelled in Russian, with only the name of the artist appearing in Latin script.

History of the Buildings and Collections

It was Peter the Great, with his bizarre purchase of 2000 embalmed 'curiosities' from Frederick Ruysch, who first introduced the concept of a museum to Russia. He also bought a number of Dutch pictures. Most were seascapes, as befitted his obssession with boat-building, but among them were important works by

Rembrandt, Van Dyck and Rubens. Peter also encouraged the preservation of the Scythian gold being uncovered at that time from burial mounds in the steppes and Siberia. These were kept in a variety of royal palaces, many of them ending up in the Winter Palace.

In the 1760s, Catherine the Great began to buy up collections of European art wholesale. She instructed Vallin de la Mothe, then head of the Academy of Arts, to design an annexe to the palace in which to house them. The result was the classical Hermitage. Here, in candle-lit privacy, she would gloat over newly arrived crates of canvasses and books. 'Only the mice and I can admire all this,' she wrote possessively on the arrival of the Walpole collection which she bought from England in 1779. To Catherine, the acquisition of these artefacts from western Europe seems to have symbolized her bringing civilization to Russia. In buying a great collection from Prussia, England or France and, if possible, provoking furore at its leaving the country, she proved the Russian monarchy more 'enlightened' than the local competition; and herself more deserving of the admiration of such great thinkers of the time as Voltaire and Diderot. Not that this vanity meant Catherine could not appreciate art for its own sake: one of the most important documents concerning the collection today is her own eight-volume catalogue.

Within five years, it was clear the collection would soon outgrow the Small Hermitage, as it is known today. Catherine commissioned Yuri Velten to extend it with the Large Hermitage, which marches on along the Neva embankment. In the late 1770s artists in Rome began the task of copying Raphael's Loggia at the Vatican onto canvas, so it could be perfectly reproduced by the Italian architect Quarenghi down the side of the Large Hermitage, overlooking the Winter Canal and Quarenghi's Imperial theatre. Catherine's grandson, Alexander I, continued to fill the walls and halls of this and other royal palaces. His largest contribution was the purchase of the collection of Josephine, wife of his vanquished enemy Napoleon.

A devastating fire in the Winter Palace in December 1837 burned for an entire day, filling the sky with flames. Thanks to the selfless behaviour of firemen and soldiers, some of whom died, it did not spread to the Hermitage. Within two years all the state rooms had been rebuilt and decorated, by a team supervised by the architect Stasov, and Nicholas I and his family were again in residence. It was during his otherwise unenlightened reign that the royal collection took the step of opening its doors to the public. Behind the Large Hermitage, building work began in 1840 on the New Hermitage. The architect was the German, Leo von Klenze, already known for his museums in Munich. From 1852 'decent citizens' could apply to enter its impressive classical interiors, which have survived to this day, and with each passing year the collection, already rich in European painting, improved with new acquisitions, particularly of classical and Egyptian antiquities.

With the Revolution the trickle turned into a flood. Aristocrats and other collectors fled from Russia, and the state lost little time in nationalizing the collections left behind. Over the next 30 years paintings, sculpture, furniture and *objets* were gradually shared out between the major state museums. Among the most important gains by the Hermitage was the collection of Modern European Painting shared with the Pushkin Gallery in Moscow, the majority of it collected by just two men, Ivan Morozov and Sergei Shchukin. Morozov reflected philosophically in exile that he had always intended to give the collection to the state, but Shchukin's heir in France has recently been making different noises. Emboldened by the collapse of the Soviet Union and its legal system, she claimed that the works had been stolen and that she intended to fight a legal battle to get them back. When the recent Matisse exhibition arrived in Paris, it did so without a number of the works from Russian museums which had been shown in New York. The Russians feared that the French courts would side with her and impound the canvases.

This is a very different attitude from that of the state in the 1920s and 30s, which regularly sold off major works of art for hard currency. The two biggest buyers were Calouste Gulbenkian, an oil magnate who helped open the world market to Soviet oil, and the American Secretary to the Treasury Andrew Mellon, who offered loans to the Soviet Union on terms which included the purchase of important works of art. These canvases, including paintings by Rubens, Rembrandt and Raphael, are now on show in Lisbon and in the USA, much to the chagrin of today's Russian curators. The Hermitage claims to have lost 52 major works through such sales, which were conducted in complete secrecy by an arm of government called the Antiquariat. More revealing still is an episode which took place in the seventies, in which several pieces of a unique imperial dinner service were broken when the then mayor of St Petersburg, the aptly named Grigory Romanov, borrowed it for his daughter's wedding banquet.

After the declaration of war in 1941 and before the German blockade of the city, three trainloads of the most valuable works were shipped to Yekaterinburg (then Sverdlovsk) in the Ural Mountains. Everything else was moved into the basement and ground floor, where thousands of statues and pieces of porcelain were buried in piles of sand. The staff continued their academic studies while living for stretches in the museum, doing their best to protect it from bombardment. If stories are to be believed, one group of soldiers drafted in to clear up glass were treated to a tour of the galleries, empty picture frames, the guide conjuring the pictures before their eyes by the sheer power of description. When the consignment returned in the autumn of 1945, only one picture, a Van Dyck, was missing.

It has recently transpired that the Hermitage cellars do contain, as has long been thought, a hoard of important Impressionist and Post-Impressionist paintings looted from Germany by Soviet soldiers in 1945. The paintings are due to go on display in the museum in March 1995, unless the simmering international row prevents their exhibition. The Russians claim that the loot is nothing compared with the damage wrought by invading German soldiers on their own cultural heritage, and that they should not therefore be returned to their former owners. Not surprisingly, the Germans think otherwise. Given the financial straits of the Hermitage and of Russia as a whole, the cynics are putting their money on the exhibition being nothing less than a vast public viewing before the sale of the century.

Special Collection (Osobaya Kladovaya—Особая Кладовая)

See Practical Hints for information on tickets for the obligatory guided tours. Following your guide to this guarded strongroom at the heart of the Large Hermitage, you will find yourself surrounded by glistering precious treasure. The exhibits divide roughly in two: firstly the best collection of Scythian, Greek and early Siberian gold anywhere in the world, mostly worked between the 7th and 2nd centuries BC, and secondly jewels and precious stones which belonged to the tsars, dating from the 16th–19th centuries.

The Scythians were a group of tribes, united by their Farsi-related language, who lived in the European southern steppe and North Caucasus, trading and fighting with the Greek colonies then established on the Black Sea coast. They have gone down in history as some of the finest early metalworkers. As well as intricate fili-gree jewellery and amulets, you will see larger golden beasts used to decorate shields, and a comb, surmounted by a fight scene, the details of which give a clear idea of Scythian clothing and weaponry. The motif of an animal, often a horse or stag, preyed upon by a magnificent lion or griffon was widespread from Greece to Persia, particularly on golden ornaments. The golden predator symbolizes the sun, a deity to these tribes, accepting an animal sacrifice. Looking at these treasures, the genesis of the myth of Jason and the Argonauts comes to mind. For it was on this Black Sea coast, so abundant with gold, that he found the Golden Fleece, the myth-ical progeny of the fleeces used in its extraction. Most of these objects were found in the burial mounds of princely warriors in the 19th century, though some were uncovered as early as the reign of Peter the Great, who gave rewards for their preservation to stop the common practice of melting them down into ingots.

Walk A: The State Rooms and Modern European Art

When Rastrelli got the commission to design the Winter Palace for the good-looking, quixotic Empress Elizabeth in the mid-18th century, the brief would have thrown most architects. The principal residence of the royal family, it needed to include living accommodation for over 1000 court officials as well as the servants required to run it. In addition, Elizabeth needed magnificent rooms in which to preside over investitures and the presentation of credentials by ambassadors, balconies from which to watch parading troops and a grand staircase down which to pass for the more idiosyncratic ceremony of the Blessing of the Waters. More personally, she required ballrooms in which to indulge her passion for dancing, an enormous boudoir for her 15,000 dresses and a church to which she could retire when her passionate religious side was in the ascendancy.

All this Rastrelli satisfied in a simple but highly decorative scheme. The ground floor was taken up with palace administration, store-rooms and servants' quarters, but once you had taken the grand staircase to the first floor, you found yourself at every turn in an enfilade of imposing state rooms, interrupted at the corners of the palace by marginally more intimate royal suites. On the second floor were bedrooms and living quarters of the courtiers. Today some of the highlights of the museum, including sculpture by Rodin and paintings by Van Gogh, Gauguin, Matisse and Picasso are housed here beneath the eaves. To get to them, this walk takes a sweep through the State Rooms, where round-faced *babushki* in scarves have replaced the giant Ethiopian royal guard, and flocks of schoolchildren the knots of well-dressed ambassadors.

> *From the ticket hall enter the long white vaulted room, the main entrance to the museum known as the* **Rastrelli Gallery.** *Its left-hand side is lined with sales desks offering a disparate selection of souvenirs and art books, but sadly no postcards of the museum's collection. This should change soon, as the new Anglo-Russian venture charged with running the museum's shops gets into gear. Straight ahead the red carpet beckons.*

It leads up the white marble steps of the **Jordan Staircase**, dividing in two beneath the watchful gaze of conically-breasted plaster angels before meeting up again between the sets of double marble pillars that line the balcony. The ornate Baroque stairwell, a confection of white and gold beneath a soaring painted ceiling depicting the gods on Mount Olympus, gives the visitor her first sense of the airy scale on which the palace was conceived. Unlike many of the other state rooms, this is one of Rastrelli's original designs. It was considered so vital an introduction to the palace that it was faithfully recreated after the 1837 fire, when many of the other rooms were rebuilt in the more classical style of the period.

The stairs owe their name to the arcane ceremony of the Blessing of the Waters, performed by the Russian tsars on 6 January since way before the capital was moved to St Petersburg. To commemorate the baptism of Jesus in the River Jordan, the entire court and leading churchmen descended the stairs and, bare-headed in the sub-zero temperatures, walked out onto the icy Neva where a hole was cut through the ice. Tsar and Metropolitan then blessed the water, which was bottled for use as baptism water in churches. Casanova, who witnessed the ceremony in the late 18th century, confirms that children were baptized in the icy waters. What amazed him, and others after him, was the reaction of the parents of children who slipped from the icy grasp of the priests never to be seen again: sure in the knowledge that their babe had gone straight to heaven, they shed not a single tear.

*Turn left at the top of the stairs, into the echoing open space of the **Field Marshals' Hall** where the 1837 fire began. This balconied white space, empty save a number of huge vases, was part of Stasov's reconstruction and once displayed pictures of Russian military leaders. The door opposite leads into the **Throne Room of Peter the Great**.*

Decorated by Montferrand, the architect of St Isaac's Cathedral, this velvet room with its church-like apse is a homage to Peter the Great, who had died over a century before it was conceived. The throne room has been perfectly restored on two occasions, once after the fire of 1837, and once after bomb damage in World War II. The walls and drapes above the throne are embroidered with silver double-headed eagles, a motif taken up with increased intensity on the roof. Here you get your first glimpse of the intricate parquet flooring which is such a leitmotif of this, and indeed all, Russian palaces; even in the most humble *kommunalka* (communal flat) the smartest thing is often the wooden floor. Both the silver and oak throne and the painting behind it have a strong London association. The throne was made there by a Huguenot silversmith, whilst the posthumous portrait of the tsar accompanied by a young woman, variously interpreted as Minerva or the Spirit of Russia, was painted by the Venetian Amiconi in 1730 for the Russian ambassador to London, Prince Antioch Kantemir.

The neighbouring **Armorial Hall** is one of the most gaudy interiors in the palace, with pairs of golden columns running right round the walls and groups of warriors with battle standards guarding the doors. It dates from Stasov's rebuilding, and was intended for balls and receptions. Its cabinets contain all manner of valuable objects exquisitely crafted from silver and semi-precious stones.

*To get to the **1812 Gallery** take the door on the left.*

This red room, an immense corridor created where six rooms had previously stood, is covered floor to ceiling in portraits of the 332 generals who fought against Napoleon. Alexander I chose Carlo Rossi, the Italian architect he consistently commissioned to give aesthetic expression to his great victory, to design the room, and he modelled it on the Waterloo Chamber at Windsor Castle. To further the similarities, Alexander imported an English artist, George Dawe, who painted over half of the portraits and oversaw the work of his Russian colleagues, Poliakov and Golik, who painted the rest. Generals who died in the course of the victory were either painted from earlier portraits and miniatures, or were represented by a blank frame

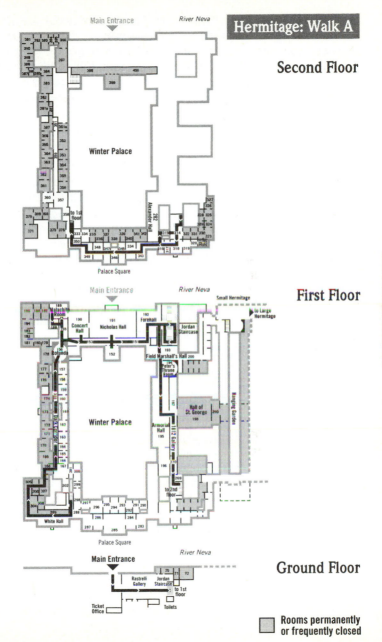

Hermitage: Walk A

Second Floor

Main Entrance

River Neva

Winter Palace

Palace Square

First Floor

Main Entrance

River Neva

Small Hermitage

to Large Hermitage

Malachite Room

Concert Hall

Nicholas Hall

Forehall

Jordan Staircase

Rotunda

Field Marshall's Hall

Peter's Throne Room

Hall of St. George

Hanging Garden

Armorial Hall

1812 Gallery

Winter Palace

to 2nd floor

White Hall

Palace Square

Ground Floor

Main Entrance

River Neva

Rastrelli Gallery

Jordan Staircase

to 1st floor

Ticket Office

Toilets

Rooms permanently or frequently closed

with their name beneath it. The majority of portraits are all one size, giving the impression of a host of romantic heroes staring in at you through a grid of small windows. Larger paintings were commissioned of the tsar himself, who presides on horseback from the end wall; of his allies Fredrick William III of Prussia and Emperor Francis I of Austria; of Field Marshals Kutuzov and Barclay de Tolly; and of Alexander's brother Grand Duke Constantine. The gallery was opened in 1826, only to burn down 11 years later. Fortunately, members of the guards regiments saved the portraits, and Stasov was able to recreate the interior with ease.

> *Directly opposite the entrance into the 1812 Gallery is an impressive gilded door leading into the Great Throne Room or* **Hall of St George***.*

The hall is used to house major travelling exhibitions like the recent hoard of Fabergé objects which did the rounds of the world's major cities, but it is otherwise closed to the public. Under the Soviet regime the throne was replaced by a giant semi-precious mosaic map of the USSR, which recent restoration may have moved elsewhere. Above it is an Italian bas-relief of St George, carved from the same Cararra marble used to decorate the rest of the room. From 1795, when the window-lined room was added on to the palace, the tsars held their most solemn receptions and delivered important speeches here. Two speeches by Nicholas II heralded key events in his downfall. In 1906 he spoke at the opening of the State Duma, the first check on the autocracy of the Russian monarchy, and in 1914 he vowed to defeat the Germans. By the time the war was over, he had been murdered.

> *If you have been able to get into the throne room, return to the 1812 Gallery and leave by the door at the far end from the equestrian painting of Alexander I. Two small rooms of badly lit European porcelain lead to a staircase on the left, which in turn takes you up to the department of* **Modern European Painting***.*

A tendency to rehang the exhibition here makes it difficult to take you through the stunning collection room by room. Its highlights include several rooms of Impressionists, the group of French painters who first ventured out of the studio to paint what they saw, *en plein air*. Rejecting the received wisdoms of academic painting, they were fascinated by what the new science of photography had revealed about the relationship between light and colour. Without the new widespread availability of tubes of oils, which freed them from mixing their own paints in the studio, the experiment would have been impossible. Startling too are the Post-Impressionists, particularly the large collection of Tahitian paintings by **Gauguin** (1848–1903), a number of **Cézanne** (1839–1906) landscapes and still lives, and a clutch of vivid, little-known **Van Goghs** (1853–90). Most famous of all are the museum's extensive collections of works by **Matisse** (1869–1954) and **Picasso** (1881–1973).

For all these paintings, and for the explosion of creativity they engendered here in the early 20th century, Russia is indebted to Sergei Shchukin and Ivan (and to a lesser extent his brother, Mikhail) Morozov. Of the two men, Shchukin was the more gifted and prolific collector. As the years went by he became increasingly sure of his own eye, and by 1917 had collected some 200 major canvases. It all began in 1897, when he fell in love with a Monet in Paris and bought it on the spot; the first Impressionist painting to come to Russia. For the next seven years he collected Impressionists, mostly Monet and, to a lesser extent, Sisley and Pissarro. The discovery of Gauguin, from whom he bought 16 Tahitian canvases to hang in his dining room, inaugurated Shchukin's Post-Impressionist phase. Sure of the value of his own taste, he bought two oils from the young Henri Matisse's studio before the painter had even been fully recognized in Paris. The two became friends, and Matisse eventually came to Russia, where he was fascinated by early icons. In 1909, Shchukin commissioned Matisse to make three paintings for his stairwell, one for each floor. Only two—*Dance* and *Music*—were painted, but they are among Matisse's greatest works. You will find them here if they are not out on loan. It must have been startling to come across them in the stucco and parquet interior of a Moscow palace. Inspired by the quality of light in the Mediterranean, particularly blues, greens and reds saturated in the light of dusk, Matisse wrote of the commission: 'I picture the visitor coming in from outside. The first floor beckons to him. He must be encouraged to make an effort, be made to feel lighter. My first panel represents dance, that ecstatic ring of dancers on the hilltop. On the second floor, you are inside the house; its spirit and silence suggest a musical scene with people listening; finally on the third floor, there is total tranquility and I will paint a restful scene: people lying on the grass, chatting or day-dreaming.'

Shchukin's last love was Picasso. Of the 51 canvases he bought between 1909 and 1914, the majority are held by the Hermitage. As well as Shchukin's own favourite Cubist period, there are also paintings from Picasso's earlier blue and pink periods.

Morozov was less sure of himself than Shchukin, and his collection was also more colour-led. It was said that he looked at a wall like a tapestry, and would leave spaces blank until he found something of exactly the right shade to fill it. The difference between Shchukin's and Morozov's style as collectors is illustrated by the following story, related by the French painter Maurice Denis. 'When Morozov visited Ambroise Vollard [the famous Paris dealer], he would say: 'I want to see a very fine Cézanne.' Whereas Shchukin would ask to see all the Cézannes and make his own choice.' Though Morozov also counted 11 Matisses and three Picassos amongst his collection, it was particularly rich in Cézanne and the Impressionists.

*During the modern European painting exhibition you will find yourself on a balcony overlooking the delicate decoration of the **Alexander Hall**,*

*commemorating the victory over Napoleon. The stucco bas-reliefs include
scenes from the war, and a portrayal of Alexander I on the far wall. It is
used for temporary exhibitions from the museum's vast stocks.*

After the works by Picasso and Matisse come a series of rooms devoted to painters associated with the movement known as Fauvism. Most typical of the group's search for expression through the simplification of composition, often reduced to a series of blocks of colour, are the canvases by **Derain** (1880–1954). The last room, Room 333 at the top of the stairs, is hung with canvases by **Kandinsky** (1866–1944), a Russian who spent most of his life in Germany. His concern was with the hidden essence of life, which he sought to express by capturing aspects of it—light, laughter, emotion and music—in his will 'o the wisp compositions.

*Taking the stairs down you will find yourself with a shock back in the
mannered world of late 18th-century France (Room 288), as portrayed by
Jean Honoré Fragonard (1732–1806).*

This suite of rooms, looking out onto Palace Square, was known as the First Guest Suite when this was a royal palace. Beneath its painted vaulted ceilings and decorative chandeliers stayed the most important guests of state.

*Turn right into the **White Hall** (Room 289), decorated after the fire using
Roman baths as a model. You are now in the west wing of the Winter
Palace, whose smaller rooms betray its use as the living quarters of the
last two tsars and their families. The southwest corner suite leading off
the hall was lived in by Maria Alexandrovna, the wife of Alexander II, and
is usually open. (If it isn't, skip to the next set of italics).*

Though the rooms are relatively small, their decor is overpowering: a surfeit of gold and silk brocade wallpaper which sums up the decorative tastes of mid-19th century Europe. The first room, with its exhibitions of seals, cameos, brooches and semi-precious gemstones, is the most vulgar in the palace and is known, for obvious reasons, as the **Gold Drawing Room**. This is followed by the **Raspberry Drawing Room**, the **Boudoir** and, thankfully, by the sombre **Blue Bedroom**, with its cabinet of fine glassware. The suite disgorges into Room 167, where a heavy Russian carnival sledge, modelled on an enormous clam shell, gives a hint of the gaiety of the afternoon promenades which took place during the week before Lent. This was known as *maslenitsa* or Butter Week; in preparation for the fast, the entire population set about feeding themselves to the limits of their purse with a surfeit of buttery pancakes. In the afternoons they would squeeze themselves into a favourite sleigh for a breath of fresh air and to see and be seen on Nevsky Prospekt.

*If the suite is out of bounds you can reach the sleigh by returning to the
staircase you recently came down, and walking through Room 302. The*

only room of **English Art** normally open, this is an embarassment to any sentient English person. The nation's heritage is represented by one measly sub-Arts and Crafts chair, while canvases by Reynolds (1723–92) and Gainsborough (1727–88), and an Imperial Wedgwood service, are hidden away behind closed doors. Having said that, when the Hermitage opened to the public in 1852, it was the only European museum outside England with an English collection at all.

The **Dark Corridor** (Room 303) which stretches beyond is hung on either wall with large French and Flemish tapestries. Behind them run more rooms lived in by Alexander II and Maria. Their displays of Russian 18th- and 19th-century applied art and paintings are rarely open to the public. The corridor opens out into the top-lit **Rotunda**, a balconied splendour whose parquet floor reflects its coffered ceiling. It was once hung with portraits of Russian rulers, but is now devoted exclusively to Peter the Great. The bronze bust of the tsar was sculpted by Carlo Bartolomeo Rastrelli, the father of the architect of the Winter Palace. You will also find locks of the tsar's hair, his death mask and a carved model of a projected triumphal column depicting the great events of his reign, topped by a statue of Peter himself.

The rooms beyond, and those inaccessible off to the left, were occupied by the last royal family, that of Nicholas and Alexandra, on their increasingly infrequent visits to the city from Tsarskoye Selo. They had all, including the Rotunda, been redecorated after the 1837 fire by the architect A. P. Bryullov, Stasov's assistant yet arguably more talented than his master. The **Moorish Dining Room** probably owes its name to the tsar's personal bodyguard of giant Ethiopians who protected the entrance to the royal suite. There is certainly nothing Moorish about its classical decoration. But then there was nothing Moorish about the Ethiopians either; Europeans were unforgivably inaccurate on such matters.

Straight ahead lies the entrance to Bryullov's masterpiece of a royal drawing room, the **Malachite Room**, *decked out in what must be the grandest of all materials.*

Nothing prepares you for the luscious sheen of the grainy, bright green malachite of these pillars, pilasters, vases and objects, set off by gold doors and the low golden vaults of the ceiling. Seams of malachite, a derivative of copper, were found in the Ural mountains by the Demidov family, granted land there by the tsars, in the 18th century. They pioneered the working of it, entailing cutting it into thin slivers and mounting it on a special clay in such a way as to create agreeable patterns. Veins of a milkier-coloured malachite have been discovered in Madagascar, but only those in the Urals had this deep imperial hue, and they are all now exhausted.

For a few months before the 1917 Revolution, the Malachite Room made a dignified backdrop for Kerensky's increasingly powerless cabinet meetings. When the

Bolsheviks began shooting at the Winter Palace from the Peter and Paul Fortress across the river on the night of 25–26 October, the politicians retreated into the **Small White Dining Room** next door. Kerensky had already escaped, but the rest of the cabinet were captured here in the early hours of the morning. This insubstantial room, a cosy, private royal dining room, hung with Russian tapestries representing Asia, Africa and America, was elevated by the Soviet propaganda machine into the site of the last stand of the reactionaries. The clock on the mantlepiece shows the time of their arrest, 2.10am.

> *A door leads from the Moorish Dining Room into a long corridor (Room 151–3) devoted to early Russian culture.*

Chronologically you are walking the wrong way down the corridor, so that the first cabinets you come to are filled with 17th- and early 18th-century telescopes and other scientific instruments which belonged to Peter the Great. Beyond them and in Room 152, which was once an interior winter garden, are religious and other artefacts from the 15th–17th centuries. Alongside icons, painted altar doors and manuscripts are palace windows of mica, portable lanterns, drinking vessels and a 17th-century map of Siberia, painted in the Oriental manner with south at the top and the rest of the compass points mapped accordingly.

> *Three doors in the left wall of the corridor lead into the three big halls that made up the second suite of State Rooms on the first floor of the palace. The doors between them are kept locked, destroying the sense of a grand thoroughfare, and you will have to pop into each separately.*

The first, the **Concert Hall** (Room 190), houses an exhibition of Russian silver dominated by the silver sarcophagus of Alexander Nevsky, crafted in the St Petersburg Mint in the mid-18th century. Brought here from the Alexander Nevsky Monastery by the Bolsheviks, the tomb is attractively tarnished, and embellished with bas-relief scenes from the life of the royal warrior-saint. As well as concerts, this was also the venue for small imperial balls.

The **Nicholas Hall** next door was used when the guest list numbered up to 5000, most of whom could dance between its towering Corinthian columns at any one time. In those days a portrait of Tsar Nicholas I, hung by his son Alexander II, made sense of the hall's name. This and the adjacent **Forehall** are now used to house temporary exhibitions. At the centre of the Fore Hall is the malachite pavilion from which champagne was served to refresh the dancers.

> *At the far end of this room, grand double doors open out onto the Jordan Staircase where this walk began. Anyone with the energy or determination to go straight on to Walk B will be able to pick it up at the bottom of the stairs.*

Walk B: Highlights of the Museum Collection

Ask a series of art historians what they would look at if they could only see one piece of West European art in the Hermitage, and the same names would come up again and again: Matisse, Picasso, Rembrandt, Leonardo, Caravaggio, Giorgione, Poussin, El Greco and Van Dyck. We came across the first two artists in the Winter Palace on the last walk, but the rest are hung in the various Hermitages attached to the palace. The aim of this walk is to seek them out while negotiating the labyrinth of halls, corridors and stairways on two floors and in three different buildings. On the way we will also pass through collections of ancient Egyptian, Italian and Greek art and a number of sumptuous interiors.

Rooms containing the supreme masterpieces of the collection are normally kept open all the time, but in the Hermitage there are no hard and fast rules. If you do get turned back, or if rooms which are normally shut open before you, use the map to negotiate yourself back onto the route of the walk. Good luck!

> *Walk through the low vaulted hallway known as the **Rastrelli Gallery** beside the ticket hall, and turn right at the bottom of the stately Jordan Staircase. Half way along this dismal corridor, constantly lined with packing cases, a left turn takes you into Room 100, the only room in the museum still exhibiting ancient Egyptian artefacts.*

Covering over 2000 years of **Ancient Egyptian** history, this dusty forgotten corner of the museum is dominated by the massive basalt sarcophagi in the middle of the room. All Egyptian collections revolve around artefacts associated with death and burial, since most of the objects to survive into the 20th century were excavated from tombs. In the third cabinet on the left you can see a series of crude wooden painted statuettes from the Middle Kingdom (2100–1788 BC), the greatest period of ancient Egyptian culture. Known as ushabti, they depict servants going about their daily tasks: the group on the plank are making beer and behind them is a cook, with a goose propped up against his legs. For a rich person to be buried without such maquettes was to risk having no-one to perform these tasks for him in the afterlife. The tombs were kitted out with everything considered vital to everyday life, including luxuries such as jewellery. The nearby alabaster pot was probably a Canopic jar, used for storing the pickled organs of the deceased.

In the far right hand corner of the room is the mummified body of a man called Padiist, who lived over a thousand years before Christ. Herodotus, in his *Histories*, gives a graphic description of the process of mummification: 'As much as possible of the brain is extracted through the nostrils with an iron hook, and what the hook cannot reach is rinsed out with drugs; next the flank is laid open with a flint knife and the whole contents of the abdomen removed; the cavity is then thoroughly cleansed and washed out, first with palm wine and again with an infusion of pounded spices.' Before being wrapped in strips of gummed linen, the body was soaked for several months in natrum. Once all this was done, the body was usually placed in three wooden cases, an inner, a middle and an outer, such as you can see here. Only then was the deceased entombed in the stone-carved sarcophagus. As you can imagine, this was an expensive process which only the rich could afford.

*The steps out of the room lead into a corridor which runs beneath Catherine the Great's first, **Small Hermitage**. Its walls are lined with 2nd- and 3rd-century AD marble reliefs from Roman sarcophagi. The first on the left depicts scenes from the Greek tragedy Hippolytus, the second stories from the Trojan war, while the third illustrates the ritual of a Roman wedding.*

*At the bottom of the stairs beyond, you find yourself in the grandiose interiors of von Klenze's **New Hermitage**, the building Nicholas I commissioned as a public museum. The highlights of the collection of **Greek and Roman sculpture** and pottery can be perused on a brief diversion to the right, but if you aren't interested in them skip to the next set of italics.*

Room 107 was specially designed to house monumental classical sculpture, in this case Roman pieces from the 1st–4th centuries AD. The most impressive is the huge cult statue of Jupiter, found at the country villa of the Emperor Domitian. His clothing, now plaster, would originally have been made of gilded wood, and gold would also have covered his hair and beard. The classical world was much more colourful than we imagine from the bleached statues that have survived. Their bright covering of paint, and that on the interior of classical temples and houses, perished long before most of them were unearthed. At the far end of the room, a gallery of portrait busts contains a number of Roman examples from the 2nd and 3rd centuries AD, with their vivid expressions of melancholia, dignity or disdain.

The next Room 108 was designed by von Klenze to resemble the courtyard of a classical villa, though with St Petersburg's foul climate he never contemplated leaving it open to the heavens or installing a central pool and fountain. It houses Roman copies of Greek sculptures, many of them featuring children. Room 109 features the first classical statue ever to be imported into Russia. Known as the Tauride Venus, after the years she spent in the nearby Tauride Palace, she is a very fine 1st- or 2nd-century AD Roman copy of a 3rd-century BC Greek original, and was bought by Peter the Great from Pope Clement IX. She stands armless on the right as you enter the room.

*From Room 110, the original entrance hall to the museum, you can look out onto the sturdy sculpted atlantes which support the porch and up the magisterial **State Staircase**. The rooms beyond are open irregularly.*

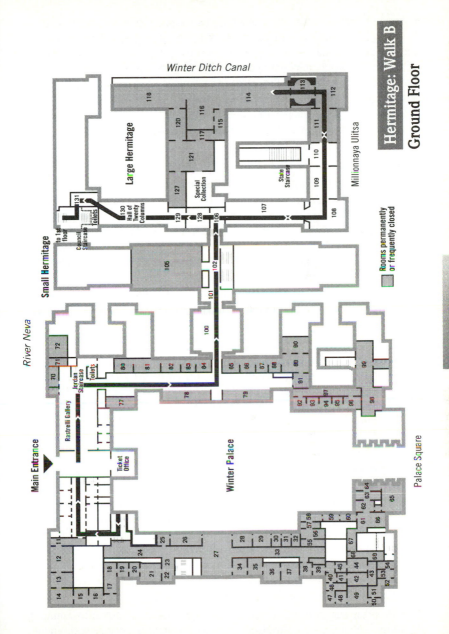

Hermitage: Walk B
Ground Floor

Winter Ditch Canal

Large Hermitage

Small Hermitage

River Neva

Winter Palace

Main Entrance

Ticket Office

Rastrelli Gallery

Jordan Staircase

Toilets

Council Staircase

to 1st floor

Hall of Twenty Columns

Special Collection

State Staircase

Millionnaya Ulitsa

Palace Square

Rooms permanently or frequently closed

Room 111 contains some exquisite early Greek pottery and terracotta figures, including the double-handled, red-figure ware urn entitled *The First Swallow*. It shows three generations of men greeting the arrival of the first swallow, harbinger of spring. The exhibition continues with fine Roman copies of important Greek statues, including works by Praxiteles and a famous, muscle-bound sculpture of Herakles (Hercules to the Romans) wrestling with the lion (Room 114). The rooms (115–7 and 121) containing works excavated from the Greek colonies on the Black Sea coast (7th century BC–3rd century AD) have long been under wraps.

> *Return to the stairs in Room 106 and carry straight on. Those who never ventured into the classical world should turn left.*

You cannot miss the vast green jasper **Kolyvan Vase** in Room 108. Made in Siberia in 1829–43, the upper bowl from a single piece of stone, it weighs 19 tons. Nearby is a 1st-century AD Roman decorative urn with a lid, whose grace puts its inflated neighbour to shame. Glancing briefly at the Roman mosaics in Room 129, you arrive in one of the museum's purpose-built rooms, the **Hall of Twenty Columns**. Painted in flat matt colours used in the ancient world, it is forested by grey granite columns alternating with purpose-built Empire cabinets. Down the left hand side are a row of tall Etruscan urns, including the **Queen of Vases**, the only one under a glass dome. Their black surfaces are so smooth and shiny they seem more like metal than ceramic. Elsewhere you will find smaller pots, bowls and metalware from the ancient Italian states of Etruria, Campania and Apulia.

> *In Room 131 we bid farewell to the ancient world, addressing it silently to the splendid multicoloured busts of the emperors Titus and Vespasian. Beyond, the **Council Staircase** leads up onto the first floor of the Large Hermitage between warm marble walls and fluted pillars. Its rich decoration and delicate iron balustrade seem to lend all who use it a sense of dignity. From the top of the stairs we make three separate forays, firstly into the neighbouring **Small Hermitage** to the left.*

You will find yourself in the dazzling white and gold elegance of the **Pavilion Hall** (Room 204) decorated in the mid-19th century, like the staircase, by the German architect Stakenschneider. He took as his well-disguised theme the orientalist poem by Pushkin, *Bakhchisaray Fountain*, the only vestige of which seems to be the shell fountains, no longer working, on the walls. The rest is a classical fantasy round a reduced copy of a floor mosaic found in an ancient bathhouse in Rome, flooded with light from full length windows on both sides. The man-sized **Peacock Clock**, which has recently been reinstalled after restoration, was given to Catherine the Great by her one-time lover Grigory Potyomkin.

The most unusual feature of Catherine's Hermitage is its so-called **Hanging Garden**, a first-floor courtyard off the Pavilion Hall, decorated with statues and fountains. Now forlorn and neglected, it is not hard to imagine a time when the empress might have sat there with Diderot, discussing the formation of St Petersburg's University, or with Prince Dmitry Golitsyn, a diplomat and Catherine's principal art buyer, working out what works they should pursue next for the collection. From time to time she would invite groups of close friends to a party here, often after a performance in the Hermitage Theatre, who would have been aware of the Rules of Conduct the empress had compiled, which included:

> Rule 1: Guests should leave every kind of rank at the door, likewise hats, and above all, swords, and

> Rule 9: Guests shall eat with pleasure, but drink in moderation, so that each can leave the room unassisted.

Beyond the Pavilion Hall, Room 259 exhibits example of West European applied art, including fine 12th- and 13th-century **enamel reliquaries** from Limoges and one of the earliest important pieces of Andalucian lustreware, the 14th-century **Fortuny Vase**. Rooms 143–6 run back through Spanish 17th- and 16th-century art, housing a temporary exhibition while the customary Spanish rooms are renovated. One of the earliest paintings is the entrancing double portrait of *The Apostles Peter and Paul*, painted by **El Greco** (1541–1614). It feels as if El Greco knew both of them well. On the right is the bald, convinced convert Paul, both hands asserting his belief in the Holy Bible. Peter, with his contemplative look and clutching the keys of the church, represents its stable foundation.

> *Return to the top of the Council Staircase and continue straight on into the large collection of Italian painting which begins in Room 207. These elaborate interiors, a bizarre contrast to the relative simplicity of the paintings, are also the work of Stakenschneider.*

The Italian collection is particularly strong in works from the height of the Renaissance in the late 15th and early 16th centuries. Walking through the rooms of earlier paintings and sculpture you will be able to follow the development of the characteristic features of the Renaissance. With the general surge of belief in the rationality and abilities of mankind came an unprecedented flood of developments in the artistic sphere: the appearance of a sense of perspective and three-dimensionality, an understanding of the true proportions of the human body, as well as the introduction of a secular reality into the religious subject matter. Viewing these paintings in Russia makes the changes particularly poignant, for this is the point at which west European art diverged from the medieval Orthodox traditions which govern religious painting here to this day.

The first room contains a fine example from early 14th-century Siena against which to measure the changes. **Simone Martini's** *Madonna of the Annunciation*, in which the Virgin is depicted alone, listening to the Angel Gabriel's news, shows an elongated figure, swathed in her traditional deep blue cloak over a red dress, silhouetted against the gold background that symbolizes the heavenly sphere. Two rooms later, a fresco by **Fra Angelico** (1387–1455), depicting the *Madonna and Child with St Dominic and St Thomas Aquinas* and painted almost exactly 100 years later, has dispensed with the symbolic golden background and replaced it with the blue sky which all four figures would have recognized from their earthly life. St Dominic, the founder of the Dominican order, is depicted holding the lily of purity, while his fellow Dominican St Thomas is distinguished by the shining star on his chest, an echo of the star which his mother is said to have seen shortly before his birth. Shading on their faces shows a deepening of the painter's sense of dimensionality. Room 213, which also contains two late paintings by **Botticelli** (1445–1510) of *St Dominic and St Jerome*, is dominated by **Filippino Lippi's** delicate *Adoration of the Infant Christ*, with its overt division of the canvas between the worldly and heavenly realms. Painted in the 1480s, its landscape background shows a well-developed sense of perspective, while the Virgin's page introduces an earthly relationship into an otherwise holy scene.

Two exquisite virgins by **Leonardo da Vinci** (1452–1519) occupy pride of place by the windows in Room 214. Although both are masterpieces of the Renaissance, they are very different from one another. The earlier *Benois Madonna* (The Madonna with a Flower) was painted in 1478 and bought by Nicholas II from the Benois family in 1914. The Benois, an artistic Russian dynasty, claimed to have acquired it in the early 19th century in Astrakhan from a travelling Italian musician. The Madonna, a young girl intrigued by her child's interest in the flower, is definitively worldly, dressed as she is in the dress of a smart 15th-century Florentine woman, her hair braided in the fashion of the day. The intriguing window with its view of the sky seems almost like a cerebral joke. By contrast the later *Litta Madonna* is once again dressed in her traditional red and blue robes and looks down at her child with an iconic serenity. And yet she and Jesus, with his fine red curls, are also fully human. While drinking from his mother's breast, the child turns his steady, all-knowing gaze on the spectator, and out of the rationally symmetrical windows you can see the earthly landscape in which Leonardo has chosen to set them.

If open, you should try to visit both Room 227 and 229 round the corner. The former houses Quarenghi's copy of Raphael's Vatican Loggie in Rome, for which a team of artists copied the original frescoes onto canvas. In the latter hang two consummate paintings by **Raphael** (1483–1520), the *Madonna Conestabile*, a study in innocence painted when he was only 17, and the *Holy Family*, a much more mature work painted a mere five years later. This room also contains Russia's only

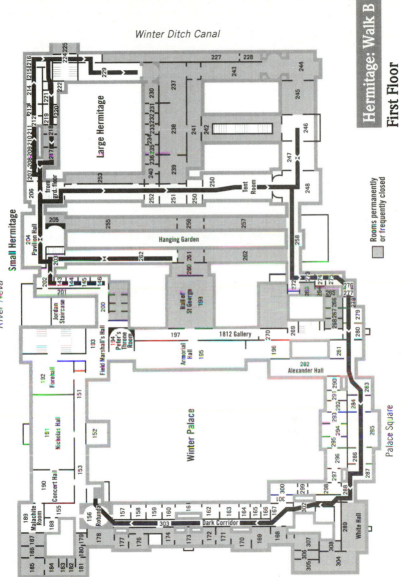

River Neva

Winter Ditch Canal

Small Hermitage

Large Hermitage

Pavilion Hall

Hanging Garden

Hall of St George

Jordan Staircase

Field Marshall's Hall

Peter's Throne Room

Armorial Hall

1812 Gallery

Alexander Hall

Forehall

Nicholas Hall

Concert Hall

Malachite Room

Winter Palace

Rotunda

Dark Corridor

White Hall

Palace Square

Tent Room

from grd. floor

Rooms permanently or frequently closed

Michaelangelo (1475–1564), an unfinished sculptu of a *Crouching Boy*, destined for a Medici tomb. Unleashed from the ston in the 1530s, the youth continues to exude an extraordinary inner strength and restlessness.

> *The Italian rooms beyond are bound to be cl sed, so you should retrace your steps and return to the Council Staircase via the suite of rooms containing paintings by the Venetian rather than Florentine Renaissance school. In Room 216 take the first turning left nto Room 222.*

A recent tendency to move things around makes it difficult to say precisely where you will find the museum's valuable hoard of canvases by **Titian** (*c.*1487–1576), last seen in Rooms 221 and 219. The masterful *Danaë* shows the ecstatic Princess Danaë being visited by Zeus disguised as a shower of golden rain. Both *The Repentant Magdalene* and *St Sebastian* are later works They show a consummate painter who not only valued mankind highly eno gh to take its depiction absolutely seriously, but also understood the innate d ma of its existence. Two other famous canvases which used to hang in the coll ction, **Giorgione's** *Judith* and Caravaggio's *The Lute Player*, have been being re tored, but apparently the **Caravaggio** (1573–1610) is on view once more.

> *Returning to the Council Staircase, we leave it for the last time, and enter the Hermitage's huge collection of Dutch and Flemish painting, beginning at the end, with Rembrandt (Room 254).*

Except in Holland itself, there is no greater collection of works by **Rembrandt Harmensz van Rijn**, the greatest painter of his age, who was born in Leiden in 1606. It is a great pity, therefore, that they are so difficult to see, with light from the huge windows pouring onto and reflecting off their complex surfaces. To get a good look at any of them you will have to duck and dive, taking peeks from a number of angles. It makes the task no easier that Rembrandt relied so much on the contrast of light and shadow for his effect, building up the emotional intensity and depth of the picture with indistinct figures in the background. The pictures down the left wall were all once attributed to Rembrandt, but are now recognized to be by his pupils.

Many of the larger canvases belong to the most successful period of Rembrandt's career, the 1630s, which coincided with his first marriage, to Saskia van Ulenburgh, whose likeness you can see disguised as *Flora*, the goddess of spring and flowers. Light is everywhere important, but nowhere more so than in Rembrandt's painting of *Danaë*, where Zeus is represented not as a shower of gold but as light itself, flooding in and saturating his welcoming beloved. In the *Descent from the Cross* it provides the focus for an event of tangible tragedy. As the years went by Rembrandt's palette became warmer, disgarding the greens and blues of the earlier years in favour of oranges, reds and golds In the small depiction of

David's Farewell to Jonathan, light falls upon the parting friends, illuminating David's hair and back as he collapses weeping against his friend, and Jonathan's tragic look of resignation. Jonathan's face bears an uncanny resemblance to the artist himself, and the painting may have been an exercise in mourning for Rembrandt, whose wife died at around this time.

Of similar tenderness is his slightly later *Holy Family*, but it is in *The Return of the Prodigal Son* that we see all the artist's talents combined. The brightest part of the canvas is occupied by the abjectly repentant son, on his knees before his father, eyes closed and head leaning into the old man's body. Gently reacquainting himself with his son, the blind old man bends over to put his inquisitive hands on his shoulders, caressing the torn and filthy garments with the lightest of touches. Only after the intensity of this image has been absorbed do you see the host of spectators in the background, getting gradually more shadowy until the ghostly female figure in the top left hand corner. A clutch of magnificent portraits hangs on the end wall. The *Portrait of an Old Man in Red* seems to sum up Rembrandt's empathetic genius cradled in his profound use of colour.

> *Take the opportunity afforded in the next three rooms of Dutch art to rest on one of the few sofas proffered to the public in the whole museum. Their age and beauty rather makes up for the lack elsewhere.*

Room 249, a huge space with a painted coffered ceiling, is known as the Tent Room and is one of the original interiors created by von Klenze in the mid-19th century. Amongst its many late 16th- and 17th-century Dutch pictures are romantic landscapes by **Jan van Goyen** (1596–1656) and **Jacob van Ruisdael** (1628–1682)—one of the greatest of the the Dutch landscape painters—and portraits by **Frans Hals** (1580–1666). They hang among a myriad of the genre paintings which reached an apogee in this golden era of Dutch creativity. In many, the exact reproduction of the subjects' clothes, their interiors and furniture seem more important than the people themselves. Vegetarians will be particularly amused by Paulus Potter's fantasy inspired by the story of St Hubert, who was converted to Christianity while out hunting when a white stag appeared before him, a shining cross between its antlers.

> *Turn left in grandly decorated Room 248.*

Room 247 is hung with a works by the Flemish painter **Peter Paul Rubens** (1577–1640), among them a copy of his acknowledged masterpiece *Descent from the Cross*, the original of which is in Antwerp Cathedral. The effect here, which emphasises the immutable deadness of Christ's physical body, is produced by the contrast between his pale body and the brightness of the clothes around him. The contrast is particularly poignant where his hand rests in Mary Magdalene's lively pink one.

Rubens is best remembered for his lively canvases saturated with people and movement, well represented here by the picture of *Perseus and Andromeda*. Having rescued Andromeda from the monster which lies at the bottom of the picture, Perseus is crowned by Glory with a laurel wreath. The question the picture seems to be asking is how long it will take him to fall, senseless for the glowing, rounded form of coy Andromeda. The limpid *Portrait of a Lady in Waiting* strikes a very different note, her face and hair a soft mass of gentle brushstrokes.

The next Room 246 is the unchallenged territory of **Anthony Van Dyck** (1599–1641), who had been one of Rubens' assistants, and had actually worked on *Feast at the House of Simon the Pharisee* next door. To get to grips with the man himself, seek out his *Self-Portrait*, painted when he was in his early twenties. Still showing signs of puppy fat, his expression betrays a lack of confidence which is completely absent in his depiction of his long, highly-prized and competent hands. Van Dyck is perhaps best known for the grand portraits he executed as court painter to Charles I of England from 1632 until his death. Aristocratic though most of his subjects are, they have not escaped Van Dyck's probing insight. Thomas Wharton, Inigo Jones and even the king and queen appear to have been caught with the effect of their own musings written on their faces.

> *Since the rooms beyond are not usually open, retrace your steps and continue straight through Room 248, passing through more Dutch 16th-century land- and seascapes which line the Room 258. You are now in the Winter Palace, at the start of the museum's hoard of French 16th–19th century painting, furniture and sculpture.*

By comparison with much of the Italian and Dutch work we have already seen, the French collection may well seem frothy and insubstantial. Its size is due to the close relationship that existed in the 18th century between the rulers of Russia and architects, sculptors, painters and men of letters from the Bourbon kingdom, many of whom were recruited to work here. Early Limoges enamel objects and paintings give way, in Room 278, to work by the Le Nain brothers whose 17th-century genre scenes seem flat by comparison with their Dutch contemporaries.

Room 279 is dominated by the extraordinary talent of **Nicholas Poussin** (1594–1665), the best known of all French 17th-century painters. Whether you like his work or not (some people decry its lack of psychological depth and humour) you have to admit that these strictly classical canvases, painted with the lustrous palette of the Venetian Renaissance, are the product of a very idiosyncratic vision. It doesn't seem surprising that Poussin's talents were more appreciated in Rome, where he lived for most of his life from 1632, than in Paris. As well as focussing attention back on the lessons of classical artists, Poussin is credited with inventing the genre of the history picture, which was to become so popular in the late 18th and 19th centuries. The next room (280) belongs to his contemporary **Claude Lorrain** (1600–82), whose landscapes, with their romantic classical scenery and obvious fascination with light, became models for Watteau and Turner.

> The **Alexander Hall**, redecorated after the 1827 fire in celebration of the victory over Napoleon, houses temporary exhibitions from the museum's stores, often on light-hearted themes. The 1993 collection of playing cards through history was an unusual and surprising aesthetic treat.

Room 284 beyond the hall is devoted to **Antoine Watteau** (1684–1721) best known for his *fêtes galantes*, conversation pieces which place well-dressed sophisticates in idyllic rural settings, as in *An Embarrassing Proposal*. Though Watteau succeeds in his intention of abandoning the exaggerated gestures and self-conscious poses of his contemporary painters, the combination of subjects is in itself so contrived that it rather cancels out the desired sense of naturalism. However an aura of charm clings to everything he paints, even the earlier painting, sketched in oil, *Actors from the Commedia dell'Arte*, which places five characterful, contrasting heads in close proximity.

The next few rooms are peppered with sculpture between the canvases. Notice the works by **Falconet** (1716–91) in Room 285. It was he who created that symbol of St Petersburg, the huge Bronze Horseman on the banks of the Neva. The seated statue of Voltaire in Room 287 was sculpted by **Jean-Antoine Houdon** (1741–1828) and shows the man months before death, sans teeth perhaps, but still possessed of a lively mind behind amused eyes.

Moving on to the full bloom of the 18th century with which this walk ends, Room 288 proffers a number of tableaux by **Jean-Honoré Fragonard** (1732–1806) and the didactic moralizing canvases of **Jean-Baptiste Greuze** (1725–1805). If you have already taken Walk A you will recognize the White Hall (Room 289) with its decorative, classical landscapes by **Hubert Robert** (1733–1808).

> By now you will probably be reeling with the accumulated impressions of over 600 years of European painting, not to mention classical statuary. Your escape from the museum lies a few hunded yards away. Return to Room 288, and turn left into the Dark Corridor (Room 303). Leaving the Rotunda by the right hand door, take the stairs to the ground floor. Turn right at the bottom and right again to the Ticket Hall where you began.

What is Where in the Hermitage

Primitive and Early Art and Culture of the Peoples on the territory of the former Soviet Union, Winter Palace Ground Floor, Rooms 11–69. Rarely open except for rooms 14–23, which include some spectacular finds, including a piece of tattooed human skin, early felt saddles, animal carvings and copies of Scythian arte-facts found in graves, including a golden headdress and hundreds of gold medallions which once decorated a king's costume. The original objects can be seen in the Special Collection.

Ancient Egyptian Art, Winter Palace Ground Floor, Room 100 (*see* p.401).

Special Collection, Large Hermitage Ground Floor (*see* p.392).

Ancient Greece, Large Hermitage Ground Floor, Rooms 111–114 (*see* Greek Department, p.402).

Art from Ancient Black Sea Cities, Large Hermitage Ground Floor, Rooms 115–7, 121. Rarely open.

Ancient Italian and Roman Art, Large Hermitage Ground Floor, Rooms 106–109, 127–131 (*see* p.402).

Department of Russian Culture, Winter Palace First Floor, Rooms 147–187. Only Rooms 151–6 and 167–8 are regularly open.

Department of Italian Art, Large Hermitage First Floor, Rooms 207–224, 229–238, 241 (*see* p.406).

Spanish Art, Winter Palace First Floor, Rooms 143–6. Moved from Rooms 239–40 which are currently being restored.

Flemish and Dutch Painting, Large Hermitage First Floor, Rooms 245–252, 254, 258, 260–262 (*see* p.408).

German Art, Winter Palace First Floor, Rooms 263–8. Currently rarely open.

French Art, Winter Palace First Floor, Rooms 272–281, 283–297. The last seven rooms have not been open for ages (*see* p.410).

English Art, Winter Palace First Floor, Rooms 298–302. Largely closed (*see* p.399).

West European 19th-20th Century Art, Winter Palace Second Floor, Rooms 314–325, 328–350 (*see* p.396).

Oriental, Byzantine and Near and Middle Eastern Departments, Winter Palace Second Floor. Rooms 351–371 cover China, Indonesia, Mongolia and India; Rooms 381–2 concentrate on Byzantium, with some fine icons and ivory carving; and Rooms 383–397 contain ceramics and metalware from Iran, Iraq, Syria, Egypt and Turkey. The only rooms that tend to be open are the Byzantine ones.

Numismatics, Winter Palace Second Floor, Rooms 398–400.

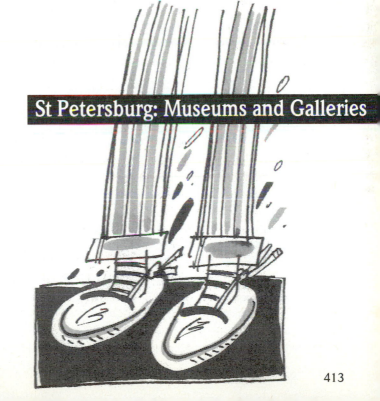

St Petersburg: Museums and Galleries

For its size, St Petersburg is studded with museums, a measure of a city that once played a greater role in the history of its country than it does now. As well as a gazetteer of places visited in the course of the walks, this listing contains a fuller description of the handful of places that could not be worked into any of them. Many of these are the former flats of figures from the cultural world—poets, journalists and composers—where a combination of personal effects and furniture blend with more objective information about the character's creative life. Depending on how interested you are in the person in question, some museums are more successful than others at evoking the era and personality of their owners. Of the other museums mentioned only here, the Alexander Nevsky Lavra allows a gentle half-hour stroll through its monument-strewn cemeteries and Baroque courtyard, while the gentle quirks of the Museum of the Arctic and the Antarctic in the Church of St Nicholas are quite unique. The Museum of the Ethnography of the Peoples of the USSR is a rambling treat for fans of costume and lifestyle, each ethnic display competing for your attention with its jewellery, stuffed animals, dioramas and model housing from tents to wooden huts. Furniture and applied arts buffs would certainly regret missing the ill-lit chasms of the Stieglitz Museum of Applied Art.

House Museums

Yussupov Palace, Naberezhnaya Reki Moyki 94, Ⓜ Nevsky Prospekt. 18th-century palace where Rasputin was assassinated. *Open for guided tours 11am–5pm (ring in advance on Ⓒ 311 5353); closed Sun (see p.326).*

Summer Palace, Summer Gardens, Ⓒ 314 0374, Ⓜ Nevsky Prospekt. Peter the Great's small summer residence. *Open 11–6; closed Tues and last Mon of the month, and from 11 Nov–30 April (see p.300).*

Peter the Great's Cabin, Petrovskaya Naberezhnaya 6, Ⓒ 232 4576, Ⓜ Gorkovskaya. The oldest surviving structure in the city. *Open 11–6; closed Tues and last Mon (see p.297).*

Pushkin's Flat Museum, Naberezhnaya Reki Moyki 12, Ⓒ 314 0006, Ⓜ Nevsky Prospekt. Shrine to Pushkin. *Open 10.30–6.30; closed Tues (see p.317).*

Dostoyevsky Memorial Flat, Kunyechny Pereulok 5/2, Ⓒ 311 4031 to arrange a tour in advance. *Open 10.30am–5.30pm; closed Mon and last Wed.*

Set up in 1971, to mark the 150th anniversary of his birth, this is not the flat as Dostoyevsky left it but a painstaking recreation of what it would have been like, using photographs and reminiscences, spiced up by the odd personal family possession. As you walk through the flat door bearing Dostoyevsky's name plaque, you enter a surreal vacuum in which two umbrellas stand to attention near the writer's top hat, lovingly preserved beneath a glass bell.

Dostoyevsky lived in this building twice. His first stay was at the beginning of his career in 1846, when he wrote *The Double*; then, over 30 years later, he escaped from the flat in which his son Alexei had died of epileptic convulsions, and returned to live here with his family from October 1878 to his death in January 1881. In the meantime, Dostoyevsky's life had gone full circle. Arrested and almost executed in 1848 for revolutionary activities, he was sentenced to four years in Siberia, married disastrously, returned to the capital and found himself perennially in debt. In 1866 he neatly used the cause of his misfortune to pull himself out of it, finding himself a more loving wife into the bargain. Faced with the penalty of losing the royalties from his previous books for nine years if he didn't produce a novel in 27 days, Dostoyevsky hired Anna Grigoryevna as a secretary. By day, she took down *The Gambler* as dictation, by night she typed it out, and in 26 days Dostoyevsky was able to deliver the book to his exploitative loan shark. Anna and Dostoyevsky were married, but financial crises dogged the couple for years. By the time they moved here, however, Dostoyevsky had finally earned security and fame with his monthly serial *The Diary of a Writer*, to which people across the nation subscribed. He was an habitué of the smartest Petersburg literary salons, where he exerted a mesmeric charm on young women. Anna left the socializing to her husband and continued to work as his secretary, looked after their surviving children, Fyodor and Liuba, and organized every detail of her husband's life, down to making sure he had a hanky in his pocket for walks. As well as *The Diary*, Dostoyevsky wrote his final masterwork, *The Brothers Karamazov* while living in this flat, but died before embarking on the envisaged sequel. The clock in his study still registers the day, date and exact time of his death.

If you become intrigued by Dostoyevsky's Petersburg, downstairs you can find out about walking tours around the locations used in *Crime and Punishment*, his quintessential Petersburg novel, and at midday on Sundays you can watch various films of Dostoyevsky's novels. Also sheltering in the building are a number of art galleries, the most interesting being the Petersburg Gallery of Naïve Art.

Rimsky-Korsakov's Flat, Zagorodny Prospect 28, flat 39, Ⓜ Vladimirskaya *Open 11–6; closed Mon and Tues (call Larissa Ivanovna on Ⓒ 113 3208 for a guided tour in English or just turn up and hope).*

The composer's flat, in the central block in the courtyard, is not well signposted. It is on the first stairwell/entrance on the left-hand side of the building. Nikolai Rimsky-Korsakov (1844–1908) lived here until his death; before his wife moved out in 1918, she made a detailed plan of their interior. Thanks to the determination of Rimsky-Korsakov's children, who kept all the furniture and objects you see here throughout the turbulent 1920s–60s, this museum was set up in 1971. Four of the rooms are just as they were when Rimsky-Korsakov lived here, right down to the wallpaper commissioned by the only son still alive when the museum opened.

The story of the composer's beginnings are highly theatrical. Rimsky-Korsakov's mother, the daughter of one of the frequent liaisons between an aristocrat and a serf, was very religious. She had her first child when she was 20, but in her early 40s, when her husband was 60, an angel came to her in a dream, carrying a candle from the heavens. She interpreted this as a sign that she had been chosen to provide a body for the flickering new soul, and Nikolai was born some months later. As her son's talents blossomed she needed no persuading that she had been right.

Over the sofa in the study where the composer worked from 9am until noon every morning, you will find an address painted by Vrubel, in the neo-Russian style, celebrating his 35th birthday. There is also a copy of the oil portrait Serov painted of him right here in the flat. On the first and third Wednesdays of the month, the drawing room would be filled with friends and admirers for the Korsakovs' regular *soirée*. It was here that the world-famous bass Fyodor Chaliapin sang both parts of the opera *Mozart and Salieri* from beginning to end, and here too that another Rimsky-Korsakov work, *The Snow Maiden*, was performed for the first time before an audience of a hundred.

Rimsky-Korsakov was part of the first great generation of Russian composers, and played an important role in establishing the nation's international musical reputation. He and his contemporaries Mussorgsky, Cui, Borodin and Balakirev, all based in St Petersburg, became known as 'The Mighty Handful' and later 'The Five'. His first symphony, indeed the first full symphony by a Russian composer, was performed when he was only 21. A prolific composer, particularly of operas, Rimsky-Korsakov was also professor of composition at the St Petersburg Conservatory and the main editor of a new publishing venture set up systematically to publish Russian music. It was in this role that he issued his own radical posthumous redraft of Mussorgsky's opera *Boris Godunov*, which has now been abandoned in favour of the original by most of the world's great opera houses.

Anna Akhmatova's Flat Museum, Lityeny Prospekt 51, ✆ 272 2211 (follow the arrows through a truly Petersburgian landscape of internal courtyards), Ⓜ Mayakovskaya. Quiet homage to one of the voices of anti-Stalinism. *Open 10.30–6.30; closed Mon and last Wed (see p.353).*

Blok's Flat Museum, Ul. Dekabristov 57, ✆ 113 8616, Ⓜ Sennaya Ploshchad/ Sadovaya and a long walk. *Open 11–6; closed Wed and last Tues of the month.*

There are two flats in this building dedicated to the memory of the Symbolist poet Alexander Blok (1880–1921). That of his mother, on the first floor, contains a chronicle of his life and career through photographs, manuscripts and objects. Blok's own flat on the third floor, where he lived with his wife Liuba Mendeleeva, daughter of the creator of the Periodic Table, has been recreated, and also contains an exhibition based on his most famous poem *The Twelve.*

Blok was born and raised in a hothouse of intellect. His father was a professor of law, his mother, with whom he stayed after the breakdown of his parents' marriage, was the well-educated daughter of a distinguished botanist, the Rector of St Petersburg University. The first room in the museum recalls these years: his early writings and drawings on his own childhood table, pictures of his family and of Liuba, his future wife, playing Ophelia opposite Blok's Hamlet at his grandparents' dacha. Even on holiday he was surrounded by St Petersburg's intellectual élite and their children.

After the 1905 revolution, Blok became preoccupied with his motherland and the theme of revolution, falling in with such distinguished Symbolists as the theoretician Vyachislav Ivanov and the journalist and poet Solovyev. His poems were first published in the Symbolist magazine, *Griffon* (Room 2). By 1910 however, Blok was beginning to turn his back on the sterile intellectualism of the Symbolists, seeking to throw his lot in with the Bolsheviks whom he felt better represented the Russian people and their future (Room 3). Unfortunately they never really took to him. His combination of eastern Orthodox spirituality and modernism was hardly proletarian fodder. Even his masterpiece *The Twelve*, written at the height of the Civil War in 1918, resonating with his unerring use of rhythm and sound, went without acclaim from the party. It follows a motley band of twelve Red Army soldiers looting and killing their way through a fierce blizzard, with a Christ figure at their head—hardly the orthodoxy the Bolsheviks were seeking to spread. Though applauded by his fellow writers, some of whose pictures (Akhmatova, Yesenin, Mayakovsky and Bely) hang in the dining room, Blok wrote that 'Dirty rotten Mother Russia has devoured me as a sow gobbles up her sucking pig.' Within three years he was dead, his depression exacerbated by the starvation and cold of the Civil War years. The last room in the first floor flat bears the poet's death mask and details of his death and funeral.

Nekrasov's Flat Museum, Lityeny Prospekt 36, ✆ 272 0165, Ⓜ Mayakovskaya.
Open 11–6; closed Mon and Tues.

Nikolai Nekrasov (1821–77) was a poet and journalist, who, with his next-door neighbour Ivan Panaev, edited the leading literary magazine *Sovremennik* (*The Contemporary*) from this flat between 1846–66. Started by the illustrious Pushkin, the magazine had lost its shine, but under Nekrasov's editorship it rose again to publish new works by Turgenev and Tolstoy. Gradually monopolized by its radical young sub-editor Chernyshevsky and his generation, it was closed down by the government for its political tone in 1866. Literary magazines, known in Russia as 'fat magazines', were a vital part of the publishing process, and most of the great works of Russian literature were first published in them, only later achieving book form. To this day much important new writing is published in the 'fat magazines', led by *Novy Mir* (*New World*), which was the first Russian publisher of Solzhenitsyn's *The Gulag Archipelago* in 1989.

Nekrasov, whose poetry mostly concerned itself with the life and hardships of the peasantry, was mad about nature and the countryside. Even in these patrician rooms he kept as many as three dogs at a time, and when his wife accidently killed one of them while out hunting he wouldn't speak to her, and developed a high temperature. The shade on the overhead light in his study continues the hunting theme. He also kept countless song birds, which were allowed to fly freely around the rooms. It was Alexandre Dumas who remarked that it was because the Russian winter was so long that the Russians so often brought birds indoors to sing. Panaev's flat next door has a convenient connecting door. Not only did the two men co-edit a magazine, they also shared a love of Panaev's wife Avdotya, a writer with whom the men campaigned for women's rights.

Historical Museums

History of Leningrad Museum, Naberezhnaya Krasnovo Flota 44, Ⓜ Sennaya Ploshchad/Sadovaya. *Open Tues 11–4, otherwise 11–6; closed Wed.*

This large and very neglected museum is housed in a 19th-century palace on what used to be called the English Embankment because of the Anglican church sited here. It may well have been rechristened since Her Majesty the Queen docked her yacht there in 1994. Walking through the rooms on the first floor, which run through the history of the city from the Revolution to the Second World War, is akin to walking through a ghostly memory. Few of the lights work and museum staff are notable by their absence, while out from the walls stare the faces of Lenin, haranguing the crowd from his armoured car in April 1917, and a thousand other Soviet heroes, demonstrating, fighting, working, educating and relaxing.

The floor above is devoted to the heroic role played by the citizens during the Seige of Leningrad in the Great Patriotic War (as the Second World War is still known in Russia). Setting the scene are photographs of women being hung and men shot under the banner 'This is Fascism'. There are pictures of children doing their lessons and eating in bomb shelters, and of women planting cabbages beneath the dome of St Isaac's Cathedral. In one display cabinet is a tiny square of bread, a day's ration at the worst moment of the seige. Its ingredients include defective rye flour, wallpaper dust, cellulose and bran. Nearby, a photograph of 11-year-old Tanya Savicheva and copies of her diary tell one of countless tragic stories. Tanya watched the deaths of her sister, grandmother, brother, uncles and mother, and the last page reads: 'The Savichevs have died. They have all died. Only Tanya remains.' Shortly after her own evacuation, Tanya also died.

Museum of Russian Political History, Ul. Kuybysheva 4, ✆ 233 7052/7050, Ⓜ Gorkovskaya. *Open 10–6; closed Thurs (see p.297).*

Peter and Paul Fortress, including the **Museum of the History of St Petersburg**, ✆ 238 4540/9454, Ⓜ Gorkovskaya. Includes the burial vaults of the tsars in its cathedral, and a gruesome prison museum. *Open 11–6, last tickets one hour before; closed Wed (see p.290).*

Cruiser Aurora, Petrogradskaya Naberezhnaya, ✆ 230 5202, Ⓜ Gorkovskaya. *Open 10.30–4; closed Mon and Thurs (see p.433).*

Monasteries and Churches

Alexander Nevsky Monastery, Ploshchad Alexandra Nevskovo, Ⓜ Ploshchad Alexandra Nevskovo. *Cemeteries open 11am–6pm; closed Thurs. Services in the cathedral at 7am, 10am and 6pm: closed 2–5pm for cleaning.*

Like most of Russia's religious buildings today, the Alexander Nevsky Monastery is in a state of flux. The Museum of Urban Sculpture which the Soviets housed in the Church of the Annunciation is closed while the church is being restored, and monks are creeping back into the Baroque courtyard. Visitors can expect a star-studded game of hunt the gravestone in two bristling cemeteries and a peaceful walk before entering the often hectic nave of the Cathedral of the Trinity, a neoclassical intruder in an otherwise Baroque ensemble.

The monastery, which became one of Russia's four great seminaries, was founded by Peter the Great in 1710 on the spot where he liked to imagine Grand Prince Alexander of Novgorod, later St Alexander Nevsky (*i.e.* of the River Neva) had defeated the Swedes in 1240. He knew quite well that the battle had actually taken place 20km upriver, but in his determination to legitimize his marsh-encircled city, he had the saint's bones brought here from Vladimir in 1724.

A neoclassical arch leads south off Ploshchad Alexandra Nevskovo into the monastery grounds. Buy tickets at the booth for the two 'museum' graveyards, which lie on either side of the path ahead. The Lazarus Cemetery on the left is the oldest extant place of burial in the city, begun when Peter I's favourite sister Natalya Alexeyevna was buried here in 1716. From then on it was the chosen resting place of imperial favourites, princesses, generals, government ministers and a host of discerning architects. Pushkin's wife is buried against the wall closest to Ploshchad Alexandra Nevskovo, just in front of the tall, black pillared monument with a cross on top of it. A gilded marble headstone, inscribed in Latin, marks the spot where the great 18th-century Renaissance man Mikhail Lomonosov lies over on the far side. In between, the jumble of funerary sculpture includes some delightful 18th-century neoclassicism, marking the graves of Starov, who built the monastery's cathedral (*see* below); Voronikhin, the architect of the Kazan Cathedral; and the favourite architects of Catherine the Great and her grandson Alexander I, Giacomo Quarenghi and Carlo Rossi. In the Tikhvin cemetery on the right , known as the Cemetery of the Masters of Art, all the important graves are signalled by bilingual Russian/English bronze markers. In Composers' Row, against the wall nearest Ploshchad Alexandra Nevskovo, a barrage of unusual gravestones commemorate Rimsky-Korsakov, Tchaikovsky, Glinka and Mussorgsky. Look out also for Dostoyevsky.

Beyond the bridge over the small Chornaya Stream, with its peaceful leafy views, lies the central monastery courtyard, a large, forested square. Immediately on the left is the earliest remaining Church of the Annunciation, designed in 1717–22 by Domenico Trezzini, a light, playful Baroque structure with a forest of pilasters and a high delicate dome from which a golden cupola emerges. After the royal mausoleum in the Peter and Paul Fortress it was the smartest place in the city to be buried, an honour lavished on Catherine the Great's inspired general, Suvorov, and on her son Paul's tutor, Nikolai Panin. It was turned into a Museum of Urban Sculpture by the Soviets, sheltering some of the most important funerary monuments in the city beside images of Lenin and Dzerzhinsky. Now it is closed while the church is repaired and state and church deliberate over its future.

The main monastery courtyard is surrounded by a series of deep red Baroque buildings, characterized by vast windows divided only by pilasters and surmounted at each corner by a cupola and cross. Built in 1756–71, these buildings include the residence of the Metropolitan of St Petersburg, the city's senior man of the cloth, directly opposite the cathedral. Littered amongst the mature trees in the courtyard are the graves of heroes of the Civil War and the Second World War, their atheist graves a provocation on such prominent holy turf. Dominating the whole ensemble is the neoclassical Cathedral of the Trinity, built for Catherine the Great by Ivan Starov in 1776–90. No church in either Moscow or St Petersburg is quite so foreign to the Russian tradition. Inside, a broad nave flanked by Corinthian pillars leads to the classical iconostasis. As is customary, the gilded wrought-iron gates, with a delicate tracery of floral bracts and swags, enclose six images, two depicting the Annunciation (the Angle Gabriel in one, the Virgin in the other) and four of the apostles. Yet these are not icons but pictures in the western European, post-

Renaissance tradition, and many of those in the rest of the iconostasis and hung in frames on the walls are copies of paintings by Dutch and Italian masters, Raphael Mengs, Rubens, Van Dyck and Perugino amongst them. Even some of the decorative marble was imported from Italy. Very fine *trompe l'oeil* architectural details adorn the ceilings and upper walls.

To the right of the iconostasis, beneath a magnificent gilded Baroque baldacchino hung with coloured oil lamps, lie the remains of St Alexander Nevsky. Though his current silver sarcophagus seems splendid enough, the original Baroque edifice, now in the Hermitage, was even better. The Empress Elizabeth donated 3250 lbs of silver for its adornment. Behind hangs a romantic painting of the saint in prayer, his rowdy jostling troops relegated to the background.

Behind the cathedral stretches the extensive Nicholas Cemetery, where churchmen and laymen lie peacefully side by side.

Chesme Church, Ul. Gastello, Ⓜ Park Pobedy. This Gothic jewel is a must for architecture buffs. *Open 10–5; closed Mon and Tues (see p.421).*

Church of the Saviour on the Blood, Naberezhnaya Kanala Griboyedova, Ⓜ Nevsky Prospekt. *Due to reopen shortly (see p.316).*

St Isaac's Cathedral, Isaakievskaya Ploshchad, Ⓜ Nevsky Prospekt. A great view of the city from the dome balcony. *Open 11–6; closed Wed (see p330).*

Kazan Cathedral, Nevsky Prospekt, Ⓜ Nevsky Prospekt. A glittering selection of church vestments, silver and icons. *Open 11–6, closed Wed (see p.333).*

Special Interest Museums

Museum of the Ethnography of the People's of the USSR, Inzhenernaya Ul. 4/1, ℗ 219 1174, Ⓜ Gostiny Dvor. *Open 10–6; closed Mon and Tues.*

Originally part of the Russian Museum, this collection of ethnographic material, housed in its purpose-built neoclassical wing (1903–10), became a separate museum in 1934. It was heavily bombed during the war, and much of its collection was destroyed, only the very best having been evacuated. The collection swelled again in 1948, however, when the ethnographic collection in Moscow was sent here. Since then it has been the home of Soviet and now Russian ethnography, with a rich store of manuscripts (some on birch bark, others in hieroglyphs) and texts in its library and research facilities. A major contribution to the museum's Siberian collections, and to the study of Siberian tribes in general, was made by the so-called 'scholar-exiles', intellectuals exiled by the tsarist regime to darkest Siberia. During the Soviet era, things were put on a more 'scientific' basis, with expeditions going out to the four corners of the empire, charged with studying, recording and plundering the applied and folk arts of the peoples.

The museum is currently beset by the usual problems, economic and political, starting with its name and scope. Exhibits in the vast hall at its centre reek of a time when one of the avowed policies was to 'reveal those processes in the lives of the peoples of the USSR that had been taking place during the formation of a new historical entity, the Soviet people.' Other rooms, organized geographically, have been closed down for a rethink; still others are suffering a lack of attention. Nevertheless its endless cabinets, photographs, models and maps reveal a wealth of material about a group of peoples who range from nomadic reindeer farmers to desert dwellers. Besides a formidable collection of costumes, you will also find methods of transport (boats, skis and sleighs), tools for weaving and hunting, fishing and harvesting, models of the interiors of Central Asian *yurts* and Eskimo igloos, ceramics, embroideries and metalware. Throughout the museum, but particularly in the Siberian section, are fascinating exhibits attesting to the folk beliefs still widespread among these peasant peoples at the time of the Revolution, and probably today. Look out for ritual wooden dolls from Russia, masks from the Caucasus, Siberian shamans' robes and headdresses aclutter with amulets, feathers, teeth and antlers, and complex Ukrainian corn dollies. Shamanism is now so in vogue that at the opening of one gallery in Moscow, a Yakutian woman shaman completely stole the show, going into a bellowing trance after several neat shots of vodka.

Kunstkamera and Museum of Anthropology and Ethnography, Universitetskaya Naberezhnaya 3, ✆ 218 1412, Ⓜ Vasileostrovskaya. Medical curios. *Open 11–5; closed Fri and Sat (see* p.384–5).

Naval Museum, Former Stock Exchange, Birzhevaya Ploshchad 4, Vasilievsky Island, Ⓜ Vasileostrovskaya. Model boats as well as the more technical. *Open 10.30–5.30; closed Mon and Tues (see* p.289).

Museum of the Arctic and Antarctic, Church of St Nicholas, corner of Kuznechny Pereulok and Ul. Marata, ✆ 311 2549, Ⓜ Vladimirskaya/Dostoyevskaya. *Open 10am–5pm; closed Mon, Tues and last Sat of the month.*

Recent talk of returning the Church of St Nicholas (1820–26) to its original purpose in 1996 has sent fans of this period museum into a tailspin. Opened in the 1930s, it has barely changed in style, and houses a series of enchanting illuminated dioramas showing life inside Arctic research stations, right down to the portrait of Lenin hanging in the tent. Downstairs there is a collection of stuffed polar wildlife and photographs of the discovery of woolly mammoth remains. Upstairs exquisite handicrafts by the indigenous peoples of the Arctic include fine carving on tusks, embroidery and clothing, some taking the 'Soviet Achievement' as their theme.

Artillery Museum, Arsenal, Kronverk Ditch, Petrograd Side, ✆ 232 0296, Ⓜ Gorkovskaya. *Open Wed–Sun, 11–6.*

Housed in the mid-19th century horseshoe-shaped arsenal building, with larger rocket launchers in its courtyard, the museum surveys advances in killing technology from the Middle Ages almost to the present.

Botany Museum, Botanical Gardens, Ul. Professora Popova 2, Apothecary's Island, north of the Petrograd Side, Ⓜ Kamennoostrovskaya. *Open 11–5; closed Fri.*

At the centre of the Botanical Gardens, which started out as a garden for medicinal herbs at the time of Peter the Great, are hothouses with exotic trees and shrubs as well as rather dusty displays covering herbal medicine and the diet of the dinosaur.

Gas-Dynamics Laboratory Museum, Peter and Paul Fortress, Ⓜ Gorkovskaya. *Open 11–6, last tickets 1 hour before; closed Wed (see p.291).*

Museum of Theatre and Musical Art, Ploshchad Ostrovskovo 6, Ⓜ Gostiny Dvor. *Open 11–6, Wed 1–7; closed Tues (see p.359).*

Zoological Museum, Universitetskaya Naberezhnaya 1, Ⓜ Vasileostrovskaya. *Open 11–6; closed Fri (see p.386).*

Off-beat Alternatives

Museum of Hygiene, Italyanskaya Ul. 25, ✆ 210 8505, Ⓜ Gostiny Dvor. *Open 10–5; closed Sat and Sun.*

Ever wondered about the effect of alcohol on foetuses, or VD on genitalia? Now is your chance to find out, painlessly, with the elucidation of plastic models. Speak Russian to convince them you are serious.

Art Galleries and Museums

The Hermitage, Dvortsovaya Naberezhnaya, ✆ 219 8625, Ⓜ Nevsky Prospekt. One of the world's great collections, started by the tsars and swelled by the wholesale confiscation of aristocratic collections after the Revolution. *Open 10.30–6; closed Mon (see Walk VII, p.387).*

The Russian Museum, Ploshchad Isskustv, ✆ 219 1615, Ⓜ Nevsky Prospekt. A bulging collection of Russian art. *Open 10–6; closed Tues (see p.341).*

Menshikov Palace, Universitetskaya Naberezhnaya 15, ✆ 213 1112, Ⓜ Vasileostrovskaya. Its period furniture, pictures, costumes and ornaments give a good idea of the aesthetics of 18th-century St Petersburg interior design. *Open 10.30–4.30; closed Mon (see p.423).*

Marble Palace, Ul. Millionaya 7, ✆ 312 9196, Ⓜ Nevsky Prospekt. The architectural highlight is the Marble Hall, where a rainbow of different coloured Ural marbles are inlaid in the walls. *Open 10–6; closed Tues (see p.312).*

Engineers' House, Ul. Sadovaya, Ⓜ Gostiny Dvor. *When showing an exhibition from the Russian Museum, open 10–6; closed Tues (see p.292).*

Tsar Paul I had this castle built and died in it, so it seems only appropriate that the Russian Museum should stage exhibitions connected with him in the few rooms so far restored.

Academy of Arts Museum, Universitetskaya Naberezhnaya, Ⓜ Vasileostrovskaya. *Open 11–7, closed Mon and Tues (see pp.380–1).*

Nothing much remains of the exhibition of students' work and ancient models that once enticed visitors here. The Academy is still a working art school, and the highlights of any visit are its round internal courtyard and senate room.

Stieglitz Museum of Applied Art, Solyanoy Pereulok 13, Ⓜ Gostiny Dvor. *Open 11–5.30; closed Sun, Mon and last Fri of the month.*

This extraordinary Renaissance building, modelled on the library of St Mark's in Venice, was commissioned in the late 1870s by the railway magnate Baron Stieglitz as an art school and museum. It has fulfilled the latter function ever since, and entrance to the museum is through the busy art school. Climb the stairs, turn right and walk through until you come to stairs on your left. The museum's dusty collection begins downstairs.

With outstanding examples of European furniture and ceramics, this dark collection, housed in a series of painted, vaulted rooms, is all the more approachable for the fact that its pieces are not all in a perfect, western museum standard state of repair. The highlight, given the museum's location, is the Russian room, to the right at the back of the central hall, where pride of place is given to 15 glorious ceramic stoves. The white ones at the far end were made in and around St Petersburg, while the earlier coloured tiles were produced in towns around Moscow. The earliest blue and white example, aping contemporary Delft designs, shows naïve representations of different Russian types.

Central Exhibition Hall, Manezh, Isaakievskaya Ploshchad, Ⓜ Nevsky Prospekt. *Open 10–6; closed Thurs.*

This cavernous former riding school houses a changing programme of exhibitions, usually by Russian artists. It has also been known to pulse to the beat of an all-night rave (*see* p.330).

St Petersburg: Peripheral Attractions

St Petersburg: Peripheral Attractions

PLOSHCHAD MUZHESTVA
PROSPEKT NEPOKORENNYKH
ПРОСПЕКТ НЕПОКОРЕННЫХ

3

CHORNAYA RECHKA

PRIMORSKY PROSPEKT
ПРИМОРСКИЙ ПРОСПЕКТ

6

Yelagin Island

4

Stone Island

5

VYBORG SIDE

Kirov Stadium

Primorsky Park Pobedy

Krestovsky Island

Gulf of Finland

Malaya Neva

PETROGRAD SIDE

River Neva

B. SAMPSONIEVSKY PROS.

Finland Station

PETROGRADSKAYA

Peter & Paul Fortress

10

VASILIEVSKY ISLAND

SREDNY PROSPEKT
BOLSHOI PROSPEKT

Winter Palace

Admiralty

St Isaac's Cathedral

Bolshaya Neva

Moyka

Griboyedov Canal

NEVSKY PROS. НЕВСКИЙ ПРОС

1

NEVSKY PROSPEKT

2

Fontanka

LITOVSKY PROSPEKT

Moscow Station

ZANEVSKY PROS. ЗАНЕВСКИЙ

NAB. REKI FONTANKI

NAB REKI FONTANKI
НАБ. РЕКИ ФОНТАНКИ

NAB. OBVODNOVO KANALA

NAB. OBVODNOVO KANALA

MOSKOVSKY PROSPEKT

LIGOVSKY PROSPEKT

PROSPEKT STACHEK

MOSKOVSKIYE VOROTA

7

STACHEK

KRASNOPUTILOVSKAYA КРАСНОПУТИЛОВСКАЯ

МОСКОВСКИЙ ПРОСПЕКТ

VITEBSKY PROSPEKT

BUKHARESTSKAYA БУХАРЕСТСКАЯ

PARK POBEDY

N

Московская Пл.
Moskovskaya Pl.

8

9

LENINSKY PROSPEKT ЛЕНИНСКИЙ ПРОСПЕКТ

TIPANOVA ТИПАНОВА

PROS. SLAVY

MOSKOVSKAYA

Пл. Победы
Pl. Pobedy

Victory Monument

3 km
2 miles

Owing to the youth of the city, and the fact that it was built on marshland that had only ever been seasonally inhabited by fishermen, there are no medieval treasures hidden amongst the towering housing developments which now surround St Petersburg. In this sense, if the weather were more reliable, St Petersburg would be the perfect tourist city, with almost everything of interest within walking distance of the centre.

A number of the things covered in this chapter are themselves central (boat rides, the *Aurora* and most of *Style Moderne*) but didn't, for one reason or another, fit into any of the walks. Otherwise it covers places for walks and picnics, and sites from the sublime (the Buddhist Temple), to the faintly ridiculous (the Lenin statue on Moskovsky Prospekt). Lovers of architecture should be sure to make a pilgrimage to the Chesme Church on Moskovsky Prospekt—it is a gem of a building, like something out of a fairytale.

Boat Rides

If the sun is shining on your first day in the city, you are in for the best possible introduction. Go to Politseisky Bridge over the River Moyka on Nevsky Prospekt, and you will find the owners of small motorboats waiting to take you on a one-hour cruise along the waterways of the city. They should not charge more than US$25, and will take up to four people for that price. Most of them speak a modicum of English, just enough to recite a litany of names as you pass Baroque palaces, churches and 18th-century naval yards. If you have a Russian speaker with you, one of the most knowledgable captains is Grigory Sergeievich Philipov (✆ 164 1623), a wizened old gnome with a poetic streak. If you want a more detailed English commentary, call Aqua Excursions, ✆ 314 5645 or 292 3054.

It is hard to imagine anyone who doesn't find this trip the best way to spend US$25 in the city. If your just don't think your purse can stretch to it, from June to September you can pick up one of the tourist motor launches which leave regularly from the pier below the Anichkov Bridge over the Fontanka River on Nevsky

Prospekt. This option has one advantage (it costs just US$1) and two big disadvantages: you cannot sit outside, and once inside you are never spared a monotonous, recorded Russian commentary. Check your purse again. One other boating option is the double-decker cruise ships that leave from the pier in front of the Hermitage Museum on the River Neva. They make a rather desultory circuit down to the Smolny Cathedral and back, but if the weather is right, it can be the perfect antidote to hours looking at paintings.

Piskarovskoye Memorial Cemetery

Пискаровское мемориальное кладбище

Getting There

Ⓜ Ploshchad Muzhestva and bus no. 123 up Prospekt Nepokorennykh. *Open daily, 9–5.*

Thankfully nothing can conjure up the horror of Leningrad's blockade to those who didn't experience it, but this cemetery, *Piskorovskoye memorialnoye kladbishche*, where over two thirds of its victims lie buried, is as good a place as any to contemplate it. As with many war cemeteries, it has an eerie, innocent tranquillity about it. The two pavilions which flank the entrance to the cemetery house exhibits giving something of the history of the blockade, which began when German troops encircled the city in early September 1941, intending 'to wipe the city of Petersburg off the face of the earth... it is proposed to tighten up the blockade of the city and level it to the ground by shelling and continuous bombing from the air.' The population of Leningrad at this time, in the absence of soldiers and the tens of thousands imprisoned in the Gulag, was some 2½ million. The city was totally unprepared for a siege, and as early as 21 November 1941 all electricity was cut off, leaving the citizens to face winter heated only by what could be scavenged. The lack of antique furniture in many homes today owes more to the blockade than anything else. On 6 December the water supply was cut. Subsisting on a daily bread ration that dipped as low as 125 grammes per person, each household had to carry buckets of water back from holes made in the ice on the canals and rivers.

Later that month all public transport in the city stopped, many people began living at their place of work and it became increasingly difficult to bury the dead individually. To get them to the chosen plot was the first problem, let alone finding someone with the strength to dig a grave in the frozen ground. An elderly friend who worked in a bakery at the time remembers feeling tremendous compassion for the 'intellectuals' who stood emaciated in the day-long queues. Their coats were good quality but it had been obvious from the start that they would be early victims, lacking the physical strength of their worker comrades. It was they who made up a disproportionate part of the heaps of corpses which began to be dragged on sledges to collection points, whence they were spirited to the then village of

Piskarov. On 20 February 1942 the cemetery records show that 10,043 bodies were delivered for burial in the vast gelignited pits. The left-hand pavilion contains an exhibition about the 'Road of Life'. This winter-only route allowed supplies to be brought into the city across the ice of Lake Ladoga, but in nothing like the quantity needed to stop wholescale starvation. Another old lady told me how her boss, a doctor, had been killed and eaten by the friendly neighbouring family in her communal flat; she called it 'the psychosis of hunger'.

Beyond the pavilions the cemetery stretches out, a vast expanse of green or white, depending on the season. Beneath flat-topped mounds the size of cricket pitches lie 490,000 Leningraders, identified only by a granite slab engraved with the year of their death, a star if they were soldiers who died on the surrounding fronts, or an oak leaf and hammer and sickle if they were civilians. At the far end of the cemetery, a towering bronze statue of Mother Russia proffers a wreath. On the sculpted memorial wall the heroic tragedy is depicted in classic realism, illuminated by the poetry of one of its survivors, Olga Bergholts:

> *We cannot remember all their noble names here,*
> *so many lie beneath the eternal granite,*
> *But of those honoured by this stone,*
> *Let no one forget*
> *Let nothing be forgotten.*

Kamenny, Yelagin and Krestovsky Islands

North of the Petrograd Side three small islands are separated one from another by tributaries of the Neva, the Small, Large and Middling Nevka rivers. Thought of as oases of calm since the foundation of the city, they are still largely green spaces, good for walks and picnics. Each has its own slightly different character.

Getting There

Kamenny Island straddles Kamennoostrovsky Prospekt ten minutes' walk south of Ⓜ Chornaya Rechka. From the small roundabout just off the Prospekt you can catch the infrequent services of bus no. 134, which wiggles round the island and over onto Krestovsky Island. There are two useful footbridges onto Yelagin Island. One is a short walk across Kamenny Island, the other, by the Buddhist Temple (see below) can be reached by buses 411 or 416 along Primorsky Prospekt from Ⓜ Chornaya Rechka, getting off at the stop called Lipova Alleya.

Kamenny Island (Stone Island), passed through the hands of a variety of courtiers in the 18th century before being bought by Catherine the Great in 1765 for her son Paul. In 1776 she commissioned a palace for him on its eastern tip,

Kamennoostrovsky Palace, one of the first strictly classical buildings in the city. Though it still stands, everything but its small Gothic chapel is out of bounds to the public, given over as a hospital for veterans. After Paul's death the island was taken over by his son Alexander I. It was here that he met with Field Marshal Kutuzov in August 1812, to plan the strategy that sent Napoleon packing later that winter.

The accessible end of the island, to the west of Kamennoostrovsky Prospekt, was colonized by the summer dachas of select aristocratic families from the early 19th century. One, the Dolgoruky Mansion, survives on the southern embankment, a couple of hundred metres from the prospekt. By the end of the century it was becoming positively suburban, and with the advent of the Soviet Union its KGB aristocrats took over. Today the mafia rules the roost, swooshing through guarded gates in smoked glass limos. Those with a taste for architectural whimsy will enjoy the combined impression these individual houses make, peeping from behind their secure walls—some traditionally wooden, some ostentatiously 'moderne', others nothing less than eclectically fairytale. At the far end of the island are two sites to enjoy: Peter's Oak, supposedly planted by the tsar in 1718, and the slightly later, classical wooden theatre by the bridge over to Yelagin Island, once a summer theatre but now sadly used as a recording and television studio.

Yelagin Island is a trafficless haven of boating ponds and leafy avenues, which fills up on summer weekends, particularly during the 'White Nights' Festival in June. On its eastern tip there is also a palace, this time open to the public and commissioned by Alexander I for his mother (built in 1818–22) on the site of an earlier palace belonging to one of Catherine the Great's courtiers. **Yelagin Palace** was the first major commission for Carlo Rossi, who so impressed the tsar that he left more buildings in St Petersburg than any other architect of the reign. Such was his favoured status that the rumour that he was actually Alexander's half-brother, son of Paul I and an Italian ballerina mother, has never died away.

The classical palace is indeed a success, if not in perfect condition. Only a number of the ground floor rooms are open but these include the Oval Hall which looks out through its bay windows onto long flights of steps leading down to the water. The room itself is surrounded by columns, interspersed with statues. The connected rooms vary in their decoration—some with painted *trompe l'oeil* in shades of grey (*grisaille*) to look like relief sculpture, others in colour against white stucco walls. None of the original furniture, all Russian, with which the empress furnished her new palace has survived the Revolution, though the parquet floors and mahogany doors with gilded fittings have been restored. The outbuildings of the palace, flanking the grand drive, consist of kitchen, stables and orangery, the former designed with the help of Signor Belardelli, the court confectioner and official taster at the time. *Open 10–6; closed Mon and Tues.*

If you have the stamina for the walk, it has long been a tradition to watch the sun set over the Gulf of Finland from the far point of Yelagin Island, where, as a certain Professor Smythe put it in 1860, you can enjoy 'on foot the pure, balmy air and the exquisite western scenery'.

Krestovsky Island, the largest of the three, is also the least pleasant, given over to sporting pursuits with its swimming pools, tennis courts, yacht clubs and indoor and outdoor stadia (*see* **Sports**, pp.545–52). The vast Kirov Stadium which crowns its western tip was hollowed out of a hill built of mud pumped out of the gulf, while the Seaside Victory Park (Primorsky Park Pobedy) which leads to it was planted by survivors of the blockade in memory of the dead and in celebration of the end of the Second World War in 1945.

Buddhist Temple (Буддийский храм—Buddiysky khram)

Getting There

The temple is at Primorsky Prospekt 91. Ⓜ Chornaya Rechka, then bus 411 or 416 along Primorsky Prospekt to Lipova Alleya stop.

While St Petersburg and its architecture have so often looked to the west and aped its styles, it is refreshing to find a building that tells of the other, Asiatic face of Russian history. The Buddhist temple was designed in a unique fusion of Tibetan Buddhist and northern Art Nouveau styles, and built between 1909 and 1915. Pyotr Badmayev, the tsar's Buddhist physician, took the initiative, collecting money from the open-minded members of turn of the century St Petersburg society, such as Nikolai Roerich who went on to champion the mystical supremacy of the Himalaya, and from the Dalai Lama himself. It is a tapering stone building, hidden from the hurtling traffic behind a secretive fence. Behind its red entrance portico lies a working monastery, revived in 1990 and run by monks from Buryatia, the small Buddhist Republic centred on Lake Baikal. In the red and yellow prayer hall monks sit cross-legged, reciting from their long thin texts, lighting incense and clanging symbols as required. It feels like a different world.

Moskovsky Prospekt

Moskovsky Prospekt, the main radial road out of St Petersburg to the airport and beyond it to Moscow, runs 9km from its start at Sennaya Ploshchad to the Victory Memorial at Ploshchad Pobedy. The buildings on either side of its motorway include educational institutions dating from tsarist times, Stalinist apartment blocks and sprawling heavy-industrial factories—this is not a place for walking.

Luckily a metro line runs the length of the prospekt, while above ground you can use bus no. 50, or trams 29 and 35 between Ⓜ Frunzenskaya and Ⓜ Moskovskaya. For a full tour of the highlights of this section of town, you should poke your nose out of Ⓜ Moskovskiye Vorota to see the Triumphal Arch, and then walk between Ⓜ Park Pobedy and Ⓜ Moskovskaya.

The **Triumphal Arch** was erected in 1838, not, as you might expect, as a posthumous tribute to Tsar Alexander I's defeat of Napoleon in 1814, but rather to celebrate the lesser military achievements of the then Tsar Nicholas I. It owes its unearthly green hue to the fact that it is made of metal, and was the largest cast-iron structure in the world when it was put up. Loosely modelled on the Brandenburg Gate in Berlin, it was taken down on Stalin's orders in 1936, only to come in handy as barricading during the siege of Leningrad. In 1960 it was re-erected.

Beyond the gate lies a no man's land of industrial depression. The factories here were among the most important in the city, and during the siege their workforce heroically continued to manufacture arms and tanks, despite daily rations of only 250 grammes of bread. The end of the Cold War has forced many factories to adapt their production lines to produce consumer electronics and machinery; they are now working well below capacity, and some are even closed for months at a time. Take the metro through Electrosila station, named after one of the largest factories, emerge at Ⓜ Park Pobedy. Turn left out of the station, walk for about seven minutes down Moskovsky Prospekt and you will come to Ul. Gastello, also on the left. You can't miss the conspicuous Zenit cinema which sits in the middle of its bulvar.

Down Ul. Gastello, beyond the cinema on the right, is an unmistakably dignified building, much altered and now a hospital for Air Force veterans. It is the **Chesme Palace**, originally built by Velten in the 1770s for Catherine the Great as a rest stop on the road to her palace at Tsarskoye Selo. It was named after the first great naval victory in Russian history, when Russia defeated the Turks at Chesme in the Aegean in 1770. The palace, a hospital since the mid-19th century, is associated more with dead royalty than with live, for it was here that the bodies of both Alexander I and his wife spent their first night back in the capital on their way for burial in the Peter and Paul Fortress. It was also in this triangular palace, which still retains its fine stone-carved Gothic windows and small towers, that Rasputin's body lay in state after his murder in 1916.

Turn right at the end of this building and you can't miss the flight of fantasy that is the **Chesme Church**, which brings a whole new meaning to the expression Perpendicular Gothic. Built in 1777–80 by Velten, it looks like a cross between a traditional Russian woman's headdress, a *kokoshnik*, a terracotta and white iced cake and a toy fort. Mesmeric stripes of white piping lead up to the five domed roof which crowns this most unusual of buildings. As if it wasn't quite extraordinary enough, inside the church houses the Museum of the Victory of Chesme, with a diorama of the 18th-century naval battle in place of the iconostasis. *Open 10am–5pm, with church services earlier on Sunday morning; closed Mon and Tues.*

Returning to Moskovsky Prospekt and walking on towards Ⓜ Moskovskaya, you come to **Moskovskaya Ploshchad**, a monumental square which lay at the centre of Stalin's 1930s plan to relocate the centre of St Petersburg away from its aristocratic past and into the heart of its proletarian future. Its centre-piece, the House of Soviets, rears its inhumane façade behind a huge statue of Lenin. All round the square are apartment blocks built on an equivalent scale, though after the expense of the war Stalin's plan was considerably scaled down and, on completion of this square, abandoned. Beyond the square and metro station, it is a few minutes walk to Ploshchad Pobedy and the **Victory Monument**, which stands in front of the Pulkovskaya Hotel. Occupying the centre of an enormous roundabout, the Monument to the Defenders of Leningrad, as it is also known, was erected in 1975 on the site of one of the siege barricades. At the bottom of its red granite obelisk, dated '1941–45', are a group of heroic black figures defending the city. The monument is best seen from a distance, and the memorial hall sunk in the ground beneath it will add little to your understanding of the siege *(open 10am–5pm, closed Wed and last Tues).*

Cruiser *Aurora* (Крейсер *Аврора*)

Ⓜ *Gorkovskaya. Open 10.30am–4pm; closed Mon and Thurs.*

Moored on the Petrogradskaya Naberezhnaya opposite the St Petersburg Hotel, this pristine battleship must rank among the world's great touristic anti-climaxes. A victim of the bogus 'crucial event' theory of history, it is billed as the ship that launched the Revolution, though its sterile, well-swabbed deck and exhibition do little to conjure up the events of that night in October 1917. The cruiser was not even moored here, but way downstream by Lieutenant Shmidt bridge leading over onto Vasilievsky Island, when it fired the blank shot at the Winter Palace which signalled the final assault on the members of Kerensky's provisional government who were still holed up inside.

Originally built in 1903, the *Aurora* was a lucky escapee from the naval disaster at Tsushima Bay during the Russo-Japanese War. Militarily obsolete, she was in St Petersburg for a refit in 1917 when the Bolsheviks managed to win over her crew. During the Second World War she was sunk, for her own safety, in the Gulf of Finland, only to be raised afterwards and turned into a museum in the 1950s. The exhibition includes photographs and biographies of the 'heroic' 1917 crew, as well as later Soviet naval good guys, and tokens of fraternal fellowship from friendly naval institutions worldwide.

Style Moderne in St Petersburg

Fans of Art Nouveau architecture will need little prompting to notice the contribution made by the genre, known in Russia as *Style Moderne*, to the city. Most of the Art Nouveau buildings are concentrated on the Petrograd side; the development of this quarter was heralded by the building of the new **Trinity Bridge**, 1897–1903, which connected with downtown St Petersburg. The bridge itself was built by a French company with strong *nouveau* influences. By the Revolution, the population of the island had more than trebled, and many of the apartment blocks built to house the explosion, still standing, are detailed from the pattern book of *Style Moderne*. Among the most remarkable and easily accessible are the **Lidval Building** and **Mathilda Kshessinskaya's house**, both a stone's throw from Ⓜ Gorkovskaya. The former (Kamennoostrovsky Prospekt 1–3) is an apartment block named after St Petersburg's most famous architect of the *moderne*, Fyodor Lidval, and was built in 1902. Its detailing is not immediately apparent, but gradually you notice fishes and owls, spiders and webs appearing out of the stone. Though most of the stained-glass staircase windows within have been destroyed in the course of this tumultuous century, a few still hang precariously in their frames. Mathilda Kshessinskaya was one of the most famous ballerinas of the turn of the century, and had also been the lover of the last tsar, Nicholas II, when he was still heir to the throne. Her mansion (Ul. Kuybysheva 4), built in 1904–6, combines the plasticity and variety of materials which were such a hallmark of the style. Today it houses the Museum of Russian Political History (*see* p.297), and the only stained glass is of a distinctly socialist hue.

South of the Neva there are also a number of buildings of note. Look out for the **Singer building**, which now houses the city's main bookstore, on Nevsky Prospekt opposite the Kazan Cathedral (*see* p.333), and **Yeliseyev's Grocery Store** at Nevsky Prospekt 58 (*see* p.357). The so-called **Tolstoy Apartment House** stretches between Ul. Rubinshteyna and the Fontanka River, the **German Embassy** is on Isaakiyevsky Ploshchad and the **Astoria Hotel** opposite it. The iron **railings of the Mikhailovsky Gardens**, next to the Cathedral of the Saviour on the Blood, and those round the cathedral itself, are the height of *nouveauté*, as is the **Vitebsk Railway Station** (Ⓜ Pushkinskaya), with curvaceous porches, tiled interiors and a glorious Royal Waiting Room on the first floor to the right.

Day Trips from St Petersburg

If Moscow is surrounded by a chain of fortified monasteries, the necklace round St Petersburg consists of a string of jewel-like royal palaces set in rolling parks. Built by the Romanovs in the last 200 years of their rule, those which you can visit today are among the most lavish of their dozens of homes. The continued existence of these palaces, with so many of their original trappings, is a miracle in itself. Contrary to Soviet propaganda, not all the Revolutionary troops in 1917 behaved with decorum as they took control of the former homes of aristocrats and royalty. The first port of call was usually the cellar, and after that paintings and sculptures were often damaged. Large-scale bureaucratic thieving by Stalin's government in the 20s and 30s enriched its own coffers while denuding the country of some of its finest works of art. They were sold secretly on the international market or exchanged in business deals with the oil magnate Calouste Gulbenkian and the US Treasury Secretary Andrew Mellon. And then in the war, all of the palaces except Oranienbaum were occupied by Nazi troops. Their pillage and wanton destruction of these pinnacles of Russian culture was judged to be a 'crime against humanity' at the Nuremburg trials. Within five weeks of the invasion, the Nazis were shipping forty or fifty freight cars of furniture, paintings and objects to Germany a day. Paintings that wouldn't easily come off the wall were cut from their frames, imperial dinner services, furniture and marble veneers were mind-lessly smashed. Before they left, the Germans set fire to each of the palaces, so that museum directors returning within hours of their retreat found only smouldering carcasses as well as booby trapped children's toys and brand new pairs of shoes, designed to maim the Russian population even after they had gone.

Few countries would have attempted to rebuild these palaces, and indeed many people in the Soviet Union regarded it a thoughtless waste of money in a war-torn country where some 27 million people had died and millions more had been made homeless. However the passion of the conservationists won out, partly out of victorious pride, partly because to allow these pre-Revolutionary palaces to die was to give in to the destruction of the war and even to collaborate with a regime (the Soviets) that had wanted to rub out the achievements of the tsarist regime. Remembering Dostoyevsky, they also felt that 'Beauty will save the world'. Work began on researching and rebuilding the palaces and reassembling their collections, work which continues to this day. As you wander through their sunburst gilded halls, bear in mind that it takes over a month to gild a piece of carving three feet long.

Choosing which palaces to see on a limited visit can be hard, though each appeals to a different taste. Peterhof is distinctive for its early, clean Baroque architecture and formal, fountain-filled gardens, while for those who like their Baroque more OTT, and gilded to boot, Tsarskoye Selo is the place. Little-visited Oranienbaum was untouched by the Germans, so that its buildings sing with age, while Gatchina is almost unknown to foreigners, with its look of a Renaissance castle. In many ways Pavlovsk is most impressive of all, a classical statement of Russia at its most powerful, set in Elysian fields. Peterhof and Oranienbaum are close to one another, as are Tsarskoye Selo and Pavlovsk, but to see two of these unique buildings in one day is to risk enjoying neither to the full.

Peterhof (Петродворец)

This, the oldest of the accessible royal palace estates, should really be thought of as a park with a number of palaces. It is the enormous formal 18th-century garden, with its straight alleys, cascades and tree-lined vistas on the banks of the Gulf of Finland that is the main attraction. The Great Palace, surveying all from its prominent bluff, is the least atmospheric of all the grandiose residences of the tsars, because none of them actually lived in it much. They preferred to stay in Peter's cosy Baroque house, Monplaisir, on the seashore, or to build less overpowering homes nearby.

Peterhof is a good place to come with children, as there are rides to be had in the children's park, and the elaborate waterworks with their golden statues are a thrill for all. The main cascade of 142 jets of water has been undergoing repairs by Polish contractors but was scheduled to be working again in 1995. More strenuous sightseers will want to wander into the naturalistic 'English' Alexandria Park with its quirky Gothic buildings, landscaped in the early 19th-century for Nicholas I and named after his wife Alexandra Fyodorovna. Ranged around the entrance to the palace are a number of other museums, one tracing the artistic talents of the Benois family, which span 19th-century architects and English comic actors, another recreating the world of an old-fashioned pharmacy.

Deciding when to go can be difficult, as all the buildings have different opening days. The park is open everyday 9am–10pm, and its fountains work May–Sept 11am–8pm. In winter many smaller buildings are shut, though the Great Palace, the Marly Palace and the Cottage Palace keep their doors open in any weather. The palaces open variously between 9am and 11am (*see* below) but the only day they are all open is weekends when the crowds can be obstructive.

Great Palace}	
Benois Museum}	Closed Mon and last Tue of the month
Cottage Palace (in winter)}	
Marly Palace	Closed Tue and last Wed of the month
Monplaisir	Closed Wed and last Thurs of the month
Catherine Wing	Closed Thurs and last Fri of the month
Cottage Palace (in summer)	Closed Fri and last Thurs of the month

Getting There/Around

In summer there are two ways of getting to Peterhof—by sea or by rail. From May–Sept, a hydrofoil (*raketa*) leaves the jetty outside the Hermitage at least every half hour 9am–6.30pm, speeding you across the gulf and slowing down to dock at the end of the palace's Marine Canal, giving you a perfect view of the palace as it was designed to be seen. Queues do build up for this as the day wears on, and you can only buy singles. If you want to go back the same way, buy your return ticket as soon as you arrive at Peterhof, as the late afternoon services get fully booked. Year round but not such fun, you can take the train from Baltic Station (Baltisky Vokzal), get out at Novy Petergof (not Stary Petergof) station, and take any of the Nos. 351–5 buses for the ten minute ride to the palace.

lunch/cafés

The most obvious place to eat is in the **self-service café** in the Lower Park (open 9am–6pm), though the food is mass-produced and the place contrasts violently with its setting. Better choices are to be found by the Great Palace and the Upper Park. There is a **café** in the Benois Museum (*open 12 noon–6pm; closed Mon and last Tues*); nearby is the **Restaurant Peterhof**, ✆ 427 9096/314 4947 (*open 12 noon–2am*), while the **Café Trapeza** (*open 12 noon–7pm; closed Mon*) is best of all

The site of Peterhof (Peter's Court) was dictated by Peter the Great's obsession with his Russian navy, part of which was based on the island fort of Kronstadt,

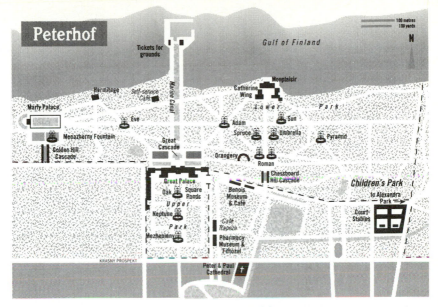

Gulf of Finland

N

100 metres
150 yards

Tickets for
grounds

Marine Canal

Hermitage

Self-service
Café

Monplaisir

Catherine
Wing

Lower   Park

Marly Palace

Eve

Adam

Sun

Menazherny Fountain

Spruce

Umbrella

Pyramid

Golden Hill
Cascade

Great
Cascade

Orangery

Roman

Chessboard
Hill Cascade

Great Palace

Oak   Square
Ponds

Upper

Benois
Museum
& Café

Children's Park

to Alexandra
Park

Neptune

Park

Café
Trapeza

Court
Stables

Mezhebinny

Pharmacy
Museum &
Fiftozal

KRASNY PROSPEKT

Peter & Paul
Cathedral

visible from the palace on a clear day. For much of the year the tsar could reach the island more easily by driving here and making the short sea crossing, than by undertaking the longer boat journey from the capital. The first building the tsar commissioned (Monplaisir) was little more than a simple Baroque bungalow. In recognition of the need for somewhere to entertain ambassadors and other guests of state, and goaded by his flamboyant advisor Alexander Menshikov, who was already building an ostentatious palace for himself down the coast at Oranienbaum, in 1715 Peter commissioned Jean Baptiste Leblond to build him a Versailles-on-sea. This palace was only as wide as the Grand Cascade, and Peter continued to live at Monplaisir, but as his reign wore on the gardens became more and more elaborate, with the tsar and his guests personally clearing alleys through the woods while architects and gardeners added pavilions and fountains according to a strict plan. The Great Palace was enlarged by Bartolomeo Rastrelli for Empress Elizabeth in the mid 18th century, and it is this version that we see today.

From early in the palace's history there was a great summer fête held here every year, when for one day in the year the population of the city and it environs were invited to share and feast in the emperor's domain, illuminated by millions of candle lamps hung from the trees. Since 1918, the palace has been open increasingly to the public (except during its Nazi occupation and the painful years of reconstruction which it entailed) so that it is easy to forget that all this was once just one of the many private estates of one family.

Assuming you opt for the novelty value and fun of the hydrofoil, this description starts with the four water's-edge palaces, then ambles through the lower park to the Great Palace, the Upper Park, the Benois and Pharmacy Museums and finally the Alexandria Park.

Monplaisir

The short walk from the jetty allows you to feast your eyes on the impressive canal which draws your attention to the multitudinous water spouts of the Grand Cascade and above it to the palace. Once you hit land, turn left at the first opportunity and wander towards Peter's first home, Monplaisir, which you enter from the back courtyard (open May–Sept 10.30am–6pm; closed Wed and last Thurs).

The house was originally commissioned from an architect named Braunstein in 1714, but it wasn't long before Leblond arrived to make his mark on this many-windowed brick building. Known as the Dutch House, this waterside home so charmed the pragmatic tsar that he gave it the whimsical name Monplaisir. A simple seven-room house flanked by wings containing picture galleries, it focuses on the central Great Hall which served as both living and dining room. Estimated by the painter Nicholas Ge to have been the site of the infamous interview between Peter and his poor son Alexei (it appears in his painting *Peter the Great Interrogating Tsarevich Alexei* in the Russian Museum, *see* p.348), this room was also the site of many a less sobering occasion. A visiting Frenchman, M. Weber, recounts how after a dinner with plenty of Hungarian wine 'it was impossible to refuse another pint glass offered by the Czarina herself. This reduced us to such pitiful circumstances that our servants chose to throw one of us into the garden'. Peter was renowned for these drunken dinners, at which he would quite often take little himself, the better to enjoy his manipulative bullying. The Danish diplomat, Just Jual, was reduced to bribery to survive. There was nothing the tsar enjoyed more than getting this light-headed foreigner legless, so Just Jual promised an influential priest that he would finance the building of an entire monastery if only he could stop the tsar insisting he should drink. Most of the room is soberly but precisely adorned in the style Peter liked, with a chequered marble floor, panelled walls and simple wooden furniture. The coffered roof is a contrasting jewel. Painted by an Italian, at its centre you can see Apollo with his lyre, surrounded by a Renaissance confection of shells, flowers and figures. The corners of the coffer appear to be supported by sculpted torsos representing the four seasons.

On either side of the hall are three small rooms—a bedroom and two studies in one direction, a kitchen, pantry and the Laquer Cabinet in the other. As well as fine wooden panelling, a number are adorned with Delft tiles and simple plasterwork chimneybreasts and ceilings. The only extravagance in the entire palace is the

Laquer Cabinet, whose orangy-red and black walls were originally executed by early 18th-century Russian icon painters copying Chinese laquerware. Today's walls are second-generation copies. When the Nazis occupied the estate, they stabled horses in Monplaisir and all but three of the panels disappeared. Peter's collection of paintings had luckily been evacuated, and now hangs throughout the palace. His first love was Dutch and Flemish art, particularly seascapes.

Catherine Wing

During the tricky years of Catherine the Great's gradual estrangement from her husband, which began in the 1750s, the future empress spent much time living in the long-demolished Tea House nearby. After her husband had threatened to divorce her and put her in a convent in 1762, it was here that Catherine's lover Grigory Orlov collected her on the day of their planned coup d'état, 28 July 1762. Peter III was living at Oranienbaum with his ugly lover, Elizaveta Vorontsova (he explained to her sister that he felt it 'safer to deal with honest blockheads like your sister and myself than with great wits who squeeze the juice out of the orange and then throw away the rind,' referring to Catherine), and Catherine processed triumphantly into the city, receiving pledges of allegiance from whole regiments of soldiers as she went. When Peter came to dine with her and could not find her, he knew he was doomed, and retreated to Oranienbaum to await his fate (see p.451).

The Catherine Wing (*open May–Sept 10.30am–6pm; closed Thurs and last Fri of the month*), whose name honours these events, was in fact built by Empress Elizabeth in the 1740s so that she could entertain from Monplaisir in her customary style. It contains a number of large rooms, including the Yellow Hall whose table is laid with places for 45 guests.

Hermitage

To find this small red and white Baroque building, surrounded by a moat and overlooking the sea, return to the Marine Canal, cross it and walk on past the café. Currently closed for restoration, its usual opening hours are May–Sept 11am–6pm; closed Wed and last Thurs of the month.

Should the situation change, you will find yourself in the private dining room which Peter commissioned Leblond to build, including a table which disappeared through the floor between courses, only to reappear covered with further delicacies. Guests marked their choice of dishes on the menu which lay by each plate. Originally even the guests were winched up and down to their waiterless meal, but after Emperor Paul was stranded between floors it was decided to install a staircase.

Marly Palace

Even if the Hermitage is closed, the walk was not wasted for you can continue on, past the vast pond which once kept the Imperial table supplied with fish, to the yellow and white Marly Palace (open 9am–5pm; closed Tues and last Wed of the month).

Built 1719–20, the Small Seaside House, as it was originally known, is one of the most important buildings in the Lower Park, since the three main alleys fan out directly from it. It became known as the Marly Palace after the nearby water cascade and fountains, which were inspired by Peter's 1717 visit to the French king's hunting lodge, Marly-le-Roi. Peter took a close interest in its construction, instructing Braunstein on the use of wood panelling, and hung more of his picture collection here. The ground floor of the palace is taken up with service rooms—an even more elaborate tiled kitchen than at Monplaisir, a pantry containing 17th- and 18th-century crockery, a bedroom and a couple of studies. Upstairs is more showy, with some of Peter's clothes displayed in the Wardrobe Room, and canvases by one of his favourite artists, Alessandro Grevenbroeck, filling the drawing room opposite with images of the sea. The dining room has a superb view along the vistas of the Lower Park, its solid English table sitting on a parquet floor exploding with dark stars. In the 18th century, during royal dinners these would have been matched by the star-bursts of fireworks let off from pontoons on the lake outside. The walls of the Oak Study in the corner are elegantly decorated with carving, while the desk in the window is said to have been made by Peter the Great himself. The bronze sundial on it was given to the tsar when he was in England by King William III.

Lower Park

Throughout the Lower Park, fountains and cascades of water form grand punctuation marks along the vistas. All of these have been recommissioned since the 1940s, when the park was crisscrossed by Nazi trenches and gun-emplacements. Not only did they decimate the trees, which have largely been replanted, but the invaders deliberately destroyed the complex web of underground pipes on which the fountains relied. All have now been reinstated, and most of the fountains' names (marked on the plan) are self-explanatory. The Menazherny Fountain by the Marly Palace gets its name from the French verb *ménager*, 'to economize'; its 40-foot jets economizing on water by being hollow. The remarkable Pyramid Fountain creates a solid pyramid from its ever-moving jets. Watch out for the fountains near Peter's palace Monplaisir; the tsar himself designed some of them after his 1717 trip to Paris when he became enchanted by trick fountains. Though he was perspicacious enough to note that 'sooner or later Paris will pay dearly for its luxury and licence' (the French Revolution was only 70 years away), the practical-joking monarch could not resist importing some of their more frivolous *jeux d'eau*.

The riotous Great Cascade, oriented down the Marine Canal to the Gulf of Finland and the Kronstadt naval base beyond, was designed to embody Peter's mastery over the Baltic following his rout of Sweden from the Gulf and at the Battle of

Poltava (1712). Its centrepiece is a gilded bronze statue of Samson, on whose saint's day the battle took place, wrenching open the mouth of a lion, the heraldic beast of Sweden. Providing the restoration is finished he will be surrounded by 38 more bright gilded figures, heros from classical mythology and watery beasts—frogs, dolphins, sirens and naiads. During the war the Nazis melted down those which had not been evacuated or hidden, including the 18th-century Samson. By 1947 it had been recreated from drawings and photographs, and was once more in place amongst the spouting, cascading waterfalls.

Before you leave the Lower Park to explore the Great Palace, you may want to drop in on the palatial Orangery, a semi-circular orange and cream building with huge windows. Originally used to cultivate the fruits, such as grapes, pineapples and oranges, which were a necessary part of any affluent table, it now houses a Museum of Wax Figures (*open 9am–5pm*). Inside you can aquaint yourself with impressive likenesses of some of the key personalities involved with Peterhof—Peter the Great, his wife Catherine I, and their successors the Empresses Anna, Elizabeth and Catherine the Great.

Great Palace

Empress Elizabeth's favourite architect Bartolomeo Rastrelli exercised considerable restraint on the exterior of Peterhof when he enlarged it in the 1740s–50s. Rather than adding his customary pillars, porticoes and deeply embellished windows, he respected the look of the smaller palace, built during Peter's time, and continued it in his extensions. Only in the gilded domes of the end pavilions can one see his Italian exuberance breaking through. Their heavy golden cupolas are topped in one instance by a cross, above the palace chapel and in the other by a huge double-headed eagle; the coat of arms of the Romanovs. Entrance to the palace is via doors in the Upper Park façade, and tickets for foreigners are on sale beyond the cloak-room (*open 11am–6pm; closed Mon and last Tues of the month*).

Inside the palace, however, Rastrelli gave free rein to his taste for gilded Baroque decoration. This can be seen on the first Ceremonial Staircase, but many of his other interiors were redecorated under Catherine the Great, whose own neoclassical taste required more restraint. Today's palace, restored from the burned-out hulk left by the Nazis in 1944, is largely as it was before the war, when rooms decorated during the reign of Peter the Great stood side by side with those redecorated in the 1840s. Intricate marquetry floors are a striking feature throughout.

At the top of the Ceremonial Staircase a series of rooms are devoted to an exhibition about the restoration work. It leads to the Blue Reception Room where the Imperial secretary would greet guests before they moved on into the state rooms. The first of these is known as the Chesma Room after its covering of canvases which depict moments from the great 1770 naval victory over the Turks at Chesma Bay. It is one of a series of rooms Catherine the Great commissioned Yuri Velten to redecorate. As well as commemorating the battle it is also a covert compliment to the Orlov brothers who were instrumental in putting Catherine on the throne, for Alexei Orlov was the highest-ranking Russian commander at the battle. When he saw the painter Philippe Hackert's preliminary work for the series, he arranged to have a battleship blown-up for him, so that he could capture the dramatic essence of the scene.

The largest room in the palace, the Throne Room, was used for balls and official receptions. Redecorated by Velten, it nevertheless betrays touches of Rastrelli in its obsession with windows, mirrors and light. Between the upper windows are bas-relief medallions portraying members of the Romanov family, but the equestrian portrait of Catherine the Great behind the throne, by the Danish painter Vigilius Erichsen, is more impressive. It shows her on the day of her coup d'état, riding her favourite horse Brilliant and wearing the green uniform of a colonel in the Preobrazhensky Regiment who supported the putsch against feeble-minded Peter III. On either side of the portrait the walls have been decorated with bas-reliefs showing Justice, and Truth and Virtue, principles which Catherine liked to think were personified by her reign. The 12 magnificent chandeliers were coloured amethyst by adding magnesium to the glass.

The neighbouring Audience Hall, also known as the Ladies-in-Waiting Room, with its riot of gilded Baroque carving, is pure Rastrelli. To widen this long thin space he hung three mirrors on each of the side walls facing one another, so that vortexes of swirling gold are caught in a series of endless perspectives. Beyond it, the White Dining Room was redecorated by Velten though its plaster moulded bas-reliefs of fruit and vegetables, upheld by putti, straddle the border between Baroque and neoclassical. Its long thin table is laid with an English cream and mauve service known appropriately as 'Queen's Ware' and produced by Wedgewood in 1770.

The centre of the suite of rooms overlooking the Lower Park is occupied by a Picture Hall, flanked by small studies decorated by Vallin de la Mothe in the chinoiserie style which was fashionable in the 1760s. The walls of both are covered in laquer panels showing stylized Chinese landscapes, post-war reproductions made to go with the two panels which had been evacuated. The floors, particularly of the Western Chinese Study, are the most complex in the entire palace and are made using about a dozen different types of wood. The walls of the Picture Hall, also known as the Room of Fashions and Graces, are completely covered by 368 portraits of Russian women by Pietro Rotari, who travelled in Russia from 1757–62. Foreigners were once told that these beauties represented the cream of Russian women from throughout the empire; in fact they were all modelled by eight of

Empress Elizabeth's women courtiers, in a fancy dress frenzy. The collection was bought by Catherine the Great from the artist's widow.

Beyond the Eastern Chinese Study, the room become rather more intimate. The Partridge Drawing Room takes its name from the pattern on the silk material on its walls. Based on an 18th-century silk from Lyons, this stuff was in fact made in the 1960s in St Petersburg. The painting on the ceiling gives a hint as to what went on in the room. It shows *Morning driving away Night*, for it was here that those close to the royal family would gather after breakfast to talk, play and plan the day. The harp is early 19th-century, from the London workshop of the French instrument maker Sebastian Erard. The Divan Room next door is covered in the most sumptuous painted Chinese silk wallpaper which has been extensively repaired. It was originally a royal bedroom, but the bed in the alcove has gone and a large, Ottoman-style divan in one corner has taken its place. Near the Divan, you can see the sculpture of one of Catherine the Great's favourite Italian greyhounds, Zemira. The next door Dressing Room with its loud silk walls contains a number of objects given to the Empress Elizabeth by Louis XV of France, including a portrait of her by Charles van Loo and a valuable mirror in a decorative silver frame. The Empresses' Study next door is thankfully plainer, its white silk walls hung with the portraits of female members of the family who lived in this suite—Elizabeth, Catherine the Great and Paul I's wife Maria Fyodorovna. Amongst them is one of Catherine's lovers, Stanislaw Poniatowski, later King of Poland.

Leaving the private female quarters, the tour moves on to two rooms connected with palace security, the Standard's Room, where the resident guard's regiment hung their standards and the Kavalerskaya, from which officers on duty protected the royal appartments. Don't miss the intricate inlaid gaming table in the Standard's Room. The next four rooms were used as guest rooms and have yet to be restored, but are used instead to display further items of furniture and objects from the palace collection. They lead to the defiantly zig-zagged floor of the Crown Room, which was redecorated by Velten in the 1770s. A door in the back wall communicates with the Divan Room, the empresses' bedroom, by means of a secret corridor, and it is thought that this was probably the emperors'. The ornate gilt bed certainly suggests a royal inhabitant. It gives directly onto my favourite wood-lined room, Peter the Great's Study, whose panels were decorated to designs by Leblond. Eight of them were evacuated before the Nazi occupation and three of the remaining four have been painstakingly recreated. We leave the palace via the Petrine Oak Staircase, watched by a portrait of the tsar as we go.

Before you leave the palace, check out any temporary exhibitions they may be holding on the Ground Floor.

Upper Park

The formal garden known as the Upper Park, with its lines of well-trimmed trees and five large sculpture-adorned ponds, was conceived during the reign of Peter the Great, but has undergone a number of decorative changes since then. Early lead statues which cracked under the strain of the northern winters were replaced with bronze ensembles, a number of which had to be recreated after the Nazi destruction. The main group is an extraordinary 17th-century survivor, older than even the idea of Peterhof itself. Depicting Neptune and his watery consorts, it was brought here from Nuremberg by the future Paul I and erected in 1799. During the Second World War it was sent back to Germany, but was found by Russian scouts afterwards and reinstalled. The Square Ponds, which once acted as reservoirs for the fountains in the Lower Park, are now presided over by statues of Apollo and Venus, while the Oak Fountain, originally in the shape of a tree, now centres on a mysterious cupid, donning the mask of tragedy. The last fountain is named after its muddled history—Mezheumny means 'indeterminate'.

Benois Family Museum, the Pharmacy Museum and Fiftozal and the Peter and Paul Cathedral

Two small museums occupy buildings within easy reach of the Upper Park. The name Benois has been linked for over a century and a half with St Petersburg's artistic life. From the loins of a French confectioner Louis Jules Benois, who arrived in Russia in 1794, came a dynasty of architects stage designers, sculptors and writers; the most famous outside Russia being the British actor Peter Ustinov. The pinnacle of the career of Nikolai Benois (1813–98), confectioner's son, was the work he did here for the tsar, which includes designing this building. The best known Benois in Russia is his son Alexander, who worked with Diaghilev on the turn of the century art magazine *Mir Isskustva* and was also a prominent stage designer, intensely involved with Diaghilev's *Russian Seasons* which took Paris by storm at the beginning of the century. The Benois Family Museum, contains work by these and the more recent members of the clan, who include more stage designers, an illustrator and a number of sculptors. Ustinov's performance as Hercule Poirot in the film *Death on the Nile* is also represented, by a poster. *Open 10.30am–6pm; closed Mon and last Tues of the month.*

On a completely different note, the Pharmacy Museum, an old-fashioned chemists, and the neighbouring herbarium (*fiftozal*), which once grew medicinal herbs for the royal family, brews a number of soothing infusions. With a less advanced (and less powerful) drugs industry, the Russians still tend a lot of natural remedies for minor ailments, and useful herbal infusions to ei e sweating, cure constipation or alleviate shock are common knowledge. (*-6; closed Sat and last*

Tues of the month. The Peter and Paul Cathedral beyond the pharmacy was built in the 1890s in the neo-Russian style, and became a cinema after the Revolution. Its interior has yet to be restored, though services are once again held here.

Alexandria Park

Entirely different in conception from the main palace gardens, the Alexandria Park is a product of the romantic era and the naturalistic English style of landscaping made popular by Catherine the Great. It was developed by Tsar Nicholas I and his wife Alexandra, after whom the park is named, with a number of romantic Gothic buildings, most of which are currently in a ruinous state. However their curious, almost suburban, Cottage Palace has been restored and forms the focus of an exploration of the area (*Open11am–6pm; closed Fri and last Thurs of the month in summer; Mon and last Tues of the month in winter*). To get to the park you take the road running from the Great Palace past the Benois Family Museum along the top of the Lower Park. On the way, the huge timbered building of the Court Stables, now a retirement home, was built by Nikolai Benois, inspired by English medieval architecture.

Both the Farm Palace and the eerie Gothic Chapel in the park have been in ruins since the Second World War, though plans are afoot to restore them soon. Continue down through wooded glades and over the ruined bridge before climbing up to the extraordinary hybrid Cottage Palace, which also has a Benois connection—a leading role in the restoration was taken by Irina Benois.

Built between 1826–9 by the architect Adam Menelaws, it was to this unpretentious three-storey house, with its exotic wrought-iron and wooden decorative flourishes, that Nicholas I and his German wife would retire to relax with their family. It was enlarged slightly in 1842 by Stakenschneider, as their family outgrew its modest proportions, and part of the interior was also remodelled at the turn of the century when Nicholas II's widowed mother, Maria Fyodorovna, spent some time here. However most of the interior has been restored to its original state, complete with an abundance of Gothic furniture. Among the more unusual objects is a clock which shows the time in all 66 of Russia's provinces, which at that point included Russian America (Alaska), which was only sold to the US in 1867.

Oranienbaum (Ораниенбаум)

This small town, known in the Soviet era as Lomonosov, grew up around the palace complex begun here in Peter the Great's reign by his right-hand man Prince Menshikov. Its exotic name conjures up the ultimate aristrocratic luxury in these northern climes—orange trees grown here in heated hot-houses. Later in the 18th century, the outstanding Russian man of science Mikhail Lomonosov built a glass and mosaic tesserae factory nearby, hence its second name.

Oranienbaum never fell into Nazi hands during the Second World War. No architectural complex, however painstakingly restored, could retain its spirit of place, its *genius loci*, after such a thorough gutting. Here, though the main palace is closed and has suffered from long use as a government office, the surprise of discovering intimate, jewel-like pavilions and mini palaces among the lush and informal gardens is undiminished. Wandering, often alone, down an avenue of 200-year-old trees towards an aquamarine gem of architecture, you can almost hear the swish of silk taffeta, the rhythmical clanking of horse-drawn carriages and the giggle of a light-headed, bewigged and courtly flirtation. Come prepared for a good long walk round the four important buildings and handful of lesser ones, leaving time for some boating before climbing back on the train. Bear in mind that the four buildings open to the public, all on guided tours, share the same opening hours: 11am–6pm, closed Tuesdays, the last Monday of the month and from early November to May Day. The park is open 9–10 in summer, but closes earlier in winter.

Getting There/Around

Trains leave Baltic Station at least every half hour for the 1-hour journey to Oranienbaum, four stops beyond Novy Peterhof on the southern bank of the Gulf of Finland. Get off as soon as you see water. Once here, take the road running straight away from the main station entrance, slightly to the right, and turn right at the T-junction to pass the church on your right. The entrance to the park is further down the road on the left, and announces itself with a colourful map and a joyless pictorial list of prohibitions.

lunch

Oranienbaum is a culinary desert, so the best advice is to bring a picnic and supplement it with delicious fresh pasties (*pirozhki*) bought in the shop near the station (buy either *s'kapoostoi*, with cabbage, or *s'myasom*, with meat). Look for the word 'Пирожковая' (*pirozhkovaya*) to identify the shop. In summer fruit can be bought in the market near the church on the way from the station. In the park itself there is a café in the Cavalry Barracks, not far from the Chinese Palace, but it's not up to much.

*The path into Oranienbaum Park leads through wild woods and over a stream to a **lake** on which pedalos and rowing boats wait for hire.*

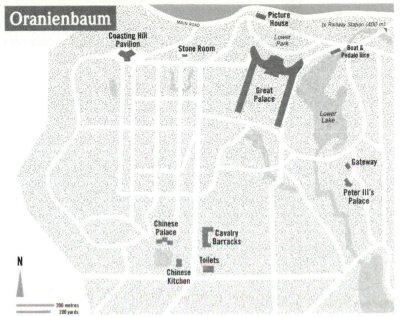

Oranienbaum

In good weather the shore is dotted with sunbathers and you can row your way up the lake, round its small island to the high rusticated bridge which crosses its feeder river, gently shattering the beams of sunlight with your bow waves.

*The copper-roofed pavilion with its lantern top, visible to the side of the lake above the trees, marks one end of the **Great Palace**. Walk along to the gates of the Lower Gardens to find yourself in its full-frontal Petrine Baroque presence. This hemisphere of formal garden contains ghostly memories of the geometric box hedges, knot gardens and topiaried yews which must have focussed attention on the formal entrance to the palace.*

Built using a natural rise in the otherwise flat coastal plain, Oranienbaum began life around 1710 as a summer residence for Prince Alexander Menshikov. He was Peter the Great's closest friend and principal political advisor, and had been made governor general of St Petersburg and its environs in 1703. Menshikov already had a grander house than his sovereign in the city, and continued to give full reign to his audacious arrogance here. For while Peter was building the humble one-storey summer palace of Monplaisir at Peterhof, work began on this grandiose palace, with its long semi-circle of wings ending in the church pavilion on the right and the Japanese pavilion on the left. In 1713, with the arrival of its principal architect Gottfried Schädel, work got fully underway, though Menshikov bankrupted himself on the project and the interior decor was never finished. Changes to the façade were made by Rastrelli in the 1750s, when he modified the palace wings, and by Rinaldi who classicized the façade for Catherine the Great. He removed gables and extended the central building, and added the zigzagging staircase which now sweeps gracefully up the stone-faced terraces.

When Menshikov fell from grace in 1728, three years after the death of his master and protector, the palace became a naval hospital. It was served by the canal and harbour excavated by Menshikov just below the Lower Gardens, at which ships could dock from Russia's main naval base opposite on Kronstadt. This phase was short-lived, for Empress Elizabeth gave the palace to her nephew and heir Grand Duke Peter and his German wife Catherine (the future Peter III and Catherine the Great respectively) and work on the complex began again. The architect Antonio Rinaldi took up the interior decoration work were it had been left off, building the Peter III Palace (*see* below) to house the Grand Duke in the meantime. Relations between the young couple were already poor, and Catherine moved to Peterhof, leaving Peter to enjoy Oranienbaum with his mistress Elizabeth Vorontsova. He was living here at the time of Catherine's coup in 1762, when he was arrested by Catherine's lover, Grigory Orlov, and his brother. Taken inland to the royal palace known as Ropsha, he was strangled by the brothers a few days later. The Grand Duke had never moved into the Great Palace. From the 1760s until the 1917 Revolution, it was constantly use by various members of the extended Romanov family. Until 1972 it housed government offices but is now occupied only by a caretaker and his cats, and a few restorers. It is derelict, and closed to visitors.

> *Walk out of the Lower Gardens by the gate below the Church Pavilion, whose gleaming new cross is almost the only sign of the restoration work. The charming but disintegrating building on the right before the gates was built by Rastrelli as a* **Picture House**. *Beyond the gate, make your way through an ill-defined car park and up the hill path which leads off to the right behind it. This becomes a mature and leafy avenue and passes another small Rastrelli pavilion, the* **Stone Room** *designed for parties and concerts, on the right, opposite a silted pair of lakes.*

The intriguing bell-topped wedding-cake of a building, which seems to grow as you walk towards it at the end of the avenue, owes its curious shape to its even more curious purpose, as a **Coasting Hill Pavilion**. The combination of steadfast winter snows and a relatively flat landscape means that Russians to this day grow up tobogganing down artificial snow mountains erected for the purpose. The passion for whooshing downhill with the wind in one's face was so ingrained in the Russians' memory of carefree childhood that Catherine the Great commissioned Rinaldi to construct the 18th-century equivalent of a roller-coaster ride here, for the summer pleasure of her guests. Leaving from the second floor terrace along what is now a long thin meadow, wooden carts hurtled up and down the three decreasing hills along the 532m track. Surrounding it was a wooden, one-storey colonnade, around the top of which spectators could promenade. After Catherine's death in 1796 her successors neglected Oranienbaum, and though the ride was used up until 1801, by the late 1850s it had become so rotten it was dismantled.

From the outside the building flirts with classicism, but perhaps inspired by its thoroughly frivolous purpose, Rinaldi subverts these with touches of whimsy. The building consists of three square wings radiating from a circular centre, all raised on a structural terrace pierced with round windows and approached via a showy double staircase. A forest of pillars, urns and diminishing tiers complete the effect. The interior, through which you will be guided, is even more successful. Much of the paint and plaster on the walls today was applied by the genius of the Barozzi brothers and Stefano Torelli in the 1760s. The ground floor now houses an exhibition of fine porcelain pieces, including important early Meissen, and a model of the Coasting Hill at the height of its glory. The pale blue walls of the curving staircase are decorated with fine white plaster bas reliefs and lead up to the first floor where light seems to flood from every direction.

The Round Hall was painted and decorated in the height of Rococo taste in 1766–7 by the Italians, but its artifical marble floor is the most astonishing feature. It was made by a Signor Spinelli to a design by Rinaldi and is composed of several concentric circles of different colours, laced with garlands and centering on a supremely delicate bird with a twig in its mouth. Very much of its time and a secret of the Italians, such high quality craftsmanship was rarely found again. Indeed it is hard to think of a more perfectly Rococo interior anywhere in Russia, informed as it is by the very essence of lightness and *rocaille*. The furniture is Russian made. The Porcelain Room off to the right was also decorated by the Barozzis, and contains several series of early 1770s Meissen or copies thereof, one of which allegorically glorifies the Russian success over the Turks in the Aegean at Chesma in 1770. To compare the real thing with their imitations, bear in mind that Neptune and Thetis, he with his strategically draped green cloak and golden crown, and the Battle Elephant are both originals. The third room upstairs, the White Room, is just that.

> *The other building which Catherine commissioned at the same time lies beyond the far end of the coasting meadow, set in its own slightly more formal enclave. Known as the **Chinese Palace** because of the abundance of Rococo chinoiserie inside, it too was built by Rinaldi and decorated by the Barozzi brothers and Stephano Torelli. The rectangular lake and venerable oaks are contemporary with the building, and the sculptures in front of it 18th-century copies of Apollo Belvedere and Artemis with a doe.*

The building, painted in its original bruised pink and deep cream, was originally single storey, the second floor having been added in the mid 19th century when several of the interiors were also altered. Guided tours begin in the suite designed for Catherine's then 7-year-old son Paul, continue through the small enfilade of state rooms which runs the length of the building and end in Catherine's suite which balances her son's, both in wings jutting out towards the lake. The Empress used the palace for diplomatic dinners during the White Nights in midsummer, but returned to her official residence at Peterhof at dawn. Neither Catherine nor her son, it is believed, ever stayed here; in fact she is only thought to have spent part of some 48 days here in her entire 34-year reign. She must have regretted that.

The first two ante-rooms in Paul's suite set the tone with their delicate decorative plasterwork set off by pastel painted walls. The ceiling of the first room shows the muses of the palace, architecture, painting and building, as women armed with their appropriate tools. Look carefully at the French tapestry in the green silk bed-room, which was redecorated in the 19th century; it is sewn onto a background of woven reeds. Entering the prince's boudoir is like walking into a wooden marquetry box. The parquet floor and walls are entirely inlaid with different woods, the latter painted.

The State Rooms begin with Stefano Torelli's paintings in the Hall of the Muses, a room shot with light from the windows on either side. Between the windows and beside the doors the rosy-cheeked and distinctly 18th-century muses tease you to identify them from the attributes they casually proffer. Passing through the Blue Drawing Room, which has been invaded by large 19th-century canvases, the Glass Bead Room is decorated on three sides by panels of fantastic birds among burgeoning trees and decorative landscapes, embroidered in silk onto a background of pearly glass beads. Known as buglework, these were made in France, possibly using Russian beads, in the early 1860s, and are divided by ornate gilded floral columns. Wisely, Rinaldi left the fourth wall simple. After that, the Great Hall seems curiously heavy, its walls decorated with artificial marble and relief medallions of Peter the Great and the Empress Elizabeth over the doors. No doubt the room would feel different had its magnificent ceiling fresco, specially commissioned for the room from Tiepolo in Italy, not vanished during the Second World War. The Lilac Drawing Room is dedicated to love, which is the theme of its 18th-century Italian oil paintings and its ceiling paintings, a Hymn to Venus. The ceiling in the Small Chinese Study beyond is held up at each corner by dragons, traditional Chinese symbols of imperial power, its walls covered in a magnificent 20th-century copy of Chinese silk wallpaper. This is merely a prelude to the Large Chinese Hall, in which the Barozzi brothers created inlaid wooden chinoiserie walls, using birch, rosewood, oak and amaranth, with a little green paint and ivory for the faces of the inhabitants of the magical landscape. The effect is like a sepia-tinted monotype of a Chinese landscape. Apart from the enormous English billiard table, made from Asian redwood and deeply carved, the rest of the furniture is original, 18th-century Chinese. The ceiling, which grows out of an oriental frieze divided by chinoiserie mouldings, is decorated with a fresco depicting The Union of Europe and Asia.

Catherine's Suite beyond is an exquisite collection of rooms, decorated with a light Elysian feel. Her bedroom combines fluid Rococo foliage and precise geometric chinoiserie, her dressing room decorated with a series of French allegorical portraits of her ladies-in-waiting symbolizing the seasons of the year and the elements. The penultimate room, known as the Portrait Room, contains 22 portraits by Pietro Rotari, whose more famous portrait series fills every inch of the vast Room of Fashions and Graces at Peterhof. The room was designed around the paintings, so that as well as being decorative, the portraits add to its physical rhythm by the inclination of their heads, the direction of their glances. The final room was Catherine's Study, whose parquet floor, as so often, is an elaborate echo of its painted walls.

To the left of the lake stand the **Chinese Kitchens**, built on the site of the original kitchens in 1870 and painted to match the Baroque exterior. Inside is an exhibition of ornate and at times heavy Chinese and Japanese furniture, and ceramics.

*Winding your way through the Upper Park towards **Peter III's Palace**, you pass the Cavalry Barracks with its depressing café, and wander through woods, open spaces and over bridges.*

You should come across an isolated gateway first, its pink arch surmounted by a lantern look-out and a spire leading into nowhere. Once it was the entrance to Peterstadt, a grown-up toy fort built for Grand Duke Peter who, while he waited to succeed his aunt on the throne, channelled his frustrations into a fixation with things military, drilling up to 1500 soldiers within its 12 pointed star-shaped fortifications. As Archbishop Coxe described: 'Everything wore a martial appearance: the hours of morning and evening parade were marked by the firing of cannon; a regular guard was stationed; the troops were taught, under his inspection, the Prussian discipline.' All that remains are ghosts of the earth ramparts. Not content with this fantasy toy, Peter also drilled thousands of toy soldiers in his palace. So obsessed was he that Catherine remembered visiting him, on a rare occasion, after he had courtmartialled and executed a rat for gnawing at his soldiers. He informed her that he intended to leave it hanging for three days as an example.

Whatever Rinaldi thought of his patron, he built him a small but perfectly formed home here. Square, but for a bite out of one corner where the main door enters, the exterior mirrors the interior with its plain lower storey and decorative first floor, with pilasters, niches and fine wrought-iron balustrades. Once servants' quarters, the ground floor now houses an exhibition of the history of Oranienbaum, but is otherwise completely bare. Upstairs a suite of six small rooms leads decoratively from one to the next. They focus on the Picture Hall, where, in the fashion of the time, oils by lesser 17th- and 18th-century west European artists have been disrespectfully cut and reframed to fit the jigsaw that covers the walls. In this particular instance however, the effect is enhanced by lacquered dados, doors and panels, painted in the Chinese idiom by the highly talented serf lacquer master Fyodor Vlasov. It is the oldest lacquer work of its type in the country.

From here, the walk back to the station via the boating pond is all downhill.

Tsarskoye Selo (Царское Цело)

In its pre-Revolutionary heyday, Tsarskoye Selo was *the* place to spend the summer. Since the 18th-century the royal family and their court had periodically decamped *en masse* from the city to imbibe its fresh country air. A nonagenarian who remembers those days explained its charms to me once—the lilac, the walks and the beneficial effects of the place. She ended with the assertion: 'It's high up you see. The altitude of the village is the same as the dome of St Isaac's Cathedral'. To Petersburgers, that is high.

The main attraction for visitors today, apart from the fabled fresh air, is the sparkling Catherine Palace and its landscaped park. Post-war restoration of this Rastrelli masterpiece continues, but plenty of the palace is open to give an idea of the gilded lifestyle led by its inhabitants. Catherine the Great's preferences, as outlined in a letter to the French philosopher Voltaire, hold true for most of the park: 'I love to distraction gardens in the English style, the curving lines, the gentle slopes, ponds like lakes, archipelagos on dry land'.

It is even truer of the neighbouring Alexander Park, which seems like the garden surrounding Sleeping Beauty's castle, 100 years on. Paths, follies and landscaped areas have grown into a nostalgic wilderness, a poignant memorial to the last royal family, who lived in the Alexander Palace under house arrest before they were taken east to their eventual execution in Yekaterinburg. The palace is closed to the public, but if you have the time, exploring the park can take the form of a seriously long walk.

Some confusion may still arise over the name of the town. During the Soviet era, it was renamed twice, first Detskoye Selo, Children's Village, because of the number of orphanages in the town, and later, to mark the centenary of the poet's death, Pushkin, for it was here that he had been educated. Today however, it is once more known as the Tsar's Village, Tsarskoye Selo, though the train station is still called Detskoye Selo. It is best to make the journey on Wed–Sun, as the Catherine Palace and the Lycée are closed on Tues and the last Mon of the month and Pushkin's Dacha is closed on Mon and Tues. If you know you want to see some royal carriages as well, be aware that the Carriage Museum is closed on Tues and Wed. If you plan to visit both the Catherine Palace and Pavlovsk in one day, they are both open on Wed, Sat, Sun and the middle Mondays of the month. On Thursdays, only the state rooms are open at Pavlovsk.

Getting There/Around

Trains leave Vitebsk Station every 20 minutes or so for the half-hour ride to Detskoye Selo. Before embarking take in a little pre-Revolutionary atmosphere at the site of Russia's first railway terminus. In 1837 track was laid from here to Tsarskoye Selo, and a model of the inaugural train which took Tsar Nicholas I and his family to their summer palace stands at the end of the platform. The present station was built in 1904, in pure *Style Moderne*, and its waiting room is painted with murals showing the old stations along the route. If you have time, go in the main triple doors and up the steps, turning right into the Royal Waiting Room (*see* p.434).

At Tsarskoye Selo, either walk 15 minutes (*see* map) or take bus Nos. 370, 378 or 382, all of which drop you near the Catherine Palace and the entrance to the park. Tickets for the park are sold opposite the entrance, and for the palace on its ground floor. Bus Nos. 370 or 280 will take you from Ul. Kominterna, beside the Orangery, to Pavlovsk.

lunch

If it isn't a day for a picnic, there are three or four possibilities around the Catherine Palace and Park. In the palace itself there is the expensive **Café Tsarskoye Selo** (entrance on the road opposite the Lycée) serving cold drinks, tea, coffee and snacks, or a cheap local cafeteria at the far end of the ground floor serving *blini* with a variety of fillings. The Admiralty building on the far side of the lake conceals a **restaurant** in its dark interior. Both service and food have recently improved dramatically (probably under private ownership), but there are no guarantees it will last. There is also a **stand-up café**, serving freshly ground coffee and open sandwiches, in the kitchen gates near the Hermitage building. For a more lavish experience, head for the **Hermitage Restaurant**, Ul. Kominterna 27, ✆ 476 6255, or **Vityaz**, Moskovskaya Ul. 20, ✆ 466 4318 (*open 11am–late*).

Catherine Palace

This site was first stumbled upon by Peter the Great who gave it to his wife Catherine. During her husband's interminable absences fighting Swedes and Turks, she decided to build a cosy summer palace here (as if they didn't already have enough), and used the architect Braunstein, already busy at Peterhof, to execute the building between 1718 and 1724. Peter was reportedly charmed by the love nest, where he and Catherine had a second honeymoon on his return, but soon returned to his own buildings beside his beloved sea.

On Catherine's death, the estate passed to her 19-year-old daughter Elizabeth, who named it in memory of her mother not, as is so often assumed, after Catherine the Great. It was during Elizabeth's reign (1741–61) that the palace took its present shape. Having tried no less than three different architects to achieve what she wanted, in 1752 she decided that Bartolomeo Rastrelli, who had already completed a number of aristocratic palaces and was in the process of building the Smolny Convent for the empress, should be commissioned to start again. In four years, incorporating parts of the earlier buildings, he had built the longest palace in the world and one of the most opulent interiors, securing himself the contract for the Winter Palace in St Petersburg in the meantime.

Catherine the Great, who was the next ruler to leave her mark on the interior, had much more sober tastes than her husband's flirtatious aunt. Her choice of architect, Charles Cameron, was inspired. Cameron was about 37 when he arrived in Russia. He had never built anything before and was never to build anywhere but Russia. His claim to fame was a book entitled the *Baths of the Roman Emperors*, which he published in London after studying the buildings in Rome. Catherine wrote excitedly of her new find—'Scottish by nationality, Jacobite by persuasion'—and of how he had been 'brought up in the Pretender's household in Rome'. In this, it was Cameron himself who was the pretender. Cameron was in fact the son of a London Scot, a master mason, but in order to attract the empress's attention he had insinuated himself into the romantic tale of the Jacobites and their quest to restore a Catholic Stuart to the British throne.

Since the empress liked to conduct her life at Tsarskoye Selo as far as possible away from the public glare, hating ceremony and even fining women who stood up when she walked into the room, Rastrelli's endless succession of state rooms were of little use to her. Cameron was commissioned to turn a number of them into cosy suites, creating a series of Adamesque neoclassical interiors that were completely new to Russia. Most original of all was his bathhouse, the Agate Pavilion. Though

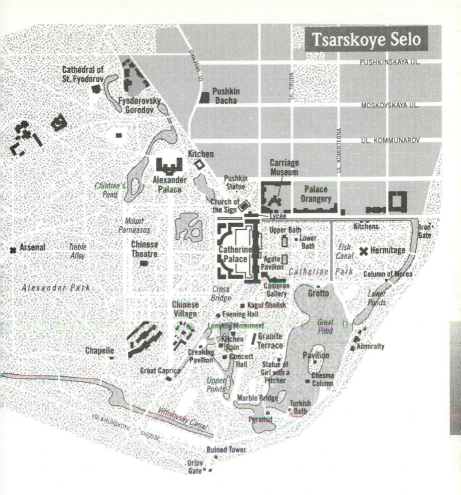

PUSHKINSKAYA UL.

MOSKOVSKAYA UL.

UL. KOMMUNAROV

Cathedral of St. Fyodorov

Pushkin Dacha

Fyodorovsky Gorodov

Kitchen

Carriage Museum

Palace Orangery

Children's Pond

Alexander Palace

Pushkin Statue

Church of the Sign

Lycée

Mount Parnassus

Upper Bath

Lower Bath

Kitchens

Iron Gate

Arsenal

Treble Alley

Chinese Theatre

Catherine Palace

Agate Pavilion

Fish Canal

Hermitage

Catherine Park

Alexander Park

Cross Bridge

Cameron Gallery

Grotto

Column of Morea

Lower Ponds

Chinese Village

Kagul Obelisk

Evening Hall

Great Pond

Lansky Monument

Kitchen Ruin

Granite Terrace

Chapelle

Creaking Pavilion

Concert Hall

Pavilion

Admiralty

Great Caprice

Statue of Girl with a Pitcher

Chesma Column

Upper Ponds

Marble Bridge

Turkish Bath

VOLKHONSKOYE SHOSSE

Vittolovsky Canal

Pyramid

Ruined Tower

Orlov Gate

many of them have been fully restored, few of Cameron's rooms are normally on show, but those you can see stand out as simple and intelligent beside those of the flouncy Rastrelli. Little of the palace was changed after this, so it stands as a monument to these two foreign architects today.

Before paying and entering the park, notice the nearest corner of the palace, crowned by a clutch of five gilded cupolas, each dressed with a cross, rising over the palace chapel beneath. Once in the park precincts, the deep turquoise façade of the palace, with mesmeric white and bronze embellishments unfolds endlessly.

You must stand back to appreciate this 300m symphony of columns, porticoes and windows. As with many of Rastrelli's façades, its success hangs on the rhythm with which these elements are distributed. One astounding feature of the building are the 60 huge figures of Atlas supporting the columns of the upper storey. Both they, the roof and elements of the window decoration were originally gilded in pure gold, dazzling visitors who arrived on sunny days, while the building itself was a greyish green. Catherine the Great who sobered the exterior by having the decorative elements painted bronze, bringing the building down to earth in the process.

The entrance is some two-thirds of the way along the façade. As an independent foreigner you will not be consigned to a group tour but will be able to wander through the palace at leisure (open 10am–6pm; closed Tues and last Mon of the month).

Begin with the **State Staircase**, one of the few rooms redesigned since the 18th century. In 1860 Ippolito Monighetti created this pure white space, decorated only by a collection of Chinese and Japanese plates, vases and pots standing on modelled wall brackets built into the walls. The orange-red curtains, red stair carpet and the ceiling paintings add a further dash of colour. The monogram over the doors, MA, belongs to Maria Alexandrovna, wife of the tsar reigning at the time, Alexander II.

Turning right at the top of the stairs, the next two rooms cover the history and restoration of the palace, with prints and plans of the palace as it was, photos of the destruction wrought by the Nazis and an exhibition of tools and methods used in the restoration.

The first restored room you find yourself in is the largest in the entire palace, the **Great Hall**. Designed by Rastrelli for Elizabeth, its opulence seems entirely fitting for a woman who is said to have owned 15,000 dresses. The hall spans the width of the palace, so that two of its walls are made largely of double sets of windows, ornately embellished with gilding and interspersed with heavily gilded mirrors. The effect is like being inside a crystal box on a glorious sunny day. On the ceiling, set among *trompe l'oeil* architectural details, is a painting of the Triumph of Russia. It is one of the few ceiling works not to have been irreparably damaged, and some of the painting, particularly round the edges, are still the original 18th-century Italian work.

*Beyond the Great Hall lie state rooms and Catherine the Great's chambers, the **Fifth Apartment**. The last set of exquisitely decorated rooms were created for her by Cameron and are said to be his finest work; one is so jewel-like that it became known as the* tabatière, *due to its similarity to the richly encrusted snuff-boxes carried by the aristocracy of the period. Tantalizingly, they are still closed to the public, though restoration of their neoclassical interiors, which also include columns of mauve glass in the bedroom and specially commissioned Wedgwood plaques, is underway.*

Instead the tour now swings round to explore the length of Rastrelli's great **Golden Enfilade,** which leads down the courtyard side of the building. From the windows you can see the single-storey wings in which court officials were housed, built by Savva Chevakinsky, Rastrelli's contemporary and the builder of the palace chapel. Sadly, nothing has yet been made of the garden within their embrace.

In the original palace the only staircase was beyond the Great Hall, so that visitors invited to the court chapel had to walk the entire length of this gilded corridor to get there. The first room they came across was the Knights' (Kavalerskaya) Dining Room, with its massive corner stove covered in Dutch tiles and reaching to the ceiling. Only special dinners, such as those honouring one of the Orders of Knighthood, were held here, illuminated by Rastrelli's great twisting branched wall lights.

Passing through the State Staircase again you come to the **Main Dining Room**, where guests ate between its gold and white walls overlooked, ironically, by a series of monumental German paintings of birds and beasts. The table is laid with the Hunters' dinner service, made in St Petersburg in 1760, of which only 50 pieces are left out of a set of 1000.

Searching for novel interior decoration, in the next two rooms, the Raspberry and the Green Pilaster Rooms, Rastrelli made pilasters from crumpled coloured foil behind glass. Perhaps the least satisfying rooms in the palace, the gilding and the recently woven silk covering the walls are very fine. The corner stove in the red room is covered in delightful Russian 18th-century tiles, each showing a figure in a different native fashion. It also contains a delicate Chinese ivory chess set, while the green room has been decorated with French furniture from the Hermitage.

The **Portrait Hall** contains paintings of all of the women involved in the 18th-century Catherine Palace. On your right as you enter you will find the likeness of Catherine I, wife of Peter the Great. Then comes a portrait of Catherine the Great before her ascent to the throne and a picture of Peter the Great's favourite sister Natalya. Last of all, on the far wall, comes Elizabeth, the patron of Rastrelli, who surveys her palace from a recently made, as yet ungilded, picture frame.

The most famous room was the **Amber Room**, decorated with a number of huge panels made entirely of Persian amber. Peter the Great had fallen for them when visiting Friedrich Wilhelm I of Prussia in 1715, and had dropped such mighty hints that the monarch felt obliged to give him them on his departure. They were used here by Rastrelli in 1755, having been carried by hand all the way from the capital by veteran soldiers, so highly did the empress esteem them. There were not enough to cover the walls entirely, but Rastrelli did his usual trick of dividing them with gilded mirrors and painting imitation amber panels at the top of the room. Today, alas, the entire room is being painted in fake amber, as the whereabouts of the panels has been uncertain since the Germans took them to Königsberg during the Second World War. Rumours claim that they were discovered buried beneath a former Soviet army base in Ordruf in Germany in the autumn of 1991. No move has been made to excavate the panels, and conspiracy theorists even link a number of recent mysterious deaths to the affair. For years it was thought they were hidden deep in a German salt mine, possibly still guarded by descendents of the dwarfs who greeted amazed Allied art experts after the war. Their families had lived and worked in the mine for generations and spoke a medieval form of German. Others insist that the amber was destroyed back in 1945.

After the Amber Room, visitors are swept into the vast magnificence of the **Picture Hall** which is plastered, walls and ceiling, with 17th and 18th-century French, Italian, Dutch and Flemish canvases. No 18th-century Russian palace was thought complete without a hall decorated in this manner, for which paintings were summarily cut to size. Before the Nazi occupation 114 of the 130 pictures were evacuated. During the restoration, paintings were taken from the unseen stores at the Hermitage Museum to fill the gaps. Two masterly Dutch tiled stoves tower up towards the cornice and the opulent swirling pattern of the floor was recreated according to Rastrelli's original design.

The next room, the **Small White Dining Room**, contains a ceiling mural of the Birth of Venus and a breathtakingly intricate inlaid wooden desk, made by one of the serfs of the Sheremetiev family. In the Reception Room of Alexander I, which heralds a series of rooms often used by the emperor and his wife Elizabeth, hang a number of portraits. Alexander I stares out from the far wall as you enter the room, with Catherine the Great opposite him. On the wall to the left of the door is the poor young Alexei, murdered by his father Peter the Great, and opposite his half-sister Anna, mother of Catherine the Great's short-lived husband Peter III.

A couple of small ante-rooms lead on to the beginning of the First Apartment, decorated by Charles Cameron, a test Catherine set him before letting him loose on her own rooms. Sadly, most of the time only the **Green Dining Room** is open to view but it shows the contrast between this style and that of Rastrelli. The powdery green walls are covered in white classical reliefs, sculpted by Ivan Martos and interspersed with pink and white Wedgwood-type plaques and medallions. To suit this more rigid style, even the parquet floor is laid in more formal patterns, and for the first time we find fireplaces and carved marble mantlepieces entering the vocabulary of Russian interior design. When it was only half done, Catherine was already crowing that 'so far only two rooms are finished, and people rush to see them because they have never seen anything like them before. I admit that I have not grown tired of looking at them for the last nine weeks; they are pleasing to the eye'.

If you are allowed further into the apartment, in which Elizabeth, the wife of Alexander I, lived for many years, the highlight is her bedroom, with its forest of porcelain pillars, painted doors and false Wedgwood medallions. Beyond lies the superb, deep blue Baroque chapel designed by Savva Chevakinsky, and its anteroom, the Predkhornaya, whose walls are covered with its original silk wallcovering from Lyon, an extra roll of which had been waiting patiently in the cellars and was luckily evacuated. Hand-embroidered by Russian serfs in the 18th-century, the intricate still lifes took several years to finish. Most likely however, you will find yourself channelled into the rooms decorated in the Russian Empire style for Alexander I by Vasily Stasov.

Created after Alexander's defeat of Napoleon, these rooms are suffused with a martial theme and a sense of empire. The walls of both the **Arched Room** and the **State Study** are made of smoothest *scagliola*, false pink marble, painted with *grisaille* murals of war trophies and allegorical scenes. The furniture here, designed by Stasov specially for the room, has been recently copied from a 19th-century watercolour. The other feature of the room, boldly offset against the pale pink walls, is its plethora of rich green malachite objects.

This begins of the **Small Enfilade**, which runs along the park side of the palace. It has proved impossible to restore the rest of its rooms, as the records are insufficient, so they are used as exhibition space. Furniture and objects from the countless other rooms of the palace include suites of Chinese laquer furniture and an entire room full of oriental carpets, metalware, furniture, a fountain and weaponry.

The exhibition, and the tour of the palace, ends by the State Staircase. Leaving the palace turn right and walk to the Agate Pavilion and the Cameron Gallery, which contains an extensive exhibition of pre-Revolutionary Russian costumes and materials.

Markedly more restrained than the main palace, Cameron's yellow stucco **Agate Pavilion**, studded with niches, sculptures and reliefs, stands on a monumental rusticated ground floor. It contained the Russian Imperial *banya*, the baths, which Catherine, as a conceit, wished the authority on Roman Imperial baths to design for her. She was able to get into them from her private rooms in this wing of the palace, via the so-called Hanging Garden on the first floor above the arches beyond the pavilion. Unfortunately, though the first floor rooms survived the Nazi occupation well, despite being used as an officers' mess, the ground floor baths were used as stabling and have not been restored. The entire building is closed to the public.

*Walk beneath the arches beyond the Agate Pavilion, and down towards the lake with the towering **Cameron Gallery** on your left.*

The long line of decreasing arches behind you was built by Cameron as a gentle ramp so that the Empress, now in her mid 50s, could walk easily in and out of the garden with her favourite greyhounds. Towards the end of her life Catherine, who was tone deaf, admitted that 'the only sounds I recognize are those of my nine dogs… each one of whom… I can recognize by his voice.'

Cunningly using the slope of the land to echo the hilltop position of temples in the ancient world, Cameron built this gallery on a massive foundation of rusticated stone. Courtiers could dine in the glazed gallery on the top floor in bad weather, taking constitutionals on the covered walkways which surrounded it. In summer, these were punctuated by 53 bronze busts, mostly copies of antique sculptures of philosophers and writers in the Hermitage. One of the few contemporaries to feature in this hall of fame was the English Whig parliamentarian Charles James Fox, whom Catherine admired for his spirited opposition to the bellicose Pitt. He did not last long however, for as soon as she heard of his approving views on the French Revolution his bust was consigned to the bin.

Taking the first of the two magnificent staircases at the far end of the gallery, the door between the embrace of the next flight leads into the **Museum of Court Dress** (*open 11am–5pm; closed Mon and Tues*). Here the world which greeted the author of the 1914 Baedeker's Guide, in which 'nearly one-tenth of the male population of St Petersburg wear some kind of uniform, including not only the numerous military officers, but civil officials, and even students, schoolboys, and others comes to life. As well as the official dress of soldiers and sailors, military cadets, pupils at lycées and gymnasiums, officers of the court and police, there are also some civvies—including magnificent women's wedding dresses of fine lace.

Catherine Park

The Catherine Park graphically illustrates the two opposing schools of 18th-century landscape gardening—the formal and the naturalistic. In front of the palace precise beds of black and red arabesque shapes made from chips of lignite and brick, symmetrical ponds, hedges and rows of trees lead into a wilder area of woodland paths around the cross-shaped **Hermitage**. This alluring structure, if you can see it for scaffolding, was built by Rastrelli as a secluded spot in which Elizabeth could entertain small groups to dinner. It is currently closed to visitors. Rastrelli's other garden pavilion, the so-called **Grotto** by the lake's edge, is about as far from most definitions of the word as you can get. The only concessions made to its organic forebears appear high up, where fish heads and sea-gods take the place of acanthus leaves in the 'Corinthian' capitals and mock stalactites drip in place of triglyphs.

The romantic, naturalistic park surrounding the various ponds was created later, by Catherine's English gardener John Bush. It is dotted with monuments, statues and follies, some of which commemorate Russian military and naval successes, others are merely embellishments on the romantic theme. The **Chesma Column** in the middle of the lake, a rostral column in the classical tradition, celebrates the naval victory over the Turks, while the **Column of Morea** celebrates a successful land victory in the same year 1770. A number of the buildings, the Gothic **Admiralty**, the neoclassical **Evening Hall** and the **Marble Bridge**, a copy of the Palladian bridge at Wilton, were designed by V. I. Neyelov and son, whom Catherine sent to England to study landscape architecture. The **Pavilion** on the island, now entirely screened by a stand of mature trees, was built by Quarenghi as a shelter for musicians, who would accompany royal boating outings. You can still hire dinghies from the prettiest of all the follies, the faded apricot and pink Moorish Baths, which was only added in the mid 19th-century.

On the other side of the Great Pond, a wide gravel path and a narrower road are separated by a host of small ponds and pavilions, including a number of buildings in the Chinese style. While in England, V. I. Neyelov and his son would have come across Sir William Chambers, who had visited China, published a book on the *Designs of Chinese Buildings*, and built the ten-storey pagoda in Kew Gardens. They were responsible for the **Creaking Pavilion**, so called after an apparently humorous appreciation of specially designed creaking floorboards, and the **Great Caprice**, a scaled down copy of the vast arch at Fukien, through which ships had been able to pass. The great artificial rock pile of the Caprice, topped by its pagoda-style summerhouse, spans the narrow road.

Not far beyond the road is the Neyelov's once colourful and now wistfully faded **Chinese Village**, an agglomeration of cottages with splayed roofs focused on a central courtyard building. Until the Revolution, courtiers lived here during the summer months while the royal family was in residence. A few of the cottages are still inhabited, though little has been done to restore them to their original form. Seeing a young inhabitant returning home from a re-established military cadet school in the town, wearing a pre-Revolutionary uniform of striped trousers tucked into cossack boots, one wonders whether a reviving sense of history might not bring restoration in its wake.

Alexander Park and Palace

Beyond the Chinese Village you stray into the Alexander Park, with its wooded paths and occasional Gothic buildings (the Arsenal and the Chapelle). Following the Cross Canal past the now overgrown formal area of the park, you arrive at the Children's Pond and beyond it at the **Alexander Palace**. Built by Giacomo Quarenghi on the orders of Catherine the Great, this archetypal Palladian building was given to her much-loved grandson, the future Alexander I, on the occassion of his marriage. Lived in by both Nicholas I and Alexander III, its most famous inhabitants were Nicholas II, Alexandra and their family, who were imprisoned here between the tsar's abdication in March and August 1917, when they were transported not to a port and then to England, as they had been led to believe, but to Siberia, where they lived until they were transported to Yekaterinburg where they were assassinated the following July. Since the war, when the building was badly damaged, it has not been open to the public, and would make for maudlin viewing anyway. The tsar's apartments were on show before the war, complete with the empress's medicine chest and the rose oil left in the icon lamp in the imperial bedroom. Its then director described how 'one had the impression that the people who had lived there had just gone into another room a minute ago.' When he returned to survey the destruction of the Second World War, he swears he met the ghost of the empress wandering through the ruins too.

Lycée and Carriage Museum

Unless you speak Russian, you may want to miss the reverential conducted tours of the **Lycée** where Alexander Pushkin studied for six years (*open 10.30am–4.30pm; closed Tues and last Mon*). He was among the first intake at the school, which began in 1811. As the poet describes it in Eugene Onegin, these were:

> *Days when I came to flower serenely*
> *in lycée gardens long ago...*

Tours begin on the second floor with the Empire-style examination room, and then move on to a semi-circular classroom with built in wooden desks, the music room and the physics laboratory. Fencing masks, accomplished drawings and musical instruments given an idea of the skills a young nobleman was expected to master. Upstairs the long pale corridor of the dormitory is lined with the small rooms of the pupils. Alexander Pushkin's name plate hangs over the door of No. 14. On the first floor, an exhibition sets the Lycée in its social context, with pictures of its more famous pupils and teachers.

The **Carriage Museum**, in the old royal stables, is open 11am–6pm; closed Tues and Wed.

Pushkin's Dacha

Not far from the Alexander Palace, you can visit the delightful, light and airy corner house which Pushkin rented with his wife for the summer of 1831. During that summer, visitors would go into the park on purpose to meet the poet, once it was established that he walked there in the early evening. In the company of Gogol and the poet Zhukovsky, Pushkin passed many an evening of readings and gentle literary banter. An English-language text in each room explains the short but charming exhibition (*open 11am–6pm; closed Mon and Tues*).

On your way to the *dacha*, take a quick look at the statue of the poet (1900) staring off into space seated on a bench in the garden near the **Church of the Sign**. The church is the oldest building in the town (1734), and looks it. Though services are once more conducted here, the building is in a terrible state of disrepair.

There is something about Pavlovsk which exudes, more than any other palace round St Petersburg, a sense of the aspirations of those who created it in the late 18th century. One of the first to undergo restoration after the war, both the palace and the park have been largely recreated, and are even beginning to show signs of maturity again. Paint peels off the façade of the palace, and looking down one of the endless avenues it is hard to believe the devastation wrought on its 150-year-old landscape only 50 years ago, when over 70,000 trees were felled or irreparably damaged. The Slavyanka River, its bridges, woods, pavilions and open meadows are once more an idyllic rural vision, while the interior of the imperious yellow and white palace has once more become an exquisite mixture of Empire grandeur and cosy proportions. Thanks to feverish activity in the months leading up to the Nazi occupation, some 14,000 pieces of furniture and fittings were evacuated, all of which have been returned to their original places, and copied where only one of a set was taken. As a monument to both 18th century Russia and Soviet restoration, Pavlovsk has no equals. The palace is open 10.30am–5.30pm; closed Fri and first Mon of every month. On Thurs only the first floor, containing the state rooms, is on view. If you are going to combine a visit to Pavlovsk and Tsarskoye Selo come on a Wed, Sat, Sun or one of the middle Mondays of the month.

Getting There/Around

It takes 40 minutes to get to Pavlovsk by train from Vitebsk Station. It is the stop after Detskoye Selo, the station for Tsarskoye Selo, and it's either a 15-minute walk or a bus ride from there to the palace. Buses No. 317, 370, 383 and 383a leaving the square in front of the station, going right to drop you at the palace in five minutes. Alternatively walk straight across the road, and buying a ticket at the gate set off straight across the park. Turn right when you can no longer go straight, cross the River Slavyanka on your left and walk up to the palace on the hill. To get to Tsarskoye Selo, take the No. 370 bus from the stop beside the palace, back to the railway station and on. It will drop you a block from the Catherine Palace.

lunch

It is sad that the spirit of faultless reconstruction governing Pavlovsk could allow such a travesty of a **buffet** (буфет) to cower in its south wing. The

Café Slavyanka over the Centaur Bridge (see map) is a great deal better, but in the right weather Pavlovsk's park is crying out for picnickers to settle down on its sloping meadows or to place themselves strategically on one of its silvan perspectives. Try living up to this description of mid-19th century pleasure-seekers 'who resort hither daily in such numbers to enjoy the country, to dine, and to drink punch and champagne'.

The Palace

As Pavlovsk's name suggests, the palace originally belonged to Emperor Paul (Pavel in Russian) and his wife Maria Fyodorovna. Catherine the Great gave them the land, undulating on either side of the lazy bends of the Slavyanka river, to commemorate the birth of their son and heir Alexander, in 1777. It was Paul's talented and energetic German wife who left a greater mark on the place. Once Paul had been given the fortress-like palace at Gatchina in 1784, he preferred to spend his time there, taking out his lust for power on a benighted regiment of soldiers.

There are three architects whose names are linked with Pavlovsk—Charles Cameron, Vincenzo Brenna and Andrei Voronykhin. The initial design belonged to Cameron, who was Catherine's favourite architect and had been 'lent' to her son and daughter-in-law as a double-edged favour. Though he was an inspired architect, he was an arrogant and stubborn man who liked to dictate the look of his buildings, right down to the last door handle. Maria Fyodorovna had strong ideas of her own, while her husband was automatically prejudiced against any favourite of his mother's. When Catherine summoned Cameron to the Crimea in 1786, the palace was habitable but not finished. The young couple took the opportunity to get rid of his services and handed the work to the assistant they had chosen for him, Vincenzo Brenna.

A battle rages in restoration circles as to exactly which interiors should be attributed to Brenna and which to Cameron, though there is no dispute over Brenna's contribution to the structure of the palace. Cameron had designed the central Palladian body and its shallow dome to be flanked by curving single storey wings ending in low pavilions. Brenna not only added a second storey to these, but he continued the embrace of the wings until they almost met to enclose an enormous, partly-arcaded oval courtyard.

In 1803 a fire damaged most of the central section of Pavlovsk. By this time Brenna had left the country and Paul had been murdered. His wife, who retired more and more to Pavlovsk, hired the Stroganov's serf-architect (*see* p.308) Andrei Voronykhin to oversee the restoration, and he continued to work at Pavlovsk until his death in 1814. Having outlived her husband by 27 years and seen two sons crowned emperor, Maria Fyodorovna finally died in 1828. After her death the

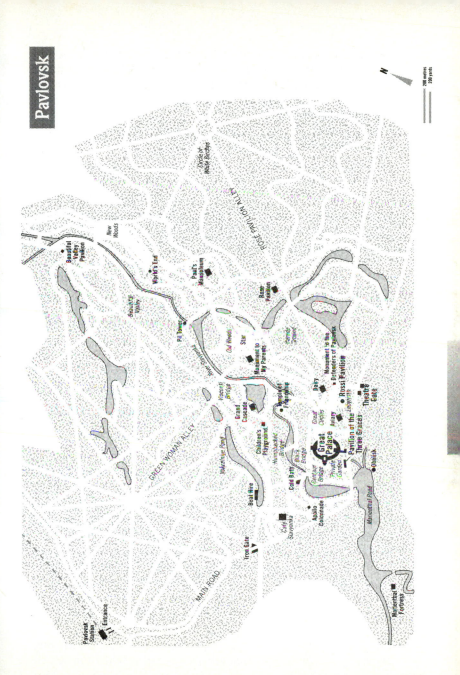

Pavlovsk

N

200 metres
200 yards

Beautiful
Valley
Pavilion

New
Woods

World's End

Paul's
Mausoleum

Circle of
White Birches

ROSE PAVILION ALLEY

Beautiful
Valley

Rose
Pavilion

Pil Tower

Old Woods

Star

Monument to
My Parents

Family
Ground

Slavyanka River

Victory
Bridge

Grand
Cascade

Children's
Playground

Temple of
Friendship

Monument to the
Defenders of Pavlovsk

Dairy

Rossi Pavilion

Humpbacked
Bridge

Great
Circles

Aviary

Theatre
Gate

Cold Bath

Black
Bridge

Centaur
Bridge

Great
Palace

Private
Garden

Pavilion of the
Three Graces

Pavilion of the Labyrinth

Obelisk

GREEN WOMAN ALLEY

Volzatnye Pond

Boat Hire

Café
Slavyanka

Apollo
Colonnade

Marienthal Pond

Front Gate

MAIN ROAD

Pavlovsk
Station

Entrance

Marienthal
Fortress

palace passed to her son Mikhail, who neglected it. The park took on a life of its own however, once the railway had been built in the 1830s and the station building became the most exciting concert hall in the St Petersburg area. For ten years Johann Strauss was the principal conductor, and the public flooded to picnic in the park before and after performances. After the Revolution, Pavlovsk opened as a museum, though Stalin managed to sell a number of its most valuable treasures. In 1957 the first of its restored halls was reopened.

> *Arriving in the embrace of the courtyard, you come face to plinth with a statue of Paul I, a copy of the one at Gatchina placed here in 1872. Tickets are on sale in the pavilion at the centre of the right wing.*

On entering the palace you will find yourself in the **Egyptian Hall** and will immediately be aware of many of the distinguishing features of the palace. Magnificent crystal lanterns hang from an intricate painted ceiling, while a *trompe l'oeil* fresco beneath the stairs creates an extraordinary sense of illusion, both originally created by Giovanni Scotti and recreated, as is all Pavlovsk's complex paintwork, by Anatoly Treskin. The 12 Egyptian sculptures were designed after the 1803 fire by Voronykhin, for Napoleon's 1790s campaign in Egypt had introduced a fashion for the aesthetics of the ancient Egyptians. Above them 12 roundels show the signs of the zodiac on a blue background.

> *Taking the staircase to the first floor, you will find yourself in the state rooms, which centre on the round **Italian Hall**.*

Under the soft natural light of the Pantheon-like dome, the false marble walls are covered in medallions, caryatids, and friezes, but the joy of the room is the Roman statues, copies of Greek originals, which fill the niches. These were too fragile to be evacuated, so in 1941 they were taken down to the vaulted cellars and packed together behind a specially built false wall. The Nazis never discovered them.

To the right of the Italian Hall, through a small dressing room and study, is **Paul's Library**, designed by Brenna in 1790 and divided by a tall arch. Books are relegated to small low bookcases and the walls are divided by tall thin tapestries illustrating La Fontaine's fables and given to the Grand Duke and Duchess by Louis XVI when they visited him in 1782. This trip, made while Cameron was building their palace, was one of the causes of Paul and Maria's quarrel with the architect. He was disgruntled when he heard his patrons were buying quantities of European furniture and objects without consulting him. Brenna on the other hand was quite happy to design a room around fine objects owned by the couple. A number of the ivory and amber objects in this room were turned and decorated by Maria Fyodorovna, who you can see in the full-length portrait. More interesting than the circular temple beneath her portrait is the square one on Paul's large mahogany desk. Like a shrine to the family, Maria painted a cameo of her husband on the pediment, whilst each face of the octagonal altar is adorned with the cipher of herself or one of her children. She even made the twelve ivory columns supporting the desk. The firescreen, also thought to have been painted by Maria Fyodorovna, has a more morbid history. It was behind this that Paul tried to hide from his assassins on the night of his murder in the Mikhailovsky Castle (*see* p.469).

Next to the library is the **Tapestry Room** in which, for the moment, the valuable Gobelins tapestry on the curving wall, from the extremely popular Don Quixote series, is flanked by two Belgian tapestries on the same subject. Restorers at Gatchina are putting immense pressure on Pavlovsk to give them back the French tapestry, since it originally hung with two others in a recently reopened room. However Pavlovsk's own magnificent set of Gobelins, given again by Louis XVI, were sold by Stalin, and as Pavlovsk was one of the earliest restored palaces, they had first choice of suitable antiques to replace gaps in the collection. The highly decorated mahogany writing desk was made in St Petersburg for Paul I, while the gilded furniture came from the workshop of the famous Henri Jacob in Paris.

A suite of three grand rooms at the end of the building looks straight out over the garden to the Apollo Colonnade on the far side of the Slavyanka.

The Halls of War and Peace, flanking the Grecian Hall, were decorated by Brenna in gold and white marble. Contrasting decorative themes are used in each, in the plaster mouldings, gilded door panels and even the ceramic stoves. In the **Hall of War**, shields, armour and weapons celebrate Russia's increasing success on the international battlefield while the eight gutsy bronze torchères are also composed on martial lines. The **Hall of Peace** is contrastingly lyrical, a sea of cornucopias overflowing with fruit, garlands of flowers and musical instruments. The blue vase with bronze chasing is known as the Tsar's Vase.

Between them lies the palatial **Grecian Hall**, surrounded by fluted deep green columns painted to look like grand *verde antico* marble. Designed by Cameron, it is decorated with special wooden, carved gilt furniture by Voronykhin. Two ornate octagonal lanterns light the centre of the room, while between each pillar hang simple marble chandeliers based on the shape of Greek oil lamps. The fireplaces are inset with bronze, lapis lazuli and jasper.

From the Hall of Peace you enter the state suite of Maria Fyodorovna, starting in her Library.

Like the Tapestry Room opposite, its wall is hung with a French tapestry. Much of the furniture, which stands on a busy parquet floor, was designed by Voronykhin, including the magnificent chair behind the desk, whose back supports are shaped like cornucopias to hold the flowers which the empress so loved. The desk was made by David Roentgen, the Prussian furniture maker who had so impressed

Catherine the Great with his gift of an incredible mechanical cabinet that he became the *ne plus ultra* of cabinet makers at the late 18th-century Russian court.

Next you find yourself in the empress's narrow, highly decorated **Boudoir**. The floor is inlaid in a complicated arabesque design to mirror the painted ceiling. As many as 50 different shades of wood might be used by Russian marquetry craftsmen, including material imported from every continent of the globe. The pilasters are painted with a series of patterns copied from Raphael's Loggia in the Vatican, and the grand porticoed fireplace is laden with jaspar and porphyry objects. The harp-backed chairs are part of the set made for Paul's library by Voronykhin.

The **Empress's Bedroom** was designed by Brenna, though not to be slept in: Versailles was responsible for the absurd concept of the state bedroom, which the Russians took to even greater excess. The bed and other pieces of furniture were made in Paris specially for this room by the Jacob studio. The exquisite Sèvres toilet set was commissioned by Marie Antoinette for her friend Maria Fyodorovna who on seeing it remarked that it was so fine it must be for the French queen herself, being too short sighted to notice her own cipher all over it. Its 64 pieces include cups with portraits of the doomed French king and queen as well as eye-baths and numerous pots for potions. Furniture in the **Empress's Dressing Room** was made by the Tula metalworkers, whose fame traditionally rested on their weaponry but who, at the end of the 18th century, began to make this delicate furniture as well.

*Leaving the empress's suite turn right into the curved **Picture Gallery**, built by Brenna in 1797 as a grand corridor leading to the Throne Room.*

The collection of mediocre 17th- and 18th-century European paintings, acquired by the royal couple on their tour of Europe, is not as interesting as the handsome brown porphyry bases which are amongst the earliest to have been carved from the newly discovered veins in the Ural Mountains.

The **Throne Room** is impossibly grand, and its restored ceiling is actually closer to what Brenna envisaged than the plain white surface that went before. By a stroke of luck Soviet researchers found part of the original design, by the brilliant theatrical designer Pietro di Gottardo Gonzaga, which had been eradicated over 100 years earlier. The principal restoration painter, Anatoly Treskin, steeped himself in Gonzaga's work in order to reinvent the missing three-quarters of the ceiling, creating a tottering edifice of crumbling architecture reaching to the open sky. The only furniture in the room are three tables loaded with dinner services. In the centre is an 18th-century French creation known as the Paris Service, while the rest is the St Petersburg Gold Dinner Service, made in the early 19th century.

Beyond the Throne Room, Paul asked Brenna to add a room known as the Hall of the Knights, in which he could entertain in his newly-found position of protector of the Knights of St John of Malta. Since his youth, Paul had been fascinated by the antiquated chivalry of this crusading order and, as it faced expulsion from Malta, he gave the order temporary sanctuary though his Orthodoxy prevented full personal membership. On his death it faced inevitable eclipse. Against the pale green walls with their white plaster reliefs are Roman copies of Greek original sculptures. You will also be able to peer into the palace chapel beyond, from the royal balcony.

Returning to the staircase, the tour continues downstairs, in the marginally less opulent private living quarters of the royal family.

The first room is the so-called **Raspberry Room**, Paul's private study dominated by views of his favourite park at Gatchina by Shchedrin. The General Study, with its portraits, was where the family used to gather. A number of the amber and ivory objects were made by Maria Fyodorovna, as were some of the miniatures in Paul's New Study next door. Above them hangs the group family portrait, with their daughter Olga, who died at the age of three, represented by a bust. The startlingly different **Corner Drawing Room** was an early design by Carlo Rossi in 1803. Rossi's time was to come under Maria Fyodorovna's son Alexander I who, perhaps mindful of this simple yet powerful and dignified mauve and yellow silk creation, chose him to give architectural voice to Russia's moment of triumph over Napoleon. Rossi also designed the furniture, made from Karelian birch, whose distinctive patina derives from its slow tortuous growth in the permafrost. Cameron designed the simple white and green **Dining Room**, though the frieze and cornice were redesigned by Voronykhin after the fire of 1803. This room, opening straight out onto the sloping lawn, was always popular, and it was here that Maria Fyodorovna chose to entertain her guests, who included many of the musical and literary luminaries of St Petersburg. The Dowager Empress was also known for her good works; with extraordinary foresight she not only did as her predecessors had done, setting up orphanages, schools and hospitals, but in the town of Pavlovsk she set up inoculation programmes and the first school for the deaf and dumb.

The corner **Billiard Room**, long ago deprived of its billiard but not its card tables, is adorned with 12 18th-century Venetian copies of Canaletto. The neighbouring Old Drawing Room is hung with three more tapestries given to the royal couple by the ill-fated Louis XVI. This time, they belong to the New Indies series, showing the fecund exoticism of the flora and fauna of newly 'discovered' lands. The four paintings by Hubert Robert in the small **Ballroom** were specially commissioned from the highly fashionable French painter for Pavlovsk. The rest of the room is as it was when Cameron designed it, a blue and pink bower with gilded ranches running along the frieze and up onto the ceiling.

The main tour of the palace ends here, since the suite of rooms on the ground floor of the southern wing are currently under repair. However on the second floor you will find an exhibition of 19th-century Russian domestic interiors, while in the southern wing of the palace, through a separate entrance from the courtyard, temporary exhibitions from the museum's collection are also shown.

The Park

The creation of Pavlovsk Park, which at the end of the 18th century was twice the size of Central Park and the largest landscaped area in the world, was undertaken by successive architects at the palace under the direction of Maria Fyodorovna. Unfounded suggestions that Capability Brown, the paramount English designer, was responsible for the overall plan merely attest to its success, greatly helped by the natural charm of the undulating landscape. The more formal areas around the palace were planned by Cameron and Brenna, while it was the stage designer and muralist Gonzaga who had the more profound effect on the outer reaches of the park, in the early 19th century. Seeing the landscape as a series of interlinking canvases, Gonzaga became more and more involved in judiciously pruning, felling and planting trees so that they became like brush strokes on his landscape. As visitors walked through the park, he felt that every so often an entirely new, perfect and yet natural-looking view should open up. The Italian was a genius with form and artifice, and his *trompe l'oeil* arcade beneath the Rossi Library, now barely visible, was so successful that dogs were known to run straight into the wall hoping to get into the room beyond. He orchestrated a number of elaborate *fêtes champêtres* for Maria Fyodorovna, including one to celebrate the triumphant return of her son Alexander I after the war with Napoleon. But his most extraordinary performance took place in 1798, when for three hours he entertained the royal family with an endless series of changing theatrical sets on an otherwise empty stage.

Apart from commissioning some 37 monuments in the park, Maria Fyodorovna's role seems to have been that of plantsman, sending seeds back from Europe, ordering bulbs from Holland and England and trees from Finland and the Baltic states. Her fame as a connoisseur was such that George III sent her 126 exotic species from Kew Gardens, with their own personal gardener.

The **Private Garden** by the palace is separated from the rest by a wrought-iron fence and can only be visited from the palace. Its formal beds were designed by Cameron, who was also called back to the palace in 1800 to complete the garden with the addition of the **Pavilion of the Three Graces**. The statue by Triscorni which it shelters, in homage to Canova, shows Joy, Flowering and Brilliance stretching to hold a vase aloft. During the 1941 evacuation, the statue was buried nearby at a depth of five metres by a team of women. When the Nazis arrived, they noticed that the earth was disturbed and dug down three metres before deciding that the Russians were just trying to waste their time.

Looking from the palace, two pavilions divide the space to the right of the Triple Lime Alley. First comes Cameron's romantic **Aviary**, draped in vines. Royal parties would eat here to the accompaniment of birdsong. Beyond it and surrounded by a labyrinth is the **Rossi Pavilion**, which though designed by Rossi was only erected in 1914 to house a statue of Maria Fyodorovna. The alley culminates in a **Monument to the Defenders of Pavlovsk**, all those people who lost their lives clearing the park of mines after the war. Many of them were adolescent girls, who did their work barefoot in warm weather, the better to feel the mines. In the morning they would set off merrily to work, singing and whistling, but in the evening, inevitably, they came back quiet, carrying a dead or wounded colleague on their stretcher.

Beyond the monument the **Rose Pavilion** is being rebuilt to Voronykhin's original plans, hopefully including the Aeolian harps which were built into the window frames, allowing the wind to play music to the assembled company. Beyond it one of Gonzaga's most ambitious pieces of landscaping, the **Circle of White Birches**, was replanted after the war and is now thriving. Closer to the monument is the rustic looking **Dairy**, with its tiled inner sanctum. In Maria Fyodorovna's day there was always a samovar of cold fresh milk awaiting passers-by. The Old Woods and New Woods on the banks of the Slavyanka are dotted with monuments erected by Maria Fyodorovna to her parents and to her husband, as well as a single column known as World's End. The star at the centre of the Old Woods is presided over by bronze statues of Apollo and the Muses. Back towards the palace from the Dairy, the **Great Circles** were laid out by Brenna, who also built the long staircase sweeping down towards the river. The sculptures at the centre of the formal parterre represent Peace, with a lion, and Justice, brandishing a sword.

Some of the most accessible park architecture sits on the banks of the Slavyanka close to the palace. Both the **Apollo Colonnade** and the **Temple of Friendship** were designed by Cameron, while the Visconti and the Centaur Bridges were built by Voronykhin. With its towering sculpture of Apollo and the tumbled down cascade beneath it, the colonnade was perfected by nature in 1817, when a landslide took part of the round portico with it, leaving the structure in a state of romantic ruin. It was Maria Fyodorovna's good judgement that it should not be repaired. The monumental round Temple of Friendship was the first building Cameron erected in the park, in 1782. Both Maria Fyodorovna and Paul intended the beautiful Doric building as a thank-you to Catherine the Great, for lending them her architect, and hoped that its theme might encourage a rapprochement between mother and son. However Catherine seems to have been oblivious to the intentions, and though she admired the building she thought it rather dark inside.

Forty-five kilometres southwest of St Petersburg, Gatchina is the furthest and least-visited of all the restored royal palace estates. With its fortress-like exterior, it has been associated with the military since Grand Duke Paul, emperor-in-waiting, took out his frustration drilling a private army of 2000 soldiers here in the late 18th century. After the Nazi destruction of the palace, the building was shored up and occupied by the Soviet military who did little to help the fabric of the building. They were finally dislodged in 1977, though there are still barracks in the neighbourhood. Restoration of the enormous and rather forbidding structure, containing a total of 500 rooms, began at once, but so far only 7 rooms have opened to the public, though a handful of others are nearing completion. *Open 11am–6pm; closed Mon and first Tues of the month.*

Gatchina's park is vast and delightfully dishevelled, with paths weaving between its Silver, White and Black Lakes. Its principal designers were a pair of Englishmen, who went by the fitting names of Mr Bush and Mr Sparrow. Two garden pavillions to look out for are both on or near the White Lake. The round Temple of Venus, on the Island of Venus, is sometimes used as a venue for summer concerts. Above it, not far from the Dubok Café is the deceptive Birch Cabin (Beryozovy Domik). Behind a classical portico stands what looks like an enormous pile of logs with a door in it. Once inside you find yourself in a room almost as grand as those in the palace.

Getting There/Around

Hourly trains leave Baltic Station (Baltisky Vokzal) for Gatchina. The palace is five minutes' walk down an avenue of trees behind the station building. The town of Gatchina lies on the far side of the park, beyond the Dubok Café, and is served by a No. 26 minibus which runs to and from Ⓜ Moskovskaya on Moskovsky Prospekt.

lunch

The only place to eat on the estate is at the Dubok Café, a dark building in the park dwarfed by oak trees. To get there take the bridge between the Black and Silver Lakes (to the right as you look from the palace out over the garden), walk past a green wooden building and up through the trees past a series of dry ponds. The food is well-prepared and tasty, and just as hearty as you would expect from a country inn. Ask for the speciality *myasa*

Gatchini, a tender piece of beef in a kind of Stroganoff sauce. *Open 12 noon–11pm; closed 5–6pm.* In summer the only problem with picnicing is the difficult choice of exactly which idyllic rural view you are going to enjoy while you eat.

Sitting on the banks of Black Lake, the village of Khotchino was first mentioned in the 15th century. After Peter the Great created St Petersburg, he granted the obscure farmstead, now known as Gatchina, to his favourite sister Natalya. In the 1760s Catherine the Great bought it for her lover Grigory Orlov, who was delighted with its rural setting, surrounded by good hunting ground and a considerable distance from the ceremony and intrigues of the court. On a high bluff above Silver Lake, he commissioned Antonio Rinaldi, author of Catherine's Chinese Palace at Oranienbaum, to build him a castle in the European idiom, far removed from the brick and stucco, porticoed buildings that had become the Russian norm. Rinaldi, who had worked on similar buildings in Italy, and studied English castles during his travels, created an austere central block from local yellowish limestone, broken only by slim pilasters and rectangular windows and ornamented on two corners by towers. Curving single-storey arcades ran on either side of the building to kitchen and stable blocks.

The building was completed in 1781, two years before the death of Orlov, whereupon Catherine bought it back from his family for one and a half million roubles and gave it to her 30-year-old son and heir Paul. He usually hated any place associated with his mother's lovers; but though Orlov had killed Paul's father, he had always been careful to treat Paul with sympathy and to spend time with the lonely young man. Paul fell immediately for the solid charms of Gatchina. By the time he had established his own mini-empire on the estate, guarded by sentries and shot through with militarism, Paul felt the palace was not grand enough to serve as the royal palace, and brought the Florentine architect Vincenzo Brenna over from his palace at Pavlovsk. As well as adding a second storey to the curved wings of the palace and a third to the central block, Brenna also raised the height of the two towers and dug a moat round the building, adding to its feudal feel. Inside, rooms decorated with Rococo flourishes by Rinaldi, fine for the empress' lover Orlov, were not considered serious enough for her heir, and Brenna redecorated many in the weighty self-important style of Imperial Rome. Sadly Gatchina drove Paul further from his loyal wife, Maria Fyodorovna, who loved Pavlovsk, the palace they had created together, better.

Apart from Alexander III, Paul's successors were not keen on Gatchina, though Nicholas I commissioned new building on the wings and a new suite of living rooms in the right-hand wing (as you look at the palace from the train station). It was here that Alexander III and his family, including the last tsar, came to live immediately after the assassination of his father had thrust him onto the throne. Alexander III, an arch-reactionary, was terrified of the revolutionary elements which he felt were running wild in society, and felt secure behind the quasi-fortified walls of Gatchina. For the first two years of his reign he lived here almost continuously, venturing to St Petersburg only for official receptions and balls, and could be seen dressed like a peasant, stalking deer with his children in the park, chopping wood and shovelling snow.

Only the 18th-century state rooms of the palace are currently open to the public, and most of what you see dates to Brenna's redecoration, though glimpses of Rinaldi's decorative touch are visible in most rooms too.

Arriving at the great, brooding palace from the train station, you find yourself dwarfed in its gravel courtyard.

Here, Paul used to drill his troops, with the aid of a cane with a watch embedded in its handle. His two-thousand strong private army were dressed in Prussian uniforms and wigs, so that with the European-looking castle in the background visitors often remarked that Paul's Gatchina felt nothing like Russia. A snub-nosed sculpture of the monarch surveys his domain to this day. On the ground floor, Gatchina's famous collection of weaponry is once again displayed in one of the curving wings, with pistols, swords and rifles describing elaborate patterns on the walls, including the Russian 'П', which stands for Paul (Pavel in Russian).

If you are lucky you may be allowed to visit the long underground tunnel which runs from the castle to a grotto on the edge of Silver Lake. Use was famously made of it by the Prime Minister of the provisional government in 1917, Alexander Kerensky, who escaped to Gatchina from the Winter Palace on the night of the October Revolution, only to avoid a revolutionary mob here six days later by fleeing down the corridor disguised as a sailor. Kerensky, who initially fled to France, was still teaching at Stanford University in the 1960s. In the lake at the end of the corridor, the first Russian submarine, which held just one man, was tested in 1879.

The rest of the rooms which have been restored are the state rooms used by Paul and his family on the first floor.

At the top of the stairs you enter the empty green and white space of the **Anteroom** in which guests would sit waiting a summons from Paul. The military symbolism of the reliefs on the walls and the ceiling were added by Brenna, for it was in this room that the Emperor's guard changed daily. However the floors and doors, consistently impressive throughout the palace, are the work, or rather the designs, of Rinaldi, executed again during the post-war restoration. In their task, Gatchina's restorers were greatly helped by an intricate series of watercolours of the interiors executed by Luigi Premazzi and Edward Hau in the 1870s and early 1880s.

A small lobby off the Anteroom aquaints you with images of the palace's two creative spirits—Rinaldi and Brenna—to personalize the competitive harmony between their two styles which seems embodied in the place.

To the left of the Anteroom the geometric world of Imperial Rome is evoked in the **Dining Room**, with its pairs of white Carrara marble columns topped by full Corinthian capitals and classical reliefs. Everything, including the stern doors and floor, was designed by Brenna to provide a suitable environment for Paul's serious pre-parade breakfasts. The cooks would bring the dishes from the kitchen and lay them out behind the low marble balustrade, now occupied by a statue of Eros. From here guards bore the dishes to their boss in a time-honoured and pompous ritual. Musicians played from the area round the balustrade and if anyone made a slip, woe betide them. Paul's punishments were summary and brutal. On a bad day an officer could be exiled to Siberia for wearing his hat at the wrong angle.

Also looking out over the palace garden to the lake is **Paul's Throne Room**, rather small considering the emperor's pretentions, but heavily gilded to make up for its size. Brenna designed the room around three of the many French tapesteries which Louis XVI had presented to the Grand Prince in Paris in 1782. Opposite one another are portrayals of the animals and people of Asia, and over the mantlepiece, itself set with semi-precious stones, the fertility goddess Ceres represents summer. Notice how the swags in the tapestery have been continued on in the relief decoration in the rest of the room, and how the motif of the dog is repeated in the clock beneath. Of the furniture, the Empire-style table with its top made of one piece of stone from Urals stands out. The most recent room to be opened is the **Raspberry Parlour**, whose name and decor depend on the magnificent French tapestries which adorn its walls. In 1782 Louis XIV gave Paul and Maria Fyodorovna three tapestries from a cycle illustrating Don Quixote, all of which originally hung here. Probably the most valuable Gobelins in Russia, they were evacuated before the war, but so far only two have been returned, causing internecine war in the normally respectful conservation world. The third hangs in the library at Paul's other palace Pavlovsk, whose own tapestries were sold by Stalin's government in 1929–30 and are now in the Getty Museum in California. Maria Fyodorovna's Throne Room is also sometimes known as the Picture Hall, for obvious reasons. An imperial dictat from her husband ruled that while his throne could rest on a platform with three or eight steps, hers must be no more than a single step off the ground.

The last room is the **White Ball Room**, the largest in the palace with an exceptional toffee-coloured floor. Beneath its floral patterns, the restorers have used the grain of the wood and its variety of tones to give an illusion of depth to the surface. Rinaldi's scagliola architraves and the plaster high-reliefs over the doors are boldly exuberant, as is his moulding round the ceiling, while Brenna's relief-strewn walls work to calm the room down. Together, their work is the embodiment of the transition between Baroque and neoclassicism—here classical pilasters are surrounded by swags and other Baroque details. Over the fireplace, further weight is given to Brenna's classicism by a number of antique reliefs, incorporated into the walls. The largest depicts the Emperor Vespasian making an offering at a temple; while the relief of a shepherd to the left of the fireplace dates from the 1st century AD.

> *The last part of the tour of the palace takes place on the second floor, which was turned into exhibition rooms as early as the 1880s.*

The second room contains portraits of a number of Gatchina's inhabitants. Grigory Orlov is resplendent in a foppish pink embroidered silk top, beside his mistress the Empress Catherine who often visited him here, calling him her 'Gatchina landlord'. On the second wall you will find Paul's wife, Maria Fyodorovna, surrounded by their three surviving daughters.

In the third room you can get acquainted with the family of Nicholas I. His favourite daughter Alexandra, who died of tuberculosis, lives on in a posthumous portrait which shows her in a white lacy dress holding a pink rose. In the background you can see the Alexander Palace at Tsarskoye Selo where she died. Highlights from the rest include marble relief portraits of Catherine the Great and snub-nosed Paul by Marie Collot, and a room of art inspired by or made specially for Gatchina, including a magnificent bureau inlaid with views of the palace. The doll, called Pandora, gives a clue as to how St Petersburg's first ladies kept abreast of European fashions in the 18th century. It was one of many sent to Maria Fyodorovna from the couture houses of Paris, modelling a dress which she could then order if she liked it. The entire transaction was carried out by post.

Food and Drink

The outside world gets a confused picture of the Russians and their food. The Japanese even made a diplomatic *faux pas* over it, initially citing the fatness of the average Russian as a reason for refusing the country food aid in 1992. The queues outside the shops, tales of meagre supplies and the *matrioshka*-shaped matriarchs simply don't add up, until you realize that an unhealthy 70% of the average Russian diet comes from starch and sugar. Cholesterol is taken to be an eccentric western obssession, odes are written on the virtues of *sala*, pure pork fat, few people believe that vodka could possibly be fattening, and once you reach 40 it is thought perfectly healthy to put on a couple of stone. This cultural climate, combined with the geographical one, adds up to an unhealthy diet.

Intourist, the former tourism monopolists provided barely adequate meals for the groups of foreigners they herded through the country, and certainly left no room for choice. Christopher Hope described the restaurant scene in Moscow in 1990 as 'the unspendable in pursuit of the inedible'.

He wouldn't know the place today. You can eat Georgian or Korean, cheaply or at great expense, quickly or at leisure, with or without music. In four years at least a hundred new restaurants have opened in the capital, and dozens in St Petersburg; with careful planning you need not eat a bad meal in either city, but to expect this dramatic improvement to be universally cheap would be too much.

Restaurants

It was the legalization of co-operative restaurants in 1986 that began the surge in good food outside the home in the Soviet Union. Now there are private restaurants as well, serving everything from Japanese to Italian (and some of the best Russian) cuisine. A few of these are difficult to book tables in, and in the case of the less commercial establishments it can be hard deciphering the menu when you get there, though it is well worth the effort. Ignore the fact that many of them are called 'café'—the word for a place which majors in coffee is normally *kofeinaya*.

If you are not feeling adventurous you will fall victim to over-priced hotel restaurants. In the new joint ventures these offer world-class imported sea-food, the very best in Russian *nouvelle cuisine* and American steak-house fare. Lesser hotels still have mediocre 'soviet'-style restaurants for the nostalgic, and often rent out space to private restaurants too. A number of the huge state restaurants lumber on, serving a well-worn combination of a Russian menu, a 'live' band and a more or less tasteful floor-show. Where groups of ordinary folk would once spin out an evening amid a growing forest of bottles to celebrate a birthday or anniversary, today only tourists and the hoods and *biznissmeny* of the new Russia can afford it.

Fast food and genuine cafés tend to be listed, where appropriate, in the walks. Some of their signs are instantly familiar—McDonald's and Pizza Hut—others have to be carefully deciphered. Look out for those advertising the following: блинная, serving sweet and savoury *blini* (pancakes); пельменная, offering *pelmeni* (meaty dumplings with a dollop of sour cream or tomato sauce); плржковая, with its stock of meat and vegetable-filled pasties; or мороженое, where welcome Russian ice-cream is dispensed.

CHAI

In both cities new restaurants are still opening, so for a full and up-to-date list you should get hold of the latest edition of the *Travellers' Yellow Pages*. Those listed below are a personal selection.

Russian, Caucasian and Central Asian Food and Menus

Despite the poverty of the Russian diet, exacerbated during the Soviet period by a piecemeal distribution system across a neglected network of roads, the Russians certainly know how to eat. A birthday celebration entails months of saving up sugar, meat, fish and alcohol, found at cheap prices earlier in the year, and turning it all into a traditional four-course feast, which also serves as the basis for menus in Russian restaurants. First come the *zakuski*: cold meats and fishes, caviar, cheese, salads and pickles, warm pancakes and mushrooms baked in sour cream. For centuries foreigners have been caught out thinking that this is the whole meal, indulging to the hilt and then being faced with soup, a main course accompanied by potatoes, and a pudding. The secret, tried and tested in the long dark northern winters, is to take your time, a practice at which the Russians are masters.

Within the ex-Soviet Union, the Georgians were renowned for their hospitality and the profusion of their feasts. True to this reputation, a lot of the very best food in Moscow and St. Petersburg is served in Georgian restaurants. While the menu follows the same basic four-course form, the *zakuski* are more elaborate, involving spicy aubergine and sheep and goats cheese; soups are mutton and bean based, and often highly spiced. Meat, particularly poultry, is set off by sauces made with nuts and coriander, or stuffed with rice into peppers and vine leaves, and puddings are laced with nuts and honey. The Central Asian republics of the former Soviet Union also have their restaurants, a mixed bunch at best, distinguished by quantity rather than quality of *plov* (a rice, meat and vegetable paella) and *shashliki*, kebabs.

A full list of items you are likely to find on restaurant menus can be found in Language (*see* pp.574–6). If you are offered any of the following do not refuse.

Russian delicacies: *gribi so smetanoy* (mushrooms in sour cream), *blini s'ikroy* (pancakes and caviar), *okroshka* (cold summer vegetable soup made with *kvas*, a fermented bread drink), good *borshch* (beetroot soup), *kulebiaka* (salmon pie), *pelmeni* (meat dumplings) and *pirozhki* (pies—often cabbage or, ideally, mushroom).

Georgian delicacies: *khachapuri* (cheesy bread), *satsivi* (walnut and coriander sauce), *khinkali*, (juicy meat dumplings with a spicy tomato sauce), and any *zakuska* with *baklazhan* (aubergine).

Prices

Now that the dollar economy has been outlawed, you only need stacks of roubles and a credit card to take full advantage of the cities' restaurants, though most of them will happily change dollar bills for you. If you are booking a table, ask how they accept payment and whether you need a passport to corroborate your credit card.

Prices range from outrageous to ludicrously little, the balance gradually tipping away from the latter as Moscow, in particular, continues its meteoric rise to become one of the most expensive capitals for business trips in the world. The price categories below apply to three- or four- course evening meals (depending whether you are eating from a western or Russian menu) with alcohol, per head.

very expensive	over $70
expensive	over $40
moderate	over $20

inexpensive	over $10
cheap	under $10

Reserving Tables and Opening Hours

Always make a reservation for the evening. Even if the restaurant is not full you may be turned away without one. You should also reserve tables in the more popular places for lunch. Many restaurants only accept evening reservations from noon on the day. Where booking policy is even more idiosyncratic it is spelled out below. The majority of places are open from about noon to midnight, with an hour's break somewhere between 4 and 6pm. Again, only variations on this are noted below.

tipping

Many restaurants now add a 10–20% service charge to their bills, leaving it for you to decide if the service merited something on top. If a service charge is not included, good service should be generously rewarded.

Vegetarians

It is not easy avoiding meat and fish in Russia, and to be certain that flesh doesn't pass your lips you will be restricted to a monotonous diet of bread, tomato and cucumber salads and mushrooms in sour cream. What is billed as *salat* never has a lettuce leaf in it, and *stolichny salat* is a concoction of potatoes, mayonnaise and chicken. Almost all soups, except summer *okroshka*, are based on a meat stock, and only in the most expensive restaurants will you find an alternative vegetarian main course. Two pieces of advice: choose Georgian restaurants and concentrate on their vegetable *zakuski*, and visit the cities in summer when vegetables are more plentiful and you can buy raspberries and other fruits on the street. Those who eat fish will be better off. *Bliny* with caviar and pickled herring are offered as *zakuski*, and there is usually a fish main course, often sturgeon, to follow.

Bars

Despite their reputation for drinking, Russian bar culture is surprisingly undeveloped. In winter, the search for oblivion takes place at home, round the kitchen table, and in summer cans of beer and bottles are consumed on park benches and in other open spaces. Bars are either stygian dumps where regulars bring their own fold-up milk cartons to drink from, or hotel piano bars serving French champagne at some $100 a bottle. At the former (normally signed **БАР** or **РЮМОЧНАЯ**) cozy, vinous friendships often lurch rapidly into punch throwing, and the only women to be found are haggard alcoholics. Unless you're with a local, these haunts are probably best avoided, except by novelists researching a Dostoyevskian opus.

Recently, a number of better-quality watering holes have opened up, independent of the hotels. The list below concentrates on these, and highlights the better hotel bars, though you will find somewhere to drink in all of the cities' hotels.

What to Drink?

Vodka (*see* p.76) is nothing like as exclusive as you might think. As well as the 'little water', you will regularly be offered Russian and imported beer, wines from Georgia and Moldova, Armenian and Azerbaijani co sweet wines known as *portvein* and a colourful host of imported liqueu recent glut of Amaretto flooded the streets, no doubt spawning a host of pote dangerous imitators. Be very wary if you buy on the street or in kiosks—mer morality is non-existant and lethal home-made spirits (*samogon*) find their into bottles, disguised behind innocuous labels. Buy familiar brands, check tops are secure and look through the bottle to see how the label has been stuck . Straight, horizontal lines of glue tend to mean factory production. More ela ate patterns should be avoided. Another obvious tell-tale sign is Spanish wine bels on bottles with plastic (*i.e.* Georgian or Russian) tops.

Long before the vine found commercial purchase on French soil, it grew on the cpes of the Caucasus, and the Georgian wines can be lelicious. Discard the prevailing western prejudice for dry wines, since the most rounded Georgian wines are ich, red and semi-sweet— look out for *Kindzmarauli*, with its deep velvety fruit, or *Akhasheni* which is less ric but much easier to find. The former holds the dubious dis inction of being known as Stalin's favourite. Of Georgia's dry table wine the white *Tsinandali* is drinkable and oaky, while *Mukuzani*, *Na areuli* and *Saperavi* are all dependable reds, the latter slightly roughe . Russian, or Soviet champagne as it is still often labelled, is reac ly available and cheap. It comes brut (*brut*), dry (*sukhoye*), sem -dry (*polu-sukhoye*), semi-sweet (*polu-sladkoye*) and sweet (*slaa oye*). Stick to the first two or three, and don't expect finest Eperr ay at these prices.

No drinking session is complete wit out a handful of Russian toasts. Give full rein to wishful think ng and sentimentality and you will get along fine. The most cc nmon toast is a simple *Na Zdaroviye*, 'your good health', which given the amount you are likely to drink is only the shad wiest of a hope.

Moscow

Restaurants and bars are listed under geographical headings, with restaurants sub-divided into categories by price. Central Moscow includes anywhere on or inside the bulvar ring. Other regions comprise West and Southwest Moscow (from Novy Arbat southwest to the river, including Kutuzovsky Prospekt and Kievsky Vokzal); Northwest Moscow (from Novy Arbat to and including Ul. Tverskaya); Northern Moscow (from Ul. Tverskaya to and including Ul. Sretenka and Prospekt Mira); Northeast Moscow (from Prospekt Mira to the Yauza River); Beyond the Yauza River (around Ploshchad Taganskaya) and Beyond the Moskva River (the southern reaches of the city). A list of central breakfast haunts is provided for those who missed it in their hotel but can't contemplate sight-seeing on an empty stomach.

Breakfast

Metropol Zal, Metropol Hotel, ✆ 927 6000. A vast breakfast buffet, from which you could construct a five-course breakfast, lies waiting beneath the mosaic splendour of this echoing dining hall ($25) *Open 7–11.*   Ⓜ Ploshchad Revolutsii

Paradise, Moskva Hotel, entrance on Okhotny Ryad opposite beginning of Ul. Pushkinskaya, ✆ 292 2030 or 924 8083, Run by a returned emigré, this Euro-Russian restaurant opens early enough to offer a hearty breakfast if you don't fancy paying Metropol prices. *Open from 10am.*   Ⓜ Teatralnaya

Bufet, Hotel Rossiya. Enter from Ul. Varvarka, take lift to 12th floor, turn left at desk and walk to end of corridor for a cheaper breakfast and a spectacular view of the Kremlin. If you can face it you could wolf down cold sausage, cheese and bread, or stick to coffee, tea and a cake. *Open from 10am.*   Ⓜ Kitai Gorod

Hotel Intourist, Ul. Tverskaya 3/5, offers the choice of a snack in its ground floor café/bar or a full breakfast in the Aztec Restaurant on Floor 20 (*from 5am*).

Ⓜ Okhotny Ryad

Café La Cantina, Ul. Tverskaya 5, ✆ 926 3684, next to the Intourist Hotel. Serves an American breakfast from 8am–12 noon.

Central Moscow

Restaurants

very expensive

Savoy, Savoy Hotel, Ul. Rozhdestvenka 3, ✆ 929 8600. The chef in this period-piece restaurant, complete with gilded walls and mirrors and frescoed ceilings, prepares menus which Tsar Nicholas II would recognize, including one served at his coronation in 1896. The sky is the limit where à la carte bills are concerned, but there is a cheaper set menu.   Ⓜ Kuznetsky Most

Lobster Grill, Metropol Hotel, entrance on Teatralnaya Proyezd 1/4, ✆ 927 6068. For seafood that isn't even fresh, this is a lot to pay, though the cooking is certainly exotic—chilled strawberry soup and lobster Thermidore enhanced by a magician who wanders between the white linen table cloths. Ⓜ Teatralnaya

expensive

Teatro Restaurant, Metropol Hotel, entrance as above, ✆ 927 6739. Almost indistinguishable from a large early-80s upper East-Side Italian restaurant, or something in Covent Garden a little later, right down to the shade of apricot. The simpler you choose the better—their salads and grilled meats are excellent, and the ambience is up-beat and lively without being noisy.

Ⓜ Teatralnaya

Tokyo, Hotel Rossiya, Red Square entrance, ✆ 298 5707. Serves heavenly Japanese food between its bamboo screens. Treat yourselves to *teppan-yaki*, where the Japanese-trained Russian chefs cook everything from starters to vegetables and rice on the flat grill in front of you. A small warning—only order squid if you like masticating. Ⓜ Kitai Gorod

Manhattan Express, Hotel Rossiya, Red Square entrance, ✆ 298 5355/54/53. From 7pm you can eat New York style at this fashionable night club.

Ⓜ Kitai Gorod

Stanislavskovo 2, Ul. Stanislavskovo 2, ✆ 291 8689. A small restaurant serving what used to be the best Russian food in the city, the major problem here is booking a table. The female owners like to keep the place exclusive and are reluctant to give a table to newcomers. Get a Russian to book for you at 6pm precisely on the evening you want to go. Since prices have recently rocketed and the food is said to have gone downhill, it is not quite so worthwhile. If you do get in and its the right time of year, indulge in the mushroom and barley soup. Ⓜ Arbatskaya

El Rincon Espagnol, Hotel Moskva, Manezhnaya Ploshchad entrance, ✆ 292 2893/0294. Intimate low-ceilinged Spanish restaurant tucked into a tiny corner of the gargantuan hotel. Service is good, the Spanish guitar-playing unobtrusive, the house wines tasty and by Moscow standards not too expensive. The tapas are better than the main courses, and come in rather larger than tapas portions. Ⓜ Okhotny Ryad

Aztec Restaurant, Hotel Intourist, Floor 20, Tverskaya Ul. 35, ✆ 956 8489. You can always get a drink and something to eat, 24 hours a day, at this cosy and popular venue right in the centre of the city. Ⓜ Okhotny Ryad

Ristorante Artistico, Kamergersky Pereulok 6/3 (opposite Moscow Arts Theatre), ✆ 292 4042 or 203 6865. Small, candle-lit Italian restaurant—pleasant but no great culinary surprises. Ⓜ Okhotny Ryad

Arkadia, Teatralnya Proezd 3 (down side alley opposite Hotel Metropole), ✆ 926 9008 or 426 9545. Serves traditional Russian food with a smattering of Caucasian dishes such as *lobio* and *dolma*, and plenty of it. The *zakuski*, including fish and caviar of various sorts, are better than the main courses. A good jazz band allows guests to talk easily above the music and dance gently on the small floor. From Thursday to Sunday the jazz gets serious after midnight, when drink and music are available until 5am to anyone paying the reasonable entry fee. Ⓜ Lubianka

Iveria, Ul. Rozhdestvenka 5/7, ✆ 928 2672. Central, welcoming and offers a good Georgian menu and wine list. The *khachapuri* is particularly cheesy, and the aubergine dishes well cooked. Ⓜ Kuznetsky Most

MB, Ul. Nemirovich-Danchenko 3, ✆ 292 9731. One of the lastest oriental additions to Moscow's restaurants, a very central Indian restaurant with an excellent tandoori oven and all the raita, nana and chutneys you could want to accompany your curry. Keep your cool with beer or soft drinks. Ⓜ Pushkinskaya

Panda, Tverskoy Bulvar 3/5, ✆ 298 6565 or 202 8313. Chinese restaurant using imported ingredients where necessary to produce food you would recognize from any provincial Chinese joint back home. They also accept take-away orders and offer a number of cheaper set lunches. Ⓜ Arbatskaya

Bwiloye, Ul. Petrovka 16, ✆ 262 0985. The name means 'the past', and the past it refers to is the Communist past. This strange commie-decorated capitalist joint dresses up its menu with jokes for the Sovietophile and hopes you are still laughing loud enough to swallow the bill.

Patio Pizza, Ul. Volkhonka 13a, ✆ 201 5000. Serves delicious wood-baked pizzas in its atrium-restaurant, plus a fresh and loaded salad bar. Ⓜ Kropotkinskays

Aragvi, Ul. Tverskaya 6, ✆ 299 3762. One of the props of the tourist circuit for years, this massive Georgian restaurant has long been surpassed in culinary terms but still offers rowdy dining and entertainment in its Marble Hall, frescoed with scenes from ancient Georgia. Avoid the tough *shashliks* and opt instead for Georgian specialities like chicken *satsivi*, with its walnut and coriander sauce and *lobio*, spicy baked beans. Ⓜ Pushkinskaya

Luchnik, Ul. Maroseika 6/8, ✆ 928 0056, offers a cheap and very Russian lunch of soup and a thin piece of indeterminate meat with a salad. By night the place transforms into a restaurant with a show, for which you must book. Agree in advance how much you want to pay per head and sit back and wait for the baked *pelmeni*, crab dishes, cold trout paté with raisin sauce and chilled Russian champagne—the big meal on offer is very, very big. Ⓜ Kitai Gorod

Pizza Hut, Ul. Tverskaya 12, ✆ 229 2031. The take-away slices are life-savers for those in a hurry and you know what to expect in the restaurant itself. Don't come here for the salad bar—you'll be disappointed. Stick to old favourites like garlic bread and pizza. **Ⓜ** Pushkinskaya

cheap

Tsentralny, Ul. Tverskaya 10, ✆ 229 0241, gives a taste of what dining in a run-of-the-mill Soviet restaurant used to be like. Major on *zakuski* and do without the main courses. **Ⓜ** Pushkinskaya

Bars

Restaurant Rossiya, Hotel Rossiya, Ul. Varvarka 6. The ultimate Moscow room with a view is this 21st floor restaurant overlooking the Kremlin. Explain that you don't want to eat and order beer, vodka or champagne. Pity the windows never get cleaned. **Ⓜ** Kitai Gorod

The News Pub, disguised by a hairdressers' sign at Ul. Petrovka 18, ✆ 921 1238/1585. Resembles an affluent 80s winebar and offers racks of foreign papers, from the International Herald Tribune to Private Eye. Try to get one of the comfortable tables in the quieter rooms at the back of the place, unless you want to be blasted by music, often mediocre jazz. *Open 12 noon–2am.* **Ⓜ** Teatralnaya

Rosie O'Grady's, Ul. Znamenka 9, ✆ 203 9087. An Irish bar complete with Guinness and Killian's on tap, rural prints on the walls, darts, crisps, toasties and other pub food. *Open 12 noon–1am.* **Ⓜ** Borovitskaya

Moscow News Bar, Ul. Tverskaya 16/2, Pushkinskaya Ploshchad, ✆ 209 0507. In the Moscow News building, this cheap bar is usually crowded out by journalists from Russia's Fleet Street outside. **Ⓜ** Pushkinskaya

La Cantina, Ul. Tverskaya 5, ✆ 926 3684. Has a long and lively bar where beer and wine are chased by nachos and guacamole. **Ⓜ** Okhotny Ryad

Lobby Bar, Metropol Hotel, Teatralny Proyezd. While the Artists' Bar tucked away at the back of the hotel fails to pull the punters, this hub is ever full of tourists and businessmen drinking round the horseshoe bar or at nearby tables. **Ⓜ** Ploshchad Revolutsii

Hermitage, Savoy Hotel, Ul. Rozhdestvenka 3, ✆ 929 8577, is a glittering bar serving drinks, tea and coffee and bar food, at a price. It was a very surprising location for the mafia hit that took place here in May 1993. But don't worry, it couldn't happen twice. **Ⓜ** Kuznetsky Most

Restaurants

expensive

Olimp, Luzhnetskaya Naberezhnaya, behind Lenin stadium, ℘ 201 0148. Looking like something out of Hicksville with its low-slung bungalow and coloured lights, this obscure co-op delivers good Russian and Central Asian food, plentiful alcohol and music to dance to after the show. Enthusiasm among the punters makes for a swinging evening.   Ⓜ Sportivnaya

Grand Imperial, Ul. Ryleeva 9, ℘ 291 6063. Velvet upholstered Empire chairs and double-headed eagles might make for elegant dining, but the Russian food isn't up to it. The different vodkas on offer are impressive, though.

Ⓜ Kropotkinskaya

Glazur, Smolensky Bulvar 12, ℘ 248 4438 or ℘/℘ 230 2319. Part-Danish restaurant serving excellent European and Russian food. Try the *baklazhany zarevshan*, an Armenian dish of aubergine, carrots, onions and garlic to start with, and then some pork. The live music varies from jazz and Russian folk to classical.   Ⓜ Smolenskaya

Tren Mos Restaurant, Komsomolsky Prospekt 21, ℘ 245 1216 or 203 2548. One of the old American favourites serving food as homely as apple pie. Try the *chili con carne* with sour cream and corn chips or the steak with jalapeno sauce, and then blow out on peanut-butter ice-cream, sliced banana and chocolate sauce with rum. *Open 12–5pm, 7–11pm.*   Ⓜ Park Kultury

Kropotkinskaya 36, Ul. Prechistenka 36, ℘ 201 7500. This was Moscow's first co-operative restaurant, started by the flamboyant capitalist Andrei Fyodoroff who now has a restaurant in New York State as well. Upstairs the decor is minimal to the point of coldness. The basement is much cosier. How they get away with charging $29 for a little caviar when you can buy a pound of the fresh stuff for less beats me, though luckily the sublimely fluffy *blinis* also come with cheaper salmon roe (red caviar). The soups, particularly the *borsch*, are excellent, and of the main dishes the spit-roasted fish and the suckling pig are both winners and come with a refreshing heap of vegetables.

Ⓜ Park Kultury

moderate

Bar Ristorante Italia, Ul. Arbat 49, ℘ 241 4342. Has the squeaky clean interior of a fast food joint, and a popular area of outdoor tables in summer. Though the place is under Italian managership and the menu is undoubtedly Italian, the food just doesn't quite taste Italian. A good selection of Italian wines and ice-creams make up for it.   Ⓜ Smolenskaya

U Pirosmani, Novodevichy Proyezd 4, ✆ 247 1926. Rumours of a price hike in this popular Georgian restaurant, named after the influential Georgian naive painter Niko Pirosmani, might take it into the expensive bracket, but with a view over the Novodevichy Monastery, good service and spicy food it's hard to resist. Order a selection of *zakuski* which may well be enough, washed down with Georgian wine. If not there are meaty main courses, delicious homebaked pastries and coffees to top it off.   Ⓜ Sportivnaya

Tren Mos Bistro, Ul. Ostozhenka 1/9, entrance on bulvar, ✆ 202 5722. Red and white check tablecloths and cheery waiters decorate this Italo-American joint where pasta comes highly recommended.   Ⓜ Kropotkinskaya

cheap

Guria, Komsomolsky Prospekt 7, ✆ 246 0378. A no reservations policy means that a formidable queue can develop outside this good value Georgian restaurant, and you'll have to have an early dinner to catch it before it closes. Private booths resound with the laughter of Caucasian groups tucking into *kharcho* and *khachapuri, lobio, pkhali, shashlik* and salad. Bear in mind that dishes begin to run out towards the end of the day. It's a bit scruffy for your maiden aunt but loaded with southern atmosphere. *Open 10am–8pm.*   Ⓜ Park Kultury.

Russky Traktir, Ul. Arbat 42, serves ordinary Russian food. The charm of this deceptively small hole in the wall lies in its nocturnal opening hours—*12 noon–5 am.*   Ⓜ Arbatskaya

Bars

Shamrock Bar, Ul. Novy Arbat 19, ✆ 291 7641. One of the first foreign-owned bars in the city, next to the Irish House supermarket, this lively Hibernian spot is still the place to be on St Patrick's Day, 17 March. *Open 12 noon–12 midnight.*   Ⓜ Arbatskaya

Tren Mos Bar, Ul. Ostozhenka 1/9, ✆ 202 3540, is a favourite American haunt where the drink is expensive and the free salted popcorn sees that you have a healthy thirst. Intimate and friendly with excellent bar food. *Open Mon–Fri 5pm–1am, Sat and Sun 3pm–1am.*   Ⓜ Kropotkinskaya

El Rincon Don Quixote, Kutuzovsky Prospekt 7/4, ✆ 297 4757, is located off the courtyard car park of the massive foreigners' ghetto at this address. Head towards the left of the courtyard and you'll see the entrance into the basement where you can wash down tapas with Spanish beer and wine.

Restaurants

very expensive

Yakor, Palace Hotel, Ul. Tverskaya Yamskaya 19, ✆ 956 3152. A strictly expense-account seafood restaurant where the ingredients are flown in, some fresh, from the US and France, and where you can choose to look out onto the busy street or in to the equally hectic kitchen. As well as predictable lobster bisque and mixed seafood grill, there are also specialities inspired by local dishes such as *kulebiaka*, a melt-in-the-mouth fish pie, not to mention the creamy puddings. ⓜ Belorusskaya

Royale, The Hippodrome, Ul. Begovaya 22, ✆ 945 1963/1854/7404. From the stable that brought you Kropotkinskaya 36 comes this upmarket casino/restaurant in the neo-classical building attached to Moscow's racing course. Russian food, including bread and *blini* like they used to make them, is combined with the freshest fish, meat, fruit and vegetables to make a lavish spread. Dress up. ⓜ Begovaya

expensive

American Bar and Grill, 1-aya Tverskaya-Yamskaya Ul. 32/1, ✆ 251 7999. Offers plain homestyle cooking 24 hours a day. ⓜ Mayakovskaya

Arlecchino, Ul. Druzhinnikovskaya 15, ✆ 205 7088. Ingredients driven all the way from Italy lend the authentic taste to this haven for pasta lovers. Obviously a good place to come after a showing at the Kino Centre in the same building. ⓜ Krasnopresnenskaya

Santa Fe, Ul. Mantulinskaya 5/1, Korp. 6, ✆ 256 1487/2126. Decorated with the mud-wall and swing-door look of the Mexican desert, this restaurant serves fast helpings of Tex-Mex food to its ritzy young clientèle. ⓜ Ul. 1905 Goda

moderate

Livan, Ul. Tverskaya 24, ✆ 299 8506. Shares a building with the Azeri Baku restaurant and provides excellent Middle Eastern food—hummus with pine-nuts, *falafel, tabuleh*, spicy salads, various kebabs and *bakhlava*. There is usually one room where you can sit in relative peace, away from the loud, semi-naked floor show. ⓜ Mayakovskaya

Delhi, Ul. Krasnaya Presnya 23B. Moscow's most well-established Indian eatery has a refined, expensive room with Indian dancing and credit card prices (✆ 255 0492), plus a huge rouble room (✆ 252 1766) where locals can enjoy the 'family' floor show, featuring contortionists, fire-eaters and other magicians. ⓜ Krasnopresnenskaya

Writers' Union Restaurant, 50 Ul. Povarskaya, ✆ 291 2169/1515. Still tries to insist on a members only policy, but try your luck. Its speciality is *pelmeni* but the *zakuski*, including crab, potato pancakes and *pirozhki* are good too. The room itself, which Tolstoy used as the headquarters of the Moscow freemasons in *War and Peace*, takes some beating, with its vast fireplace, mosaic decoration and Bechstein piano. In summer you can take advantage of the kitchen via the outdoor kiosks and cluster of tables, where groceries, drink, delicious cakes and ordinary sandwiches are on sale. *Open 12 noon–last orders at 9.30.* Ⓜ Barrikadnaya

Jam Club, Ul. Zholtovskovo 7, ✆ 299 4547. Across Patriarch's Pond from the well-known Café Margarita this tiny eatery, is a vital, if bizarre, late night option. The menu is hard to decipher as it comes in code. Order Stendhal's Scarlet and Black for salmon and sturgeon caviar, Griboyedov Soup for mushroom soup and in summer steamed fresh-water crayfish, *raki. Evenings only, open till 3am.* Ⓜ Mayakovskaya

Peking, Hotel Peking, Ul. Bolshaya Sadovaya 1/2, ✆ 209 2124/2456, has such a tendency to charge too much for its Russo-Chinese (with an emphasis on the Russo-) food it really isn't worth trying. The floor show in the soaring, imitation laquer hall is utterly middle-of-the-road. Ⓜ Mayakovskaya

inexpensive

Moskovskiye Zory, Maly Kozikhinsky Pereulok 11, ✆ 299 5725. Choose between the welcoming panelled interior or the outside garden at this small co-op restaurant whose Russian food, though not exciting, is always presented with friendly attention. Champagne, imported beer and Georgian wine usually available. Ⓜ Mayakovskaya

Café Margarita, Ul. Malaya Bronnaya 28, ✆ 299 6534 (reservations recommended). It's hard to linger long in this tiny, convivial restaurant where the service verges on express and the evening jazz drowns out conversation. The menu is short but faithful, with stuffed tomatoes, soups and Russian mushroom stews among the perennial favourites. *Open from 2pm.* Ⓜ Mayakovskaya

Northern Moscow

Restaurants

expensive

La Cipollo d'Oro, Ul. Gilyarovskovo 39, ✆ 281 8906. A delightful breath of Italian air in northern Moscow. A la carte takes prices into this bracket, though the menu of the day brings the bill down a notch. Pasta of course, is a mainstay of the menu, but the grilled meats, particularly the sausages, are better.

Ⓜ Prospekt Mira

Sapporo, Prospekt Mira 14, ℗ 207 0198/7093, ✆ 207 7869. Ousted from its position as Moscow's best Japanese restaurant by Tokyo, Sapporo still offers a good if expensive meal and the city's only karaoke room. Ⓜ Sukharevskaya

moderate

Pescatore-90, Prospekt Mira 36, ℗ 280 2406/3582. Busy trattoria for those times when all the bones in your body are crying out for pasta. If you choose from the entrées as well, your meal will probably jump into the expensive bracket.
Ⓜ Prospekt Mira

Kolkhida, Sadovaya-Samotyochnaya 6, Stroyenie 2, ℗ 299 6757. A Georgian restaurant which has not sunk into apathy, safe in the knowledge that hundreds of rich foreigners live in the nearby block. It sings and dances for its roubles, and excels in mutton dishes and the juicy *khinkali*, meat-filled dumplings, which you must order in advance. Bring your own alcohol. Ⓜ Tsvetnoy Bulvar

inexpensive

Moosh, Ul. Oktyabrskaya 2/4, ℗ 284 3670. A must for Armenians and sympathizers with the fate of this embattled nation. The food is acceptable but it is the chance of a display of expatriate Armenian nostalgia, which of course includes singing and dancing, that makes the trip worthwhile. Ⓜ Rizhskaya

cheap

Kombi's, Prospekt Mira 46/48, ℗ 280 6402. One of a chain of American-style delis for a quick and filling pit-stop. Milkshakes or freshly-squeezed OJ wash down sandwiches and cheesecake. Ⓜ Prospekt Mira

Northeast Moscow

Restaurants

very expensive

Sirena, Ul. Bolshaya Spasskaya 15, ℗ 208 1412. So many of Moscow's expensive restaurants are not worth the bill, that you may need your faith restoring in this wood-panelled restaurant or, in summer, in its vine-covered courtyard. Try the smoked chicken roll with apricot sauce and fresh fruits to start and follow with giant shrimp from the Russian far east. Ⓜ Sukharveskaya

moderate

Don Quixote, Pokrovsky Bulvar 4/17, ℗ 297 4757 is, surprise, surprise, Spanish. Located in a building full of foreign firms, its clientèle tends to follow suit. Wallow in the strange luxury of simple Spanish peasant food, *gazpacho* and *tortilla*, followed by *paella*, while you put back pitchers of *sangria*. The lunchtime menu even more reasonable. Ⓜ Chistiye Prudy

Razgulyai, Ul. Staraya Basmannaya 11, ✆ 267 7613, offers straightforward Russian food and a good selection of alcohol in its vaulted basement rooms, one painted the blue and white of Gzhel pottery, the other red and gold like *khokhloma* painted wooden spoons. The gypsy singers are fun and extravagant, the service attentive without being fussy. **Ⓜ** Baumanskaya

Bars

Jack's Piano Bar, Leningradskaya Hotel, Ul. Kalanchovskaya 21/40, ✆ 975 1967. Attached to the Casino Moscow, this cheap bar is one of the most convenient late night drinking haunts in the city. *Open 8pm–5am.*

Beyond the Yauza River

Restaurants

expensive

Moscow Commercial Club, Ul. Bolshaya Kommunisticheskaya 2A, ✆ 271 0707, offers a pair of restaurants, Russian and European, neither of which is really worth the prices charged. If you happen to be nearby, the three-course lunch special is good value however. **Ⓜ** Taganskaya

Skazka, Tovarishchevsky Pereulok 1, ✆ 271 0998. Friendly, cosy candle-lit interior with authentic, almost home-style Russian food, including *pelmeni*, mushroom noodle soup and good home-baked puddings. **Ⓜ** Taganskaya

moderate

Taganka Café, Zemlyanoy Val 76, ✆ 272 7320. A café downstairs with a restaurant above. After the *zakuski* put some exellence in your tummy in the form of baked *pelmeni*. Attached to the eponymous theatre, this place attracts a healthy late-night crowd. **Ⓜ** Taganskaya

cheap

Café Union, Bernikov Pereulok 2/6, ✆ 227 2805. A quasi-American joint offering chef's salad, frankfurters and chocolate brownies.

Bars

U Petra, Zemlyanoy Val 72, ✆ 298 3248, is a lively basement dive with dancing, and entertainment which often includes a stripper.

Restaurants

very expensive

Le Romanoff, Baltschug Kempinski Hotel, Ul. Balchuga 1, ℗ 230 6500, has an imaginative chef who in the course of his research has blended traditional Russian ingredients in an ingenious late 20th-century menu. For a real celebration come here and be waited on hand and foot. The wine list is superb—choose carefully to accompany such delicacies as salad of warm venison, prawns in a caviar and Pernod sauce and duck with pomegranate. Ⓜ Novokuznetskaya

expensive

Baltschug, Baltschug Kempinski Hotel, Ul Balchuga 1, ℗ 230 6500. The alternative to Le Romanoff is a menu offering imaginative Russian variations like beetroot roulade stuffed with mushrooms or a groaning buffet table laden with European and Russian starters, cold meats and salads, hot dishes, sumptuous puddings and cornucopias of fruit.

Atrium, Leninsky Prospekt 44, ℗ 137 3008. Undergoing restoration when last tried, this unlikely Imperial Roman interior is hidden beneath a huge apartment block. Look out for the pedimented entrance, dwarfed by the rest of the building. Familiar Russian soups (*staromoskovsky*—mushroom with meat) and stews with a few twists. Try the delicious cheese baked with herbs and the smoked pork. Ⓜ Leninsky Prospekt and a few stops by bus or trolleybus

Seoul Plaza, Serpukhovsky Val 14, ℗ 254 0303. With a largely Korean staff, and a menu in Korean, English and photographs, you are in good hands. Settle down and enjoy the food grilled at your table, accompanied by dips, garlic and onion, salad, rice and noodles, or plump for a stew-like soup instead. Ask to see the additional menu otherwise your options are reduced. Ⓜ Tulskaya

Danilovsky, Danilovsky Hotel Complex, Bolshoy Stary Danilov Pereulok 5, ℗ 954 0566. The restaurant in this monastery hotel offers a long, exotic menu including many old Russian dishes and even *kvas*, a refreshing slightly fermented drink made from bread that used to be readily available in summer. Use this opportunity to taste baked Russian dishes such as the rich *pelmeni* with sour cream, chicken with apricots and beef stew. Ⓜ Tulskaya

moderate

Lazagna, Ul. Pyatnitskaya 40, ℗ 231 1085. If you inadvertently order the overpriced bread and home-made juice this mock-Italian venture, with its tomato salad and wide choice of pasta dishes, might slip up into the expensive category. Dining is elegant and quiet by night and in summer you can eat outside on the terrace—both rarities in Moscow. Ⓜ Novokuznetskaya

Traktir Zamoskvarechye, Ul. Bolshaya Polyanka 54, ✆ 230 7333. Good, plain Russian fayre in this dark basement is better at night than by day, when the darkness can seem dismal. The menu seems to be universally well-cooked, offering fluffy *bliny* and a filling potato and mushroom casserole. The ubiquitous meat stew *zharkoe* distinguishes itself with its bread pie-crust.

U Babushki, Ul. Bolshaya Ordynka 42/44, ✆ 230 2797 or 239 1484. Book well in advance to get a table at this bright, clean establishment in the evening. Swift yet unostentatious service makes a delightful change and the food is exquisite. Try any herring (*seld*) dish or the soups, pies (*pirozhki*) or *pelmeni*, and leave room for a delicate pudding. Probably the best value Russian food in the city.

St Petersburg

Here restaurants and bars are divided into five regional lists. In the main part of the city south of the Neva they are split between those inside the Fontanka River, and those beyond it. The rest of the city divides into Vasilievsky Island, the Petrograd Side and the Islands, and the Vyborg Side.

Breakfast

Angleterre, Astoria Hotel, Isaakiyevskaya Ploshchad (entrance closest to St Isaac's Cathedral). Offers an all-you-can-eat buffet, including delicious *aladi* pancakes. *Open from 7.30.* Ⓜ Sennaya Ploshchad

Café/Bar, Astoria Hotel, Isaakiyevskaya Ploshchad (entrance furthest from St Isaac's Cathedral). For those whose breakfast appetite barely stretches beyond an espresso or cappucino. Ⓜ Sennaya Ploshchad

Evropeisky Restaurant, Grand Hotel Europe, Ul. Mikhailovskaya 1/7. Serves a much more expensive buffet breakfast in its elegant hall. *Open 7–10 Mon–Sat; jazz brunch Sun 12–3.* Ⓜ Nevsky Prospekt

Pevchesky Mostik, Naberezhnaya Reki Moyki 26. Excellently situated just off Palace Square, this café makes a good cheap breakfast alternative for the later riser. Choose from tea and coffee, soft drinks, pastries, biscuits and open sandwiches. *Open 10–10.* Ⓜ Nevsky Prospekt

Inside the Fontanka

Restaurants

very expensive

Evropeisky Restaurant, Grand Hotel Europe, Ul. Mikhailovskaya 1/7, ✆ 312 0072, is reckoned to be the best in town by those who can afford it. Proceedings are very formal beneath the towering glass ceiling of its Art Nouveau dining room, the service exemplary, the fillet of salmon stuffed with cream cheese melt-in-the-mouth. *Open 6–11pm, Sun 12–3 for an extravagant champagne and jazz brunch.* Ⓜ Nevsky Prospekt

Dvorianskoye Gnezdo, Ul. Dekabristov 21, ☎ 312 3205. To make a real night of it, try this new restaurant in a restored garden pavilion. The food and surroundings are reputed to be outstanding. Ⓜ Sennaya Ploshchad

Restaurant St Petersburg, Kanal Griboyedova 5, ☎ 314 49 47. A spotless tourist restaurant, with an unusually imaginative menu and a historic (and histrionic) cabaret from 7pm, followed by Russian folk music. Candle-light helps to disguise the artificiality of the wooden-boothed intimacy. Well-behaved staff, but very touristy. *Open 12–5, 7–2.* Ⓜ Nevsky Prospekt

expensive

Brasserie, Grand Hotel Europe, Ul. Mikhailovskaya 1/7, ☎ 312 0072, serves good continental brasserie food, from steaks and hamburgers, to seafood and pasta. *Open 11–11, Sun 3–11.* Ⓜ Nevsky Prospekt

Chopsticks, Grand Hotel Europe, Ul. Mikhailovskaya 1/7, ☎ 312 0072, serves the best Chinese food in the city, and by far the most expensive, prepared by the Hong Kong-trained chef. *Open daily 12–12.* Ⓜ Nevsky Prospekt

Tandoor, Voznesensky Prospekt 2, ☎ 312 3886, is a brand new Indian restaurant in the centre of town, a godsend for vegetarians, which specializes in tandoori-cooked dishes. *Open 12 noon–11pm.* Ⓜ Nevsky Prospekt

Bistro Le Français, Ul. Galernaya 20, ☎ 315 2465. Smallish Parisian-style bistro with red checked tablecloths, a bar and mouth-watering French food.
Ⓜ Nevsky Prospekt

moderate

Restaurant Na Fontanke, Naberezhnaya Reki Fontanki 77, ☎ 310 2547. Icy blue bordello-style swathes of material decorate St Petersburg's first co-operative restaurant, which opened in 1988. The menu is extensive, and generally good. Try cold *borshch* in summer, hot in winter, followed by beef Stroganov or delicious *pelmeni*. Quiet piano at lunchtime is replaced by a floorshow of folk dancing and singing and then something with a few less clothes in the evening. *Open 1–5, 7.30–11.30.* Ⓜ Sennaya Ploshchad

1001 Nights, Millionaya Ul. 21/6 (entrance on Zaporozhsky Pereulok), ☎ 312 2265/314 5266. A fun Uzbek restaurant which serves belly-dancers and snake charmers with your *plov* and *manti*.

Nevsky 40, Nevsky Prospect 40. Two restaurants in this German establishment serve the same microwave menu, but for aesthetics choose the recently restored turn-of-the-century chinoiserie tea room, with its fine silk embroidered panels of birds. Bizarre menu stretches itself too wide, with herring and sauerkraut competing with Malaysian *nasi goreng*, and tastes of nothing much as a result. *Open 12 noon–12 midnight.* Ⓜ Gostiny Dvor

Metropol, Ul. Sadovaya 22, ✆ 310 1845. If you must have a Soviet nostalgia trip do it here, in the oldest restaurant in the city, which first opened its doors in 1898. Stick to *zakuski* and be warned, you can't talk when the music gets going. Ⓜ Gostiny Dvor

Senat Bar, Galernaya Ul. 1–3, ✆ 314 9253. A cavernous basement joint with low lighting, decorated with freshly commissioned paintings of the 18th-century city and plaster busts. Mostly a drinking haunt; there is a small restaurant although eating here feels rather claustrophobic. *Open 11am–5am.*

Winter Garden, Astoria Hotel, Isaakiyevskaya Ploshchad (entrance furthest from Cathedral), ✆ 311 4206. There is an old-world charm about this conservatory restaurant, where a grand piano tinkles in the background and traditional Russian food is served on pre-war plates. A great place to while away the afternoon over buttery *blini*, *borshch* and beef Stroganoff. Ⓜ Sennaya Ploshchad

Literaturnoye Café, Nevsky Prospekt 18, ✆ 312 6057/8543, is ideal for those who like rowing with waiters. Whether by surly service or over-charging, they are sure to infuriate you in their frilly shirts and 19th-century frock-coats. Only the endless wave of tourists, drawn by the fact that Pushkin set out for his fatal duel from a completely different establishment on this spot, allows them to get away with it. Saving graces? Delicate metal tree chandeliers and live classical music downstairs. *Open 12 noon–4.30pm, 7–11pm.* Ⓜ Nevsky Prospekt

Assambleya, Ul. Bolshaya Konyushennaya 13, ✆ 314 1537, serves good and unpretentious Russian food in its coldly decorated interior. *Open 24 hours.*
Ⓜ Nevsky Prospekt

inexpensive

Chaika, Kanal Griboyedova 14, ✆ 312 4631, is a German pub serving cold beer and snack food. *Open 11am–3am.* Ⓜ Nevsky Prospekt

Sadko, Grand Hotel Europe, Ul. Mikhailovskaya 1/7, ✆ 119 6000 ext 6390, has a simple blackboard menu which changes daily, offering a choice of three dishes for each course. By day the view of life on Nevsky Prospekt, just a pane of glass away, cannot be bettered. In the evenings they have live music and the joint gets considerably more lively. *Open 11am–2pm.* Ⓜ Nevsky Prospekt

01, Ul. Karavannaya 7, is a tiny restaurant serving plentiful food and alcohol. Soups and stews are particularly recommended, often laced with the southern flavour of coriander. Gets full and you can't reserve, so you just have to try your luck. Afternoon and early evening are best. *Open 12 noon–4pm, 5–11pm.* Ⓜ Gostiny Dvor

Dom Arkhitektorov, Ul. Gertsena 52, ☏ 311 4557. The restaurant in this grand town house was once the exclusive preserve of the Union of Architects. Since opening its doors to all-comers, it has become one of the most popular dining-rooms in the city. Its not the food that attracts, nor the erratic supply of alcohol or the lack of English spoken by the staff. It's the ambience in the two rooms—one plastered with dark embossed leather wallpaper and quasi-historical paintings, the other airy and lightly painted. The menu is short and verbal, and the main courses usually include a choice of meat or fish, both of which often turn up *pod mayonaisom*, baked under mayonnaise. *Open Mon–Fri 12 noon–10pm.*   Ⓜ Sennaya Ploshchad

cheap

Café St Petersburg, Kanal Griboyedova 5. Round the side of the restaurant of the same name (above), this small café serves decent homemade food, most of it laid out on the counter so you can choose. *Open 4–9pm (weekends 12 noon–9pm). Closed 3–4pm.*   Ⓜ Nevsky Prospekt

Art Club Café, Kanal Griboyedova 3, opposite the Cathedral of the Saviour on the Blood, ☏ 314 5273. Mostly drinks and coffee, this gallery café on the top floor also serves simple snack-like cucumber and tomato salads, and a munchy cheese and egg toasted sandwich. *Open 12 noon 11pm.*

Ⓜ Nevsky Prospekt

House of Scholars Café, Dvortsovaya Naberezhnaya 26. Closest café for a quick breather from the Hermitage. Walk across the hall, past the huge chinoiserie urns, and through the door beyond the grand staircase. Before the Revolution, this Renaissance-style palace belonged to the Grand Duchess Maria Pavlovna, and it was here that members of the Romanov family gathered to write a letter of warning to Tsar Nicholas II in 1916.

Vika, Ul. Soyuza Pechatnikov 8, is a steamy cheap little café, ideally situated for a sober dinner before ballet or opera at the Mariinsky. Food is generally good, the *pelmeni* and soups especially so. *Open 12–9; closed Sun.*

Café Premyera, Ul. Dekabristov, just round the corner from the Mariinsky Theatre. This café offers coffee and cakes, but also stocks copious quantities of alcohol and a simple hot snack menu.

Bars

Most of the places to drink have been mentioned above since they also offer food. Any café which is not specifically described as without alcohol will also serve you a drink. In addition however, there is a very dull, expensive bar in the Astoria Hotel (St Isaac's Cathedral entrance) and a more lively, more expensive one in the Grand Hotel Europe.

Restaurants

expensive

Afrodite, Nevsky Prospekt 86, ✆ 275 7620, has the strange feeling of being part of a chain of seafood restaurants, perhaps because of the colourful menu. The wine list is surprisingly large, and the food rather a disappointment. The fish just isn't fresh. Its location, in the basement of the actors' union, means that at weekends you can continue the evening dancing upstairs.

Izmailov, 6-aya Krasnoarmeiskaya 22, ✆ 292 6838, is the sort of place to go with a large, hungry group. They lay on an impressive spread, which is best discussed, and a price agreed, beforehand. From 11pm the entertainers begin to wear fewer and fewer clothes. *Open 1–4pm, 8pm–late.*

Ⓜ Tecknologichesky Institut

Club Ambassador, Naberezhnaya Reki Fontanki 14, ✆ 272 9181/3791. Extremely expensive, clubby restaurant with an ever-changing short menu and one of the most romantic mock 17th-century vaulted Russian interiors. Service in the candle-lit rooms is immaculate.

Troika, Zagorodny Prospekt 27, ✆ 113 5343, the self-proclaimed 'Moulin Rouge of St Petersburg', is the more traditional place to go for a slap-up meal and opulent floor-show. *Open 7pm–12 midnight.* Ⓜ Pushkinskaya

moderate

Daddy's, Moskovsky Prospekt 73, ✆ 298 9552/7744, is neither subtle nor refined, just heaven for steak lovers. *Open 12 noon–11pm.* Ⓜ Frunzenskaya

inexpensive

Café Fontanka, Fontanka Naberezhnaya 14. Deservedly popular thanks to its imaginative menu, huge main courses and late-night hours. You may have to queue for a table. Place your order at the bar, pick up your own cutlery and cold dishes. The rest will be brought to you, quickly. Staff speak some English. *Open 2pm–5am, with a break from 10–11pm.* Ⓜ Gostiny Dvor

Korean House, Fontanka Embankment 20, through the courtyard, ✆ 275 7203 (moving in 1995). A little piece of Korea in the northern wastes, you can even choose to sit on mats round a low wooden table if you want. Cold salads tend to be quite spicy. Otherwise try dumpling soup and marinated beef cooked on a griddle at your table. Bring your own alcohol. *Open 12 noon–10pm.*

Ⓜ Gostiny Dvor

Pizza House, Ul. Podolskaya 23, ✆ 292 2666, will do you steak or Weiner Schnitzel as well as one of its 13 flavours of pizza. As you might have gathered from this eclectic menu, they are not part of the huge American chain, but a Finnish-Russian joint venture. Call them on this number to order a delivery. *Open 10am–12 midnight.*   Ⓜ Tekhnologichesky Institut

cheap

Café Iveria, Ul. Marata 35, ✆ 164 7478. Down a few steps off busy Ul. Marata, you walk into a simple clean Georgian restaurant with wild flowers on each table. Order at the bar and then sit down at a table and wait for a minute or two for your food to appear at the hatch. Cold dishes on show, hot ones you will have to decipher on the menu. A good bet to start with is the spicy meat soup, *kharcho,* with *khachapuri* bread. *Open 11am–10pm.*   Ⓜ Vladimirskaya

Zakusnitsa, Ul. Rubinshteyna 2. Conveniently close to Nevsky Prospekt, this tiny hole in the basement cooks exceptionally tender meat dishes. It is not a place to linger over your food however. There is normally someone hovering to take your place. *Open 11am–10pm.*   Ⓜ Mayakovskaya

Metekhi Café, Ul. Belinskovo 3. A good choice for vegetarians, this cheap Georgian restaurant often has salted cheese (like the Greek *halloumi*) called *sir sulu-guni,* and *lobio* (beans in a spicy tomato sauce). Add more heat with a judicious sprinkling of *adjika,* the pepper mix you will find on each table. If *khachapuri* is not on the menu, you can always buy it and bring it with you from Vodi Lagidzi, the café next door. *Open 11am–9pm.*   Ⓜ Gostiny Dvor

Bagdad, Ul. Fushtadtskaya 35, ✆ 272 3533. Small basement café not far from the German and American consulates, serving Central Asian and Georgian food to the over-loud beat of MTV. The best place in this book to eat *plov,* the only thing to avoid is the sometimes overly greasy soup. Look over fellow diners shoulders to check. *Open 12 noon–11pm.*   Ⓜ Chernyshevskaya

Elf Café, Stremyannaya Ul. 11, bizarrely decorated with characters from Walt Disney, remains a popular hangout for the 70s generation. Depending on the time of day, choose between typical Russian food, coffee, cakes, ice-cream and alcohol.

Bars

John Bull Pub, Nevsky Prospekt 79, ✆ 164 9877, is much as it suggests, a place for consuming draught beer in familiar saloon bar surroundings. Also serves a cold snack menu. *Open 12–12.*

Mollie's Irish Bar, Ul. Rubinshteina 36, ✆ 319 9768/314 9768. The drink, not the food, is the point of this busy and popular watering hole. *Open 11am–3am.*

Beer Garden, Nevsky Prospekt 86, in the courtyard, is open 1pm–3am daily in the summer, serving snacks with beer. In winter you should be able to get a drink and something to eat in the building itself, the Actors' Union, and Wed–Sun you can continue dancing until 5am.

Vasilievsky Island

Restaurants

moderate

Hotelship Peterhof, Naberezhnaya Makarova, ✆ 213 6321, has a Russo-European restaurant, the Peterhof, whose chef delights in regular food festivals, featuring food from different countries. Ordering à la carte is distinctly expensive, but there is a good inexpensive set lunch. In the height of summer, the best place to eat is outside, at the grill bar on deck.

inexpensive

Venice, Ul. Korablstroitely 21, ✆ 352 1432. If you happen to be nearby, patronize the rouble pizzeria here but leave the over-priced and under-imaginative Italian restaurant alone.   Ⓜ Primorskaya

plus tram (11 and 63) bus (41, 42 and 47) and trolleybus (10,10a and 46).

cheap

Café Fregat, Bolshoi Prospekt 39/11-ya Liniya 14, is a long, thin, dark restaurant, with a plain Russian menu enlivened by daily specials and the rare opportunity to drink the late lamented Russian favourite, *kvas*.   Ⓜ Vasileostrovskaya

Petrograd Side

Restaurants

expensive

Bubnovy Valet, Ul. Lenina 32, ✆ 230 8830. Russian food served in a cosy interior. Food and service are fine, but the company, attracted by the telephones on the table, are sharp operators.   Ⓜ Petrogradskaya and a 15-minute walk.

moderate

Café Tet-a-Tet, Bolshoi Prospekt 65, ✆ 232 7548, is best described as the most suitable restaurant in St Petersburg to make a proposal of marriage. The small Empire tables barely seat more than two, the tinkly piano music is just loud enough to camouflage your conversation from the other diners, the lighting is perfect. Sad then that the food is no better than average. When you book, which you should, they may ask you to bring round a deposit. This is a bore. Try and wriggle out of it. *Open 1pm–12 midnight, closed 5–7pm.*

Ⓜ Petrogradskaya

Pirosmani, Bolshoi Prospekt 14, ✆ 235 6456. Apart, perhaps, from the very expensive hotel restaurants, this reclusive Georgian restaurant serves the best food in the city in its bizarre restaurant. For a once in a lifetime experience, ask if you can dine at the table in the middle of the pond, and order a selection of starters. As is so often the case with Georgian food, these are better than the main courses. Even if you think you don't like semi-sweet wine, try the Georgian red, Kinsmarauli, Stalin's and everyone else's favourite. *Open 12 noon–11pm; reservations (a must) 2–5pm.* Ⓜ Petrogradskaya is at the far end of Bolshoi Prospekt, a considerable walk.

Vostok, Yuzhnaya Alleya, Primorsky Park Pobedy, Krestovsky Island, ℗ 235 5984. Ring to make a reservation and for once stress your foreignness to make sure you are not put into the large hall with the smoke-obscured mafiosi. The Indian food is well-cooked, and it makes a great change to order one of the lamb dishes you get so rarely elsewhere, or the vegetarian lentil *dhal* and *samosas*. Come and go by taxi, and negotiate with your driver to wait. Taxis out here come very expensive. *Open 12 noon–4.30am, closed 6–9.*

Imperial, Kamennoostrovsky Prospekt 53, ℗ 234 1742. Reservations are a must in this rather formal nostalgic haven, popular with groups of tourists who want a more sedate evening than that offered by Troika (see above). Music is classical and background, and you will be watched by portraits of the former royal family as you eat. Ⓜ Petrogradskaya and a short walk north

inexpensive

Tbilisi, Ul. Sytninskaya 10, ℗ 232 9391. This Georgian restaurant, with its elderly doorman in Georgian dress, is dark and well-designed for secret rendezvous and caucasian cabals in its nooks and crannies. Order *kharcho* and *khacha-phuri* to start, and anything after that will be pure profit. The service is excellent and friendly. Ⓜ Gorkovksaya

Fortetsia, Ul. Kuybysheva 7, ℗ 233 9468, is a small, louchly-upholstered Belgian joint-venture serving good Russian food, though it is best to avoid the fish. The private room and its perennial celebration is intriguing. *Open Mon 7pm–12 midnight, Tues–Sun 12 noon–12 midnight.* Ⓜ Gorkovskaya

Demyanovaya Ukha, Pr. Maxim Gorky 53, on corner with Ul. Markina, ℗ 232 8090, hides behind windows of stained-glass fish. Though variable, this fish restaurant can serve some of the best value food in the city. You can start with caviar or fresh crab in mayonnaise, follow it with the eponymous *ukha* (fish soup) and continue with delicately stuffed *sudak* (pike). It would be a pity to order sturgeon (*osetrina*) here, since you are offered a choice. The owner has a boat on Lake Ladoga, which off-loads fish for the restaurant twice a week in summer. Either book, or ring persistently at the door. *Open 12 noon–10pm.*

Austeria, Peter and Paul Fortress, ℗ 238 4262. Set in the defensive out-ravelin of the fortress, this state-run place takes its name from the first hostelry that opened nearby in St Petersburg. The sombre almosphere and institutional food is only slightly enlivened by small touches of individuality—witness the unusual pastry top on the cabbage soup (*Petrovsky Shchi*).

Hebei, Bolshoi Prospekt 61, ✆ 233 2046. A reputation that changes with the week makes this Chinese restaurant a second-string if the other choices on this long avenue are full or too expensive. *Open 12 noon–11pm.* Ⓜ Petrogradskaya

Troitsky Most, Ul. Malaya Possadkaya 2. It is left to devotees of Hari Krishna to provide St Petersburg with its only vegetarian restaurant, and the word is that the food is good. *Open 10am–9pm, closed 2–3pm.* Ⓜ Gorkovskaya

Grill Diez, Kamennoostrovsky Prospekt 16, ✆ 232 4255, is a very popular joint selling spit-roast chickens, prepared with a peppery coating and quite unlike their scrawny Russian relations. Ideal as part of a summer picnic, but come early in the day to be sure of success. *Open 10am–9pm.* Ⓜ Gorkovskaya

Vyborg Side

Restaurants

expensive

Nevsky Melody, Sverdlovskaya Naberezhnaya 62, ✆ 227 1596 or 222 5180. Nighttime complex combining restaurant, casino and nightclub plus erotic shows at midnight and one. The food in the smart chrome interior is fine. Save yourself the hassle and take a taxi. *Open 12 noon–1am, nightclub until 4am.*

moderate

Schwabski Domik, Krasnogvardeisky Prospekt 28/19, ✆ 528 2211. No-nonsense German food, wurst and schnitzel, served either at tables or in a stand-up bar where it is considerably cheaper. *Open 11am–2am.*

Ⓜ Novocherkasskaya (Krasnogvardeiskaya)

inexpensive

Polesye, Sredneokhtinsky Prospekt 4, ✆ 244 2917, is a small co-operative specialising in Belorussian food, with black forest style wood-lined interior and only slightly too loud folk and gypsy singing. Food is excellent and service is fast, and it is a relaxed place for women on their own. Order поросёнок молочный (*parasyonok molochny*, roast suckling pig) or котлеты с грыбами (*kotlyety s gribami*, rissoles stuffed with mushrooms) for the main course.

Where to Stay

Change has erupted onto the Russian hotel scene, at least if you can afford it. Joint-ventures with international hotel chains have refurbished many of the best old hotels and built new ones. Both cities have long suffered a shortage of hotel rooms, and with the increase in western businessmen in Russia since the late 80s, something had to change. Enter the expense-account hotel with Burberry, American Express and neo-Fabergé boutiques nestling on the ground floors (or the first floor as they call it here), while lobster and caviar bars, Italian trattorias, business service and health centres cater to other needs.

For the average sightseer, these hotels are astronomically expensive, though if you arrive on a package tour you may find your operator has managed to do an affordable deal with the management. Intourist, the Soviet travel dinosaur, has lost its near monopoly on running hotels. Many have been privatized, and the concept of service with a smile is slowly filtering through. Even that infamous institution, the battle-axe *concièrge* (*dezhurnaya*) who ruled her floor with withering condescension, seems headed for extinction. Keeping an eye on every passing capitalist is no longer top priority. Parts of some hotels have been leased by independent restaurants serving Italian, German or Spanish food, and some refurbishment has taken place. Many of the hotels in the moderate and cheap brackets are better than they used to be.

For those for whom enjoying the ambience of a hotel is part of the fun of a holiday, Moscow and St Petersburg are not highly-starred destinations. Not even the most expensive places have avoided the decorative blandness of the international style. Both cities are almost completely lacking in small, characterful hotels, which add so much to other European cities, and cheap bed-and-breakfast type accommodation. The only substitute is a microscopic youth hostel association (with a couple of establishments in each city), the occasional ex-student dorm accommodation, motels and campsites on the city fringes and a pubescent business in flat and room rentals.

For those on a low budget, bear in mind that Moscow, in particular, is an enormous city with an increasingly erratic transport system, and an unwritten law makes sure that cheap accommodation often goes hand in hand with inconvenience. Weigh up what it is worth to you not to be ripped off by taxi drivers or to have to brave 1½ hours of frustrating public transport every time you want to go out. It really is worth staying as close to the centre of the city as you can afford. With that in mind, the following listings have been divided by price, but within each band hotels nearest the centre are listed first, getting further out as the list continues.

Most hotels in Russia, and particularly the more expensive ones, charge dollars and will accept all major credit cards (and to a lesser extent travellers' cheques) as payment. Since even dollar inflation manages to be high here, the following price guide can only be approximate, and things are bound to get yet more expensive. For a double room occupied by two people, reckon on:

luxury	over $290
expensive	over $150
moderate	$60–$150
cheap	under $60

Renting a room in a flat, bed and breakfast, will cost you from $20 a night; a whole flat that much more.

Moscow

luxury

Baltschug-Kempinski, Ul. Balchuga 1, ☎ 230 6500, 🖅 230 6502 (7 501 230 9500 and 7 501 230 9502 respectively from outside Russia). Newest of the central joint venture hotels, managed by the Swiss. This one has an enviable location across the river from the Kremlin. Ask for a room with a view. The amenities include a 20-metre swimming pool, three restaurants, bars and a café. You'll have to walk or taxi across the river to most of the city's sights, except for the Tretyakov Gallery and the village atmosphere of Zamoskvarechye. Its name, Balchug, ironically means mud in Tatar.   Ⓜ Novokuznetskaya

Metropol, Teatralny Proezd 1–4, ☎ 927 6000/2, 🖅 927 6010 (using the code 7 501 in front of either number from outside Russia gives you the satellite line). The city's most famous hotel was built at the turn of the century by a British architect, Walcott, in the *Style Moderne* and decorated with a ceramic frieze by Vrubel. The interior meets late 20th-century hotel standards, while managing to keep some of the original feel. Rooms are spacious and the Metropol Hall dining room is a three-storey mosaic atrium.   Ⓜ Pl. Revolutsii/Teatralnaya

Savoy, Ul. Rozhdestvenskaya 3, ✆ 929 8500/8558, 📠 230 2186. Far from the cool modernism of the Metropol is the gilded interior of this small hotel just across the road. The only hotel in the capital you could call cosy, those with a penchant for grandeur might well call the rooms poky. Ⓜ Kuznetsky Most

Moscow Palace, Ul. Pervaya Tverskaya Yamskaya 19, Moscow 125047, ✆ 956 3152, 📠 956 3151. With its marble mosaic of Moscow in the lobby, this palatial addition to Moscow's smart hotels boasts an astronomical seafood restaurant, Yakor, and excellent service.Not quite as central as the aforementioned, but still only a five-minute drive from the Kremlin. Ⓜ Belorusskaya

Radisson-Slavyanskaya, Berezhkovskaya Naberezhnaya 2, ✆ 941 8020, 📠 941 8000 (fax from outside Russia 7 502 224 1225). Specifically designed as a home-from-home for American businessmen, many of whom live here, you really wouldn't know you were in Moscow until you stepped out into the motley crowd at the nearby Kiev railway station. Ⓜ Kievskaya

Olympic Penta Renaissance, Olimpisky Prospekt 18–1, ✆ 971 6101, 📠 230 2597. Run by the Penta group to generally high standards, the distinguishing feature of this hotel, appropriately, is its fitness centre. In an ideal world it's a bit far out, but if you're on business you won't mind the taxi bills. Ⓜ Prospekt Mira

Mezhdunarodnaya, Krasnopresnenskaya Naberezhnaya 12, ✆ 253 7136, 📠 253 2051. Miles from public transport, and a hoodish-looking bunch of taxi drivers outside make this an unattractive option for the price. When first opened it became the centre of ex-pat life in the city, with chemists, supermarkets and a video rental store. Since then other establishments have made its cavernous brown mall redundant and businessmen, who have worn out the Italian furniture, have moved elsewhere. Ⓜ Krasnopresnenskaya and bus no. 4

expensive

National, 14/1 Okhotny Ryad, ✆ 203 6539. Scheduled to reopen in 1995 as the flagship state hotel, one can only hope that in the extensive refurbishment they rediscover the qualities and service that made this the best pre-Revolutionary hotel in the city. It was here that Lenin chose to stay while moving the government back into the Kremlin in 1918. The location, overlooking Manezh Square and the Kremlin Walls, is sensational. Ⓜ Okhotny Ryad

Marco Polo Presnya, Spiridonyevsky Pereulok 9, ✆ 503 956 3010, 📠 503 956 6306. Originally built for visiting Communist big-wigs, the Austrian Marco-Polo chain have done their best to give its 68 rooms some style. Clean and comfortable, though lacking glamour, it is located in one of Moscow's best-loved residential areas near the Patriarch's Ponds. For peace and quiet this is the place. Ⓜ Pushkinskaya/Tverskaya, Mayakovskaya or Barrikadnaya.

Daniilovsky Hotel Complex, Bolshoy Staryodanilovsky Pereulok 5, ℰ 954 0503, ℰ 954 0559. Owned by the Orthodox church and often full of visiting prelates, this is a quiet and pleasantly eccentric place to spend your holiday, with the metro a ten-minute walk away. Ask for a room overlooking the monastery or splash out on an apartment with a vast dining room and an unclerical, painted four-poster bed. Ⓜ Tulskaya

Inflotel, aboard the *Alexander Blok*, Krasnopresnenskaya Naberezhnaya 12, ℰ 255 9287, ℰ 253 9578. Transport is poor, the taxi drivers are crooks and the clientèle in the bar are their rich equivalent at this 'boatel'. True, you can get cheap 4-birth cabins here, but is it really worth it? The only real plus point is the Thursday evening all-you-can-eat fish buffet in the Greek restaurant, but that will cost you. Ⓜ Krasnopresnenskaya a long walk away

Aerostar, Leningradsky Prospekt 37, Korp 9, ℰ 155 5030, ℰ 155 6614. The Canadians have picked up a not very promising Russian development and turned it into a respectable hotel with excellent service for businessmen at a location half-way between city and international airport. Ask for a room looking towards the rather distant red-brick Gothic Petrovsky Palace, at which the tsars would rest in preparation for their triumphal entry into Moscow after the long journey from St Petersburg. Ⓜ Aeroport 10 minutes walk

Pullman Iris, Korovinskoye Shosse 10, ℰ 488 8000, ℰ 906 0105 (502 220 8000 and 220 8888 respectively from outside Russia). A long way from the centre of town, and partly built to house western visitors to the adjacent Fyodorov's Eye Clinic, where pioneering work has been done in correcting short-sight by laser surgery. It is a bright, cheerful oasis in a grim urban landscape, though the free hourly shuttle service to Red Square eases the pain of the location.

Novotel, Sheremetyevo-II Airport, ℰ 578 9401/9110, ℰ 578 2794. No surprises from this international chain. It goes without saying that this is a perverse place to stay unless you are in transit.

moderate

Rossiya, Ul. Varvarka 6, ℰ 298 5531, ℰ 298 5541. Why anyone except extras from 'The Prisoner' should be expected to stay in this smelly labyrinth of threadbare red carpets beats me. And to think they thought it a selling point to be the largest hotel, with some 5000 rooms, in the world. Problem is, the location and views of the Kremlin are second to none. Ⓜ Kitai Gorod

Moskva, Okhotny Ryad 2, ℰ 292 1100, ℰ 292 9217. Opinion divides as to whether this hotel is too overbearingly Soviet or worth putting up with for the location. The latter is probably the more balanced assessment, given that the rooms are spacious and the hotel is surrounded by bars and restaurants were you can escape the (lack of) Soviet-style service. Ⓜ Okhotny Ryad/Pl. Revolutsii

Intourist, Ul. Tverskaya 3, ✆ 956 4426. Good location but the rooms are uninspiring, and until you get used to them the assorted bouncers, taxi drivers, gypsies and hobos round the door can be off-putting. They are here to prey on the largest concentration of foreign tour groups in central Moscow. Ⓜ Oknotny Ryad

Hotel Budapesht, Ul. Petrovskiye Linii 2/18, ✆ 921 1060 or 924 8820, 📠 921 1266. Tucked away behind the Bolshoi Theatre, this hotel is a brisk 15-minute walk from the Kremlin, and its rooms are fine as long as you aren't going to spend all day in them. A recent sign that service is on the up is the offer of breakfast in your room. Ⓜ Teatralnaya

Belgrade, Smolenskaya Ploshchad 8, ✆ 248 1906/3236/3232. The location may be good, but the decor and service are poor. The twin tower opposite, which used to be the Belgrade II, has been sold to private operators. Now known as the **Zolotoye Koltso**, Smolenskaya Ploshchad 5, ✆ 248 6734, 📠 248 7395, its prices are about the same as the Belgrade. Ⓜ Smolenskaya

Ukraina, Kutuzovsky Prospekt 2/1, ✆ 243 2596, 📠 243 2896/243 3092. The hotel for those with a nostalgia for socialist realism. Housed in one of the Seven Sisters, Stalin's Gothic skyscrapers, the public parts are all red carpet and high painted ceilings, and rooms are clean (with Soviet empire furniture) but worn. Metro 10 minutes away. Events across the river at the White House and city beyond made compulsive viewing for newshounds in October 1993—ask for a room with a view. Ⓜ Kievskaya, or bus 89 and trolleybus 2 to the Kremlin.

Leningradskaya, Ul. Kalanchovskaya 21/40, ✆ 975 1815/1750. Another of the Seven Sisters, the Leningradskaya is if anything more opulent than the Ukraina, but the location, next to three major railway stations is not as calm or interesting. A good place for night-birds who can while away the hours in Jack's Piano Bar, which stays open till 5am. Ⓜ Komsomolskaya

Sovietskaya, Leningradsky Prospekt 322, ✆ 250 7255/53, 📠 250 8003. Once the stamping ground of the Communist Party's central committee, the palatial interiors are now notably absent. Few tourists stay here, there's no excursion bureau and the only restaurant just does breakfast. A last resort. Ⓜ Dinamo

Kosmos, Prospekt Mira 150, ✆ 217 0785/8680, 📠 215 7991. From the number of prostitutes in the bars you would have thought the entire towering golden crescent was a brothel. In fact the rooms aren't bad, and though it is far out the French-built hotel is right opposite the metro station and is well-equipped to cater to the needs of tourists. Ⓜ VDNKh

Soyuz, Ul. Levoberezhnaya 12, ✆ 457 2088, 📠 457 2096. This hotel near the River Moskva is a relative bargain, with clean, cheery rooms and a recent overhaul, but it is way out of town—15 minutes on a 90, 200, 205, 270 or 551 bus will take you to Ⓜ Rechnoy Vokzal, the last stop on this metro line.

Veshnyaky Hotel, Vtoroy Pyatigorsky Proezd (behind 53 Ryazansky Prospekt), ✆ 174 2500, 🖨 174 2599. Ⓜ Ryazansky Prospekt, front carriage. Trolleybus 63, or bus 46, 169 or 143 (four stops). If you plan to be here for a while and the easterly location suits, investigate this small hotel, advertised as a 'discreet bed and breakfast for businessmen'.

cheap/motels, youth hostels and campsites

Artists' Union Hotel, Gogolievsky Bulvar 8, ✆ 291 8744. Ideally located on one of the quietest stretches of the bulvar ring, a couple of minutes from the metro, this hostel for painters and sculptors visiting the capital now accepts foreigners when there are rooms to spare. They have cottoned on to the financial implications, and a room will cost $25 or so. Don't expect luxury, but the rooms are perfectly good. Either go in person and use a phrase book (entrance at back of building), or get a Russian speaker to book you in. Ⓜ Kropotkinskaya

Travellers Guesthouse, Ul. Bolshaya Pereyaslavskaya 50, floor 10, ✆ 971 4059, 🖨 280 7686. Set up as a partner to the Youth Hostel in St Petersburg, this efficiently run guesthouse has clean doubles, dormitory rooms and bathrooms and also serves breakfast. Ⓜ Prospekt Mira and a 15 minute walk

Izmailovo, Izmailovskoye Shosse 69a, ✆ 166 0109. A series of five bleak tower blocks raised to house visitors for the Olympics, this vast hotel has a little of what you fancy and a funfare of a flea market on its doorstep at weekends. There is also a nearby park and the metro station is no distance, but most tourists will feel shortchanged to find themselves so far from the centre of the Moscow of their imaginations. Ⓜ Izmailovsky Park

Tsentralny Dom Turista, Leninsky Prospekt 146, ✆ 434 6482, 🖨 434 3197. Way out along Leninsky Prospekt this large hotel has long processed tourists efficiently through a few days Moscow sightseeing, but its location makes it a bore for the independent-minded. Rooms are clean with bathrooms, the service bureau can book you into excursions or restaurants but to get there you have to take any bus two stops from Ⓜ Yugo-Zapadnaya

Molodyozhnaya, Dmitrovskoye Shosse 27, ✆ 210 4565. Originally used by the Soviet youth travel organisation Sputnik, hence the name, meaning simply 'youth', this multi-storey hotel is low on creature comforts and aesthetics but cheap. Three- and five-person suites here offer probably the cheapest deal in the city, and the metro station is not far away. Ⓜ Timiryazevskaya

Of the two Moscow motels the **Mozhaisky Motel**, Mozhaiskoye Shosse 165, ✆ 447 3434, is the smaller and better located. Bus 139 will take you to it, outside the Moscow ring road, in 25 minutes from Ⓜ Filyovsky Park.

Resist the offer of the **Solechnaya Motel and Campsite**, Varshavskoe Shosse km 21, ✆ 119 7100, as hard as you can. Among its neighbours are a spaghetti junction, a power station and a railway line.

Renting Rooms and Flats

The easiest way to do this is probably via one of the agencies at home, listed on p.561. But if you find yourself in Moscow and decide you have to stay longer, try the following options:

Hotel Tsaritsino, Shipilovsky Prospekt 47/1, ✆ 343 4343/73, reservations 3434356/17, ✉ 343 4363, is miles out in the southern suburbs and rents furnished apartments at reasonable rates. Ⓜ Orekhovo

Unifuturer, ✆ 203 5843, ✉ 343 4363, promises to find apartments for long and even short stays.

The Moscow Times and **Moscow Tribune** (if it is still going) always have flat rental propositions in their classified sections. See also the chapter on Living and Working in Moscow and St Petersburg.

St Petersburg

luxury

Grand Hotel Europe, Ul. Mikhailovskaya 1/7, ✆ 119 6000, ✉ 119 6001. The renovation of this central hotel overlooking Nevsky Prospekt and the Russian Museum has put it at the heart of St Petersburg tourism, even if you can only afford to pop in for the occasional coffee or a meal in its cheapest restaurant, Sadko. It is a pity that the Swedish hotel group Reso have reinvented much of the Art Nouveau interior, and not very well at that. The rooms, decorated in pastel shades with spotless tiled bathrooms, can be stuffy—ask for an outside room or one overlooking the covered atrium. Ⓜ Nevsky Prospekt

Nevsky Palace, Nevsky Prospekt 57, ✆ 311 6366/112 5238, ✉ 850 1501. From the Austrian Marco Polo group comes the latest offering in St Petersburg, a renovation of the former Baltiskaya Hotel building on Nevsky Prospekt. Service was a bit hesitant in its first few months, but the will is there as well as the amenities, including a pool and sauna. Ⓜ Mayakovskaya/Pl. Vostaniya

expensive

Astoria and **Angleterre**, Ul. Gertsena 39, ✆ 210 5032, ✉ 315 9668. Once two hotels, now bashed together into one. Fears for their fabric during renovation prompted a challenge by conservation pressure groups. Though the exterior was saved, from the interior it would seem their fears were justified, with just the dining room in the glass-ceilinged Winter Garden left to remind you how it must once have been. That said this is an efficient, modern hotel at the heart of the city, with clean rooms and adequate service.   Ⓜ Nevsky Prospekt

Hotelship Peterhof, Pier Makarov Embankment, by Tuchkov Bridge, Vasilievksy Ostrov, ☎ 213 6321, ✉ 213 3158. For reservations from abroad, contact the Swiss head office of I.C.H. Management in Switzerland, ☎ 55 27 56 17, ✉ 55 27 31 74 or telex 876 371 ICH CH. By the time you stay here the tiny cabins will have been doubled in size, but you will still find yourself asking how a shoe-box could cost so much a night. The staff are helpful, the *à la carte* dining room distinctly expensive. This company runs two other hotelships which cruise around the Baltic and regularly make the fascinating journey by river and canal from St Petersburg to Moscow (*see* p.8).

Neptun, Nab. Obvodnovo Kanala 93a, ☎ 210 1707, ✉ 311 2270. This new hotel includes everything you would expect from a recently built establishment of this price, but nothing can change the industrial location.
Ⓜ Pushkinskaya 15 minutes' walk away

Pulkovskaya, Ploshchad Pobedy 1, ☎ 264 5122, ✉ 264 5844. Behind its dark glass front this Finnish-Russian hotel looks and feels like a nightclub. Built with the business traveller in mind, halfway to the airport, facilities include a business centre, a sauna and tennis courts.   Ⓜ Moskovskaya 10 minutes' walk away

Petrodin, Pervy Berozovaya Alleya 7, ☎ 234 4588. Though it is fun staying in this small hotel, formerly for high-ranking Communist officials, housed in a *dacha* on pretty Kamenny Ostrov, there's a funny atmosphere in the former corridors of power. Rooms are huge but echoingly empty.   Ⓜ Chyornaya Rechka
or Petrogradskaya, bus 46 or 65 to the island and then by foot.

Pribaltiskaya, Ul. Korablestroiteley 14, Vasilievsky Ostrov, ☎ 356 0001, ✉ 356 0094. Miles from the centre of town on the edge of the Gulf of Finland, this massive concrete ship of a hotel may be fine for large groups with their own buses but it makes no attempts to be attractive to the individual tourist, unless (s)he has a particular *penchant* for early 70s psychedelic interior design, Russian-style. To get there pack a lot of time, head for Ⓜ Primorskaya and take tram 11 or 63, bus 41, 42 or 47 or trolleybus 10, 10a or 46.

moderate

Sankt Peterburg, Vyborgskaya Naberezhnaya 5/2, ☎ 542 9123, ✉ 248 8002. The best choice in this category has to be this hideous 1970's building on the Vyborg side of the River Neva, on the principle that if you're in it you can't see it. You can, if you ask for a river view, see the wide expanse of the Neva slipping past, between you and the showy Palace Embankment. The hotel is feeling its age a bit, and the top floors still haven't been repaired after the 1991 fire, but you'll want for nothing important here, as long as you don't mind the uninspiring walk to the metro. **Ⓜ** Ploshchad Lenina

Mercury, 39 Ul. Tavricheskaya, ✆/🖨 278 1977. This tiny hotel tucked away in one of the city's nicest residential areas originally hosted regional party members only. The English-speaking manager, Alexander Leonov, is keen to lure foreigners to its clean, quiet rooms, and bar/buffet. Rates are a bit stiff at the moment but try negotiating by fax beforehand. **Ⓜ** Chernyshevskaya

Moskva, Ploshchad Aleksandra Nevskovo 2, ✆ 274 2115, 🖨 274 2130. Close to the metro station and St Petersburg's most important monastery is about the most one can say about this drab, brown hotel. Its also got a reasonable shop selling imported goods on the ground floor. **Ⓜ** Pl. Aleksandra Nevskovo

Helen (sometimes called the **Fontanka**), Lermontovsky Prospekt 45, ✆ 251 6101, 🖨 113 0859. Marginally better than her high-rise sister the Sovietskaya beside her, thanks to a refurbishment. Both establishments suffer from out-dated lack of service and a worn-out air. They are also a good ten minutes' walk from the nearest metro. **Ⓜ** Baltiskaya

Sovietskaya, Lermontovsky Prospekt 43/1, ✆ 259 2552, 🖨 251 8890. *See* above. **Ⓜ** Baltiskaya

Okhtinskaya, Bolsheokhtinsky Prospekt 4, ✆ 227 3767/4438, 🖨 227 2618. If it wasn't for the isolated location on the Vyborg side of the river opposite the Smolny Cathedral, this would undoubtedly be St Petersburg's best value hotel. Rooms are small but clean and service really exists, though the restaurant retains an exclusively group tourism feel. Ask for a room overlooking the river and Rastrelli's sublime cathedral, and stock up at the excellent Italian deli on the ground floor. **Ⓜ** Novocherkasskaya and tram 7, 23 or 46

Karelia, Ul. Tukhachevskovo 27, ✆ 226 3515, 🖨 226 3511. As an independent traveller, resist being put here at all costs. Though the staff are friendly it is in an endlessly depressing area of town and local transport takes hours.

Octavian, Sredny Prospekt 88, Vasilievsky Ostrov, ✆ 356 8516, is currently undergoing a Russian-British overhaul which may manage to dispel the gloomy air which makes this isolated high-rise feel more like a morgue than a place you would pay to go on holiday to. **Ⓜ** Vasileostrovskaya and tram 11 or 40

---

cheap/motels, youth hostels and campsites

Akademicheskaya, Ul. Millionnaya 27, ✆ 315 8986, go straight through the courtyard. If you can talk your way in to this hotel which used to be reserved for guests of the Academy of Sciences you are laughing. The rooms are rather shoddy, there isn't always water, let alone hot water, but you are on millionaire's row, the road leading from the Hermitage, in which the cream of St Petersburg society lived until the Revolution.   Ⓜ Nevsky Prospekt

Oktyabrskaya, Ligovsky Prospekt 10, ✆ 277 6330. This cheap and central option offers no decor to look forward to and a smelly warren of endless corridors to negotiate. An uninviting room is fine for a city like this however—you should want to be outside all the time. Those interested in enemas should check out the medical kiosk from hell in the lobby.   Ⓜ Ploshchad Vosstaniya

St Petersburg Youth Hostel, Ul. Tretaya Sovyetskaya (or Rozhdestvenskaya) 28, ✆ 277 0569, ✆ 277 5102. Pioneered by an American, who came here to learn acting and became a businessman, the hostel has 50 beds and more in the summer.   Ⓜ Ploshchad Vosstaniya.

Holiday Hostel, Ul. Mikhailova 1, ✆/✆ 542 7364. Sits right on the River Neva, next door to the infamous Kresty Prison. Prices include breakfast, though other meals are also served in the café.   Ⓜ Finlandsky Vokzal

Mir, Ul. Gastello 17, ✆ 108 5165. Small low-rise Russian hotel right next to one of St Petersburg's most original pieces of architecture, the Chesme Church. Staff are friendly considering that foreigners are a rarity, but rooms are small.

Ⓜ Moskovskaya

Of the two campsites on offer, the **Retur Motel-Camping**, 29km from the city on Primorskoye Shosse towards Finland is infinitely preferable to the crime-ridden **Olgino Motel-Camping** only 18km out on the same road. It is a long ride to both from Chornaya Rechka metro station, on buses 110, 411 or 416. You can also get to the Retur by train from Finland Station. Take the line to Sestroretsk and get off at Aleksandrovsky.

Renting Rooms and Flats

If you are in this bracket you will probably have already booked your accommodation through one of the operators listed on p.561. However, if you do want to rent on the ground ring the following:

Lena Topichkanova, ✆ 310 7132, or to speak English Natasha Ostrovskaya ✆ 156 4525.

Libra-Tours, Grivtsovsky Pereulok 22, flat 26, ✆ 310 9186, ✆ 552 5631 will also arrange bed and breakfast, or a more comprehensive holiday with personal guide and car. Ask for the dependable, English-speaking Valentine, who can also issue you with the invitation needed to obtain a visa.

Lingva, 7ya liniya 36, Vasilievsky Ostrov, ✆ 218 7339. One of the better established independent tourist companies under the banner of an English-language school. Also tour guides, transport, visa support and airport collection, as well as language courses and sightseeing programmes.

Yuzhny Dvor, ✆ 315 0438, finds flats for rent for anything over three days.

Host Families Association, Tavricheskaya Ul. 5–25, ✆ 275 1992, ✆ 552 6086, can provide both bed and breakfast and full board accommodation with Russian families.

Entertainment and Nightlife

517

Theatre, classical music, ballet and opera have long been the mainstay of evenings in Moscow and St Petersburg, but with liberalization a healthy rash of music clubs, discotheques and a dubious dose of casinos have emerged. Rock music used to be rationed and used cynically by the regime to keep young people away from church on Good Friday—the only televised rock concert coincided with the most important Orthodox service of the year. Today top Russian bands like Zvuky Moo, Liuki and the indefinable shows of Sergei Kuriokhin's Pop Mekhanika fill vast auditoria and sports stadiums, Russian rapper Bogdan Titomir encourages the whole of Red Square to 'Look at Me' and less well-known talents play in rock clubs in both cities. Jazz too has its own space in both cities, though it tends to be traditional or Dixieland. It's come a long way from its hooligan reputation under Communism, when Maxim Gorky claimed that 'from saxophone to the knife is just one step'.

But if the days of political censorship are over, those of economic censorship have only just begun. After years of state subsidies, the government has turned off the tap and theatres, the film business and even two of the world's most famous ballet companies have been forced to confront the realities of the free market. As a result, the Mariinsky and Bolshoi ballet companies are now on tour abroad, earning foreign currency, for a large part of the year, and film production has dropped from over 800 a year to around 60. Though ballet performances continue, you are as likely to see the stars of the company in New York, Sydney or London as you are here, and most cinemas now show a staple diet of cheap American films. On top of this, the freedom to disagree has brought simmering differences of approach to the surface, and artistic battles are raging over many an institution, notably the Taganka and Bolshoi Theatres in Moscow. Never has there been such chaos in Russia's performing arts.

Something that hasn't changed is the summer break which most theatres take between mid-July and mid-September. Beware that if you come during that time your options will be severely diminished. For listings, those who read Russian should look out for *Dosug v Moskve* (Leisure in Moscow), which comes out on Saturdays, and *Pyatnitsa* in St Petersburg, which is published, as its name suggests, on Fridays. Alternatively the English-language *Moscow Times* and *St Petersburg Press*, available in hotels, shops and restaurants frequented by foreigners, carry a comprehensive cultural listings on

Fridays. Films are always dubbed into Russian rather than subtitled, often by one man playing men, women and children. They are advertised on huge posters which list all the films showing in the city. Keep your eyes open near cinemas.

Tickets

An Illustration: one night in 1993, I was invited by Alex to the Bolshoi. We stood outside the stage door where a ballerina friend was going to give him two tickets. Instead of the ballerina, the only member of the company we saw was a man with tickets for three German VIPs. Performance time drew closer and we went reluctantly towards the touts, sussing what was on offer and getting a few preliminary prices. Just as we were about to part with the dollars, the man from the stage door ran up. Only two Germans had turned up, did I want to buy his front-row of the stalls ticket, at face value? Fifty cents! Getting face-value tickets for the Bolshoi in Moscow or the Mariinsky (Kirov) in St Petersburg only happens in dreams. Alex's stalls ticket cost $25.

As you will gather, getting tickets in Russia is no straightforward matter unless you are happy to pay 50 times the proper price, though compared with the west this is still not a fortune. In that case go through the Intourservice bureau in your hotel, call IPS Theatre Box Office in the lobby of the Metropol Hotel, Moscow, ℗ 927 6728/9 or the service desk in the Grand Hotel Europe in St Petersburg, ℗ 312 0072. The other alternative is simply to buy from touts operating outside popular venues—the Bolshoi and Mariinsky Theatres, circuses, pop concerts and well-reviewed plays. For a good choice get there half an hour before and try for tickets in the *parterre* (stalls) or *amphiteatr* (circle). Unless you know the theatre well, beware of *balkon* (balcony) tickets, as you may find yourself with a limited view.

The obvious place, the box office of the venue in question, will have sold all its tickets, probably to racketeers, weeks before a popular performance. The only case in which the box office might deliver is if you want to go see a play which has been in rep at one of the theatres for a while, or if you want to listen to classical music.

There are also a number of theatre ticket kiosks, Teatralnaya Kassa (marked either Театральная Касса or simply Театр, theatre) all over both cities, which you will identify by the chaos of printed tickets stuck to the windows. The system by which they receive tickets is random, but it is worth checking the windows for anything you might fancy in the central ones. In Moscow head for the junction of Pushkinskaya Ploshchad and Ul. Chekhova, the kiosk in front of Intourist's main office at Mokhovaya Ul. 13 on Manezhnaya Ploshchad and that on Ul. Tverskaya opposite the Yermolova Theatre. In St Petersburg the most helpful are the Central Ticket Office, sandwiched between cafés at Nevsky Prospekt 42, the office in the detached temple where Ul. Dumskaya meets Nevsky Prospekt and in the ticket hall of the Hermitage Museum, where you should look out particularly for tickets to performances in Catherine the Great's Hermitage Theatre.

Ballet and Opera

Bolshoi Theatre, Teatralnaya Ploshchad 1, ℗ 292 9986. If you want to go once to the Bolshoi Theatre, opt for ballet rather than opera, since that is its strength. Don't expect many surprises though, as the Russian school is the most traditional. Things haven't changed since Harold Wilson complained of having seen *Swan Lake* seven times in the Soviet Union. Director Yuri Grigorevich's last great hit was *Spartacus* in the 1960s, still running now. It's highly theatrical, a showcase for strong male dancing, and since you are less likely to see it in the west it makes a good choice. Alternatively try the love story *Raymonda*, by Glazunov. Behind the sumptuous red and gold, the theatre is suffering serious subsidence, dancers change and warm up in appalling conditions and there is talk of having to shut for renovations.   Ⓜ Teatralnaya

Stanislavsky and Nemirovich-Danchenko Musical Theatre, Ul. Pushkinskaya 17, ℗ 229 8388. Performances of the ballet and opera here are often of a higher standard than at the Bolshoi, as emphasis is put on acting as well as dancing and singing.   Ⓜ Chekhovskaya

Kremlin Palace of Congresses, in the Kremlin, ℗ 926 7901 or 929 7726. Try to find out beforehand whether the Moscow Ballet Company will be dancing to a live orchestra or gramophone in this terrible performance space, designed for the gargantuan Congress of People's Deputies. Don't sit further back than Row 30 in the stalls. Box office at Ul. Vozdvizhenka 1 (building behind the Manezh), near the Trinity Gate entrance to Kremlin.   Ⓜ Aleksandrovsky Sad

Classical Music

Tchaikovsky Conservatoire, Ul. Gertsena 13, © 229 8183. It is not that the standard of performance is necessarily better here than in the west, though concerts are often excellent. What gives an evening at the conservatoire its buzz is the impassioned attention of the knowledgable, mostly elderly audience. During the Soviet period it was, for many people, their only access to art, as it was difficult to apply the dogma of social realism to, say, Beethoven. Tickets for the big hall, with its bas-relief portraits of great composers, on sale at the box office *2–7.30; closed Mon and Tues.*   Ⓜ Okhotny Ryad

Tchaikovsky Concert Hall, Triumfalnaya Ploshchad 4/31, © 299 0378/5362, is the home of the State Symphony Orchestra and gives a full programme of concerts from September to July.   Ⓜ Mayakovskaya

Gnessin Academy of Music, corner of Ul. Paliashvili and Ul. Povarskaya, © 290 6737. During term time students at the academy give seasons of concerts ranging from chamber music to opera.   Ⓜ Barrikadnaya or Arbatskaya

Theatre

Serious theatre lovers with no Russian may wish to find out for themselves what has happened to the great Russian theatrical tradition. It used to be easy to say where to go and where not to—some theatres had radical directors, others simply toed the line. Nowadays standards vary from play to play. This list includes places to see traditional theatre and some which have recently shown flair.

Maly Theatre, Teatralnaya Ploshchad 1/6, © 923 2621/924 4083. One of the oldest in Moscow, this theatre mounts conventional stagings of popular Russian plays. The 19th-century playwright Ostrovsky's plays about the mores of Moscow's merchant class are still a firm favourite here.   Ⓜ Teatralnaya

Moscow Arts Theatre named after Chekhov (MKhAT), Kammergersky Per 3, © 229 8760, is the founding theatre of the Russian realist tradition of acting, started by Stanislavsky and Nemirovich-Danchenko (*see* p.168). Here too they still perform plays by one of the founding playwrights Chekhov, as well as modern western playwrights such as Shaffer.   Ⓜ Okhotny Ryad

Taganka Theatre, Zemlyanoy Val 76, © 271 2826/2825. Moscow's leading radical theatre, but recent disputes between the old and new guard have closed it on occasion. The more difficult it is to get a ticket, the better the show—it's worth approaching a tout outside before the performance.   Ⓜ Taganskaya

Teatr U Nikitskikh Vorot, Ul. Bolshaya Nikitskaya 23/9, © 202 8219. Director Mark Rozhovsky, his ardour undiminished by 15 years of official censure, set this place up in 1981 when he became acceptable again. Since Gorbachev, facilities have been improved. If *Uncle Vanya* is on, go see it.   Ⓜ Arbatskaya

Teatr na Krasnoy Presnye, 9a Ul. Stankevicha, 290 2! 57. One of the better small studio theatres with a fringy feel. Ⓜ Tverskaya/Pushkinskaya

Teatr Na Yugo-Zapade, Prospekt Vernadskovo 125, ʼⅅ 434 7483. Beliakovich's company caused a stir with their radical improvis ʼions and ensemble performances in this small suburban space in the 19 ;0s. The clamour has died down but the quality is still excellent. Ⓜ Yugo-Zapadnaya

Mossoviet, Ul. Bolshaya Sadovaya 16, ℗ 299 2035/20(5943. Performances range from *Jesus Christ Superstar* to Bulgakov's *White Ꞡuard*, and from the incompetent to the excellent. Ⓜ Mayakovskaya

Lenkom Theatre, Ul. Chekhova 6, ℗ 299 9668. Dire tor Mark Zakharov, something of a populist, has had recent successes with Jewish plays and a musical based on Beaumarchais' *The Marriage of Figaro*. Ⓜ Tverskaya/Pushkinskaya

Theatr na Maloy Bronnoy, Ul. Malaya Bronnaya 4, ℗ .:90 4093. Recent work has been variable. One play here by Sergei Zhenovac ꞧ was a sell-out, the next a critical flop. Find out before you go. Ⓜ Tverskaya/Pushkinskaya

Both the **Sovremmenik**, Chistoprudny Bulvar 19A, ℗ 9 !1 6473/6629 (Ⓜ Chistiye Prudy), and the **Teatr Vakhtangova**, Ul. Arbat !6, ℗ 241 1679, have also had recently acclaimed shows. Ⓜ Arbat

---

Circus

Old Moscow Circus, Tsvetnoy Bulvar 13, ℗ 200 68ꞷ 9/4949. A favourite with Muscovite children and visitors alike, the new bui ding opened in 1989 under the directorship of the well-loved old clown Yuri Ⱦiꞣulin. If you can't get hold of them beforehand, tickets are normally easy to ϼ rocure outside the building before performances. *Shows daily at 7, plus at 3 ϲ n Sat and 3 and 11 on Sun; closed Tues.* Ⓜ Tsvetnoy Bulvar

New Moscow State Circus, Prospekt Vernadskovo 7, ℗ 930 2815. A more breathtaking show than at the old circus includes dizzy ꞧrapeze acts. The circus has four interchangeable floors including a pool and ar ice-rink, with *shows Mon–Fri at 7, Sat and Sun at 11.30 and 3 as well*. Ch ldren will enjoy the funfair and elephant rides on offer beforehand. Ⓜ Universitet

---

Cinema

Only two cinemas in the city regularly show interesting fil ns:

Kinocenter, Ul. Druzhinnikovskaya 15, ℗ 205 7306/255 9237, is the only place to see good Soviet films and contemporary Russian f lms, though they also show world cinema from America to Zimbabwe. Ⓜ Barrikadnaya

Illuzion, in the Stalinist skyscraper at Kotelnicheskaya Ⲛ aberezhnaya 1/15, ℗ 227 4339, concentrates on foreign, largely European, ꝟorks. Ⓜ Taganskaya

Jazz and Rock Music

Big concerts take place on Red Square and in stadiums at Luzhniki (Ⓜ Sportivnaya) and the Olympiisky Sports Complex, Olimpiisky Pr 16 (Ⓜ Prospekt Mira). At the smaller venues listed below burly bouncers and metal detectors, and a check your weapon policy, is thankfully standard. All charge an entry fee and there are often specialist records on sale within.

All-Star Jazz Club, Ul. Generala Yermolova 6, call Oleg Chernayev on ✆ 973 3474 or 923 9292 for tickets in advance of the weekly session. If it's good, in Moscow, and jazz, it's likely to be here. A bar serves minimal snacks; intimate clubby feel and great atmosphere. *Open from 7.30 on Wed.* Ⓜ Kutuzovskaya

Arkadia Jazz Club, Teatralny Proyezd 3, opposite the Metropol Hotel and through the arch, ✆ 926 9008. A restaurant all week until midnight, after which, Thurs–Sun, you pay a cover fee which gets you a free drink, and enter a late-night haven for jazz fans. Music until 5am. Ⓜ Lubianka

Bunker Club, Basement, Trifonovskaya Ul. 56, ✆ 278 7043/284 3578, Leading light of the recent spate of new live music clubs, not least because design of the club as a whole has been deemed important, a rare thing in Moscow. Neither are the management slack in choosing their bands, who represent the cream of Russia's second stream rock bands. *Open Wed, Fri and Sat, 8–till the neighbours in the block complain.* Ⓜ Rizhskaya

Akustica Club, Khamovnichesky Val 2, ✆ 242 1707, is the closest the Bunker Club gets to a rival, and to some tastes a whole lot nicer. As the name suggests it is often quieter, less rabid than most of the other clubs in the city. Housed in what used to be the second stage of the Mossoviet Theatre, there is plenty of room away from the music, and a bar selling drink and sandwiches. *Open Fri and Sat from 7.* Ⓜ Sportivnaya

Arbat Blues Club, Theatre Studio on Arbat, Pereulok Aksakova 11, house 2, ✆ 291 1546. This is a two room dive, one big enough for a band and dancing, the other, with the bar, *almost* quiet enough to talk. The eclectic (confused?) music policy ranges from ear-splitting local heavy-metal to American journalists side-lining in nostalgic blues. *Open Fri & Sat from 7.30.* Ⓜ Arbatskaya

Sexton Fozd, Pervy Baltiisky Proyezd 6, korp. 2, ✆ 151 1218. Opened by Russian Hell's Angels, the Night Wolves, who curiously played a vital role in keeping democracy activists in touch with one another during the August 1991 coup. It's their club, leathers are in and the metal is heavy. *Open almost round the clock, with a break from 10am–12 noon, live music sets from 7.* Ⓜ Sokol

Rock Club at Kievskaya, Ul. Berezhkovskaya 28, ✆ 300 7609 (ask for Dima), is quite a large venue attracting some of the better known bands.
Ⓜ Kievskaya and bus 91, 119 or 505.

Jerry Rubin Club, Profsoyuznaya Ul. 31, korp. 2, ✆ 120 7006 (ask for Sveta). Another venue for local rock, heavy metal and post-punk. Ⓜ Profsoyuznaya

Nightclubs

The only nightclubs foreigners used to visit were in their hotels, and there was always a quota of prostitutes in the mix. This formula has been taken on by certain private discotheques now operating in the city (reluctantly listed at the end), and those sensitive to sexploitation may find some of the offerings here hard to take.

To get an idea of what the average young Muscovite wants of an evening out, visit the vast mafia-run discotheques held in the city's indoor stadia. If that isn't your scene there are a handful of smaller places to go dancing, where the crowd, if raketeers have not muscled in, is rather more laid-back. Unless otherwise stated, entry is around the $15 mark.

Manhattan Express, Hotel Rossiya (Red Square entrance), ✆ 298 5354/5355, is the latest hip opening, started by a pair of NY club owners. Entry around $25, a small price to pay for dancing shoulder to shoulder with the city's happening crowd, both pats and ex-pats. Open daily 7pm–4am. Ⓜ Ploshchad Revolutsii

Hermitage, Hermitage Theatre, Karetny Ryad 3, ✆ 299 7519/1160. When the theatre crowd has left, the artsy crowd takes over to boogie. Extraordinary plastic sculptures by provocative group Art Blya lead down a corridor to the dance floor (no rap), and the lasers mesmerise. Cheap entry and drinks. *Open Fri, Sat, Sun 10pm–6am; plans to extend during the week.* Ⓜ Chekhovskaya

0–11 Club, Ul. Sadovaya Kudrinskaya 19 behind American Express, is a cheap Serbian club with some of the liveliest dancing in town and not so loud you can't talk. Ⓜ Barrikadnaya

Russkaya Troika, Orlyonok Hotel, Kosygina Ul. 15, reserve a comfortable table on 939 8609/8683. A spectacular floor show, Follies Bergères Moscow-style (*i.e.* more naked), with dancing afterwards. Drinks, hors d'oeuvres and snappy service. *Open Thurs–Sun 11.30–late.*

M & S, Ul. Ostozhenka 40–42, ✆ 291 3232. For those who like comfy surroundings with their dancing, this is the up-market, friendly place. Vast selection of drinks and miraculous absence of mafiosi account for the slightly more expensive entry and prices. Snacks too. *Open daily 8–5.* Ⓜ Park Kultury

Arlecchino, Ul. Druzhinnikovskaya 15, ✆ 255 9759. Expensive entrance and live music distinguish this old dancing haunt next to the Italian restaurant. *Open Thurs–Sun 11–5.30.* Ⓜ Krasnopresnenskaya

Jump, Universalny Sportivny Zal, Luzhniki Sports Complex, ✆ 247 0343. Stage shows and a video screen are the only distractions from a night of techno-pop for teeny boppers. *Open 11–5.30; closed Mon and Tues.* Ⓜ Sportivnaya

U Lisa, Olympic Stadium, Olimpiisky Prospekt 16, ✆ 288 4027 or 923 3436. The wide range of distractions to choose from in this vast space include a casino, a stage show, food stalls and bars, but most people choose to dance. *Open Fri and Sat 11–6.* Ⓜ Prospekt Mira

Night Flight, Tverskaya Ul. 17, ✆ 229 4165. Centrally located with a small two-floor bar and dance floor, this place should be ideal. The management's policy of flooding the place with twice as many prostitutes as customers and playing atrocious music kills, that dead, however. No sports gear or trainers, men must be over 30, women over 21. *Open daily 9–5.*

Red Zone, TsSKA Ice Palace, Leningradsky Prospekt, ✆ 213 5098. The gulag theme would be interesting if the designers hadn't fallen into the S&M trap of the creators of the gulag itself. Vast dance floor beneath strippers in suspended cages... need I say more. *Open 11–6, closed Mon.* Ⓜ Aeroport

Banzai, Ul. Novopeschannaya 12, ✆ 157 7552 to reserve that ringside table. Another bizarre product of the modern Moscow psyche, featuring boxing, karate, dancing and stripping. *Open Fri–Sun 9–5.*

Casinos

All the rage in Moscow's wild west economy at the moment, gambling dens range from places which rival Monte Carlo for turnover to those where a beginner can happily spend an evening throwing chips at roulette and Black Jack and emerge with enough money for the taxi ride home. Most hotels have their own casinos, but it's much more fun to go out and see Moscow's new rich squander their gains.

Casino Royale in the magnificent neoclassical Hippodrome, Ul. Begovaya 22, ✆ 945 1410, is the queen of casinos. The manager, who has seen a thing or two, says he's never experienced amounts like it. With Fyodoroff's famous restaurant on the premises this is the best place in Moscow to get rid of it all in one night. Dress smart, and bring your passport or hotel registration card to get in. *Restaurant open 12 noon–4am, gaming tables from 8pm.* Ⓜ Begovaya

Golden Ostrap, Shmitovsky Prospekt 3, ✆ 259 4795. This is a new Russian-German venture started by a Georgian actor attracting its share of Moscow's thespians. A Georgian chef creates for the expensive restaurant, and there is also a cheaper bistro open until 11. *Open 8–4.* Ⓜ Ul. 1905 Goda

Alexander's, Kolonny Zal, Ul Pushkinskaya 1, entrance 6, ✆ 292 7123. It seems strange to gamble in the very room where tens of thousands of weeping Russians paid their last respects to Stalin. Aiming for the same clientele as the Royale, this club includes a small dance floor for its expensive entrance fee.

Casino Moscow, Leningradskaya Hotel, Ul. Kalanchovskaya 21/40, ✆ 975 1967. One of the best aspects of this hotel is the friendly mixed crowd who visit its casino and late night bar *Open 2pm–5am.* Ⓜ Komsomolskaya

Casino Arbat, Novy Arbat 29, ✆ 291 1172. The best place for novices. The stakes are low, and when even they get too much there are plenty of tables to sit out at among the potted plants. *Open 9–5.*

St Petersburg

Social life in St Petersburg remains truer to the tradition of getting together over the kitchen table, and the choice of evening entertainment lags behind that in the capital. When Petersburgers do go out however, it tends to be zanier, for longer, and to get drunker. Locals attribute any misdemeanours to the climate. One vital factor governing your decisions between April and November, when the Neva runs through the city free of ice, is the bridges. To let shipping into the network of rivers, lakes and canals that leads right through Russia to the Black Sea, they are opened for nearly three hours in the middle of the night. If you get stuck on the wrong side you face either a long, cold wait or, if you are lucky, an extortionately expensive boat ride. There are respites over various bridges around 3am:

Dvortsovy Most	1.35–3.05 and 3.15–4.45
Birzhevoy Most	2.25–3.20 and 3.40–4.40
Troitsky Most	2–4.40
Most Leytenanta Shmita	1.55–4.50
Tuchkov Most	2.00–3.10 and 3.40–4.40
Liteyny Most	2.10–4.40
Kamennoostrovsky Most	2.15–3 and 4.05–4.55
Bolsheokhtinsky Most	2.45–4.55
Alexandra Nevskovo Most	2.35–4.50
Sampsonievsky Most	2.10–2.45 and 3.20–4.25
Bolshoykrestovsky Most	2.05–2.55 and 4.45–5.20
Grenadersky Most	2.45–3.45 and 4.20–4.45

Ballet and Opera

Mariinsky Theatre, Teatralnaya Ploshchad 2, ✆ 314 9083 or 114 1211. Known as the Kirov ballet during the Soviet period, this charming building with its delicate blue and gold interior has been home to some of the greatest dancers of all time—Nureyev, Baryshnikov and Pavlova amongst them. It premiered Tchaikovsky's Sleeping Beauty in 1890. It is a measure of quite how traditional Russian ballet is that the very same choreography is danced today. The main company tours a great deal but is most likely to be at home in winter. Secondary companies perform during the rest of the year, except July and August when the theatre closes. The Mariinsky is also currently reputed to be the best place to see opera. Ⓜ Nevsky Prospekt and bus 22 or 27

Maly Theatre, Pl. Isskustv 1, ✆ 219 1978, is St Petersburg's second ballet and opera stage, on which everyone descends in July and August when the Mariinsky is closed.

It is well worth keeping an eye open for performances in both the **Hermitage Theatre**, Dvortsovaya Naberezhnaya 34, ✆ 311 9025, and the **Yusupov Palace Theatre**, Naberezhnaya Reki Moyki 94, ✆ 314 9883. Both are small, private affairs, the former built for Catherine the Great, and though performances tend to be extracts, the buildings themselves and their intimate proportions make the occasions a great treat.

Yubileyny Sports Palace, Pl. Dobrolyubova 18, Petrograd Side, ✆ 238 4049, often stages ballet on ice in winter.

Hotel Astoria has its own theatre, where the private Valentina Ganibalova Ballet Company performs every night at 10 except Mondays.

Classical Music

Glinka Capella, Naberezhnaya Reki Moyki 20, ✆ 314 1159, used to produce the choir for the tsar's chapel in the Hermitage, and classical choral music is what it is still best at though you can hear folk music here too.

Shostakovich Philharmonia, Ul. Mikhailovskaya 2, ✆ 311 7333/110 4290. Tickets for concerts in both the featureless big hall, with its entrance on Pl. Isskustv, and the small hall at Nevsky Prospekt 30 can be bought at this address. Large posters outside advertise the programme; inside is a good secondhand music, record and compact disc emporium.

Oktyabrskaya Concert Hall, Ligovsky Pr. 6, ✆ 277 6960, is used equally for important Russian and foreign classical and rock concerts.

Rimsky-Korsakov's Flat, Zagorodny Prospekt 28, ✆ 210 5226, continues the composer's tradition of musical evenings on Wednesdays and Saturdays.

Theatre

Bolshoy Dramatichesky Teatr, Nab Reki Fontanki 65, ✆ 310 9242. St Petersburg's premier theatre is largely known for it traditional staging of traditional Russian plays. Ⓜ Gostiny Dvor

Pushkin Drama Theatre, Pl. Ostrovskovo 2, ✆ 312 1545. A beautiful neoclassical theatre, part of one of Rossi's ensembles built to aggrandize the city after the victory over Napoleon. The theatre stretches occasionally to ballet, and productions, again, are very traditional. Ⓜ Gostiny Dvor

Maly Dramatichesky Teatr, Ul. Rubinshteyna 18, ✆ 113 2028. Of all the mainstream theatres, this is the place to come to see more experimental staging and controversial new Russian plays. Ⓜ Vladimirskaya/Dostoyevskaya

Baltisky Dom, Aleksandrovsky Park 4, ✆ 232 4490 or 6244. Known as a youth the-atre, attracting the more innovative but lesser known St Petersburg companies who perform raw plays appealing to a younger audience.   Ⓜ Gorkovskaya

Circus and Puppetry

The Circus, Naberezhnaya Reki Fontanki 3, ✆ 210 4411 or 314 8478. The oldest extant circus in Russia, the performances can often feel rather the same. Closed mid-July to mid-Sept.

Sharmanka Theatre, Moskovsky Pr. 151a, ✆ 297 2666 or 294 6311, calls itself kinetic theatre and uses monstrous automated metal puppets to explore recent Russian experience. Beguiling theatre of the mind for adults and older children.

Cinema

To find out what is on look out for the cinema posters, one of which is always posted inside the archway at Nevsky Prospekt 60.

If you want to relax with very soft porn or violence, Nevsky Prospekt's cinemas offer a selection of familiar American fare, dubbed into Russian.

Dom Kino, Karavansaya Ul. 12, ✆ 314 8118, is the club of the union of cinema workers, and you are supposed to be a member to enter, but try your luck. They show classic Russian films, dubbed foreign films and retrospective sea-sons by geniuses of the order of Paradzhanov.   Ⓜ Gostiny Dvor

Spartak, Ul. Saltykova Schedrina 8, ✆ 272 7897. This converted church shows dubbed foreign films.   Ⓜ Chernyshevskaya

Dostoyevsky Museum, Kuznechny Pereulok 5, arranges showings of film adapta-tions of the novelist's work, in Russian, at around midday most Sundays.

Ⓜ Vladimirskaya/Dostoyevskaya

Jazz and Rock Music

St Petersburg was the fount of underground rock in the 1970s and 1980s, though Moscow seems to have stolen the limelight now. Big names include Boris Grebinshikov and his famous St Petersburg band *Akvarium*, the Pop Mekhanika music, movement, design ensemble led by the talented and versatile Sergei Kuriokhin, and DDT, a rock band led by the poetic lyricist, Shavchuk. Bands of this stature are likely to fill auditoria like the **Oktyabrsky** and **Yubileyny** (above) or the **Sport and Culture Complex**, Prospekt Yura Gagarina 8, by Ⓜ Park Pobedy.

Jazz Club, Zagorodny Prospekt 27, ✆ 164 8565, invites you to book a table and listen to jazz star David Goloshchukhin and his band. If you want to listen to modern jazz, the only chance is during the late night sets on Fri and Sat *Open 8–11, later on Fri and Sat.* A good night out but rather sedate and no dancing.

New Jazz Club, Tavricheskaya Ul. 4, ☎ 275 6090. Challenging the monopoly long held by the Jazz Club this new venue also tends to stick to classic jazz rather than modern. *Open Wed–Sun 7.30–11pm.*

Tam Tam Club, 16ya liniya and Maly Prospekt, Vasilievsky Ostrov. Resting precariously on its reputation, this is still the place to listen to live music in the city, with a penchant for hard core and punk. There is a bar and small snack bar on the premises *Open Fri and Sat 8–11.* Ⓜ Vasileostrovskaya

Rok Klub, Ul. Rubinshteyna 13, ☎ 312 3483, was the only officially sanctioned rock club in the city for a long time, hence its imaginative Soviet-style name. Still open and fronting a wide range of indie bands, but ignored by the hard-core St Petersburg music scene. *Open 8–3.* Ⓜ Mayakovskaya

Indie Club, Lenin House of Culture, Pl. Obukhovskoy Oborony 233. Foreign and out-of-town groups share the stage with locals in this heavy metal hang out. *Open 2nd and 4th Friday of the month.*

Roksi, Ul. Tushina, attracts a number of popular and more famous bands with its big hall. *Open Sat from 7.* Ⓜ Ligovsky Prospekt

Nightclubs

The urge to rave in Moscow was imported from St Petersburg where a number of companies, Tanzpol and MX amongst them, have been set up specifically to organize one-off parties in bizarre locations. For a while the place to dance was in a swimming pool on the Petrograd Side, and during the White Nights festival in 1993 those who could get in got down amongst the military hardware in the courtyard of the Museum of Military History. The only way to find out about these extravaganzas is to keep an eye on posters and an ear to the ground.

It's a measure of their hold on things in St Petersburg that the mafia even tried muscling in here. One party planner had his arm broken after refusing the 'protection' of the powerful Tambov Group. But don't worry, as an outsider you are unlikely to get involved. All of these clubs charge an entrance fee of around $15.

Tunel, Liubansky Pereulok 1, on the corner of Zverinskaya Ul. This discotheque in a converted bomb shelter is the place to dance on a regular basis. *Open Thurs and Sat.* Ⓜ Gorkovskaya and quite a walk.

Arts Club Café, Kanal Griboyedova 3, ☎ 314 5273, stages live bands and dance parties from 10pm. Ⓜ Nevsky Prospekt

Dom Aktyorov, the actor's club, at Nevsky Prospekt 86, ☎ 273 3189, hosts dancing Wed–Sun from 12–5. Ⓜ Mayakovskaya

Lis's, Sport and Culture Complex, Prospekt Yura Gagarina 8. Huge dance floor with dubious naked entertainment but always plenty of people dancing. Not for those who dislike mass activities. A body frisk at the entrance keeps out weapons. Keep your wits about you. *Open Fri and Sat 11–dawn.* Ⓜ Park Pobedy

Nevsky Melody, Naberezhnaya Sverdlovskaya 62, ℗ 227 1596. Discotheque attached to an expensive restaurant and casino, attracting a richer mix of businessmen and their molls. *Open 9–4.* Ⓜ Novocherkasskaya plus tram 7, 23 or 46

Grand Hotel Europe nightclub top floor, Ul. Mikhailovskaya 1/7, ℗ 312 0072, has great views of the city, but its cosy interiors are principally a pick-up joint for single business men. For this the hotel requests jacket and tie.

Casinos

The gambling bug, or perhaps the money to make it profitable, has yet to hit St Petersburg. Addicts should head for:

Spielbank Casino, Hotel Pribaltiskaya, Ul. Korablestroiteley 14. *Open 10–4.* Ⓜ Primorskaya plus tram 11 or 63, bus 41, 42 or 47 or trolleybus 10, 10a or 46

Nevsky Melody, Neberezhnaya Sverdlovska 62, ℗ 227 2676. *Open 9pm–3am.* Ⓜ Novocherkasskaya plus tram 7, 23 or 46

White Nights in St Petersburg

Though touted as a major event in St Petersburg's calendar, it is quite easy to miss the cultural events which mark the longest days of the year over the summer solstice on June 21. Ask your hotel service desk or Russian friends to give you the low down. To appreciate nature's performance, which keeps the skies light from 5am to 3am and the city ghostly in its silvery grip, take a walk on the banks of the river. There is a light-headed, 24-hour party atmosphere of guitar playing and drinking; boats buzz up and down, music blaring, champagne bottles held aloft, and on the solstice itself vast scroll paintings may be let down from the suspended bridges.

Rock concerts are held at Palace Square, the Peter and Paul Fortress and Yelagin Island, together with other outdoor events. Those on for a marathon with the Russians can catch a boat at midnight at Anichkov Most which sails round the canals and rivers until 5am. The one hour trip from in front of the Hermitage leaving at 10 is too sedate, and it is too early to see the bridges going up. Best of all, arrange during the day for a private boat near Nevsky Prospekt on the Moyka Canal to meet up with you later and scud beneath the opening bridges, or call Akva Express, ℗ 237 1436 or 110 1192, between 9–11am and 6–11pm, to arrange a night-time sight-seeing cruise in English.

Shopping

531

The most visible effect of the *perestroika* revolution has been on shopping. In place of a lack of goods you will find a rampant market economy, with salesmen and women hawking anything they can make a profit from on pavements outside metro stations, department stores and museums. The phenomenon of the kiosk is legendary. Over a period of months hundreds of thousands of these metal boxes appeared on the streets, filling the gaping hole in state supply with everything from condoms to clothes. On top of these there is a healthy sprinkling of shops run in partnership with foreign companies, selling western goods (food, clothes and electrical items) in an environment you would recognize, at a price. Most tourists will easily be able to satisfy their needs from these sources.

The more demanding shopper and those on a low budget, like the majority of the Russian population, face trickier terrain. The difficulty lies in finding something interesting and good-looking at a reasonable price. To be successful you should learn a number of Russian habits. Pop into shops as you pass for a quick look and glance into kiosk windows. Always keep an *avoizka*, a 'just-in-case' bag, traditionally a string one, somewhere about your person as you never know when you are going to find what's needed. There is nothing more satisfying than coming back from an excursion with the very thing the city is currently in *defitsit*. Never think you will come back and buy something later. Quality flies out of the shops.

As for handing over the money and getting the goods in return; if you are in a Russian shop this too has its own logic. Take pencil and paper with you if your Russian is not strong. First identify what you want and how much it will cost. If it entails weighing, have the assistant do so so that you know the exact price. Next, bearing in mind also the number of the counter (*otdel*), go to the cashier at the till (*kassa*) and tell her (it usually is) the price and counter. Pay and take your receipt back to the counter where you hand it over in exchange for your purchase. This may entail three separate queues. One final piece of advice—think laterally if you are determined to find something in the Russian shops. Logic like selling loo paper in stationary departments defeats most western minds.

Art and Antique Export

You should be aware that it is illegal to export anthing pre-1945. They may simply be taken from you at the airport on your departure. On top of this you are *supposed* to get permission from the Ministry of Culture to export more recent painting and sculptures. So many tourists do so without permission that it is hard to believe the process of getting a letter from the artist, two photographs of the work and greasing the palm of the bureaucrat is worth it. If you are buying a serious piece however, the artist or gallery owner will help you.

Opening Times

Russian shops are mostly closed on Sundays, and universally take an hour's lunch break somewhere between 1 and 3. They open between 8 and 10 and do not close until 8 or 9. Supermarkets and shopping centres run in partnership with western firms tend to eschew the lunch hour and open for 12 hours—8–8 or 10–10. Times have only been given where they do not correspond to these outlines, or are also closed on Saturdays or Mondays.

Antiques

As well as the export difficulties mentioned above, watch out for fakes, particularly icons. The antiques market is not large. Families treasure the one old tea-cup or chair to have survived the upheavals of the last 80 years, while the rest of the set are beign cherished by the descendants of KGBisti who helped themselves during the wholesale confiscations which accompanied arrests before the war. However, incomprehensible inflation is causing people to surrender their valuables to *kommissionny*, shops which sell them for a small percentage. This is where the fun is to be had, as long as you think of the money you are providing the owners with, not their sentimental loss.

Moscow

Ul. Arbat contains the greatest concentration of *kommissionny* in the city, providing hours of fertile hunting. Look out for signs starting with the letters 'Антиквар' (antikvar), and don't miss **Unisat**, at Ul. Vakhtangova 5 leading off the Arbat. It is a must for fans of 19th-century ceramics and a curiosity for anyone, with its old French horns and '50s radio sets. Ⓜ Arbatskaya

Knigolyuba Lavka, Ul. Tverskaya Yamskaya 22, is one of the top *kommissionny* in Moscow, specializing in books but also selling an eclectic range of objects, from old embroidered *tubetyekas* (Central Asian men's hats) to Art Deco watches. Ⓜ Belorusskaya

Antikvariat, Ul. Krasina 16, offers everything from old pianos to silver, including icons and occasional pieces of Soviet ceramic. Ⓜ Mayakovskaya

St Petersburg

Kommissionny, Ul. Bolshaya Konyushennaya 13, is a two-room treasure trove, from hideous '50s lamps to exquisite Indian miniatures. Ⓜ Nevsky Prospekt

Sankt Peterbourg, Nevsky Prospekt 54, is the city's most exclusive *kommissionny*, selling fine objects, and less good paintings and furniture, at inflated prices.

Ⓜ Gostiny Dvor

Kommissionny, Kamenoostrovsky Prospekt 4, is worth keeping an eye on as well.

Ⓜ Gorkovskaya

Staraya Kniga, Nevsky Propekt 18, is better known for books but also sells bric-a-brac and fine old prints of bizarre subjects. Prints of Moscow and St Petersburg are infinitely easier to find in Portobello Road.

Art

There is a danger of killing your aesthetic sense with an overdose of mediocre painting in the streets and galleries of both cities. Ever since the idea of the starving 'underground' artist first gripped the tourist imagination in the early 80s, those of dubious talent have been encouraged to expect good money for their efforts, displayed at Izmailovo and Krimsky Val in Moscow, and on Nevsky Prospekt and Klenovaya Alleya in St Petersburg (*see* souvenirs). The following list highlights the better galleries in which you can regain a sense of perspective. Those in Moscow far outstrip the ones in St Petersburg for professionalism.

Moscow

Contemporary Art Centre, Ul. Bolshaya Yakimanka 2/6, is housed in a peaceful two-strorey building round a courtyard. Plans are afoot to develop the centre with a café and restaurant, but for the moment it consists of some six galleries, ranging from naive and primitive art at Gallery Dar to contemporary Russian conceptual art at Shkola.

Ⓜ Polyanka

L Gallery, Ul. Oktyabrskaya 26, ✆ 289 2491, is the leading gallery for contemporary Russian sculpture and installations. *Open 12–8 Wed and Thurs, 11–7 Fri–Sun; closed Mon and Tues.*

Ⓜ Rizhskaya

Atrium-V, Museum of the History of Moscow, Novaya Ploshchad 12, ✆ 489 7253 or 925 4660, specializes in high quality lithographs, watercolours and prints of Moscow, to save the agony of trying to find something good from the stalls at Izmailovo or Krimsky Val.

Ⓜ Lubianka

Photo Centre, Gogolievsky Bulvar 8, ✆ 290 4188, hosts a specialist outlet for genuine Soviet posters and memorabilia. These people know what they're doing and stock only the best; consequently prices are high, but the stock is magnificent—bombs reigning down on wicked capitalists, Stalin smiling up at Soviet planes flying in a formation spelling his name. *Open 12–8; closed Mon.*

Ⓜ Kropotkinskaya

A-3 Gallery, Starokonyushenny Pereulok 39, ✆ 291 8484, is at the intelligeable cutting edge of the contemporary Moscow arts scene—where Art-Blya, who did the obscene yet humorous sculptures at the Hermitage Nightclub, started out. *Open 11–7, closed Mon and Tues.* Ⓜ Arbatskaya

Alfa Art Auctions, Central House of Artists, Krymsky Val 10, ✆ 230 0091, is the leader of a new fashion in the Moscow art world for auctions. They put together exhibitions of late-19th and early-20th century Russian art and auction them monthly. Ⓜ Oktyabrskaya

Art Moderne Gallery, Ul. Bolshaya Ordynka 39, ✆ 233 1551. The eclectic range of its exhibitions, from photography to glass, suggest a generalist, market-oriented approach and aesthetic quality varies considerably. *Open 11–7; closed Mon.* Ⓜ Tretyakovskaya

Mars Gallery, Ul. Malaya Filyovskaya 32, ✆ 146 2029, used to house the best selection of contemporary Russian art, but has been overtaken by the expansion of the market in the last two years. *Open 12–6; closed Mon.* Ⓜ Pionerskaya

St Petersburg

Gallery 10–10, Ul. Pushkinskaya 10, was originally at the heart of the vibrant St Petersburg underground art scene, attached to this huge artistic squat. Today their shows are no better than hit or miss. Pushkinskaya 10 holds an iconic position in the history of Underground St Petersburg, for it was here that many of the leading painters, poets and thinkers of the early 1980s came together to live. If you manage to catch one of the parties/concerts held in the courtyard in summer you will get a whiff of the tail end of that artistic anarchy. *Closed Sat and Sun.* Ⓜ Mayakovskaya

The Modern Art Gallery, Naberezhnaya Reki Moyki 83, ✆ 314 4734, is a new gallery associated with the St Petersburg Union of Artists, which attempts to represent the city's artistic traditions from realism to avant garde. The gallery also intends to buy important pieces of Petersburg art to serves as the foundation for a Museum of Modern Art. Ⓜ Nevsky Prospekt

Palitra Gallery, Nevsky Prospect 166, ✆ 277 1216, exhibits a mixed bag of painters in its peaceful courtyard rooms. The directors have a good eye, the gallery a good café. Ⓜ Ploshchad Alexandra Nevskovo

Dostoyevsky Museum, Kuznechny Pereulok 5/2, houses a number of galleries in its building, including one which specializes in characterful naive painting. *Open 10.30–5.30; closed Mon.* Ⓜ Vladimirskaya

Lavka Khudozhnikov, Nevsky Prospekt 8, ✆ 312 6193, concentrates less on paintings than on ceramics, jewellery and even printed silk. Ⓜ Nevsky Prospekt

Books

Well-printed colour art books are still one of the bargains to be had in Russia, and you will find them for sale outside any of the major tourist sights—the Kremlin,

Novodevichy Monastery, the Hermitage Museum and Nevsky Prospekt. Second-hand bookshops sometimes turn up old English-language books and magazines which have arrived there through their own mysterious history and could end up being taken back to the land of their birth by you. They often share space with yet more *kommissionny*.

Moscow

Ul. Arbat has a number of second-hand bookstores, called *bukinist*, notably at **No. 9** and **No. 36**. Ⓜ Arbatskaya

Souvenir, Ul. Arbat 4, includes the best counter for art books in Moscow, when you take the selection and the price together. Ⓜ Arbatskaya

Innostraniye Knigi, Ul. Kachalova 16, has a second-hand English-language department where you can pick up kid's books, non-fiction (often with a Russian angle) and novels. They also sell Russian-English dictionaries. Ⓜ Barrikadnaya

Akademkniga, Ul. Tverskaya 19, has an impressive selection of art books and paperbacks in English on the first (second) floor. Ⓜ Pushkinskaya

Dom Knigi, Ul. Novy Arbat 26, was once the place for cheap book but is now a waste of time. The hawkers on the steps outside have a much better selection.
  Ⓜ Arbatskaya

Progress Books, Zubovsky Bulvar 17, is the cheap outlet for English translations of Russian classics. Beware poor quality translations—the assistants are happy to let you read a bit to check. Don't think you can come here with a particular book in mind; they have what they have when they have it. Ⓜ Park Kultury

Zwemmers, Kuznetsky Most 18, is a bit of Covent Garden in downtown Moscow, an English-language bookshop. Its concentrates on expensive art books (like the parent-shops in London), classics of world literature, particularly English and Russian, and non-fiction on Russian subjects. Ⓜ Kuznetsky Most

Beriozka, Ul. Prechistenka 37, used to be the best place for foreigners to buy art books, and it still has a good selection behind the food and drink section.
  Ⓜ Park Kultury

Shkolnik, Leninsky Prospekt 21, always piled high with notebooks, papers of all weights, colouring books, crayons and pens, is the place to head if you want to write your own book. Ⓜ Leninsky Prospekt

St Petersburg

Staraya Kniga, Nevsky Prospekt 18, sells a small, high-quality selection of books, displaying the most valuable in mahogany, glass fronted book shelves from a bye-gone age. Ⓜ Nevsky Prospekt

Bukinist, Lityeny Prospekt 57/59 contains yards of dusty old books on all manner of subjects, plus a few antique objects. Ⓜ Mayakovskaya

Dom Knigi, Nevsky Prospekt 28, the so called 'House of Books' contains little to interest English speakers except stationary and the small foreign language arts' section to the right on the first floor.   Ⓜ Nevsky Prospekt

Kniga, Nevsky Prospekt 16, and the shop in the **Russian Museum**, Pl. Isskustv, share the best selection of art books and postcards.   Ⓜ Nevsky Prospekt

Clothes

If fashion is what you are after on holiday, you've chosen the wrong place to come. There was a journalistic flurry of excitement in the 1980s when Raisa Gorbachova became the first Soviet leader's wife to take an interest in such a bourgeois concern. Her couturier was Slava Zaitsev, whose latest collection can be viewed and bought at Dom Mody, Prospekt Mira 21, Moscow (Ⓜ Prospekt Mira). Don't rush there with high expectations.

Since then the Russian fashion scene has hit the headlines from time to time, mostly when artists have created sculptural costumes so outrageous you couldn't actually wear them. If something vital is missing from your wardrobe and you have the stamina, you could scour the Russian department stores for items, but you are far more likely to find what you want at the expensive boutiques selling imported clothing. That just leaves fur hats and coats, a Russian speciality. Hats appear wherever tourists congregate. Coats can be found, if your conscience allows, at the fur shops listed below.

Moscow

Mekha, at Ul. Pyatnitskaya 13 (Ⓜ Novokuznyetskaya) and Stoleshnikov Pereulok, at the corner with Ul. Petrovka (Ⓜ Teatralnaya) both specialize in fur. Supply is erratic.

Kiosks selling imported clothes and shoes are concentrated at certain locations. Two of the most central are at the junction of Ul. Nikolskaya and Bogoyavlinsky Pereulok in Kitai Gorod and at the junction of Ul. Petrovka and Kuznetsky Most behind TsUM. Here you will find trainers, chinese silk shirts, Turkish-made shell-suits, quilted Chinese jackets and shoes of all kinds.

Sadko Arcade, Krasnogvardyeisky Proyezd, shelters boutiques selling labels such as Charles Jourdan and Max Mara. *Open 10–10.*   Ⓜ Ul. 1902 Goda

GUM, Red Square, has sold out spectacularly to capitalism, renting space to Escada, Galeries Lafayette, Benetton and Karstadt.   Ⓜ Ploshchad Revolutsii

Stockmann Fashion and Office Store, Leninsky Prospekt 73, ✆ 134 3546, was one of the first to address itself to the problem of clothes for the foreign community and the increasingly rich Russians. It has the largest selection of designer labels in the city.

Moscow is Paris compared to St Petersburg where fashion is concerned. In desperation search the department stores. Otherwise:

Lenwest, Nevsky Prospekt 119, ✆ 277 0635, is the best shoe shop in the city, and tries to ensure it stocks good warm boots in winter.   Ⓜ Ploshchad Vosstaniya

Burberry, Grand Hotel Europe, Ul. Mikhailovskaya 1/7, has a moderate selection of the label's classic clothing range.   Ⓜ Nevsky Prospekt

Mekha, Bolshoy Prospekt 64, Petrograd Side, is stuffed with fur coats and hats, including ones to transform your toddlers into teddy bears.   Ⓜ Petrogradskaya

Department Stores

Known as *univermag* and mostly built in the 19th-century as emporia for the sale of piles of exotic goods, Russia's department stores became a showcase for the dreary state consumerism of the Soviet Union. Today the bright colours of Benetton are pitched next to the increasingly competitive offerings of Russian manufacturers. The more traditional still offer a 'universal' range of goods from clothes and shoes, household goods and stationary to musical instruments and souvenirs.

Moscow

GUM, Red Square, is the king of the stores, its three long arcades attracting a never-diminishing throng of shoppers and watchers. Imported clothes now rank high, but you can still find rouble bargains in the bed-linen and souvenir departments.   Ⓜ Ploshchad Revolutsii

TsUM, Ul. Petrovka 2, started life behind its Gothic façade as the Scottish store Muir and Merrilees. The back extension is interesting too, built in 1933 and one of the earliest constructivist buildings in Russia. The interior is a haven of cheap goods, everything from *matrioshkas* to socks.   Ⓜ Teatralnaya

Petrovsky Passage, Ul. Petrovka 10, has had a massive face-lift which mysteriously seems to have lessened its appeal. There are consistently fewer customers in its gleaming mall, where Fuji develop photographs, and a range of stalls sell souvenirs, clothes and electrical goods.   Ⓜ Teatralnaya

St Petersburg

Gostiny Dvor, Nevsky Prospekt 35. In its present state of dereliction, approaching Gostiny Dvor in a bad mood can be a recipe for serious depression. The one side of this enormous quasi-triangular 18th-century building still operating runs along Ul. Sadovaya. Dull neon fails to highlight the few consumer peaks—childrens toys, stationery and hand-knitted scarves. The British store *Littlewoods* monopolizes the far end of the store, selling the cheap end of its clothing range as well as food and electrical goods.   Ⓜ Gostiny Dvor

Passazh, Nevsky Prospekt 48, is undergoing a piecemeal modernisation. Highlights
include a small *kommissionny* section, bed linens on the top floor and the odd
stall of imported clothing.

Apraksin Dvor, Ul. Sadovaya, is another 18th-century umbrella of separate shops.
For a modern-day descent into the world of a Dostoyevskian market seek out
the arched entrance to *Veschovy Rynok*, the penny-pinching, underworld flea-
market which takes place inside the courtyard.

Food and Drink

There are three ways of buying food in Moscow and St Petersburg: in the state
shops, at the markets and in the supermarkets part-owned and run by foreign partners. The easier the experience, the more expensive the produce. Queues still form
at cheap state shops, no longer so much because of poor supply but simply because
they are all most people can afford. The one Russian shop you should not miss is
the bread shop. Russian bread, the normal brown rye loaf, is delicious, and if you
are lucky you will find an aromatic (*aromatny*) loaf in stock, the king of which is
known as 'Borodinsky'. There is a bread shop in every neighbourhood, simply
called хлеб (*khleb*—bread).

More affluent Russians, foreigners and—on special occasions—everyone else, head
for the markets, where fruit and vegetables, dairy products and better, more varied
cuts of meat are available in abundance. They are exclusively Mafia-controlled,
often by gangs from the southern borders between Russia, Azerbaijan and Georgia.
The rule here is to bargain. Even if you manage to talk your way out of the foreigners' premium, the salesman will still be making a healthy profit.

There is a rash of foreign-run supermarkets in Moscow, and a couple of really good
ones in St Petersburg. Each has its own strengths and weaknesses, and language
can be an initial problem (is this Finnish for flour or sugar?). Russian food shops,
the best of which are called 'Gastronom', are open 8–9, the markets are open 9–5
and the supermarkets 10–8. Most are open 7 days a week. Some supermarkets
only accept credit cards and you must have your passport with you as identity.

Gastronoms and Specialist Russian Shops

Moscow

Novy Arbat Gastronom, Ul. Novy Arbat 19, is located beneath and managed by the
Irish House supermarket. An efficient and reliable supplier of cheap tinned
caviar and other more basic ingredients, if you have the patience to queue.

Yeliseyev's, Gastronom No. 1, Ul. Tverskaya 14. The Fortnum and Mason's of pre-
Revolutionary Russia still has its grandiose interior, not matched, sadly, by the
selection of food it sells.

Taganka Gastronom situated on Taganskaya Square, between Uls. Taganskaya and Marksistskaya, sells bread, chicken, pizza, fish, meat and dairy products.

Praga Deli, Ul. Arbat beneath the Praga Restaurant at No. 2. Pre-prepared dishes such as chicken Kiev and exotic gateaux can be bought here after a little wait.

St Petersburg

Yeliseyev's, Nevsky Prospekt 58, is the original branch of Yeliseyev's 19th-century grocery empire. As at the Moscow branch, the decor is uplifting, the crowds queuing for the mediocre stock less so.

Troika Deli, Zagorodny Prospekt 27, sells delicious cakes and pre-cooked dishes to massive queues.

Mechta, Nevsky Prospekt 46, hides a selection of cakes and biscuits in the basement of this Moderne-style building.

Pirozhnoye Ul. Bolshaya Konyushennaya 7, is another place to try for cakes.

Gastronom, corner Ul. Millionaya and Zaporozhny Pereulok, is very crowded, but on good days you can find smoked salmon and caviar here.

Honey. Call ✆ 164 4765 for your supply of addictive organic Siberian honey.

Markets

Moscow

Tsentralny (Central) Rynok, Tsvetnoy Bulvar 15 (*see* p.183), is the most extravagant and expensive of the capital's markets, but is temporarily closed. Everyday groceries are supplemented by fresh caviar from March to June, smoked eel and crayfish. For caviar the guy on the left, top of the stairs after the flower hall is reliable. Aim to pay $20 for a big jam jar, though without a modicum of joking Russian you may be charged more.   Ⓜ Tsvetnoy Bulvar

Cheryomushkinsksy Rynok, Lomonosovsky Prospekt 1, is very good for spices, flowers and potted plants, all at lower prices than at the central market.

Ⓜ Universitet and tram 14, 26 or 39

St Petersburg

Kuznechny Rynok, Kuznechny Pereulok 3, is the city's best market and sells healthy fat chickens, vegetables, fruit and mouth-watering pickled garlic and cucumbers. *Closed Mon.*

Depending where you are, you may prefer to buy veg and fruit from:

Nekrasovsky Rynok, Ul. Nekrasova 52

Sytny Rynok, Sytninskaya Ploshchad 3/5, Petrograd Side, or

Vasileostrovsky Rynok, Bolshoy Prospekt and 4/5 Liniya on Vasilievsky Ostrov.

Supermarkets

Colognia, Ul. Bolshaya Sadovaya 5/1, ℗ 200 5200, is run in partnership with the Germans, and has a particularly good deli for cheese and cold meats.

Ⓜ Mayakovskaya

Garden Ring Supermarket, Ul. Bolshaya Sadovaya 1, ℗ 209 1572, is Irish run for those from Great Britain wanting familiar brands. Ⓜ Mayakovskaya

Sadko, Ul. Bolshaya Dorogomilovskaya 16, ℗ 243 6659, specializes in Japanese ingredients—seaweed, soy, rice—on top of European groceries. Ⓜ Kievskaya. There is also a branch in Sadko Arcade, Krasnogvardeisky Proyezd.

Tito Fontana, Mezhdunarodnaya Hotel, Krasnopresnenskaya Naberezhnaya 12, is where Italian food lovers satisfy cravings for Amaretto biscuits, seafood pasta.

Ⓜ Krasnopresnenskaya

Stockmann's, Zapetsky Val 4/9, ℗ 233 2602, has one of the most exotic fruit stalls in town. Ⓜ Paveletskaya

All the above sell wine, beer and spirits as well, but for specialists try:

Begemot, Ul. Malaya Bronnaya, the only place where among the bottles you can find French wine in a box. Ⓜ Pushkinskaya

Galerie du Vin, Kutuzovsky Pr 1/7, ℗ 243 0365/7256, the closest Moscow gets to a wine warehouse. *Open Mon–Fri 2–7.30, Saturday 10–7.30.* Ⓜ Kievskaya

St Petersburg

Stockmann's, Finlandsky Prospekt 1, ℗ 542 2297, is a Finnish joint venture with by far the best selection of imported food in the city. *Open daily 10am–10pm.*

Babylon Super, Maly Prospekt 54–6, Petrograd Side, ℗ 230 8096, includes fresh fruit and vegetables, fresh bread, frozen foods and an extensive delicatessen counter. *Open Mon–Sat 10am–9pm, Sun 12 noon–8pm.*

Music

Keep your eyes constantly skinned for cheap classical CDs on the Melodiya label, as their normal outlets are increasingly unreliable. You are as likely to have them sold to you in the streets or in a bookshop as you are in record shops.

Moscow

Dom Muzikhi, Ul. Sadovaya Triumfalnaya, sells Russian folk songs and classical recordings among its instruments and sheet music. For rock music, the stalls outside are as good as anywhere. Ⓜ Mayakovskaya

Melodiya, Ul. Novy Arbat 40, seems to be erratically supplied: sometimes it's a treasure trove, at others a wash-out. Ⓜ Arbatskaya

Melodia, Nevsky Prospekt 32/34, has little of interest unless you want a hi-fi system.
 Nevsky Prospekt

Gramplastinka, 7th Liniya 40, Vasilievsky Ostrov, has stacks of classical LPs and as good a selection of CDs as you will find in the city.  Vasileostrovskaya

Philharmonia Ul. Mikhailovskaya 2. Fight your way past the ticket office for the concert hall to find a secondhand record, tape and CD emporium with surprising finds for the connoisseur.

Souvenirs

Unless you are fussy there is no need to plan your shopping in this department. The stock items will find you—again and again. The delightful wooden Russian nest-dolls, *matrioshkas*, are so numerous they become nightmarish, but they are great when you get them back home. If you are serious about quality look for one in which all the figures are slightly different, with a wealth of detail in their costume. Themes include political leaders, fairytales, or women carrying different icons or aspects of domestic life. You can pay the equivalent of hundreds of dollars for the best. Other items which turn up consistently at tourist sites include old Soviet flags, banners and badges, gem-like painted Palekh (and fake Palekh) boxes, tin trays, floral scarves and brooches.

RUSSIAN COMPUTER

Moscow

Izmailovo Market, Izmailovo Park, makes the best expedition on a weekend morning. If you don't feel like buying you can just watch the snake of people searching, finding, bargaining and buying. The huge market includes about an acre of old and new Central Asian carpets, stalls selling antiques and junk, paintings, watches, fur hats, home-made children's clothes, patchwork quilts and toys. *Open 9–5 Sat and Sun.*  Izmailovsky Park

Krimsky Val, outside Central House of Artists, Krimsky Val 10, has the largest selection of souvenir paintings in the city.  Oktyabrskaya

Central Salon of the Russian Artistic Fund, Ukrainsky Bulvar 6. These dismal halls hide some of the most original ceramics, painted boxes and jewellery by contemporary masters in the city.  Kievskaya

Art Salon of the Moscow Cultural Fund, Ul. Pyatnitskaya 16. The woman who runs this tiny shop has a good eye for objects and talented craftsmen. As well as paintings, jewellery and hand-made items of clothing, there is usually a small hoard of antiques for sale. Ⓜ Novokuznetskaya

Arbatskaya Lavka, Ul. Arbat 27, is a good place to buy a lot of presents on a small budget. With *matrioshkas* at about a dollar a piece, you can't expect great quality, but you could stock up for children's parties. Ⓜ Arbatskaya

Russkiye Suveniry, Kutuzovsky Prospekt 9, is warren of interconnected shops selling all the usual souvenirs plus brightly knitted socks and Central Asian hats.

Yantar, 14 Gruzinsky Val, is a good outlet for amber from the Baltic. While much that you see at markets is plastic, this should be the real thing. The styling of necklaces and earrings are sadly uninspired.

St Petersburg

Klenovaya Alleya, Manezhnaya Ploshchad, is an open-air compound of paintings and souvenirs where you will find everything on offer in one place. *Open daily 9–dusk.* Ⓜ Gostiny Dvor

Naslediye (Heritage), Nevsky Propekt 116, ℗ 279 5067, 219 2129, sells good quality *matrioshkas*, painted trays, *khokhloma* (painted cups and spoons) and scarves as well as enamelled eggs and the occasional inviting piece of one-off craftsmanship. *Open daily.* Ⓜ Ploshchad Vosstaniya

Khudozhestvenny Promysli, Nevsky Prospekt 51, is a cheap shop sometimes selling embroidered linen, traditional Russian shirts and socks. Ⓜ Nevsky Prospekt

Ananov, Grand Hotel Europe, Ul. Mikhailovskaya 1/7. You have to be seriously rich to consider buying the exquisite jewellery or *objets d'art*. Andrei Ananov has taken up the mantle of Carl Fabergé, the famed jeweller who made his name creating intricate Easter eggs for European royalty before the Revolution. Ananov claims many of his best customers are also royal. Fine enamelled easter eggs (small enough to hang on necklaces) are made by a skilled team of retrained veterans disabled in the Afghan war. Ⓜ Nevsky Prospekt

Polar Star, Nevsky Prospekt 158, sells basic gold rings and necklace chains but of more interest are the pretty necklaces threaded with semi-precious stones. Ⓜ Ploshchad Alexandra Nevskovo

Sports Gear

Moscow

Sporting Goods, Ul. Tverskaya-Yamskaya 27, is one of the few Russian outlets worth visiting for tennis rackets and sports' clothes. Ⓜ Belorusskaya

Olimp, Ul. Krasnopresnendskaya 23, is good for football boots, tennis shoes, speedo swimwear, soccer and volley balls and, if you are lucky, some Fischer downhill and cross-country skis. Outside, entrepreneurs sell anything the shop has failed to stock.   Ⓜ Ul. 1905 Goda

Reebok, Novinsky Bulvar. Everything you ever wanted to put on your feet in order to get fit, and image-enhancing clothes, all at astronomic prices. Ⓜ Barrikadnaya

World Class Moscow, Ul. Zhitnaya 14, korp. 2, ✆ 239 1994, supplies most of the clothing you might need in its fitness centre—swimming costumes, leggings, leotards and shorts.   Ⓜ Oktyabrskaya

Top Sport, Sadko Arcade, Krasnogvardeisky Proyezd 1, is another address to try for imported sportswear.

St Petersburg

World Class Gym, Grand Hotel Europe, Ul. Mikhailovskaya 1/7, ✆ 312 0072 ext. 6500, includes a small Nike sportswear shop.   Ⓜ Nevsky Prospekt

Sporttovary, Nevsky Prospekt 122, has an erratic supply of Russian sporting equipment, particularly for fishing.   Ⓜ Ploshchad Vosstaniya

Miscellaneous

Moscow

Coins and Medals, Ul. Pushkinskaya 9. *Closed Sat and Sun.*   Ⓜ Teatralnaya

Ptichy Rynok (Bird Market), Ul. Bolshaya Kalitnikovskaya 42a. Animals of many sorts, furry, feathery and scaly, are on sale here. Choose between snakes, terrapins, songbirds, cats, fish, monkeys and a host of different dog breeds. Don't forget to stock up on accessories as well—hand-crafted wooden birdcages, leads and pet food. Some of the sales people are almost as endearing as their charges. *Open Sat and Sun 9–5.*   Ⓜ Taganskaya and trolleybus 16.

Zoomagazin Ul. Arbat 30, for when you run out of birdseed and it isn't a weekend.

St Petersburg

Kondratievsky Market, Polyustrovsky Prospekt 45, is St Petersburg's pet market, where they logically if inconsiderately do a huge line in fur hats as well. *Sat best for pets; closed Sun*   Ⓜ Ploshchad Lenina plus trolleybuss 3, 12 or 43.

Pet Boutique, Entrance 13, Ul. Bucharestskaya 23, ✆ 174 8746, specializes in winter clothes for cats and dogs. *Open daily 12–8.*

Sports and Outdoor Activities

With pompous, straight-faced slogans such as Stalin's 'trained muscles and bodies have military uses,' a cult of sport was encouraged during the Soviet period. Team sports, right up to national level, took place under the auspices of the workplace; footballers playing for Spartak received their salary from the aviation industry, while those on the Dinamo team were paid as, but never did the work of, the political police. As with most things Soviet there was always a healthy dose of scepticism round a nearby corner, with poets coining doggerel such as 'A healthy mind in a healthy body!/Come on, get real, it's one or the other'.

Today there is a plethora of sporting activities on offer in both cities. Particularly fun for visitors are the winter opportunities for cross-country skiing and skating. Retailers of sports equipment are listed in the chapter on shopping, though anyone coming to live here would be well advised to bring skates and ski boots with them as rentals are universally toe-crunching. Residents may also want to get into the Russian version of aerobics, called shaping. Following an assessment of fitness and fatness and a discussion about diet, you are encouraged to attend the exercise classes which can be found in every district.

Banyas

Not strictly a sport, but central to the Russian body beautiful, is the tradition of visiting the bath house, or *banya*. Foreigners either love it or hate it—being stark staring naked and beetroot-red in front of countless other members of their own sex. If you can't make up your mind, remember that you will feel a million dollars after a few hours in and out of the heat. The routine is simple. Take your own towel, wash things, creams and, if you want, a pair of flip-flops (you can often hire these there). Before entering the building, look aroud for someone selling bundles of birch and oak twigs, complete with leaves. Do the most traditional thing and buy a switch of birch (*veniki*) and then enter and pay the fee. Undress in the changing room and give any valuables to the attendants (better still, leave them at home). In the washing room find a bowl (*tazik*), fill it with very hot water and soak your *veniki* for several minutes while you shower or slosh yourself with water as often as you care. With your switch, head for the steam room (*parilka*) where the sight of piles of rolled flesh surmounted by woolly hats worthy of Rastafarians awaits. The heat is not supposed to be good for exposed hair. There is usually a staircase leading to an infernal balcony. Sit or stand as high as you can bear, flicking yourself and your friends gently with the *veniki* once the pores begin to open. Go in and out of the heat, relax for a while with a cup of herbal tea in the changing room, and give yourself a really good scrub before leaving. The best *banya* in each city offers massage, facials and pedicures.

Moscow

Sandunovskaya Banya, behind the Bolshoi Theatre at Pervy Neglinny Pereulok, ✆ 925 4631. The most exotic and accessible of Moscow's bathhouses is about to undergo a renovation, though it is quite fun as it is, with heavy 19th-century benches, kitsch plastic flowers and long marble slabs on Empire-style legs in the wash room. *Open 8–10; closed Tues.* Ⓜ Kuznetsky Most

St Petersburg

Banya 43, Fonarny Pereulok and Naberezhnaya Reki Moyki 82, ✆ 312 3151, is central, 19th-century and the most atmospheric in the city. *Open 8–10; closed Mon. Women get the plunge pool, massage and* parilka *on Wed, Fri and Sun, men on Tues, Thurs and Sat.* Ⓜ Sadovaya/Sennaya Ploshchad

Nevskiye Bani, Ul. Marata 5/7, ✆ 312 1279, is a large modern complex with pools for both sexes. Ⓜ Mayakovskaya

Boating

Moscow

Central (Gorky) Park, Ul. Krimsky Val 9, ✆ 237 1112, has rowing boats and pedalos to rent in summer. Ⓜ Park Kultury

Filyovsky Park, has a rental station for rowing boats on the Moskva River.
Ⓜ Filyovsky Park

New Russians Corporation, Gals Water Sports' Base, ✆ 901 6551 and ask for Artur or Vasily. Reserve a catamaran or windsurfing board; instructors available.

St Petersburg

Yelagin Island, near the bridge over to the Buddhist Temple. Rowing boats for rent on the lake. Ⓜ Chyornaya Rechka and bus 411 or 416 to Lipovaya Alleya

Neva Yacht Club, Martinova Nab. 94, Krestovsky Ostrov, ✆ 235 2722 or Kostya Klimov, captain of the Argus, on ✆ 166 0222. Yachts sleeping 6–8 can be rented for the weekend at rates of around $100–$150 a day including crew and catering. Ⓜ Petrogradskaya, plus tram 17 or 18

Bowling

Moscow

Kosmos Hotel, Prospekt Mira 150, ✆ 217 0196, has bowling alleys in the basement. Tickets from the service bureau in the lobby. *Open from 3–10.* Ⓜ VDNKh

Hotel Pribaltiskaya, Ul. Korablestroiteley 14, ✆ 356 1663. There are tenpin bowling alleys in this out-of-the-way hotel. *Open daily 12–10.*

Ⓜ Primorskaya, plus tram (11, 63)/bus (41, 42, 47)/trolleybus (10, 10a, 46).

Fitness Gyms

Moscow

World Class Moscow, Ul. Zhitnaya 14, korp. 2, ✆ 239 1994, is the newest of a series of fitness centres set up and run by a Swedish joint-venture. Facilities include weights rooms, tennis and squash court, aerobics hall and swimming pool. Entry and memberships will cost you. *Open 9–9.*   Ⓜ Oktyabrskaya

Olympiisky Stadium, Olympisky Prospekt 16, ✆ 288 3777, has a gym, a health club and a pool.

Dinamo Stadium, Leninsky Prospekt 36, ✆ 212 7092, has a gym and a pool.

Of the hotels the **Radisson Slavyanskaya**, Berezhhovskaya Nab. 2, ✆ 941 8020, and the **Olympic Penta**, Olimpisky Prospekt 18/1, ✆ 971 6101, have the best facilities, though unless you are staying there you pay through the nose. The **Metropol Hotel**'s gym, sauna and small pool are slightly cheaper, ✆ 927 6148.

St Petersburg

World Class (*see* above) have gyms and saunas in a number of locations. The smallest is at the **Hotel Astoria**, ✆ 210 5010, *Open 7.30–10am, 3–10pm, 9.30am–9pm on Sat and Sun*. Better equipped is the Fitness Centre in the **Grand Hotel Europe**, ✆ 113 8066. *Open 7am–10pm, 9am–9pm on Sat and Sun)*. For a more local environment head for their facilities in the **Sport-Klass Co-op**, Kamennoostrovsky Prospekt 26/28, ✆ 232 7581. *Open 9am–10, 11–8 on Sat and Sun.*

Flying

Moscow

Fly With Us! offer courses, Ul. Grekova 1/128, ✆ 387 2979/473 3463.

St Petersburg

Airlen, ✆ 104 1676, offers helicopter rides in and around the city.

Golf

Moscow

Tumba Golf Course, Ul. Dovzhenko 1, ✆ 147 8330, ▨ 147 6254, was built and is run by Finns; it also offers tennis courts, saunas and a restaurant. *Open 8am–8pm.*

Moscow Country Club Golf Course, ℗ 564 3467/3471, is Russia's only 18-hole golf course and comes, at a price, with a luxurious club house.

Hot Air Ballooning

Andrei Afefiev, ℗ 458 9371, can fix you up with an hour's sightseeing tour, floating over the city for around $200 if you have got cash to burn.

Ivan Bolon Inc., ℗ 193 8393, offers the same service.

Hunting and Fishing

Russia's enviable possession of some of the most remote pieces of country on the globe has made it the target of adventure and sporting holiday companies. Local hunting organizations on the ground include:

Moscow

IntourService. You should speak to Felix Nefedov, Director of Special Interest Tours on ℗ 292 2361 or Vladimir Vraginsky on 925 5096.

Moscow Society of Hunting and Fishing, Stroiteley Ul. 6, korp. 7, ℗ 930 4978, offers a choice of 120 local hunting lodges and provides all the help you need.

Brezhnev's Hunting Dacha can be hired by the day, but privileges like this don't come cheap if you aren't the General Secretary, ℗ 203 4820.

St Petersburg

Versam, Rizhskaya Ul. 16, ℗ 221 2489 ℘ 223 5823, organize trips with English-speaking guides to the Kola Peninsula on the Arctic circle to fish for salmon and hunt duck, elk or bear.

Prostor-Sever, Nevsky Prospekt 179, ℗ 274 6483, will arrange excursions of various sorts in the Leningrad and Karelia regions.

Ice Skating

Moscow

Central (Gorky) Park, Ul. Krimsky Val 9, transforms in winter into an outdoor skating mecca with two rinks and specially iced tarmac lanes. It then tries to kill the fun by renting you torturing skates. Troika rides (three horses pulling a sleigh) can also be picked up here at weekends in winter *Open 10–10*.

You can also skate on **Chistoprudny Bulvar** (Ⓜ Chistiye Prudy) and **Patriarch's Ponds** (Ⓜ Mayakovskaya).

Sokolniki Park also has skating and renting facilities, which you will find near the metro station of the same name.

Tauride Park, ✆ 272 6044, is designated for children who ski, sledge and skate here in winter in profusion.

Kronwerk Canal, behind the Peter and Paul Fortress is a great place to head if you have your own skates.

If not, go to the lake on **Yelagin Island**, near the Buddhist Temple, ✆ 239 0911 (*see* Boating above).

In summer you can skate on the rink at the **Letny Sportklub**, Naberezhnaya Reki Fontanki 112, ✆ 292 2081/2128.

Parachuting

Moscow

Moscow Parachute Club, ✆ 111 3315, 🕿 111 4475. Bear in mind before you call that several ex-pats broke legs on a sponsored jump in 1993.

Riding

Moscow

Riding Clubs, Hippodrome, Ul. Begovaya 22, ✆ 945 4516 or 5872. The Moscow Race Course shelters two private stables with their own indoor arenas, in which you can ride in winter when the grounds of the racecourse are too cold. Trainers include Olympic team trainers and the horses are far superior to those in most riding clubs. As well as Arabs you can try out Trakheners, bred for the East Prussian cavalry, and Akhal-Tekes, the 'horse equivalent of a Porsche' according to the owner. Ⓜ Begovaya

Bittsa Equestrian Centre, Balaklavsky Prospekt 33, ✆ 318 0744, is also well-equipped, with show-jumping stadium and indoor riding school.

Moscow Tourist Club, Ul. Sadovo-Kudrinskaya 4, ✆ 203 1094.

St Petersburg

Prostov-Park, Krestovsky Ostrov 20, ✆ 230 7873, offers riding in nearby Primorsky Park as well as lessons in dressage and show-jumping.

Olgino Motel and Campsite, ✆ 238 3132, is the only place used to renting horses on a regular basis, apart from those horses you find trotting about on Nevsky Prospekt and Palace Square in the city centre. They can arrange troika rides in winter. *Open 10–12 and 3–6; closed Mon.* Elektrichka from Finlandsky Vokzal to Olgino station.

Moscow

An astronomically expensive weekend could be spent at the **Villa Peredelkino Hotel**, Pervy Chobotovskaya Alleya 2, Peredelkino (*see* p.271) where, providing it has survived the tussle with the Komsomol, you could ski between bouts of Italian food and sessions in the sauna.

Bittsa Park, **Sokolniki Park** and **Luzhniki Park** all have ski stations where equipment can be rented for cross-country skiing by the day.

St Petersburg

One of the best places to ski in the vicinity of St Petersburg is at **Tsarskoye Selo** (*see* p.455). You can rent skis and sledges from an office in the semi-circular wing of the main Catherine Palace.

Swimming Pools

Health certificates from a Russian doctor are required before you can use most municipal pools, so check before you go. The same does not apply to club pools.

Moscow

Chaika Sports Club, Prechistenskaya Naberezhnaya 3/5, ✆ 202 0474 or 246 1344, has a huge pool and a membership system. Ⓜ Park Kultury

Of the hotels, the **Radisson Slavyanskaya** and the **Olimpic Penta** have the best pools.

St Petersburg

Dinamo Sports Centre, Dinamo Prospekt 44, ✆ 235 2944, has a huge pool amongst its many facilities. *Open 6am–12pm.* Ⓜ Krestovsky Ostrov

Delfin, Ul. Dekabristov 38, ✆ 114 2054, contains a pool *open 6am–12pm.*

There are also tiny pools in the **Hotel Pribaltiskaya** and **Hotel St Petersburg**.

Tennis

Moscow

Keen players can practice year-round on the indoor courts at **Chaika Sports Club**, Prechistenskaya Naberezhnaya 3/5, ✆ 202 0474 or 246 1344.

Outdoor courts can be hired at **Petrovsky Park Tennis Club**, Leningradsky Prospekt 36, ✆ 212 7956/7392 (Ⓜ Dinamo), and at the **Luzhniki Sports Complex**, Luzhnetskaya Naberezhnaya 10, ✆ 201 1655 (Ⓜ Sportivnaya).

St Petersburg

There are tennis courts for rent at the **Lawn Tennis Club**, Pr Metallistov 116, ✆ 540 1886, and at two locations on Krestovsky Ostrov. Phone ✆ 235 2077 to reserve a court in **Primorsky Park Pobedy**, or ✆ 235 0407 for one at the smart **Tennis Club** at Konstantinovsky Proezd 23. Both lie on bus route 71a from Ⓜ Krestovsky Ostrov.

Spectator Sports

Moscow

Football is Russia's most important spectator sport, and Moscow shelters a third of the premier league clubs. The season is from March to November.

Russia's best team is Spartak, who share the Central Lenin Stadium at Luzhniki with the army team, CSKA Moscow. Dinamo, Torpedo and Lokomotiv all have their own eponymous stadiums, and Asmaral play at Sokolniki.

Horse Racing takes place at the Hippodrome, Ul. Begovaya 22, ✆ 945 4516, and includes not only flat racing but also races in *kachalki*, lightweight carriages, and in winter the occasional troika race, all accompanied by much drinking and betting. *Races from 6pm on Wed and Sat, from 1pm on Sun.*

Ice Hockey matches are held throughout the year at both the Central Lenin Stadium (Ⓜ Sportivnaya), ✆ 246 5515 and the Dinamo Stadium, Leningradsky Prospekt 36 (Ⓜ Dinamo), ✆ 212 7092.

St Petersburg

Football. The choice in St Petersburg is limited to the uninspiring team Zenit Leningrad, which plays between March and October in the Kirov Stadium on Krestovsky Ostrov, ✆ 235 5435.

Ice Hockey. The city's best team SKA St Petersburg play throughout the year at the Yubileiny Sports Palace on Petrograd Side, ✆ 293 4049.

"SNEGOVICK"

Children's Moscow & St Petersburg

If you can avoid it, don't bring children on holiday here unless they are small enough to carry for long periods or big enough to enjoy city sightseeing. They will probably prefer St Petersburg, with its water and gilded empresses' palaces, to the more cerebral charms of Moscow. Baby-sitters can be arranged through your hotel, although foreigners complain that their children are spoiled by them.

Beaches

Both cities have nearby beaches where you can indulge in sun, sand castles and gritty sandwiches. If it is hot, children may want to swim. At the Moscow beach they should keep their mouths shut; in St Petersburg persuade them just to paddle, as the unfinished flood barrier has created a back-up of polluted water in the gulf.

Moscow

Serebryanny Bor, Moscow River upstream (*see* p.246)—crowded at weekends.

St Petersburg

Ss. Peter and Paul Fortress (*see* p.290) is good for a quick paddle.

Parks and Boats

Boat trips along the Moscow River (*see* p.245) and the canals of St Petersburg (*see* p.427) are an enjoyable way to pass a summer's afternoon without tiring tiny legs.

Moscow

Central (Gorky) Park, Ul. Krimsky Val, Ⓜ Oktyabrskaya/Park Kultury. The new funfair by the river looks less risky than old rides inland. In summer you can rent rowing boats and pedalos on the ponds, and in winter paths are specially iced for skating. Skates for hire are painful: buy some or bring them with you.

Tsaritsyno and **Kolomenskoye** both make interesting picnic trips on balmy days. You can rent boats on the lake at Tsaritsyno as well (*see* p.240).

St Petersburg

Tauride Children's Park (Tavrichesky Sad) is the official children's park, though there is nothing much there to show for it. They descend in droves with sledges and skis in winter; rumour has it there are skates for rent. (*see* p.367).

Letny Sad, with its musicians and neoclassical sculptures beneath the leafy canopy, can be fun at weekends in summer (*see* p.298).

Tsarskoye Selo has an extensive park where you can play hide and seek, go boating and picnic in summer, or hire skis and sledges in winter (*see* p.455).

Yelagin Island is nearer to hand and also offers opportunities to skate and boat on its ponds (*see* p.430).

Museums

Moscow

Polytechnical Museum, Novaya Ploshchad 3/4, ✆ 923 0756, is perfect for children in the 'how does it work' phase (*see* p.228).　　　　　　　Ⓜ Lubianka

Cosmonauts Museum, Aleeya Kosmonavtov, ✆ 283 7914. Astronauts have rather faded as role models for children, but worth a visit. (*see* p.227).　　Ⓜ VDNKh

Cat Museum, Ul. Malaya Gruzinskaya 15. Where else to see a genuine cat-walk in action? (*see* p.228).　　　　　　　　　　　　Ⓜ Krasnopresnenskaya

Puppet Museum, Obraztsov Puppet Theatre, Ul. Sadovaya-Samotyochnaya 3, ✆ 299 0904. Open before puppet shows (*see* below).

Toy Museum at Sergeyev Possad (*see* p.265).

St Petersburg

Naval Museum, Old Stock Exchange, Pushkinskaya Ploshchad 4, Vasilievsky Ostrov, will be popular with model makers, one entire room being stuffed with model wooden boats and their elaborate rigging (*see* p.289).

Zoological Museum, Universitetskaya Naberezhnaya 1, Vasilievsky Ostrov, ✆ 218 0112, has a collection of stuffed animals and an exhibition on the discovery of woolly mammoths in the Siberian permafrost (*see* p.386).

Clothes and Toys

Moscow

Detsky Mir, Teatralny Proezd 5, ✆ 926 2152. After a lean period of echoing corridors and empty shelves, this store is coming back into its own.　　Ⓜ Lubianka

Benetton 0–12, GUM on Red Square, middle row on ground floor.

Karstadt Kids, GUM on Red Square, 1st Floor, ✆ 926 3263. Clothes and toys.

Boys and Girls, Sadko Arcade, Krasnogvardeisky Proyezd 1, ✆ 253 9592. Imported clothes and toys, including Matchbox cars and Barbie. *Open 10–10*.

St Petersburg

Dom Leningradskoy Torgovli, Ul. Bolshaya Konushennaya 21/3, ✆ 312 2627, can have a good selection of children's clothes and toys.　　Ⓜ Nevsky Prospekt

Detsky Mir, Bolshoy Prospekt 25, Petrograd Side, ✆ 233 5636, has a wide selection of Russian and foreign-made toys and clothes.　　　Ⓜ Petrogradskaya

Theatres and Circuses

Children enjoy the magic of circuses and the ballet from a very young age (*see* **Entertainment and Nightlife**, p.528). Other venues of particular interest include:

Clown Theatre of Teresa Durova, Dom Kultury Zavoda Vladimira Ilicha, Ul. Pavlovskaya 6, ✆ 237 1689. As well as several clown acts, tricks are taught in the intervals. Programmes change every three weeks. Ⓜ Tulskaya

Obraztsov Puppet Theatre, Ul. Sadovaya-Samotyochnaya 3, ✆ 299 0904. Before taking your child to a performance, check it's suitable—one of the first nudes on the Moscow stage was a puppet. Museum in foyer. Ⓜ Tsvetnoy Bulvar

St Petersburg

Sharmanka Puppet Theatre (*see* p.528). Ⓜ Moskovskiye Vorota

Maly Theatre, Pl. Isskustv 1, ✆ 219 1978. Young members of the Vaganova Ballet School often perform here to a largely juvenile audience. Ⓜ Nevsky Prospekt

Puppet Theatre for Children, Moskovsky Prospekt 121, ✆ 298 0031.
Ⓜ Moskovskiye Vorota

Zazerkale Children's Theatre, Shamsheva Ul. 8, Petrograd Side, ✆ 238 1205. Opera and ballet for kids. Ⓜ Petrogradskaya

Zoos

Neither of the zoos in these cities are suitable for the soft-hearted, though children may still enjoy the pony rides.

Moscow

Zoo, Bolshaya Gruzinskaya Ul. Ⓜ Barrikadnaya

Aquarium World, 22 Novinsky Bulvar, ✆ 202 0906. 150 species of fish and turtles inhabit exotic, well-kept aquariums. *Open Sat, Sun 11–6.* Ⓜ Barrikadnaya

St Petersburg

Zoo, Park Lenina, Petrograd Side. Ⓜ Gorkovskaya

Miscellaneous

Moscow

The Children's Railway, is run by children aged 11–16. The miniature train, called the *Little Bee*, slowly travels 4km over 40 minutes through *dacha*-dotted countryside. Buy round trip tickets and if the weather is fine picnic by the lake near Kratovo station. To get there take the train from Kazansky Vokzal to Kratovo, an hour from Moscow on the line to Pl. 47km.

Ostankino TV Tower contains an observation platform and a revolving restaurant, Sedmoye Nebo (Seventh Heaven). If the weather is good and the windows have been cleaned, views are impressive. Don't expect a culinary treat, and bring your passports which, in homage to a bygone era, are required for entry.

Living and Working

Like a 27-piece *matrioshka*, life in Russia never stops throwing out one more surprise: the sudden glut of pineapples in your local shop in April, the babysitter with a PhD, the late-night realization that everyone round the table except you lost relatives at Stalin's whim, the wads of dollars bandied around in the casino, the legless beggar jumping nimbly off the trolleybus on his skateboard. Here intellectuals in poverty, there thugs in clover, here mindless brutality, there ineffable, selfless kindness and suddenly, at the height of summer, not a drop of water out of the taps for a month.

There is one rule to recommend—try to have as little to do with officialdom as possible. Until the 1990s all foreigners living in Russia were nannied by UPDK, a government department which doled out apartments and repairs, cars and chauffeurs, cooks and nannies and thereby knew every detail of your life. Today it is possible to live here without anyone knowing, though you are not supposed to.

Visas and Registering

There is nothing more infuriating than being invited by someone in St Petersburg to spend a weekend in Finland, three hours away, and realizing you can't go because you only have a single-entry visa and would not be allowed back into Russia in time for the meeting on Monday morning. Try as hard as you can to get the organization that officially invites you to Russia to make sure you are furnished with a multiple-entry visa straight away. If not, and you are going to be here for a long stretch, it is worth getting your visa status changed in Russia. You will need a letter from your sponsoring organization, reiterating all the details of your current visa and passport, your local residential address and region (plus militia district), including somewhere the phrase that your 'personal and property security is guaranteed'. This should be stamped with their all-important round, registered stamp. Then go to a branch of Sperbank, fill in a *kvitantsia* and pay the fee requested into OVIR's account, No. 101–308–02 at the Kommerchesky Narodny Bank. Take the receipt from the bank with your passport, current visa, two photos and the letter to OVIR's office, and perhaps a Russian to hold your hand.

OVIR's main offices are:

Ul. Pokrovka 42, Moscow, ✆ 208 2358/2091

Ul. Saltykova-Schedrina 4, St Petersburg, ✆ 273 9038

Ring first for the ever-changing opening hours.

There is no longer any need to register your presence with OVIR if you are not staying in a hotel, but you might want to register with your nearest embassy or consulate (*see* p.26). In an emergency they will be able to advise you, and most also run clubs for ex-pats, counselling and a variety of other community services.

Useful Publications

The Moscow Times, published daily except Sunday, and its occasional magazine *Moscow Guide* are invaluable aids in finding out where, how, when and what. Though *The Moscow Times* obviously concentrates on the capital, it also carries news and occasional listings covering St Petersburg, and the magazine always has a section on the city. It is free, distributed through most hotels, supermarkets and restaurants frequented by foreigners, and can also be picked up in the major St Petersburg hotels a day late. St Petersburg's *Neva News* and *St Petersburg Press* are pale imitations, though the latter has recently become much more useful.

The Traveller's Yellow Pages to St Petersburg and *The Traveller's Yellow Pages to Moscow* have been produced by the gargantuan efforts of an American-led team. Aside from bars, restaurants, hotels and airlines, they list addresses and phone numbers for a host of other potentially useful services, such as television repair shops, local government offices and food radioactivity testing. These are on sale in hotel shops and supermarkets. If you don't see them around, get in touch with their offices either at Naberezhnaya Reki Moyki 64, ✆ 315 6412, 🖷 312 7341 in St Petersburg or Putinkovsky Per. 2/1, ✆ 200 2110, 🖷 209 5465 in Moscow. Their US phone number is (516) 549 0064.

Russia Survival Guide, published by Russian Information Services Inc., is a regularly updated guide to doing business and travelling in Russia. They also publish a number of other useful fact sheets. For more information call them in Vermont, USA on ✆ (802) 223 4955, 🖷 (802) 223 6105 or in Moscow on ✆/🖷 (095) 254 9275.

Studying Russian

There are a plethora of organizations offering to teach Russian, providing anything from month-long intensive group courses to private tutors who come to your home. Try the following to find out what's on offer and for how much. For something cheaper, try your luck with the offers in the classifieds in the *Moscow Times* and *St Petersburg Press*, though you may not always get value for money that way.

Moscow

Moscow International School of Translation and Interpreting, PO Box 51, Moscow 123103, ✆ 208 7387, 161 5319, 🖷 947 9387.

Moscow Institute of Social and Political Studies, Ul. Volgina 6, ✆ 335 6192.

Interdialect, Ul. Lunacharskovo 1, Moscow 121002, ✆ 241 6307/7436/5298, 🖷 241 9970.

Fortuna Centre of Russian Study, ✆ 941 0776.

Russian Language Centre, Vtoroy Minayevsky Per 2, room 7418, ✆ 258 9101 or 972 6200.

IBS Foreign Language School, ✆ 251 5447.

Julia Marchi-Intensive, ✆ 455 4162, specializes in one-month intensive courses for beginners, and offers follow-up as well.

The following concentrate on providing you with a private tutor:

Russian Intensive, ✆ 253 8301 or 930 3268.

Russian Lessons, ✆ 398 1675.

Private Tutoring, ✆ 946 0428 or 128 1465.

St Petersburg

St Petersburg State University, Russian Language Centre, Naberezhnaya Universitetskaya 7/9, ✆ 213 3256.

Vneshvus-Centre, Naberezhnaya Morskaya 9, Vasilievsky Ostrov, ✆ 356 9905, 🖷 355 6987, claim to be able to give you survival Russian in two weeks.

AsLantis, ✆ 297 2614, 🖷 298 9007.

Lingra, ✆ 218 7339.

Finding a Job

The job market for non-Russians is not yet extensive, but there are more personnel adverts in the English-language papers mentioned abov⟨ ⟩y the day. If you have not got a job before you arrive, a couple of useful ca⟨l⟩ ⟨wo⟩uld be to your nearest embassy or consulate, and to the English-language ⟨⟩ng schools listed in the *Traveller's Yellow Pages*, *see* above.

Finding Somewhere to Live

Living on a pittance, which was perfectly possible as r⟨ece⟩ntly as 1992, is a thing of the past. Domestic real estate, previously all owned ⟨by⟩ the state and of nominal value, is in the process of being privatized, acquiring a ⟨ ⟩narket value. Prices are in free-rise, with Moscow far outstripping St Petersbur⟨g⟩ though a large flat in the latter with a view of canal or river also comes at a prem⟨i⟩um. Once privatized, a flat can be rented and, in theory, sold to a foreign individ⟨u⟩al. If you decide to do the latter, make sure you hire the services of an established ⟨fi⟩rm as the legal niceties are not obvious.

To do it the Russian way, start looking at the ingenious ⟨a⟩dverts people stick up near metro stations. Their fringed ends bear the telephone n⟨u⟩mber and can be torn off. Flats will be advertised as 2-, 3- or 4-room, meaning ap⟨a⟩rt from bathroom, loo and

kitchen, and will give the square meterage of the whole space. Many of the ads are looking to swap flats in different neighbourhoods, but some will be simple sales (продажа). Another possible route is the classifieds in the English-language papers, or via one of the following agencies, most of which deal in both sales and rentals.

Moscow

Catherine Mamet Agency, Tverskoy Bulvar 25, Moscow 103104, ✆ 291 1941/61, 🖃 202 0449. A rarity here, a real walk-in agency.

Unifuturer, ✆ 203 5843/9440, 🖃 213 7210.

Home Sweet Home, Ul. Nikolaeva 4, apt. 53, ✆ 205 6122/0129.

House Service Ltd, Vakhtangova Ul. 7, 241 7402/3485.

St Petersburg

Dom Plus, Dvortsovaya Nab. 16, ✆ 312 8873.

K-keskus, ✆ 232 0723, 233 4833.

Lena Topichkanova, ✆ 310 7132, or to speak English call Natasha Ostrovskaya on ✆ 156 4525.

Registering with a Doctor

Western-run family practices in both Moscow and St Petersburg run a variety of schemes for long-term residents, including local insurance schemes. Call them to compare.

Moscow

American Medical Centre, 2-ya Tverskaya Yamskaya 10, ✆ 956 3366.

European Medical Centre, Gruznisky Per. 3, korp. 2, ✆ 253 0703.

St Petersburg

American Medical Centre, Nab. Reki Fontanki 77, ✆ 119 6101.

Insurance

Three of the largest all-purpose insurance companies in Russia have offices in both Moscow and St Petersburg. Call them to compare policies and premiums on buildings, contents and medical insurance.

Moscow

ASKO, Bol. Norodmitrovskaya Ul. 14, ✆ 120 1183.

Ingosstrakh, Pyatnitskaya Ul. 12, ✆ 233 1759/0550.

Rossiya, Sadovaya-Spasskaya Ul. 21, ✆ 262 1731.

St Petersburg

Asko-Peterburg, Pr. Yuriya Gagarina 1, 7th floor, ✆ 294 8881.

Ingosstrakh, Zakharevskaya Ul. 17, ✆ 275 7710.

Rossiya, Ul. Gertsena 33, ✆ 314 4621.

Useful Addresses

Moscow

Alcoholics Anonymous shares in English at Ul. Dmitrya Ulyanova 37, korp. 1. Call ✆ 243 4260 for times and more information.

Alphagraphics, Tverskaya Ul. 50, Moscow 125047, ✆ 251 1208/15, ✉ 230 2207/17, for printing, photocopying and Apple Mac design.

Cable TV can be installed by Kosmos TV, ✆ 282 3360.

Dry Cleaning. Sadly, interesting items, and almost all of yours will count as that, tend to go missing in the ubiquitous local *khimchistkas*. To safeguard your clothes call Mayers International, ✆ 242 8946 or ✉ 145 7426 and they will pick up and return your load the following day if you call before 2. Alternatively try Moscow Laundry Service, ✆ 480 9452.

Film Development There are Kodak processing booths in Passazh Department Store, Ul. Petrovka 10, and in GUM on Red Square. The Fuji Film Centre is at Ul. Novy Arbat 17, ☎ 203 7307. For anything complicated (slides or b&w) go to the Photo Centre, Gogolievsky Bulvar 8, ☎ 290 4188, where the professionals lurk.

Library of Foreign Literature, Ulyanovskaya Ul. 1, ☎ 915 3636, just over the Yauza between Ⓜ Taganskaya and Kitai Gorod, contains the American Cultural Centre and the British Council Resource Centre (☎ 917 3499) with current magazines, newpapers and reference sections. To get a library card and take out books, bring a photo, your passport, and proof of residency.

Hairdressers and Beauty Parlours are scattered all over the city. Some of the better ones include City Looks Hair Salon, Ul. Pokrovka 2/1, ☎ 928 7084/7235; Yves Rocher, Ul. Tverskaya 4, ☎ 923 5885; Wella, Ul. Myaskovskovo 12, ☎ 290 5137 and the beauty parlours inside the Mezhdunarodnaya and Metropol Hotels.

Home Delivery Food is not extensive, but you can get Chinese from Panda, ☎ 298 6565, burgers from McDonald's, ☎ 200 1655 and pizzas from Pizza Hut, ☎ 229 2013.

Household Goods. Stockmann's Home and Car Store at Ul. Lyusinovskaya 70/1, ☎ 954 8234, accepts only credit cards so remember your passport for ID. The Russian version is called a *Khozyaistvenny Magazin* (хозяйственный магазин), and can be found in every district. You will find a well-supplied example at Ul. Bolshaya Dorogomilovskaya 10. Ⓜ Kievskaya

Clubs. International Women's Club, call ☎ 253 2508, 238 3014. Moscow Country Club, offering all-round facilities, even long-term accommodation and a golf course, ☎ 561 2977. Most embassies have their own social clubs which meet on certain days of the week. Call your own embassy for information.

Limousines. Someone you want to impress coming to town? Take them to the Bolshoi in a stretch Lincoln with bar and VCR. Call Sunrise Limousines, ☎ 366 4656, 🖷 292 6511.

Mail Order Catalogues offer everything the ex-pat could ever want, from carry cots to vintage claret. The best two are Peter Justensen, Ul. Chetvyortaya Marinoy Roschi 12, ☎ 292 5110, 🖷 971 1178, and Osterman, Ul. Sadovaya-Samotyochnaya 5, apt. 12, ☎ 292 5110, 🖷 230 2142.

Parties. Not enough going on? Rent Annushka, the restaurant/tram. Food and booze can all be arranged, but sadly it doesn't stretch to a loo. Call Armen on ☎ 236 8272.

Passport Photos. Polaroid Express booths can be found at a number of locations, including their new shop at Leninsky Prospekt 70/2, ☎ 930 5203.

Alphagraphics, Ul. Tverskaya Yamskaya 20, ✆ 251 1208, will also take them when their camera is working. Local photographic studios, such as that at Ul. Pushkinskaya 16, will take black and white photos ready for collection on the same day at 7pm.

Pets. Once you have bought it at Ptichny Rynok (*see* p.544), get food and other accessories either there or at one of the Zoo Magazin (зоомагазин) scattered across the city. They tend to be better stocked with the wherewithal to kill animals, but do have birdseed and basic leads. There is one at Ul. Arbat 30.

Video Rental, Video Force, Korovy Val 7, Entrance 1, ✆ 238 3136. Open daily 11am–8pm, with a lunch break 1–2. The Garden Ring Supermarket, Ul. Bolshaya Sadovaya 1, ✆ 209 1572, also has a selection of quality movies, as does the American Video Store, Bol. Gnezdnikovsky Per. 16, ✆ 229 7459.

St Petersburg

Cable TV is provided by Peter the Great, Sredneokhtinsky Prospekt 52, ✆ 526 6631, 🖷 526 6624.

Film Developing can be done in one hour at the Agfa Shop, Nevsky Prospekt 20, ✆ 311 9974, and is also handled at the Astoria and St Petersburg hotels. Fuji processing lab at Naberezhnaya Reki Fontanki 23, ✆ 314 4936.

Hairdressers and Beauty Salons. Apart from the hotel facilities, Wella at Nevsky Prospekt 54, ✆ 312 3026, does a reliable job.

Home Delivery Food. Not a lot of choice here. It's Pizza Express, Podolskaya Ul. 23, ✆ 292 2666.

Passport Photos for those nagging visa requirements, from Express Photo, Malaya Konushennaya Ul. 12, ✆ 312 0122.

Pet Shops. The best selection is on Saturdays at Kondryatevsky Pet Market, Polyustovsky Prospekt 45, ✆ 540 3039. Otherwise try Zoo Magazin, Ligovsky Prospekt 63, ✆ 164 7674.

Photocopies. Outside the extortionate hotel business centres, try Informatika, Naberezhnaya Reki Moyki 64/1, ✆ 314 0632, or the Copy-Centre, Prospekt Morisa Toreza 30, ✆ 552 5420.

Printers. For your stationary and business cards, printed in Russian on one side, English on the other, go to Kella Design and Printing, Kronverkskaya Ul. 10, ✆/🖷 232 1890.

862	Swedish Vikings under Rurik found state of Rus at Novgorod
880	Oleg makes Kiev the capital of the Rus
988	Under Vladimir I, Kievan Rus adopts Christianity
1223	First Mongol raid
1240	Kiev Sacked by Mongols
1242	Alexander Nevsky defeats Teutonic Knights on Lake Peipus
1327	Metropolitan of Russian Orthodox Church moves to Moscow
1328	Ivan I is created Grand Prince of Muscovy
1380	Dmitry Donskoy leads the first victory against the Mongols at Kulikovo
1480	Ivan III stops paying the annual tribute to the Mongols
1547	Ivan IV adopts the title 'tsar'
1563–7	Ivan IV's terror, carried out by the *oprichniki*
1571	Crimean Tartars raid Moscow for the last time
1588	Russia is granted her own Patriarch
1605–13	The Time of Troubles
1613	The Romanovs ascend the throne of Russia
1649	Russia's gets her first rationalized Law Code, the *Ulozheniye*
1660	Patriarch Nikon is deposed
1697–8	Peter the Great visits Europe
1700–21	Great Northern War
1703	Foundation of St Petersburg
1712	St Petersburg becomes capital of Russia
1722	Table of Ranks adopted
1772	First Partition of Poland
1773–4	Pugachev Uprising
1783	Potemkin annexes the Crimea
1792	Second Partition of Poland
1795	Third Partition of Poland
1805–7	First war with Napoleon

Chronology and List of Russian Rulers

| 1812 | Napoleon invades Russia and is driven out |

1814	Congress of Vienna
1825	Decembrist Uprising
1853–6	Crimean War
1861	Emancipation of the Serfs
1881	Assassination of Alexander II, the 'Tsar-Liberator'
1903	Pogroms against Russia's Jewish communities
1904–5	Russo-Japanese War
1905	The 1905 Revolution
1906	Russia's first elected *duma* meets
1911	Prime Minister Stolypin assassinated in Kiev
1913	300th anniversary of the Romanov dynasty
1914	First World War begins
1916	Rasputin is murdered
1917	Nicholas II abdicates in February
	Bolsheviks seize power in October Revolution
1918	Russia bows out of First World War at Treaty of Brest-Litovsk
	Romanovs murdered
	Government returns to Moscow
1918–20	Civil War
1922	Formation of the Soviet Union
1924	Lenin dies
1928	First Five Year Plan introduced
1934	Murder of Kirov; the purges begin
1939	Nazi-Soviet Pact
1939–40	War with Finland
1940	Soviet Union annexes Baltic Republics and Bessarabia
1941	Germans attack the Soviet Union
1941–4	Seige of Leningrad
1945	Second World War ends: Yalta and Potsdam conferences
1956	Khrushchev denounces Stalin in secret speech at 20th Party Congress
	Hungarian Uprising crushed
1961	Contruction of Berlin Wall
1962	Cuban Missile Crisis
1968	'Prague Spring' put down by Soviet troops
1979	Invasion of Afghanistan
1985	Gorbachev introduces *glasnost* and *perestroika*

1986	Chernobyl nuclear reactor blows up
1989	Soviets pull out of Afghanistan
	East European satellite states declare independence of Soviet Union, culminating in fall of Berlin Wall
	Yeltsin tears up Communist Party card on TV
1990	Baltic Republics gain independence
	Yeltsin voted President of Russian Republic
	Conservative August coup fails
	Ukraine, Belarus and Georgia declare independence
	Gorbachev resigns as head of a non-existent Soviet Union
1992	Radical PM Gaidar replaced by more conservative Chernomyrdin
1993	Yeltsin disolves parliament in September
	October—he defeats his parliamentary opposition, led by Khasbulatov and Rutskoi, in bloody Moscow shoot-out
	December parliamentary elections yield high nationalist vote
1994	Treaty of Civil Accord

Selected List of Russian Rulers

The Rurik Dynasty

Rurik	862–879
Oleg	879–912
Vladimir I	978–1015
Vladimir Monomakh	1113–25
Alexander Nevsky	1252–63
Ivan I ('Kalita')	1328–40
Dmitry Donskoy	1359–89
Vasily I	1389–1425
Vasily II	1425–62
Ivan III ('the Great')	1462–1505
Vasily III	1505–33
Ivan IV ('the Terrible')	1533–84
Fyodor I	1584–98
Boris Godunov	1598–1605
Fyodor II	1605
The Time of Troubles	1605–13

The Romanov Dynasty

Mikhail	1613–45
Alexei	1645–76
Fyodor III	1676–82
Ivan V & Peter I (Sophia regent to 1689)	1682–98
Peter I ('the Great')	1698–1725
Catherine I	1725–27
Peter II	1727–30
Anna	1730–40
Ivan VI	1740–41
Elizabeth	1741–1761
Peter III	1761–62
Catherine II ('the Great')	1762–96
Paul	1796–1801
Alexander I	1801–25
Nicholas I	1825–55
Alexander II	1855–81
Alexander III	1881–94
Nicholas II	1894–1917

Prime Ministers of Provisional Government

Prince Lvov	Feb–May 1917
Alexander Kerensky	May–Oct 1917

People's Chairman

Vladimir Ilich Lenin	1917–24

General Secretaries of the Communist Party

Joseph Stalin	1924–53
Georgi Malenkov	1953–55
Nikital Khrushchev	1955–64
Leonid Brezhnev	1964–82
Yuri Andropov	1982–84
Konstantin Chernenko	1984–85
Mikhail Gorbachev	1985–91

Presidents of the Russian Republic

Boris Yeltsin	1991–

There is no point pretending that Russian is an easy language, with its strange alphabet, nouns and adjectives declining in seven cases and verbs of motion with perfective and imperfective aspects in all tenses. However you will get an immense sense of satisfaction, not to mention great orientational benefit, if you learn to read the cyrillic script. Cosmopolitan Russians will always applaud your efforts to actually speak a few words, though country folk can be remarkably unsympathetic at your communication difficulties. Both Moscow and St Petersburg are full of English-speakers, and one will nearly always appear when you need one.

If you are going to be in the country for some time and want to do rather better, you will find lists of Russian language courses in both cities in the Living and Working chapter. In London the Britain-Russia Centre, ✆ 0171 235 2116, will give you a list of recommended courses and private tutors. A good teach-yourself course is to be found between the covers of *The Penguin Russian Course* for which cassettes are also available. Langenscheidt produce both a pocket and a mini English-Russian, Russian-English dictionary, one of which you may wish to take with you as well.

Language

The Russian Alphabet

		Transliteration	*Pronunciation*
А	а	a	as in 'car'
Б	б	b	as in 'book'
В	в	v	as in 'van'
Г	г	g	as in 'good'
Д	д	d	as in 'day'
Е	е	ye/e	as in 'yes'
Ё	ё	yo/o	as in 'yonder' (often not accented)
Ж	ж	zh	like 'g' in massage
З	з	z	as in 'zone'
И	и	i	like 'ee' in 'feet'
Й	й	y	as in 'boy', but silent at end of word
К	к	k	as in 'kin'
Л	л	l	as in 'lamp'
М	м	m	as in 'man'
Н	н	n	as in 'nut'
О	о	o	as in 'pot' when stressed; like 'a' in 'aloud' when unstressed
П	п	p	as in 'pen'
Р	р	r	as in 'red' (rolled)
С	с	s	as in 'sing'
Т	т	t	as in 'top' (sometimes written as *m*)
У	у	u	like 'oo' in 'fool'
Ф	ф	f	as in 'fat'
Х	х	kh	like 'ch' in Bach
Ц	ц	ts	as in 'lots'
Ч	ч	ch	as in 'chair'
Ш	ш	sh	as in 'ship'
Щ	щ	shch	as in 'fresh cheese'
Ъ	ъ	{none}	unpronounced hard sign
Ы	ы	y/i	like 'ey' in 'chop suey', pronounced from the back of the throat
Ь	ь	{none}	unpronounced soft sign
Э	э	e	as in 'set'
Ю	ю	yu	like 'u' in 'use'
Я	я	ya	as in 'yard'

Note on Transliteration

This book largely follows the transliteration set out above, except for a few proper names, the standard English spelling of which has been established by the media: *e.g.* Gorbachev, not Gorbachov.

The common masculine adjective endings -ый, -ий have both been rendered into Engish with a single -y, as the nuances of sound are not important to a new Russian speaker.

Many masculine and neuter adjective in the genitive singular end in -ого (ogo) and -его (ego), but are confusingly pronounced -ovo and -evo. They have been transliterated with a 'v' as they are pronounced, but in these cases, which often occur in street names, there will be a discrepancy between the written Russian and the transliteration, *e.g.* Площадь Островского = Ploshchad Ostrovskovo.

Essential Phrases

English	Pronunciation	Russian
Yes	da	да
No	nyet	нет
Please	pazhálsta	пожалуйста
Thank you	spasíba	спасибо
Not at all	nyé za shto	не за что
Hello	zdrávstvuitye/privét	здравствуите/привет
Goodbye	da svidániya	до свидания
See you later	poká	пока
Good Morning	dóbroye útra	доброе утро
Good Evening	dóbry vyécher	добрый вечер
Glad to meet you	óchen priyátno	очень приятно
How are you?	kak delá?	как дело?
Fine/good	kharashó	хорошо
Bad	plókha	плохо
Do you speak English?	vy govorítye pa-anglísky?	Вы говорите по-английски?
I don't understand	ya nye ponimáiyu	Я не понимаю
I don't speak Russian	ya nye gavaryú pa-rússky	Я не говорю по-русски
Slowly, please	máidlyenna, pazhálsta	Медленно пожалуйста
I am English (m/f)	ya anglichánin/anglichánka	Я англичанин/англичанка
American (m/f)	ya amerikánets/amerikánka	Я американец/американка
Canadian (m/f)	ya kanádets/kanádka	Я канадец/канадка

Australian (m/f)	ya avstrályets/avstralíka	Я австралец/австралийка
Please help me	pamagítye mnye pazhálsta	Помогите мне пожалуйста
Go away!	von otsúda!	Вон отсюда!
Help!	pamagí!	Помоги!

Common Signs

Entrance	vkhod	Вход
Exit	výkhod	Выход
Toilet	tualyét	Туалет
Men	múzhi	Мужи
Women	zhení	Жены
Open	otkríta	Открыто
Closed (for repairs)	zakríta (na remont)	Закрыто (на ремонт)
Out of Order	nye rabótayet	Не работает
No entry	vkhóda nyet	Входа нет
No smoking	nye kúrit	Не Курить
Ticket Office	kássa	Касса

Buying and Selling

How much is it?	skólka stóit?	Сколько стоит?
Too expensive	éta dóroga	Это дорого
I would like	ya khachú	Я хочу
This one	éta	Это
More/Less	yeshchó/ménshe	Ещё/меньше
(Very) Big	(óchen) bolshóy	(Очень) большой
(Very) Small	(óchen) mályenky	(Очень) маленкий
Old/New	stáry/nóvy	старый/новый
Hot/Cold	goryáchy/khalódny	горячий/холодный
What is it?	shto éta?	что это?
Please show me	pakazhítye mnye pazhálsta	Покажите мне пожалуйста

Numbers

0	nol	ноль
1	adín	один
2	dva	два
3	tree	три
4	chetíry	четыре

5	pyat	пять
6	shest	шесть
7	syem	семь
8	vósyem	восемь
9	dévyat	девять
10	décyat	десять
11	adínnadtsat	одиннадцать
12	dvyenádtsat	двенадцать
13	treenádtsat	тринадцать
14	chetírnadtsat	четырнадцать
15	pyatnádtsat	пятнадцать
20	dvádtsat	двадцать
21	dvádtsat adín	двадцать один
22	dvádtsat dva	двадцать два
30	tréedtsat	тридцать
40	sórok	сорок
50	pyatdecyát	пятьдесят
60	shestdecyát	шестьдесят
90	dycvyenósta	девяносто
100	sto	сто
200	dvyésti	двести
300	trísta	триста
400	chetírysta	четыреста
500	pyatsót	пятьсот
600	shestsót	шестьсот
1000	týsyacha	тысяча
5000	pyat týsyach	пять тысяч
1,000,000	millión	миллион

Directions

(On the) left	(na) lyéva	(На) лево
(On the) right	(na) práva	(На) право
Straight on	pryáma	Прямо
Street	úlitsa	Улица
Square	plóshchad	Площадь
Lane	pereúlok	Переулок

| Boulevard | bulvar | Булвар |
| Avenue | prospékt | Проспект |

Transport

Train	póyezd/elektríchka	Поезд/электричка
Bus	avtóbus	Автобус
Metro	metró	Метро
Trolleybus	trolléibus	Троллейбус
Tram	tramvái	Трамвай
Taxi	taksí	Такси
Car	mashína	Машина
Where is…?	gdye…?	Где…?
…the bus stop	…avtastántsiya	…автостанция?
…the tram stop	…tramváinaya stántsiya	…трамвайнная станция?
…the trolleybus stop	…trolleistántsiya	…троллейстанция?
…the train station	…vokzál	…вокзал?
When is the next train?	kogdá slyéduyushchy póyezd?	Когда следующий поезд?
Ticket, please	bilyét, pazhálsta	Билет, пожалуйста
Return	tudá i abrátna	Туда и обратно

Food and Drink

Restaurant	restorán	Ресторан
Café	kafé	Кафе
Bar	bar	Бар
Food Shop	gastronóm	Гастроном
Market	rýnok	Рынок
Breakfast	závtrak	Завтрак
Lunch	abéd	Обед
Supper/Dinner	úzhin	Ужин
Knife	nozh	Нож
Fork	vílka	Вилка
Spoon	lózhka	Ложка
Glass	stakán	Стакан
Cup	cháshka	Чашка

Useful Phrases

I am vegetarian (m/f)	ya vegetariánets/ vegetariánka	Я вегетарианец/ вегетарианка
I don't eat meat or fish	ya myása i rýbu ne yem	Я мясо и рыбу не ем
Please bring me…	prinesítye pazhálsta…	Принесите пожалуйста…
…the bill	…schot	…счёт
…an ashtray	…pépelnitsu	…пепельницу
…more…	…yeshchó…	…ещё…
I would like…	ya khachú	Я хочу

Basic Foods

Bread	khleb	хлеб
Butter	másla	масло
Milk	malakó	молоко
Egg	yáitsa	яйцо
Omelette	yáichnitsa	яйчница
Meat	myása	мясо
Fish	rýba	рыба
Sugar	sákhar	сахар
Salt	sol	соль
Pepper	pyérets	перец
Sour Cream	smyetána	сметана
Drinking Yoghurt	kefír	кефир
Cheese	seer	сыр

Vegetables

Potato	kartófel	картофель
Rice	riz	риз
Tomato	pomidór	помидор
Cucumber	agouryéts	огурец
Onion	luk	лук
Pepper	pyérets	перец
Cabbage	kapusta	капуста
Carrot	markóv	морковь
Beetroot	svyókla	свёкла
Mushrooms	gribý	грибы
Aubergine	baklazhán	баклажан

Fruits

Apples	yábloky	яблоки
Plums	slivý	сливы
Cherries	vishný	вишны
Orange	apelsín	апельсин
Lemon	limón	лимон
Grapes	vinogrády	винограды
Strawberries	klúbniky	клубники
Raspberries	malíny	малины
Berries	yágada	ягода

Drinks

(Mineral) water	(minerálnaya) vodá	(минеральная) бода
Tea	chai	чай
Coffee	kófye	кофе
Fruit Juice	sok	сок
Fruit Drink	napítok	напиток
Wine	vinó	вино
Beer	píva	пибо
Vodka	vódka	водка
Cognac	kanyák	коньяк
Champagne	shampánskoye	шампанское

Dishes from the Menu

Russian	*Pronunciation*	*English*
Супы	**Supi**	**Soups**
щи	shchi	Cabbage soup
борщ	borshch	Beetroot soup
окрошка	akróshka	Cold vegetable soup
уха	úkha	Fish soup
харчо	kharchó	Spicy mutton soup
солянка	solyánka	Soup with pickles
Закуски	**Zakuski**	**Appetizers**
икра (красная/ чёрная	ikrá (krásnaya/ chórnaya)	Caviar (red/ black)
баклажанная икра	baklazhánnaya ikrá	Cold baked aubergine

блины	bliný	Pancakes/blini
грибы со сметаной	gribý so smetánoi	mushrooms in sour cream
ассорти мясное/ рыбное	assórti myásnoe/ rýbnoe	assorted cold meats/ fish
сельдь	seld	herring
столичный салат	stolíchny salát	cold chicken & vegetables in mayonnaise
салат из огурцов	salát iz ogúrtsov	cucumber salad
салат из помидоров	salat iz pomidórov	tomato salad
хачапури	khachapúri	cheesy Georgian bread
лаваш	lavásh	flat Georgian bread

Вторые Блюда — Vtoriye Bliuda — Main Courses

говядина	govyádina	beef
свинина	svínina	pork
курица	kúritsa	chicken
телятина	telyátina	veal
баранина	baránina	mutton/lamb
лососина/сёмга	losósina/cyómga	salmon
щука	shchúka	pike
осетрина	osetrína	sturgeon
антрекот	antrekót	entrecote steak
бефстроганов	befstroganóv	beef stroganov
бифштекс	bifshtéks	beef steak
бастурма	bastúrma	cured meat
цыпляата табака	tsiplyáta tabáka	flat, grilled chicken
долма	dólma	vine leaves stuffed with rice & meat (Central Asian)
сосиски	sosíski	Frankfurter-type sausages
биточки	bítochki	meatballs
ачма	achmá	noodles & cheese (Georgian)
голубцы	golubtsý	cabbage leaves stuffed with mince
котлеты	kotléty	meat croquettes
кулебяка	kulebyáka	pie with cabbage or fish
пхали	pkháli	aubergine with walnut sauce (Georgian)

манти	mánti	giant meat dumplings (Central Asian)
жаркое	zhárkoye	beef stew
шницель	shnítsel	Schnitzel
шашлык	sháshlik	kebab
плов	plov	pilaf (Central Asian)
люла-кебаб	liúla-kebáb	spiced, minced kebab
пельмени	pelméni	meat-filled dumplings
пирожки	pirozhkí	pies
сациви	satsívi	Walnut & coriander sauce, with poultry (Georgian)

Десерт	**Dessert**	**Desert**
мороженое	morózhenoye	ice cream
пирожное	pirózhnoye	pastry
вареники	varéniki	jam or fruit dumplings

atlantes	male human figures supporting architectural features in place of columns
banya	communal Russian steam bath
boyar	senior Russian nobles below princes (the class was abolished by Peter the Great)
caryatids	female human figures supporting architectural features in place of columns
Cheka	earliest name for Bolshevik secret police (1917–21)
constructivism	Soviet name for the Modernist architecture of the 1920s
cupola	dome above a church or belltower, often onion-shaped in Russia
dacha	wooden country house
drum	cylindrical base on which a cupola sits
dvorets	palace
futurism	avant-garde movement in art, which sought to incorporate technological imagery
grisaille	mural in shades of grey and white, resembling plaster relief
icon	religious painting, traditionally encaustic on wood
iconostasis	wall of icons dividing nave from sanctuary in Russian churches
KGB	Soviet secret police between 1954–91, short for the Committee for State Security
kokoshniki	ornamental gables on the roof of Russian churches and palaces, often semi-circular or ogee shaped
kremlin	medieval fortress at the heart of traditional Russian town
krepost	military fortress
lavra	highest level of monastery
muzei	museum
NKVD	name given to the secret police in 1934–46
ogee	arch or gable shaped like the top part of a spade in a pack of playing cards
sobor	cathedral
Style Moderne	Russian word for Art Nouveau style in architecture and design
tent roof	steep sided, almost conical roof, as seen on Russian churches; known as a *shatyor* in Russian
terem	women's quarters in traditional palace, at the top of the house

Glossary and Name Changes

tserkov	church
zakomar	semi-circular gable on top of wall

The dissolution of the Soviet Union has led to the reversal of one of its absurder policies: the renaming of streets, squares, metro stations and indeed whole cities after Communist heroes and work-forces. The process of reversal began in June 1991, when the citizens of Leningrad voted to change the name of their city back to St Petersburg, and has been going on, not without controversy, every since. Some of the names chosen by the Communists included Pushkin Square, Chekhov Street. Indignant citizens are now asking why dishonour should be done to these respectable Russian heroes in order to change back to a name commemorating a church which no longer exists. A definitive list of name changes has been announced by both city governments, but their use is distinctly piecemeal, and the putting up of new street signs even more so. The list below features the names in common use in December 1994 on the left, followed by their alternatives on the right. In most cases, more so in St Petersburg than Moscow, the 'new' (infact pre-Revolutionary) names have caught on, and you will find the old Communist name on the right. The lines indicated by an asterisk indicate that the old Communist names still prevail, and the 'new' names are given on the right, in case they come into use soon. Bear in mind that whatever the common usage, when talking to people, particularly taxi drivers, you may need to know that what is Tverskaya Ul. to one citizen is still Ul. Gorkovo to another.

Moscow

Streets and Squares

Pr Akademika Sakharova	Novokirovsky Pr
Arbatskaya Ploshchad	Arbatskiye Vorota*
Barrikadnaya Ul.	Kudrinskaya Ul.*
Bogoyavlinsky Per	Kuybyshevsky Per
Bolotnaya Pl	Pl Repina
Bolshaya Lubianka Ul.	Ul. Dzerzhinskovo
Ul. Chekhova	Malaya Dmitrovka Ul.*
Pokrovka Ul.	Ul. Chernyshevskovo
Ul. Gertsena	Ul. Bolshaya Nikitskaya*
Granatny Per	Ul. Shchuseva
Ul. Ilinka	Ul. Kuybysheva

Internatsionalnaya Ul.
Ul. Kachalova
Kaluzhskaya Pl
Kamergersky Per
Kharitonevsky Maly Per
Ul. Kachalova
Ul. Korovy Val
Lermontovskaya Pl
Lubianskaya Pl
Pr Serova
Maly Patriarshy Per
Maly Rzhevsky Per
Manezhnaya Pl
Ul. Marksa i Engelsa
Ul. Maroseika
Mokhovaya Ul.
Teatralny Proyezd
Ul. Okhotny Ryad
Nab Morisa Toreza
Myasnitskaya Ul.
Ul. Nemirovicha-Danchenko
Nikitsky Bulvar
Nikolskaya Ul.
Nikolsky Proyezd
Pl Nogina
Novinsky Bulvar
Ul. Ogaryova
Okhotny Ryad
Ul. Ostozhenka
Ul. A N Ostrovskovo
Ul. Ostuzheva
Pervy Neglinny Per
Ul. Prechistenka
Prechistenskaya Nab
Pushkinskaya Ul.
Ul. Rozhdestvenka
Ul. Ryleeva
Serpukhovskaya Pl
Ul. Spiridonovka
Ul. Stanislavskovo

Yauzskaya Ul.*
Ul. Malaya Nikitskaya*
Oktyabrskaya Pl
Per Khuchozhestvennovo Teatra
Ul. Griboyedova
Malaya Nikitskaya Ul.*
Dobrininskaya Ul.
Krasnovorotskaya Pl*
Pl Dzerzhinskovo
Lubiansky Pr*
Maly Pionersky Per
Ul. Paliashvili
Pl 50-letiya Oktyabrya
Starovagankovsky Ul.*
Ul. Bogdana Khmelnitskovo
}   Pr Marksa
}
}
Sofiiskaya Nab*
Ul. Kirova
Glinishchevsky Per*
Suvorovsky Bulvar
Ul. 25 Oktyabrya
Proyezd Vladimirova
Slavyanskaya Pl
Ul. Tchaikovskovo
Gazetny Per*
Pr Marksa
Metrostroyevskaya Ul.
Ul. Malaya Ordynka*
Bolshoy Kozikhinsky Per*
Sandunovsky Per
Kropotkinskaya Ul.
Kropotkinskaya Nab
Bolshaya Dmitrovka Ul.*
Ul. Zhdanova
Gagarinsky Per*
Dobryninskaya Pl
Ul. Aleksaya Tolstovo
Leontyevsky Per*

Ul. Stankevicha	Voznesensky Per*
Ul. Staraya Basmannaya	Ul. Karla Marksa
Sukharevskaya Pl	Kolkhoznaya Pl
Teatralnaya Pl	Pl Sverdlova
Telegrafny Per	Arkhangelsky Per*
Triumfalnaya Pl	Pl Mayakovskovo
Tverskaya Pl	Sovietskaya Pl
Tverskaya Ul.	} Ul. Gorkovo
Tverskaya Yamsakaya Ul.	}
Ul. Vakhtangova	Bolshoy Nikolopeskovsky Per*
Ul. Varvarka	Ul. Razina
Ul. Vesnina	Denezhny Per
Ul. Volodarskaya	Povarskaya Ul.*
Povarskaya Ul.	Ul. Vorovskovo
Pl Vosstaniya	Kudrinskaya Pl*
Vozdvizhenka Ul./Novy Arbat	Pr Kalinina
Bolshaya Yakimanka Ul.	Ul. Dmitrovka
Yelokhovskaya Ul.	Spartakovskaya Ul.
Zemlyanoy Val	Ul. Chkalova
Ul. Zholtovsksovo	Yermolayevsky Per*
Ul. Znamenka	Ul. Frunza

Metro Stations

Ⓜ Tverskaya	Ⓜ Gorkovskaya
Ⓜ Lubianka	Ⓜ Dzerzhinskaya
Ⓜ Kitai-Gorod	Ⓜ Pl Nogina
Ⓜ Vykhino	Ⓜ Zhdanovskaya
Ⓜ Teatralnaya	Ⓜ Pl Sverdlova
Ⓜ Okhotny Ryad	Ⓜ Pr Marksa
Ⓜ Tsaritsyno	Ⓜ Lenina
Ⓜ Alexandrovsky Sad	Ⓜ Kalininskaya
Ⓜ Chistiye Prudy	Ⓜ Kirovskaya
Ⓜ Sukharevskaya	Ⓜ Kolkhoznaya
Ⓜ Novo-Alekseyevskaya	Ⓜ Shcherbakovskaya

St Petersburg

Streets and Squares

Angliskaya Nab	Nab Kraznovo Flota
Birzhevaya Pl	Pushkinskaya Pl

Bolshoy Sampsonievsky Pr	Pr Karla Marksa
Bolshaya Konyushennaya Ul.	Ul. Zhelyabova
Pl Dekabristov	Senatskaya Pl*
Furshtadtskaya Ul.	Ul. Petra Lavrova
Galernaya Ul.	Krasnaya Ul.
Ul. Gertsena	Bolshaya Morskaya Ul.*
Ul. Gogolya	Malaya Morskaya Ul.*
Prospekt Maxima Gorkovo	Kronverksky Prospekt*
Gorokhovaya Ul.	Ul. Dzerzhinskovo
Italyanskaya Ul.	Ul. Rakova
Kamennoostrovsky Pr	Kirovsky Pr
Karavannaya Ul.	Ul. Tolmacheva
Konnogvardeysky Bulvar	Bulvar Profsoyuzov
Malaya Konyshennaya Ul.	Ul. Sofi Perovskoy
Ul. Mikhailovskaya	Ul. Brodskovo
Millionnaya Ul.	Ul. Khalturina
Pl Ostrovskovo	Aleksandriyskaya Pl*
Ul. Pestelya	Panteleymonovskaya Ul.*
Pochtamtskaya Ul.	Podbelskovo Per
Ul. Saltykova Shchedrina	Kirochnaya Ul.*
Sennaya Pl	Pl Mira
Shpalernaya Ul.	Ul. Voinova
Troitskaya Pl	Pl Revolutsii
Pl Truda	Blagoveshchenskaya Pl*
Ul. Truda	Blagoveshchenskaya Ul.*
Pl Vosstaniya	Znamenskaya Pl*
Voznesensky Pr	Pr Mayorova

Bridges

Troitsky Most	Kirovsky Most
Most Leytenanta Shmidta	Nikolayevsky Most*
Birzhevoy Most	Stroiteley Most
Politseysky Most	Narodny Most
Lityeiny Most	Aleksandrovsky Most*
Panteleymonovsky Most	Most Pestelya

Metro Stations

Ⓜ Sennaya Ploshchad	Ⓜ Ploshchad Mira
Ⓜ Devyatkino	Ⓜ Komsomolskaya
Ⓜ Novocherkasskaya	Ⓜ Krasnogvardeyskaya

Maps and Useful Reference Books

Northern Cartographic/Russian Information Services currently produce the most up-to-date maps of Moscow and St Petersburg, available from hotels in the cities and by ordering from a good bookshop abroad.

Victor and Jennifer Louis, *The Moscow Street Atlas* (Collets). Moscow's very own A–Z.

Michael R. Dohan (ed.), *The Traveller's Yellow Pages for St Petersburg* and *The Traveller's Yellow Pages for Moscow* (InfoServices International Inc.) are invaluable chronicles of the phone numbers and addresses you are most likely to need in both cities.

Paul E. Richardson, *Russia Survival Guide* (Russian Information Services 1993), is a regularly updated guide to doing business in Russia.

In both Moscow and St Petersburg you will find maps showing the routes of overground public transport for sale on the street or in kiosks. In Moscow, the *Plan of the Passenger Transport* comes in Latin script, while in St Petersburg you will only find the Cyrillic *Маршрути Городского Транспорта* (*Marshruty Gorodskovo Transporta*).

Travel

Marquis de Custine, *Letters from Russia* (Penguin 1991) is the classic 19th-century account of Moscow and St Petersburg through the eyes of a conservative Frenchman.

Robert Byron, *First Russia, Then Tibet* (Penguin 1985). After a slow start Byron develops a remarkable discourse on the Bolshevik system and Russian aesthetics in the 1930s. One of the books which established his reputation.

John Steinbeck and Robert Capa, *A Russian Journal* (Paragon House, NY 1989). In 1948 this renowned US writer/photographer team recorded their impressions of Russia during the austerity of the post-war Stalinist period.

Truman Capote, *The Muses are Heard* (from *A Capote Reader*, Hamish Hamilton 1987). A wickedly amusing piece of reportage describing the journey to Russia and reception of a 1956 American touring production of *Porgy and Bess*.

Colin Thubron, *Among the Russians* (Penguin 1985). Thubron's book, a perceptive description of travels in Russia and the Caucasus in the early 1980s

Further Reading

with chapters on Moscow and St Petersburg, is a testament to how much can change in 10 years, and yet how much the Russians remain the same.

William and Jane Taubman, *Moscow Spring* (Summit Books 1989) is a fascinating account of life in the heart of Russia's political, cultural and intellectual élite during the spring of 1988, when Gorbachev's words were beginning to be transformed into tentative action.

Bruce Chatwin, *What am I Doing Here* (Picador 1989) contains a couple of short pieces, about meetings with Nadezhda Mandelstam and the constructivist architect Konstantin Melnikov in Moscow.

Christopher Hope, *Moscow! Moscow!* (Minerva 1990). A brilliant, vibrant series of observations by this South African writer suggest that it takes someone brought up under one repressive regime to recognize the insidious power behind the petty ironies of another.

Susan Richards, *Epics of Everyday Life* (Viking 1990). An English woman's encounters in Moscow and other cities of the Soviet Union, capturing the enduring charm of the Russians during a period of constant change.

History

Tibor Szamuely, *The Russian Tradition* (Fontana 1988) traces the roots of revolution in Russia back to medieval times in a sweeping and engrossing account of the country's social history.

Geoffrey Hosking, *A History of the Soviet Union* (Fontana 1990). The second edition of this comprehensive survey of Soviet history runs well into Gorbachev's term as General Secretary.

Barbara B. Green, *The Dynamics of Russian Politics* (Praeger Publishers, Westport, Conneticut, 1994) gives the economic and political background to the Revolution, before launching into an acute analysis of Soviet politics and ending in the chaos of disintegration which accompanied the Union's demise. The most up-to-date general account available.

Lawrence Kelly, *Moscow: a traveller's companion* and *St Petersburg: a traveller's companion* (Constable 1983 & 1981) trace the history and social mores of each city through exerpts from contemporary documents. From the earliest accounts to the Revolution.

Biography and Autobiography

Robert K. Massie, *Peter the Great* (Abacus 1993) is a Pullitzer Prize-winning 850-page masterpiece of historical biography. The pages fly by as the giant epileptic tries to haul Russia out of a vividly-portrayed Middle Ages and into the modern world.

John T. Alexander, *Catherine the Great* (OUP 1989). Unlike many of her biographers, Alexander's analysis of Catherine the myth takes an intelligent probing attitude which only adds to his portrayal of Catherine the empress.

Christine Sutherland, *The Princess of Siberia* (Robin Clark Ltd 1988) is the breathy, romantic account of Princess Maria Volkonskaya's journey to and life in Siberia in the 1820s, to join her husband who was exiled for his leading role in the Decembrist Uprising.

Robert K. Massie, *Nicholas and Alexandra* (Atheneum 1967) is the standard, very readable portrait of the last of the Romanovs, now somewhat overtaken by the opening of archives and discovery of the bodies of the family near Yekaterinburg.

Michael Glenny and Norman Stone, *The Other Russia* (Faber & Faber 1991). Takes the form of a series of interviews with members of the greatest Russian diaspora, those who fled their native land in the aftermath of the Revolution.

Michael Ignatieff, *The Russian Album* (Penguin 1988). In this endearing volume, Ignatieff digs back to reveal the anti-Semitic skeletons in his family cupboard and to provide a vivid depiction of the Revolution and exile from an aristocratic perspective.

Osip Mandelstam, *The Noise of Time* (in **The Prose of Osip Mandelstam**, Quartet Encounter 1988). Memoirs of life in St Petersburg by the poet who died a victim of Stalin in the Gulag in 1938.

Nadezhda Mandelstam, *Hope against Hope* and *Hope Abandoned* (Collins Harvill 1989 & 1961) together chronicle a life of internal exile in constant opposition to the Soviet system, during which the author's primary concern was the preservation of her husband, Osip Mandelstam's poetic works and his rehabilitation. Nadezhda is a writer of brilliance in her own right, and has produced the definitive chronicle of life under Stalin.

Isaac Deutscher, *Stalin* (Penguin 1976). The classic biography, its relatively sympathetic analysis ever more questionable in the light of new revelations.

Rosamond Richardson, *The Long Shadow* (Little Brown 1993). Badly written but fascinating account of the effect Stalin had on his own family.

Evgenia S. Ginzburg, *Into the Whirlwind* and *Within the Whirlwind*, (Collins Harvill 1989). A terrifying account of life in the gulag in the 30s and 40s by one of the survivors.

Joseph Brodsky, *In a Room and a Half* and *A guide to a Renamed City* (essays from *Less than One*, Farrar Straus Giroux 1986). Fascinating, evocative memoires of life in Leningrad in the 1950s and 60s.

Art and Architecture

Christopher Marsden, *Palmyra of the North* (Faber and Faber 1942). An enthusiastic and intimate account of the architectural and artistic birth of St Petersburg in the 18th century.

Tamara Talbot Rice, *A Concise History of Russian Art* (Thames and Hudson 1974). A superficial romp through the art and architecture of Russia from medieval Kievan Rus to the explosion of talent in the early 20th century.

Camilla Gray, *The Russian Experiment in Art 1863–1922* (Thames and Hudson 1993). Exhaustive survey of the 'great experiment' which profoundly influenced the course of 20th-century painting world-wide.

Suzanne Massie, *Pavlovsk—The Life of a Russian Palace* (Little Brown 1990). By tracing the two-hundred year history of one of Russia's most perfect palaces, the author has managed to write not only a architectural history but also a social history, embracing everyone from the 19th-century royal inhabitants to the palaces 20th-century restorers, including a thorough and comprehensive account of the heroic efforts to preserve the country's heritage during the seige of Leningrad in the Second World War. Brilliant.

John Freeman & Kathleen Berton, *Moscow Revealed* (Doubleday 1991). A pictorial survey of Moscow's outstanding surviving interiors.

Zoia Belyakova, *The Romanov Legacy* (Hazar 1994). Latest of many coffee-table books about the stunning 18th- and 19th-century palaces of St Petersburg.

Sociology

Hedrick Smith, *The New Russians* (Vintage 1991). Absorbing study of Russian society on the eve of glasnost and of the momentous political, social, economic and psychological changes 1985–1991.

Francine du Plessix Gray, *Soviet Women—Walking the Tightrope* (Virago 1991). Taking as its central paradox the official equality yet unofficial inequality of the country's women, these interviews paint a grim picture of ignorance and social injustice.

Thomas Lahusen (ed.), *Late Soviet Culture* (Duke University Press 1993) gives a taste of post-*perestroika* academic thinking, in fields as diverse as 'Saint' Alexander Pushkin, Soviet film and women's studies.

Russian Cuisine

Anya von Bremzen and John Welchman, *Please to the Table* (Workman Publishing, NY 1990). This enchanting book covers the whole of the former Soviet Union and is more a bible of domestic mores than a cook book. Peppered amongst the recipes are mouth-watering quotes from Russian literature, notes on favourite dishes, menu suggestions and host of other enlightening culinary trivia.

Moscow and St Petersburg in Literature

Mikhail Bulgakov, *The Master and Margerita* (Collins Harvill 1988) is a master-piece, a fantastical tale in which the devil comes to 1930s Moscow. Short stories set in Moscow by the same author include *The Heart of a Dog*.

Lev Tolstoy, *War and Peace* and *Anna Karenina* (Penguin Classics). For Moscow in the 19th century, you can hardly do better. Tolstoy hated St Petersburg.

Anatoly Rybakov, *Children of the Arbat* (Hutchinson 1988) is a flawed novel examining the effect of living through the Stalinist purges on a bunch of young hoodlums. Much better on the moral morrass of life in Moscow in the same period is **Yuri Trifonov's**, *House on the Embankment.*

Fyodor Dostoyevsky is the classic 19th-century St Petersburg novelist, with *Crime and Punishment* perhaps the most evocative of his *oeuvre*.

Andrei Bely, *Petersburg* (Penguin 1983) not just a taste of Russian symbolism and an evocation of the turbulence beneath the surface of St Petersburg in 1905, Bely's novel is one of the great experimental works of this century.

Sacheverell Sitwell, *Valse des Fleurs* (Faber and Faber 1941) is a whimsical evo-cation of a ball at the Winter Palace in St Petersburg in 1868, complete with court runners delivering invitations and Ethiopian palace guards.

Daniil Kharms, *The Plummeting Old Women* (Lilliput 1989) is a collection of short pieces by one of the great absurdist modernists of the early Soviet period. Kharms died under Stalin; though well known as a writer for chil-dren, his other works are only now receiving the attention they deserve.

Anna Akhmatova, *Selected Poems* (Collins Harvill 1989). Pained, strained and painfully moving, even in translation, Akhmatova's is the voice of St Petersburg speaking through the period of Leningrad.

Glas is a quarterly of new Russian writing in translation, available from Dr. Arch Tait, Dept. of Russian Literature, University of Birmingham B15 2TT.

Note: Chapter headings and main references are in **bold** type; page numbers of maps are in *italic*

Index